ADO.NET

IN A NUTSHELL

ADO.NET

IN A NUTSHELL

Bill Hamilton and Matthew MacDonald

O'REILLY®

Beijing • Cambridge • Farnham • Köln • Paris • Sebastopol • Taipei • Tokyo

ADO.NET in a Nutshell

by Bill Hamilton and Matthew MacDonald

Published by O'Reilly & Associates, Inc., 1005 Gravenstein Highway North, Sebastopol, CA 95472.

O'Reilly & Associates books may be purchased for educational, business, or sales promotional use. Online editions are also available for most titles (*safari.oreilly.com*). For more information, contact our corporate/institutional sales department: 800-998-9938 or *corporate@oreilly.com*.

Editor:	Brian Jepson
Production Editor:	Mary Anne Weeks Mayo
Cover Designer:	Emma Colby
Interior Designer:	Bret Kerr

Printing History:

April 2003:	First Edition.

ISBN: 0-596-00361-7
[M]

Table of Contents

Part II. ADO.NET Core Classes

Part III. API Quick Reference

Part IV. Appendixes

Preface

Almost every software application is driven by data. Usually, this data is centralized in a relational database system such as SQL Server, Oracle, or DB2. In the .NET world, you access this information using Microsoft's latest data access technology: ADO.NET.

Like many other .NET technologies, ADO.NET bears some superficial similarities to its predecessor (in this case, ADO). However, ADO.NET also includes some dramatic changes and a few surprising innovations. It has a disconnected programming model tailored for distributed applications and the Web, built-in support for XML serialization, practical data binding, and an extensible set of interfaces that let you create custom data providers.

Learning to use ADO.NET takes a little work, but the rewards are well worth it. With the help of this reference, you'll be up and running before you know it.

Audience

This book is intended primarily as a reference and learning tool for experienced developers who need to master ADO.NET. You don't need experience with ADO, but you should be familiar with .NET basics such as assemblies, events, metadata, and the Common Language Runtime. If you are new to .NET, you'll be well served by starting with an introductory work such as *.NET Framework Essentials* by Thuan L.Thai and Hoang Lam (O'Reilly and Associates, Inc.).

This book also assumes you know the basics of developing database applications. The examples in this book use the Northwind sample database, which is automatically installed with SQL Server and available with the freely installable, scaled-down version, Microsoft Data Engine (MSDE). If you use a different database product, you won't be able to run all the examples as written, although all the concepts will still apply.

Finally, to get the most out of this book, it's strongly recommended that you know the SQL language. If you're new to SQL, you should supplement this book with such books as *SQL in a Nutshell* by Kevin Kline and Daniel Kline (O'Reilly). You may also want to read books that target the specific SQL extensions used by your database product, such as *Oracle PL/SQL Programming* by Steven Feuerstein and Bill Pribyl and *Transact-SQL Programming* by Kevin Kline, Lee Gould, and Andrew Zanevsky (both O'Reilly books).

Contents of This Book

This book consists of a tutorial section that explains ADO.NET concepts, a class library references that describes every ADO.NET type, and several appendixes with supplementary information.

The best place to begin your exploration of ADO.NET is with the foundation chapters in Part I, *ADO.NET Tutorial*. Here's a brief description of those chapters:

Chapter 1, *Introduction*
Introduces the basic ADO.NET objects and their roles.

Chapter 2, *.NET Data Providers*
Describes the classes that make up an ADO.NET data provider and the providers available with the .NET framework.

Chapter 3, *Connections*
Describes how to create a connection to a data source using ADO.NET and handle connection pooling.

Chapter 4, *Commands*
Describes the first level of ADO.NET: connection-based programming to perform live record updates, inserts, and deletions. Also shows how to interact with stored procedures and create parameterized commands.

Chapter 5, *DataReaders*
Explains how to retrieve the results of a query from a data source using a read-only, forward-only cursor. Also briefly demonstrates how you can write provider-agnostic ADO.NET code

Chapter 6, *DataSets*
Introduces the heart of ADO.NET's disconnected data features: the DataSet.

Chapter 7, *DataTables*
Introduces the DataTable object that stores one or more rowsets in a DataSet.

Chapter 8, *DataColumns*
Explains the DataColumn object, which together with Constraint objects defines the schema for a DataTable.

Chapter 9, *DataRows*
Explains the DataRow object, which contains an individual row of data in a DataTable.

Chapter 10, *Constraints*
Describes Constraint objects, which enforce unique and foreign key constraints of data.

Chapter 11, *DataRelations*

Describes the DataRelation, which helps you navigate parent-child relationships and maintain referential integrity within the DataSet.

Chapter 12, *DataViews and Data Binding*

Describes the DataView object, which represents a custom view of the data within a DataTable. The chapter discusses using the DataView to sort, filter, and edit data and to perform data binding in both Web and Windows Forms.

Chapter 13, *Strongly Typed DataSets*

Describes strongly typed DataSet classes, how to generate and use them, and considerations about their use.

Chapter 14, *DataAdapters*

Describes how the DataAdapter class bridges the disconnected classes in ADO.NET with the underlying data source. The chapter explains how to retrieve data from the data source, place that data into a DataSet, and subsequently update modifications to the DataSet back to the underlying data source.

Chapter 15, *Updating the Data Source*

Describes how to commit updates made in a DataSet to the original data source.

Chapter 16, *Transactions*

Describes how to start and manage client-initiated transactions, and compares them with stored procedure transactions and distributed COM+ transactions.

Chapter 17, *XML and the DataSet*

Explains how ADO.NET works with XML. You'll learn what you can and can't control with ADO.NET's XML serialization, how DiffGrams store versioning information, and how web services encode the DataSet for transmission. Also introduces the XML features built into SQL Server 2000.

Part II, *ADO.NET Core Classes*, documents the core ADO.NET classes. A separate chapter is provided for each class, with an essential description of its properties, methods, and events.

Part III, *API Quick Reference*, provides a high-level reference of the ADO.NET namespaces. When you design or code an application, you'll often find it useful to refer to this condensed class information.

Namespaces described in the reference include:

```
System.Data
System.Data.Common
System.Data.OleDb
System.Data.SqlClient
System.Data.SqlTypes
```

Part IV, *Appendixes*, encompasses the following:

Appendix A, *ADO.NET Providers*

Includes provider tables that show the key types for each provider, the data type mappings, and other miscellaneous details. Also describes some providers that aren't included with .NET.

Appendix B, *ADO.NET XML Extensions*

Explains the custom XML namespaces used when serializing a DataSet with versioning information or creating a typed DataSet schema.

Appendix C, *Microsoft Data Engine (MSDE)*

Briefly describes MSDE, the freely distributable scaled-down version of SQL Server that can be used for desktop applications.

Appendix D, *Type, Method, Property, and Field Index*

Contains an alphabetic listing of the types and members found in Part III. You can use it to determine the namespace to which a particular type or member belongs.

What's on the CD-ROM

The CD-ROM that accompanies this book contains a copy of *ADO.NET in a Nutshell for Microsoft Visual Studio .NET*. This software plugs directly into Microsoft Visual Studio .NET and makes the contents of Part III of this book, *API Quick Reference*, available to you as a fully integrated member of Visual Studio . NET Dynamic Help.

By making *ADO.NET in a Nutshell* a part of your Visual Studio .NET development environment, you gain the following benefits:

- Constantly updated Dynamic Help links to relevant *Quick Reference* entries as you write C# code (these links appear in a separate Dynamic Help window link group named O'Reilly Help)
- Links to both *Quick Reference* topics and Microsoft documentation topics when you use either the Help Search facility or interactive Index
- Access to the O'Reilly web site, *http://www.oreilly.com*, for additional books and articles on Visual Basic .NET, C#, and the .NET Framework
- Cross links from Quick Reference topics to related topics in MSDN documentation.

For more information on *ADO.NET in a Nutshell for Microsoft Visual Studio .NET*, please read the release notes on the CD-ROM.

To use *ADO.NET in a Nutshell for Microsoft Visual Studio .NET*, you must be running a version of Visual Basic .NET or Visual Studio .NET on your computer or laptop. To install *ADO.NET in a Nutshell* for Microsoft Visual Studio .NET:

1. Place the CD-ROM in the CD-ROM player.
2. If you are running Visual Studio .NET 2003, double-click on the file named *ADONETinaNutshell2003.msi*. If you are still running Visual Studio .NET 2002, double-click on the file named *ADONETinaNutshell2002.msi*.
3. Follow the instructions contained in the install program windows. Be sure to read and accept the terms of the software license before proceeding.

To uninstall *ADO.NET in a Nutshell for Microsoft Visual Studio .NET*, repeat the previous procedure, but click on the Remove button when the program prompts you to select an install option.

Making the *ADO.NET in a Nutshell* Quick Reference section available as a Visual Studio .NET plug-in is a new venture for O'Reilly & Associates and Microsoft. We want very much to hear your comments and ideas. Please send any comments to:

> *bookquestions@oreilly.com*

If you discover errors in content or encounter any problems in using this product, please report them to:

> *bookquestions@oreilly.com*

Conventions Used in This Book

The following typographic conventions are used in this book:

Italic is used for:

- Pathnames, filenames, program names, and utilities
- Internet addresses, such as domain names and URLs
- New terms where they are defined

Constant width is used for:

- Command lines and options that should be typed verbatim
- Names and keywords in C# programs, including method, variable, and class names
- Events, event handlers, objects, properties, classes, methods, controls, values, operators, and namespaces
- Code samples
- XML element tags

 This icon designates a note, which is an important aside to the nearby text.

 This icon designates a warning relating to the nearby text.

Comments and Questions

Please address comments and questions concerning this book to the publisher:

> O'Reilly & Associates, Inc.
> 1005 Gravenstein Highway North
> Sebastopol, CA 95472
> (800) 998-9938 (in the United States or Canada)
> (707) 829-0515 (international/local)
> (707) 829-0104 (fax)

There is a web page for this book that lists errata, examples, or any additional information. You can access this page at:

> *http://www.oreilly.com/catalog/adonetian*

To comment or ask technical questions about this book, send email to:

> *bookquestions@oreilly.com*

For more information about books, conferences, Resource Centers, and the O'Reilly Network, see the O'Reilly web site at:

> *http://www.oreilly.com*

Acknowledgments

This book couldn't have been written without the help of many individuals at O'Reilly, including Robert Denn, Nancy Kotary, John Osborn, and Brian Jepson, who kept the book on track through its revision process. We also owe heartfelt thanks to the technical reviewers, including Shawn Wildermuth, who offered valuable comments throughout.

Without the support of these people and many more at O'Reilly, the book would never have been written.

Bill

I would like to thank Molly for her encouragement and support. I love you Molly—you're the best! I would also like to thank my friends and family who not only put up with me, but cheer me on.

Matthew

I'd like to thank my parents (all four of them) and my endlessly supportive wife Faria, whom I love dearly. Without them all, this book would never have been written!

CD-ROM Acknowledgments

ADO.NET in a Nutshell for Visual Studio .NET is the work of many individuals. Mike Sierra of O'Reilly converted the ADO.NET namespace API references to Microsoft Help 2.0 format and added the XML tags needed to integrate their content with the Visual Studio .NET Dynamic Help system. He was assisted by Lenny Muellner and Erik Ray. Greg Dickerson and the O'Reilly Tech Support group tested each prerelease build of the software. Kipper York and Shane McRoberts of the Microsoft Help team provided invaluable technical assistance at critical moments, and Erik Promislow of Active State built the install package that makes our Help files an integral part of the Visual Studio .NET developer environment. John Osborn managed the development and release of the product. Frank Gocinski of the Visual Studio .NET third-party integration program was instrumental in making us full VSIP partners. A special tip of the hat as well to Rob Howard who understood our original vision and helped us make the right connections to get this project off the ground

ADO.NET Tutorial

Introduction

ADO.NET is a new programming model built upon the .NET Framework, sharing a common type system, design patterns and naming conventions. The stated goals of ADO.NET are to:

- Provide a disconnected (offline) data architecture in addition to supporting connected operation
- Integrate tightly with XML
- Interact with a variety of data sources through a common data representation
- Optimize data source access

ADO.NET is designed to provide consistent access to data sources. This is accomplished through ADO.NET data providers that provide methods for connecting to data sources as well as retrieving, manipulating, and updating data in both connected and disconnected environments.

ADO.NET Data Providers

An ADO.NET data provider connects to a data source such as SQL Server, Oracle, or an OLE DB data source, and provides a way to execute commands against that data source in a consistent manner that is independent of the data source and data source-specific functionality. However, aside from a core set of similar capabilities, there is no guarantee that identical functionality will be available in each data provider. This is due to differences between data sources (for example, SQL Server provides many more capabilities than Access) and provider implementations (for example, both Microsoft and Oracle offer ADO.NET providers for Oracle's data server with slight implementation differences).

A complete .NET data provider includes the following classes:

Connection
    Connects to the data source.

`Command`
> Executes commands against the data source.

`DataReader`
> A forward-only, read-only connected result set.

`ParameterCollection`
> Stores all parameters related to a `Command` and the mappings of both table and column names to the `DataSet` columns.

`Parameter`
> Defines parameters for parameterized SQL statements and stored procedures.

`Transaction`
> Groups statements modifying data into work units that are either committed in their entirety or cancelled.

`DataAdapter`
> Bridges the connected components to the disconnected components, allowing a `DataSet` and `DataTable` to be filled from the data source and later reconciled with the data source.

The classes for the different providers inherit from a common set of classes and implement a common set of interfaces to provide consistent functionality regardless of the provider. Each data provider uses a unique namespace to logically name and group the classes in the data provider and prevent collisions in the assemblies.

The .NET Framework Version 1.0 ships with SQL Server and OLE DB data providers. The .NET Framework Version 1.1 also ships with both ODBC and Oracle data providers; these providers must be downloaded and installed separately with .NET Framework Version 1.0. Other .NET data providers can be downloaded and installed separately with either version of the .NET Framework. Specific data providers are discussed in more detail in Chapter 2.

Because all .NET data providers present a consistent interface, porting an ADO. NET application from one provider to another is a straightforward task. The examples in this book use the .NET SQL Server data provider except when discussing OLE DB specific functionality (e.g., schema views). Any significant differences between the SQL Server and OLE DB data providers are also discussed throughout the book.

Connected and Disconnected Data

As mentioned earlier, ADO.NET supports two different programming environments: connected and disconnected.

The *connected* environment provides forward-only, read-only access to data in the data source and the ability to execute commands against the data source. The connected classes provide a common way to work with connected data regardless of the underlying data source. They include `Connection`, `Command`, `DataReader`, `Transaction`, `ParameterCollection`, and `Parameter` classes.

The *disconnected* environment allows data retrieved from the data source to be manipulated and later reconciled with the data source. The disconnected classes provide a common way to work with disconnected data regardless of the underlying data source. They include the `DataSet`, `DataTable`, `DataColumn`, `DataRow`, `Constraint`, `DataRelationship`, and `DataView` classes.

Finally, ADO.NET introduces the connected `DataAdapter` class to bridge the data source and disconnected classes by way of the connected classes. The `DataAdapter` is an abstraction of the connected classes that simplifies filling the disconnected `DataSet` or `DataTable` classes with data from the data source and updating the data source to reflect any changes made to the disconnected data. Figure 1-1 shows the relationship between the connected and disconnected classes in ADO.NET.

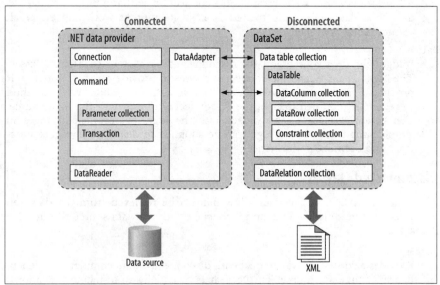

Figure 1-1. The connected and disconnected ADO.NET classes

Connected Classes

The following classes are used by ADO.NET to communicate directly with the data source:

`Connection`
> Maintains information required to connect to the data source through a connection string. The connection string contains information such as the name of the data source and its location, and authorization credentials and settings. The `Connection` class has methods to open and close the connection, for transactions to be initiated on the connection, as well as control other properties of the connection.

`Command`
> Executes SQL statements or stored procedures against the data source. The command class has a `ParameterCollection` object containing `Parameter` objects that allow parameterized SQL statements and stored procedures to be used against the data source.

DataReader

> Provides connected forward-only, read-only access to the data source. It is optimized for speed. The DataReader is instantiated through a Command object.

Parameter

> Allows parameters for both parameterized queries and stored procedures to be defined and set to appropriate values. The Parameter class is accessed through the ParametersCollection object within a Command object. It supports input and output parameters as well as return values from stored procedures.

Transaction

> Allows transactions to be created on a connection so that multiple changes to data in a data source are treated as a single unit of work and either all committed or cancelled.

DataAdapter

> Bridges the data source and the disconnected DataSet or DataTable classes. The DataAdapter wraps the connected classes to provide this functionality. It provides a method to retrieve data into a disconnected object and a method to reconcile modified data in the disconnected object with the data source. The CommandBuilder class can generate the logic to reconcile changes in simple situations; custom logic can be supplied to deal with complex situations and optimize performance.

Disconnected Classes

The following ADO.NET classes allow data to be retrieved from the data set, examined and modified offline, and reconciled with the data source through the DataAdapter:

DataSet

> Provides a consistent way to deal with disconnected data completely independently of the data source. The DataSet is essentially an in-memory relational database, serving as a container for the DataTable, DataColumn, DataRow, Constraint, and DataRelation objects.
>
> The XML format serializes and transports a DataSet. A DataSet can be accessed and manipulated either as XML or through the methods and properties of the DataSet interchangeably; the XmlDataDocument class represents and synchronizes the relational data within a DataSet object with the XML Document Object Model (DOM).

DataTable

> Allows disconnected data to be examined and modified through a collection of DataColumn and DataRow classes. The DataTable allows constraints such as foreign keys and unique constraints to be defined using the Constraint class.

DataColumn

> Corresponds to a column in a table. The DataColumn class stores metadata about the structure of the column that, together with constraints, defines the schema of the table. The DataColumn can also create expression columns based on other columns in the table.

DataRow

Corresponds to a row in a table and can examine and update data in the DataTable. The DataTable exposes DataRow objects through the DataRowCollection object it contains. The DataRow caches changes made to data contained in its columns, storing both original and current values. This allows changes to be cancelled or to be later reconciled with the data source.

Constraint

Allows constraints to be placed on data stored within a DataTable. Unique and foreign key constraints can be created to maintain data integrity.

DataRelation

Provides a way to indicate a relationship between different DataTable objects within a DataSet. The DataRelation relates columns in the parent and child tables allowing navigation between the parent and child tables and referential integrity to be enforced through cascading updates and deletes.

DataView

Allows data, once retrieved into a DataSet or DataTable, to be viewed in different ways. It allows data to be sorted based on column values and for a subset of the data to be filtered so that only rows matching specified criteria are displayed.

Chapter 2 examines .NET data providers in more detail and describes the way in which they provide connected functionality and serve as a bridge to disconnected functionality.

2

.NET Data Providers

The .NET Framework 1.0 ships with the Microsoft SQL Server .NET data provider and OLE DB .NET data provider. The .NET Framework 1.1 also includes both the Oracle and ODBC .NET data providers. A .NET data provider connects to the data source and executes commands, either to retrieve results or to modify the data in the data source. It is possible to create a .NET data provider for practically any data source: Exchange servers, XML documents, and SQL databases other than those .NET supports out of the box. Figure 2-1 shows the relationship between the ADO.NET data providers that ship with .NET, the data sources that they access, and the disconnected ADO.NET classes.

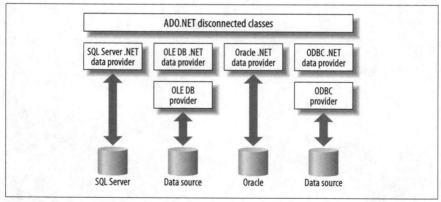

Figure 2-1. ADO.NET data providers

Data Providers

The most commonly used .NET data providers are described in the following sections.

Microsoft SQL Server

The SQL Server .NET data provider ships with the .NET Framework. It uses the Tabular Data Stream (TDS) protocol to send requests to and receive responses from the SQL Server. This provider delivers very high performance because TDS is a fast protocol that can access Microsoft SQL Server directly without an OLE DB or ODBC layer and without COM interop. The SQL Server .NET data provider can be used with Microsoft SQL Server 7.0 or later. To access earlier versions of Microsoft SQL Server, the OLE DB .NET data provider with the SQL Server OLE DB provider (SQLOLEDB) should be used. The SQL Server .NET data provider classes are located in the `System.Data.SqlClient` namespace.

OLE DB

The OLE DB .NET data provider ships with the .NET Framework. It communicates with a data source using a data source-specific OLE DB provider through COM interop. The OLE DB provider, in turn, communicates directly with the data source using native OLE DB calls.

The OLE DB .NET data provider supports OLE DB interfaces later than Version 2.5. As a result, some OLE DB providers, including those for Microsoft Exchange Server and Internet Publishing, aren't supported. Also, the OLE DB .NET data provider can't be used with the OLE DB provider for ODBC (MSDASQL). To access ODBC data, use the ODBC .NET data provider discussed later in this chapter.

The OLE DB.NET data provider classes are located in the `System.Data.OleDb` namespace.

ODBC

The ODBC .NET data provider is installed as an add-in component to the .NET Framework Version 1.0 and ships with the .NET Framework Version 1.1. The provider communicates with the data source using native ODBC drivers through COM interop.

The following ODBC drivers are guaranteed compatible with the ODBC .NET data provider:

- Microsoft SQL Server ODBC Driver
- Microsoft ODBC Driver for Oracle
- Microsoft Access (Jet) ODBC Driver

The ODBC .NET data provider classes are located in the `Microsoft.Data.Odbc` namespace in Version 1.0 of the .NET Framework. In Version 1.1, the namespace changes to `System.Data.Odbc`.

The Microsoft ODBC .NET data provider can be downloaded from the .NET Framework section of *http://msdn.microsoft.com/downloads*.

Oracle

The Oracle .NET data provider is installed as an add-in component to the .NET Framework Version 1.0 and ships with the .NET Framework Version 1.1. This provider accesses an Oracle database using the Oracle Call Interface (OCI). The Oracle .NET data provider can be used with Oracle 8i Release 3 (8.1.7) or later. Use the OLE DB .NET data provider with the Oracle OLE DB provider (MSDAORA) for earlier versions of Oracle. Oracle 9i is required to access UTF16 databases because UTF16 is a new feature in Oracle 9i.

The Microsoft Oracle .NET data provider classes are located in the System.Data.OracleClient namespace in both Versions 1.0 and 1.1 of the .NET Framework.

The Microsoft Oracle .NET data provider can be downloaded from the .NET Framework section of *http://msdn.microsoft.com/downloads*.

Additionally, Oracle has a .NET data provider available at *http://otn.oracle.com/software/tech/windows/odpnet/content.html*.

SQLXML Managed Classes

The SQLXML Managed Classes can access the functionality of SQLXML 3.0 from within .NET applications. Using SQLXML Managed Classes, XML data can be retrieved from a SQL Server, processed, and sent back to the SQL Server to apply updates. The SQLXML Managed Classes can't be considered a full .NET data provider because only partial implementations of the Command, Parameter, and DataAdapter classes are included.

The SQLXML Managed Classes are located in the Microsoft.Data.SqlXml namespace.

The SQLXML Managed Classes can be downloaded from the SQL Server Development section of *http://msdn.microsoft.com/downloads*.

Other Providers

In addition to the data providers mentioned earlier, there are many other native managed providers available or under development. Table 2-1 lists sources for more information about other native .NET data providers.

Table 2-1. Other native .NET data providers

Organization	Data source	URL
Core Lab	Oracle, MySQL	*http://crlab.com*
DataDirect Technologies	Oracle and Sybase	*http://www.datadirect-technologies.com*
dataWeb	TurboDB	*http://www.turbodb.com*
Enterprise Information Designs	MySQL	*http://www.einfodesigns.com*
MySQL	MySQL	*http://www.mysql.com*
PostgreSQL	PostgreSQL	*http://gborg.postgresql.org*
SourceForge	MySQL, Firebird	*http://sourceforge.net*

As mentioned, many databases and data sources that currently don't have native managed providers, including DB2, Informix, and Interbase, can be accessed using the .NET OLE DB data provider and an OLE DB provider.

Selecting a Data Provider

The Microsoft SQL Server .NET data provider is recommended for all applications using Microsoft SQL Server 7.0 or later, or Microsoft Data Engine (MSDE) applications.

The Microsoft OLE DB .NET data provider is recommended for applications using Microsoft SQL Server 6.5 and earlier with the OLE DB provider for SQL Server (SQLOLEDB). It is also recommended for applications using Microsoft Access databases. Additionally, it can access any data source that has an OLE DB provider that supports OLE DB interface greater than Version 2.5. However, if a data source-specific provider is available, that is likely to be a preferred solution.

The ODBC .NET data provider can be used for any data source that is accessible through ODBC but doesn't have either a .NET data provider, an OLE DB provider, or a vendor-supplied .NET data provider.

Creating a Custom Data Provider

ADO.NET provides a set of interfaces that allow you to build a custom .NET data provider. While most DBMSs can be accessed through a specific .NET data provider or through the OLE DB .NET data provider, some reasons to implement a custom data provider include:

- To access proprietary data sources that have neither a specific .NET data provider nor an OLE DB provider that can be accessed through the .NET OLE DB data provider.

- To expose specific functionality of the data source that is accessed through a general-purpose provider. For example, a database that is accessed through the OLE DB .NET data provider might have functionality that isn't available through that provider. A custom data provider can be written to expose the database-specific functionality.

- To provide application-specific data access architecture to improve performance, simplify programming, and improve maintainability.

An alternative to writing a custom data provider for a proprietary data source is to write an OLE DB provider for the data source and use the OLE DB .NET data provider to access the data through that OLE DB provider. This approach might make sense in situations when broad access to a full set of database features is required. Once the OLE DB provider is written, the data source can also be accessed not only with the OLE DB .NET data provider but by any application or tool that supports OLE DB provider data access.

A custom .NET data provider must at least support the DataSet through the IDataAdapter interface, and possibly the IDataParameter interface for parameterized queries. Such a minimal data provider allows a DataSet to be loaded with data from the data source, the modification of data within the DataSet, and the reconciliation of the changed DataSet with the data source. A minimal provider can support clients that deal primarily with a disconnected data, thereby functioning as a bridge between the DataSet and data source.

A complete .NET data provider supports the minimum functionality described here, as well as connected data access using connections, commands, and transactions. A complete .NET data provider implements the complete set of IData* and IDb* interfaces.

When developing a custom provider, you must first identify the ADO.NET interfaces and classes that must be implemented to achieve the required functionality. Unsupported classes and methods should raise a NotSupportedException or a NotImplementedException as appropriate.

Table 2-2 describes the available ADO.NET interfaces.

Table 2-2. ADO.NET interfaces

Interface	Description
IDbConnection	A unique session that communicates with the data source.
IDbTransaction	A local transaction. This interface supports nested transactions, although providers aren't required to support them.
IDbCommand	Represents a query, stored procedure, or command against the data source.
IDataParameter	Exposes properties and methods required to define parameters for commands. Implementing this interface is optional for an IDataAdapter-only provider.
IDataParameterCollection	Allows a user to implement a parameter to a command and its mapping to DataSet columns.
IDataReader	A read-only, forward-only stream of data from the data source.
IDataAdapter	A DataAdapter that populates a DataSet and reconciles any changes to the DataSet back to the data source. This is the only interface required for every .NET data provider implementation.
IDbDataAdapter	A DataAdapter for use with a relational database that inherits from IDataAdapter. It populates a DataSet and reconciles any changes to the DataSet back to the data source. The .NET Framework also includes a utility class called DbDataAdapter that can be inherited along with IDbDataAdapter, which helps implement the IDbDataAdapter interface.

A custom adapter can provide access to data stored in a relational database. It is important to remember that there are no constraints as to how the ADO.NET disconnected classes are filled and how the changed data is updated back to the data source. Consider a solution other than developing a custom .NET data provider, if it is appropriate.

For more information about implementing a custom .NET data provider and about the interfaces described in Table 2-2, consult the .NET Development documentation at *http://msdn.microsoft.com/library*.

3

Connections

Before you can perform any task with an ADO.NET data source, you need to open a connection. In ADO.NET, this means creating and using a Connection object. Connection objects are one of the simplest components in ADO.NET, but they encapsulate a fair bit of lower-level functionality, including user authentication information, a connection pooling mechanism, and a network connection (assuming the data source is located on a separate computer).

In this chapter, we'll examine the basics of the ADO.NET Connection object and the connection string settings you can configure. We'll also consider some finer points, including connection pooling—a key to highly scalable database applications—and connection events.

Connection Object Overview

The Connection object, like all provider-specific ADO.NET objects, comes in more than one version. You use the version that's tailored for your specific data source. Here are two examples:

- System.Data.SqlClient.SqlConnection allows you to connect to a SQL Server database (Version 7.0 or later).

- System.Data.OleDb.OleDbConnection allows you to connect to almost any data source with an associated OLE DB provider.

Every Connection object that accesses relational databases implements the common System.Data.IDbConnection interface. By looking at the IDbConnection interface, you'll quickly see the small set of properties and methods that every Connection object is guaranteed to support (see Tables 3-1 and 3-2). The most important of these are the Close( ) and Open( ) methods, and the ConnectionString property, which specifies a variety of options about the data source and how to connect to it. All IDbConnection properties are read-only, except ConnectionString.

Table 3-1. IDbConnection properties

Member	Description
ConnectionString	A string with name-value pairs of connection settings. These settings often include information such as the user to log in and the location of the database server. This is the only writeable property.
ConnectionTimeout	The time to wait for a connection to open before failing with a provider-specific exception (such as SqlException or OleDbException). The default is 15 seconds; 0 waits indefinitely. This value must be set through the connection string; the property is read-only.
Database	The name of the database to use once the connection is open. This can be set in the connection string and changed with the ChangeDatabase( ) method. Oracle databases don't support this property.
State	A bitwise connection of values from the ConnectionState enumeration. Currently, only Open and Closed are supported, and information isn't provided about whether the connection is currently retrieving data or executing a query.

Table 3-2. IDbConnection methods

Member	Description
BeginTransaction( )	Programmatically starts a database transaction. Database transactions are detailed in Chapter 16.
ChangeDatabase( )	Sets a new database to be used for subsequent operations. Alternatively, you can execute the SQL USE command with SQL Server. Oracle databases don't support this method.
CreateCommand( )	Returns a provider-specific IDbCommand object that is set to use this connection. This method is primarily useful when writing provider-agnostic code.
Open( ) and Close( )	Attempts to connect to or disconnect from the data source.

Other providers add additional members. For example, most Connection objects add the ServerVersion property (which contains a string with version information for the database product) and two events: StateChange (which fires when the connection is opened or closed) and InfoMessage (which fires when warning or error messages are received). SqlConnection also adds a WorkstationId and PacketSize property with additional information. For complete information about provider-specific members, refer to Part III.

The Connection String

When creating a connection, you must specify several pieces of required information. Typically, this includes the type of authentication or user to authenticate, the location of the database server, and the name of the database. In addition, OLE DB connection strings specify an OLE DB provider, and ODBC connection strings specify an ODBC driver. To specify this information, use the ConnectionString property.

The ConnectionString contains a series of name/value settings delimited by semicolons (;). The order of these settings is unimportant, as is the capitalization. Taken together, they specify the information needed to create a connection.

Table 3-3 describes some settings you can use. Parameters that are used for connection pooling are omitted; they are discussed later in this chapter.

 Connection strings are data source-specific, although they tend to have broad similarities. Most parameters in Table 3-2 are supported by the SQL Server, OLE DB, and Oracle providers, although some exceptions apply. Consult the documentation for your particular database product or your OLE DB or ODBC driver for more information.

Table 3-3. Basic connection string parameters

Parameter	Description
AttachDBFilename / Initial File Name	Used only if you want to connect to an attachable database file (for example, an *.mdf* file that isn't registered with the database system). Normally, you use the Initial Catalog parameter instead.
Connect Timeout / Connection Timeout	The length of time (in seconds) to wait for a connection to the server before terminating the attempt and generating an error. Defaults to 15 seconds, and 0 seconds represents an infinite wait.
Data Source / Server / Address / Addr / Network Address	The server name or network address of the database product to connect to. Use localhost for the current computer.
Initial Catalog / Database	The name of the database to use for all subsequent operations (insertions, deletions, queries, and so on).
Integrated Security / Trusted_Connection	Defaults to false. When set to true or SSPI, the .NET provider attempts to connect to the data source using Windows integrated security.
Persist Security Info	When set to false (the default), security-sensitive information such as the password is removed from the ConnectionString property as soon as the connection is opened. Thus, you can't retrieve this information in your code.
User ID	The database account user ID.
Password/Pwd	The password corresponding to the User ID.

Table 3-4 lists some connection string settings that are specific to SQL Server.

Table 3-4. SQL Server connection string parameters

Parameter	Description
Current Language	The SQL Server language record name.
Network Library / Net	The network library used to establish a connection to an instance of SQL Server. Supported values include dbnmpntw (Named Pipes), dbmsrpcn (Multiprotocol), dbmsadsn (Apple Talk), dbmsgnet (VIA), dbmsipcn (Shared Memory), dbmsspxn (IPX/SPX), and dbmssocn (TCP/IP), which is the default.
Packet Size	The size in bytes of the network packets that communicate with an instance of SQL Server (defaults to 8192).
Workstation ID	The name of the workstation connecting to SQL Server. Defaults to the local computer name.

Setting Connection String Parameters

The following code snippet shows how you might set the ConnectionString property on a SqlConnection object. The actual connection string details are omitted.

```
SqlConnection con = new SqlConnection();
con.ConnectionString = "...";
```

All standard ADO.NET Connection objects also provide a constructor that accepts a value for the ConnectionString property. For example, the following code statement creates a SqlConnection object and sets the ConnectionString property in one statement. It's equivalent to the previous example.

```
SqlConnection con = new SqlConnection("...");
```

The next few sections present some sample connection strings with commonly used settings. Because the connection string varies depending on the provider, these examples are separated into provider-specific sections.

The SQL Server connection string

When using a SQL Server database, you need to specify the server name using the Data Source parameter (use localhost for the current computer), the Initial Catalog parameter (the database name), and the authentication information.

You have two options for supplying the authentication information. If your database uses SQL Server authentication, you can pass a user ID and password defined in SQL Server. This account should have permissions for the tables you want to access:

```
SqlConnection con = new SqlConnection("Data Source=localhost;" +
        "Initial Catalog=Northwind;user id=userid;password=password");
```

If your database allows integrated Windows authentication, you can signal this fact with the Integrated Security=SSPI connection string parameter. The Windows operating system then supplies the user account token for the currently logged-in user. This is more secure because the login information doesn't need to be visible in the code (or transmitted over the network):

```
SqlConnection con = new SqlConnection("Data Source=localhost;" +
        "Initial Catalog=Northwind;Integrated Security=SSPI");
```

Keep in mind that integrated security won't always execute in the security context of the application user. For example, consider a distributed application that performs a database query through a web service. If the web service connects using integrated authentication, it uses the login account of the ASP.NET worker process, not the account of the client making the request. The story is similar with a component exposed through .NET remoting, which uses the account that loaded the remote component host.

The MSDE connection string

MSDE is a scaled-down, freely distributable version of SQL Server you can use to develop very small systems with less than five users (see Appendix C for a brief overview). MSDE uses the same connection string format as SQL Server (in fact,

MSDE uses the SQL Server engine under the hood). Like SQL Server, MSDE supports integrated authentication and SQL authentication. The only difference is found in the Data Source parameter, which consists of two parts: the computer name and the data source name, separated by a backslash character. The data source name will be NetSDK if MSDE was installed from the .NET framework SDK, or VSdotNET if installed as part of Visual Studio .NET. If you are using MSDE on the local machine, the server name should be set to localhost.

Here's an example that connects to an MSDE instance on the local computer that was installed from the .NET framework SDK:

```
SqlConnection con = new SqlConnection("Data Source=localhost\\NetSDK;" +
        "Initial Catalog=Northwind;Integrated Security=SSPI");
```

The OLE DB connection string

The OLE DB connection string resembles the SQL Server connection string. However, the support for some parameters depends on the OLE DB provider you use. Typically, an OLE DB connection string requires a Data Source parameter (use localhost for the current computer), the Initial Catalog parameter (the database name), and the user id and password parameters. It also requires a Provider setting that indicates which OLE DB provider to use.

The following code snippet shows a sample connection string that connects to a SQL Server database through the OLE DB provider. This is the only way to connect to a version of SQL Server earlier than 7.0:

```
OleDbConnection con = new OleDbConnection("Data Source=localhost;" +
        "Initial Catalog=Northwind;user id=sa;password=secret;" +
        "Provider=SQLOLEDB");
```

Here's an example that connects to an Access database file through the Jet provider:

```
OleDbConnection con = new OleDbConnection("Data Source=localhost;" +
        "Initial Catalog=c:\Nortwdind.mdb;" +
        "Provider=Microsoft.Jet.OLEDB.4.0");
```

The ODBC .NET connection string

The ODBC connection string resembles the SQL Server and OLE DB connection strings. However, the support for some parameters depends on the ODBC driver used. Typically, an ODBC connection string requires a Data Source parameter (use localhost for the current computer), the Initial Catalog parameter (the database name), and the user id and password parameters. It also requires a Driver setting that indicates the ODBC driver to use, or its data source name (DSN), which associates a symbolic name with a group of database settings that otherwise goes into the connection string. The DSN must be enclosed in curly braces and match exactly.

Here is an example that accesses an Excel file:

```
OdbcConnection con = new OdbcConnection(
        "Driver={Microsoft Excel Driver (*.xls)};" +
        "DBQ=c:\book1.xls");
```

Here's an example that uses the ODBC driver for MySQL (available from *www. mysql.com*). It adds a new connection string setting, Option, which configures certain low-level behaviors to support specific clients. For more information, refer to the MySQL documentation.

```
OdbcConnection con = new OdbcConnection(
        "Driver={MySQL ODBC 3.51 Driver};" +
        "Database=test;UID=root;PWD=secret;Option=3");
```

Use the Data Sources icon (in the Administrative Tools portion of the Control Panel) to configure ODBC DSN settings or add new drivers.

The Oracle .NET connection string

The Microsoft Oracle provider supports a smaller subset of connection-string options, as shown in Table 3-3. The Oracle provider also includes connection string settings that allow you to configure connection pooling. These are described in Chapter 5.

Here's how you can create an OracleConnection with a connection string:

```
OracleConnection con = new OracleConnection(
        "Data Source=Oracle8i;Integrated Security=true");
```

Security Risks of the Connection String

Be careful if you are constructing a connection string dynamically based on user input. For example, make sure you check that the user has not inserted any extra semicolons (or that all semicolons are contained inside apostrophes). Otherwise, the user can add additional connection string parameters, possibly tricking your code into connecting to the wrong database.

For example, you might request a password and place it in a connection string as follows:

```
connectionString = "Data Source=localhost;" +
  "Initial Catalog=Northwind;user id=" + txtUser.Text +
  ";password=" + txtPassword.Text;
```

In this case, a problem occurs if the user submits a password in the form ValidPassword;Initial Catalog=ValidDatabase. The connection string will now have two Initial Catalog parameters, and it will use the second one, which the user appended to the end of the password!

To overcome this sort of problem, you should never allow a user to specify connection string parameters directly. Consider storing this information in a configuration file.

Opening and Closing Connections

You've now seen all the ingredients you need to create and use a connection. You simply create the Connection object required for your data source, apply the appropriate connection string settings, and open the connection. In Example 3-1,

---

a connection is created to a SQL Server database on the local computer using integrated authentication. The code opens the connection, tests its state, and closes it.

Example 3-1. Opening and testing a connection

```
// ConnectionTest.cs - Opens and verifies a connection

using System;
using System.Data.SqlClient;

public class ConnectionTest
{
    public static void Main()
    {
        SqlConnection con = new SqlConnection("Data Source=localhost;" +
            "Initial Catalog=Northwind;Integrated Security=SSPI");

        con.Open();
        Console.WriteLine("Connection is " + con.State.ToString());

        con.Close();
        Console.WriteLine("Connection is " + con.State.ToString());
    }
}
```

The output clearly indicates whether the connection test is successful:

```
Connection is Open
Connection is Closed
```

Connection Events

Connection objects expose only two events. The InfoMessage event can retrieve warnings and other messages from a data source. Generally, you use this event if you wish to receive specific information messages that don't correspond to errors (in SQL Server, these are messages with a severity of 10 or less). You can't use this event to be informed about errors, which simply causes the Connection object to throw an exception.

The message information is wrapped into a provider-specific EventArgs object, such as OleDbInfoMessageEventArgs or SqlInfoMessageEventArgs.

You can examine this object for the error number and message text, as well as the additional provider-specific information. For example, SQL Server provides information about the database, stored procedure, and line number where the message originated.

Here's an example event handler for the InfoMessage event:

```
    private void OnInfoMessage(object sender, SqlInfoMessageEventArgs args)
    {
        foreach (SqlError err in args.Errors)
        {
            Console.WriteLine("The {0} has received a severity {1}, " +
                "state {2} error number {3} on line {4} of procedure {5} " +
```

```
                "on server {6}", err.Source, err.Class, err.State, err.Number,
            err.LineNumber, err.Procedure, err.Server);
    }
}
```

You can connect the event handler any time after creating the Connection object:

```
con.InfoMessage += new SqlInfoMessageEventHandler(OnInfoMessage);
```

Connection objects also provide a StateChange event that fires when the connection is opened or closed. This event provides a StateChangeEventArgs object with information about the current and previous state as a value from the System.Data. ConnectionState enumeration. Currently, the StateChange event fires only when the connection is opened or closed (not to inform you about other ConnectionState values), which reduces its usefulness dramatically.

Connections and Exception Handling

Exception handling is critical when accessing an external resource such as a database, as you can't guarantee the success of your operations. Problems such as a heavy user load, a misbehaving network connection, or invalid connection string parameters can derail your attempts to use or open a connection. However, because database connections are a finite resource, you also need to make sure you close a connection after a problem occurs. For example, consider this poorly written ADO.NET code:

```
try
{
    con.Open();
    // (Execute an ADO.NET command here.)
    con.Close();
}
catch (Exception err)
{
    Console.WriteLine(err.ToString());
}
```

If an error occurs after opening the connection but before closing it, the connection is left open. This potentially locks out other users until the garbage collector finds the Connection object and disposes it (at which point any outstanding transactions are rolled back, and the Dispose( ) method is invoked automatically). In a large, heavily used distributed application, this mistake can have a serious detrimental effect on user concurrency.

The correct approach is to create your ADO.NET objects outside the exception handler, open the connection inside the exception handler, and use the finally block to close the connection. This ensures that the Connection will always be closed, even if an error occurs.

```
try
{
    con.Open();
    // (Execute an ADO.NET command here.)
}
catch (err)
```

```
{
    Console.WriteLine(err.ToString());
}
finally
{
    con.Close();
}
```

If an exception such as SqlException, OleDbException, or OdbcException is thrown by a Connection or Command object, it's provider-specific. This exception can represent invalid query syntax, invalid user credentials, the inability to find the specified data source, or any one of a host of other problems. Provider-specific exceptions don't derive from a common base class that identifies them as ADO. NET exceptions, which can make it difficult to write generic code that works with different providers.

Disposing Connections

Instead of using an exception handling block, you can use the C# using statement with the Connection object. This ensures that Dispose( ) will be called on the Connection when code inside the using block ends. The Dispose( ) method is always called, regardless of whether the statements conclude successfully or an unhandled exception is thrown.

```
using (con)
{
    con.Open();
    // (Execute an ADO.NET command here.)
}
// (con.Dispose() is called automatically.)
```

This approach is similar to the previous example because the Dispose( ) method also closes the connection. However, it's *not* equivalent because the Dispose( ) method also releases all the unmanaged resources associated with the Connection object and removes it from the connection pool. This distinction means that this approach isn't suitable for most large-scale applications because it removes the key benefits of connection pooling (discussed in the next section).

Connection Pooling

Connection pooling recycles a set of open connections to save time—a key requirement in enterprise-level database applications. Without connection pooling, your application might be able to support a large throughput but will provide poor scalability. For example, you might find that your system can easily handle 10 simultaneous clients performing 1,000 transactions/minute but falters with 1,000 clients performing 10 transactions/minute, even though the overall transaction throughput is the same.

The problem is that acquiring a database connection automatically imposes some overhead. This is because the process of establishing a connection requires several lower-level operations, including a verification of security credentials. If your system is characterized by a large number of clients that frequently connect, perform a single operation, and then disconnect, the overhead required to create connections can become a crippling bottleneck. This is typical in a large stateless distributed application, such as an ASP.NET web site or web service.

To counteract this effect, most database access frameworks support connection pooling. Connection pooling works by retaining a pool of available connections. When a client requests a connection, it's served directly from the available pool, rather than recreated. In a large system with a quick turnover of database connections, this automatic reuse can save CPU cycles and network bandwidth.

ADO.NET doesn't include a connection-pooling mechanism. However, most ADO.NET providers do implement some form of connection pooling. In the case of the SQL Server and Oracle providers, this connection pooling mechanism is written entirely in managed code. In the case of the OLE DB and ODBC providers, this connection pooling depends on a lower level and has a few limitations. Most providers enable connection pooling automatically. However, you may be able to use connection string parameters to configure pool size settings.

All forms of connection pooling work by examining the connection string. A connection is reused only if the connection string matches exactly. Most ADO. NET providers use a case-sensitive full-text matching algorithm. This means that even if you have the same connection string parameters, but they are in a different order, the connections isn't reused. (The ODP .NET provider from Oracle is one exception.) To ensure that your connections can be reused, store the connection string in a single location (such as a configuration file) and don't enter it directly in your code.

The following example demonstrates how connection pooling works with a single Connection object:

```
string conString1 = "Data Source=localhost;" +
  "Initial Catalog=Northwind;Integrated Security=SSPI");

string conString2 = "Data Source=localhost;" +
  "Initial Catalog=pubs;Integrated Security=SSPI");

SqlConnection con = new SqlConnection();

con.ConnectionString = conString1;
con.Open();
// The initial pool is created (we'll call it pool A).

con.Close()
// The connection is returned to pool A.

con.ConnectionString = conString2;
con.Open();
// A new pool is created (pool B), because the connection strings differ.

con.Close()
// This connection is returned to pool B.
```

```
con.ConnectionString = conString1;
con.Open();
// The open connection from pool A is reused. This saves time.

con.Close()
// The connection is returned to pool A.
```

You'll notice several important factors in this example:

- It doesn't matter whether you are using one Connection object or several Connection objects. When you call Close( ), the underlying connection is placed in the pool. When you call Open( ), the provider searches the pool for available connections.

- Connections are reused only if the parameters match. This makes sense—in the previous example, you wouldn't reuse a connection to the Northwind database if the client thinks it is opening a connection to the pubs database. Similarly, a change in security information (for example, the user account and password) or the location of the database server would cause problems if connections were reused indiscriminately.

- If no pool exists, it is created the first time you call Open( ). Depending on connection string settings, the pool may be initially populated with a set number of connections, or it may be limited to a certain maximum number.

SQL Server and Oracle Connection Pooling

With SQL Server, Oracle, and MSDE, connection pooling is implemented by the managed provider, unless you have specifically disabled it with a connection string parameter.

Both the SQL Server and Oracle .NET providers give you some control over connection pooling with the connection string parameters in Table 3-5. Note that if you require a minimum pool size, the application incurs a small performance overhead when the first client connects, and the initial pool of connections is created. Note also that the connections are created one after the other, ensuring that the database server isn't flooded with simultaneous requests when the pool is first created.

Table 3-5. Connection string parameters for connection pooling

Parameter	Description
Connection Lifetime	Specifies a time interval in seconds. If a connection is returned to the pool, and it is older than the specified Connection Lifetime, it is destroyed. The default is 0, which disables this behavior. This feature is useful primarily when you need to recycle a large number of connections at once, such as when you want to balance the load with a new server that has just been brought online.
Connection Reset[a]	If true (the default), the connection state is reset when a pooled connection is reused. This setting requires an extra round trip but makes for easier programming (and is recommended). State includes session-level SET statements and the currently selected database.
Enlist	When true (the default), the connection is enlisted in the current transaction context of the creation thread.
Max Pool Size	The maximum number of connections allowed in the pool (defaults to 100).

Table 3-5. Connection string parameters for connection pooling (continued)

Parameter	Description
Min Pool Size	The minimum number of connections always retained in the pool (defaults to 0).
Pooling	When `true` (the default), the connection object is drawn from the appropriate pool or, if necessary, is created and added to the appropriate pool.

a This property isn't supported by the Oracle .NET provider.

As with all forms of connection pooling, every pool is divided into multiple transaction-specific pools (and one pool for connections that aren't currently enlisted in a transaction). Fortunately, this process is managed transparently, and threads associated with a particular transaction context automatically receive a connection from the appropriate pool. However, it does mean that using client-initiated transactions can reduce the efficacy of connection pooling.

OLE DB and ODBC Connection Pooling

OLE DB connection pooling doesn't need to be explicitly enabled because it uses the built-in OLE DB session pooling features. However, OLE DB connection pooling doesn't support explicit configuration of thresholds and pool sizes. Thus, it is technically possible to actually achieve better performance by disabling connection pooling and implementing COM+ object pooling in its place. However, this is a complex task, and isn't recommended unless you are comfortable with terms such as *manual transaction enlistment*.* Microsoft provides OLE DB developer documentation that includes more information about this low-level process. The first step is to disable OLE DB resource pooling and automatic transaction enlistment by including OLE DB Services=-4 in the connection string.

The ODBC .NET provider uses the connection pooling that's implemented by the ODBC driver. You can configure pooling settings for ODBC drivers using the Connection Pooling tab in the Data Sources window.

Connection Pooling and Application Domains

One caveat applies with the managed connection pooling mechanisms in the SQL Server and Oracle providers: connections can be pooled only in a single application domain. In other words, if your system is made up of Windows clients that use your custom data access class locally, they can't share a pool of connections. Instead, they each have their own local pool of connections, which is far less useful. Figure 3-1 shows this situation.

To allow connection pooling, you need to host the custom data class out-of-process on a separate server, using ASP.NET, web services, or .NET remoting. In the case of ASP.NET and web services, the ASP.NET worker threads share a common pool of connections. With remoting, every component host shares a connection pool. Figure 3-2 diagrams this approach.

---

* If you'd still like to dive right into to this topic, try the excellent OLE DB developer documentation on MSDN at *http://msdn.microsoft.com/library/en-us/oledb/htm/oledbresourcepooling.asp.*

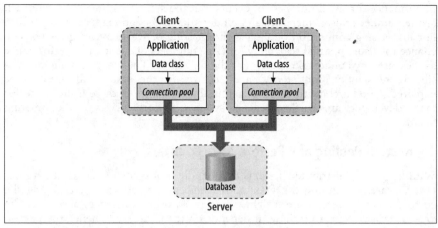

Figure 3-1. Direct database access: no connection pooling

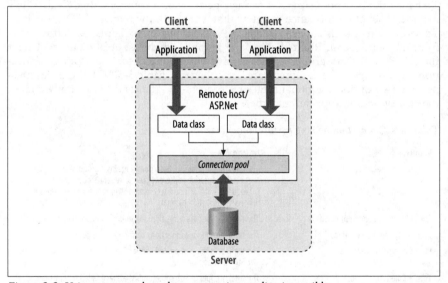

Figure 3-2. Using a remote data class: connection pooling is possible

Of course, that doesn't mean you should replace local data classes with a more complex architecture based on web services or remoting. In fact, if you do, you could actually harm performance in a small-scale system. Communicating with an out-of-process component is an order of magnitude slower than communicating with a local in-memory object. When you also factor in the time taken to send a call over a network or serialize a message to XML, the latency becomes a notice-able drag on performance.

What you are faced with is a tradeoff between sheer performance for small numbers and scalability. Using clients with local data classes ensures the best performance for small numbers of clients, but the system will reach a bottleneck as the number of users increases and, under a large enough load, start to perform horribly. Using connection pooling with remoting or web services gives you the chance to ensure optimal scalability for large numbers of clients. But performance as measured by application speed isn't the only issue. The maintainability, extensibility, reusability, consistency, and security of the system all need to be explored. Good architecture and design is about balance of these factors, and for many developers architecting mid-size systems, performance isn't a key driving factor.

Connection Pooling and Performance Counters

With large-scale distributed systems that handle thousands of clients, it's important to carefully choose the maximum connection pool size. Determining the correct size requires a little insight, some real-world experience, and a healthy dose of trial-and-error profiling. It depends on the number of clients, the pattern of usage, and the server hardware. This section will help with the insight.

To gauge the best pool size, you can use performance counters. By default, .NET includes a set of performance counters that work with the managed SQL provider. To work with them, choose Programs → Administrative Tools → Performance from the Start menu. Right-click on the graph, and choose Add Counter. Under the .NET CLR Data group is a series of useful counters for monitoring connection pool usage. The counters are described in Table 3-6. All these counters provide two options: a global total or a process-specific total (you simply choose the corresponding application name).

Table 3-6. Connection pooling performance categories

Counter	Description
Current # connection pools	Current number of pools. Each pool contains a group of connections that can be reused for different clients. Separate pools will be created for requests with different connection strings or for connections in different transaction contexts.
Current # pooled and nonpooled connections	The total number of connections, including those in the pool.
Current # pooled connections	The total number of connections currently in the pool.
Peak # pooled connections	The highest number of pooled connections that was reached since the .NET process was started.
Total # failed commands	The total number of SQL commands that have failed for any reason. Not directly related to connection pooling, but can suggest other problems.
Total # failed connects	The total number of connection attempts that have failed for any reason. Not directly related to connection pooling, but can suggest other problems.

The .NET data counters can be added to the graph and logged through the MMC Performance snap-in, or you can use a dedicated testing tool such as Microsoft Application Center Test. In a typical test, you might measure the pool-usage statistics and record the performance of your application using a machine-specific counter simultaneously. This test allows you to see how the performance is affected by different numbers of users and usage patterns.

 If you use SQL Server, you can also use counters in the SQLServer:GeneralStatistics category, which includes a User Connections counter that lists the total number of current connections.

4

Commands

Every interaction between a client and a data source, whether it is to retrieve information, delete a record, or commit a change, is governed by a Command object. In this chapter, we introduce the Command object in detail. You'll learn how to define a command and use it to execute nonquery commands such as direct record updates, insertions, and deletions. You'll also learn how to use parameterized commands and commands that access stored procedures.

Command Object Overview

The Command object is the heart of data processing with ADO.NET. Typically, the Command object wraps a SQL statement or a call to a stored procedure. For example, you might use a Command object to execute a SQL UPDATE, DELETE, INSERT, or SELECT statement. However, ADO.NET providers that don't represent databases may use their own nomenclature. The only rule is that the Command.CommandText property, which defines the command, must be a string.

As with the Connection object, the Command object is specific to the data provider. Two examples are:

- System.Data.SqlClient.SqlCommand executes commands against SQL Server Version 7.0 or later.

- System.Data.OleDb.OleDbCommand executes commands against an OLE DB data provider.

Each Command object implements the System.Data.IDbCommand interface. That means it is guaranteed to support the members shown in Tables 4-1 and 4-2. At a minimum, you must set the CommandText and a reference to a valid Connection before using a Command. In addition, you must modify the CommandType default value if you wish to invoke a stored procedure.

Table 4-1. IDbCommand properties

Member	Description
CommandText	Contains the SQL statement, stored procedure name, or table name. For an unusual provider (one that doesn't work with a database), this can contain something entirely different and proprietary; the only requirement is that is must be formatted as a string.
CommandTimeout	The amount of time (in seconds) to wait for a command to complete before giving up and throwing an exception. The default is 30 seconds.
CommandType	Indicates the format used for the CommandText property. You can use Text (the default) for a SQL command, StoredProcedure for a stored procedure call, or TableDirect for one or more tables (which is a poor scalability choice because it returns all rows and columns from the named table).
Connection	References the IDbConnection object to use for this command. The connection must be open before you execute the command.
Parameters	A collection of input, output, or bidirectional parameter objects. This is used only for parameterized queries or stored procedure calls.
Transaction	Gets or sets the transaction that this command is part of. Transactions are examined in Chapter 16.
UpdatedRowSource	Specifies how this command updates a data source when it is used with a DataSet and IDbDataAdapter. We'll return to this topic in the next chapter.

Table 4-2. IDbCommand methods

Member	Description
Cancel( )	Tries to stop a running command. In order to invoke this method, you must start the command on a separate thread, because all commands execute synchronously. Otherwise, your code will be stalled and won't have a chance to call the Cancel( ) method.
CreateParameter( )	Creates a new Parameter object, which can be added to the Command.Parameters collection.
ExecuteReader( )	Executes the command and returns a forward-only read-only cursor in the form of a DataReader.
ExecuteNonQuery( )	Executes the command and returns the number of rows that were affected. Often used with record UPDATE, DELETE, or INSERT statements.
ExecuteScalar( )	Executes the command, and retrieves a single value. Used with aggregate functions and in cases where you want to return the first column of the first row of a result set.
Prepare( )	If CommandType is StoredProcedure, you can use this method to precompile the command in the data source. If you perform this task before calling the same stored procedure with different parameters, you may achieve a small performance increase, depending on the provider. However, it requires an additional roundtrip to the data source, so don't use it unless you have tested it and are sure it actually provides a measurable benefit.

Creating and Executing a Command

When creating a Command object, you have the choice of several constructors. The most useful accepts a CommandText value and a Connection. Here's an example with the SqlCommand class:

```
SqlConnection con = new SqlConnection(connectionString);
SqlCommand cmd = new SqlCommand(commandText, con);
```

For standard providers, there are three ways to execute a command: ExecuteNonQuery( ), ExecuteReader( ), and ExecuteScalar( ). You choose one of these methods, depending on the type of command you are executing. For example, ExecuteReader( ) returns a DataReader and provides read-only access to query results. We examine the DataReader in Chapter 5.

Some providers include additional members. For example, the ADO.NET SQL Server provider includes an ExecuteXmlReader( ) method that retrieves data as an XML document. We'll examine this specialized version in Chapter 17, which considers ADO.NET's support for XML.

Executing a Command That Doesn't Return Rows

The SQL language includes several nonquery commands. The best known include UPDATE, DELETE, and INSERT. You can also use other commands to create, alter, or drop tables, constraints, relations, and so on. To execute any of these commands, just set the CommandText property with the full SQL statement, open a connection, and invoke the ExecuteNonQuery( ) method. The next sections consider examples that update, delete, and insert records.

Updating a record

The UPDATE statement, at its simplest, uses the following syntax:

```
UPDATE table SET update_expression WHERE search_condition
```

The UPDATE expression can thus modify a single record, or it can apply a change to an entire batch of records in a single table. Example 4-1 puts the UPDATE statement to work with a simple command that modifies a single field in a single category record in the Northwind database.

Example 4-1. Updating a record

```
// UpdateRecord.cs - Updates a single Category record

using System;
using System.Data.SqlClient;

public class UpdateRecord
{
    public static void Main()
    {
        string connectionString = "Data Source=localhost;" +
                "Initial Catalog=Northwind;Integrated Security=SSPI";
        string SQL = "UPDATE Categories SET CategoryName='Beverages'" +
                "WHERE CategoryID=1";

        // Create ADO.NET objects.
        SqlConnection con = new SqlConnection(connectionString);
        SqlCommand cmd = new SqlCommand(SQL, con);

        // Execute the command.
        con.Open();
        int rowsAffected = cmd.ExecuteNonQuery();
```

Example 4-1. Updating a record (continued)

```
        con.Close();

        // Display the result of the operation.
        Console.WriteLine(rowsAffected.ToString() + " row(s) affected");
    }
}
```

Note that the ExecuteNonQuery( ) method returns the number of rows affected, not the row itself. In order to see the results of the change, you need to either query the row or use a tool such as SQL Server's Enterprise Manager to browse the database.

If the UPDATE statement fails to update any records because the WHERE clause is too restrictive, an error isn't generated. You must examine number of affected rows to determine if this is this case. If you are adding this logic to a custom data access component, you might want to raise an exception if this happens, because it indicates that no update took place.

Deleting a record

The SQL DELETE statement simply specifies a search condition that selects one or more records to be removed:

```
DELETE FROM table WHERE search_condition
```

You can modify the previous example to delete a record simply by changing the SQL variable:

```
string SQL = "DELETE FROM Categories WHERE CategoryID=1";
```

Inserting a record

Finally, you can insert a record using a list of column names, followed by a list of column values in the same order:

```
INSERT INTO table (column_list) VALUES (value_list)
```

Once again, the console example can be adapted to insert a category record just by modifying the SQL text:

```
string SQL = "INSERT INTO Categories (CategoryName, Description) " +
    "VALUES ('Beverages', 'Soft drinks, coffees, teas, beers, and ales')";
```

Note that the category table includes a CategoryID column that is configured as a unique identity value. That means the CategoryID number is created by the data source, which ensures that duplicate IDs don't occur. For that reason, the INSERT statement doesn't include a CategoryID value. As a side effect, this code will always succeed and create a new row with identical information, but with a new CategoryID. (If you want to replace a row you deleted in the previous example, you can manually specify a CategoryID with the value of 1).

Executing a Command That Returns a Single Value

ExecuteScalar( ) method returns a single value. If you perform a query, this will be the first value in the first column of the first row. More likely, you'll use ExecuteNonQuery( ) to return an aggregate value, which is the result of a calculation using a subset of rows.

An aggregate function must be part of a SQL SELECT statement, which indicates the table and (optionally) a search filter and sort order:

```
SELECT aggregate_expression FROM tables [WHERE search_condition]
    [ORDER BY order_expression ASC | DESC]
```

Example 4-2 shows how an aggregate command can retrieve the total number of orders for the year 1996.

Example 4-2. Executing an aggregate function

```
// TotalOrders.cs - Gets the number of order records from 1996

using System;
using System.Data.SqlClient;

public class TotalOrders
{
    public static void Main()
    {
        string connectionString = "Data Source=localhost;" +
                "Initial Catalog=Northwind;Integrated Security=SSPI";
        string SQL = "SELECT COUNT(*) FROM Orders WHERE " +
                "OrderDate >= '1996-01-01' AND OrderDate < '1997-01-01'";


        // Create ADO.NET objects.
        SqlConnection con = new SqlConnection(connectionString);
        SqlCommand cmd = new SqlCommand(SQL, con);

        // Execute the command.
        con.Open();
        int result = (int)cmd.ExecuteScalar();
        con.Close();

        // Display the result of the operation.
        Console.WriteLine(result.ToString() + " rows in 1996");
    }
}
```

Here's the sample output for this code:

```
152 rows in 1996
```

Parameter Object Overview

In the examples shown so far, the SQL command text and the data values have been embedded in a single string. This approach is easy, and convenient for writing data access code. However, it also has significant drawbacks that make it unsuitable for a production-level application. These include inflexibility, poor performance, and potential security problems when using user-supplied values.

To overcome these problems, you need to use another feature of the Command object: parameters. Command parameters are conceptually the same as method parameters in an ordinary piece of .NET code. The most common type of parameter is an *input parameter*, which carries information from your application to the data source. You can use an input parameter when calling a stored procedure or when coding a parameterized query. In addition, you can use *output parameters*, which return information from the data source to your code, or *bidirectional parameters*, which transmit values in both directions. Output and bidirectional parameters are used only when you are making stored procedure calls.

Every Command object has an associated collection of Parameter objects (referenced by its Parameters property). The Parameter object is a provider-specific object, which means a SqlCommand uses a SqlParameter, an OleDbCommand uses an OleDbParameter, and so on.

Creating Parameters

In order to create a Parameter object, you must specify a parameter name, and the exact data type for the information it will contain. For the managed OLE DB provider, you specify data types using the System.Data.OleDb.OleDbType enumeration. For the SQL Server data provider, you use the System.Data.SqlDbType enumeration. If the data type is a variable-length field such as a string or binary field, you also need to indicate the field length.

For example, the following code snippet shows how to create a SqlParameter object named @MyParam with a SQL Server integer type. Note that the name is preceded with an @ symbol; this is a convention of stored procedure programming with SQL Server, but it is by no means a necessity in your code.

```
SqlParameter param = new SqlParameter("@MyParam", SqlDbType.Int);
```

To use a variable-length data type, you need to use a different constructor that accepts a field length, as shown here:

```
SqlParameter param = new SqlParameter("@MyParam", SqlDbType.NVarChar,
                                      15);
```

Once you've created a Parameter, you will probably want to assign a value and add it to an existing Command:

```
SqlCommand cmd = new SqlCommand(commandText, con);

SqlParameter param = new SqlParameter("@Description", SqlDbType.VarChar,
                                      88, "Description");
param.Value = "This is the description";

cmd.Add(param);
```

Alternatively, you can create the `Parameter` and add it to the `Command` in one step using an overloaded version of the `Add( )` method. This method returns a reference to the newly created `Parameter` object, allowing you to quickly set a value.

```
SqlCommand cmd = new SqlCommand(commandText, con);

SqlParameter param = cmd.Add("@Description", SqlDbType.VarChar,
                             88, "Description");
param.Value = "This is the description";
```

By default, when you create a parameter, it is configured as an input parameter, meaning that the `Parameter.Direction` property is set to `ParameterDirection.Input`.

You can retrieve parameters from the `Parameters` collection by index number or by the assigned parameter name:

```
// Select the first parameter.
param = cmd.Parameters[0];

// Select the parameter with the name "@Description".
param = cmd.Parameters["@Description"];
```

Now that you can create and configure `Parameter` objects, it's time to consider how to use them to build a parameterized command.

Parameterized Commands

Parameterized commands are executed in the same way as normal commands. They simply use placeholders to separate literal values from the query itself. For example, consider the following dynamically constructed command (used in Example 4-1):

```
UPDATE Categories SET CategoryName='Beverages'
  WHERE CategoryID=1
```

As a parameterized command with the SQL Server provider, it takes this form:

```
UPDATE Categories SET CategoryName=@CategoryName
  WHERE CategoryID=@CategoryID
```

You then add two `Parameter` objects to the `Command`, with the names `@CategoryName` and `@CategoryID`. Now set the values for both these `Parameter` objects to Beverages and 1, respectively, and invoke the command. Example 4-3 shows a full example that rewrites Example 4-1 to use a parameterized command.

Example 4-3. Updating a record with a parameterized command (SQL Server)

```
// ParameterizedUpdateSQL.cs - Updates a single Category record

using System;
using System.Data;
using System.Data.SqlClient;

public class UpdateRecord
{
```

Example 4-3. Updating a record with a parameterized command (SQL Server) (continued)

```
public static void Main()
{
    string connectionString = "Data Source=localhost;" +
                "Initial Catalog=Northwind;Integrated Security=SSPI";
    string SQL = "UPDATE Categories SET CategoryName=@CategoryName " +
                "WHERE CategoryID=@CategoryID";

    // Create ADO.NET objects.
    SqlConnection con = new SqlConnection(connectionString);
    SqlCommand cmd = new SqlCommand(SQL, con);

    SqlParameter param;
    param = cmd.Parameters.Add("@CategoryName", SqlDbType.NVarChar, 15);
    param.Value = "Beverages";

    param = cmd.Parameters.Add("@CategoryID", SqlDbType.Int);
    param.Value = 1;

    // Execute the command.
    con.Open();
    int rowsAffected = cmd.ExecuteNonQuery();
    con.Close();

    // Display the result of the operation.
    Console.WriteLine(rowsAffected.ToString() + " row(s) affected");
}
}
```

Note that in order for this to work, the Command.CommandType property must be CommandType.Text, which is the default.

The SQL Server provider matches the parameter values to the query placeholders by using the parameter name. With the OLE DB provider, parameterized queries take a slightly different syntax. Instead of using named parameters, you use question-mark placeholders:

```
SELECT * FROM Customers WHERE CustomerID = ?
```

If you have more than one question mark in the same query, the OLE DB provider matches them to the question marks based on their order. Thus the first parameter you add should correspond to the first question mark in your query. Example 4-4 shows how you would approach the same task using the OLE DB provider. In this case, both Parameter objects are still assigned the same names, but these names aren't used in the query. The position alone is significant.

Example 4-4. Updating a record with a parameterized command (OLE DB)

```
// ParameterizedUpdateOLEDB.cs - Updates a single Category record

using System;
using System.Data.OleDb;
```

Example 4-4. Updating a record with a parameterized command (OLE DB) (continued)

```
public class UpdateRecord
{
    public static void Main()
    {
        string connectionString = "Data Source=localhost;" +
                    "Initial Catalog=Northwind;Provider=SQLOLEDB;" +
                    "Integrated Security=SSPI";
        string SQL = "UPDATE Categories SET CategoryName=? " +
                    "WHERE CategoryID=?";

        // Create ADO.NET objects.
        OleDbConnection con = new OleDbConnection(connectionString);
        OleDbCommand cmd = new OleDbCommand(SQL, con);

        OleDbParameter param;
        param = cmd.Parameters.Add("@CategoryName", OleDbType.VarWChar, 15);
        param.Value = "Beverages";

        param = cmd.Parameters.Add("@CategoryID", OleDbType.Integer);
        param.Value = 1;

        // Execute the command.
        con.Open();
        int rowsAffected = cmd.ExecuteNonQuery();
        con.Close();

        // Display the result of the operation.
        Console.WriteLine(rowsAffected.ToString() + " row(s) affected");
    }
}
```

Parameterized commands have several benefits:

They are less error-prone. You can code the SQL statement in a single long string, rather than piece it together, where it is notoriously easy to mistype.

They are more secure. Metacharacters within parameters are escaped automatically, reducing the risk of some classes of SQL injection attacks.

They prevent syntax errors with different data types. In SQL, you need to escape different data types (strings, numbers, and dates) differently. In a parameterized query, this is performed automatically.

They are reusable. Parameterized queries make it easy to reuse Command objects. For example, you can use the Command in Example 4-3 to update multiple category records, simply by modifying the value of the parameters and executing the query again.

A parameterized command *won't* improve performance as compared to the original dynamic SQL statement. Unlike a stored procedure, a parameterized query isn't stored in the database and isn't precompiled. The difference is simply one of syntax.

Commands with Stored Procedures

Stored procedures—SQL scripts stored in the database—are a key ingredient in any successful large-scale database applications. One advantage of stored procedures is improved performance. Stored procedures typically execute faster than ordinary SQL statements because the database can create, optimize, and cache a data access plan in advance. Stored procedures also have a number of other potential benefits. They:

- Improve security. A client can be granted permissions to execute a stored procedure to add or modify a record in a specify way, without having full permissions on the underlying tables.

- Are easy to maintain, because they are stored separately from the application code. Thus, you can modify a stored procedure without recompiling and redistributing the .NET application that uses it.

- Add an extra layer of indirection, potentially allowing some database details to change without breaking your code. For example, a stored procedure can remap field names to match the expectations of the client program.

- Reduce network traffic, because SQL statements can be executed in batches.

Of course, stored procedures aren't perfect. Most of their drawbacks are in the form of programming annoyances:

- Using stored procedures in a program often involves importing additional database-specific details (such as parameter data types) into your code. You can control this problem by creating a dedicated component that encapsulates all your data access code.

- Stored procedures are created entirely in the SQL language (with variations depending on the database vendor) and use script-like commands that are generally more awkward than a full-blown object-oriented language such as C# or VB .NET, particularly with respect to error handling and code reuse. Microsoft promises that the next version of SQL Server (code-named Yukon) will allow stored procedures to be written using .NET languages like C#.

Stored procedures can be used for any database task, including retrieving rows or aggregate information, updating data, and removing or inserting rows.

Executing a Stored Procedure

Using a stored procedure with ADO.NET is easy. You simply follow four steps:

1. Create a Command, and set its CommandType property to StoredProcedure.

2. Set the CommandText to the name of the stored procedure.

3. Add any required parameters to the Command.Parameters collection.

4. Execute the Command with the ExecuteNonQuery( ), ExecuteScalar( ), or ExecuteQuery( ) method (depending on the type of output generated by the stored procedure).

For example, consider the generic update command defined earlier:

```
UPDATE Categories SET CategoryName=@CategoryName
  WHERE CategoryID=@CategoryID
```

You can encapsulate this logic in a stored procedure quite easily. You'll probably use Visual Studio .NET or a third-party product (like SQL Server's Enterprise Manager) to create the stored procedure, but the actual stored procedure code will look something like this:

```
CREATE PROCEDURE UpdateCategory
(
    @CategoryID int,
    @CategoryName nvarchar(15)
)
AS
    UPDATE Categories SET CategoryName=@CategoryName
    WHERE CategoryID=@CategoryID

GO
```

You'll notice that the actual SQL statement is unchanged. However, it is now wrapped in a SQL stored procedure called UpdateCategory that requires two input parameters. The stored procedure defines the required data types for all parameters, and you should pay close attention: your code must match exactly.

Example 4-5 rewrites Example 4-3 to use this stored procedure. The only two changes are found in the CommandText and CommandType properties of the Command object.

Example 4-5. Updating a record with a stored procedure

```
// SProcUpdateSQL.cs - Updates a single Category record

using System;
using System.Data;
using System.Data.SqlClient;

public class UpdateRecord
{
    public static void Main()
    {
        string connectionString = "Data Source=localhost;" +
                    "Initial Catalog=Northwind;Integrated Security=SSPI";
        string SQL = "UpdateCategory";

        // Create ADO.NET objects.
        SqlConnection con = new SqlConnection(connectionString);
        SqlCommand cmd = new SqlCommand(SQL, con);
        cmd.CommandType = CommandType.StoredProcedure;

        SqlParameter param;
        param = cmd.Parameters.Add("@CategoryName", SqlDbType.NVarChar, 15);
        param.Value = "Beverages";

        param = cmd.Parameters.Add("@CategoryID", SqlDbType.Int);
        param.Value = 1;
```

Example 4-5. Updating a record with a stored procedure (continued)

```
        // Execute the command.
        con.Open();
        int rowsAffected = cmd.ExecuteNonQuery();
        con.Close();

        // Display the result of the operation.
        Console.WriteLine(rowsAffected.ToString() + " row(s) affected");
    }
}
```

Output Parameters

One common use of a stored procedure is to insert a record in a table that uses a unique identity field. This type of stored procedure accepts several input parameters that identify the data for new row and one output parameter that returns the automatically generated unique ID to your .NET code. This saves you re-querying the database to find this information.

The Northwind sample database doesn't use this technique; the database used by the IBuySpy e-commerce store does. You can install the store database with IBuySpy code download from Microsoft's *http://www.ibuyspy.com* site or just refer to the following example.

Here is the `CustomerAdd` stored procedure code in the store database:

```
CREATE Procedure CustomerAdd
(
    @FullName    nvarchar(50),
    @Email       nvarchar(50),
    @Password    nvarchar(50),
    @CustomerID int OUTPUT
)
AS

INSERT INTO Customers
(
    FullName,
    EMailAddress,
    Password
)

VALUES
(
    @FullName,
    @Email,
    @Password
)

SELECT
    @CustomerID = @@Identity

GO
```

Commands

This stored procedure defines three input parameter and one output parameter for the generated ID. The stored procedure begins by inserting the new record and sets the output parameter using the special global SQL Server system function @@Identity.

Using this routine in code is just as easy, but you need to configure the @CustomerID parameter to be an output parameter (input is the default) (see Example 4-6).

Example 4-6. Using a stored procedure with an output parameter

```
// AddCustomer.cs - Runs the CustomerAdd stored procedure.

using System;
using System.Data;
using System.Data.SqlClient;

public class AddCustomer
{
    public static void Main()
    {
        string connectionString = "Data Source=localhost;" +
                    "Initial Catalog=store;Integrated Security=SSPI";
        string procedure = "CustomerAdd";

        // Create ADO.NET objects.
        SqlConnection con = new SqlConnection(connectionString);
        SqlCommand cmd = new SqlCommand(procedure, con);

        // Configure command and add input parameters.
        cmd.CommandType = CommandType.StoredProcedure;
        SqlParameter param;

        param = cmd.Parameters.Add("@FullName", SqlDbType.NVarChar, 50);
        param.Value = "John Smith";

        param = cmd.Parameters.Add("@Email", SqlDbType.NVarChar, 50);
        param.Value = "john@mydomain.com";

        param = cmd.Parameters.Add("@Password", SqlDbType.NVarChar, 50);
        param.Value = "opensesame";

        // Add the output parameter.
        param = cmd.Parameters.Add("@CustomerID", SqlDbType.Int);
        param.Direction = ParameterDirection.Output;

        // Execute the command.
        con.Open();
        cmd.ExecuteNonQuery();
        con.Close();

        Console.WriteLine("New customer has ID of " + param.Value);

    }
}
```

Your stored procedure is free to return any type of information in an output parameter, as long as it uses the correct data type. There's also no limit to the number of parameters, output or otherwise, that you can use with a stored procedure.

Stored Procedure Return Values

Stored procedures can also return information through a return value. The return value works in much the same way as an output parameter, but it isn't named, and every stored procedure can have at most one return value. In SQL Server stored procedure code, the return value is set using the RETURN statement.

Here's how the CustomerAdd stored procedure can be rewritten to use a return value instead of an output parameter:

```
CREATE Procedure CustomerAdd
(
    @FullName   nvarchar(50),
    @Email      nvarchar(50),
    @Password   nvarchar(50),
)
AS

INSERT INTO Customers
(
    FullName,
    EMailAddress,
    Password
)

VALUES
(
    @FullName,
    @Email,
    @Password
)

RETURN @@Identity

GO
```

This revision carries no obvious advantages or disadvantages. It's really a matter of convention. Different database developers have their own system for determining when to use a return value; many use a return value to provide ancillary information such as the number of rows processed or an error condition.

As with input and output parameters, the return value is represented by a Parameter object. The difference is that the Parameter object for a return value must have the Direction property set to ReturnValue. In addition, some providers (e.g., the OLE DB provider) require that the Parameter object representing the return value is the first in the Parameter collection for a Command.

Example 4-7 shows how to call the revised CustomerAdd stored procedure.

Example 4-7. Using a stored procedure with a return value

```
// AddCustomerReturn.cs - Runs the CustomerAdd stored procedure.

using System;
using System.Data;
using System.Data.SqlClient;

public class AddCustomer
{
    public static void Main()
    {
        string connectionString = "Data Source=localhost;" +
                        "Initial Catalog=store;Integrated Security=SSPI";
        string procedure = "CustomerAdd";

        // Create ADO.NET objects.
        SqlConnection con = new SqlConnection(connectionString);
        SqlCommand cmd = new SqlCommand(procedure, con);

        // Configure the command.
        cmd.CommandType = CommandType.StoredProcedure;
        SqlParameter param;

        // Add the parameter representing the return value.
        param = cmd.Parameters.Add("@CustomerID", SqlDbType.Int);
        param.Direction = ParameterDirection.ReturnValue;

        // Add the input parameters.
        param = cmd.Parameters.Add("@FullName", SqlDbType.NVarChar, 50);
        param.Value = "John Smith";

        param = cmd.Parameters.Add("@Email", SqlDbType.NVarChar, 50);
        param.Value = "john@mydomain.com";

        param = cmd.Parameters.Add("@Password", SqlDbType.NVarChar, 50);
        param.Value = "opensesame";

        // Execute the command.
        con.Open();
        cmd.ExecuteNonQuery();
        con.Close();

        param = cmd.Parameters["@CustomerID"];
        Console.WriteLine("New customer has ID of " + param.Value);

    }
}
```

Deriving Parameters

So far, the stored procedure examples suffer in one respect: they import numerous database-specific details into your code. Not only do you need to hardcode exact parameter names, but you need to know the correct SQL Server data type, and the field length for any text data.

One way to get around these details is to use a CommandBuilder class. This class is used with DataSet updates (which we'll consider in Chapter 5), but it also is useful when dealing with stored procedures. It allows you to retrieve and apply all the parameter metadata for a command. The disadvantage of this approach is that it requires an extra round trip to the data source. This is a significant price to pay for simplified code, and as a result, you won't see it used in enterprise-level database code.

Once the parameter information is drawn from the database, all you need to do is set the parameter values. You can retrieve individual parameter objects either by index number or by parameter name from the Command.Parameters collection. Example 4-8 shows how the AddCustomer code can be rewritten to use this technique.

Example 4-8. Retrieving parameter information programmatically

```
// DeriveParameter.cs - Retrieves stored procedure parameter information

using System;
using System.Data;
using System.Data.SqlClient;

public class AddCustomer
{
    public static void Main()
    {
        string connectionString = "Data Source=localhost;" +
                "Initial Catalog=store;Integrated Security=SSPI";
        string procedure = "CustomerAdd";

        // Create ADO.NET objects.
        SqlConnection con = new SqlConnection(connectionString);
        SqlCommand cmd = new SqlCommand(procedure, con);

        // Configure command and add input parameters.
        cmd.CommandType = CommandType.StoredProcedure;

        // Execute the command.
        con.Open();

        SqlCommandBuilder.DeriveParameters(cmd);

        cmd.Parameters[1].Value = "Faria MacDonald";
        cmd.Parameters[2].Value = "joe@mydomain.com";
        cmd.Parameters[3].Value = "opensesame";
        cmd.Parameters[4].Value = DBNull.Value;

        cmd.ExecuteNonQuery();
        con.Close();
```

Example 4-8. Retrieving parameter information programmatically (continued)

```
        Console.WriteLine("New customer has ID of " +
                            cmd.Parameters[4].Value);
    }
}
```

 Note that though most .NET providers include a `CommandBuilder` class, they aren't in any way generic. Different `CommandBuilder` classes don't inherit from a common base class or implement a common interface, which means you can't use this class generically.

Because deriving parameters adds extra overhead, it's not suitable for a performance-critical application. It's a much better idea to create a dedicated database component that encapsulates the code that creates and populates stored procedure parameters and all the database-specific details.

Commands and Data Definition Language (DDL)

Most data-access code focuses on Data Manipulation Language (DML) commands. These instructions change, delete, or retrieve information about the values in tables. Typically, a database administrator creates the tables as part of a separate process, using a dedicated tool. This isn't always the case. Sometimes you want to create or modify table structure directly from your code. To do this, you need Data Definition Language (DDL) commands. SQL defines many basic commands various database vendors use to implement and sometimes extend. These include old standbys such as DROP TABLE and CREATE DATABASE.

ADO, the previous generation of data-access technology, had a sibling called ADOX that provided an object-oriented wrapper for the DDL commands. ADO. NET doesn't have any such niceties. However, you can still modify table structure or create new tables programmatically; you just have to do it the hard way, by constructing a `Command` and executing it with the `ExecuteNonQuery( )` method. Example 4-9 shows a trivial example that uses the CREATE TABLE statement to create a single table with two columns. In this case, the table is created in the Northwind database because that's the initial database selected when the connection is opened.

Example 4-9. Inserting a new table programmatically

```
// DDL.cs - Inserts a new table

using System;
using System.Data.SqlClient;

public class UpdateRecord
{
    public static void Main()
    {
        string connectionString = "Data Source=localhost;" +
                    "Initial Catalog=Northwind;Integrated Security=SSPI";
```

Example 4-9. Inserting a new table programmatically (continued)

```
    string SQL = "CREATE TABLE Users ("+
                "UserName nvarchar(20), Password nvarchar(20) )";


    // Create ADO.NET objects.
    SqlConnection con = new SqlConnection(connectionString);
    SqlCommand cmd = new SqlCommand(SQL, con);

    // Execute the command.
    con.Open();
    int rowsAffected = cmd.ExecuteNonQuery();
    con.Close();

    // Display the result of the operation.
    Console.WriteLine(rowsAffected.ToString() + " row(s) affected");
  }
}
```

In this case, rowsAffected will be −1 because the Command didn't execute an UPDATE, DELETE, or INSERT statement.

5

DataReaders

In the previous chapter, you learned to execute simple nonquery commands to update the data source and retrieve calculated values. You can also use queries to fetch a set of rows from a data source in a single operation. In ADO.NET, there are two ways to use query commands: with the disconnected DataSet object, as discussed in later chapters, and with the DataReader, which is the focus of this chapter.

The DataReader is little more than a thin wrapper over a cursor that retrieves query results in a read-only, forward-only stream of information. The DataReader won't let you perform updates, see the results of live updates, or move back and forth through a result set as a server-side cursor does in traditional ADO programming. However, what you sacrifice in flexibility, you gain in performance. Because this cursor consumes few server resources and requires relatively little locking, the DataReader is always a performance-optimal way to retrieve data.

In this chapter, you'll learn how to use a DataReader to retrieve data and schema information, how to handle specialized data types such as binary large objects (BLOBs), and how to write code that can access any type of data source with the DataReader.

DataReader Object Overview

As with all connection-specific objects, there is a DataReader for every data provider. Here are two examples:

- System.Data.SqlClient.SqlDataReader provides forward-only, read-only access to a SQL Server database (Version 7.0 or later).
- System.Data.OleDb.OleDbDataReader provides forward-only, read-only access to a data source exposed through an OLE DB provider.

Every DataReader object implements the System.Data.IDataReader and the System.Data.IDataRecord interfaces. The IDataReader interface provides the core methods shown in Table 5-1, such as Read( ), which retrieves a single row from the stream. The IDataRecord interface provides the indexer for the DataReader and allows you to access the column values for the current row by column name or ordinal number.

Table 5-1. IDataReader methods

Member	Description
Close( )	Closes the DataReader but not the underlying Connection. This allows you to use the Connection for another task.
GetSchemaTable( )	Retrieves a DataTable object with information about the schema for the current result set.
NextResult( )	When executing a Command that returns multiple result sets, you must use NextResult( ) to move from one result set to another. This method returns true if there are more result sets.
Read( )	Loads the next row into the DataReader. This method returns true if there are more rows left to be read.

The key to understanding the DataReader is to understand that it loads only a single row into memory at a time. This ensures that memory use is kept to a minimum. It's also important to realize that the DataReader represents a live connection. Thus, you should read the values, close the connection as quickly as possible, and then perform any time-consuming data processing.

You can't create a DataReader directly. Instead, a DataReader must be generated by the ExecuteReader( ) method of a Command object. You won't need to manually open the DataReader; it will be initialized as soon as you execute the Command. You can begin using it immediately by calling the Read( ) method.

Typical DataReader access code follows five steps:

1. Create a Command object with an appropriate SELECT query.

2. Create a Connection, and open it.

3. Use the Command.ExecuteReader( ) method, which returns a live DataReader object.

4. Move through the returned rows from start to finish, one at a time, using the DataReader.Read( ) method. You can access a column in the current row by index number or field name.

5. Close the DataReader( ) and Connection( ) when the Read( ) method returns false to indicate there are no more rows.

The DataReader is limited in scope and thus extremely simple to use. For example, the DataReader also has no intrinsic support for table relations, so you will need to perform a JOIN query if you want to see combined information from more than one table.

Performing a Query with a DataReader

To retrieve records with a `Command` and `DataReader`, you need to use the SELECT statement, which identifies the table and rows you want to retrieve, the filter and ordering clauses, and any table joins:

```
SELECT columns FROM tables WHERE search_condition
        ORDER BY order_expression ASC | DESC
```

When writing a SELECT statement with a large table, you may want to limit the number of returned results to prevent your application from slowing down dramatically as the database grows. Typically, you accomplish this by adding a WHERE clause that limits the results.

Example 5-1 shows a sample Windows application that fills a list box with the results of a query. The designer code is omitted.

Example 5-1. Using a fast-forward DataReader

```csharp
// DataReaderFillForm.cs - Fills a ListBox

using System;
using System.Windows.Forms;
using System.Data.SqlClient;

public class DataReaderTest : Form
{
    private ListBox lstNames;
    private string connectionString = "Data Source=localhost;" +
        "Initial Catalog=Northwind;Integrated Security=SSPI";

  public DataReaderTest()
  {
    lstNames = new ListBox();
    lstNames.Dock = DockStyle.Fill;
    Controls.Add(lstNames);
    Load += new EventHandler(DataReaderTest_Load);
  }

  public static void Main()
  {
    DataReaderTest t = new DataReaderTest();
    Application.Run(t);
  }
    private void DataReaderTest_Load(object sender, System.EventArgs e)
    {
        string SQL = "SELECT ContactName FROM Customers";

        // Create ADO.NET objects.
        SqlConnection con = new SqlConnection(connectionString);
        SqlCommand cmd = new SqlCommand(SQL, con);
        SqlDataReader r = null;
```

Example 5-1. Using a fast-forward DataReader (continued)

```
        // Execute the command.
        try
        {
            con.Open();
            r = cmd.ExecuteReader();

            // Iterate over the results.
            while (r.Read())
            {
                lstNames.Items.Add(r["ContactName"]);
            }
        }
        catch (Exception err)
        {
            MessageBox.Show(err.ToString());
        }
        finally
        {
            if (r != null) r.Close();
            con.Close();
        }
    }

}
```

The results are shown in Figure 5-1.

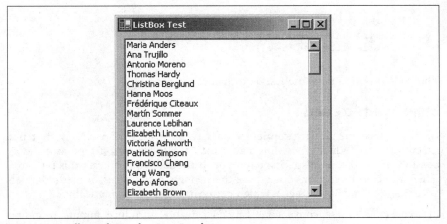

Figure 5-1. Filling a list with a DataReader

Using Column Ordinals

The previous example retrieved field values using a column name. Internally, however, the DataReader stores field information using a zero-based index. When you supply a column name, the DataReader performs a lookup in a Hashtable collection behind the scenes and then determines the appropriate ordinal. This adds a slight overhead, which increases the time required to read a column by up to 30%.

You can avoid this overhead by using the column ordinal when selecting a column:

```
// Display the value from the first column.
Console.WriteLine(r[0]);
```

Of course, this adds a tighter level of coupling between the data source and your code. For example, imagine you are writing your code as part of an enterprise-level distributed application. You are probably retrieving your query through a stored procedure. The order of DataReader columns is determined by the order of column names in the SELECT statement that the stored procedure uses. If the stored procedure changes, your code could fail. (A similar problem occurs if you are using name-based lookup, and the column names are changed, but this problem is typically easier to spot.)

To manage the possible confusion, you can retrieve the column ordinals after executing the query. This way, you perform the name lookup once and can use the better-performing index numbers for the remainder of your code, without exposing your code to unnecessary risk if the database changes. The DataReader provides a GetOrdinal( ) method for this purpose:

```
// Read and store all the ordinals you need.
int ID = r.GetOrdinal("CustomerID");
int Name = r.GetOrdinal("ContactName");

while (r.Read())
{
    // Use the ordinals when retrieving field values.
    Console.Write(r[ID]);
    Console.WriteLine(r[Name]);
}
```

This code realizes a fairly modest performance increase.

Using Typed Accessors

Databases use their own proprietary data types, which map closely, but not exactly, to .NET data types. Internally, the DataReader uses a type as close as possible to the database-specific data type. If needed, you can cast this type to a .NET framework type, or you can use the strongly typed accessor methods such as GetInt32( ) and GetString( ), which perform this step automatically.

In some cases, these conversions can conceivably introduce minute rounding errors, loss of precision, or a minor performance slowdown. To circumvent these problems, some DataReader implementations provide additional methods that let you retrieve data types in their native form. For example, the SQL Server provider includes the types in the System.Data.SqlTypes namespace. These types map directly to SQL Server database types (such as money, smalldatetime, and varchar). To see the exact mapping, refer to Appendix A.

The SqlDataReader also provides corresponding methods for each data type, such as GetSqlMoney( ) and GetSqlDataTime( ). To use this method, you must supply the column index (the column name isn't supported).

Example 5-2 shows how you might retrieve information from the Orders table using native SQL Server data types.

Example 5-2. Using native SQL Server data types

```
// NativeSqlServer.cs - Retrieves data as native SQL Server types.

using System;
using System.Data.SqlClient;
using System.Data.SqlTypes;

public class NativeSqlServer
{
    public static void Main()
    {
        // Query string to get some records from Orders table
        string SQL = "SELECT OrderID, CustomerID, " +
                     "OrderDate, Freight FROM Orders";

        // First column OrderID is int datatype in SQL Server.
        SqlInt32 orderID;

        // Second column CustomerID is nchar in SQL Server.
        SqlString customerID;

        // Third column OrderDate is datetime in SQL Server.
        SqlDateTime orderDate;

        // Fourth column Freight is money in SQL Server.
        SqlMoney freight;

        // Create the ADO.NET objects.
        SqlConnection con = new SqlConnection("Data Source=localhost;" +
                "Initial Catalog=Northwind;Integrated Security=SSPI");
        SqlCommand cmd = new SqlCommand(SQL, con);
        SqlDataReader r;

        con.Open();

        // Perform the query.
        r = cmd.ExecuteReader();

        // Read the rows from the query result.
        while (r.Read())
        {
            // Get the columns as native SQL types.
            orderID = r.GetSqlInt32(0);
            customerID = r.GetSqlString(1);
```

Example 5-2. Using native SQL Server data types (continued)

```
                orderDate = r.GetSqlDateTime(2);
                freight = r.GetSqlMoney(3);

                // You can now do something with the data.
                // This example just prints out the row.
                Console.Write(orderID.ToString() + ", ");
                Console.Write(customerID + ", ");
                Console.Write(orderDate.ToString() + ", ");
                Console.Write(freight.ToString() + ", ");
                Console.WriteLine();
            }
        }
}
```

In this example, the advantage of using the SQL Server-specific types is minimal. In fact, all the SQL Server types map quite closely to their .NET equivalents. However, if you use a data source that exposes data in a unique format, this approach may become very important.

 Each SQL data type provides a set of methods for comparison, data conversion, and (for numeric data) mathematical manipulations. See Part III for more information.

The managed Microsoft Oracle provider includes some specialized structures (e.g., OracleDateTime) in the System.Data.OracleClient namespace. You can use these structures to retrieve data using the dedicated methods of the OracleDataReader class.

The OLE DB managed provider doesn't include any specialized structures for OLE DB types. Refer to Appendix A for more information about the mapping between OLE DB types and .NET framework types.

Retrieving Null Values

A common database convention is to use the null value to represent missing data. Some fields may refuse nulls, while others may allow them, indicating that data doesn't need to be entered for this column.

.NET value types can't legally contain a null value. Thus, if you try to retrieve a null value through a DataReader and assign it to a value type, you will receive an InvalidCastException. However, the data types in the DataReader can contain null values. (Otherwise, simply trying to read a row that contains a null value generates an error, rendering the DataReader useless).

There are several ways to code around the null value problem:

- If you use SQL Server, you can retrieve native SQL Server data types with the appropriate DataReader methods. Every SQL Server data type implements the System.Data.SqlTypes.INullable interface, allowing them to legally contain a null value. However, a problem will occur if you try to cast a null value to a base .NET type.

- You can call the ToString( ) method on the value, as shown in Example 5-2. Types that contain the null value simply return an empty string. This approach works well when you only need to display the data.
- You can explicitly check the value before attempting to assign it to another variable.

The final approach is useful if you need to store the value in another variable. However, you can't just test the field for a null reference. The problem here is that the column value does in fact exist: it isn't null. However, it represents a null value because it doesn't contain any information. The .NET framework includes the System.DBNull class for this purpose, which allows you to distinguish between a null reference and a null database value. If the column value is equal to DBNull. Value, it represents a null database field. The syntax is shown here:

```
int rowVal;

if (r[i] != DBNull.Value)
{
    // Use default value. Row is null.
    rowVal = 0;
}
else
{
    // Use database value.
    rowVal = (int)r[i];
}
```

There's another way to explicitly test for a null value: using the IsDbNull( ) method of the DataReader. This code is equivalent:

```
int rowVal;

if (r.IsDbNull(i))
{
    // Use default value. Row is null.
    rowVal = 0;
}
else
{
    // Use database value.
    rowVal = (int)r[i];
}
```

Returning Multiple Result Sets

It is possible to execute a query that returns multiple result sets. This technique can improve performance because you need to contact the database only once to initiate the query. All data is then retrieved in a read-only stream from start to finish.

There are two ways to return more than one result set. You might be executing stored procedures that contain more than one SELECT statement. Alternatively, you might set up a batch query to execute multiple SQL statements by separating them with a semicolon:

```
// Define a batch query.
string SQL = "SELECT * FROM Categories; SELECT * FROM Products";

SqlConnection con = new SqlConnection(connectionString);
SqlCommand cmd = new SqlCommand(SQL, con);

con.Open();

// Execute the batch query.
SqlDataReader r = cmd.ExecuteReader();
```

You need only one DataReader to process multiple result sets. To move from the first result set to the second, use the DataReader.NextResult( ) method:

```
while (reader.Read())
{
    // (Process the category rows here.)
}

reader.NextResult();

while (reader.Read())
{
    // (Process the product rows here.)
}
```

Showing All Columns with the DataReader

The OLE DB, ODBC, Oracle, and SQL Server providers all add a FieldCount property to the DataReader. This property allows you to retrieve the number of fields in the current row. Using this information, you can write a generic code routine to display the results of a query by index number, rather than by hard-coding field names. The disadvantage of this approach is that you are forced to use the order in which the columns were retrieved, which may not make the most sense for display purposes. Generally, the more your application knows about the structure of your data, the better it can present it—and the more difficult your life becomes when the database changes.

Example 5-3 shows an example that fills a ListView details grid with the results of the current query, regardless of the number or type of columns.

Example 5-3. Filling a ListView with all columns

```
// ListViewFillForm.cs - Fills a ListView

public class DataReaderTest : System.Windows.Forms.Form
{
    private System.Windows.Forms.ListView lvCustomers;
```

Example 5-3. Filling a ListView with all columns (continued)

```csharp
private string connectionString = "Data Source=localhost;" +
    "Initial Catalog=Northwind;Integrated Security=SSPI";

// (Windows designer code omitted.)

private void DataReaderTest_Load(object sender, System.EventArgs e)
{
    string SQL = "SELECT * FROM Customers";
    lvCustomers.View = View.Details;

    // Create ADO.NET objects.
    SqlConnection con = new SqlConnection(connectionString);
    SqlCommand cmd = new SqlCommand(SQL, con);
    SqlDataReader r = null;

    // Execute the command.
    try
    {
        con.Open();
        r = cmd.ExecuteReader();

        // Add the columns to the ListView.
        for (int i = 0; i <= r.FieldCount - 1; i++)
        {
            lvCustomers.Columns.Add("Column " + (i + 1).ToString(),
                                    100, HorizontalAlignment.Left);
        }

        // Add rows of data to the ListView.
        while (r.Read())
        {
            // Create the ListViewItem row with the first column.
            ListViewItem lvItem = new ListViewItem(r[0].ToString());

            // Add the data for the other columns.
            for (int i = 1; i <= r.FieldCount - 1; i++)
            {
                lvItem.SubItems.Add(r[i].ToString());
            }

            // Add the completed row.
            lvCustomers.Items.Add(lvItem);
        }
    }

    catch (Exception err)
    {
        MessageBox.Show(err.ToString());
    }
```

DataReaders

Example 5-3. Filling a ListView with all columns (continued)

```
        finally
        {
            if (r != null) r.Close();
            con.Close();
        }
    }
}
```

The results for this example are shown in Figure 5-2.

Figure 5-2. Filling a ListView with every column

Reading Single Rows with a DataReader

Command objects also provide another variation of the ExecuteReader( ) method that accepts a combination of values from the CommandBehavior enumeration. These values provide additional information about how the command should be executed.

The CommandBehavior enumeration is useful if you need to read large binary data sequentially, as described in the next section. However, it can also offer some performance improvement in cases when you know a SELECT statement will return only a single record (for example, if you include a WHERE clause specifying a value from a unique column). In this case, you can use CommandBehavior. SingleRow to inform the provider:

```
    r = cmd.ExecuteReader(CommandBehavior.SingleRow);
```

This extra step certainly won't harm performance, but its potential benefit depends on the specific implementation in the data provider.

Retrieving BLOB Data

The CommandBehavior enumeration is useful if you need to retrieve a BLOB from the database. In this situation, the DataReader's default behavior, which is to load the entire row into memory before providing it to your code, is dangerously inefficient. By specifying CommandBehavior.SequentialAccess, you indicate that your code will read through the data in a row sequentially, from start to finish. Thus, only a single field of data is read into memory at a time, instead of the entire row, reducing the memory overhead of your code. This benefit is trivial if row sizes are small but important if they are large.

When using CommandBehavior.SequentialAccess, you must read the fields in the same order they are returned by your query. For example, if your query returns three columns, the third of which is a BLOB, you must return the values of the first and second fields before accessing the binary data in the third field. If you access the third field first, you can't access the first two fields.

When dealing with binary data, you typically use the DataReader.GetBytes() method, which fills a byte array with a portion of the data, according to the buffer size and starting position you specify. The GetBytes() method returns an Int64 value that indicates the number of bytes that were retrieved. To determine the total number of bytes in the BLOB, pass a null reference to the GetBytes() method.

Example 5-4 demonstrates a console application that reads a list of records, and then reads a large binary field and writes it to disk as a bitmap file. This example uses the pubs database.

Example 5-4. Writing a BLOB to a file

```
// BLOBTest.cs - Writes binary data to a file

using System;
using System.Data.SqlClient;
using System.Data;
using System.IO;

public class ConnectionTest
{
    private static string connectionString = "Data Source=localhost;" +
        "Initial Catalog=pubs;Integrated Security=SSPI";
    private static string SQL = "SELECT pub_id, logo FROM pub_info";

    public static void Main()
    {
        int bufferSize = 100;                  // Size of the BLOB buffer.
        byte[] bytes = new byte[bufferSize];   // The BLOB byte[] buffer.
        long bytesRead;                        // The number of bytes read.
        long readFrom;                         // The starting index.

        SqlConnection con = new SqlConnection(connectionString);
        SqlCommand cmd = new SqlCommand(SQL, con);

        // Open the connection and execute a sequential DataReader.
        con.Open();
        SqlDataReader r =
          cmd.ExecuteReader(CommandBehavior.SequentialAccess);
```

Example 5-4. Writing a BLOB to a file (continued)

```
        while (r.Read())
        {
            string filename = "logo" + r.GetString(0) + ".bmp";
            Console.WriteLine("Creating file " + filename);

            // Create a file stream and binary writer for the data.
            FileStream fs = new FileStream(filename, FileMode.OpenOrCreate,
                              FileAccess.Write);
            BinaryWriter bw = new BinaryWriter(fs);

            // Reset the starting position for the new BLOB.
            readFrom = 0;

            // Read the field 100 bytes at a time.
            do
            {
                bytesRead = r.GetBytes(1, readFrom, bytes, 0, bufferSize);

                bw.Write(bytes);
                bw.Flush();

                readFrom += bufferSize;

            } while (bytesRead == bufferSize);

            // Close the output file.
            bw.Flush();
            bw.Close();
            fs.Close();
        }

        r.Close();
        con.Close();
    }
}
```

Stored Procedures with the DataReader

Using a command to execute a stored procedure query isn't much different from using one to execute a stored procedure that wraps a nonquery command such as INSERT, UPDATE, or DELETE.

The Northwind database includes a small set of stored procedure queries. One example is the CustOrderHist procedure, which returns the total number of products a given customer has ordered, grouped by product name.

Here's the SQL code to create the CustOrderHist stored procedure. It defines one parameter (shown in the first line), called @CustomerID:

```
CREATE PROCEDURE CustOrderHist @CustomerID nchar(5)
    AS
    SELECT ProductName, Total=SUM(Quantity)
```

```
        FROM Products P, [Order Details] OD, Orders O, Customers C
        WHERE C.CustomerID = @CustomerID AND
               C.CustomerID = O.CustomerID AND
               O.OrderID = OD.OrderID AND OD.ProductID = P.ProductID
        GROUP BY ProductName

    GO
```

Example 5-5 executes this stored procedure for the customer "ALFKI" and displays the results in a console window.

Example 5-5. Using a stored procedure query

```
// TotalOrders.cs - Runs the CustOrderHist stored procedure.

using System;
using System.Data;
using System.Data.SqlClient;

public class TotalOrders
{
    public static void Main()
    {
        string connectionString = "Data Source=localhost;" +
                "Initial Catalog=Northwind;Integrated Security=SSPI";
        string procedure = "CustOrderHist";

        // Create ADO.NET objects.
        SqlConnection con = new SqlConnection(connectionString);
        SqlCommand cmd = new SqlCommand(procedure, con);
        SqlDataReader r;

        // Configure command and add parameters.
        cmd.CommandType = CommandType.StoredProcedure;
        SqlParameter param;
        param = cmd.Parameters.Add("@CustomerID", SqlDbType.NChar, 5);
        param.Value = "ALFKI";

        // Execute the command.
        con.Open();
        r = cmd.ExecuteReader();
        while (r.Read())
        {
            Console.WriteLine(r["Total"].ToString() + " of " +
                            r["ProductName"].ToString());
        }

        con.Close();
    }
}
```

Here's the sample output for this code:

```
20 of Vegie-spread
15 of Raclette Courdavault
```

```
17 of Rössle Sauerkraut
15 of Lakkalikööri
16 of Grandma's Boysenberry Spread
20 of Flotemysost
2 of Original Frankfurter grüne Soße
2 of Spegesild
21 of Chartreuse verte
6 of Aniseed Syrup
40 of Escargots de Bourgogne
```

 If you use a stored procedure that returns information through output parameters or a return value, this information won't be available until after you close the `DataReader` because the stored procedure will still be executing.

DataReaders and Schema Information

Schema information is information about the structure of your data. It includes everything from column data types to table relations.

Schema information becomes extremely important when dealing with the ADO. NET `DataSet`, as you'll learn in the following chapters. However, even if you aren't using the `DataSet`, you may want to retrieve some sort of schema information from a data source. With ADO.NET, you have two choices: you can use the `DataReader.GetSchemaTable()` method to retrieve schema information about a specific query, or you can explicitly request a schema table from the data source.

Retrieving Schema Information for a Query

As long as a `DataReader` is open, you can invoke its `GetSchemaTable()` method to return a `DataTable` object with the schema information for the result set. This `DataTable` will contain one row for each column in the result set. Each row will contain a series of fields with column information, including the data type, column name, and so on.

Example 5-6 shows code to retrieve schema information for a simple query.

Example 5-6. Retrieving the schema information for a query

```
// GetSchema.cs - Retrieves a schema table for a query

using System;
using System.Data;
using System.Data.SqlClient;

public class GetSchema
{
    public static void Main()
    {
        string connectionString = "Data Source=localhost;" +
                    "Initial Catalog=Northwind;Integrated Security=SSPI";
        string SQL = "SELECT * FROM CUSTOMERS";
```

Example 5-6. Retrieving the schema information for a query (continued)

```
        // Create ADO.NET objects.
        SqlConnection con = new SqlConnection(connectionString);
        SqlCommand cmd = new SqlCommand(SQL, con);
        SqlDataReader r;
        DataTable schema;

        // Execute the query.
        try
        {
            con.Open();
            r = cmd.ExecuteReader();
            schema = r.GetSchemaTable();
        }
        finally
        {
            con.Close();
        }

        // Display the schema table.
        foreach (DataRow row in schema.Rows)
        {
            foreach (DataColumn col in schema.Columns)
            {
                Console.WriteLine(col.ColumnName + " = " + row[col]);
            }
            Console.WriteLine();
        }
    }
}
```

If you run this test, you'll find that it returns a significant amount of information. Here's the output for just a single column in the query (omitting columns that don't return any information):

```
ColumnName = CustomerID
ColumnOrdinal = 0
ColumnSize = 5
NumericPrecision = 255
NumericScale = 255
IsUnique = False
BaseColumnName = CustomerID
DataType = System.String
AllowDBNull = False
ProviderType = 10
IsIdentity = False
IsAutoIncrement = False
IsRowVersion = False
IsLong = False
IsReadOnly = False
```

Although you must retrieve the schema DataTable while the DataReader is open, you can store it in a variable and access it later, after the connection is closed.

That's because the `DataTable` is a disconnected data container. For more information about the `DataTable` object, refer to Chapter 7.

Retrieving Schema Tables

The `GetSchemaTable()` method is ideal if you need schema information based on a query, but it won't allow you to retrieve anything else. For example, you might want to retrieve a list of databases, tables and views, constraints, or stored procedures from a data source. The `DataReader` has no built-in support for this type of information. However, it is possible to retrieve schema information directly with a specialized command, depending on the data source and data provider you use.

Retrieving schema tables with SQL Server

SQL Server exposes schema information through dedicated stored procedures and informational schema views. Informational schema views allow you to retrieve metadata as a table, using a SQL SELECT statement. However, the information is generated internally by the data source, not stored in a table. For example, the code in Example 5-7 shows how you can use one of the information schema views (TABLES) to retrieve a list of all the tables and views in the Northwind database. Though it appears to be querying information from a table, there is no physical table named INFORMATION_SCHEMA.TABLES in the data source.

A full description of information schemas is beyond the scope of this book, but they are described in detail in the SQL Server Books Online (just search for INFORMATION_SCHEMA).

Example 5-7. Retrieving a list of tables using an information schema

```
// GetTableList.cs - Retrieves a list of tables in a database

using System;
using System.Data.SqlClient;

public class GetTableList
{
    public static void Main()
    {
        string connectionString = "Data Source=localhost;" +
                "Initial Catalog=Northwind;Integrated Security=SSPI";
        string SQL = "SELECT TABLE_TYPE, TABLE_NAME FROM " +
                "INFORMATION_SCHEMA.TABLES";

        // Create ADO.NET objects.
        SqlConnection con = new SqlConnection(connectionString);
        SqlCommand cmd = new SqlCommand(SQL, con);
        SqlDataReader r;

        // Execute the query.
        try
        {
            con.Open();
            r = cmd.ExecuteReader();
```

```
        while (r.Read())
        {
            Console.WriteLine(r[0] + ": " + r[1]);
        }

    }
    finally
    {
        con.Close();
    }
  }
}
```

Here's a partial listing of the information this code returns:

```
VIEW: Alphabetical list of products
BASE TABLE: Categories
VIEW: Category Sales for 1997
VIEW: Current Product List
VIEW: Customer and Suppliers by City
BASE TABLE: CustomerCustomerDemo
BASE TABLE: CustomerDemographics
BASE TABLE: Customers
BASE TABLE: Employees
BASE TABLE: EmployeeTerritories
...
```

If you want to include only tables (not views), you can modify the query by adding an extra WHERE clause as follows:

```
SELECT TABLE_TYPE, TABLE_NAME FROM INFORMATION_SCHEMA.TABLES
  WHERE TABLE_TYPE = 'BASE TABLE'
```

Other views provide information about stored procedure parameters, columns, keys, constraints, user privileges, and more. You can also use specialized system stored procedures to perform tasks that the informational schema views can't, such as retrieving a list of all databases (via sp_catalog). All system stored procedures start with "sp_" and are documented in the SQL Server Books Online.

Retrieving schema tables with the OLE DB provider

Information views are limited to SQL Server and won't work with other data sources. However, if you use the OLE DB provider, you have another option. The OleDbConnection object provides a GetOleDbSchemaTable( ) method that can return various types of schema information, similar to what SQL Server accomplishes with its built-in informational views. Each data source handles this task differently, depending on the data source, but the ADO.NET code is generic.

GetOleDbSchemaTable( ) takes two parameters. The first is a value from the OleDbSchemaGuid class that specifies the type of schema information you want to return. The second is an array of objects that represent column restrictions. You apply these in the same order as the columns of the schema table.

Each field in the OleDbSchemaGuid class maps to an OLE DB schema rowset. Your OLE DB provider doesn't necessarily support all values from the OleDbSchemaGuid class. Refer to your database documentation for specific information.

GetOleDbSchemaTable( ) returns the schema information as a DataTable, similar to the GetSchemaTable( ) method of the DataReader. Example 5-8 uses GetOleDbSchemaTable( ) to retrieve a list of tables and views, similar to Example 5-7.

Example 5-8. Retrieving a list of tables using the OleDbSchemaGuid

```
// GetOleDbTableList.cs - Retrieves a list of tables in a database

using System;
using System.Data;
using System.Data.OleDb;

public class GetSchema
{
    public static void Main()
    {
        string connectionString = "Data Source=localhost;" +
            "Provider=SQLOLEDB;Initial Catalog=Northwind;" +
            "Integrated Security=SSPI";

        // Create ADO.NET objects.
        OleDbConnection con = new OleDbConnection(connectionString);

        DataTable schema;

        // Execute the query.
        try
        {
            con.Open();
            schema = con.GetOleDbSchemaTable(OleDbSchemaGuid.Tables,
                        new object[] {null, null, null, null});

        }
        finally
        {
            con.Close();
        }

        // Display the schema table.
        foreach (DataRow row in schema.Rows)
        {
            Console.WriteLine(row["TABLE_TYPE"] + ": " +
                            row["TABLE_NAME"]);
        }
    }
}
```

The resulting output is similar to the previous example. To create a list that includes only tables, you would need to realize that the TABLE_NAME column is the fourth column returned from the GetOleDbSchemaTable( ) method. You can then specify a restriction by supplying a filter string as the fourth element of the restriction array:

```
schema = con.GetOleDbSchemaTable(OleDbSchemaGuid.Tables,
            new object[] {null, null, null, "TABLE"});
```

For more information about the type of schema information you can retrieve with the OLE DB provider, refer to the OleDbSchemaGuid in the class library reference at the end of this book.

6

DataSets

The DataSet is a memory-resident representation of data including tables, relationships between the tables, and both unique and foreign key constraints. It is used for working with and transporting data in a disconnected environment.

There are four important characteristics of the DataSet:

It's not provider-specific. It's impossible to tell by looking at the DataSet, or at the objects contained within the DataSet, which provider was used to retrieve the data or what the original data source was. The DataSet provides a consistent programming model regardless of the data source.

It's always disconnected. Information is retrieved from the data source and placed in the DataSet using another ADO.NET object—the DataAdapter. At no point does a DataSet directly reference a Connection object.

It can track changes made to its data. The DataSet contains multiple versions of each row of data in the tables, which allows changes to be updated back to the data source using a DataAdapter object, changes to be cancelled, and XML DiffGrams of the changes to be created.

It can contain multiple tables. Unlike the traditional ADO Recordset, the DataSet approximates a relational database in memory.

DataSets exist as both untyped and strongly typed. Strongly typed DataSets are a collection of automatically generated classes that inherit from the DataSet, DataTable, and DataRow classes, and provide additional properties, methods, and events based on the DataSet schema. A strongly typed DataSet can make programs more intuitive to write and allows the Visual Studio .NET IDE to provide functionality such as autocomplete and for the compiler to detect type mismatch errors and misspelled names during compilation rather than at runtime. Strongly typed DataSets are discussed in detail in Chapter 13.

The data stored in the DataSet can be manipulated programmatically and populated using a DataAdapter or from XML documents or streams. The actual DataSet schema can be created programmatically, read from a data source, read from an XML schema, or inferred from an XML document or stream. The DataSet can easily be serialized to XML for marshalling between processes with .NET remoting or to meet persistent storage requirements.

Figure 6-1 shows the structure of the DataSet and the contained classes.

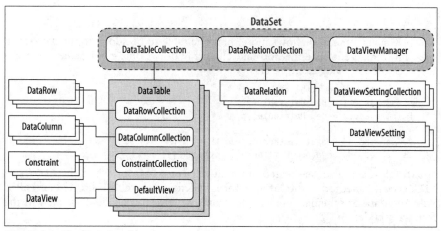

Figure 6-1. The DataSet class

Creating an Untyped DataSet

There are several ways a DataSet can be created. In the simplest case, a DataSet is created using the new keyword. The constructor accepts on optional argument that allows the DataSetName property to be set. If the DataSetName argument isn't supplied, the default name of the DataSet will be NewDataSet.

```
DataSet ds = new DataSet("MyDataSet");
```

A DataSet can also be created from another DataSet. The Copy( ) method can create a new DataSet containing both the schema and data from the original DataSet. The Clone( ) method creates a new DataSet with the same schema, but none of the data of the original. Finally, the GetChanges( ) method creates a new DataSet containing data that has changed since the DataSet was last loaded or the pending changes were accepted. These methods will be discussed in more detail later in this chapter.

Working with Tables in the DataSet

Tables belonging to the DataSet are stored as DataTable objects in a DataTableCollection object and accessed through the Tables property of the DataSet. This section examines some methods and properties of the DataTableCollection.

Tables are added to the DataSet using the Add( ) method of the DataTableCollection. The Add( ) method takes an optional table name argument.

If this argument isn't supplied, the tables are automatically named Table, Table1, and so on. The following example adds a table to a DataSet:

```
DataSet ds = new DataSet("MyDataSet");
DataTable dt = new DataTable("MyTable");

// ... code to define the schema for the newly constructed DataTable

ds.Tables.Add(dt);
```

The AddRange( ) method allows more than one table to be added to the DataSet in the same statement. The method takes an array of DataTable objects as the argument, as the following example shows:

```
// create two new tables
DataTable dt1 = new DataTable();
DataTable dt2 = new DataTable();

// use the AddRange() method to add them to the DataSet.
ds.Tables.AddRange(new DataTable[] {dt1, dt2});
```

A DataTable can also be created automatically in a DataSet when the Fill( ) or FillSchema( ) method of the DataAdapter is called. A new table is created and filled with the data or schema, respectively, from the data source, as illustrated in the following code:

```
// connection and select command strings
String connString = "Data Source=(local);Integrated security=SSPI;" +
    "Initial Catalog=Northwind;";
String selectSql = "SELECT * FROM Orders";

// create a new DataSet to receive the data
DataSet ds = new DataSet();

SqlDataAdapter da = new sqlDataAdapter(selectSql, connString);
// an empty table named OrdersSchema will be created in the DataSet
da.FillSchema(ds, SchemaType.Mapped, "OrdersSchema");

// a table named Orders will be created in the DataSet
// filled with data as specified by the SQL statement
da.Fill(ds, "Orders");
```

The DataAdapter class and the Fill( ) and FillSchema( ) methods are discussed in detail in Chapter 14.

Existing tables within the DataSet can be accessed by an indexer, which usually is passed the table name or the position of the table within the DataTableCollection as an argument as shown in the following examples:

```
// using the table name
DataTable dt = ds.Tables["MyTable"];

// using the table ordinal
DataTable dt = ds.Tables[0];
```

The Count property returns the number of tables within the DataSet:

```
Int32 tableCount = ds.Tables.Count;
```

The `Contains( )` method determines whether a table with a specified table name exists within a DataSet:

```
// Boolean tableExists = ds.Tables.Contains("MyTable");
```

The `IndexOf( )` method returns the index of the table within the collection using either a reference to the table object or the name of a table. The following example demonstrates both techniques:

```
// get the index using the name of the table
Int32 tableIndex = ds.Tables.IndexOf("MyTable");

// get the index using a reference to a table
DataTable dt = ds.Tables.Add("MyTable")

// ... build the table and do some work

// get the index of the table based on the table reference
Int32 tableIndex = ds.Tables.IndexOf(dt);
```

The `Remove( )`, `RemoveAt()`, and `Clear( )` methods remove tables from the DataSet. The `Remove( )` method takes an argument that specifies either a table name or a reference to the table to be removed, as shown in the following example:

```
DataTable dt = ds.Tables.Add("MyTable");

// remove by table reference
ds.Remove(dt);

// remove using the table name
ds.Remove("MyTable");
```

The `RemoveAt( )` method removes the table at the specified index from the `DataTableCollection` object, as shown in the following example:

```
// removes the first table from the tables collection in the DataSet
ds.RemoveAt[0];
```

The `Clear( )` method removes all tables from the DataSet, as shown here:

```
ds.Tables.Clear();
```

Adding and Removing Relations

Relations belonging to the DataSet are stored as `DataRelation` objects in a `DataRelationCollection` object and are accessed through the `Relations` property of the DataSet. Each `DataRelation` object represents the relationship between a parent and child table in the DataSet. This section examines some methods and properties of the `DataRelationCollection`.

Relations are added to the DataSet using the `Add( )` method of the `DataRelationCollection`, as shown in the following example:

```
ds.Relations.Add("MyDataRelation", parentTable.Columns["PrimaryKeyField"],
    childTable.Columns["ForeignKeyField"]);
```

The Remove( ) method removes a relation matching the relation-name argument. The following example removes the relation added in the previous example:

```
ds.Relations.Remove("MyDataRelation");
```

The Contains( ) method can determine if a specific relation exists as shown in the following example:

```
Boolean exists = ds.Relations.Contains("MyRelation");
```

Relations and the DataRelationCollection are discussed in detail in Chapter 11.

Adding Custom Information

The DataSet contains a PropertyCollection that is exposed through the ExtendedProperties property. This collection allows a user to add custom information to the DataSet such as the date and time when the DataSet should be refreshed. The following example sets an extended property indicating that the DataSet should be refreshed in 20 minutes:

```
ds.ExtendedProperties.Add("RefreshDateTime",
    DateTime.Now.AddMinutes(20).ToString());
```

The following code can then check that value to see if the DataSet needs to be refreshed:

```
if(DateTime.Now>Convert.ToDateTime(
    ds.ExtendedProperties["RefreshDateTime"].ToString( ) ))
{
    // ... code to refresh the DataSet
}
```

Extended properties must be of type String, or else they will not persist when the DataSet is written as XML.

The DataTable, DataColumn, DataRelation, and Constraint objects also have a similar collection of extended properties.

Cloning the Schema

The Clone( ) method creates a new DataSet with the same structure, including table schemas and relations, as the original but containing none of the data in the original DataSet. The following example uses the Clone( ) method to create a new DataSet:

```
// create a DataSet object variable to receive the clone
DataSet cloneDs;
cloneDs = ds.Clone();
```

Copying the DataSet

The Copy( ) method of the DataSet creates a new DataSet with the same structure, including tables schemas and relations, and data as the original DataSet. The following example uses the Copy( ) method to create a new DataSet:

```
// create a DataSet object variable to receive the copy
DataSet copyDs;
copyDs = ds.Copy();
```

Merging Two DataSets

The Merge() method combines the data and structure of a second, or source, DataSet into a specified target DataSet with a similar structure. The Merge() method is typically used in a client application to update a DataSet with the latest changes to the underlying data in the data source.

When the Merge() method is called, the schemas of the source and target DataSet are compared. If there are schema differences, the MissingSchemaAction argument determines whether the target schema is updated to include the missing schema and data or whether an exception is raised. If the MissingSchemaAction is specified as Add or AddWithKey, the schema is extended to accommodate the new data, and the primary key information added in the case of the later value. Specifying Ignore results in the data for the missing schema being ignored; specifying Error results in an exception being raised.

During the merge operation, source rows with a RowState of Unchanged, Modified, or Deleted are matched to rows in the target DataSet with the same Current primary key values. Source rows with RowState of New are created in the target DataSet with the same primary key values as the Current value in the source because the Original version doesn't exist in the source. Figure 6-2 shows the result of merging two tables with similar schemas, accepting the default MissingSchemaAction value of Add.

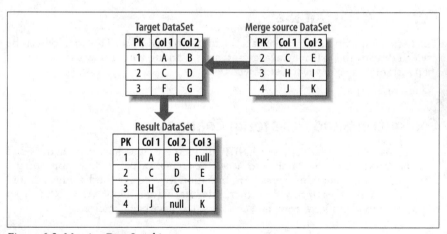

Figure 6-2. Merging DataSet objects

If the optional PreserveChanges argument is set to true, incoming values from the source doesn't overwrite Current values in the target DataSet rows. Data in the target Original row version is overwritten with the Original row version of the source row, and the target RowState is set to Modified. There are two exceptions. If

DataSets

the target RowState is Deleted, it remains deleted and isn't set to Modified. If the source RowState is Added, the target existing row isn't overwritten because it doesn't exist.

If PreserveChanges is false, both the Current and Original rows of the target are overwritten with the source data, and the RowState of the target row is set to the RowState of the source row. Again, there are two exceptions. If the source RowState is Unchanged, and the target RowState is Unchanged, Modified, Added, or Deleted, the RowState of the target row is set to Modified. If the source RowState is Added, the Original version of the target isn't overwritten because it doesn't exist.

During the merge operation, constraints are disabled. If constraints can't be enabled after the merge, the EnforceContraints property of the DataSet is set to false, and all invalid rows are marked as having errors.

The following example demonstrates the most complete form of the Merge() method:

```
Boolean preserveChanges = true;
Boolean missingSchemaAction = MissingSchemaAction.Add;

ds.Merge(mergeDs, preserveChanges, missingSchemaAction);
```

Removing All Data

The Clear() method removes all rows from all tables in the DataSet:

```
ds.Clear();
```

Resetting the DataSet

The Reset() method returns the DataSet to its original state. This method can be used to discard the existing DataSet and start working with a new DataSet rather than instantiating a new DataSet object:

```
ds.Reset();
```

Committing and Discarding Changes

When a DataRow is modified, ADO.NET marks the row as having a changes and sets the RowState of the DataRow to Added, Modified, or Deleted, as appropriate. ADO.NET also maintains version information by storing both Original and Current versions of each row. Together, this information allows ADO.NET or an application to identify the rows and columns that have been changed.

AcceptChanges and RejectChanges

The AcceptChanges() and RejectChanges() methods either accept or reject the changes that have been made to the DataSet since it was last loaded from the data source or since AcceptChanges() was last called.

The AcceptChanges( ) method commits all pending changes within the DataSet. Calling AcceptChanges( ) changes the RowState of Added and Modified rows to Unchanged. Deleted rows are removed. The Original values for the DataRow are set to the Current values. Calling the AcceptChanges( ) method has no effect on the data in the underlying data source.

The AcceptChanges( ) method is implicitly called on a row when the DataAdapter successfully updates that row back to the data source when the Update( ) method is called. As a result, when a DataAdapter is used to update the data source with the changes made to the DataSet, AcceptChanges( ) doesn't need to be called. Calling AcceptChanges( ) on a DataSet filled using a DataAdapter effectively removes all information about how the DataSet has been changed since it was loaded. This makes it impossible to reconcile those changes back to the data source using the Update( ) method of the DataSet.

The following example demonstrates the AcceptChanges( ) method:

```
ds.AcceptChanges();
```

The RejectChanges( ) method cancels any pending changes within the DataSet. Rows marked as Added are removed from the DataSet. Modified and Deleted rows are returned to their Original state. The following example demonstrates the RejectChanges( ) method:

```
ds.RejectChanges();
```

The following example illustrates the concepts just explained:

```
// create a table with one column
DataTable dt = new DataTable();
dt.Columns.Add("MyColumn",  typeof(System.String));

// add three rows to the table
DataRow row;

row = dt.NewRow();
row["MyColumn"] = "Item 1";
dt.Rows.Add(row);

row = dt.NewRow();
row["MyColumn"] = "Item 2";
dt.Rows.Add(row);

row = dt.NewRow();
row["MyColumn"] = "Item 3";
dt.Rows.Add(row);

dt.AcceptChanges();

// modify the rows

dt.Rows[0]["MyColumn"] = "New Item 1"; // DataRowState=Modified
dt.Rows[1].Delete();                   // DataRowState=Deleted
//dt.Rows[2]                           // DataRowState=Unchanged
```

```
dt.Rows[0].AcceptChanges();           // DataRowState=Unchanged,
                                      // MyColumn value="New Item 1";
dt.Rows[1].RejectChanges();           // DataRowState=Unchanged,
                                      // row not deleted
```

The DataTable and DataRow objects also expose an AcceptChanges() method and a
RejectChanges() method. Calling these methods on the DataSet implicitly calls
these methods for all DataRow objects in the DataSet.

HasChanges and GetChanges

The HasChanges() method of the DataSet indicates whether the DataSet has
changes, including Added, Deleted, or Modified rows. The method accepts an
optional DataRowState argument that causes the method to returns a value from
the DataSetRow enumeration if the DataSet has changes:

```
// check if there are any changes to the DataSet
Boolean hasChanges = ds.HasChanges();

// check if there are modified rows in the DataSet
Boolean hasModified = ds.HasChanges(DataRowState.Modified);
```

The GetChanges() method creates a copy of the DataSet containing all the changes
that have been made since it was last loaded or since AcceptChanges() was called.
The method takes an optional DataRowState argument that specifies the type of
row changes the DataSet should include. The GetChanges() method can select the
data that has been modified in a DataSet so that only the changed data rather than
the entire DataSet is returned. This subset of the DataSet that contains just the
changed data can improve performance of disconnected applications by reducing
the amount of information that needs to be transmitted between different application domains.

The HasChanges() method can be called first to determine whether GetChanges()
needs to be called. The following example show how to use the HasChanges() and
GetChanges() methods:

```
// check to see whether GetChanges needs to be called
if (ds.HasChanges())
{
    // create a DataSet containing all changes made to DataSet ds
    DataSet dsChange = ds.GetChanges();

    // create a DataSet containing only modified rows in DataSet ds
    DataSet dsModified = ds.GetChanges(DataRowState.Modified);
}
```

7

DataTables

The DataTable is an in-memory data store that contains DataColumn and Constraint objects that define the schema of the data. The actual data is stored as a collection of DataRow objects within the DataTable. Both the schema and the data can be created entirely programmatically, retrieved as the result of a query against a data source using a .NET managed data provider, or loaded from an XML document or stream through the DataSet to which it belongs.

The DataTable and the DataReader are similar because they both provide access to the results of a query that can then be exposed through collections of row and column objects. The primary difference is that the DataTable is a disconnected class that places little restriction on how the data within it is accessed and allows that data to be filtered, sorted, and modified. The DataReader is a connected class that provides little functionality beyond forward-only, read-only access to the results of the query.

Creating a DataTable

There are a number of ways a DataTable can be created. In the simplest case, a DataTable is created using the new keyword. The constructor accepts an optional argument that allows the TableName property to be set. If the TableName argument isn't supplied, the default name of the table is Table; subsequent tables are named Table1, Table2, and so on. The following example demonstrates how to create a table named MyTable:

```
DataTable dt = new DataTable("MyTable");
```

A DataTable can also be created automatically in a DataSet when the Fill() or FillSchema() method of the DataAdapter is called specifying a table that doesn't already exist in the DataSet. The DataAdapter class and the Fill() and FillSchema() methods are discussed in detail in Chapter 14.

DataTable objects can also be created from other DataTable objects. A new DataTable can be created from either the table schema alone, the schema and the data, or a subset of the DataTable based on if and how the data has been modified. Methods to do this are discussed later in this chapter.

Working with Columns

The schema for a table is defined by the columns in the table and the constraints on those columns. Columns belonging to the DataTable are stored as DataColumn objects in a DataColumnCollection object and are accessed through the Columns property of the DataTable. This section examines some methods and properties of the DataColumnCollection.

There are two methods that can add a column to a table. The Add( ) method optionally takes arguments that specify the name, type, and expression of the column to be added. An existing column can be added by passing a reference to an existing column. If no arguments are passed, the default names Column1, Column2, Column3, and so on are assigned to the new columns. The following examples show how to create columns within the table:

```
// adding a column using a reference to an existing column
DataColumn col = new DataColumn("MyColumn, typeof(System.Int32));
dt.Columns.Add(col);

// adding and creating a column in the same statement
dt.Columns.Add("MyColumn", typeof(System.Int32));
```

The second method for adding columns is the AddRange( ) method, which allows more than one column stored in a DataColumn array to be added to the table in a single statement, as shown in the following example:

```
DataTable dt = new DataTable("MyTable");

// create and add two columns to the DataColumn array
DataColumn[] dca = new DataColumn[]
    {new DataColumn("Col1", typeof(System.Int32)),
    new DataColumn("Col2", typeof(System.Int32))};

// add the columns in the array to the table
dt.Columns.AddRange(dca);
```

There are several properties and methods that interrogate the collection of columns within a table. The Count property returns the number of columns in a table:

```
Int32 colCount = dt.Columns.Count;
```

The Contains( ) method returns a value indicating whether a column with a specified name exists in the collection. The method takes a String argument containing the column name:

```
Boolean colExists = dt.Columns.Exists("MyColumn");
```

The IndexOf( ) method returns the zero-based index of a column with a specified name within the collection. The method returns the index if the specified column exists or −1 if the column doesn't exist in the collection. The method takes a single argument containing the column name.

```
Int32 colIndex = dt.Columns.IndexOf("MyColumn");
```

The Remove( ), RemoveAt( ), and Clear( ) methods remove columns from the DataSet. The Remove( ) method takes an argument that specifies either a column name or a reference to the column to be removed, as shown in the following example:

```
// remove a column by specifying the name of the column
dt.Columns.Remove("MyColumn")

// remove a column by specifying a reference to the column
DataColumn col = new DataColumn("MyColumn");
dt.Columns.Add(col);

// ... do some work

dt.Columns.Remove(col);
```

The RemoveAt( ) method removes a column with a specified column index from the collection as shown in the following example:

```
// remove the first column from the collection
dt.Columns.RemoveAt(0);
```

The Clear( ) method removes all columns from the column collection:

```
dt.Columns.Clear();
```

Constraints

As mentioned earlier, schema for a table is defined by the columns in the table and the constraints on those columns. There are two types of constraints that can be placed on a table. Unique constraints define a column or group of columns for which the value in the column or columns must be unique in each data row. Foreign key constraints define and restrict the action performed when a value in a column or columns is updated or deleted. Constraints belonging to the DataTable are stored as either UniqueConstraint or ForeignKeyConstraint objects in a ConstraintCollection object and are accessed through the Constraints property of the DataTable. This section examines some methods and properties of the ConstraintCollection.

To add a constraint to a table, the Add( ) method takes an argument specifying a reference to an existing constraint or takes specific arguments if a unique or foreign-key constraint is added. The following example demonstrates adding both a unique and foreign-key constraint by specifying a reference to an existing constraint:

```
// add a unique constraint by reference
UniqueConstraint uc =
  new UniqueConstraint(dt.Columns["MyColumn"]);
dt.Constraints.Add(uc);
```

```
// add a foreign key constraint by reference (wxh - test)
ForeignKeyConstraint fc = new ForeignKeyConstraint(
    dtParent.Columns["ParentColumn"],
    dtChild.Columns["ChildColumn"]);
dt.Constraints.Add(fc);
```

Two overloads of the Add( ) method create and add UniqueConstraint objects in one statement. The methods take a constraint name, a reference either to a DataColumn or a DataColumn array, and an argument indicating whether the column or columns are a primary key.

```
// add a unique constraint that is also a primary key
dt.Constraints.Add("MyUniqueConstraint", dt.Columns["MyColumn"], true);
```

The other two overloads of the Add( ) method create and add a ForeignKeyConstraint in one statement. The methods take a constraint name and either two DataColumn references or two DataColumn arrays, as shown in the following example:

```
// add a foreign key constraint based on two columns
dt.Constraints.Add("MyForeignKeyConstraint",
    new DataColumn(dtParent.Columns["ParentCol1"],
    new dtParent.Columns["parentCol2"]),
    new DataColumn(dtChild.Columns["ChildCol1"],
    dtChild.Columns["ChildCol2"]));
```

There are several properties and methods that interrogate the collection of constraints within a table. The Count property returns the number of constraints in a table:

```
Int32 constraintCount = dt.Constraints.Count;
```

The Contains( ) method returns a value indicating whether a column with a specified name exists in the collection. The method takes an argument containing the column name:

```
Boolean colExists = dt.Columns.Exists("MyColumn");
```

The Remove( ), RemoveAt( ), and Clear( ) methods remove constraints from the DataTable. The Remove( ) method takes an argument that specifies either a constraint name or a reference to the constraint to be removed, as shown in the following example:

```
// remove a constraint by specifying the name of the constraint
dt.Constraints.Remove("MyConstraint");

// remove a constraint by specifying a reference to the constraint
DataConstraint constraint = new DataConstraint("MyConstraint");
dt.Constraints.Add(constraint);

// ... do some work

dt.Constraints.Remove(constraint);
```

The RemoveAt( ) method removes a constraint with a specified index from the collection, as shown in this example:

```
// remove the first constraint from the collection
dt.Constraints.RemoveAt(0);
```

The Clear( ) method removes all constraints from the constraint collection:

```
dt.Constraints.Clear();
```

Constraints are discussed in detail in Chapter 10.

Primary Key

The primary key is a column or collection of columns that uniquely identify each row in the table. The PrimaryKey property accesses one or more DataColumn objects that define the primary key of the DataTable. The primary key acts both as a unique constraint for the table and allows records to be located using the Find( ) method of the DataTableRows collection, as discussed in the next section.

The primary key for a table is set by specifying an array of DataColumn objects from the table. The following example illustrates creating a primary key based on two columns:

```
// set the primary key based on two columns in the DataTable
DataTable dt = new DataTable("MyTable");
dt.Columns.Add("PK_Field1", typeof(System.Int32));
dt.Columns.Add("PK_Field2", typeof(System.Int32));

// ... add other table columns

// set the primary key
dt.PrimaryKey = new DataColumn[] {dt.Columns["PK_Field1"],
    dt.Columns["PK_Field2"]};
```

To remove the primary key, simply set the primary key object to null.

```
// remove the primary key
dt.PrimaryKey = null;
```

Rows

A DataRow object represents a row of data in the table stored in a collection of columns. Rows belonging to the DataTable are stored as DataRow objects in a DataRowCollection object and are accessed through the Rows property of the DataTable. The Rows property accesses methods and properties that can add, remove, and examine the DataRow objects in a DataTable. This section examines some of the methods and properties of the DataRowCollection.

There are two methods that can add a row to a table. The Add( ) method takes either a DataRow argument or an object array of columns of the row to be added:

```
DataTable dt = new DataTable("MyTable");
dt.Columns.Add("Column1", typeof(System.Int32));
dt.Columns.Add("Column2", typeof(System.String));
```

```
DataRow newrow = dt.NewRow();
newrow["Column1"].Value = 1;
newrow["Column2"].Value = "DataRow 1";

// add a row using a reference to a DataRow
dt.Rows.Add(dr);

// add and create a DataRow in one statement
dt.Rows.Add(new Object[] {2, "DataRow 2"});
```

Additionally, a DataRow can be inserted at a specific point in the DataRowCollection using the InsertAt( ) method, which in addition to a reference to a DataRow, takes an argument specifying the zero-based index at which to insert the row.

```
// create a new row
DataRow row = dt.NewRow();
row.ItemArray = new Object[] {1, "DataRow 1"};

// insert a new row as the first item of the collection
dt.Rows.InsertAt(row, 0);
```

There are two methods that can examine and locate rows within the DataRow collection. The Contains( ) method returns a value indicating whether the primary key exists in the collection of rows. The method has two overloads that take an object or an array of objects and allow primary keys based on one or more columns to be examined.

```
// look for a primary key that is based on a single column
Boolean exists = dt.Rows.Contains("PK Value 1");

// look for a primary key that is based on multiple columns
Boolean exists = dt.Rows.Contains(new Object[] {"PK Field1 Value",
    "PK Field2 Value"});
```

The Find( ) method is the second method that can locate a row based on the primary key. The Find( ) method differs from the Contains( ) method in that it returns the matching row rather than just indicating if a matching row was found. Like the Contains( ) method, the Find( ) method has two overloads that take an object or an array of objects and allow primary keys based on one or more columns to be examined. A null reference is returned if a matching row isn't found:

```
// get the row for a primary key that is based on a single column
DataRow row = dt.Rows.Find("PK Value 1");

// get the row for a primary key that is based on multiple columns
DataRow row = dt.Rows.Find(new Object[] {"PK Field1 Value",
    "PK Field2 Value"});
```

The Remove( ), RemoveAt( ), and Clear( ) methods remove rows from the DataTable. The Remove( ) method takes a DataRow argument and removes that row from the collection:

```
// remove the row matching the primary key value, if found
DataRow row = dt.Rows.Find("PK Value 1");
```

```
if(row! = null)
    dt.Rows.Remove(row);
```

The `RemoveAt( )` method takes an argument that specifies the index within the collection at which to remove the row:

```
// remove the first row from the collection
dt.Rows.RemoveAt(0);
```

Finally, the `Clear( )` method removes all rows from the table:

```
// remove all rows from the table
dt.Rows.Clear();
```

Rows are discussed in detail in Chapter 9.

Loading Data

There are three methods that can add new rows to the `DataTable`. The `NewRow( )` method creates a new empty `DataRow` with the same schema as the `DataTable`. After creating the row, it can be added to the `DataTable` using the `Add( )` method of the `DataRowCollection`:

```
// create the target table
DataTable dt = new DataTable("MyTable");
dt.Columns.Add("Column1", typeof(System.Int32));
dt.Columns.Add("Column2", typeof(System.String));

// create and add a new row to the table
DataRow newrow = dt.NewRow();
newrow["Column1"] = 1;
newrow["Column2"] = "Row 1";
dt.Rows.Add(newrow);
```

The `LoadDataRow( )` method takes an array of values and attempts to find a row with a matching primary key. If the primary key is found, the values replace the existing data for the row; otherwise a new row is added. The `LoadDataRow( )` method takes a Boolean `AcceptChanges` argument. If the `AcceptChanges` value is true, `AcceptChanges` is called to accept all changes for both inserted and modified rows. If `AcceptChanges` is `false`, the `DataRowState` fields of newly added rows are marked as insertions, while changes to existing rows are marked as modifications.

The `BeginLoadData( )` method turns off all constraints, notifications, and index maintenance for the `DataTable` while data is loaded; the `EndLoadData( )` method turns them back on. Calling `BeginLoadData( )` and `EndLoadData( )` methods might result in performance improvements when adding a series of `DataRows` to the `DataTable` using the `LoadDataRow( )` method. If there are constraint violations when the `EndLoadData( )` method is called, a `ConstraintException` is raised. The following example illustrates these methods:

```
// create the target table
DataTable dt = new DataTable("MyTable");
dt.Columns.Add("Column1", typeof(System.Int32));
dt.Columns.Add("Column2", typeof(System.String));
```

```
// add two rows to the DataTable dt
dt.BeginLoadData();
dt.LoadDataRow(new Object[]{1,"Row 1"}, false);
dt.LoadDataRow(new Object[]{2,"Row 2"}, false);
dt.EndLoadData();
```

Finally, the ImportRow( ) method accepts a DataRow object argument and either adds the row to the table or updates an existing row with a matching primary key in the table, using the existing schema and preserving the existing DataRowState of the row:

```
// create the target table
DataTable dt = new DataTable("MyTable");
dt.Columns.Add("Column1", typeof(System.Int32));
dt.Columns.Add("Column2", typeof(System.String));

DataRow newrow = dt.NewRow();
newrow["Column1"] = 1;
newrow["Column2"] = "Row 1";
dt.Rows.ImportRow(newrow);
```

Committing and Discarding Changes

When a DataRow is modified, ADO.NET marks the row as having a pending change and sets the RowState of the DataRow to Added, Modified, or Deleted as appropriate. ADO.NET also maintains version information by tracking both Original and Current versions of each row. Together, this information allows ADO.NET to identify the rows and columns that have been changed.

The DataTable has three methods—GetChanges( ), AcceptChanges( ), and RejectChanges( )—that can commit or discard the changes made to a DataTable since it was last loaded or since AcceptChanges( ) was last called. These methods function identically to the same methods for the DataSet as they are described in Chapter 6. Also, when these methods are called on a DataSet, they are implicitly called on all tables contained within the DataSet.

Cloning the Schema of the Table

The Clone( ) method creates a new DataTable with the same schema as the original, but it contains none of the data in the original DataTable. The following example uses the Clone( ) method to create a new DataTable:

```
// create a DataTable object variable to receive the clone
DataTable cloneDt;
cloneDt = dt.Clone();
```

Copying the Table

The Copy( ) method creates a new DataTable with the same structure and data as the original. The following example uses the Copy( ) method to create a new DataTable:

```
// create a DataTable object variable to receive the copy
DataTable copyDt;
copyDt = dt.Copy();
```

Selecting a Subset of Rows

The Select( ) method returns a subset of rows from the DataTable and returns the result as a DataRow array. The four overloads take optional arguments specifying the filter criteria, sort order, and DataViewRowState of the rows to be returned. The following example illustrates this concept:

```
// all rows with order amount > 100, sorted on the order date descending
DataRow[] dra = dt.Select("OrderAmount>100.00", "OrderDate DESC");
```

The following example returns all modified rows in the table:

```
DataRow[] dra = dt.Select(null, null, DataViewRowState.ModifiedCurrent);
```

Performing Aggregate Calculations

The Compute( ) method computes the result of an aggregate query on the rows in the table that meet the filter criteria. Here's an example that illustrates this:

```
DataTable dt = new Table();
dt.Columns.Add("OrderId", typeof(System.Int32));
dt.Columns.Add("OrderAmount", typeof(System.Decimal));

// ... add some rows

// computes the sum of order amounts for all orders with Id less than 10
Decimal totalOrderAmount = dt.Compute("SUM(OrderAmount)", "OrderId<10")
```

Removing All Data

The Clear( ) method removes all rows from the DataTable:

```
dt.Clear();
```

Resetting the Table

The Reset( ) method returns the DataTable to its original state. This method can discard the existing DataTable and start working with a new DataTable rather than instantiating a new DataTable object.

```
dt.Reset();
```

Identifying Errors in the Table

The GetErrors( ) method returns an array of the rows that contain errors, whether they are constraint violations or failed update attempts. The RowError property or the SetColumnError( ) method of the DataRow object can be used to set an error, or an error can be set by the DataAdapter in response to errors that occur while data is being reconciled with the data source. The HasErrors( ) method should be called prior to calling GetErrors( ) to determine whether the call to GetErrors( ) is necessary. The following example shows how to use these methods:

```
DataRow[] errorRow;
if(dt.HasErrors())
{
    errorRows = dt.GetErrors();
    for(Int32 i = 0; i<errorRows.Length; i++)
    {
        // ... resolve the error for the row

        // clear the error for resubmitting
        errorRows[i].ClearErrors();
    }
}
```

DataTable Events

The following section describes DataTable events.

ColumnChanged and ColumnChanging

The ColumnChanged and ColumnChanging events can be handled to validate data or control user interface elements. The ColumnChanging event is raised when a value is being changed in a specified column; the ColumnChanged event is raised after the value in the column has been changed. Both events pass a DataColumnChangeEventArgs argument to the event handler that provide information specific to the event.

The following code demonstrates handling the ColumnChanging and ColumnChanged events to perform data validation and logging:

```
DataTable dt = new DataTable();

dt.ColumnChanged += new DataColumnChangeEventHandler(dt_ColumnChanged);
dt.ColumnChanging += new DataColumnChangeEventHandler(dt_ColumnChanging);

private static void dt_ColumnChanging(object sender,
    DataColumnChangeEventArgs e);
{
    if (e.Column.ColumnName == "MyColumn")
    {
        if(e.ProposedValue.Equals("Invalid Data")
        {
            e.Row.RowError = "Invalid data.";
            e.Row.SetColumnError(e.Column, "Column value " +
                "cannot be " e.ProposedValue.ToString());
        }
    }
}

private static void ds_ColumnChanged(object sender,
    DataColumnChangeEventArgs e);
```

```
{
    System.IO.TextWriter tw = System.IO.File.AppendText("colchange.log");
    tw.WriteLine("ColumnChanging: Name = {0}; ProposedValue = {1}; " +
        "Row Id = {2}", e.ColumnName, e.ProposedValue.ToString(),
        e.Row["Id"].ToString());
    tw.Close();
}
```

RowChanged, RowChanging, RowDeleted, and RowDeleting

The DataTable raises four events in response to actions performed on rows. These events are RowChanging and RowChanged, which are raised, respectively, before and after a row is edited; RowDeleting and RowDeleted are raised, respectively, before and after a row is marked for deletion. These events can support custom validation logic similar to the ColumnChanging and ColumnChanged events described earlier. All four events pass a DataRowChangeEventArgs argument to the event handler providing information specific to the event.

The following code demonstrates handling the RowChanged, RowChanging, RowDeleted, and RowDeleting events:

```
DataTable dt = new DataTable();

dt.RowChanged+= new DataRowChangeEventHandler(dt_RowChanged);
dt.RowChanging+= new DataRowChangeEventHandler(dt_RowChanging);
dt.RowDeleted+= new DataRowChangeEventHandler(dt_RowDeleted);
dt.RowDeleting+= new DataRowChangeEventHandler(dt_RowDeleting);

private void dt_RowChanged(object sender, DataRowChangeEventArgs e);
{
    MessageBox.Show("RowChanged: Action  =  " + e.Action + "; " +
        "Row Id  =  " + e.Row["Id"].ToString());
}

private void dt_RowChanging(object sender, DataRowChangeEventArgs e);
{
    MessageBox.Show("RowChanging: Action  =  " + e.Action + "; " +
        "Row Id  =  " + e.Row["Id"].ToString());
}

private void dt_RowDeleted(object sender, DataRowChangeEventArgs e);
{
    MessageBox.Show("RowDeleted: Action  =  " + e.Action + "; " +
        "Row Id  =  " + e.Row["Id"].ToString());
}

private void dt_RowDeleting(object sender, DataRowChangeEventArgs e);
{
    MessageBox.Show("RowDeleting: Action  =  " + e.Action + "; " +
        "Row Id  =  " + e.Row["Id"].ToString());
}
```

8

DataColumns

The DataColumn defines the schema for a single column in a DataTable. The DataTable schema is defined by a collection of columns in the table along with any constraints. The DataColumn defines:

- The type of data that can be stored in the column
- The length of the column for text-based column types
- Whether the data in the column can be modified
- Whether the column values for each row must be unique
- Whether the column in rows can contain null values
- Whether the column values are automatically generated and the rules for generating those values
- Whether the column value is calculated based on an expression

As with all disconnected classes, the DataColumn is independent of the column in the underlying data source. As a result, its data type is defined as a .NET Framework data type that is matched to the data type in the data source.

Creating DataColumns

When creating a new DataColumn, the overloaded constructor allows up to four optional arguments to be specified to initialize the ColumnName, DataType, Expression, and ColumnMapping properties. The following example creates a column and specifies both its name and data type:

```
// create the column and set the name and data type using properties
DataColumn col = new DataColumn();
col.ColumnName = "MyTextColumn";
col.DataType = typeof(System.String);
```

```
// the code below is identical to the above three lines
DataColumn col = new DataColumn("MyTextColumn", typeof(System.String));

// set the maximum length in characters of the new column
col.MaxLength = 50;
```

The following example demonstrates another overloaded constructor and subsequently sets some properties of the column:

```
// create another column
DataColumn col = new DataColumn("Id", typeof(System.Int32));
col.AllowDBNull = false;    // the column doesn't allow null values
col.DefaultValue = -1;      // set the default value
col.Caption = "ID #";       // column title used by certain bound controls
col.Unique = true;          // the column value is each row must be unique
col.ReadOnly = true;        // the column value cannot be changed once the
                            // the row is added to a table
```

If the column name isn't supplied, the names Column1, Column2, Column3, and so on, are assigned when the column is added to the table. An exception is raised if the name of the column being added to the table is the same as the name of an existing column in the table.

Creating AutoIncrement Columns

ADO.NET supports columns that increment automatically to ensure that values are unique when new rows are added to the table. These properties are AutoIncrement, AutoIncrementSeed, and AutoIncrementStep. The following code demonstrates creation of an AutoIncrement column:

```
DataColumn col = new DataColumn("Id", typeof(System.Int32));
col.AutoIncrement = true;
col.AutoIncrementSeed = -1;
col.AutoIncrementStep = -1;
```

The code uses seed and step values of −1. This causes the values for the added rows to start at −1, with subsequent values of −2, −3, and so on, which ensures that the automatically generated values will not already exist in a data source with an AutoIncrement key containing only positive values. When the data is updated back to the data source, the added records are correctly identified as new records, inserted into the data source, and at that point the AutoIncrement value can be returned from the data source and update the negative value in the DataSet. Returning the AutoIncrement values generated from the data source is discussed in more detail in Chapter 15.

Creating Expression Columns

An expression column can be created to perform calculations on columns in the row or aggregations on a collection of rows. No data is actually stored in the column, and the expression value is evaluated when the column is read. Setting the Expression property to anything other than an empty string automatically sets the ReadOnly property of the column to true. If the expression isn't valid, an EvaluateException is raised.

```
// calculate the extended price for the the order detail line
DataColumn col1 = new DataColumn("Quantity", typeof(System.Int32));
DataColumn col2 = new DataColumn("Price", typeof(System.Decimal));

// create a column calculating the extended price
DataColumn col3 = new DataColumn("ExtendedPrice", typeof(System.Decimal));
Col3.Expression = "Quantity * Price";
```

Handling Null Values

The AllowDBNull property determines whether null values can be stored in the column in rows. This value is true by default.

The System.DBNull class must be used to set a column value to null and can test whether a column contains a null value. Using the null keyword results in a runtime error. The following code demonstrates this concept:

```
DataRow row;
// ... retrieve the DataRow

// set the value of the first column in the row to null
row[0] = DBNull.Value;

// test the first column to determine if it contains a null value
Boolean isNull = (row[0] == DBNull.Value);
```

The IsNull( ) method also allows the columns in the DataRow to be tested for null values using a more convenient syntax. The method returns a Boolean value indicating whether the value for the specified column in the row is null.

```
DataRow row;
// ... retrieve the DataRow

// test the first column to determine if it contains a null value
Boolean isNull = row.IsNull(0);
```

Mapping .NET Data Provider Types to .NET Framework Types

ADO.NET disconnected classes are data-source independent. When data is retrieved from a data source into the .NET objects, the data is stored as .NET Framework types rather than data types specific to the data source. When data is retrieved, either by using the Fill( ) method of the DataAdapter or the GetValue( ) method of the DataReader, the .NET Framework type is inferred from the type returned from the .NET data provider. When specifying the data type for a column, a .NET Framework type compatible with the data type in the underlying data source must be specified. Appendix A lists the .NET Framework Types corresponding to Microsoft SQL Server types and OLE DB types.

9

DataRows

The DataRow class represents a single row of data in the DataTable. The DataRow class can retrieve, update, insert, and delete a row of data from the DataTable. Using the DataRow class, each column value for the row can be accessed.

The DataRow maintains the RowState property that is used by ADO.NET to track the changes that have been made to a DataRow. This property allows changed rows to be identified, and the appropriate update command to be used to update the data source with the changes.

Creating a DataRow

A DataRow is created by calling the NewRow( ) method of a DataTable, a method that takes no arguments. The DataTable supplies the schema, and the new DataRow is created with default or empty values for the fields:

```
// create a table with one column
DataTable dt = new DataTable();
dt.Columns.Add("MyColumn", typeof(System.String));

// create a row with the same schema as DataTable dt
DataRow row = dt.NewRow();
row["MyColumn"] = "Item 1";

// add the row to the table
dt.Rows.Add(row);
```

Updating Rows

There are three ways to modify the contents of a row. First, you can simply replace the values of the column with a new value:

```
DataRow row;
// ... code to retrieve data into the row
```

```
// access the column by its ordinal and update the value
row[0] = "New Value";

// access the column by its name and update the value
row["MyColumn"] = "New Value";
```

You can also buffer the updates to a row by calling the BeginEdit( ), EndEdit( ), and CancelEdit( ) methods. The BeginEdit( ) method turns off all constraints and suspends events used to enforce validation rules. If CancelEdit( ) is called, the changes in the buffer are discarded. When EndEdit( ) is called, the data is validated against the constraints, and the appropriate events are raised. BeginEdit( ) is called implicitly when a user changes the value of a data-bound control. EndEdit( ) is called implicitly when AcceptChanges( ) is called.

```
DataTable dt = new DataTable();

// ... code to retrieve data into the DataTable object

DataRow row = dt.Rows[0];

row.BeginEdit();
foreach(DataColumn col in dt.Columns)
{
    // ...modify the column value
}

bool rowValid = true;

// ...check the values in the row to make sure that they are valid

if(rowValid)
{
    row.CancelEdit();
}
else
{
    row.EndEdit();
}
```

Finally, a row can be updated by accessing the row through the ItemArray property. When this method is called, an attempt is made to locate the row matching the primary key. If the row is found, it is updated with the values in the ItemArray; otherwise, a new row is created. Any columns with an array element set to null are set to the default value for the column. The value for AutoIncrement columns should be set to null in the ItemArray.

```
// create a table with two columns
DataTable dt = new DataTable();
DataColumn colId =
  new DataColumn("ProductId", typeof(System.Int32));
DataColumn colDesc =
  new DataColumn("Description", typeof(System.String));
dt.Columns.AddRange(new DataColumn[] {colId, colDesc});
```

```
dt.Rows.Add(new object[] {1, "Widget"});

// get the data for the row using the ItemArray property
object[] row = dt.Rows[0].ItemArray;

// set the ProductId to be AutoIncrement
colId.AutoIncrement = true;
// pass null for the AutoIncrement value
dt.Rows.Add(new object[] {null, "Thing"});

// let the description be null
colDesc.AllowDBNull = true;
// add a row with a null description, and AutoIncrement Id
dt.Rows.Add(new object[] {null, null});
```

Deleting Rows

The Delete( ) method deletes rows from the DataTable. If the RowState is Added, the row is removed; otherwise the RowState of the existing DataRow is changed to Deleted. The row is permanently removed from the table only when AcceptChanges( ) is called on the row either explicitly or implicitly when the Update( ) method of the DataAdapter successfully updates the changes to the row back to the data source.

```
// delete the first row from the table
DataRow row = dt.Rows[0];
row.Delete();          // RowState changed to Deleted

row = dt.NewRow();
// ... code to set the data for the row

// add the row to the table
dt.Rows.Add(row);

// delete the row
row.Delete();          // Newly inserted row is removed from the table
```

When you iterate through the rows of a DataTable, it is important to remember that rows are only marked for deletion and are still present in the collection of rows for the table. If you might be accessing Deleted rows in the DataTable, you need to explicitly check the state of the row and ignore it if it is Deleted. This is shown in the following example:

```
// Iterate over the results (and ignore deleted rows).
foreach (DataRow dr in ds.Tables["Customers"].Rows)
{
    if (dr.RowState != DataRowState.Deleted)
    {
        // ... process the row
    }
}
```

If you try to access the current value of a field in a row that has been deleted, you'll receive the RowNotInTableException or DeleteRowInacessibleException.

DataRows

Using Row State Information

The RowState property is used by ADO.NET to track the changes that have been made to a DataRow, which allows changes made to the data while disconnected to be updated back to the data source. The RowState property indicates whether the row belongs to a table, and if it does, whether it's newly inserted, modified, deleted, or unchanged since it was loaded.

The value of the RowState property can't be set directly. ADO.NET sets the row state in response to actions that affect the DataRow. The AcceptChanges( ) and RejectChanges( ) methods, whether explicitly or implicitly called, both reset the RowState value for the row to Unchanged. The following code illustrates this idea:

```
// create a table with one column
DataTable dt = new DataTable();
dt.Columns.Add("MyColumn", typeof(System.String));

// create a new row
DataRow row = dt.NewRow();          // RowState = Detached

// add the row to the table
dt.Rows.Add(row);                   // RowState = Added
dt.AcceptChanges();                 // RowState = Unchanged

// modify the row
row["MyColumn"] = "MyFieldValue"; // RowState = Modified

// reject the changes
row.RejectChanges();                // RowState = Unchanged

// delete the row
row.Delete();                       // RowState = Deleted
row.AcceptChanges();                // row no longer exists
```

Using Row Version Information

ADO.NET maintains up to three versions of each DataRow object. The DataAdapter reconciles changes made since the data was loaded from the data source, thereby making changes to the disconnected data permanent. Two versions of each row are maintained to allow the DataAdapter to determine how to perform the reconciliation. The Original version contains the values that were loaded into the row. The Current version contains the latest version of the data, including the changes made since the data was originally loaded. The Original version isn't available for newly created rows.

ADO.NET also allows a row to be put into edit mode which temporarily suspends events for the row and allows the user to make multiple changes to the row without triggering validation rules. The BeginEdit( ) method of the DataRow puts the row into edit mode, while the EndEdit( ) and CancelEdit( ) methods take the row out of edit mode. AcceptChanges( ) also takes the row out of edit mode because it implicitly calls EndEdit( ), as does RejectChanges( ), which implicitly calls CancelEdit( ).

A `Proposed` row version is made available while the row is in edit mode and contains the changes that have been made to the row while it was in edit mode. If the `EndEdit( )` method is called, the changes made are copied from the `Proposed` row to the `Current` row. If the `CancelEdit( )` method is called, the values in the `Proposed` version are simply discarded. In either case, once the editing is completed, the `Proposed` version of the row is no longer available.

Finally, a `Default` row version returns the `Current` version if the row isn't being edited or the `Proposed` row if it is.

The `HasVersion( )` method of the `DataRow` can determine whether a specific version of the row exists. If the version exists, column values for it can be retrieved using one of the three overloads of the `DataRow` indexer. The following example shows how to check for and retrieve the `Proposed` version of a row:

```
DataRow dr;

// ... code to build, fill, and modify the row

object objColVal;

// check if the Proposed version of the row exists
if (dr.HasVersion(DataRowVersion.Proposed))
{
    // retrieve the value for the first column in the Proposed row
    objColVal = dr[0, DataRowVersion.Proposed];
}
```

Accepting or Rejecting Changes to Rows

When a `DataRow` is modified, ADO.NET marks the row as having a pending change and sets the `RowState` of the `DataRow` to `Added`, `Modified`, or `Deleted` as appropriate. ADO.NET also maintains version information by tracking both `Original` and `Current` versions of each row. Together, this information allows ADO.NET to identify both the rows and columns that have been changed.

The `DataRow` has three methods—`GetChanges( )`, `AcceptChanges( )`, and `RejectChanges( )`—that can commit or discard the changes made to a `DataRow` since it was last loaded or since `AcceptChanges( )` was last called. These methods function identically to the same methods for the `DataSet` that are described in Chapter 6. Also, when these methods are called on a `DataSet`, they are implicitly called on all tables contained within the `DataSet` and from there are called implicitly on all rows in the table.

Navigating Parent and Child Rows

A `DataRow` can have both parent and child rows if the `DataTable` that it belongs to has a `DataRelation` set up with another table. There are three methods that allow these relationships to be navigated. The `GetParentRow( )` method returns the parent row as a `DataRow` object. The `GetParentRows( )` method returns the parent rows as an array of `DataRow` objects. Both methods require either the name of the

DataRows

`DataRelation` or a reference to the `DataRelation` as an argument. An optional argument specifying the `DataRowVersion` allows control over the version of the rows returned.

The `SetParentRow( )` method changes the parent row for the `DataRow`. This method simply takes a reference to the new parent `DataRow` and an optional `DataRelation` argument, if required.

Finally, the `GetChildRows( )` method returns the child rows as an array of `DataRow` objects. The name of the `DataRelation` or a reference to the `DataRelation` is required as an argument. An optional argument specifying the `DataRowVersion` allows control over the version of rows returned.

Navigating parent and child rows is explored in detail in Chapter 11.

Using Row Error Information

The `HasErrors` property returns a Boolean value indicating whether an error is set on any of the columns in the row. This value can determine whether error-handling code needs to be executed or set custom error information based on custom validation rules. Rather than iterating over the entire collection of rows to locate errors, the `GetErrors( )` method of the `DataTable` can return the array of rows containing errors within the table. The `HasErrors` property of the `DataTable` indicates whether there are any rows with errors and should be checked to determine whether calling `GetErrors( )` is necessary.

Error information for the row can be set for the entire row or for a specific column in the row. The `RowError` property sets and retrieves an error description that applies to the entire row. The `GetColumnError( )` and `SetColumnError( )` methods set and get the error description for a particular column specified with either a column name, column ordinal, or a reference to the column object.

Finally, the `ClearErrors( )` method clears all error information for the row and for all columns in the row.

The following example demonstrates how to work with `DataRow` errors:

```
DataRow row;

// ... code to set up the row

if(row.HasErrors)
{
    String rowErrorText = row.RowError;

    foreach(DataColumn colError in row.GetColumnsInError())
    {
        String colErrorColumnName = colError.ColumnName;
        String colErrorText = row.GetColumnError(colError);

        // ... processing for column errors
    }
```

```
        // ... processing for row error

        // clear the errors, once processed
        row.ClearErrors();
    }
    else
    {
        // no errors in the row
    }
```

As mentioned, errors can also be set on columns, as shown in this example:

```
    DataRow row;

    // ... code to set up the row

    // using the column name
    row.SetColumnError("MyColumn", "Custom error text, based on name.");

    // using the ordinal
    row.SetColumnError(1, "Custom error text, based on ordinal.");
```

10

Constraints

One key to successfully using disconnected data is minimizing the possibility for invalid information. If invalid values are entered in the DataSet, the error won't be caught until you commit changes to the data source. At this point, the problem can be much more difficult to track down and resolve.

In order to reduce the possibility of invalid data, you can use properties of the DataColumn object, as explained in Chapter 8. For example, if your DataSet is correctly configured with schema information, you'll receive an error if you try to insert a null value into a non-null column, use an invalid data type, or exceed the column length restrictions. Another way to prevent data errors is by using Constraint objects.

Constraint objects are required to enforce specialized rules that involve comparing column values in more than one row. ADO.NET currently provides two types of constraints:

- The UniqueConstraint, which represents a rule forbidding duplicate values in a column (or across multiple columns)
- The ForeignKeyConstraint, which represents a relationship that links a column (or set of columns) in one table to a column (or set of columns) in another table and defines the type of action to take for updates or deletions

In this chapter, you'll learn how to create these classes, enforce constraint checking, and enforce referential integrity in the DataSet.

Constraint Object Overview

The System.Data.Constraint type is an abstract class with two derived classes: UniqueConstraint and ForeignKeyConstraint. In order to use a constraint, you must create the appropriate class and add it to the DataTable.Constraints collection.

Constraints are enforced only if the EnforceConstraints property of the containing DataSet is true, which it is by default. If you attempt to modify, delete, or insert data in such a way that it violates an existing constraint, and EnforceConstraints is true, a ConstraintException is thrown, and the change is rejected. Similarly, if the DataTable already contains data, and you add a new Constraint, all the rows are checked to ensure they agree with the new rule. If any row violates the constraint, an InvalidConstraintException is thrown, and the Constraint object isn't added.

Here are a few more rules of thumb that come into play when working with Constraint objects:

- If you have set DataSet.EnforceConstraints to false, you will never encounter a ConstraintException or InvalidConstraintException. However, if you later change DataSet.EnforceConstraints to true, all the rows will be examined to ensure that they don't violate the existing constraints. If a discrepancy is found, an InvalidConstraintException is thrown, and EnforceConstraints is set to false.

- When merging a DataSet, constraints are applied and verified after the merge is complete.

- There is no limit to how many Constraint objects a DataTable can contain; you are free to define as many unique rows and foreign key restrictions as you need.

 It doesn't seem possible for .NET developers to create custom .NET constraint classes. The Constraint object defines several abstract methods that have assembly-level protection, so they can be overridden only by classes in the System.Data.dll assembly. However, you can create a class that handles the DataTable.ColumnChanging event to implement custom validation, as explained in Chapter 7.

The UniqueConstraint

The UniqueConstraint prevents duplication in a single column or the combined value of a group of columns. The UniqueConstraint object adds two properties: Columns, which defines one or more DataColumn objects that, when taken together, must be unique; and IsPrimaryKey, which indicates whether the UniqueConstraint is required to guarantee the integrity of the primary key for the table.

The UniqueConstraint provides several overloaded constructors. Here's how you might create a UniqueConstraint that prevents duplicate CustomerID values:

```
// Create the UniqueConstraint object.
UniqueConstraint uc = new UniqueConstraint("ID", dt.Columns["CustomerID"]);

// Add the UniqueConstraint to the table's Constraints collection.
dt.Constraints.Add(uc);
```

You can also define a UniqueConstraint that encompasses several columns, such as this first and last name combination:

```
// Create an array with the two columns.
DataColumn[] cols = new DataColumn[] {dt.Columns["LastName"],
  dt.Columns["FirstName"]};

// Create the UniqueConstraint object.
UniqueConstraint uc = new UniqueConstraint("FullName", cols);

// Add the UniqueConstraint to the table's Constraints collection.
dt.Constraints.Add(uc);
```

To create a primary key UniqueConstraint, use an overloaded version of the constructor that accepts a Boolean parameter, and specify true. Once created, you can't change the IsPrimaryKey property of a UniqueConstraint.

```
// Create a UniqueConstraint object that represents the primary key.
UniqueConstraint uc = new UniqueConstraint("ID", dt.Columns["CustomerID"],
  true);

// Add the UniqueConstraint to the table's Constraints collection.
dt.Constraints.Add(uc);
```

You can also pass constructor arguments to several overloads of the Add( ) method of a ConstraintCollection to create a UniqueConstraint. In this case, the false parameter indicates that this UniqueConstraint should not be designated as the primary key for the table.

```
// Add a new UniqueConstraint to the table's Constraints collection.
dt.Constraints.Add("ID", dt.Columns["CustomerID"], false);
```

However, it's quite possible that you won't use any of these approaches to generate UniqueConstraint objects because ADO.NET provides an even easier approach through the DataColumn object. As soon as you set the DataColumn.Unique property to true, a new UniqueConstraint is generated and added to the collection. Similarly, setting the Unique property of a column to false removes the UniqueConstraint. This process is transparent to your application, unless you need to modify the IsPrimaryKey property or create a UniqueConstraint that acts on multiple columns.

Having a UniqueConstraint in place doesn't mean you won't receive an error when updating data back to the data source. Remember, the DataSet almost always contains a subset of the total information in the database. If a unique column value conflicts with another value in the data source (but not the DataSet), the problem won't be detected until you attempt to commit changes.

 If you add a UniqueConstraint on a DataColumn in which AllowDbNull is set to true, you will get only a single row with a null value in the column. If there are multiple rows with null values, ADO.NET considers it to be a duplication and a violation of the UniqueConstraint.

Constraints and FillSchema( )

If you fill a DataSet without using the FillSchema( ) method, ADO.NET doesn't create any Constraint objects automatically. However, you can still create and apply Constraint objects manually, as shown earlier.

If you use the FillSchema( ) to retrieve schema information, UniqueConstraint objects are created to match the restrictions you have defined in the data source. The FillSchema( ) method also attempts to designate a primary key. If a primary key column (or group of columns) is found in the result set, it's used to create a UniqueConstraint with IsPrimaryKey set to true. Otherwise, FillSchema( ) uses any non-nullable unique column returned by the query.

To see how this works, you can run the simple test in Example 10-1, which displays the automatically generated UniqueConstraint objects.

Example 10-1. Add unique constraints to a data source

```
// FillWithConstraints.cs - Create UniqueConstraints defined in data source

using System;
using System.Data;
using System.Data.SqlClient;

public class FillWithConstraints
{
    static string connectionString = "Data Source=localhost;" +
        "Initial Catalog=Northwind;Integrated Security=SSPI";
    static string SQL = "SELECT * FROM Categories";

    public static void Main()
    {
        // Create ADO.NET objects.
        SqlConnection con = new SqlConnection(connectionString);
        SqlCommand comSelect = new SqlCommand(SQL, con);
        SqlDataAdapter adapter = new SqlDataAdapter(comSelect);
        DataSet ds = new DataSet();

        // Execute the command.
        try
        {
            con.Open();

            adapter.FillSchema(ds, SchemaType.Mapped, "Categories");
            adapter.Fill(ds, "Categories");
        }
        catch (Exception err)
        {
            Console.WriteLine(err.ToString());
        }
        finally
        {
            con.Close();
        }
```

Example 10-1. Add unique constraints to a data source (continued)

```
    foreach (UniqueConstraint uc in
      ds.Tables["Categories"].Constraints)
    {
        Console.WriteLine("*** " + uc.ConstraintName + " ***");

        Console.Write("Primary Key: \t");
        Console.WriteLine(uc.IsPrimaryKey);
        Console.Write("Column: \t");
        Console.WriteLine(uc.Columns[0].ColumnName);
    }
  }

}
```

If you omit the FillSchema( ) method call, you'll find that no constraint information is retrieved. With FillSchema( ), you'll find that exactly one UniqueConstraint has been added to the DataSet:

```
*** Constraint1 ***
Primary Key:    True
Column:         CategoryID
```

 ForeignKeyContraint objects are never created automatically, regardless of whether you use FillSchema( ) when populating the DataSet.

The ForeignKeyConstraint

The ForeignKeyConstraint provides an easy way to impose referential integrity rules on records in a DataSet. The ForeignKeyConstraint serves two purposes: it prevents you from making DataSet changes that violate referential integrity, and it allows you to define what action to take with child rows when parent rows are updated or deleted.

When creating a ForeignKeyConstraint, you specify the parent and child DataColumn and optionally name the constraint. You add the ForeignKeyConstraint to the child DataTable . For example, the following code creates and applies a ForeignKeyConstraint that relates product records to a specific category:

```
ForeignKeyConstraint fc = new ForeignKeyConstraint("CategoryID",
    ds.Tables["Categories"].Columns["CategoryID"],
    ds.Tables["Products"].Columns["CategoryID"]);

ds.Tables["Products"].Constraints.Add(fc);
```

Before performing this step, you should add a UniqueKeyConstraint on the CategoryID column in the parent (Categories) table to ensure that every relation can be resolved.

You can also pass constructor arguments to several overloads of the Add( ) method of a ConstraintCollection to create a ForeignKeyConstraint. The following code is equivalent to the previous example:

```
// Add a new ForeignKeyConstraint to the table's Constraints collection.
dt.Constraints.Add("CategoryID",
    ds.Tables["Categories"].Columns["CategoryID"],
    ds.Tables["Products"].Columns["CategoryID"]);
```

When a ForeignKeyConstraint is in place, and constraint checking is enabled for the DataSet, all child column values (except nulls, if they are allowed) must point to an existing parent row.

Referential Integrity with ForeignKeyConstraint Rules

The ForeignKeyConstraint doesn't just restrict changes; it can also propagate them depending on the value of three key properties: DeleteRule, UpdateRule, and AcceptRejectRule:

- The DeleteRule determines what happens to child rows when a parent is deleted. By default, this is Cascade, which means all child rows are deleted along with the parent.
- The UpdateRule determines what happens if the parent's key column is modified. The default is Cascade, which means that the child rows are updated to point to the new value.
- The AcceptRejectRule determines what happens when the DataRow. AcceptChanges( ) method is called (usually as part of a data source update). By default, this is None.

Generally, DeleteRule is the most important of these settings. The UpdateRule isn't frequently used because you rarely change the value in a primary key column. In fact, this field often corresponds to an identity value that is generated by the data source. Tables 10-1 and 10-2 present the options for the Rule enumeration when used to set the DeleteRule and UpdateRule properties,

Table 10-1. Values for the DeleteRule

Value	Used for DeleteRule
Cascade	If the parent row is deleted, the child rows are also deleted.
None	No action is taken on child rows. Thus, if you try to delete a parent that has linked children, an exception will be thrown. This is the default SQL Server behavior.
SetDefault	If the parent row is deleted, the child rows have the default value placed in their foreign key column, if allowed (otherwise an exception is thrown).
SetNull	If the parent row is deleted, the foreign key column of all children is set to null. If the DataColumn.AllowDbNull property disallows this, an exception is thrown.

Table 10-2. Values for the UpdateRule

Value	Used for UpdateRule
Cascade	If the linked column is changed in the parent, the foreign key column in all child rows is updated accordingly.
None	No action is taken on child rows. Thus, if you change the linked column of a parent that has children, an exception is thrown. This is the traditional SQL Server behavior.

Table 10-2. Values for the UpdateRule (continued)

Value	Used for UpdateRule
SetDefault	If the linked column of a parent row is changed, the foreign key column in the child rows is reset to the default value, if allowed (otherwise an exception is thrown).
SetNull	If the linked column of the parent row is changed, the foreign key column of all children is set to null. If the DataColumn.AllowDbNull property disallows this, an exception is thrown.

The AcceptRejectRule, on the other hand, can accept a value of Cascade or None from the AcceptRejectRule enumeration. If you set this value to Cascade, the AcceptChanges( ) method is called on child rows when the parent row is updated. This is rarely the behavior you want. In fact, because the AcceptChanges( ) method resets the DataRow.RowState to Unchanged, this technique may actually prevent child rows from being updated when you merge changes back into the data source! Thus, it's strongly recommended that you use the default of None, unless you aren't intending to commit DataSet changes.

Like UniqueConstraints, the usefulness of ForeignKeyConstraints may be limited by the fact that the DataSet contains only a subset of information from the DataSet. Thus, if you use a ForeignKeyConstraint, you can't insert child rows that don't have corresponding parent rows in the DataSet, even if these parent rows legitimately exist in the data source. However, you can still create and use DataRelation objects, as described in Chapter 11.

11

DataRelations

Chapter 10 showed how to use ForeignKeyConstraint rules to help ensure the integrity of relational data. Though ForeignKeyConstraint objects are important for data validation, they don't provide any benefit when it comes to navigating the DataSet. For example, even if you define a link between two tables with a ForeignKeyConstraint, you can't use this link to create a master-detail list.

ADO.NET provides another object that can help in this situation: the DataRelation. You can use a DataRelation to automatically generate and apply a ForeignKeyConstraint, or you can use it simply as a navigational aid. The benefit of the DataRelation is that it allows you to navigate disconnected data using a defined relationship between tables. For example, if you select a single parent row, you can use the DataRelation to retrieve a list of child records. Conversely, you can use the DataRelation to discover the parent of any child row.

This chapter explains how to create a DataRelation, use it for record navigation, and build a master-detail list.

DataRelation Object Overview

Every DataSet contains a DataRelationCollection object, which contains DataRelation objects. Each DataRelation defines a relationship between two tables. There are two reasons why you might define DataRelation objects:

- To provide better error checking (for example, spotting an orphaned child before you reconnect to update the data source). This functionality is provided through the ForeignKeyConstraint, which the DataRelation can create implicitly.

- To provide better navigation.

A typical DataRelation requires three pieces of information: a descriptive name of your choosing (which doesn't signify anything or relate to the data source), a reference to the parent DataColumn, and a reference to the child DataColumn. You can add this information with the DataRelation constructor:

```
DataRelation relation = new DataRelation("Name", ParentCol, ChildCol);
```

Once you've defined the DataRelation object, you need to add it to the DataSet:

```
ds.Relations.Add(relation);
```

For example, to create a relationship between product categories and products, use the following code:

```
DataColumn parentCol = ds.Tables["Categories"].Columns["CategoryID"];
DataColumn childCol = ds.Tables["Products"].Columns["CategoryID"];
DataRelation relation = new DataRelation("Cat_Prod", parentCol, childCol);

ds.Relations.Add(relation);
```

If you attempt to create a DataRelation, and the parent record column isn't unique, or there are child records that refer to nonexistent parents, an exception is thrown.

 Currently, there is no way to automatically add a DataRelation object based on the relationships defined in the data source. That means that if you want to use relations, either to enforce data integrity or provide parent-child navigation, you need to create them yourself.

DataRelations and Constraints

At first glance, the DataRelation seems to duplicate some of the functionality provided by the ForeignKeyConstraint to enforce referential integrity. However, this isn't really the case. The DataRelation actually uses the Constraint classes. By default, when you create a new DataRelation, a UniqueConstraint is created automatically for the parent column and added to the parent table if it doesn't already exist. At the same time, a ForeignKeyConstraint is created for the child column and added to the child table. Thus, the rules governing relational integrity are exactly the same as those discussed in Chapter 10.

In some cases, you might want to create a DataRelation without generating any constraints. This allows you to use a relation to aid navigation but not enforce it as a data validation rule. One reason why you might not want to enforce a relationship could be because you have queried only a subset of the total parent rows in the data source. Consequently, there may be child rows that reference a valid parent row that isn't a part of the DataSet.

To make sure constraints are generated, you must use the DataRelation constructor that accepts an additional Boolean value. If you supply false, the Constraint objects aren't generated.

```
DataRelation relation = new DataRelation("Name", ParentCol,
                                         ChildCol, false);
```

You can still use the DataRelation for navigation, but referentially integrity will not be enforced on the DataSet.

As explained in Chapter 10, you can configure the ForeignKeyConstraint to specify if deletes and updates are cascaded. When using a DataRelation, you can still use this feature; you simply need to modify the automatically generated ForeignKeyConstraint, which is available through the DataRelation.ChildKeyConstraint property.

Navigating Relational Data

Once a relation is established, you can use it navigate from a parent row to the associated child rows or from a child row to the parent. Use the GetChildRows() or GetParentRow() method of the DataRow object:

```
foreach (DataRow parent in ds.Tables["Categories"].Rows)
{
    // (Process the category row.)

    foreach (DataRow child in parent.GetChildRows("Cat_Prod"))
    {
        // (Process the products in this category.)
    }
}
```

Similarly, the reverse logic branches from a child to the related parent:

```
foreach (DataRow child in ds.Tables["Products"].Rows)
{
    // (Process the product row.)

    DataRow parent = child.GetParentRow("Cat_Prod");
    // (Process category for this product.)
}
```

This syntax presents an easy and elegant way to traverse hierarchical data. However, it isn't the only way to handle relational data. You can simply use the DataTable.Select() method to extract matching rows from another table. The Select() method returns an array of DataRow objects based on a SQL expression (and optionally the DataViewRowState). For example, to traverse relational data, use the Select() method to retrieve rows from the child table that match the parent's key field. It's a little more work, but accomplishes the same task without requiring a DataRelation.

```
foreach (DataRow parent in ds.Tables["Categories"].Rows)
{
    // (Process the category row.)

    DataRow[] rows =
        ds.Tables["Products"].Select("CategoryID=" +
                                    parent["CategoryID"].ToString());

    foreach (DataRow row in rows)
    {
```

```
        // (Process the products in this category.)
    }
}
```

Of course, you have another option that doesn't rely on `DataRelation` objects or the `DataTable.Select()` method: using a join query to combine multiple tables in the data source into a single retrieved table. This approach is useful if you want to display some sort of aggregate data but don't need to access the tables separately or perform updates.

When developers begin ADO.NET programming, they commonly ask whether they should design with join queries or `DataRelation` objects in mind. One factor in making a decision is whether you plan to update the retrieved data. If so, separate tables and a `DataRelation` object offers the most flexibility. If you don't need to deal with the data separately or update it later, a join query can be more efficient, although it can introduce additional complications.

Modeling a One-to-Many Relationship

Our next example demonstrates `DataRelation` objects in action with a simple master-detail view. Figure 11-1 shows the example, which presents a list of categories of the left and a list of the products in the currently selected category on the right.

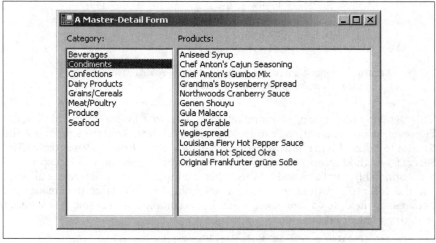

Figure 11-1. Using relationships with a master-detail form

To implement this design, you simply need to fill a `DataSet` with both tables and define a `DataRelation`. Then when an item is selected in the first list, the corresponding rows are added to the second. The full code is shown in Example 11-1.

Example 11-1. A master-detail form

```
using System;
using System.Data;
```

Example 11-1. A master-detail form (continued)

```
using System.Drawing;
using System.Data.SqlClient;
using System.Windows.Forms;


public class MasterDetail : Form
{
    // (Designer code omitted.)

    private ListBox lstCategories = new ListBox();
    private ListBox lstProducts = new ListBox();
    private DataSet ds = new DataSet();
    private DataRelation relation;

    string connectionString = "Data Source=localhost;" +
                  "Initial Catalog=Northwind;Integrated Security=SSPI";
    string categorySQL = "SELECT * FROM Categories";
    string productSQL = "SELECT * FROM Products";

    private void MasterDetail_Load(object sender, System.EventArgs e)
    {
        // Create ADO.NET objects.
        SqlConnection con = new SqlConnection(connectionString);
        SqlCommand com = new SqlCommand(categorySQL, con);
        SqlDataAdapter adapter = new SqlDataAdapter(com);

        // Execute the command.
        try
        {
            con.Open();
            adapter.Fill(ds, "Categories");
            adapter.SelectCommand.CommandText = productSQL;
            adapter.Fill(ds, "Products");
        }
        catch (Exception err)
        {
            MessageBox.Show(err.ToString());
        }
        finally
        {
            con.Close();
        }

        // Add the relation.
        DataColumn parentCol =
                    ds.Tables["Categories"].Columns["CategoryID"];
        DataColumn childCol = ds.Tables["Products"].Columns["CategoryID"];
        relation = new DataRelation("Cat_Prod", parentCol, childCol);
        ds.Relations.Add(relation);

        // Show the category list.
        foreach (DataRow row in ds.Tables["Categories"].Rows)
```

Example 11-1. A master-detail form (continued)

```
        {
            lstCategories.Items.Add(row["CategoryName"]);
        }
    }

    private void lstCategories_SelectedIndexChanged(object sender,
                                                    System.EventArgs e)
    {
        lstProducts.Items.Clear();

        // Find the corresponding parent row.
        DataRow[] rows = ds.Tables["Categories"].Select("CategoryName='" +
                        lstCategories.Text + "'");
        DataRow parent = rows[0];

        // Browse through all the children.
        foreach (DataRow child in parent.GetChildRows(relation))
        {
            lstProducts.Items.Add(child["ProductName"]);
        }
    }
}
```

Note that this code deliberately avoids data binding, which we'll consider in Chapter 12. Data binding can simplify the code used to fill the control, but our approach offers more flexibility, particularly if you need to use an unusual control that doesn't really support data binding. One such control is the TreeView (see Figure 11-2).

Figure 11-2. Using relationships with a TreeView

In Example 11-2, we put similar code and the same relation to work by filling a TreeView with a hierarchical list of products grouped by categories.

Example 11-2. A hierarchical TreeView

```
using System;
using System.Data;
using System.Data.SqlClient;
using System.Windows.Forms;

public class HierarchicalTreeView : System.Windows.Forms.Form
{
    // (Designer code omitted.)

    private TreeView tree = new TreeView();

    string connectionString = "Data Source=localhost;" +
                "Initial Catalog=Northwind;Integrated Security=SSPI";
    string categorySQL = "SELECT * FROM Categories";
    string productSQL = "SELECT * FROM Products";

    private void HierarchicalTreeView_Load(object sender,
                                        System.EventArgs e)
    {
        // Create ADO.NET objects.
        SqlConnection con = new SqlConnection(connectionString);
        SqlCommand com = new SqlCommand(categorySQL, con);
        SqlDataAdapter adapter = new SqlDataAdapter(com);
        DataSet ds = new DataSet();

        // Execute the command.
        try
        {
            con.Open();
            adapter.Fill(ds, "Categories");
            adapter.SelectCommand.CommandText = productSQL;
            adapter.Fill(ds, "Products");
        }
        catch (Exception err)
        {
            MessageBox.Show(err.ToString());
        }
        finally
        {
            con.Close();
        }

        // Add the relation.
        DataColumn parentCol =
                ds.Tables["Categories"].Columns["CategoryID"];
        DataColumn childCol = ds.Tables["Products"].Columns["CategoryID"];
        DataRelation relation = new DataRelation("Cat_Prod", parentCol,
                                            childCol);
        ds.Relations.Add(relation);

        // Fill the tree.
        foreach (DataRow parent in ds.Tables["Categories"].Rows)
```

Example 11-2. A hierarchical TreeView (continued)

```
    {
        TreeNode nodeParent =
                tree.Nodes.Add(parent["CategoryName"].ToString());
        foreach (DataRow child in parent.GetChildRows(relation))
        {
            nodeParent.Nodes.Add(child["ProductName"].ToString());
        }
    }
  }
}
```

Modeling a Many-to-Many Relationship

So far, the examples have focused on one-to-many relationships. In a one-to-many relationship, a single parent (in this case, a category) can be linked to multiple child records (such as products). In a many-to-many relationship, categories can pertain to more than one product, and products can belong to more than one category.

A many-to-many relationship is actually built out of two one-to-many relationships with an intermediate table. One example is in the pubs database, which uses a many-to-many relationship between books and authors. In this case, there is a one-to-many relationship between authors and the records in the TitleAuthor table, and another one-to-many relationship between titles and the records in that table. Thus, to model this type of relationship in ADO.NET code, you simply need to create two DataRelation objects.

Example 11-3 shows a full example that uses two DataRelation objects to navigate a many-to-many relationship.

Example 11-3. Navigating a many-to-many relationship

```
// ManyToMany.cs - Navigate a many-to-many relationship.

using System;
using System.Data;
using System.Data.SqlClient;

public class ManyToMany
{
    public static void Main()
    {
        string connectionString = "Data Source=localhost;" +
                "Initial Catalog=pubs;Integrated Security=SSPI";
        string SQL = "SELECT au_lname, au_fname, au_id FROM Authors";

        // Create ADO.NET objects.
        SqlConnection con = new SqlConnection(connectionString);
        SqlCommand cmd = new SqlCommand(SQL, con);
        SqlDataAdapter adapter = new SqlDataAdapter(cmd);
        DataSet ds = new DataSet();
```

Example 11-3. Navigating a many-to-many relationship (continued)

```
try
{
    con.Open();
    adapter.Fill(ds, "Authors");

    cmd.CommandText = "SELECT au_id, title_id FROM TitleAuthor";
    adapter.Fill(ds, "TitleAuthor");

    cmd.CommandText = "SELECT title_id, title FROM Titles";
    adapter.Fill(ds, "Titles");
}
catch (Exception err)
{
    Console.WriteLine(err.ToString());
}
finally
{
    con.Close();
}

// Create the relationships between the tables.
// Connect Titles to TitleAuthor.
DataRelation titles_titleAuthor;
titles_titleAuthor = new DataRelation("",
  ds.Tables["Titles"].Columns["title_id"],
  ds.Tables["TitleAuthor"].Columns["title_id"]);

// Connect TitleAuthor to Authors.
DataRelation authors_titleAuthor;
authors_titleAuthor = new DataRelation("",
  ds.Tables["Authors"].Columns["au_id"],
  ds.Tables["TitleAuthor"].Columns["au_id"]);

// Add the relations to the DataSet.
ds.Relations.Add(titles_titleAuthor);
ds.Relations.Add(authors_titleAuthor);

// Navigate through the results.
foreach (DataRow rowAuthor in ds.Tables["Authors"].Rows)
{
    Console.WriteLine(rowAuthor["au_fname"] + " " +
                      rowAuthor["au_lname"]);

    foreach (DataRow rowTitleAuthor in
     rowAuthor.GetChildRows(authors_titleAuthor))
    {
        foreach (DataRow rowTitle in
         rowTitleAuthor.GetParentRows(titles_titleAuthor))
        {
            Console.WriteLine("\t" + rowTitle["title"]);
        }
    }
}
```

Example 11-3. Navigating a many-to-many relationship (continued)

```
            Console.WriteLine();
        }
    }
}
```

The output for this application shows the list of books written by every author, grouped by author. Because some books are written by more than author, they appear more than once in the listing. Here's a partial excerpt of the output:

```
    ...

    Sylvia Panteley
            Onions, Leeks, and Garlic: Cooking Secrets of the Mediterranean

    Albert Ringer
            Is Anger the Enemy?
            Life Without Fear

    Anne Ringer
            The Gourmet Microwave
            Is Anger the Enemy?

    ...
```

Creating Expression-Based Columns Using Relations

One interesting application of the DataRelation object is the use of calculated columns. Once you have defined a DataRelation, you can use the relationship to create a calculated column that incorporates values from a related table. This allows you to create a column in a child table that contains information about the parent, or a column in a parent table with aggregate information about all children.

First, create a new DataColumn object with an Expression property that uses the syntax Child(RelationName).ColumnName or Parent(RelationName).ColumnName. For example, the following DataColumn could be used in the Products table in Examples 11-1 or 11-2 to retrieve the corresponding CategoryID. (The last parameter sets the DataColumn.Expression property.)

```
    ds.Tables["Products"].Columns.Add("ProductCount", typeof(Int32),
      "Parent(Cat_Prod).CategoryID");
```

On the other hand, if you want to return information about a child, you need to use a SQL aggregate function such as COUNT, MIN, MAX, SUM, or AVG to process the information from all rows. Here's a DataColumn that can be used in the Categories table to retrieve the total number all products in a category:

```
    ds.Tables["Categories"].Columns.Add("ProductCount", typeof(Int32),
      "Count(Child(Cat_Prod).ProductID)");
```

Example 11-4 incorporates this technique into a full example that outputs information about the total price and average price of products in a category.

Example 11-4. Creating expression-based columns with a relation

```
// CaclulatedColumn.cs - Use a relationship with a calculated column

using System;
using System.Data;
using System.Data.SqlClient;

public class CalculatedColumn
{
    public static void Main()
    {
        string connectionString = "Data Source=localhost;" +
                "Initial Catalog=Northwind;Integrated Security=SSPI";
        string SQL = "SELECT * FROM Categories";

        // Create ADO.NET objects.
        SqlConnection con = new SqlConnection(connectionString);
        SqlCommand cmd = new SqlCommand(SQL, con);
        SqlDataAdapter adapter = new SqlDataAdapter(cmd);
        DataSet ds = new DataSet();

        try
        {
            con.Open();
            adapter.Fill(ds, "Categories");

            cmd.CommandText = "SELECT * FROM Products";
            adapter.Fill(ds, "Products");
        }
        catch (Exception err)
        {
            Console.WriteLine(err.ToString());
        }
        finally
        {
            con.Close();
        }

        // Create the relationships between the tables.
        DataColumn parentCol =
                ds.Tables["Categories"].Columns["CategoryID"];
        DataColumn childCol = ds.Tables["Products"].Columns["CategoryID"];
        DataRelation relation = new DataRelation("Cat_Prod", parentCol,
                                                 childCol);
        ds.Relations.Add(relation);

        // Create a calculated column showing average product price.
        ds.Tables["Categories"].Columns.Add("AveragePrice",
          typeof(Decimal), "AVG(Child(Cat_Prod).UnitPrice)");

        // Create a calculated column showing total price for all products
        // in a category.
```

Example 11-4. Creating expression-based columns with a relation (continued)

```
        ds.Tables["Categories"].Columns.Add("TotalPrice",
          typeof(Decimal), "SUM(Child(Cat_Prod).UnitPrice)");

        // Display table information.
        foreach (DataRow row in ds.Tables["Categories"].Rows)
        {
            Console.WriteLine(row["CategoryName"]);
            Console.Write("\tAverage price in this category: ");
            Console.WriteLine(row["AveragePrice"]);
            Console.Write("\tPrice to purchase one of everything: ");
            Console.WriteLine(row["TotalPrice"]);
            Console.WriteLine();
        }
    }
}
```

Here's a partial sampling of output from this example:

```
...
Confections
        Average price in this category: 25.16
        Price to purchase one of everything: 327.08

Dairy Products
        Average price in this category: 28.73
        Price to purchase one of everything: 287.3

Grains/Cereals
        Average price in this category: 20.25
        Price to purchase one of everything: 141.75
...
```

> Relational expressions can also be used to define a custom sort order. This technique is explored in Chapter 12.

12

DataViews and Data Binding

Data binding, a technique for displaying data without writing any code, has suffered from a poor reputation. In the past, the only applications that could use it successfully were simple report-generating tools or thin database wrappers that were typically written in a high-level language such as Visual Basic or Microsoft Access Basic. These applications were easy to program but notoriously limited, inflexible, and performed poorly.

Almost every data-binding solution suffered from the same well-known problems:

Continuous connection requirements. With traditional data binding, connections are required for long periods of time, usually as long as a window is being displayed. This might be acceptable for a small client-server application, but it won't work in a distributed environment or with a web-based application.

Little customizability. The developer can't control any part of the data binding process, has little ability to apply validation logic, and can't customize the display of most of the controls that support data binding.

Tight coupling. Data binding breaks down the separation needed for good three-tier design. Not only is it hard to reuse and likely to stop working if the structure of the data source changes, data binding code also can't be ported from one programming language or environment to another.

ADO.NET addresses these issues with a customizable and reusable data-binding framework that centers on two classes: the DataView and DataViewManager. This chapter examines these classes and explores the two data-binding models used in .NET: Windows Forms and ASP.NET.

The DataView and DataViewManager

Data binding depends on two classes in the System.Data namespace: DataView and DataViewManager. These classes provide an important layer of indirection between your data and its display format, allowing you to apply sorts and filter rows without modifying the underlying information—that is, to have different views on the same data. ADO.NET binding is always provided through one of these objects.

 Both ASP.NET and Windows Forms allow you to bind other types of objects to controls, including custom classes, arrays, and some collection types. However, ADO.NET binding always uses DataView and DataViewManager, so this chapter focuses on these two classes.

The DataView class acts as a view onto a single DataTable. When creating a DataView object, you specify the underlying DataTable in the constructor:

```
// Create a new DataView for the Customers table.
DataView view = new DataView(ds.Tables["Customers"]);
```

Every DataTable also provides a default DataView through the DataTable. DefaultView property:

```
// Obtain a reference to the default DataView for the Customers table.
DataView view = ds.Tables["Customers"].DefaultView;
```

The DataViewManager represents a view of an entire DataSet. As with the DataView, you can create a DataViewManager manually, passing in a reference to a DataSet as a constructor argument, or you can use the default DataViewManager provided through the DataSet.DefaultViewManager property.

The DataView and DataViewManager provide three key features:

- Sorting based on any column criteria
- Filtering based on any combination of column values
- Filtering based on the row state (such as deleted, inserted, and unchanged)

Binding to a DataView

To make all this a little clearer, it helps to consider a simple example with the Windows DataGrid control. In Example 12-1, three tables are queried and added to a DataSet. By setting its DataSource property, the Customers table is then bound to the DataGrid in a single highlighted line.

Example 12-1. Binding a single table from a DataSet

```
private void DataTest_Load(object sender, System.EventArgs e)
{
    string connectionString = "Data Source=localhost;" +
      "Initial Catalog=Northwind;Integrated Security=SSPI";

    string SQL = "SELECT * FROM Customers";
```

Example 12-1. Binding a single table from a DataSet (continued)

```
// Create ADO.NET objects.
SqlConnection con = new SqlConnection(connectionString);
SqlCommand com = new SqlCommand(SQL, con);
SqlDataAdapter adapter = new SqlDataAdapter(com);
DataSet ds = new DataSet("Northwind");

// Execute the command.
try
{
    con.Open();
    adapter.Fill(ds, "Customers");

    com.CommandText = "SELECT * FROM Products";
    adapter.Fill(ds, "Products");

    com.CommandText = "SELECT * FROM Suppliers";
    adapter.Fill(ds, "Suppliers");
}
catch (Exception err)
{
    MessageBox.Show(err.ToString());
}
finally
{
    con.Close();
}

// Show the customers table in the grid.
dataGrid1.DataSource = ds.Tables["Customers"];
}
```

On the surface, it looks as though this code is binding the grid directly to a DataTable object. However, behind the scenes, .NET retrieves the corresponding DataTable.DefaultDataView and uses that. You can replace the highlighted line with the following equivalent syntax:

```
dataGrid1.DataSource = ds.Tables["Customers"].DefaultView;
```

Similarly, you can create a new DataView object and use it for the binding:

```
DataView view = new DataView(ds.Tables["Customers"]);
dataGrid1.DataSource = view;
```

This technique is particularly useful if you want to display different views of the same data in multiple controls. Figure 12-1 shows the result of binding the view. The DataGrid automatically creates a column for each field in the table and displays all the data in the order it was retrieved from the data source. By default, every column is the same width, and the columns are arranged according to the order of fields in the SELECT statement; you'll learn how to customize the view later in this chapter.

There is one reason why you should bind directly to the view rather than use the table name. If you specify an invalid table name when binding directly to a table, you don't receive an error; the DataGrid just appears empty. However, if you make the same mistake when binding to a view, you receive a more informative NullReferenceException.

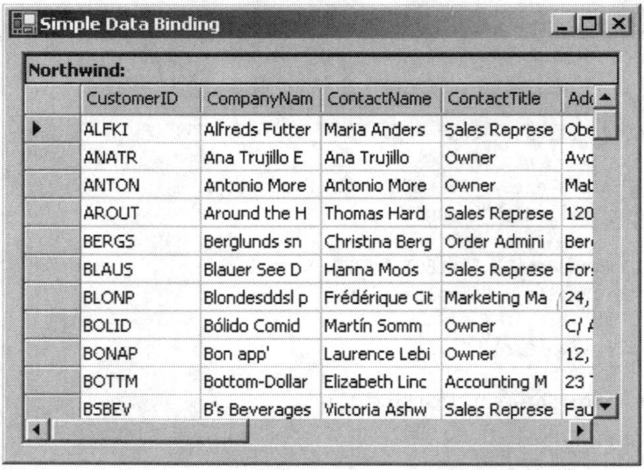

Figure 12-1. Binding a DataView to a DataGrid

Binding to a DataViewManager

The DataGrid is the only Windows Forms control that supports binding to an entire DataSet as well as a single table, although many other third-party controls follow suit. When binding a DataSet, .NET automatically uses the corresponding DataViewManager provided through the DataSet.DefaultViewManager property:

```
// Bind to the DefaultViewManager explicitly.
dataGrid1.DataSource = ds.DefaultViewManager;

// Bind to the DefaultViewManager implicitly. This code is equivalent.
dataGrid1.DataSource = ds;

// Bind to an identical DataViewManager you create manually.
// This code has the same effect, but isn't exactly the same
// (because it creates a new object).
dataGrid1.DataSource = new DataViewManager(ds);
```

Figure 12-2 shows the initial appearance of a DataGrid when bound to a DataSet. A separate navigational link is provided for every table in the DataSet. When the user clicks on one of these links, the corresponding table is shown, as in Figure 12-2.

There is one important difference between the DataViewManager and the DataView approach, however. When you use the navigational links to display a table, .NET

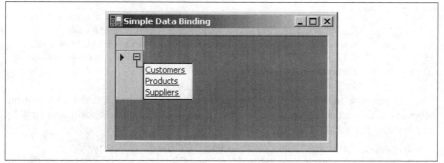

Figure 12-2. Binding a DataViewManager to a DataGrid

doesn't use the `DefaultView` to configure the appearance of the that table. Instead, every `DataViewManager` provides a collection of `DataViewSetting` objects. When the user navigates to a table through a `DataViewManager`, a new `DataView` is created according to the settings in the corresponding `DataViewSetting` object.

Sorting and Filtering

The `DataView` object also gives you the opportunity to apply sorting and filtering logic that customizes how data will appear without modifying the underlying data itself.

Sorting with the DataView

To apply a sort to bound data, you simply set the `DataView.Sort` property with a string with the corresponding sort information. ADO.NET sorting uses the same syntax as the ORDER BY clause in a SQL query. For example, you might use the following SQL statement to order results by country:

```
SELECT * FROM Customers ORDER BY Country ASC
```

The equivalent ADO.NET code is shown here:

```
ds.Tables["Customers"].DefaultView.Sort = "Country ASC";
dataGrid1.DataSource = ds.Tables["Customers"];
```

The sort is according to the sort order of the data type of the column. For example, string columns are sorted alphanumerically without regard to case (assuming the `DataTable.CaseSensitive` property is `false`). Numeric columns are ordered using a numeric sort. Columns that contain binary data can't be sorted. Add ASC after a column name for an ascending sort (with smallest values first) or DESC for a descending sort.

Keep in mind that if you want to bind a control to the full `DataSet`, setting the `DataView.Sort` property will have no effect because the default `DataView` isn't used. Instead, you must modify the `DataViewSetting.Sort` property exposed through the `DataViewManager`:

```
ds.DefaultViewManager.DataViewSettings["Customers"].Sort = "Country ASC";
dataGrid1.DataSource = ds;
```

DataGrid binding is dynamic and updateable. If you change a value that affects the sort order, the affected row is automatically repositioned. Similarly, if you programmatically modify a DataView while it is in use (or the underlying data), the linked controls update themselves immediately.

You can also use nested sorts. To sort using multiple columns, just add a comma between each sort specification. For example, the following code sorts first by country and then orders all rows that have the same country by city:

```
ds.Tables["Customers"].DefaultView.Sort = "Country ASC, City ASC";
dataGrid1.DataSource = ds.Tables["Customers"];
```

Alternatively, instead of setting the DataView.Sort property, you can set the DataView.ApplyDefaultSort property to true. In this case, ADO.NET automatically creates a sort order in ascending order based on the primary key column of the DataTable. ApplyDefaultSort applies only when the Sort property is a null reference or an empty string, and when the table has a defined primary key.

Filtering by Column

To filter a DataView, you set a filter expression in the DataView.RowFilter property. Filtering by column works similarly to the SQL WHERE clause: it allows you to select rows that match the filter criteria. For example, consider the following SQL query, which filters rows based on two column values:

```
SELECT * FROM Customers WHERE Country='Argentina' AND City='Buenos Aires'
```

This translates into the ADO.NET code shown here:

```
ds.Tables["Customers"].DefaultView.RowFilter =
    "Country='Argentina' AND City='Buenos Aires'";
dataGrid1.DataSource = ds.Tables["Customers"];
```

If you use this code with the Northwind table, you receive three rows. The other rows are still present in the underlying DataTable, but they are hidden from view.

Filter operators

Like the WHERE clause, the RowFilter property allows a wide range of operators and functions for both numeric and string data types. Consider some of the following examples:

```
// Find all the rows that match one of the three specified countries.
ds.Tables["Customers"].DefaultView.RowFilter =
    "Country IN ('Argentina', 'Canada', 'Japan')";

// Find all the rows where a Country isn't specified.
ds.Tables["Customers"].DefaultView.RowFilter = "Country IS NULL";

// Use alphabetic comparison to find all the rows where the Country
// starts with S or any letter after it in the alphabet
// (including Switzerland, USA, UK, Venezuela, and so on).
ds.Tables["Customers"].DefaultView.RowFilter = "Country > 'S'";
```

After you apply a sort, you can read the `DataView.Count` property to determine how many rows meet the criteria and will be displayed in data bound controls.

With numeric values, you can use ranges or mathematical operators to filter rows. For example, here are some filters for the `Products` table:

```
// Find all the rows where UnitPrice is greater than 10.
ds.Tables["Products"].DefaultView.RowFilter = "UnitPrice > 10";

// Find all the rows where UnitPrice is above 10 but below 15.
// This is an exclusive range.
ds.Tables["Products"].DefaultView.RowFilter =
    "UnitPrice > 10 AND UnitPrice < 15";

// Find all the rows where UnitPrice is anywhere from 10 to 15.
// This is an inclusive range.
ds.Tables["Products"].DefaultView.RowFilter =
    "UnitPrice BETWEEN 10 AND 15";

// Find all prodcuts where the total stock value is at least $1000.
ds.Tables["Products"].DefaultView.RowFilter =
    "UnitPrice * UnitsInStock > 1000";
```

Table 12-1 lists the most common filter operators.

Table 12-1. Filter operators

Operator	Description
AND	Combines more than one clause. Records must match all criteria to be displayed.
OR	Combines more than one clause. Records must match at least one of the filter expressions to be displayed.
NOT	Reverses an expression. Can be used in conjunction with any other clause.
<, >, <=, and >=	Performs comparison of values. These comparisons can be numeric (with numeric data types) or alphabetic dictionary comparisons (with string data types).
BETWEEN	Specifies an inclusive range. For example, `Units BETWEEN 5 AND 15` selects rows that have a value in the Units column from 5 to 15.
<> and =	Performs equality testing.
IS NULL	Tests the column for a `null` value.
IN(a,b,c)	A short form for using an OR clause with the same field. Tests for equality between a column and the specified values (a, b, and c).
LIKE	Performs pattern matching with string data types.
+	Adds two numeric values, or concatenates a string.
-	Subtracts one numeric value from another.
*	Multiplies two numeric values.
/	Divides one numeric value by another.
%	Finds the modulus (the remainder after one number is divided by another).

Pattern-matching filters

The LIKE keyword performs pattern matching on strings. Pattern matching is akin to regular-expression syntax but is much less powerful. Unfortunately, the pattern matching provided by ADO.NET, while similar to that provided in SQL Server, lacks a few features. Notably, the _ character (which represents a single variable character) and the [ ] brackets (which specify a character from a range of allowed values) aren't supported. However, you can use the % character to specify zero or more characters.

Here are two examples of pattern matching with ADO.NET:

```
// Use pattern matching to find all the countries that start with
// the letter "A" (includes Argentina, Austria, and so on.)
ds.Tables["Customers"].DefaultView.RowFilter = "Country LIKE 'A%'";

// Matches contacts that contain the word "Manager"
// (includes Sales Manager, Marketing Manager, and so on).
ds.Tables["Customers"].DefaultView.RowFilter =
    "ContactTitle LIKE '%Manager%'";
```

Filter-supported functions

Finally, you can also use a few built-in SQL functions to further refine a column sort. These features (detailed in Table 12-2) allow you to perform comparisons that include null values, parse a portion of a string, or even perform an aggregate query on related child rows.

```
// Display records where the country name is longer than eight characters
// (includes Venezuela, Argentina, and Switzerland).
ds.Tables["Customers"].DefaultView.RowFilter =    "Len(Country) > 8";

// Display records where the second and third letter are "ra"
// (includes Brazil and France).
// Note that this expression uses 1-based counting.
ds.Tables["Customers"].DefaultView.RowFilter =
    "Substring(Country, 2, 2) = 'ra'";

// Display all the columns that have a region code of SP, or a null value.
ds.Tables["Customers"].DefaultView.RowFilter =
    "IsNull(Region, 'SP') = 'SP'";
```

Table 12-2. Filter-supported functions

Function	Description
Sum, Avg, Min, Max, and Count	These aggregate functions return a single calculated number by examining several. They are used in conjunction with child rows.
Convert(value, type)	Allows you to modify the data type of a column. This is useful if you need to perform a numeric operation with a string column or vice versa.
Len	Returns the number of characters in a string.
IsNull(exp, replacement)	Returns the replacement value if the column is null or the column value otherwise.

Table 12-2. Filter-supported functions (continued)

Function	Description
IIF(exp, trueval, falseval)	Returns one of two values, depending on whether the specified condition evaluates to true or false.
SubString(string, start, length)	Retrieves a portion of a string field. The start value uses 1-based counting (the first letter is designated as 1, not 0).

Aggregate functions and relations in filters

You can also use aggregate functions to create a filter that restricts related child rows. For example, you can look at all customers that have total orders greater than a certain dollar figure. You can also return all the region records that have at least 20 matching customers. In order to use this technique, however, you need to create a DataRelation between the related tables first.

The basic syntax is Child(RelationName).ColumnName or Parent(RelationName).ColumnName. Here are a few examples that use the Suppliers and Products tables, which are linked on the SuppliersID column using a relation named Suppliers_Products:

```
// Only display products for a specific supplier.
ds.Tables["Products"].DefaultView.RowFilter =
    "Parent(Suppliers_Products).CompanyName='Tokyo Traders'";
dataGrid1.DataSource = ds.Tables["Products"];

// Display suppliers that have at least five related products.
ds.Tables["Suppliers"].DefaultView.RowFilter =
    "Count(Child(Suppliers_Products).SupplierID) >= 5";
dataGrid1.DataSource = ds.Tables["Suppliers"];

// Display suppliers that have at least one product with more than 50 units
// in stock.
ds.Tables["Suppliers"].DefaultView.RowFilter =
    "Max(Child(Suppliers_Products).UnitsInStock) > 50";
dataGrid1.DataSource = ds.Tables["Suppliers"];
```

Example 12-2 presents the full code needed to create a relationship, add it to the DataSet, and then use it with a relational filter expression.

Example 12-2. Using a relational filter expression

```
private void RelationTest_Load(object sender, System.EventArgs e)
{
    string connectionString = "Data Source=localhost;" +
      "Initial Catalog=Northwind;Integrated Security=SSPI";

    string SQL = "SELECT * FROM Suppliers";

    // Create ADO.NET objects.
    SqlConnection con = new SqlConnection(connectionString);
    SqlCommand com = new SqlCommand(SQL, con);
```

Example 12-2. Using a relational filter expression (continued)

```csharp
SqlDataAdapter adapter = new SqlDataAdapter(com);
DataSet ds = new DataSet("Northwind");

// Execute the command.
try
{
    con.Open();
    adapter.Fill(ds, "Suppliers");

    com.CommandText = "SELECT * FROM Products";
    adapter.Fill(ds, "Products");
}
catch (Exception err)
{
    Console.WriteLine(err.ToString());
}
finally
{
    con.Close();
}

// Create references to the parent and child columns.
DataColumn parentCol = ds.Tables["Suppliers"].Columns["SupplierID"];
DataColumn childCol = ds.Tables["Products"].Columns["SupplierID"];

// Create the DataRelation object.
DataRelation relation = new DataRelation("Suppliers_Products",
  parentCol, childCol);

// Add the relation to the DataSet.
ds.Relations.Add(relation);

// Define the filter expression for the Suppliers table.
ds.Tables["Suppliers"].DefaultView.RowFilter =
  "Count(Child(Suppliers_Products).SupplierID) > 3";

// Display the table.
dataGrid1.DataSource = ds.Tables["Suppliers"];
}
```

When you try this code, you'll find that as a side effect, the DataGrid automatically adds navigation links that allow you to view the related child rows of a supplier. These navigational links (shown in Figure 12-3) use the name of the corresponding DataRelation.

Filtering by Row State

The DataView.RowStateFilter property allows you to hide or show rows based on their state. Table 12-3 shows the DataViewRowState enumeration values that set the RowStateFilter. You can use any one of these values or a bitwise combination of values.

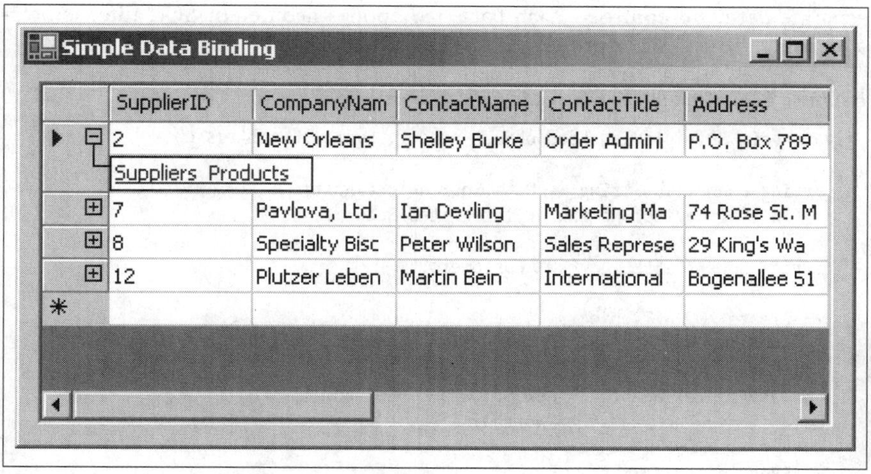

Figure 12-3. Relational data in the DataGrid

```
// Show only deleted rows.
ds.Tables["Products"].DefaultView.RowStateFilter =
    DataViewRowState.Deleted;

// Show deleted and added rows.
ds.Tables["Products"].DefaultView.RowStateFilter =
    DataViewRowState.Deleted | DataViewRowState.Added;
```

By default, the RowStateFilter is set to CurrentRows and shows everything except rows that are scheduled for deletion.

Table 12-3. Values from the DataViewRowState enumeration

Value	Description
Added	A new row that will be inserted into the data source when the next update is performed.
CurrentRows	Current rows, including unchanged, new, and modified rows. This is the default.
Deleted	A deleted row that is removed from the data source when the next update is performed.
ModifiedCurrent	A row that exists in the DataSet but has been modified.
ModifiedOriginal	The original version (although it has since been modified and is available as ModifiedCurrent).
None	No rows will be shown.
OriginalRows	Original rows including unchanged and deleted rows.
Unchanged	A row that exists in the DataSet and has not been modified.

Displaying Multiple Views

One of the most useful aspects of the DataView is the ability to create multiple DataView objects to provide different representations of the same data: This technique is quite straightforward and is shown in Example 12-3 with three separate DataGrid controls. Each DataView applies a different SQL filter expression using the RowFilter property.

Example 12-3. Binding the same data with different views

```
private void MultipleView_Load(object sender, System.EventArgs e)
{
    string connectionString = "Data Source=localhost;" +
      "Initial Catalog=Northwind;Integrated Security=SSPI";

    string SQL = "SELECT * FROM Customers";

    // Create ADO.NET objects.
    SqlConnection con = new SqlConnection(connectionString);
    SqlCommand com = new SqlCommand(SQL, con);
    SqlDataAdapter adapter = new SqlDataAdapter(com);
    DataSet ds = new DataSet("Northwind");

    // Execute the command.
    try
    {
        con.Open();
        adapter.Fill(ds, "Customers");
    }
    catch (Exception err)
    {
        Console.WriteLine(err.ToString());
    }
    finally
    {
        con.Close();
    }

    // Create views.
    DataView viewArgentina = new DataView(ds.Tables["Customers"]);
    DataView viewBrazil = new DataView(ds.Tables["Customers"]);

    // Filter views.
    viewArgentina.RowFilter = "Country = 'Argentina'";
    viewBrazil.RowFilter = "Country = 'Brazil'";

    // Perform data binding.
    gridArgentina.DataSource = viewArgentina;
    gridBrazil.DataSource = viewBrazil;
    gridAll.DataSource = ds.Tables["Customers"].DefaultView;
}
```

Notice that if you modify a row in one view, the changes appear automatically in all other views. Remember, there is only one data source—the linked DataTable.

Figure 12-4 shows the three views, each of which contains only a subset of the full data in the DataTable.

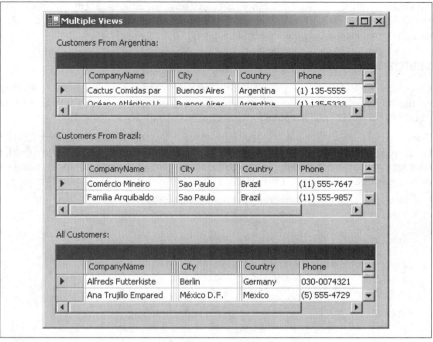

Figure 12-4. Multiple views of the same data

Accessing Data Through a DataView

A DataView isn't just for data binding. You can also use it when making program-matic changes. For example, you might create a DataView that contains rows that match certain criteria and then apply a global change to these rows. For example, the following code creates a view that includes all rows with a null value in the Country field and then deletes them:

```
// Find all the rows where a Country isn't specified.
DataView view = new DataView(ds.Tables["Customers"]);
view.RowFilter = "Country IS NULL";

// Delete these rows.
foreach (DataRowView row in view)
{
    row.Delete();
}

// Display the results.
dataGrid1.DataSource = ds.Tables["Customers"].DefaultView;
```

This example uses the indexer for the DataView, which accesses the collection of DataRowView objects. Each DataRowView represents a single row from the original DataTable. The DataRowView provides most of the same features as the underlying

DataRow object, including the ability to begin and end editing, access values using the field name, and delete the row. You can also access the underlying DataRow directly through the DataRowView.Row property.

Searching a DataView

Once you have defined a sort order for a DataView, either by setting the RowFilter or the ApplyDefaultSort properties, you can use criteria to search for rows. The DataView provides two methods for this task: Find( ) and FindRows( ).

For example, if you have a sort defined on the ContactName column of the Customers table, you can use the Find( ) method to search for a row with the ContactName Roland Mendel. If a match is found, Find( ) returns the index number of the row in the DataView. If no match is found, it returns –1.

```
DataView view = new DataView(ds.Tables["Customers"]);
view.Sort = "ContactName";

int rowIndex = view.Find("Roland Mendel");

if (rowIndex == -1)
{
    Console.WriteLine("No match found.");
}
else
{
    Console.WriteLine(view[rowIndex]["CustomerID"].ToString() +
                    " is a match.");
}
```

The only limitation is that the string you use to search must match the sort fields exactly. The Find( ) and FindRows( ) methods don't support partial matches or wildcards (in the previous example, you can't search for just "Roland").

If there is a possibility that more than one row will match the criteria you use, you should use the FindRows( ) method instead of Find( ). It returns an array of DataRowView objects that reference the matching rows. If no match is found, FindRows( ) returns an empty array.

```
DataView view = new DataView(ds.Tables["Customers"]);
view.Sort = "Country";

DataRowView[] rows = view.FindRows("Germany");

if rows.Length == 0
{
    Console.WriteLine("No match found.");
}
else
{
    foreach (DataRowView row in rows)
    {
```

```
            Console.WriteLine(row["CustomerID"].ToString() + " is a match.");
        }
    }
```

Finally, if you've created a sort expression that incorporates information from multiple columns, you must use an overloaded version of the Find( ) or FindRows( ) methods that accepts an array with search values for all columns, in the same order:

```
DataView view = new DataView(ds.Tables["Customers"]);
view.Sort = "Country, City";

DataRowView[] rows = view.FindRows(new object[] {"Germany", "Berlin"});
```

 The case-sensitivity of search values for the Find( ) and FindRows( ) methods is determined by the CaseSensitive property of the underlying DataTable.

Navigating Relations with a DataView

Unlike the DataRow object, the DataRowView doesn't include methods such as GetChildRows( ) and GetParentRow( ). However, you can still use DataRelations with the DataView, thanks to the CreateChildView( ) method. CreateChildView( ) accepts a reference to a DataRelation object and creates a new DataView that contains the appropriate child rows.

```
// Define a DataRelation.
DataColumn parentCol = ds.Tables["Categories"].Columns["CategoryID"];
DataColumn childCol = ds.Tables["Products"].Columns["CategoryID"];
DataRelation relation = new DataRelation("Cat_Prod", parentCol, childCol);
ds.Relations.Add(relation);

// Create a view on the Categories table.
DataView viewCategories = new DataView(ds.Tables["Categories"]);
view.Sort = "CategoryName";

// Select a specific category row through the DataRowView.
DataRowView rowCategory = viewCategories.Find("Beverages");

// Find products in this category using a new DataView.
DataView viewProducts = rowCategory.CreateChildView(relation);

// Display the products.
foreach (DataRowView row in viewProducts)
{
    Console.WriteLine(row["ProductName"]);
}
```

This navigation works in one direction only. There is no direct way to retrieve a reference to the parent row of a DataRowView.

Windows Data Binding

So far, the examples have concentrated on a single control designed specifically for data binding: the Windows DataGrid. But the Windows Forms platform also supports data binding with just about any control (as demonstrated a little later in this section) and automatically synchronizes multiple data-bound controls. This ability goes far beyond just ADO.NET and the DataSet. In fact, the ability to bind a data object to a Windows control depends on the small set of interfaces shown in Table 12-4.

Table 12-4. Data binding interfaces

Interface	Description
IList	Allows simple data binding to a collection of objects of the same type. For example, you can data bind to an ArrayList that contains only one type of object because it implements this interface.
IBindingList	Provides additional features for notification. This notification includes when the list itself changes (for example, the number of items in the list increases) and when the list items change (for example, the third item in a list of customers has a change to its FirstName field). This interface is implemented by DataView and DataViewManager.
IEditableObject	Provides support for editing. In other words, when the user modifies the control, the changes are applied to the data object. This is implemented by the DataRowView class.
IDataErrorInfo	Allows a data object to offer error information a control can bind to. This information consists of two strings: the Error property, which returns general error message text (for example, "An error has occurred") and the Item property, which returns a string with a specific error message from the column (for example, "The value in the Cost column can't be negative"). This is implemented by the DataRowView class.

Some collection classes, such as the Array and ArrayList, support data binding because they implement the IList interface. This is the minimum requirement for simple read-only data binding. The ADO.NET data objects implement three additional interfaces, giving them the ability to support notification, editable binding, and error information.

The CurrencyManager and BindingContext

These interfaces don't tell the whole data binding story, however. Windows Forms can also synchronize multiple controls. This allows you to (for example) choose a record using a list control and see the related field information automatically appear in other data-bound text or label controls on the same form. This ability isn't directly derived from ADO.NET; in fact, unlike the ADO Recordset, classes such as the DataSet and DataView don't store any positional information that would allow them to "point" to a single row. Instead, this ability comes from the Windows Forms architecture and is provided by two classes: CurrencyManager and BindingContext.

When you bind a data object to a control, it is automatically assigned a CurrencyManager object. The CurrencyManager keeps track of the position in the data source. If you are binding to more than one data object, each has a separate CurrencyManager. If several controls are bound to the same data source, they share the same CurrencyManager.

Every form has a `BindingContext` object. The `BindingContext` object keeps track of all the `CurrencyManager` objects on the form. It is possible to create and use more than one `BindingContext` object (as discussed a little later) but, by default, every form is given a single `BindingContext`. Figure 12-5 diagrams this relationship.

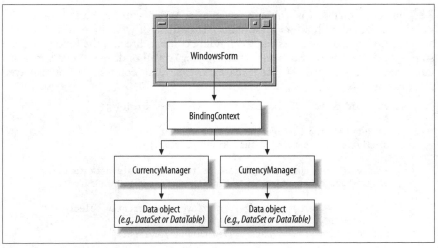

Figure 12-5. The binding context of a form

The next few sections show how to use Windows Forms data binding with the common set of .NET controls.

List Binding

All controls that derive from `ListControl` (including `ListBox` and `ComboBox`) support read-only data binding to a `DataTable` object. Indicate the desired `DataTable` by setting the `DataSource` property, much as you would with the `DataGrid` control. However, list controls can track only two pieces of information, and they can display only a single field. Specify the field to display by setting the `DisplayMember` property to the field name.

For example, the following code binds a `DataTable` to a `ComboBox` and shows the CustomerID field. (You can add this code to the end of Example 12-1 to test it.)

```
cboCustomerID.DataSource = ds.Tables["Customers"].DefaultView;
cboCustomerID.DisplayMember = "CustomerID";
```

You can also use the `ValueMember` property to store additional information (technically, an instance of any .NET type) with each list item:

```
cboCustomer.DataSource = ds.Tables["Customers"].DefaultView;
cboCustomer.DisplayMember = "ContactName";
cboCustomer.ValueMember = "CustomerID";
```

You can then retrieve the value of the currently selected item using the `SelectedValue` property. For example, here's the event handler for a button that displays the CustomerID of the currently selected record:

```csharp
private void button1_Click(object sender, System.EventArgs e)
{
    // Display the CustomerID of the currently selected record.
    MessageBox.Show(cboCustomer.SelectedValue.ToString());
}
```

Keep in mind that this is only a convenience. When you bind a DataTable, the object is retained with all its information, regardless of what item you choose to show in the control. By accessing the binding context directly, the following code snippet accomplishes the same task, relying on the display member. This approach is useful if you need to retrieve several columns of undisplayed information.

```csharp
private void button1_Click(object sender, System.EventArgs e)
{
    // Retrieve the binding context for the form.
    BindingContext binding = this.BindingContext;

    // Look up the currency manager for the appropriate data source.
    BindingManagerBase currency = binding[cboCustomer.DataSource];

    // Using the currency manager, retrieve the currently selected
    // DatRowView.
    DataRowView drView = (DataRowView)currency.Current;

    // Display the CustomerID of the currently selected record.
    MessageBox.Show(drView["CustomerID"].ToString());
}
```

Single-Value Binding

Most controls don't provide a DataSource property. For example, common .NET controls such as the TextBox, Label, and Button don't provide any special data-binding member. However, they can display a single value of bound information. This functionality is inherited from the base Control class.

The Control class provides a DataBindings collection that allows you to link any control property to a field in the data source. Usually, you'll add a data binding that binds information to a display property like Text. However, much more exotic designs are possible—such as binding a color name to the Control.ForeColor property.

To connect a TextBox to the ContactName field of a DataTable, use the following code:

```csharp
txtContact.DataBindings.Add("Text", ds.Tables["Customers"].DefaultView,
                        "ContactName");
```

The first parameter is the name of the control property. .NET uses reflection to find the matching property at runtime (although it can't catch mistakes at design time). The second parameter is the data source. The third parameter is the property or field in the data source that will be bound—in this case, the ContactName field. The Add( ) method is a shorthand that allows you to create and add a

Binding object in one step. Here's the equivalent code that creates the Binding object manually:

```
Binding propertyFieldBinding; = new Binding("Text",
    ds.Tables["Customers"].DefaultView, "ContactName");

txtContact.DataBindings.Add(propertyFieldBinding);
```

You can use a similar approach to link the CustomerID value to the TextBox.Tag property. The Tag property isn't used by .NET but is available for information storage you might want later. This way, you can determine the CustomerID for the current customer, just as you did with the list control.

```
txtContact.DataBindings.Add("Tag", ds.Tables["Customers"].DefaultView,
                            "CustomerID");
```

Unlike the list binding, single-value binding provides no way to move from record to record. However, if you've followed the previous examples, you will now have a form with multiple synchronized controls. When you choose a record in a list control or DataGrid control, the corresponding information is shown in any linked single-value controls such as the Label or TextBox (see Figure 12-6).

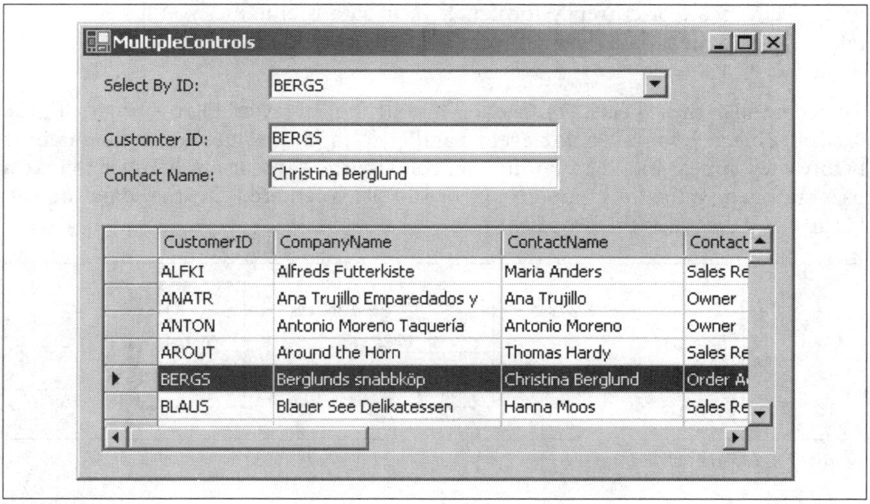

Figure 12-6. Multiple bound controls

Single-value binding is also useful with list controls. When you bind a list control by setting the DataSource property, you create a read-only navigational control. When a value is selected from the list, the CurrencyManager moves to the appropriate record, and all other controls are updated appropriately. When you use single-value binding with a list, you create an editable value that allows you to modify the bound field for the current record.

To use a list control in this fashion, follow these two steps:

1. Fill the list control with all possible choices. You can do this using the Add( ) or AddRange( ) method. Do *not* use data binding.

2. Bind the `Text` or `SelectedValue` property to the appropriate field in the data source using single-value binding.

 If you use this technique with a `ListBox` or `ComboBox` that uses the `DropDownList` style, you must ensure there is an item added for every possible value. Otherwise, an exception is thrown when the user navigates to a record that has a value not included in the list. You don't need to follow this restriction when using a `ComboBox` that has the `DropDown` or `Simple` style.

Now, the list control shows the bound field automatically when you navigate to a record. However, the user can also select a new value to modify the field.

Format and Parse

One of the traditional limitations with data binding was that it provided relatively few opportunities to format the data. Unfortunately, the raw data drawn directly from a database may contain numeric codes or short forms that need to be replaced with more descriptive equivalents or numbers that need to be formatted to a specific scale or currency format. If your data is editable, you'll also need to take user-supplied data and convert it to data that can be inserted into the database.

To accomplish these tasks, you need to handle the `Format` and `Parse` events for the `Binding` object. Use the `Format` event handler to modify values from the database before they appear in a data bound control. Use the `Parse` event handler to take a user-supplied value and modify it before it is entered in the data object. Figure 12-7 diagrams the process.

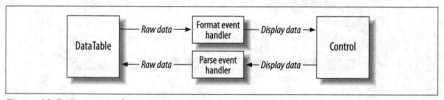

Figure 12-7. Format and parse

For example, the `Products` table in the Northwind database includes a `UnitPrice` column. By default, this displays a number in ordinary decimal format as shown here:

```
21.3
12
14.33
```

A more consistent representation looks like this:

```
$21.30
$12.00
$14.33
```

The following code shows how you might write the data binding code to support this conversion. This code binds the UnitPrice field to a TextBox and registers to handle the Format and Parse events:

```
// Create the binding.
Binding dataBinding = new Binding("Text",
    dsStore.Tables["Products"].DefaultView, "UnitPrice");

// Connect the methods for formatting and parsing data.
dataBinding.Format += new ConvertEventHandler(DecimalToCurrencyString);
dataBinding.Parse += new ConvertEventHandler(CurrencyStringToDecimal);

// Add the binding.
txtUnitCost.DataBindings.Add(dataBinding);
```

The Format and Parse event handlers access the value to convert from the ConvertEventArgs.Value property. They replace this value with the converted value. It's also good practice for the Format and Parse event handlers to verify the expected data type using the ConvertEventArgs.DesiredType property. For example, in a TextBox, every value is converted to a string. However, the reverse conversion expects a decimal. If the desired type doesn't meet expectations, the event handlers leave the value untouched. See Example 12-4.

Example 12-4. Formatting and parsing values

```
private void DecimalToCurrencyString(object sender, ConvertEventArgs e)
{
    if (e.DesiredType == typeof(string))
    {
        // Use the ToString method to format the value as currency ("c").
        e.Value += ((decimal)e.Value).ToString("c");
    }
}

private void CurrencyStringToDecimal(object sender, ConvertEventArgs e)
{
    if (e.DesiredType == typeof(decimal))
    {
        // Convert the string back to decimal using the static Parse()
        // method.
        e.Value = Decimal.Parse(e.Value.ToString(),
                System.Globalization.NumberStyles.Currency, null);
    }
}
```

Controlling Navigation

So far, we've considered only one way to control navigation: using a navigational control such as a ListBox or DataGrid. However, you can also control navigation programmatically by directly interacting with the CurrencyManager.

Example 12-5 shows the event handlers for Next and Previous buttons. When one of these buttons is clicked, a new record is selected, and all bound controls are updated automatically. In this case, the CurrencyManager is retrieved every time it is needed. It might be a better approach to store a reference to it in a private form-level variable.

Example 12-5. Changing record position programmatically

```
private void cmdPrev_Click(object sender, System.EventArgs e)
{
    // Retrieve the binding context for the form.
    BindingContext binding = this.BindingContext;

    // Look up the currency manager for the appropriate data source.
    BindingManagerBase currency = binding[dataGrid1.DataSource];

    // Move to the previous record.
    currency.Position--;
}

private void cmdNext_Click(object sender, System.EventArgs e)
{
    // Retrieve the binding context for the form.
    BindingContext binding = this.BindingContext;

    // Look up the currency manager for the appropriate data source.
    BindingManagerBase currency = binding[dataGrid1.DataSource];

    // Move to the next record.
    currency.Position++;
}
```

In this example, the code doesn't bother to check whether it's reached the limits of the data source. For example, if the user clicks the previous button while positioned on the first record, it tries to set the Position property to the invalid value −1. Fortunately, the CurrencyManager simply ignores invalid instructions, and the Position remains unchanged.

Example 12-6 shows the event handler you'll need.

Example 12-6. Handling the PositionChanged event

```
private void Binding_PositionChanged(object sender, System.EventArgs e)
{
    // Retrieve the binding context for the form.
    BindingContext binding = this.BindingContext;

    // Look up the currency manager for the appropriate data source.
    BindingManagerBase currency = binding[dataGrid1.DataSource];

    if (currency.Position == currency.Count - 1)
    {
        cmdNext.Enabled = false;
    }
    else
    {
```

Example 12-6. Handling the PositionChanged event (continued)

```
        cmdNext.Enabled = true;
    }

    if (currency.Position == 0)
    {
        cmdPrev.Enabled = false;
    }
    else
    {
        cmdPrev.Enabled = true;
    }
}
```

And here is some of the data binding code, which now also hooks up the required event handler:

```
// Bind a DataGrid.
dataGrid1.DataSource = ds.Tables["Customers"].DefaultView;

// Hook up the PositionChanged event handler.
BindingContext binding = this.BindingContext[dataGrid1.DataSource];
currencyPositionChanged += new EventHandler(Binding_PositionChanged);
```

Master-Detail Forms

The `PostionChanged` event also makes it easy to create master-detail forms (see Figure 12-8). A master-detail binds two data objects and uses two `CurrencyManager` objects. When the parent record changes, the child data must also be modified. This modification can be accomplished by configuring the `DataView.RowFilter` property.

Example 12-7. Master-detail data binding

```
public class MasterDetail : System.Windows.Forms.Form
{
    private System.Windows.Forms.DataGrid gridSuppliers;
    private System.Windows.Forms.DataGrid gridProducts;

    // (Designer code omitted.)

    DataSet ds = new DataSet("Northwind");

    private void MasterDetail_Load(object sender, System.EventArgs e)
    {
        string connectionString = "Data Source=localhost;" +
            "Initial Catalog=Northwind;Integrated Security=SSPI";

        string SQL = "SELECT * FROM Products";

        // Create ADO.NET objects.
        SqlConnection con = new SqlConnection(connectionString);
```

Example 12-7. Master-detail data binding (continued)

```
        SqlCommand com = new SqlCommand(SQL, con);
        SqlDataAdapter adapter = new SqlDataAdapter(com);

        // Execute the command.
        try
        {
            adapter.Fill(ds, "Products");

            com.CommandText = "SELECT * FROM Suppliers";
            adapter.Fill(ds, "Suppliers");
        }
        finally
        {
            con.Close();
        }

        // Display the results.
        gridSuppliers.DataSource = ds.Tables["Suppliers"].DefaultView;
        gridProducts.DataSource = ds.Tables["Products"].DefaultView;

        // Handle the PositionChanged event for the Suppliers table.
        BindingManagerBase currency;
        currency = this.BindingContext[gridSuppliers.DataSource];
        currency.PositionChanged += new
            EventHandler(Binding_PositionChanged);
    }

    private void Binding_PositionChanged(object sender, System.EventArgs e)
    {
        string filter;
        DataRowView selectedRow;

        // Find the current category row.
        selectedRow = (DataRowView)this.BindingContext[
                    gridSuppliers.DataSource].Current;

        // Create a filter expression using its SupplierID.
        filter = "SupplierID='" + selectedRow["SupplierID"].ToString() +
                "'";

        // Modify the view onto the product table.
        ds.Tables["Products"].DefaultView.RowFilter = filter;
    }

}
```

Example 12-7 uses two DataGrid controls: one that displays Suppliers (the parent table) and one that displays the Products offered by the currently selected supplier. The DataGrid controls are bound as before. The difference is that the PositionChanged event handler dynamically builds a filter string based on the currently selected supplier and uses it to filter the product list.

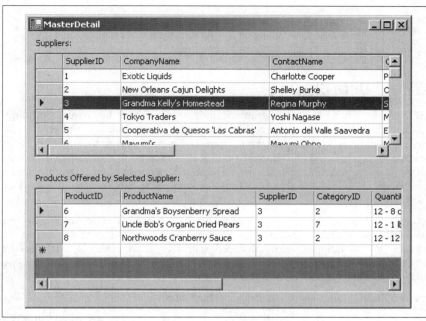

Figure 12-8. A master-detail form

Another equivalent option is to use the `CreateChildView( )` method discussed earlier in this chapter to generate a new `DataView` object based on a `DataRelation` each time the position changes.

Creating New Binding Contexts

Every form provides a default `BindingContext` object. As you've seen, you can access this object to determine the currently selected item or change the current position. However, what happens if you want to create a form that has more than one `BindingContext`? For example, imagine you show two differently filtered views of the same data. In this case, when the user selects an item in one view, you don't want the same item selected in the second view, even if it is available. Fortunately, you can create new binding contexts with these three steps:

1. Create one container control for each binding context you want. (Forms and container controls are the only controls that can host a `CurrencyManager`.) A common choice is the `GroupBox`.

2. Organize all the data-bound controls into the container control according to the desired binding context. For example, if you have two `DataGrid` controls that should not be synchronized, you can place each `DataGrid` in a separate `GroupBox`.

3. Create a new binding context for each container control. You do this by assigning a new `BindingContext` object to the `BindingContext` property of the container control, as shown here:

```
        // Create two new binding contexts.
        grpNormalView.BindingContext = new BindingContext();
        grpSortedView.BindingContext = new BindingContext();
```

4. Bind all the controls as you would ordinarily.

ASP.NET Data Binding

ASP.NET data binding differs dramatically from Windows Forms data binding. The key difference is that ASP.NET data binding takes place on the server side when the page is loaded. However, there is no mechanism to apply the data binding to the rendered HTML page that is sent to the user. Thus, there is no way to implement synchronized controls or editable data objects (although this can be simulated). ASP.NET binding is strictly one-way; data can flow from a DataSet into a control but not vice versa.

Because of a web application's stateless nature, ASP.NET data binding is less powerful than Windows Forms data binding. However, ASP.NET makes up for the loss by including several advanced template-based controls, such as the DataGrid, DataList, and Repeater. These controls have a much more customizable interface and offer many features the Windows DataGrid doesn't.

The data binding process in an ASP.NET page works like this:

1. You define the bindings, using similar syntax to what you use when binding a Windows form.

2. You trigger data binding for individual controls or the entire page by calling the DataBind( ) method. At this point, the information moves from the data objects to the controls.

3. The final page is rendered to HTML. The data objects are discarded.

4. The page is posted back at a later point, perhaps in response to an editing action the user has performed with a data-bound control. At this point, you must requery the database, re-create the ADO.NET objects, and rebind the page before returning it to the user. Optionally, your program can issue an update statement to the database.

It helps to think of ASP.NET data binding as a quick and flexible way to populate controls with information from a database. It can't create the same sort of "record-browsers" that are possible with Windows Forms because there is no synchronization method for the controls. To implement functionality similar to what is available in Windows Forms, you have to handle control events and continuously post back the page whenever a selection changed.

List Binding

ASP.NET list binding works with the ListBox, DropDownList, CheckBoxList, and RadioButtonList web controls, and the HtmlSelect server-side HTML control (which represents the HTML <select> element). The syntax required is similar to Windows Forms list binding, but the DisplayMember property is replaced with the equivalent DataTextField property. The ValueMember property is replaced with the equivalent `DataValueField` property. The `DataValueProperty` property is typically much more important for web programmers than the `ValueMember` property is for Windows programmers, because there is no way to access the original data source of a control (for example, the original `DataSet` used to fill the control) during a postback.

Here's an example that binds data to a list control when a page is first loaded. Figure 12-9 shows the page.

```
private void Page_Load(object sender, System.EventArgs e)
{
    string connectionString = "Data Source=localhost;" +
        "Initial Catalog=Northwind;Integrated Security=SSPI";

    string SQL = "SELECT * FROM Customers";

    // Create ADO.NET objects.
    SqlConnection con = new SqlConnection(connectionString);
    SqlCommand com = new SqlCommand(SQL, con);
    SqlDataAdapter adapter = new SqlDataAdapter(com);
    DataSet ds = new DataSet("Northwind");

    // Execute the command.
    try
    {
        con.Open();
        adapter.Fill(ds, "Customers");
    }
    finally
    {
        con.Close();
    }

    // Display the results.
    lstContactName.DataSource = ds.Tables["Customers"];
    lstContactName.DataTextField = "ContactName";
    lstContactName.DataValueField = "CustomerID";
    lstContactName.DataBind();

}
```

One important difference with this data-binding code is that you must call the `DataBind()` method of the `ListBox` to activate the binding. It's at this point that the information is copied from the `DataTable` to the list control. If you omit this step, the page is rendered without any information in the `ListBox`. Alternatively, you can call the `DataBind()` method of the web page, which triggers the `DataBind()` method of every contained control.

If you look at the source code for this HTML page, you'll see that it includes names and ID hidden values. The following code is the shortened HTML markup for the list control.

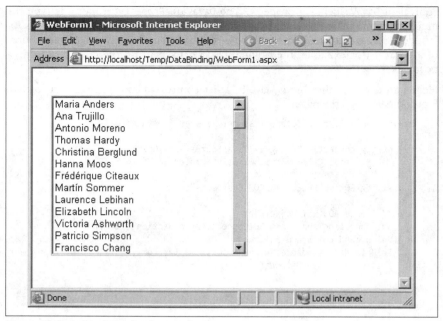

Figure 12-9. A data-bound web control

```
<select name="lstContactName" id="lstContactName">

    <option value="ALFKI">Maria Anders</option>
    <option value="ANATR">Ana Trujillo</option>
    <option value="ANTON">Antonio Moreno</option>
    <option value="AROUT">Thomas Hardy</option>
    <option value="BERGS">Christina Berglund</option>
    <option value="BLAUS">Hanna Moos</option>
    <option value="BLONP">Fr&#233;d&#233;rique Citeaux</option>

    <!-- Other items omitted. -->

</select>
```

On a postback, you can retrieve the text of the selected item from the ListBox.
SelectedItem.Text property and the value attribute from the ListBox.
SelectedItem.Value property.

ASP.NET Templated Data Controls

ASP.NET does a lot with its small set of advanced data-binding controls: the
DataList, DataGrid, and Repeater, which are outlined in Table 12-5. These
controls allow you to provide repeating lists or grids that can display more than
one column of information at a time. These controls also give you the ability,
through templates, to incorporate any other ASP.NET controls, such as a TextBox,
Label, and so on. You can bind these controls to a field in the current row using
embedded data-binding expressions in the *.aspx* markup code.

Table 12-5. ASP.NET data controls

Control	Description
DataList	Displays a list of items in an HTML table. By default, each item is contained in a single column on a single row. Because of this, the DataList is ideal for customized displays in which multiple fields are grouped and formatted in one block of HTML. The DataList supports automatic selection and editing events.
DataGrid	Displays a multicolumn table. Every item in a list has a single row with multiple columns. Typically, each column corresponds to information in an individual database field, although templates allow you to precisely configure the content. The DataGrid supports automatic paging (breaking a table into multiple pages for separate display), sorting, selecting, and editing events.
Repeater	Displays a custom layout by applying a template for each value. It makes no assumption about the formatting of the content it contains, and it provides no default format. The DataList and DataGrid, on the other hand, supply a basic HTML table to delimit items.

The full range of features of these three controls is beyond the scope of this book. The remainder of this chapter presents an example of how you can implement a simple data-bound DataList control with basic selection ability. For more information about ASP.NET data binding, refer to *ASP.NET In a Nutshell* by G. Andrew Duthie and Matthew MacDonald, or *Programming ASP.NET* by Jesse Liberty and Dan Hurwitz, both of which are available from O'Reilly.

The DataList

The DataList works using templates. A template is a block of HTML that allows you to define the content and formatting for part of a control. For example, you might create an item template to define how each item in the list should be formatted, and what data should be inserted. This item template is reused for each DataRow in a DataTable.

You must enter template information manually in script form. This means you have to modify the user interface code in the *.aspx* portion of your web page. Currently, Visual Studio .NET doesn't include any wizards or tools that can automate this task.

For example, the *.aspx* markup for a blank DataList is shown next. The item template is defined, but no content has been added.

```
<asp:DataList id=listCustomers runat="server">
  <ItemTemplate></ItemTemplate>
</asp:DataList>
```

To transform this into a more useful control, you need to define the exact HTML tags and controls that should be used for every item. To do this, you use data-binding expressions, which identify the fields that will be displayed from the database. Data binding expressions are enclosed and delimited by special characters: <%# and %>. Here's a simple example that shows a DataList displaying the CustomerID field:

```
<asp:DataList id=listCustomers runat="server">
  <ItemTemplate>
```

```
<%# DataBinder.Eval(Container.DataItem, "CustomerID") %>

    </ItemTemplate>
  </asp:DataList>
```

If you execute this code and examine the rendered HTML code, you'll discover a simple list of customer ID values delimited inside an HTML table:

```
<table id="listCustomers" cellspacing="0" border="0"
  style="border-collapse:collapse;">

  <tr><td>ALFKI</td></tr>
  <tr><td>ANATR</td></tr>
  <tr><td>ANTON</td></tr>
  <tr><td>AROUT</td></tr>
  <tr><td>BERGS</td></tr>
  <tr><td>BLAUS</td></tr>

  <!-- Other entries omitted. -->

</table>
```

You can also define a more appealing display format and combine several pieces of information:

```
<asp:DataList id=listCustomers runat="server">
  <ItemTemplate>

    <font face="Verdana" size="2"><b>
    <%# DataBinder.Eval(Container.DataItem, "CustomerID") %>
    <%# DataBinder.Eval(Container.DataItem, "CompanyName") %>
    </b></font><br>

    <font face="Verdana" size="1">    Contact Title:
    <%# DataBinder.Eval(Container.DataItem, "ContactTitle") %><br>
            Contact Name:
    <%# DataBinder.Eval(Container.DataItem, "ContactName") %><br>
            Address:
    <%# DataBinder.Eval(Container.DataItem, "Address") %>
    </font><br><br>

  </ItemTemplate>
</asp:DataList>
```

Figure 12-10 shows the rendered output.

Templates and Styles

The item template isn't the only template offered by the DataList control. To further specify formatting, you can add up to seven different templates, as described in Table 12-6.

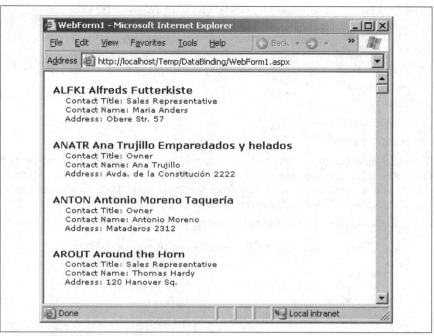

Figure 12-10. DataList output

Table 12-6. ASP.NET data control templates

Template	Description
AlternatingItemTemplate	Similar to ItemTemplate. If defined, items alternate between the ItemTemplate and the AlternatingItemTemplate, with ItemTemplate being used for the first item and every second item after that.
EditItemTemplate	Specifies how items will appear while they are edited.
FooterTemplate	If defined, this is a single row that is added to the end of the control.
HeaderTemplate	If defined, this is a single row that is added to the beginning of the control.
ItemTemplate	The default appearance of all items. The DataList creates one instance of the ItemTemplate for each item in the data source (unless you are using alternating items).
SelectedItemTemplate	Specifies how items will appear when they are selected. Only one item can be selected at a time.
SeparatorTemplate	Defines special content that will appear in a row between each item (or between an item and an alternating item).

Templates aren't the only way to configure the appearance of the DataList. You can also use *styles*. Styles define a broad range of formatting information that applies to all the content in a given template. For example, you can configure the appearance of a header template by using a header style. Each style has a significant amount of associated information, allowing you to set background and foreground colors, borders, fonts, and alignment.

Every template has a corresponding style. The available DataList styles are:

- AlternatingItemStyle
- EditItemStyle
- FooterStyle
- HeaderStyle
- ItemStyle
- SelectedItemStyle
- SeparatorStyle

A simple style tag looks like a single tag, with a number of formatting-related attributes. Each attribute corresponds to a property of the TableItemStyle class, which inherits most of its properties from the Style class. Both classes are found in the System.Web.UI.WebControls namespace.

```
<asp:DataList id=listCustomers runat="server">

  <HeaderStyle Font-Bold="True" ForeColor="White" BackColor="#A55129">

  <ItemTemplate>
    <!-- Content omitted. -->
  </ItemTemplate>

</asp:DataList>
```

You can configure styles using *.aspx* code (as with templates), or you can configure them using the Properties Window in Visual Studio .NET, which adds the corresponding information to your code automatically. In fact, you can even use a built-in wizard that allows you to choose a DataList "theme" and sets multiple related style properties. To use this feature, click the Auto Format link at the bottom of the Properties Window when the DataList is selected.

The next example shows a DataList that displays the same information but uses multiple templates and styles to apply the more exotic formatting shown in Figure 12-11. All styles inherit basic appearance properties (such as color and font) from the containing control (in this case, the DataList). In addition, the styles used for alternating items, selected items, and edited items all inherit the formatting you apply to the item style.

```
<asp:DataList id=listCustomers runat="server"
    BorderColor="#DEBA84" BorderStyle="None" CellSpacing="2"
    BackColor="#DEBA84" CellPadding="3" GridLines="Both"
    BorderWidth="1px">

<!-- Define templates. -->

  <ItemTemplate>
    <font face="Verdana" size="2"><b>
    <%# DataBinder.Eval(Container.DataItem, "CustomerID") %>
    <%# DataBinder.Eval(Container.DataItem, "CompanyName") %>
    </b></font><br>
```

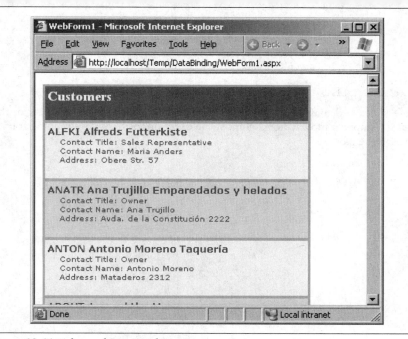

Figure 12-11. Advanced DataList formatting

```
        <font face="Verdana" size="1">    Contact Title:
        <%# DataBinder.Eval(Container.DataItem, "ContactTitle") %><br>
                Contact Name:
        <%# DataBinder.Eval(Container.DataItem, "ContactName") %><br>
                Address:
        <%# DataBinder.Eval(Container.DataItem, "Address") %>
        </font><br><br>
    </ItemTemplate>

    <HeaderTemplate>
        <h2>Customers</h2>
    </HeaderTemplate>

    <FooterTemplate>
        <br>This list provided on <%# System.DateTime.Now %>
    </FooterTemplate>

<!-- Define styles. -->

    <HeaderStyle Font-Bold="True" ForeColor="White" BackColor="#A55129" />
    <ItemStyle Font-Size="Smaller" Font-Names="Verdana" ForeColor="#8C4510"
            BackColor="#FFF7E7" />
```

```
<AlternatingItemStyle BackColor="#FFE0C0" />
<FooterStyle ForeColor="#8C4510" BackColor="#F7DFB5" />

</asp:DataList>
```

These styles and templates provide fine-grained control over every aspect of the DataList's appearance, which is almost the exact opposite of data binding frameworks in the past.

13

Strongly Typed DataSets

Strongly typed DataSets are a collection of classes that inherit from the DataSet, DataTable, and DataRow classes, and provide additional properties, methods, and events based on the DataSet schema. These methods, properties, and events allow, among other things, named properties and methods to be used to retrieve column values, access parent and child records, find rows, and handle null column values.

It is important to remember that strongly typed DataSets are in fact just a collection of classes. Because the strongly typed DataSet classes inherit from DataSet, DataTable, and DataRow, all the functionality present in those classes can be used just as it is for the untyped classes. The development environment just provides a way to automatically generate consistent and efficient strongly typed DataSet classes.

Using a strongly typed DataSet has a number of advantages over using untyped DataSet:

- Schema information is contained within the strongly typed DataSet. This results in an improvement in performance over retrieving schema information at runtime. Of course, the schema of an untyped DataSet can also be defined programmatically.

- Programming is more intuitive, and code is easier to maintain. Table and field names are accessed through properties rather than indexer arguments. The Visual Studio .NET IDE provides autocomplete functionality for these names. As an example, the following code demonstrates accessing data using both an untyped and strongly typed Northwind DataSet:

```
// untyped
String categoryName =
    (String)dsNorthwind.Tables["Categories"].Rows[0]["CategoryName"];

// strongly typed
String categoryName = dsNorthwind.Categories[0].CategoryName;
```

- Type mismatch errors and errors resulting from either misspelled or out-of-bounds indexer arguments to retrieve tables and columns can be detected during compilation rather than at runtime.

There are some drawbacks to using strongly typed `DataSet` objects:

- Using typed classes adds some overhead to code execution. If the strongly typed functionality isn't required, application performance can be improved slightly using an untyped `DataSet`.
- The strongly typed `DataSet` will need to be regenerated when the data structure changes. Applications using the strongly typed `DataSet` will need to be rebuilt using a reference to the new strongly typed `DataSet`. This can be especially significant in a multitier application or distributed where any clients that use the strongly typed `DataSets` will have to be rebuilt using a reference to the updated version, even those that would not otherwise have been affected by the change if an untyped `DataSet` was used.

This chapter discusses how to create strongly typed `DataSets` and describes some of their added functionality. Examples that demonstrate how to use the extended functionality are presented.

Creating a Strongly Typed DataSet

There are three ways a strongly typed `DataSet` class can be generated. The easiest method is to drop one or more `DataAdapter` objects from the Data tab in the Visual Studio .NET Toolbox onto a design surface such as a form or a component. Configure each `DataAdapter` to select data from one table. Right-click on the design surface and select Generate DataSet. Provide a name for the `DataSet`, select the tables to be included, and generate the new strongly typed `DataSet`. To relate the two tables, double-click on the XSD file for the new `DataSet` in the Solution Explorer window to open it. Right-click on the child table in XSD schema designer, select Add/New Relation... from the shortcut menu, and complete the dialog. Instances of the strongly typed `DataSet` can now be created programmatically or by using the `DataSet` object from the Data tab in the Visual Studio.NET Toolbox.

The other two methods are more involved, and both require an XSD schema file, which can be generated in a number of ways, e.g., using Visual Studio IDE tools, third-party tools, or the `DataSet` `WriteXmlSchema( )` method. The following example shows a utility that uses the `WriteXmlSchema( )` method to create an XSD schema based on the `Categories` and `Products` tables in the Northwind database:

```
String connString = "Data Source=localhost;" +
    "Initial Catalog=Northwind;Integrated Security=SSPI";

SqlDataAdapter daCategories = new SqlDataAdapter(
    "SELECT * FROM Categories", connString);
SqlDataAdapter daProducts = new SqlDataAdapter(
    "SELECT * FROM Products", connString);
SqlDataAdapter daOrders = new SqlDataAdapter(
    "SELECT * FROM Orders", connString);
SqlDataAdapter daOrderDetails = new SqlDataAdapter(
    "SELECT * FROM [Order Details]", connString);
```

```
DataSet ds = new DataSet("Northwind");

// load the schema information for the tables into the DataSet
daCategories.FillSchema(ds, SchemaType.Mapped, "Categories");
daProducts.FillSchema(ds, SchemaType.Mapped, "Products");
daOrders.FillSchema(ds, SchemaType.Mapped, "Orders");
daOrderDetails.FillSchema(ds, SchemaType.Mapped, "Order Details");

// add the relations
ds.Relations.Add("Categories_Products",
    ds.Tables["Categories"].Columns["CategoryID"],
    ds.Tables["Products"].Columns["CategoryID"]);
ds.Relations.Add("Orders_OrderDetails",
    ds.Tables["Orders"].Columns["OrderID"],
    ds.Tables["Order Details"].Columns["OrderID"]);
ds.Relations.Add("Products_OrderDetails",
    ds.Tables["Products"].Columns["ProductID"],
    ds.Tables["Order Details"].Columns["ProductID"]);

// output the XSD schema
ds.WriteXmlSchema(@"c:\Northwind.xsd");
```

The following code is a partial listing of the XSD schema for the Categories and
Products tables in the Northwind database. Note that the msdata namespace is
defined to add Microsoft-specific extensions, including the read-only and autoincrement column properties. These attributes are described in more detail later in
Appendix B.

```
<?xml version="1.0" standalone="yes"?>
<xs:schema id="Northwind" xmlns=""
    xmlns:xs="http://www.w3.org/2001/XMLSchema"
    xmlns:msdata="urn:schemas-microsoft-com:xml-msdata">
  <xs:element name="Nortdwind" msdata:IsDataSet="true">
    <xs:complexType>
      <xs:choice maxOccurs="unbounded">
        <xs:element name="Categories">
          <xs:complexType>
            <xs:sequence>
              <xs:element name="CategoryID" msdata:ReadOnly="true"
                  msdata:AutoIncrement="true" type="xs:int" />
              <xs:element name="CategoryName">
                <xs:simpleType>
                  <xs:restriction base="xs:string">
                    <xs:maxLength value="15" />
                  </xs:restriction>
                </xs:simpleType>
              </xs:element>
              <xs:element name="Description" minOccurs="0">
                <xs:simpleType>
                  <xs:restriction base="xs:string">
                    <xs:maxLength value="1073741823" />
                  </xs:restriction>
                </xs:simpleType>
              </xs:element>
```

```
                 <xs:element name="Picture" type="xs:base64Binary"
                        minOccurs="0" />
                 </xs:sequence>
               </xs:complexType>
             </xs:element>
             <xs:element name="Products">

             <!-- Product definition omitted. -->

             </xs:element>
           </xs:choice>
         </xs:complexType>
         <xs:unique name="Constraint1" msdata:PrimaryKey="true">
           <xs:selector xpath=".//Categories" />
           <xs:field xpath="CategoryID" />
         </xs:unique>
         <xs:unique name="Products_Constraint1"
             msdata:ConstraintName="Constraint1" msdata:PrimaryKey="true">
           <xs:selector xpath=".//Products" />
           <xs:field xpath="ProductID" />
         </xs:unique>
         <xs:keyref name="Categories_Products" refer="Constraint1">
           <xs:selector xpath=".//Products" />
           <xs:field xpath="CategoryID" />
         </xs:keyref>
       </xs:element>
     </xs:schema>
```

From this schema, a strongly typed DataSet can be created using Visual Studio .NET or the XML Schema Definition Tool.

To create a strongly typed DataSet from the XSD schema using Visual Studio .NET, right-click on the project in the Solution Explorer window, choose Add / Existing Item... from the shortcut menu, and select the XSD file to add it to the project. Double-click on the XSD file to open it in the designer window. Right-click on the designer window and select Generate DataSet. To see the strongly typed DataSet file in the Solution Explorer window, select Show All Files from the Project menu. The strongly typed DataSet class Northwind.cs lists as a child of the Northwind.xsd node.

The second way to create a strongly typed DataSet from an XSD schema is to use the XML Schema Definition Tool (XSD.EXE) found in the .NET Framework SDK *bin* directory. To generate the class file from *Northwind.xsd*, issue the following command from the command prompt:

```
xsd Northwind.xsd /d /l:CS
```

The /d switch specifies that source code for a DataSet should be created, while the /l switch specifies that the utility should use the C# language, which is the default if not specified. The XML Schema Definition Tool offers additional options that are documented in the .NET Framework SDK documentation.

The resulting class file for the strongly typed DataSet is named using the DataSet name in the XSD schema and an extension specifying the language. In this case, the file is named *Northwind.cs* because the DataSet was named *Northwind* when it was constructed. The strongly typed DataSet is ready to be added to a project.

Discussion of Underlying Classes

As mentioned before, the strongly typed DataSet is simply a collection of classes extending the functionality of the untyped DataSet. Specifically, three classes are generated for each table in the DataSet: one for each DataTable, DataRow, and DataRowChangeEvent. This section provides a brief overview of the classes generated and discusses the more commonly used methods, properties, and events of those classes.

A class called *TableName*DataTable is created for each table in the DataSet. This class inherits from DataTable and implements the IEnumerable interface. Table 13-1 lists the commonly used methods of this class specific to strongly typed DataSet objects.

Table 13-1. TableNameDataTable methods

Method	Description
Add*TableName*Row( )	Adds a row to the table. The method has two overloads and takes an argument of either a *TableName*Row object or a set of arguments, one for each of the column values.
FindBy*PrimaryKeyField1* ... *PrimaryKeyFieldN*( )	Takes *N* arguments that are the values of the primary key fields of the row to find. Returns a reference to a *TableName*Row object.
New*TableName*Row( )	Takes no arguments and returns a reference to a new *TableName*Row object with the same schema as the table to be used for adding new rows to the table in the strongly typed DataSet.

A class called *TableName*Row is created for the DataRow in each table. This class inherits from DataRow. The class also exposes a property for each column in the table with the same name as the column. Table 13-2 lists the commonly used methods of this class.

Table 13-2. TableNameRow Class methods

Method	Description
Typed Accessor	For each column, a typed accessor to set and get the value of a column that is a property with the same name as the underlying column.
Is*ColumnName*Null( )	Returns a Boolean value indicating whether the value of the field is null.
Set*ColumnName*Null( )	Sets the value of the underlying field to DBNull.
Get*ChildTableName*Rows( )	Returns an array of *ChildTableName*Row objects comprising the child rows.
*Parent*TableNameRow( )	Returns an object of type *ParentTableName*Row providing access to the parent row.

Finally, a class called *TableName*RowChangeEvent is created for each table in the DataSet. This class inherits from EventArgs. Table 13-3 lists the method of this class.

Table 13-3. TableNameChangeEvent method

Property	Description
*TableName*Row	Returns a reference to a *TableName*Row object representing the row that caused the event to be raised.

Adding a Row

As with untyped DataSet objects, there are two ways to add a new row to a strongly typed DataSet. The first uses the New*TableName*Row( ) method of the strongly typed DataSet to return a reference to a *TableName*Row object. The accessor properties are then used to assign values to the columns of the new row. Finally, the Add*TableName*Row( ) method adds the new row to the DataTable. The following example demonstrates this method:

```
// strongly typed DataSet called Northwind containing the Orders table
Northwind.OrdersDataTable ordersTable = new Northwind.OrdersDataTable();
// create a new row object
Northwind.OrdersRow ordersRow = ordersTable.NewOrdersRow();
// use property accessors to set the column values for the row
ordersRow.CustomerID = "VINET";
ordersRow.EmployeeID = 1;

// ... set the rest of the fields

// add the row to the table
ordersTable.AddOrdersRow(ordersRow);
```

The following code sample shows how the same thing can be accomplished with an untyped DataSet:

```
DataTable ordersTable = new DataTable("Orders");
// ... code to define or retrieve the schema for the DataTable
DataRow ordersRow = ordersTable.NewRow();
ordersRow["CustomerID"] = "VINET";
ordersRow["EmployeeID"] = 1;

// ... set the rest of the fields

ordersTable.Rows.Add(ordersRow);
```

The second way to add a new row to a strongly typed DataSet is to use the Add*TableName*Row( ) method. This method allows a row to be added to the DataSet using a single statement similar to the Add( ) method of the DataRowCollection when dealing with untyped DataSet objects. The main difference, aside from the simpler syntax, is that the method is strongly typed, allowing parameter data type errors to be caught at compilation time. The following example illustrates the second method for adding a row:

```
// strongly typed DataSet
Northwind.OrdersDataTable ordersTable = new Northwind.OrdersDataTable();

// add the row to the table
ordersTable.AddOrdersRow("VINET", 1, ... );
```

Again, the following code sample shows how the same thing can be accomplished using an untyped DataSet:

```
// untyped DataSet
DataTable ordersTable = new DataTable("Orders");

// ... code to define or retrieve the schema for the DataTable

// add the row to the table
ordersTable.Rows.Add(new Object[] {"VINET", 1, ...});
```

Editing a Row

Editing a row in a strongly typed DataSet is nearly the same as editing a row in an untyped DataSet. The only real difference is that columns for the rows are accessed using properties of the strongly typed DataSet. The following example illustrates editing data using a strongly typed DataSet:

```
// strongly typed DataSet called Northwind containing the Orders table
Northwind.OrdersDataTable ordersTable = new Northwind.OrdersDataTable();

// ... code to add new rows to, or Fill the Orders table

// modify the employee ID for the first Order
Northwind.OrdersRow ordersRow = ordersTable[0];
ordersRow.EmployeeID = 2;
```

This example shows editing the same data using an untyped DataSet:

```
// untyped DataSet containing the Orders table
DataSet ds = new DataSet("Northwind");
DataTable ordersTable = ds.Tables.Add("Orders");

// ... code to define or retrieve the schema for the Orders table
// ... code to add new rows to, or Fill the Orders table

// modify the employee ID for the first Order
DataRow ordersRow = ordersTable.Rows[0];
ordersRow["EmployeeID"] = 2;
```

Finding a Row

The strongly typed DataSet has a FindBy( ) method to locate a row in a DataTable based on the primary key. The method accepts one argument for each of the columns that make up the primary key. The method has named arguments, making it easier to work with than similar untyped DataSet code. Additionally, the arguments are typed, allowing mismatch errors to be caught at compilation time rather than at runtime. The following example demonstrates using the strongly typed DataSet FindBy( ) method and also shows comparable code using an untyped DataSet.

```
// strongly typed DataSet called Northwind containing the Orders table
Northwind.Order_DetailsDataTable table =
  new Northwind.Order_DetailsDataTable();

// ... code to add new rows to, or Fill the Orders table

// locate the row based on its primary key value
Northwind.Order_DetailsRow orderDetailsRow
    = table.FindByOrderIDProductID(10248, 11);
if(orderDetailsRow != null)
{
    // ... code to process the row
}
```

This example shows comparable code using an untyped DataSet:

```
// untyped DataSet containing the Orders table
DataSet ds = new DataSet("Northwind");
DataTable ordersTable = ds.Tables.Add("Orders");

// ... code to define or retrieve the schema for the DataTable
// ... code to add new rows to, or Fill the Orders table

// locate the row based on its primary key value
DataRow orderDetailsRow = ordersTable.Find(new Object[] {10248, 11});
if(orderDetailsRow != null)
{
    // ... code to process the row
}
```

Null Data

The strongly typed DataSet adds two methods for each column,
Is*ColumnName*Null( ) and Set*ColumnName*Null( ), to make it easier and more intuitive to work with null values in DataRow columns. Is*ColumnName*Null( ) returns a
Boolean value indicating whether the underlying field value is null, while
Set*ColumnName*Null( ) sets the value of the underlying field to DBNull. The
following sample demonstrates using the strongly typed DataSet null handling
methods:

```
// strongly typed DataSet called Northwind containing the Orders table
Northwind.OrdersDataTable ordersTable = new Northwind.OrdersDataTable();

// ... code to add new rows to, or Fill the Orders table

// check whether the CustomerID of the first row is null
Northwind.OrdersRow ordersRow = ordersTable[0];
if(ordersRow.IsCustomerIDNull())
{
    // ... code to handle the null CustomerID condition
}

// set the EmployeeID to null
ordersRow.SetEmployeeIDNull();
```

This example shows comparable code using an untyped DataSet:

```
// untyped DataSet containing the Orders table
DataSet ds = new DataSet("Northwind");
DataTable ordersTable = ds.Tables.Add("Orders");

// ... code to define or retrieve the schema for the DataTable
// ... code to add new rows to, or Fill the Orders table

// check whether the CustomerID of the first row is null
DataRow ordersRow = ordersTable.Rows[0];
if(ordersRow.IsNull("CustomerID"))
{
    // ... code to handle the null CustomerID condition
}

// set the EmployeeID to null
ordersRow["EmployeeID"] = Convert.DBNull;
```

Navigating Hierarchical Data

Strongly Typed
DataSets

The strongly typed DataSet provides two methods for each DataRelation, *TableName*Row( ) and *TableName*Rows( ), to facilitate navigating records in parent child relationships. These methods are similar to the GetParentRow( ) and GetChildRows( ) methods in the untyped DataSet. The *TableName*Row( ) method is defined for the child table and retrieves the parent row for a DataRow. The *TableName*Rows( ) method is defined for the parent table in a relationship and retrieves the child rows for a DataRow.

The strongly typed DataSet methods encapsulate the DataRelations defined within the DataSet so a reference to the DataRelation or the name of the DataRelation isn't required when navigating the hierarchy of records. The following sample demonstrates using the strongly typed DataSet methods to navigate a hierarchy of records:

```
// strongly typed DataSet called Northwind containing Orders table and
// OrderDetails table, related through the OrderID field
Northwind ds = new Northwind();

// ... code to fill the Orders and Order Details tables in the DataSet

foreach(Northwind.OrdersRow ordersRow in ds.Orders)
{
    // iterate the collection of order details for the order through
    // the GetOrderDetailsRow accessor
    foreach(Northwind.Order_DetailsRow orderDetailsRow in
        ordersRow.GetOrder_DetailsRows())
    {
        // get the CustomerID from the parent row, through the
        // OrdersRow property of the child row
        String customerId = orderDetailsRow.OrdersRow.CustomerID;
```

```
        // get the ProductID
        Int32 productId = orderDetailsRow.ProductID;
    }
}
```

This example shows comparable code using an untyped DataSet:

```
// untyped DataSet containing Orders table and
// OrderDetails table, related through the OrderID field
DataSet ds = new DataSet();

// ... code to define or retrieve the schema for the Orders and
// [Order Details] tables schemas including creating DataRelation objects
// ... code to add new rows to the Orders and [Order Details] tables

foreach(DataRow ordersRow in ds.Tables["Orders"].Rows)
{
    foreach(DataRow orderDetailsRow in
        ordersRow.GetChildRows("Order_OrderDetails"))
    {
        // get the CustomerID from the parent row
        String customerId =
            orderDetailsRow.GetParentRow("Order_OrderDetails")
            ["CustomerID"].ToString();

        // get the ProductID
        Int32 productId = (Int32)orderDetailsRow["ProductID"];
    }
}
```

Annotations

By default, strongly typed DataSet classes use names from the underlying tables and columns in the data source to generate the names of methods, properties, and events. Annotations allow the names of elements in the typed DataSet to be changed without modifying the underlying schema. The names can be made more meaningful, making the strongly typed DataSet easier to use and the code using it more readable.

To use annotations, the codegen namespace declaration must be added to the XSD file. This can be placed directly after the msdata namespace declaration at the beginning of the file:

```
<?xml version="1.0" standalone="yes"?>
<xs:schema id="NewDataSet" xmlns=""
    xmlns:xs="http://www.w3.org/2001/XMLSchema"
    xmlns:msdata="urn:schemas-microsoft-com:xml-msdata"
    xmlns:codegen="urn:schemas-microsoft-com:xml-msprop">
```

Annotations can be used to change the names of elements in the strongly typed DataSet. Using the Categories table in Northwind as an example, the default schema results in a DataRow name of CategoriesRow and a DataRowCollection name of Categories in the strongly typed DataSet. Here's an excerpt from the default schema:

```
<xs:element name="Categories">
```

Specifying the typedName and the typedPlural in the schema element changes the name of the DataRow to Category and the name of the DataRowCollection to Categorys. Here's the new XSD schema:

```
<xs:element name="Categories"
    codegen:typedName="Category" codegen:typedPlural="Categorys">
```

Annotations can also change the names of methods that navigate relationships. Here's the automatically generated code relating Categories to Products:

```
<xs:keyref name="Categories_Products" refer="Constraint1">
    <xs:selector xpath=".//Products" />
    <xs:field xpath="CategoryID" />
</xs:keyref>
```

Adding the typedParent and typedChildren attributes to the relationship allows the method Category.Products( ) to be used instead of the default Category. GetProductsRows( ) to retrieve the child records for a product:

```
<xs:keyref name="Categories_Products" refer="Constraint1"
    codegen:typedParent="Categories" codegen:typedChildren="Products">
    <xs:selector xpath=".//Products" />
    <xs:field xpath="CategoryID" />
</xs:keyref>
```

Annotations can also control the way null values in the underlying data source are handled. The default schema element for the Description field of the Categories table in Northwind is a null value as shown here:

```
<xs:element name="Description" type="xs:string" minOccurs="0" />
```

By specifying a nullValue annotation, the default value for the Description field in the typed DataSet will be an empty string when the value for the Description is null in the underlying data source. Here's the annotated schema element for the field:

```
<xs:element name="Description" type="xs:string" minOccurs="0"
    codegen:nullValue="" />
```

This section introduced the use of annotations with strongly typed DataSet objects. Appendix B provides complete coverage of the available annotations in the codegen namespace.

14

DataAdapters

The DataAdapter class serves as a bridge between a disconnected ADO.NET objects and a data source. The DataAdapter retrieves data into a DataSet or a DataTable from a data source using the Fill( ) method. Schema information can be retrieved using the FillSchema( ) method. The DataAdapter updates any changes made to the DataSet or DataTable back to the data source using the Update( ) method.

In simple scenarios, the updating logic that the DataAdapter uses to reconcile changes made to the DataSet can be generated automatically from the query used to retrieve the data by using a CommandBuilder object. For more complex scenarios, custom update logic can be written to control the logic the DataAdapter uses when adding, deleting, and modifying records in the data source in response to changes made to the DataSet. In either case, the updating logic is used when the Update( ) method is called.

Once data is retrieved using the DataAdapter, no information about the connection, database, tables, columns, or any other details about the source of the data is available in the disconnected objects. The data can be persisted or passed between applications without the risk of exposing details about the location or structure of the data source or access credentials used. Figure 14-1 shows the structure of the DataAdapter and the contained classes.

Creating DataAdapter Object

The overloaded constructor for the DataAdapter allows four different ways to create the data adapter, of which two are most commonly used. The following example creates a DataAdapter specifying the SELECT statement and connection string in the constructor.

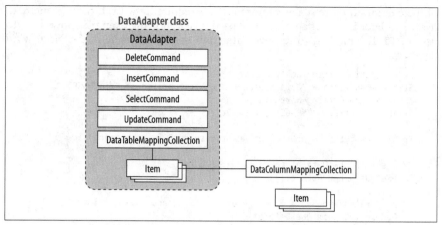

Figure 14-1. The DataAdapter class

```
String connString = "Data Source=(local);Integrated security=SSPI;" +
    "Initial Catalog=Northwind;";
String selectSql = "SELECT * FROM Orders";

SqlDataAdapter da = new SqlDataAdapter(selectSql, connString);
```

While this approach is common, it is awkward when using parameterized queries or stored procedures. The following example creates a DataAdapter specifying a Command object for the SelectCommand property of the DataAdapter in the constructor:

```
// create the Connection
String connString = "Data Source = (local);Integrated security = SSPI;" +
    "Initial Catalog = Northwind;";
SqlConnection conn = new SqlConnection(connString);

// create a Command object based on a stored procedure
String selectSql = "MyStoredProcedure";
SqlCommand selectCmd = new SqlCommand(selectSql, conn);
selectCmd.CommandType = CommandType.StoredProcedure;

SqlDataAdapter da = new SqlDataAdapter(selectCmd);
```

It should be noted that there is no best way to create a DataAdapter, and it makes no real difference how it is created.

Retrieving Data from the Data Source

The Fill( ) method of the DataAdapter retrieves data from the data source into a DataSet or a DataTable. When the Fill( ) method for the data adapter is called, the select statement defined in the SelectCommand is executed against the data source and retrieved into a DataSet or DataTable. In addition to retrieving data, the Fill( ) method retrieves schema information for columns that don't exist. This schema that it retrieves from the data source is limited to the name and data type of the column. If more schema information is required, the `FillSchema( )` method, described later in this chapter, can be used. The following example shows how to use the `Fill( )` method to retrieve data from the `Orders` table in the Northwind database:

```
// connection string and the select statement
String connString = "Data Source=(local);Integrated security=SSPI;" +
    "Initial Catalog=Northwind;";
String selectSQL = "SELECT * FROM Orders";

SqlDataAdapter da = new SqlDataAdapter(selectSQL, connString);

// create a new DataSet to receive the data
DataSet ds = new DataSet();

// read all of the data from the orders table and loads it into the
// Orders table in the DataSet
da.Fill(ds, "Orders");
```

A `DataTable` can also be filled similarly:

```
// ... code to create the data adapter, as above

// create the DataTable to retrieve the data
DataTable dt = new DataTable("Orders");

// use the data adapter to load the data into the table Orders
da.Fill(dt);
```

Notice that a connection object is never opened and closed for the data adapter. If the connection for the data adapter isn't open, the `DataAdapter` opens and closes it as required. If the connection is already open, the `DataAdapter` leaves the connection open.

The same set of records can be retrieved more efficiently using a stored procedure. Stored procedures have a number of benefits over SQL statements:

- Stored procedures allow business logic for common tasks to be consistently implemented across applications. The stored procedure to perform a task can be designed, coded, and tested. It can then be made available to any client that needs to perform the task. The SQL statements to perform the task need to be changed in only one place if the underlying business logic changes. If the parameters for the stored procedure don't change, applications using the stored procedure will not even need to be recompiled.

- Stored procedures can improve performance in situations where a group of SQL statements are executed together with conditional logic. A stored procedure allows a single execution plan to be prepared for the SQL statements together with the conditional logic. Rather than having the client submit a series of SQL statements based on client-side conditional logic, both the SQL statements and conditional logic are executed on the server, requiring only one round trip. Additionally, when a stored procedure is executed, only the parameters need to be transmitted to the server rather than the entire SQL statement.

- Stored procedures are more secure. Users can be granted permission to execute stored procedures that perform required business functions rather than having direct access to the database tables.
- Stored procedures provide a layer of abstraction for the data, making performing business function more intuitive and, at the same time, hiding database implementation from the users.

SQL Server Stored Procedures

In SQL Server Version 6.5 and earlier, stored procedures were more efficient than T-SQL statements because a partially compiled execution plan for the stored procedure was stored in a system table when the stored procedure was created. SQL Server only had to optimize the stored plan. Additionally, the fully compiled plan was stored in the procedure cache so that subsequent executions of the stored procedure could use the precompiled execution plan.

SQL Server Version 7.0 and later doesn't store a partially compiled execution plan for stored procedures. Stored procedures and T-SQL statements are compiled at execution time, and these execution plans are then stored in the procedure cache and reused for subsequent statements. Extending execution plan reuse to all SQL statements reduces the relative performance benefit of stored procedures compared to T-SQL statements.

The following example shows the stored procedure used to select records from the Orders table in the Northwind database. The stored procedure takes a CustomerID parameter that results in only orders for that customer being retrieved.

```
// the stored procedure
CREATE PROCEDURE GetOrders
    @CustomerID nchar(5)
AS
    SET NOCOUNT ON

    SELECT * FROM Orders WHERE CustomerId=@CustomerID

    RETURN
```

The code to retrieve the data using the stored procedure has some differences compared with the code using the SQL statements directly. The CommandText property of the SelectCommand is set to the name of the stored procedure rather than to a SQL statement. The CommandType is set to StoredProcedure rather than specifying or accepting the default value of Text. The following example illustrates retrieving orders for a specific customer using a stored procedure:

```
// connection string and the stored procedure
String connString = "Data Source=(local);Integrated security=SSPI;" +
    "Initial Catalog=Northwind;";
String selectSql = "GetOrders";
```

```
// create a DataSet to receive the data
DataSet ds = new DataSet();

SqlConnection conn = new SqlConnection(connString);

// create a command object based on the stored procedure
SqlCommand selectCmd = new SqlCommand(selectSql, conn);
selectCmd.CommandType = CommandType.StoredProcedure;

// create and set the CustomerID parameter for the stored procedure
selectCmd.Parameters.Add("@CustomerID", SqlDbType.NChar, 5);
selectCmd.Parameters["@CustomerID"].Value = "VINET";

// create and fill the DataSet
SqlDataAdapter da = new SqlDataAdapter(selectCmd);
da.Fill(ds, "Orders");
```

The same result could be accomplished with a parameterized query, as shown in
the following example:

```
// connection string and parameterized query
String connString = "Data Source=(local);Integrated security=SSPI;" +
    "Initial Catalog=Northwind;";
String selectSql = "SELECT * FROM Orders WHERE CustomerID=@CustomerID";

DataSet ds = new DataSet();
SqlConnection conn = new SqlConnection(connString);

// create a command object based on the SQL select statement
SqlCommand selectCmd = new SqlCommand(selectSql, conn);

// create and set the CustomerID parameter for the select statement
selectCmd.Parameters.Add("@CustomerID", SqlDbType.NChar, 5);
selectCmd.Parameters["@CustomerID"].Value = "VINET";

// create and fill the DataSet
SqlDataAdapter da = new SqlDataAdapter(selectCmd);
da.Fill(ds, "Orders");
```

There are several options available to load more than one table into the same
DataSet using a DataAdapter:

- The Fill( ) method can be called several times on the same DataAdapter,
  specifying a different DataTable in the same DataSet. The SelectCommand is
  modified to select the records for a different table each time Fill( ) is called.
- Multiple DataAdapter objects, each returning one table, can be created. Fill( )
  is called on each DataAdapter, specifying the appropriate DataTable in the same
  DataSet.
- Either a batch query or a stored procedure that returns multiple result sets
  can be used.

In the last option, the DataAdapter automatically creates the required tables and
assigns them the default names Table, Table1, Table2, if a table name isn't specified. If a table name is specified, for example MyTable, the DataAdapter names the

tables MyTable, MyTable1, MyTable2, and so on. The tables can be renamed after the fill, or table mapping can map the automatically generated names to names of the underlying tables in the DataSet. The following example shows how to use a batch query with a DataAdapter to create two tables in a DataSet:

```
// connection string and batch query
String connString = "Data Source=(local);Integrated security=SSPI;" +
    "Initial Catalog=Northwind;";
String selectSql = "SELECT * FROM Customers;" +
    " SELECT * FROM Orders";

// create the data adapter
SqlDataAdapter da = new SqlDataAdapter(selectSql, connString);

// create and fill the DataSet
DataSet ds = new DataSet();
da.Fill(ds);
```

The DataSet is filled with two tables named Table and Table1, respectively, containing data from the Customers and the Orders tables in data source.

Finally, the DataAdapter provides an overloaded Fill( ) method that retrieves a subset of rows from the query and loads them into the DataSet. The starting record and maximum number of records are specified to define the subset. For example, the following code statement retrieves the first 10 records and inserts them into a DataTable named Categories:

```
da.Fill(ds, 0, 10, "Categories");
```

It is important to realize that this method actually performs the original query and retrieves the full set of results. It then discards those records that aren't in the specified range. As a result, this approach performs poorly when selecting from large result sets. A better approach is to limit the amount of data that must be transferred over the network and the work that must be performed by the data source by fine-tuning a SQL SELECT statement using a TOP *n* or WHERE clause.

Retrieving Schema Information from the Data Source

Schema information can be retrieved from a data source using the FillSchema( ) method, which retrieves the schema information for the SQL statement in the SelectCommand. The method adds a DataTable to the DataSet and adds DataColumn objects to that table. Finally, it configures the AllowDBNull, AutoIncrement, MaxLength, ReadOnly, and Unique properties of the DataColumn, based on the data source. While it configures the AutoIncrement property, it doesn't set the AutoIncrementSeed and AutoIncrementStep properties. The FillSchema( ) method also configures the primary key and unique constraints for the DataTable. It doesn't configure the DefaultValue property.

In addition to an argument specifying the DataSet argument, the FillSchema( ) method takes an argument specifying whether the schema is transformed by the table mappings for the data adapter. Mapping tables and columns is discussed in more detail later in this chapter

If the FillSchema( ) method is used with a table that already has schema defined, the original schema isn't overwritten. Rather, new columns are added if they are part of the schema retrieved but don't exist in the table.

Finally, if a query returning multiple result sets is specified in the SelectCommand, only the schema from the first result set is used. To fill schemas based on queries with multiple result sets, use the Fill( ) method with the MissingSchemaAction set to AddWithKey.

The following example demonstrates the FillSchema method:

```
// connection and select command strings
String connString = "Data Source=(local);Integrated security=SSPI;" +
    "Initial Catalog=Northwind;";
String selectSql = "SELECT * FROM Orders";

// create the data adapter
SqlDataAdapter da = new SqlDataAdapter(selectSql, connString);

// create a new DataSet to receive the table schema
DataSet ds = new DataSet();
// read the schema for the Orders table from the data source and
// create a table in the DataSet called "Orders" with the same schema
da.FillSchema(ds, SchemaType.Source, "Orders");

// create a new DataTable to receive the schema
DataTable dt = new DataTable("Orders");
da.FillSchema(dt, SchemaType.Source);
```

As with the Fill( ) method, the DataAdapter connection must be valid, but doesn't have to be open. If it is closed when FillSchema( ) is called, it is automatically opened to retrieve the data and then closed. If it is open when FillSchema( ) is called, it is left open after the data is retrieved.

Updating the Data Source

The Update( ) method can submit DataSet changes back to the data source. It uses the statements in the DeleteCommand, InsertCommand, and UpdateCommand objects to attempt to update the data source with records that have been deleted, inserted, or updated in the DataSet. Each row is updated individually and not as part of a batch process. Furthermore, the order in which the rows are processed is determined by the indexes on the DataTable and not by the update type. Figure 14-2 illustrates how the DataAdapter is used both to reconcile changed data in the DataSet with the data source using the Update() method and to retrieve data from the data source using the Fill() method.

The delete, insert, and update statements can be automatically generated using the CommandBuilder object, but this is probably not the best approach for production systems. The CommandBuilder object is discussed in more detail in Chapter 15. Alternatively, custom update logic can be used where the DeleteCommand,

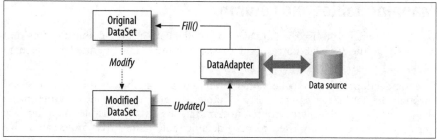

Figure 14-2. Retrieving and updating data using the DataAdapter

InsertCommand, and UpdateCommand are each defined. Compared with using the CommandBuilder, custom logic can significantly improve performance and can implement solutions to complex updating and conflict-resolution scenarios. Custom update logic is also examined in detail in Chapter 15.

The following example demonstrates the Update( ) method. For simplicity, a CommandBuilder generates the update logic.

```
// connection and select command strings
String connString = "Data Source=(local);Integrated security=SSPI;" +
    "Initial Catalog=Northwind;";
String selectSql="SELECT * FROM Orders";

// create a new DataSet to receive the data
DataSet ds = new DataSet();

SqlDataAdapter da = new SqlDataAdapter(selectSql, connString);

// create the command builder
// this creates SQL statements for the DeleteCommand, InsertCommand,
// and UpdateCommand properties for the data adapter based on the
// select command that the data adapter was initialized with
SqlCommandBuilder cb = new SqlCommandBuilder(da);

// read all of the data from the orders table and load it into the
// Orders table in the DataSet
da.Fill(ds, "Orders");

// ... code to modify the data in the DataSet

// update the data in the Orders table in the DataSet to the data source
da.Update(ds, "Orders");
```

As with the Fill( ) and FillSchema( ) methods, opening and closing the connection are performed by the data adapter, if necessary.

Mapping Tables and Columns

By default, when you use the DataAdapter to fill a DataSet, the column names that are used in the DataSet correspond to the column names defined in the data source.

The data adapter has a collection of table-mapping objects that are accessed through the TableMappings property. A table-mapping object maps a table in the data source to a table with a different name in the DataSet. Table mappings are perhaps most commonly used to map default table names that are created as a result of filling a DataSet from a query that returns multiple result sets. When multiple result sets are added to a DataSet using the Fill( ) method of the DataAdapter, they are assigned the default names Table, Table1, Table2, and so on. Mapping the table names ensures that the data is updated to the correct tables in the data source. Of course, the table objects can also be renamed with the same result.

Each table-mapping object has a collection of column-mapping objects that are accessed through the ColumnMappings property. A column-mapping object maps a column in the data source to a column with a different name in the DataSet, within the table defined by the containing table-mapping object. Figure 14-3 shows how tables and columns in the DataSet and data source are mapped to each other using mapping classes in the DataAdapter.

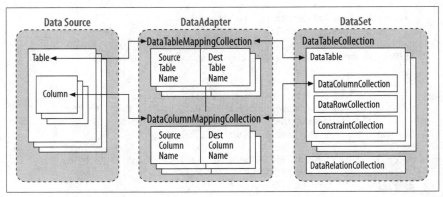

Figure 14-3. Table and column mapping classes

Both table and column mappings can be used by the Fill( ) and FillSchema( ) methods when retrieving data, and by the Update( ) method when submitting DataSet changes back to the data source. The Fill( ) method always uses mapping information, if present. The FillSchema( ) method lets you choose whether to use mapping information.

The following example shows how to set up a table mapping and a column mapping:

```
SqlDataAdapter da;

// ... code to set up the data adapter
```

```
// map the DataSet table MyOrders to the data source table Orders
DataTableMapping dtm = da.TableMappings.Add("Orders", "MyOrders");

// map the DataSet column MyOrderID (in the DataSet MyOrders table)
// to the data source column OrderID (in the data source Orders table)
dtm.ColumnMappings.Add("MyOrderID", "OrderID");
```

If incoming data source table and column names don't match DataSet object names and mapping can't be performed, the MissingMappingAction property of the DataAdapter determines what action is taken when data is retrieved using the Fill( ) method. The default value Passthrough results in the creation of the missing objects in the DataSet. The MissingMappingAction property can also be set to ignore missing objects or to raise an exception if missing objects are encountered.

Similarly, the MissingSchemaAction property of the DataAdapter determines what action is taken when the schema is retrieved using the FillSchema( ) or Fill( ) method. As with the MissingMappingAction property, options allow the missing objects to be added, ignored, or to cause an exception to be raised. Additionally, the MissingSchemaAction can be set to add the missing objects along with the primary key information.

AcceptChangesDuringFill

The AcceptChangesDuringFill( ) controls whether AcceptChanges( ) is implicitly called on new rows when they are added to a DataTable by the Fill( ) method. If AcceptChangesDuringFill is true, the rows added as a result of the Fill( ) have a RowState of Unchanged after they are added to the DataSet. If AcceptChangesDuringFill is false, the RowState of the newly added rows is Added. The following example demonstrates this:

```
// connection and select command strings
String connString = "Data Source=(local);Integrated security=SSPI;" +
    "Initial Catalog=Northwind;";
String selectSql = "SELECT * FROM Orders";

// create a new DataSet to receive the data
DataSet ds = new DataSet();

SqlDataAdapter da = new SqlDataAdapter(selectSql, connString);

da.Fill(ds, "Orders");
// each row in the Orders table has RowState = Unchanged

ds.Tables["Orders"].Clear();

da.AcceptChangesDuringFill = false;
da.Fill(ds, "Orders");
// each row in the Orders table has RowState = Inserted

// manually call AcceptChanges
ds.AcceptChanges();
// each row in the Orders table has RowState = Unchanged
```

The default value for AcceptChangesDuringFill is true. Because the records already exist in the data source, the records retrieved during the Fill( ) operation should not be considered new records when the data source is eventually updated with the DataSet.

Setting AcceptChangesDuringFill to false can be useful, for example, to transfer data between data sources. Records retrieved from a data source are marked as New, and the DataSet can then insert these records into another data source using the Update( ) method of a DataAdapter.

ContinueUpdateOnError

The ContinueUpdateOnError property controls whether an Update( ) continues with remaining rows or stops processing if an error is encountered during the updating. If ContinueUpdateOnError is true, and an error is encountered during the update, an exception isn't raised, the RowError property of the DataRow causing the error is set to the error message that would have been raised, and the update continues processing the remaining rows. A well-designed application uses the RowError information to present the user with a list of the failed and possibly the current values in the data source for those rows. It also provides a mechanism to correct and resubmit the failed attempts, if required.

If ContinueUpdateOnError is false, the DataAdapter raises a DBConcurrencyException when a row update attempt fails. Generally, ContinueUpdateOnError is set to false when the changes made to the DataSet are part of a transaction and must be either completely applied to the data source or not applied at all. The exception handler rolls back the transaction.

DataAdapter Events

The FillError event is most commonly raised when the data being added violates a constraint in the DataSet or when the data being added can't be converted to a .NET Framework data type without a loss of precision. When a FillError event occurs, the current row isn't added to the DataTable. Handling the FillError event allows the error to be resolved and the row to be either added or ignored before resuming the Fill( ) operation with the next row.

The FillError event handler receives an argument of FillErrorEventArgs, which contains specific data about the event that can effectively respond to and handle the error. The Continue property of the FillErrorEventArgs argument determines whether an exception is thrown or processing continues because of the error.

The following example demonstrates handling the FillError event when filling a table containing three columns:

```
SqlDataAdapter da;

// ... code to set up the data adapter
```

```
da.FillError += new FillErrorEventHandler(da_FillError);
DataSet ds = new DataSet();
da.Fill(ds, "MyTable");

private void da_FillError(object sender, FillErrorEventArgs e)
{
    // ... code to identify and correct the error

    // add the fixed row to the table
    DataRow dr = e.DataTable.Rows.Add(new object[] {e.Values[0],
        e.Values[1], e.Values[2]});

    // continue the Fill with the rows remaining in the data source
    e.Continue = true;
}
```

The RowUpdating event is raised before changes to a row are submitted to the data source. The RowUpdating event handler can modify update behavior, providing additional handling or canceling the update for the row. The RowUpdated event is raised after the update command is executed against the data source and is used to respond to exceptions that occur during the update.

The RowUpdating and RowUpdated event handlers receive arguments of SqlRowUpdatingEventArgs and SqlRowUpdatedEventArgs, respectively, containing data specific to each event. The arguments contain among other properties, a reference to the Command object that performs the update, a DataRow object containing the updated data, a StatementType property containing the type of update being performed, an Errors property containing any errors generated, and a Status property. The Status property returns a value of ErrorsOccurred if an error occurred while updating the row. The Status property can control the action to be taken with the current and remaining rows to be updated after an error; an error can be thrown, the current row can be skipped, or all remaining rows can be skipped by setting the Status property after an error.

The following code demonstrates handling the RowUpdating and RowUpdated events:

```
SqlDataAdapter da;

// ... code to set up the data adapter

// add the event handlers
da.RowUpdating += new SqlRowUpdatingEventHandler(da_RowUpdating);
da.RowUpdated += new SqlRowUpdatedEventHandler(da_RowUpdated);

DataSet ds = new DataSet();

// ... code to fill the DataSet
// ... code to modify the data in the DataSet

da.Update(ds, "Orders");

private void da_RowUpdating(object sender, SqlRowUpdatingEventArgs e)
{
```

```
        // Write the date, OrderID, and type of update to a log
        System.IO.TextWriter tw = System.IO.File.AppendText("update.log");
        tw.WriteLine("{0}: Order {1} {2}.", DateTime.Now, e.Row["OrderID",
            DataRowVersion.Original], e.StatementType.ToString());
        tw.Close();
    }

    private void da_RowUpdated(object sender, SqlRowUpdatedEventArgs e)
    {
        if(e.Status == UpdateStatus.ErrorsOccurred)
        {
            // set the error information for the row
            e.Row.RowError = e.Errors.Message;
            // skip peocessing the current row and continue with the rest
            e.Status = UpdateStatus.SkipCurrentRow;
        }
    }
```

An alternative to processing each error in response to the RowUpdated event as shown in this example is to set the DataAdapter ContinueUpdateOnError property to true, allowing all errors to be handled once the update of all rows is complete.

15

Updating the Data Source

This chapter discusses how to use the DataAdapter object to submit changes made to a DataSet back the data source. First, the CommandBuilder object, which is easy to use but provides only limited functionality, is introduced, and an overview of using it to submit changes is presented. Following that, using custom command logic to submit the updates is described. Finally, techniques to handle common tasks such as retrieving new AutoIncrement values, refreshing updated data, updating data in related tables, and handling concurrency issues are discussed.

SqlCommandBuilder Class Overview

The command builder can automatically generate commands used by the data adapter to update changes made to a DataSet back to the data source. The class is limited to single-table updates using SQL statements.

The command builder uses the SelectCommand object of the DataAdapter to retrieve the metadata required to build the update command objects DeleteCommand, InsertCommand, and UpdateCommand. If the SelectCommand is changed, the RefreshSchema( ) method should be called to generate new update commands. This forces the command builder to regenerate its updating logic when the Update( ) method of the DataAdapter is called or when one of the update commands is retrieved from the command builder using GetDeleteCommand, GetInsertCommand, or GetUpdateCommand.

The SelectCommand must contain a primary key, or at least one unique column, so that records can be located by the generated DeleteCommand and UpdateCommand. The SelectCommand must also contain all the required columns without default values in the DataRow for the generated InsertCommand to work. Also, as previously mentioned, the SelectCommand must return data from only one table. An InvalidOperation exception is raised otherwise, and the commands aren't generated.

The command builder is useful because it lets you update the data source with changes made to the DataSet using very little code. It also lets you create update logic without understanding how to code the actual delete, insert, and update SQL statements. There are drawbacks, however, including slower performance because of the time that it takes to request metadata and construct the updating logic, updates that are limited to simple single-table scenarios, and a lack of support for stored procedures.

Updating a Data Source Using Command Builder

To use a CommandBuilder, create it supplying a reference to the DataAdapter you used to retrieve the results:

```
SqlDataAdapter da = new sqlDataAdapter(sqlSelect, connString);

SqlCommandBuilder cb = new SqlCommandBuilder(da);
```

Once you create CommandBuilder, it registers itself as a listener for the DataAdapter RowUpdating event, which fires just before a row is updated in the data source. In the event handler, CommandBuilder creates and supplies the Command object required to perform the update, if it has not been specified.

The following example demonstrates how to use a CommandBuilder to generate the update logic for a data adapter:

```
// connection and select command strings
String connString = "Data Source=(local);Integrated security=SSPI;" +
    "Initial Catalog=Northwind;";
String sqlSelect = "SELECT * FROM Orders";

// create a new DataSet to receive the data
DataSet ds = new DataSet();

SqlDataAdapter da = new SqlDataAdapter(sqlSelect, connString);

// create the command builder
// this creates SQL statements for the DeleteCommand, InsertCommand,
// and UpdateCommand properties for the data adapter based on the
// select command that the data adapter was initialized with
SqlCommandBuilder cb = new SqlCommandBuilder(da);

// read all of the data from the orders table and load it into the
// Orders table in the DataSet
da.Fill(ds, "Orders");

// ... code to modify the data in the DataSet

// update the data in the Orders table in the DataSet to the data source
da.Update(ds, "Orders");
```

To see the logic that the CommandBuilder generates, examine the CommandText property and the Parameters collection of the DeleteCommand, InsertCommand, and UpdateCommand objects returned by the GetDeleteCommand( ), GetInsertCommand( ),

and GetUpdateCommand( ) methods, respectively, of the CommandBuilder. Some points become evident once the generated commands are examined:

- The generated commands are modeled as parameterized SQL statements that use inline parameters.
- Both current and original values are used for parameter values. For example, to update a record, the command searches for a record with the original value of the primary key and updates it using the new values for the fields.
- When matching a row for DELETE or UPDATE operations, ADO.NET searches for an exact match. It isn't satisfied with a record that has the same primary key unless all the other columns also match. This can add significant overhead when updating tables with a large number of fields, many of which aren't indexed.

The CommandBuilder is convenient, but it also suffers from some significant limitations. Instead of using the CommandBuilder, custom update logic can be defined to overcome those limitations. The next section examines how to define and use custom updating logic to update the data source.

Updating a Data Source Using Custom Logic

The CommandBuilder provides an extremely convenient way to create the required Command objects, but it has definite limitations. Here are some reasons to avoid the CommandBuilder and use your own custom updating logic:

Stored procedures
Most significant applications use stored procedures because of their benefits, which include maintainability, security, and performance over SQL statements.

Table joins
In some cases, table joins are needed to retrieve aggregate information. However, even if you edit only fields from a single table, the CommandBuilder can't automatically generate the Command objects.

More flexible concurrency handling
The UPDATE and DELETE statements generated by the CommandBuilder search the data source for a row that matches all fields in the original row exactly. If any original values have changed, the update will fail for that row. In some cases, this approach isn't ideal.

There is only one real difference between using the CommandBuilder and custom update logic. The CommandBuilder generates the DeleteCommand, InsertCommand, and UpdateCommand objects used by the DataAdapter to reconcile changes made to the DataSet with the data source. With custom update logic, those update objects have to be defined.

The SourceColumn and SourceVersion properties of the Parameter object bind associate a Parameter with a DataColumn. The DataAdapter uses these properties to determine the source of the values within the DataRow; these values are loaded into the Parameter for the appropriate update Command for the DataRow before the update is performed for the row. The default value for SourceVersion is the Current row, so this value needs to be set only when a different version is required. The following two examples illustrate the effect of the SourceColumn and SourceVersion properties. The first example maps the CustomerID column from the Current version of the DataRow to the Parameter named @CustomerID:

```
params.Add("@CustomerID", SqlDbType.NChar, 5, "CustomerID");
```

The second example maps the OrderID column from the Original version of the DataRow to the Parameter named @OrderID:

```
params.Add("@OrderID", SqlDbType.Int, 0, "OrderID");
params["@OrderID"].SourceVersion = DataRowVersion.Original;
```

It's important to understand that this mapping occurs each time a row is updated and is defined separately for each update Command object. The actual Command object that updates a particular row when the Update( ) method is called is based on the DataRowState of that row.

The update Command objects can be based on parameterized SQL statements, as is demonstrated by CommandBuilder, or on stored procedures, as is more commonly the case. One obvious drawback to using SQL statements is that updated values in the data source can't be returned back to the DataSet. Refreshing the DataSet after an update using stored procedures is discussed in more detail later in this chapter.

The following example uses the Orders table from Northwind database to demonstrate how to use stored procedures to define the update Command objects and then how to use these custom update Command objects. The stored procedures are presented first followed by the code that uses these stored procedures.

Example 15-1 uses the stored procedures that delete, select, insert and update the data source.

Example 15-1. Stored procedures for commands

```
-- stored procedure for DeleteCommand
CREATE PROCEDURE DeleteOrders
    @OrderID int
AS
    SET NOCOUNT ON

    delete
    from
        Orders
    where
        OrderID=@OrderID

    return
GO


--stored procedure for SelectCommand
CREATE PROCEDURE GetOrders
AS
    SET NOCOUNT ON
```

Example 15-1. Stored procedures for commands (continued)

```
    select
        OrderID,
        CustomerID,
        EmployeeID,
        OrderDate,
        RequiredDate,
        ShippedDate,
        ShipVia,
        Freight,
        ShipName,
        ShipAddress,
        ShipCity,
        ShipRegion,
        ShipPostalCode,
        ShipCountry
    from
        Orders

    return
GO

--stored procedure for InsertCommand
CREATE PROCEDURE InsertOrders
    @OrderID int output,
    @CustomerID nchar(5),
    @EmployeeID int,
    @OrderDate datetime,
    @RequiredDate datetime,
    @ShippedDate datetime,
    @ShipVia int,
    @Freight money,
    @ShipName nvarchar(40),
    @ShipAddress nvarchar(60),
    @ShipCity nvarchar(15),
    @ShipRegion nvarchar(15),
    @ShipPostalCode nvarchar(10),
    @ShipCountry nvarchar(15)
AS
    SET NOCOUNT ON

    insert Orders(
        CustomerID,
        EmployeeID,
        OrderDate,
        RequiredDate,
        ShippedDate,
        ShipVia,
        Freight,
        ShipName,
        ShipAddress,
        ShipCity,
        ShipRegion,
```

Updating the
Data Source

Example 15-1. Stored procedures for commands (continued)

```
        ShipPostalCode,
        ShipCountry)
    values (
        @CustomerID,
        @EmployeeID,
        @OrderDate,
        @RequiredDate,
        @ShippedDate,
        @ShipVia,
        @Freight,
        @ShipName,
        @ShipAddress,
        @ShipCity,
        @ShipRegion,
        @ShipPostalCode,
        @ShipCountry)

    if @@rowcount=0
        return 1

    set @OrderID=Scope_Identity()

    select @OrderId OrderId

    return
GO

--stored procedure for UpdateCommand
CREATE PROCEDURE UpdateOrders
    @OrderID int,
    @CustomerID nchar(5),
    @EmployeeID int,
    @OrderDate datetime,
    @RequiredDate datetime,
    @ShippedDate datetime,
    @ShipVia int,
    @Freight money,
    @ShipName nvarchar(40),
    @ShipAddress nvarchar(60),
    @ShipCity nvarchar(15),
    @ShipRegion nvarchar(15),
    @ShipPostalCode nvarchar(10),
    @ShipCountry nvarchar(15)
AS
    SET NOCOUNT ON

    update
        Orders
    set
        CustomerID = @CustomerID,
        EmployeeID = @EmployeeID,
        OrderDate = @OrderDate,
```

Example 15-1. Stored procedures for commands (continued)

```
        RequiredDate = @RequiredDate,
        ShippedDate = @ShippedDate,
        ShipVia = @ShipVia,
        Freight = @Freight,
        ShipName = @ShipName,
        ShipAddress = @ShipAddress,
        ShipCity = @ShipCity,
        ShipRegion = @ShipRegion,
        ShipPostalCode = @ShipPostalCode,
        ShipCountry = @ShipCountry
    where
        OrderID = @OrderID

    if @@rowcount = 0
        return 1

    return
GO
```

Example 15-2 demonstrates how to create the update Command objects that retrieve and update the data, configure the stored procedure parameters, create the DataAdapter, and assign the command objects to the data adapter.

Example 15-2. Creating update objects

```
// connection and select command strings
String connString = "Data Source=(local);Integrated security=SSPI;" +
    "Initial Catalog=Northwind;";
SqlConnection conn = new SqlConnection(connString);

// create command objects using stored procedures
SqlCommand selectCommand = new SqlCommand("GetOrders", conn);
selectCommand.CommandType = CommandType.StoredProcedure;
SqlCommand deleteCommand = new SqlCommand("DeleteOrders", conn);
deleteCommand.CommandType = CommandType.StoredProcedure;
SqlCommand insertCommand = new SqlCommand("InsertOrders", conn);
insertCommand.CommandType = CommandType.StoredProcedure;
SqlCommand updateCommand = new SqlCommand("UpdateOrders", conn);
updateCommand.CommandType = CommandType.StoredProcedure;

// set up the parameters
SqlParameterCollection cparams;

// delete command parameters
cparams=deleteCommand.Parameters;
cparams.Add("@OrderID", SqlDbType.Int, 0, "OrderID");
cparams["@OrderID"].SourceVersion=DataRowVersion.Original;

// insert command parameters
cparams = insertCommand.Parameters;
cparams.Add("@OrderID", SqlDbType.Int, 0, "OrderID");
cparams["@OrderID"].Direction = ParameterDirection.Output;
cparams["@OrderID"].SourceVersion = DataRowVersion.Original;
```

Updating the
Data Source

Example 15-2. Creating update objects (continued)

```
cparams.Add("@CustomerID", SqlDbType.NChar, 5, "CustomerID");
cparams.Add("@EmployeeID", SqlDbType.Int, 0, "EmployeeID");
cparams.Add("@OrderDate", SqlDbType.DateTime, 0, "OrderDate");
cparams.Add("@RequiredDate", SqlDbType.DateTime, 0, "RequiredDate");
cparams.Add("@ShippedDate", SqlDbType.DateTime, 0, "ShippedDate");
cparams.Add("@ShipVia", SqlDbType.Int, 0, "ShipVia");
cparams.Add("@Freight", SqlDbType.Money, 0, "Freight");
cparams.Add("@ShipName", SqlDbType.NVarChar, 40, "ShipName");
cparams.Add("@ShipAddress", SqlDbType.NVarChar, 60, "ShipAddress");
cparams.Add("@ShipCity", SqlDbType.NVarChar, 15, "ShipCity");
cparams.Add("@ShipRegion", SqlDbType.NVarChar, 15, "ShipRegion");
cparams.Add("@ShipPostalCode", SqlDbType.NVarChar, 10, "ShipPostalCode");
cparams.Add("@ShipCountry", SqlDbType.NVarChar, 15, "ShipCountry");

// update command parameters
cparams = updateCommand.Parameters;
cparams.Add("@OrderID", SqlDbType.Int, 0, "OrderID");
cparams["@OrderID"].SourceVersion=DataRowVersion.Original;
cparams.Add("@CustomerID", SqlDbType.NChar, 5, "CustomerID");
cparams.Add("@EmployeeID", SqlDbType.Int, 0, "EmployeeID");
cparams.Add("@OrderDate", SqlDbType.DateTime, 0, "OrderDate");
cparams.Add("@RequiredDate", SqlDbType.DateTime, 0, "RequiredDate");
cparams.Add("@ShippedDate", SqlDbType.DateTime, 0, "ShippedDate");
cparams.Add("@ShipVia", SqlDbType.Int, 0, "ShipVia");
cparams.Add("@Freight", SqlDbType.Money, 0, "Freight");
cparams.Add("@ShipName", SqlDbType.NVarChar, 40, "ShipName");
cparams.Add("@ShipAddress", SqlDbType.NVarChar, 60, "ShipAddress");
cparams.Add("@ShipCity", SqlDbType.NVarChar, 15, "ShipCity");
cparams.Add("@ShipRegion", SqlDbType.NVarChar, 15, "ShipRegion");
cparams.Add("@ShipPostalCode", SqlDbType.NVarChar, 10, "ShipPostalCode");
cparams.Add("@ShipCountry", SqlDbType.NVarChar, 15, "ShipCountry");

// create the data adapter
SqlDataAdapter da = new SqlDataAdapter(selectCommand.CommandText, conn);

// assign the custom update logic to the DataAdapter
da.DeleteCommand = deleteCommand;
da.InsertCommand = insertCommand;
da.UpdateCommand = updateCommand;

// create a new DataSet to receive the data and load the data
DataSet ds = new DataSet();
da.Fill(ds, "Orders");

// ... code to modify the DataSet

// update the data source using the custom update logic
da.Update(ds, "Orders");
```

Refreshing Data After Updating

The `DeleteCommand`, `InsertCommand`, and `UpdateCommand` objects submit the changes made to a `DataSet` back to a data source. This is however a one-way process; the updated data isn't automatically returned back to the `DataSet`. Often this is acceptable because after the update, the data in the data source implicitly matches the data in the `DataSet`. This isn't, however, the case for some data such as `AutoIncrement` columns when rows are inserted into the data source and `timestamp` columns, which are updated with a new value whenever the row is updated in the data source. In both cases, a new value must be retrieved from the data source row when it's inserted, or in the case of the `timestamp` column, updated or inserted.

The `UpdatedRowSource` property of each `Command` object that submits updates to the data source determines how data is returned back to the `DataSet`. By default, this property is set to `Both`, resulting in both the data in the first returned row and the return values for stored procedures updating the `DataSet` after the update. The property can be set so that only the first returned record or only the return parameters update the `DataSet`, or so that the `DataSet` isn't updated.

Retrieving Updated Values from the Data Source

There are three techniques that can retrieve updated data from the data source.

The first technique is to use a batch query to return the new value using a query after the update command has executed. Example 15-3 demonstrates this for an `AutoIncrement` column by creating a batch insert statement containing the statements:

```
"SET @OrderID = Scope_Identity();" +
"SELECT @OrderID OrderID;";
```

If the row also contains a `timestamp` column named `rowversion`, the following code can be used with the insert statement to retrieve the new timestamp value:

```
"SET @OrderID=Scope_Identity();" +
"SELECT @OrderID OrderId, rowversion WHERE OrderID = @OrderID;";
```

This technique requires that the `UpdatedRowSource` property update commands be set to either `Both` or `FirstReturnedRecord`.

The second technique uses output parameters to retrieve updated data. Example 15-3 demonstrates the use of this method with an `AutoIncrement` column by creating an output parameter for the `OrderID` on the `InsertCommand`:

```
params.Add("@OrderID", SqlDbType.Int, 0, "OrderID");
params.Direction = ParameterDirection.Output;
```

This technique requires that the `UpdatedRowSource` property for the update command be set to either `Both` or `OutputParameters`.

The third technique handles the `DataAdapter` `RowUpdated` event. An event handler is first attached to the data adapter:

```
da.RowUpdated += new SqlRowUpdateEventHandler(da_RowUpdated);
```

The event handler retrieves the new AutoIncrement value and stores it in the OrderID field if the update was a successful insert. AcceptChanges( ) is called so that the row doesn't appear to be modified:

```
private void da_RowUpdated(object sender, SqlRowUpdatedEventArgs e)
{
    if(e.Status == UpdateStatus.Continue &&
        e.StatementType == StatementType.Insert)
    {
        e.Row["OrderId"] = (Int32)cmdIdentity.ExecuteScalar();
        e.Row.AcceptChanges();
    }
}
```

Example 15-3 demonstrates the three techniques for returning updated data from the data source described earlier. All three techniques have been included in the same example in the interest of saving space. Normally, only one technique is used.

Example 15-3. Returning updated data

```
// following variable has class scope
private SqlCommand insertCommand;

// ...

// the SQL statements, select and update
String sqlSelect = "SELECT OrderID, CustomerID, EmployeeID, " +
    "OrderDate, RequiredDate, ShippedDate, ShipVia, Freight, " +
    "ShipName, ShipAddress, ShipCity, ShipRegion, " +
    "ShipPostalCode, ShipCountry FROM Orders";
String sqlDelete = "DELETE FROM Orders WHERE OrderID=@OrderID";
String sqlInsert = "INSERT Orders(CustomerID, " +
    "EmployeeID, OrderDate, RequiredDate, ShippedDate, ShipVia, " +
    "Freight, ShipName, ShipAddress, ShipCity, ShipRegion, " +
    "ShipPostalCode, ShipCountry) " +
    "VALUES (@CustomerID, @EmployeeID, @OrderDate, @RequiredDate, " +
    "@ShippedDate, @ShipVia, @Freight, @ShipName, @ShipAddress, " +
    "@ShipCity, @ShipRegion, @ShipPostalCode, @ShipCountry);" +
    "SET @OrderID=Scope_Identity();" +
    "SELECT @OrderID OrderID;";
String sqlUpdate = "UPDATE Orders SET " +
    "CustomerID=@CustomerID, EmployeeID=@EmployeeID, " +
    "OrderDate=@OrderDate, RequiredDate=@RequiredDate, " +
    "ShippedDate=@ShippedDate, ShipVia=@ShipVia, Freight=@Freight, " +
    "ShipName=@ShipName, ShipAddress=@ShipAddress, ShipCity=@ShipCity, " +
    "ShipRegion=@ShipRegion, ShipPostalCode=@ShipPostalCode, " +
    "ShipCountry=@ShipCountry WHERE OrderID=@OrderID";

// build the connection
String connString = "Data Source=(local);Integrated security=SSPI;" +
    "Initial Catalog=Northwind;";
SqlConnection conn = new SqlConnection(connString);
```

Example 15-3. Returning updated data (continued)

```
// create command objects using SQL statements
// UpdatedRowSource property of Command objects defaults to Both
SqlCommand selectCmd = new SqlCommand(sqlSelect, conn);
SqlCommand deleteCommand = new SqlCommand(sqlDelete, conn);
insertCommand = new SqlCommand(sqlInsert, conn);
SqlCommand updateCommand = new SqlCommand(sqlUpdate, conn);

// set up the parameters
SqlParameterCollection cparams;

// delete command parameters
cparams = deleteCommand.Parameters;
cparams.Add("@OrderID", SqlDbType.Int, 0, "OrderID");

// insert command parameters
cparams = insertCommand.Parameters;
SqlParameter orderid =
  cparams.Add("@OrderID", SqlDbType.Int, 0, "OrderID");
orderid.Direction = ParameterDirection.Output;
cparams.Add("@CustomerID", SqlDbType.NChar, 5, "CustomerID");
cparams.Add("@EmployeeID", SqlDbType.Int, 0, "EmployeeID");
cparams.Add("@OrderDate", SqlDbType.DateTime, 0, "OrderDate");
cparams.Add("@RequiredDate", SqlDbType.DateTime, 0, "RequiredDate");
cparams.Add("@ShippedDate", SqlDbType.DateTime, 0, "ShippedDate");
cparams.Add("@ShipVia", SqlDbType.Int, 0, "ShipVia");
cparams.Add("@Freight", SqlDbType.Money, 0, "Freight");
cparams.Add("@ShipName", SqlDbType.NVarChar, 40, "ShipName");
cparams.Add("@ShipAddress", SqlDbType.NVarChar, 60, "ShipAddress");
cparams.Add("@ShipCity", SqlDbType.NVarChar, 15, "ShipCity");
cparams.Add("@ShipRegion", SqlDbType.NVarChar, 15, "ShipRegion");
cparams.Add("@ShipPostalCode", SqlDbType.NVarChar, 10, "ShipPostalCode");
cparams.Add("@ShipCountry", SqlDbType.NVarChar, 15, "ShipCountry");

// update command parameters
cparams = updateCommand.Parameters;
cparams.Add("@OrderID", SqlDbType.Int, 0, "OrderID");
cparams.Add("@CustomerID", SqlDbType.NChar, 5, "CustomerID");
cparams.Add("@EmployeeID", SqlDbType.Int, 0, "EmployeeID");
cparams.Add("@OrderDate", SqlDbType.DateTime, 0, "OrderDate");
cparams.Add("@RequiredDate", SqlDbType.DateTime, 0, "RequiredDate");
cparams.Add("@ShippedDate", SqlDbType.DateTime, 0, "ShippedDate");
cparams.Add("@ShipVia", SqlDbType.Int, 0, "ShipVia");
cparams.Add("@Freight", SqlDbType.Money, 0, "Freight");
cparams.Add("@ShipName", SqlDbType.NVarChar, 40, "ShipName");
cparams.Add("@ShipAddress", SqlDbType.NVarChar, 60, "ShipAddress");
cparams.Add("@ShipCity", SqlDbType.NVarChar, 15, "ShipCity");
cparams.Add("@ShipRegion", SqlDbType.NVarChar, 15, "ShipRegion");
cparams.Add("@ShipPostalCode", SqlDbType.NVarChar, 10, "ShipPostalCode");
cparams.Add("@ShipCountry", SqlDbType.NVarChar, 15, "ShipCountry");
```

Example 15-3. Returning updated data (continued)

```
// create the data adapter and an event handler for after row inserts
SqlDataAdapter da = new SqlDataAdapter(sqlSelect, conn);
da.RowUpdated += new SqlRowUpdatedEventHandler(da_RowUpdated);

// load all of Orders data from the data source into the DataSet
DataSet ds = new DataSet();
da.Fill(ds, "Orders");

// ... code to modify the data in the DataSet

// update the data source
da.Update(ds, "Orders");

//...

private void da_RowUpdated(object sender, SqlRowUpdatedEventArgs e)
{
  if(e.Status == UpdateStatus.Continue &&
    e.StatementType == StatementType.Insert)
  {
    e.Row["OrderId"] = (Int32)insertCommand.ExecuteScalar();
    e.Row.AcceptChanges();
  }
}
```

Updating Data in Related Tables

To avoid referential integrity problems when updating the data source from a DataSet containing related rows, especially in situations involving batch updates, the rows must be updated in the following order:

1. Deleted grandchild rows
2. Deleted child rows
3. Deleted parent rows
4. Updated parent rows
5. Inserted parent rows
6. Updated child rows
7. Inserted child rows
8. Updated grandchild rows
9. Inserted grandchild rows

To obtain the set of deleted rows, pass DataViewRowState.Deleted to the DataTable.Select() method. To obtain the set of inserted rows, pass DataViewRowState.Added to the DataTable.Select() method. To obtain the set of modified rows, pass DataViewRowState.ModifiedCurrent to the DataTable.Select() method.

There are few other considerations involving the primary key. If the primary key can't be modified once added, the updated and inserted rows can be processed in the same statement. If, on the other hand, the primary key can be modified, the database must cascade the updated primary key values to the child records; otherwise a referential integrity violation will occur. The UpdateCommand property of child tables must accept either the Original or the Current value of the foreign key if it is used as part of a concurrency handling process. Finally, if the primary key is an AutoIncrement value, and the value is generated by the database, the InsertCommand must return the primary key value from the data source and use it to update the value in the DataSet. The DataSet then automatically cascades this new value to the child records.

Example 15-4 demonstrates the ordering of updates using a parent and child table; because there are no grandchild records, only six update commands instead of nine are required. As discussed earlier, the code uses the Select( ) method of the tables with the DataViewRowState argument to select the subset of records to update.

Example 15-4. Update ordering

```
SqlDataAdapter daOrders;
SqlDataAdapter daOrderDetails;

// setup data adapters, and the SelectCommand and UpdateCommands for the
// parent Orders table and the child Order Details table

// load the data for parent and child tables into the DataSet
DataSet ds = new DataSet();
daOrders.Fill(ds, "Orders");
daOrderDetails.Fill(ds, "Order Details");

// ... code to modify the data in the DataSet

// update the modified data in the DataSet back to the data source
daOrderDetails.Update(ds.Tables["Order Details"].Select(null, null,
    DataViewRowState.Deleted));
daOrders.Update(ds.Tables["Orders"].Select(null, null,
    DataViewRowState.Deleted));
daOrders.Update(ds.Tables["Orders"].Select(null, null,
    DataViewRowState.ModifiedCurrent));
daOrders.Update(ds.Tables["Orders"].Select(null, null,
    DataViewRowState.Added));
daOrderDetails.Update(ds.Tables["Order Details"].Select(null, null,
    DataViewRowState.ModifiedCurrent));
daOrderDetails.Update(ds.Tables["Order Details"].Select(null, null,
    DataViewRowState.Added));
```

Handling Concurrency Issues

It is important to handle concurrency issues that almost inevitably result when multiple users access data simultaneously. Updates from one user should not inadvertently overwrite changes made by another user.

Because ADO.NET uses optimistic concurrency, two users can request the same data and then subsequently update the same data. Without managing concurrency, the changes made by the first user will be overwritten by the second user's changes and, to make matters worse, no one will know that this has happened.

There are several ways that concurrency can be managed in an optimistic locking environment. As discussed earlier, the CommandBuilder object attempts to match all original fields to the row data source to determine if the row has changed since it was retrieved. That approach suffers from several significant drawbacks that limit its usefulness.

The best approach to managing concurrency is to add a timestamp column to the table. The timestamp type is supported by most databases and doesn't actually contain a time and date; it's a binary value that is unique within the database. When updating a record in the data source, the timestamp value is used in addition to the primary key to locate a record in the data source. If a row has been modified by another user since it was last retrieved, it will not be found because the timestamp value will have changed. The second user can be notified of the failure, shown the new data in the row, and presented with options to deal with the concurrency violation that are suitable for the application. Figure 15-1 shows how a timestamp column can be used to handle the concurrency violation that results when a user retrieves a disconnected record, modifies it, and tries to reconcile it to the data source in which the row has been modified since it was retrieved. The timestamp values don't match, the user is notified of the error resulting from the update attempt, and the row in the data source isn't updated.

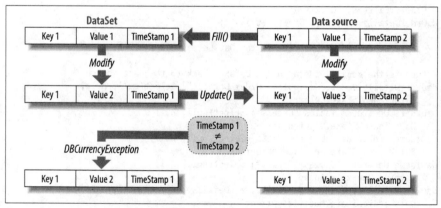

Figure 15-1. Using a timestamp column to handle data concurrency

 Technically, you can match a record in SQL Server just by using the timestamp column because every timestamp value is unique. However, a primary key provides faster lookup because it is indexed. You should never create an index on a timestamp value because it changes frequently.

Example 15-5 uses a `timestamp` field called rowversion to help manage concurrency issues. Further, each concurrency violation is added to a table in a DataSet of conflicts.

Example 15-5. Managing concurrency

```
private SqlDataAdapter daConflict;
private DataSet dsConflict;

// ...

// connection and select command strings
String connString = "Data Source=(local);Integrated security=SSPI;" +
    "Initial Catalog=Northwind;";
SqlConnection conn = new SqlConnection(connString);
SqlCommand cmd = new SqlCommand("SELECT * FROM Orders ", conn);

daConflict = new SqlDataAdapter(cmd);

// create the DataSet to store concurrency exceptions and retrieve the
// schema from the data source
dsConflict = new DataSet();
daConflict.FillSchema(dsConflict, SchemaType.Source);

// create command objects using SQL statements
SqlCommand selectCmd = new SqlCommand("SELECT OrderID, CustomerID, " +
    "EmployeeID, OrderDate, RequiredDate, ShippedDate, ShipVia, " +
    "Freight, ShipName, ShipAddress, ShipCity, ShipRegion, " +
    "ShipPostalCode, ShipCountry, rowversion FROM Orders", conn);
SqlCommand updateCommand = new SqlCommand("UPDATE Orders SET " +
    "CustomerID=@CustomerID, EmployeeID=@EmployeeID, " +
    "OrderDate=@OrderDate, RequiredDate=@RequiredDate, " +
    "ShippedDate=@ShippedDate, ShipVia=@ShipVia, Freight=@Freight, " +
    "ShipName=@ShipName, ShipAddress=@ShipAddress, ShipCity=@ShipCity, " +
    "ShipRegion=@ShipRegion, ShipPostalCode=@ShipPostalCode, " +
    "ShipCountry=@ShipCountry " +
    "WHERE OrderID=@OrderID AND rowversion=@rowversion;" +
    "SELECT rowversion WHERE OrderID=@OrderID", conn);

// ... code for delete and insert commands

// set up the parameters
SqlParameterCollection cparams;

// update command parameters
cparams = updateCommand.Parameters;
cparams.Add("@OrderID", SqlDbType.Int, 0, "OrderID");
cparams.Add("@CustomerID", SqlDbType.NChar, 5, "CustomerID");
cparams.Add("@EmployeeID", SqlDbType.Int, 0, "EmployeeID");
cparams.Add("@OrderDate", SqlDbType.DateTime, 0, "OrderDate");
cparams.Add("@RequiredDate", SqlDbType.DateTime, 0, "RequiredDate");
cparams.Add("@ShippedDate", SqlDbType.DateTime, 0, "ShippedDate");
cparams.Add("@ShipVia", SqlDbType.Int, 0, "ShipVia");
cparams.Add("@Freight", SqlDbType.Money, 0, "Freight");
```

Example 15-5. Managing concurrency (continued)

```
cparams.Add("@ShipName", SqlDbType.NVarChar, 40, "ShipName");
cparams.Add("@ShipAddress", SqlDbType.NVarChar, 60, "ShipAddress");
cparams.Add("@ShipCity", SqlDbType.NVarChar, 15, "ShipCity");
cparams.Add("@ShipRegion", SqlDbType.NVarChar, 15, "ShipRegion");
cparams.Add("@ShipPostalCode", SqlDbType.NVarChar, 10, "ShipPostalCode");
cparams.Add("@ShipCountry", SqlDbType.NVarChar, 15, "ShipCountry");
cparams.Add("@rowversion", SqlDbType.Timestamp, 0, "rowversion");
cparams["@rowversion"].SourceVersion=DataRowVersion.Original;

// ... create parameters for delete and insert commands

// create the data adapter
SqlDataAdapter da = new SqlDataAdapter(selectCmd.CommandText, conn);

// set the ContinueUpdateOnError property so that all records are
// processed regardless of exceptions
da.ContinueUpdateOnError = true;

// add the event handler so that the concurrency exceptions can be added
// to the DataSet containing the conflicts
da.RowUpdated += new SqlRowUpdatedEventHandler(da_RowUpdated);

// set the update commands for the data adapter
da.DeleteCommand = deleteCommand;
da.InsertCommand = insertCommand;
da.UpdateCommand = updateCommand;

// create a new DataSet to receive the data and load the data
DataSet ds = new DataSet();

// load all of the data for the Orders table into the DataSet
da.Fill(ds, "Orders");

// ... code to modify the DataSet

// update the data in the Orders table in the DataSet to the data source
da.Update(ds, "Orders");


private void da_RowUpdated(object sender, SqlRowUpdatedEventArgs e)
{
    if (e.Status == UpdateStatus.ErrorsOccurred &&
        e.Errors.GetType() == typeof(DBConcurrencyException))
    {
        // retrieve the data for the row with concurrency
        // exception and store it to the DataSet with an error message
        daConflict.SelectCommand.Parameters["@ID"].Value
            = (String) e.Row["ID"];
        if(daConflict.Fill(dsConflict, "Orders") == 1)
```

Example 15-5. Managing concurrency (continued)

```
            e.Row.RowError = "Row has been changed in the database";
        else
            e.Row.RowError = "Row has been deleted from database";

        e.Status = UpdateStatus.Continue;
    }
}
```

There are really two practical ways to deal with the row updates that have failed as a result of a concurrency exception:

- If partial updates are acceptable, handle the RowUpdated event. When an exception is encountered, set the RowError for the failed row and retrieve new values from the data source. Continue processing the update for remaining rows by setting the UpdateStatus to Continue. Once all rows in the update have been processed, present the user with the new data source values for the failed rows along with the data that failed. Allow the user the opportunity to modify or correct the failed updates and resubmit as appropriate to the application. Example 15-5 demonstrates most of this technique.

- If the update requires that all rows successfully update back to the data source, wrap the entire update in a transaction. If a concurrency error is raised, roll back the transaction. This prevents rows that have been updated prior to the exception from being persisted to the data source, thereby leaving the data source in a state that is known to be valid. This approach works well with small batches where multiple users are unlikely to be accessing the same data.

> The RowUpdated event occurs while an update is in progress and, hence, while your application has a live connection to the database. For that reason, you should be extremely careful not to perform any time-consuming logic in your event handler (or even worse, delay the code by requesting user input). A good approach is to log errors and display them in a user interface control once the update is complete.

Optimization

To maximize performance and use of bandwidth in multitier or distributed applications, it is important to minimize the amount of data passed back and forth between components. The GetChanges( ) method can select the data that has been modified in a DataSet so that only the changed data is passed rather than the entire DataSet. The GetChanges( ) method returns a new DataSet with the same schema as the original DataSet, but it contains only changed records and any related records required so that foreign key constraints aren't violated. These related records can be omitted by setting the EnforceConstraints property of the DataSet to false prior to calling GetChanges( ).

If the data being updated contains changes after the update is called, in cases such as AutoIncrement field inserts and timestamp updates, the updated data must also be returned to the client and reintegrated with the original DataSet. This is done by merging the returned updated data back into the original DataSet and accepting the changes to set the RowState of the modified and successfully updated rows back to Unchanged.

The merge doesn't, however, remove the originally inserted rows that now have data source-generated AutoIncrement values. This is because the Merge( ) method uses the primary key to synchronize the rows. The solution is to delete inserted rows from the original DataSet prior to merging.

Example 15-6 demonstrates using the GetChanges( ) method to optimize data updating between a client and a web service and merging the data back into the original DataSet.

Example 15-6. Optimizing data updates

```
// Client code

MyWebService ws = new MyWebService();

DataSet ds = new DataSet();
ds = ws.GetData();

// ... code to modify the data in the DataSet

// create the DataSet of changes
DataSet dsChanges = ds.GetChanges();

// update the DataSet to the client and store the returned DataSet
dsChanges = ws.UpdateData(dsChanges);

// primary key OrderID is AutoIncrement. Delete the inserted rows from the
// original DataSet to prevent duplicate rows due to the OrderID changing
// to the data source generated value
foreach(DataRow row in ds.Tables("Orders").Select("", "",
    DataRowViewState.Added)
{
    ds.Tables("Orders").Remove(row);
}

// merge the returned DataSet back into the original changed DataSet
ds.Merge(dsChanges);
ds.AcceptChanges();
```

Example 15-7 shows the web service code.

Example 15-7. Web service code

```
// Web Service MyWebService

// connection and select command strings
String connString = "Data Source=(local);Integrated security=SSPI;" +
    "Initial Catalog=Northwind;";
String sqlSelect = "SELECT * FROM Orders";

// create a new DataSet to receive the data
```

Example 15-7. Web service code (continued)

```
DataSet ds = new DataSet();

SqlDataAdapter da = new sqlDataAdapter(sqlSelect, connString);

// create the command builder
SqlCommandBuilder cb = new SqlCommandBuilder(da);

// read all of the data from the orders table and load it into the
// Orders table in the DataSet
da.Fill(ds, "Orders");

public DataSet GetData()
{
    return ds;
}


public DataSet UpdateData(DataSet dsWS)
{
    // update the changed data from the client to the data source
    da.Update(dsWS, "Orders");

    // return the updated DataSet to the client
    return dsWS;
}
```

16

Transactions

Transactions ensure that a set of related operations are all completed or are aborted, leaving the involved resources in the state that they were in when the transaction was started. Transactions are most commonly used when all related operations must be completed successfully (e.g., debiting and crediting respective bank accounts when funds are transferred from one to the other). The related operations are bound together into a transactional unit of work that must either completely succeed or completely fail. This is referred to as committing or aborting the transaction.

ADO.NET supports manual transactions whose bounds are defined by the application using explicit commands to begin and end the transaction. Manual transactions are easy to code and offer both performance and flexibility, but can't span multiple data resources. Instances of a .NET Framework class can also be registered with COM+ component services to enlist in and participate in automatic transactions. Automatic transactions are the only choice when a transaction spans multiple data resource.

When selecting a transaction model, DBMS transactions are another option. DBMS transactions contain all transaction logic within a stored procedure; they offer the best performance but are more difficult to code than ADO.NET manual transactions. The DBMS transaction model is also the most limited model. If more than one stored procedure needs to be called within the context of a single transaction, either the manual or automatic transaction model must be used. DBMS transactions can be used together with manual transactions, but code must be written to deal with transactions that are rolled back from within the stored procedures.

Finally, it's important to understand that transactions should be used only when required. Using transactions imposes a performance penalty due to the system overhead in managing the transaction. Transactions can also block the work of other users in the system, which causes performance problems. For that reason, if transactions are required, the isolation level of the transactions should be carefully considered.

Manual Transactions

Manual transactions use explicit statements to control the boundaries of a transaction. Transactions are started, and subsequently either committed or rolled back. The SQL .NET data provider allows savepoints to be defined that allow a transaction to be partially rolled back. The OLE DB .NET data provider allows new, or nested, transactions to be started within the boundaries of the parent transaction. If transactions are nested, the parent can't commit until all nested transactions have committed.

A Transaction is started by calling the BeginTransaction( ) method of a Connection object. You can set a Command object to run in a transaction by setting its Transaction property to a Transaction object connected to the same Connection as the Command object. An overloaded constructor for the Command object allows this to be done in a single statement.

Once running in a Transaction, commands can be executed on the Command object within a try/catch block. If an exception is raised, the Rollback( ) method can be called on the Transaction to roll back all changes; otherwise, the Commit( ) method persists the changes.

The following example demonstrates these concepts. Order and order detail records are inserted within a transaction, thereby ensuring that either both or neither record is added:

```
String connString = "Data Source=(local);Integrated security=SSPI;" +
    "Initial Catalog=Northwind;";

SqlConnection conn = new SqlConnection(connString);
conn.Open();
SqlTransaction tran = conn.BeginTransaction();

//create command and enlist in transaction
SqlCommand cmdOrder = new SqlCommand("InsertOrder", conn, tran);
cmdOrder.CommandType = CommandType.StoredProcedure;
SqlCommand cmdOrderDetail = new SqlCommand("InsertOrderDetail",
    conn, tran);
cmdOrderDetail.CommandType = CommandType.StoredProcedure;

SqlParameterCollection orderParams = cmdOrder.Parameters;
orderParams.Add("@OrderID", SqlDbType.Int, 0, "OrderID");
orderParams["@OrderID"].Direction = ParameterDirection.InputOutput;
orderParams.Add("@CustomerID", SqlDbType.NChar, 5, "CustomerID");
// ... code to define remaining parameters

SqlParameterCollection orderDetailParams = cmdOrderDetail.Parameters;
orderDetailParams.Add("@OrderID", SqlDbType.Int, 0, "OrderID");
orderDetailParams.Add("@ProductID", SqlDbType.Int, 5, "ProductID");
// ... code to define remaining parameters
```

```
String result = "";
try
{
    // insert order
    cmdOrder.Parameters["@OrderID"].Value = -1;
    cmdOrder.Parameters["@CustomerID"].Value = "ALFKI";
    // ... set the other parameters
    cmdOrder.ExecuteNonQuery();

    // insert order detail with OrderID from the inserted order
    cmdOrderDetail.Parameters["@CustomerID"].Value =
        (Int32)cmdOrder.Parameters["@OrderID"].Value;
    cmdOrderDetail.Parameters["@ProductID"].Value = 20;
    //... set the other parameters
    cmdOrderDetail.ExecuteNonQuery();

    //if okay to here, commit the transaction
    tran.Commit();
    result = "Transaction commit.";
}
catch (SqlException ex)
{
    tran.Rollback();
    result = "ERROR: " + ex.Message + "; Transaction rollback.";
}
catch (FormatException ex)
{
    tran.Rollback();
    result = "ERROR: " + ex.Message + "; Transaction rollback.";
}
finally
{
    conn.Close();
}
```

Isolation Levels

The transaction isolation level specifies the transaction locking level for a connection. It determines the extent to which changes to data within a transaction are visible outside that transaction while uncommitted.

Table 16-1 lists and describes problems that might occur if several users access data concurrently without locking.

Table 16-1. Concurrency problems

Condition	Description
Lost update	Two or more transactions select the same row and subsequently update the row. The transactions are unaware of each other and, as a result, updates overwrite one another, resulting in lost data.
Uncommitted dependency (dirty read)	A second transaction selects a row that has been updated, but not committed, by another transaction. The data being read might be further updated or rolled back by the original transaction, resulting in invalid data in the second transaction.

Table 16-1. Concurrency problems (continued)

Condition	Description
Inconsistent analysis (nonrepeatable read)	A second transaction reads different data each time the same row is read. The second transaction reads data that has been changed and committed by another transaction between the reads.
Phantom read	An insert or delete is performed for a row belonging to a range of rows being read by a transaction. The rows selected within the transaction are missing the newly inserted rows and contain deleted rows that no longer exist.

Locks ensure transactional integrity and maintain database consistency by controlling how resources can be accessed by concurrent transactions. A lock is an object that indicates a user has some dependency on a resource. Other users are prevented from performing operations that would adversely affect the dependency of the user with the lock. Locks are managed internally by system software and acquired and released as a result of actions taken by users. Table 16-2 lists and describes resource lock modes used by ADO.NET.

Table 16-2. Resource lock modes

Lock mode	Description
Shared	Allows concurrent transactions to read the locked resource. Another transaction can't modify the locked data while the lock is held.
Exclusive	Prevents access, both read and modify, to a resource by concurrent transactions.

Isolation level is the level at which a transaction is prepared to accept inconsistent data; it is the degree to which one transaction must be isolated from other transactions. As the isolation level increases, access to current data increases at the expense of data correctness. Table 16-3 lists and describes the different isolations supported by ADO.NET. The first four levels are listed in order of increasing isolation.

Table 16-3. IsolationLevelEnumeration

Name	Description
ReadUncommitted	No shared locks are issued, and exclusive locks aren't honored. A dirty read is possible.
ReadCommitted	Shared locks are held while data is read by the transaction. Dirty reads aren't possible, but nonrepeatable reads or phantom rows can occur because data can be changed before it is committed.
RepeatableRead	Shared locks are placed on all data used in a query preventing other users from updating the data. Nonrepeatable reads are prevented, but phantom reads are still possible.
Serializable	A range lock, where the individual records and the ranges between records are covered, is placed on the data preventing other users from updating or inserting rows until the transaction is complete. Phantom reads are prevented.
Chaos	Pending changes from more highly isolated transactions can't be overwritten. Not supported by SQL Server.
Unspecified	A different isolation level than the one specified is being used, but that level can't be determined.

The isolation level can be changed programmatically at any time. If it is changed within a transaction, the new locking level applies to all remaining statements within the transaction.

The following example demonstrates how to set the isolation level for a transaction:

```
String connString = "Data Source=(local);Integrated security=SSPI;" +
    "Initial Catalog=Northwind;";

SqlConnection conn = new SqlConnection(connString);
conn.Open();
SqlTransaction tran =
    conn.BeginTransaction(IsolationLevel.RepeatableRead);

// returns IsolationLevel.RepeatableRead
IsolationLevel il = tran.IsolationLevel;
```

Savepoints

Rolling back a transaction cancels the effect of all statements in that transaction. In some cases, it is only necessary to roll back a portion of the transaction. This can be done using savepoints.

A savepoint is created using the Save( ) method of the Transaction object. The method takes a string argument specifying the name of the savepoint. A transaction is rolled back to the savepoint by calling the RollBack() method and specifying the name of the savepoint as the optional argument. Savepoints are supported only by the SQL .NET managed data provider; nested transactions can be used with the OLE DB data provider to accomplish a similar result. The following example demonstrates how to use savepoints:

```
String connString = "Data Source=(local);Integrated security=SSPI;" +
    "Initial Catalog=Northwind;";

SqlConnection conn = new SqlConnection(connString);
conn.Open();
SqlTransaction tran = conn.BeginTransaction();

//create command and enlist in transaction
SqlCommand cmd = new SqlCommand("InsertCustomer", conn, tran);
cmd.CommandType = CommandType.StoredProcedure;

SqlParameterCollection cparams  = cmd.Parameters;
cparams.Add("@CustomerID", SqlDbType.NChar, 5, "CustomerID");
cparams.Add("@CompanyName", SqlDbType.NVarChar, 40, "CompanyName");
// ... code to define remaining parameters

try
{
    // insert a record into the table
    cmd.Parameters["@CustomerID"].Value="CUST1";
```

```
    // ... set the other parameters
    cmd.ExecuteNonQuery();
}
catch (Exception ex)
{
    tran.Rollback();
    Console.WriteLine(
      "ERROR: {0}: Transaction rollback (CUST1).", ex.Message);
    conn.Close();
    return;
}

tran.Save("SavePoint1");

try
{
    // insert a second record into the table
    cmd.Parameters["@CustomerID"].Value = "CUST2";
    // ... set the other parameters
    cmd.ExecuteNonQuery();

    //if okay to here, commit the transaction
    tran.Commit();

    Console.WriteLine("Transaction commit (CUST1 and CUST2).");
}
catch (SqlException ex)
{
    tran.Rollback("SavePoint1");
    tran.Commit();
    Console.WriteLine(
      "ERROR: {0} Transaction commit (CUST1); " +
      "Transaction rollback (CUST2).", ex.Message);
}
finally
{
    conn.Close();
}
```

Nested Transactions

Nesting allows one transaction to initiate other transactions. These nested transactions are initiated using the Begin( ) method of the Transaction object, which returns a reference to a new transaction object. However, rolling back this transaction rolls back only the nested transaction and not the entire transaction.

Nested transactions aren't supported by the SQL Server .NET data provider although savepoints can be used with that data provider to accomplish a similar result. The OLE DB provider for SQL Server also doesn't support nested transactions.

Transactions Using a DataAdapter

The DataAdapter uses its Command objects DeleteCommand, InsertCommand, and UpdateCommand to update changes back to the data source. As a result, using transactions from a DataAdapter isn't very different from using them with the Command object directly. If custom updating logic is being used with the DataAdapter, simply create the transaction and assign it to the three update Command objects for the DataAdapter. The following example illustrates how to use transactions with the DataSet and the DataAdapter objects with custom update logic:

```
String connString = "Data Source=(local);Integrated security=SSPI;" +
    "Initial Catalog=Northwind;";

String sqlSelect = "SELECT * FROM Orders";

SqlConnection conn = new SqlConnection(connString);
conn.Open();

SqlDataAdapter da = new SqlDataAdapter(sqlSelect, conn);
DataSet ds = new DataSet();

// define update logic for the data adapter

// load  data from the data source into the DataSet
da.Fill(ds, "Orders");

// start the transaction
SqlTransaction tran = conn.BeginTransaction();

// associate transaction with the data adapter command objects
da.DeleteCommand.Transaction = tran;
da.InsertCommand.Transaction = tran;
da.UpdateCommand.Transaction = tran;

// ... modify the data in the DataSet

// submit changes, commit or rollback, and close the connection
try
{
    da.Update(ds, "Orders");

    // commit if successful
    tran.Commit();
}
catch (Exception)
{
    tran.Rollback();
}
finally
{
    conn.Close();
}
```

When the CommandBuilder generates the updating logic used by the DataAdapter, it doesn't generate updating logic when it is instantiated. Good design dictates minimizing data interaction within a transaction. This means that the updating logic for the CommandBuilder should be generated before the transaction is started, rather inside the transaction. This is accomplished by calling the GetDeleteCommand(), GetInsertCommand(), and GetUpdateCommand() methods of the CommandBuilder object prior to using it with a transaction the first time. The following example illustrates how to use a transaction with a DataAdapter object that uses a CommandBuilder object to provide update logic:

```
// ... create the connection and data adapter as with custom update logic

// use a command builder to define updating logic
SqlCommandBuilder cb = new SqlCommandBuilder(da);
// generate updating logic for command objects
cb.GetDeleteCommand();
cb.GetInsertCommand();
cb.GetUpdateCommand();

// load  data from the data source into the DataSet
da.Fill(ds, "Orders");

// start the transaction
SqlTransaction tran = conn.BeginTransaction();
// associate transaction with command builder command objects
cb.GetDeleteCommand().Transaction = tran;
cb.GetInsertCommand().Transaction = tran;
cb.GetUpdateCommand().Transaction = tran;

// ... modify the data in the DataSet

// submit changes, commit or rollback, and close the connection
try
{
    da.Update(ds, "Orders");

    // commit if successful
    tran.Commit();
}
catch (Exception)
{
    tran.Rollback();
}
finally
{
    conn.Close();
}
```

Automatic Transactions

Microsoft Transaction Server (MTS), COM+ 1.0, and the .NET CLR support the same automatic distributed transaction model. The .NET Framework provides support for transactional components through COM+ services. There are two key benefits to COM+ transactions:

- They allow distributed transactions that span multiple data sources.
- Objects that can participate in COM+ transactions are free from having to anticipate how they might be used within a transaction. A client can perform different tasks with multiple objects, all in the context of a single transaction without the participating objects being aware of the transaction.

Instances of a .NET Framework class can participate in automatic transactions. Once an object is marked to participate in a transaction, it automatically executes within a transaction. This transactional behavior is controlled by the value of the transaction attribute for the .NET class, ASP.NET page, or XML web service method using the object. This allows the instantiated object to be configured programmatically to participate automatically in an existing transaction, to start a new transaction, or to not participate in a transaction.

When a transactional object accesses a data resource, a transaction occurs according to the value of the declarative transaction attribute of the object. When the transactional object accesses a data resource, the data driver enlists in the transaction through the distributed transaction coordinator (DTC).

During the lifetime of an automatic transaction, the objects participating in it can vote to either commit the transaction they are participating in by calling the static SetComplete() method of the ContextUtil class or to abort the transaction by calling the static SetAbort() method of the ContextUtil class. In the absence of an explicit vote, the default is to commit the transaction. The transaction is committed once it completes if none of the participating objects have voted to abort.

Alternatively, you can apply the AutoCompleteAttribute attribute to a transactional method. This attribute instructs .NET to automatically commit the transaction, provided no exceptions are encountered. If an unhandled exception is thrown, the transaction is automatically rolled back.

For a .NET Framework object to participate in an automatic transaction, it must be registered with COM+ component services. The following steps will prepare a class to participate in an automatic transaction:

1. Apply the TransactionAttribute to the class, and specify the transaction behavior, timeout, and isolation level.
2. Derive the class from ServicedComponent allowing access to COM+ services.
3. Sign the assembly with a strong name. Use the *sn.exe* utility to create a key pair with the following syntax:

    ```
    sn -k MyApp.snk
    ```

    Add the AssemblyKeyFileAttribute or AssemblyKeyNameAttribute assembly attribute specifying the file containing the key pair, for example:

    ```
    [assembly: AssemblyKeyFileAttribute("MyApp.snk")]
    ```

4. Register the assembly containing the class with the COM+ catalog* by executing the .NET Services Registration Tool (*regsvcs.exe*) with the following syntax:

```
regsvcs /appname:MyApp MyAssembly.dll
```

This step isn't strictly required. If a client calling the class is managed by the CLR, the registration is performed automatically.

This example is a simple .NET class that participates automatically in transactions:

```
using System.EnterpriseServices;
using System.Runtime.CompilerServices;
using System.Reflection;

namespace ServicedComponentCS
{
    [Transaction(TransactionOption.Required)]
    public class ServicedComponentTest : ServicedComponent
    {
        [AutoComplete]
        public void TranTest()
        {
            bool success = true;

            // ... do work and store the outcome to success variable

            if(success)
            {
                // don't need the next line since AutoComplete
                // ContextUtil.SetComplete();
            }
            else
            {
                ContextUtil.SetAbort();
                throw new System.Exception("Error in Serviced " +
                    "Component. Transaction aborted.");
            }
        }
    }
}
```

The `TransactionOption.Required` attribute in this example indicates that every method in this class must be used in a transaction, but the method can use the existing transaction if one has already been started in the caller's context. The full list of `TransactionOption` values is featured in Table 16-4.

---

* COM+ services are explored in detail in *COM and .NET Component Services*, by Juval Löwy (O'Reilly).

Table 16-4. Values for the TransactionOption enumeration

Value	Description
Disabled	Indicates that transactions aren't created or used automatically with this object.
NotSupported	Indicates that the object doesn't run within the scope of transactions. When a request is processed, its object context is created without a transaction, regardless of whether there is a transaction active.
Supported	Indicates that the object runs in the context of an existing transaction, if one exists. If no transaction exists, the object runs without a transaction.
Required	Indicates that the object requires a transaction. It runs in the scope of an existing transaction, if one exists. If no transaction exists, the object starts one.
RequiresNew	Indicates that the object requires a transaction, and a new transaction is started for each request.

17

XML and the DataSet

In the rush to capitalize on the promise of the XML format, Microsoft and other technology vendors have introduced a variety of different options for converting relational data into XML. Unfortunately, no single approach so far has combined ease-of-use with the flexibility developers require. For example, later versions of ADO introduced XML as a format for persisting a stream to disk. However, the developer had little control over the structure of the XML document. Around the same time, SQL Server 2000 introduced the new FOR XML query syntax. This technique was more flexible, but proved difficult to manage, could complicate queries horribly, and limited solutions to a single database product.

ADO.NET improves upon this picture. With ADO.NET, you can easily convert data into XML. It's also easy to generate a matching XSD schema, perform an XPath search on a result set, or even interact with an ordinary XML document through the ADO.NET data objects. All these features of ADO.NET's support for XML far exceed previous Microsoft data-access technologies.

Things aren't as straightforward if you need to use XML for cross-platform use (for example, sharing data between a .NET web service and a Java client). If you can write a Java client to accommodate the default ADO.NET XML structure, your task is easy. However, if you have an existing client that expects information in a different format, you may need to perform some tedious processing with the .NET XML classes. You'll also need to master the DiffGram schema if you want a non-.NET client to use the DataSet to submit batch changes.

This chapter introduces all these concepts, focusing on three topics:

- Using XML as a format to store and share DataSet information, even across process and platform boundaries.
- Using ADO.NET as a wrapper to allow convenient editing of otherwise ordinary XML documents.

- Synchronizing XML and the ADO.NET representation of a DataSet with the XmlDataDocument object. This also makes it easy to use XPath, XSLT, and other XML-specific technologies with an ADO.NET DataSet.

We'll conclude with a quick look at the XML extensions available in SQL Server 2000.

DataSet XML Methods

The ADO.NET DataSet stores information internally in a proprietary binary format that's optimized for XML representation. This means that data can be retrieved in XML format seamlessly, without any data loss or conversion errors. Table 17-1 lists the DataSet methods that work with XML.

Table 17-1. ADO.NET DataSet XML methods

Method	Description
GetXml( )	Retrieves the XML representation of the data in the DataSet as a single string.
GetXmlSchema( )	Retrieves the XSD schema for the DataSet XML as a single string. No data is returned.
ReadXml( )	Reads XML data from a file or a TextReader, XmlReader, or Stream object, and uses it to populate the DataSet. The XML document can include an inline schema.
ReadXmlSchema( )	Reads an XML schema from a file or a TextReader, XmlReader, or Stream object, and uses it to configure the DataSet (for example, creating Constraint and DataColumn objects).
WriteXml( )	Writes the contents of the DataSet to a file or a TextWriter, XmlWriter, or Stream object. You can choose to write the schema inline.
WriteXmlSchema( )	Writes just the XSD schema describing the contents of the DataSet to a file or a TextWriter, XmlWriter, or Stream object.
InferXmlSchema( )	Infers the XML schema and applies it to the DataSet by reading through an XML document supplied by a file or a TextReader, XmlReader, or Stream object.

If you need to manipulate or serialize the XML, the best choice is the direct WriteXml( ) method. Using the GetXml( ) method to retrieve a string containing the XML content (and then using the string to create a new object or write the data to disk) is inherently less efficient.

The key decision you make when dealing with the XML representation of a DataSet is deciding how to handle the schema, which defines the allowed structure and data types for the XML document. If you save the schema, you can use it as a basic form of error checking. Simply reload the schema into the DataSet before you insert any data.

Another reason to use an XML schema is to make your database code more efficient. For example, you can use ReadXmlSchema( ) to preconfigure your DataSet instead of the FillSchema( ) method discussed in Chapter 5, which requires a separate trip to the database. Alternatively, you can use a strongly typed DataSet.

Example 17-1 shows a console application that writes the retrieved XML to a file, reads it back, and then displays the XML for the retrieved DataSet using the GetXml() method. Note that this code doesn't provide any error handling for its file operations (i.e., the WriteXml() and ReadXml() methods).

Example 17-1. Writing a DataSet to XML with a schema

```
using System;
using System.Data;
using System.Data.SqlClient;

public class SaveDataSet
{
    private static string connectionString = "Data Source=localhost;" +
        "Initial Catalog=Northwind;Integrated Security=SSPI";

    public static void Main()
    {
        string SQL = "SELECT CategoryID, CategoryName, " +
                    "Description FROM Categories";

        // Create ADO.NET objects.
        SqlConnection con = new SqlConnection(connectionString);
        SqlCommand com = new SqlCommand(SQL, con);
        SqlDataAdapter adapter = new SqlDataAdapter(com);
        DataSet ds = new DataSet("Nortwind");

        // Execute the command.
        try
        {
            con.Open();
            adapter.FillSchema(ds, SchemaType.Mapped, "Categories");
            adapter.Fill(ds, "Categories");
        }
        catch (Exception err)
        {
            Console.WriteLine(err.ToString());
        }
        finally
        {
            con.Close();
        }

        // Save DataSet to disk (with schema).
        ds.WriteXmlSchema("mydata.xsd");
        ds.WriteXml("mydata.xml");

        // Reset DataSet.
        ds.Reset();

        // Read schema and reload data.
        ds.ReadXmlSchema("mydata.xsd");
        ds.ReadXml("mydata.xml");
```

Example 17-1. Writing a DataSet to XML with a schema (continued)

```
        // Display DataSet.
        Console.WriteLine("DataSet retrieved.");
        Console.WriteLine(ds.GetXml());
    }
}
```

Dissecting the DataSet XML

The DataSet XML follows a predefined format that follows a few simple rules:

- The root document element is the DataSet.DataSetName (in our example, Northwind).

- Each row in every table is contained in a separate element, using the name of the table. In our example with one table, this means multiple Categories elements. If there are two tables, these rows are followed by a list of other elements (such as Customers elements).

- An element for every column is included in each table row element. The actual column value is recorded as text inside the tag (although this is configurable).

Here's the default XML (excerpted to the first two rows) created by Example 17-1 for the Categories table:

```
<?xml version="1.0" standalone="yes"?>
<Northwind>
  <Categories>
    <CategoryID>1</CategoryID>
    <CategoryName>Beverages</CategoryName>
    <Description>Soft drinks, coffees, teas, beers, and ales</Description>
  </Categories>
  <Categories>
    <CategoryID>2</CategoryID>
    <CategoryName>Condiments</CategoryName>
    <Description>Sweet and savory sauces, relishes, spreads, and
      seasonings</Description>
  </Categories>
  <!-- Other categories omitted. -->
</Northwind>
```

It's possible to modify this representation without resorting to additional code or an XSLT transform. You'll learn how you can alter the structure of the XML data with ADO.NET a little later in this chapter.

Dissecting the DataSet XML Schema

The rules for the schema document are a little more subtle. First of all, a complexType is defined for each type of table row. Complex types define a structure that is composed of several separate pieces of information. In the following example, the Categories element is a complex type that contains several subtags:

```
<?xml version="1.0" standalone="yes"?>
<xs:schema id="Northwind" xmlns=""
```

```
xmlns:xs="http://www.w3.org/2001/XMLSchema"
xmlns:msdata="urn:schemas-microsoft-com:xml-msdata">

  <xs:element name="Northwind" msdata:IsDataSet="true">

    <xs:complexType>
      <xs:choice maxOccurs="unbounded">
        <xs:element name="Categories">
          <xs:complexType>

          <!-- Definition of Categories type omitted. -->

          </xs:complexType>
        </xs:element>
      </xs:choice>
    </xs:complexType>

    <!-- Additional code omitted. -->

  </xs:schema>
```

The XSD sequence element is nested inside the complexType element, indicating that the fields must occur in a set order:

```
<xs:element name="Categories">
  <xs:complexType>
    <xs:sequence>

    <!-- Definition of Categories type omitted. -->

    </xs:sequence>
  </xs:complexType>
</xs:element>
```

Every field in a row is declared using the corresponding XSD data type. If the field is optional (in other words, DataColumn.AllowDbNull is True), the minOccurs attribute is set to 0, indicating that this element isn't necessary. Similarly, a maxLength restriction element is added to a type if the DataColumn.MaxLength property is set.

```
<xs:element name="Categories">
  <xs:complexType>
    <xs:sequence>

      <xs:element name="CategoryID" msdata:ReadOnly="true"
          msdata:AutoIncrement="true" type="xs:int" />

      <xs:element name="CategoryName">
        <xs:simpleType>
          <xs:restriction base="xs:string">
            <xs:maxLength value="15" />
          </xs:restriction>
        </xs:simpleType>
      </xs:element>
```

XML and the
DataSet

```
<xs:element name="Description" minOccurs="0">
  <xs:simpleType>
    <xs:restriction base="xs:string">
      <xs:maxLength value="1073741823" />
    </xs:restriction>
  </xs:simpleType>
</xs:element>
</xs:sequence>

</xs:complexType>
</xs:element>
```

Additional database-specific information is added using the `msdata` namespace, which allows attributes such as `ReadOnly` and `AutoIncrement` that aren't part of the XSD standard but are recognized by ADO.NET.

Finally, the XSD document ends with a definition of unique elements to represent `DataSet` constraints. In the next snippet, a single unique element represents the primary key definition for the `CategoryID` field. Two XPath elements are also contained: a selector element that indicates how to find the table this constraint applies to and a field element that indicates how to find the relevant column.

```
<xs:unique name="Constraint1" msdata:PrimaryKey="true">
  <xs:selector xpath=".//Categories" />
  <xs:field xpath="CategoryID" />
</xs:unique>
```

Remember, the XSD schema is created based on the characteristics of the `DataColumn` and `Constraint` objects in the `DataSet`. To make sure you have as much information as possible, use the `FillSchema()` method before the `WriteXmlSchema()` method (or a strongly typed `DataSet`).

 For more information about Microsoft's `msdata` and `codegen` XML namespaces and what elements and attributes they define, refer to Appendix B.

XML Write and Read Modes

By default, the `WriteXml()` method simply outputs the XML data. You must create the XSD document separately. However, you can use an overloaded version of the `WriteXml()` method, which accepts a value from the `XmlWriteMode` enumeration. These values are described in Table 17-2.

Table 17-2. XmlWriteMode values

Value	Description
IgnoreSchema	Writes the current contents of the DataSet as XML data, without an XML Schema. This is the default.
WriteSchema	Writes the current contents of the DataSet as XML data with the relational structure as inline XML schema.
DiffGram	Writes the entire DataSet as a DiffGram, which includes information about original and current values. We'll examine DiffGrams in the next section.

For example, you can choose to write the XSD inline with the XML. This shortens the coding but can waste some disk space if you store multiple DataSet files with the same schema. It can also lead to versioning problems if you modify the DataSet structure later on, and it no longer matches the schema.

```
// Save DataSet to disk (with schema).
ds.WriteXml("mydata.xml", XmlWriteMode.WriteSchema);

// Reset the DataSet.
ds.Reset();

// Read schema and reload data.
ds.ReadXml("mydata.xml", XmlReadMode.ReadSchema);
```

The *mydata.xml* file now has the following structure:

```
<?xml version="1.0" standalone="yes"?>
<Northwind>

  <!-- Inline XSD schema document goes here. -->

  <Categories>
    <CategoryID>1</CategoryID>
    <CategoryName>Beverages</CategoryName>
    <Description>Soft drinks, coffees, teas, beers, and ales</Description>
  </Categories>

  <!-- Other rows omitted. -->

</Northwind>
```

In this case, you don't need to specify the XmlReadMode.ReadSchema when retrieving the data. The default, XmlReadMode.Auto, inspects the file and uses ReadSchema mode if it contains a schema. On the other hand, the default when saving data is XmlWriteMode.IgnoreSchema, which uses only the data. The full list of XmlWriteMode values is shown in Table 17-3.

Table 17-3. XmlReadMode values

Value	Description
Auto	Inspects the XML file and tries to perform the most appropriate action, depending on whether the file is a DiffGram or contains an inline schema. (Note that the inline schema is ignored if the DataSet already has a schema or the file contains a DiffGram.)
DiffGram	Reads a DiffGram, which specifies the contents of the DataSet and uses additional attributes to indicate changed values and inserted and deleted rows. These changes are applied to the DataSet automatically. However, it must have the same schema as the DataSet used to create the DiffGram, or an exception will be thrown.
Fragment	Reads partial XML documents, such as those generated by executing FOR XML queries with SQL Server 2000. The default namespace is read as the inline schema.
IgnoreSchema	Ignores any inline schema and reads data into the existing DataSet (preserving any schema information it already has). If any data doesn't match the existing schema, it is discarded. You can also use this mode to read a DiffGram.

Table 17-3. XmlReadMode values (continued)

Value	Description
InferSchema	Ignores any inline schema, loads the data, and infers the schema from the XML document. If the DataSet already contains a schema, the current schema is extended by adding new tables or adding columns to existing tables. An exception is thrown if the inferred table already exists but with a different namespace or if any of the inferred columns conflict with existing columns.
ReadSchema	Reads any inline schema and loads the data. If the DataSet already contains schema, and the schema refers to the same table, an exception is thrown. Otherwise, the new schema information extends the current DataSet schema by adding new tables.

Dissecting the DiffGram

The DataSet doesn't just contain schema information and a single set of data, it also tracks the state of each row and, if modified, the current and original values. In order to record this information in XML, ADO.NET defines a special Diff-Gram format.

The DiffGram format is divided into three sections: the current data, the original data, and any errors:

```
<?xml version="1.0"?>
<diffgr:diffgram
        xmlns:msdata="urn:schemas-microsoft-com:xml-msdata"
        xmlns:diffgr="urn:schemas-microsoft-com:xml-diffgram-v1"
        xmlns:xsd="http://www.w3.org/2001/XMLSchema">

    <DataInstance>
    </DataInstance>

    <diffgr:before>
    </diffgr:before>

    <diffgr:errors>
    </diffgr:errors>

</diffgr:diffgram>
```

The DataInstance element contains the actual DataSet information. Rows that have been changed are marked with the diffgr:hasChanges attribute. The diffgr:before element lists the information about the original values, while elements in diffgr:errors represent the DataRow.RowError property. Elements are matched between these three sections using the diffgr:id attribute.

Example 17-2 creates a DiffGram (and displays it in a console window). The DataSet is made up of three rows retrieved from the database. The first row is modified, the second is deleted, and a fourth row is created and added programmatically.

Example 17-2. Writing a DataSet DiffGram

```
using System;
using System.Data;
using System.Data.SqlClient;
```

Example 17-2. Writing a DataSet DiffGram (continued)

```
public class SaveDiffGram
{
    private static string connectionString = "Data Source=localhost;" +
        "Initial Catalog=Northwind;Integrated Security=SSPI";

    public static void Main()
    {
        string SQL = "SELECT TOP 3 CategoryID, CategoryName, " +
                     "Description FROM Categories";

        // Create ADO.NET objects.
        SqlConnection con = new SqlConnection(connectionString);
        SqlCommand com = new SqlCommand(SQL, con);
        SqlDataAdapter adapter = new SqlDataAdapter(com);
        DataSet ds = new DataSet("Nortwind");

        // Execute the command.
        try
        {
            con.Open();
            adapter.FillSchema(ds, SchemaType.Mapped, "Categories");
            adapter.Fill(ds, "Categories");
        }
        catch (Exception err)
        {
            Console.WriteLine(err.ToString());
        }
        finally
        {
            con.Close();
        }

        // Modify the DataSet (change first row, delete second,
        // and add a fourth).
        DataRow row = ds.Tables["Categories"].Rows[0];
        row["CategoryName"] = "Pastries";
        row["Description"] = "Danishes, donuts, and coffee cake";

        ds.Tables["Categories"].Rows[1].Delete();

        row = ds.Tables["Categories"].NewRow();
        row["CategoryName"] = "Baked goods";
        row["Description"] = "Bread, croissants, and bagels";
        ds.Tables["Categories"].Rows.Add(row);

        // Save DataSet diffgram to disk.
        ds.WriteXml("mydata.xml" , XmlWriteMode.DiffGram);

        // Display DataSet diffgram.
        ds.WriteXml(Console.Out , XmlWriteMode.DiffGram);
    }
}
```

The DiffGram includes all four rows. However, the deleted row appears only in the diffgr:before section:

```xml
<?xml version="1.0" standalone="yes"?>
<diffgr:diffgram
        xmlns:msdata="urn:schemas-microsoft-com:xml-msdata"
        xmlns:diffgr="urn:schemas-microsoft-com:xml-diffgram-v1">

  <Nortwind>
    <Categories diffgr:id="Categories1" msdata:rowOrder="0"
     diffgr:hasChanges="modified">
      <CategoryID>1</CategoryID>
      <CategoryName>Pastries</CategoryName>
      <Description>Danishes, donuts, and coffee cake</Description>
    </Categories>
    <Categories diffgr:id="Categories3" msdata:rowOrder="2">
      <CategoryID>3</CategoryID>
      <CategoryName>Confections</CategoryName>
      <Description>Desserts, candies, and sweet breads</Description>
    </Categories>
    <Categories diffgr:id="Categories4" msdata:rowOrder="3"
     diffgr:hasChanges="inserted">
      <CategoryID>4</CategoryID>
      <CategoryName>Baked goods</CategoryName>
      <Description>Bread, croissants, and bagels</Description>
    </Categories>
  </Nortwind>

  <diffgr:before>
    <Categories diffgr:id="Categories1" msdata:rowOrder="0">
      <CategoryID>1</CategoryID>
      <CategoryName>Beverages</CategoryName>
      <Description>Soft drinks, coffees, teas, beers,
       and ales</Description>
    </Categories>
    <Categories diffgr:id="Categories2" msdata:rowOrder="1">
      <CategoryID>2</CategoryID>
      <CategoryName>Condiments</CategoryName>
      <Description>Sweet and savory sauces, relishes, spreads, and
       seasonings</Description>
    </Categories>
  </diffgr:before>

</diffgr:diffgram>
```

Without the DiffGram, the XML file resembles the first section, without the added msdata and diffgr attributes. In other words, the deleted row isn't saved, and no distinction is made between the original rows and the inserted row. When you reload the non-DiffGram XML into a DataSet, every row is set to DataRowState.Unchanged. If you tried to update the data source with this DataSet, no changes are made.

You can read the DiffGram using XmlReadMode.DiffGram or the default XmlReadMode.Auto. However, the DataSet must already have the correct schema in place, or an exception is thrown. There is no way to create an XML file with a DiffGram *and* inline schema.

The default output generated with WriteXml( ) and WriteXmlSchema( ) includes the current contents. The DiffGram output, on the other hand, generates the information needed to use the DataSet change tracking.

If you use a DataSet as a return value from a method in a web service or a component exposed through .NET remoting, the DiffGram is automatically returned. For example, consider what happens if you modify the code in Example 17-2 to become a rudimentary web service in Example 17-3.

Example 17-3. A web service that returns a modified DataSet

```
<%@ Webservice Class="ADOService" Language="C#" %>

using System;
using System.Web.Services;
using System.Data;
using System.Data.SqlClient;

public class ADOService : System.Web.Services.WebService
{
    private string connectionString = "Data Source=localhost;" +
        "Initial Catalog=Northwind;Integrated Security=SSPI";

    [WebMethod]
    public DataSet GetCategoriesTest()
    {
    string SQL = "SELECT TOP 3 CategoryID, CategoryName, " +
                    "Description FROM Categories";

        // Create ADO.NET objects.
        SqlConnection con = new SqlConnection(connectionString);
        SqlCommand com = new SqlCommand(SQL, con);
        SqlDataAdapter adapter = new SqlDataAdapter(com);
        DataSet ds = new DataSet("Nortwind");

        // Execute the command.
        con.Open();
        adapter.FillSchema(ds, SchemaType.Mapped, "Categories");
        adapter.Fill(ds, "Categories");
        con.Close();

        // Modify the DataSet.
        DataRow row = ds.Tables["Categories"].Rows[0];
        row["CategoryName"] = "Pastries";
        row["Description"] = "Danishes, donuts, and coffee cake";

        ds.Tables["Categories"].Rows[1].Delete();
```

Example 17-3. A web service that returns a modified DataSet (continued)

```
row = ds.Tables["Categories"].NewRow();
row["CategoryName"] = "Baked goods";
row["Description"] = "Bread, croissants, and bagels";
ds.Tables["Categories"].Rows.Add(row);

// Return DataSet
return ds;
}
}
```

If you try this web method using the Internet Explorer test page, you'll find that the retrieved result includes a schema (at the beginning of the message), followed by a DiffGram containing the DataSet contents and recording all changes Figure 17-1 shows a partially collapsed view of this information.

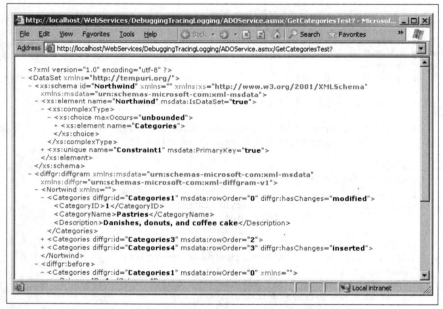

Figure 17-1. A DataSet schema and DiffGram returned by a web method

Thus, a .NET client can capture this information and automatically recreate an identical DataSet instance. A third-party client, however, needs to prepare for this information and handle it accordingly.

Shaping DataSet XML

The default format used for the DataSet XML works perfectly well when you create a new cross-platform application. However, most systems include legacy clients that require data in a set format. Unfortunately, even a minute difference between the expected and the actual XML file format can prevent a client from successfully reading the data.

ADO.NET offers limited ways to customize the generated XML for a DataSet. Before writing your own custom code, you should begin by examining these features. If you need to perform more significant changes, you need to perform these additional operations using the .NET XML classes or XLST transformation.

Attributes and Elements

One recurring question in XML modeling is the question of whether to use attributes to store data or contained elements. For example, here's a category row that uses only elements:

```
<Categories>
  <CategoryID>1</CategoryID>
  <CategoryName>Beverages</CategoryName>
  <Description>Soft drinks, coffees, teas, beers, and ales</Description>
</Categories>
```

And here's the same row with attributes:

```
<Categories CategoryID="1" CategoryName="Beverages"
 Description="Soft drinks, coffees, teas, beers, and ales" />
```

With ADO.NET, you can configure whether column values are stored in attributes or elements. Best of all, you can do it on a per-column basis (for example, storing the unique identity column as an attribute and all other columns as elements). All you need to do is set the DataColumn.ColumnMapping property to one of the values shown in Table 17-4.

Table 17-4. MappingStyle values

Value	Description
Element	The column is written as an XML element. The column name becomes the name of the element, and the contents of the column are written as the text of the element. This is the default. <ColumnName>ColumnContent</ColumnName>
Attribute	The column is written as an XML attribute of the XML element for the current row. The column name becomes the name of the attribute, and the contents of the column become the value of the attribute. <RowElement ColumnName="ColumnContent" />
SimpleContent	The contents of the column are written as text in the XML element for the current row. Note that only one column in a table can be set to SimpleContent, and SimpleContent can't be used for a table that has other MappingStyle.Element columns or nested relations. <RowElement>ColumnContent</RowElement>
Hidden	The column isn't written as part of the XML output.

The following code snippet iterates through all the column objects in a DataSet and configures them to use attribute-based representation. You can add this code to Example 17-1 earlier in this chapter to try out the technique.

```
foreach (DataColumn col in ds.Table["Categories"].Columns)
{
```

```
        col.ColumnMapping = MappingStyle.Attribute;
}
```

Unfortunately, there is no easy way to use a different element or attribute name. If you don't want to use the default `DataColumn.ColumnName`, you have to create an export routine that manually renames columns before serializing the `DataSet`.

Relational XML Data

Relational databases organize information into tables, in which each row represents an independent item. To relate different types of items (such as customers and orders), table relations are added. XML, on the other hand, often uses a hierarchical model. For example, you can model a list of products by creating product elements inside category elements. This type of organization is more efficient for some operations (for example, finding all the products in a given category), and less flexible for others (for example, creating a composite list of products).

By default, when writing a `DataSet` with multiple tables to XML, ADO.NET places the row elements for each table consecutively. For example, in XML, a table with rows from the Categories and Products tables is stored with the following format:

```
<?xml version="1.0" standalone="yes"?>
<Northwind>
  <Categories>
    <CategoryID>1</CategoryID>
    <CategoryName>Beverages</CategoryName>
    <Description>Soft drinks, coffees, teas, beers, and ales</Description>
  </Categories>
  <Categories>
    <CategoryID>2</CategoryID>
    <CategoryName>Condiments</CategoryName>
    <Description>Sweet and savory sauces, relishes, spreads, and
      seasonings</Description>
  </Categories>

  <!-- Other categories omitted. -->

  <Products>
    <ProductID>1</ProductID>
    <ProductName>Chai</ProductName>
    <CategoryID>1</CategoryID>
  </Products>
  <Products>
    <ProductID>2</ProductID>
    <ProductName>Chang</ProductName>
    <CategoryID>1</CategoryID>
  </Products>

  <!-- Other products omitted. -->

</Northwind>
```

Alternatively, you can create XML using a tree-based structure with relations. All you need to do is create the `DataRelation` and set the `DataRelation.Nested` property to true. In this case, the format is hierarchical, based on the parent-child relationship, and products are grouped by categories:

```xml
<?xml version="1.0" standalone="yes"?>
<Northwind>

  <Categories>
    <CategoryID>1</CategoryID>
    <CategoryName>Beverages</CategoryName>
    <Description>Soft drinks, coffees, teas, beers, and ales</Description>

    <Products>
      <ProductID>1</ProductID>
      <ProductName>Chai</ProductName>
      <CategoryID>1</CategoryID>
    </Products>
    <Products>
      <ProductID>2</ProductID>
      <ProductName>Chang</ProductName>
      <CategoryID>1</CategoryID>
    </Products>

    <!-- Other products in this category omitted. -->

  </Categories>

  <Categories>
    <CategoryID>2</CategoryID>
    <CategoryName>Condiments</CategoryName>
    <Description>Sweet and savory sauces, relishes, spreads, and
      seasonings</Description>

    <Products>
      <ProductID>3</ProductID>
      <ProductName>Aniseed Syrup</ProductName>
      <CategoryID>2</CategoryID>
    </Products>

    <!-- Other products in this category omitted. -->

  </Categories>

  <!-- Other categories omitted. -->

</Northwind>
```

Figure 17-2 diagrams the difference.

This is all well and good for a one-to-many relationship, but what about a many-to-many relationship, which is always implemented by three tables? For example, in the Northwind database, there are Territories, Employees, and linking EmployeeTerritories tables.

The hierarchical tree-based model isn't well suited to show this relationship. If you nest Territory elements in EmployeeTerritory elements, which in turn are

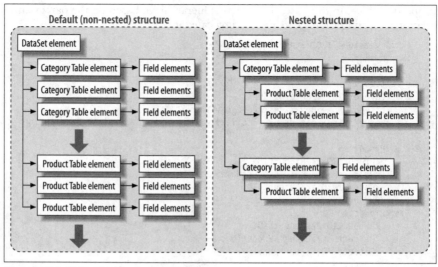

Figure 17-2. Related tables in an XML document

placed inside Employee elements, you quickly end up with duplicate Territory elements. If you use a tree starting with Territory elements, you end up with a duplicate employee under more than one territory branch. ADO.NET avoids this problem by disallowing it. If you try to set the Nested property on both columns, you receive an ArgumentException.

Other .NET XML Classes

The .NET framework provides a full complement of classes for XML manipulation, which are found in the System.Xml family of namespaces (see Table 17-5).

Table 17-5. XML classes in .NET

Class	Description
XmlDocument	An in-memory representation of an XML document. You can navigate freely through its structure, adding, removing, inserting, or modifying nodes.
XmlSchema	An in-memory representation of an XML schema document.
XmlTextReader and XmlTextWriter	Allows you to quickly retrieve XML data from or save it to a file or stream. These classes provide optimized forward-only access.
XmlValidatingReader	Similar to XmlReader in that it provides read-only, forward-only access to an XML file or a stream. Unlike XmlReader, XmlValidatingReader throws an exception if the XML document violates the rules in a specified schema.
XslTransform	Allows you to perform XSLT transformations to change an in-memory XML document to another XML document.

These classes offer XML-specific functionality that isn't directly available through the ADO.NET objects. For example, if you load a serialized DataSet using an XML file and XSD schema, you may not receive a warning if the XML document violates the schema; typically, you'll just lose some of the data. In cases in which you aren't sure if the XML file fits a given schema (or, in other words, you aren't sure that the data in an XML file pertains to a given table or a given version of that table), you can run through the XML file with the `XmlValidatingReader` before loading it into the `DataSet`.

XmlDataDocument Object Overview

There is one .NET object that combines an XML view with a `DataSet`—the `XmlDataDocument`. The `XmlDataDocument` inherits from `XmlDocument`, so it provides the same node-based iteration ability and XPath querying methods. It also provides a single additional property, `XmlDataDocument.DataSet`, which provides the relational representation of XML data.

When using the `XmlDataDocument`, you can start with either an XML document or a `DataSet`. To create an `XmlDataDocument` based on a `DataSet`, use the overloaded constructor that accepts a `DataSet` instance:

```
XmlDataDocument dataDoc = new XmlDataDocument(ds);
```

Although you can use the `XmlDataDocument.Nodes` collection to modify the information in the `DataSet`, it becomes much more difficult to take into account referential integrity and other database-specific concepts. It can be useful if you want to execute an XPath query or perform an XSLT transform (as shown in the next two examples) or take advantage of some other XML-specific feature. However, it won't replace the tasks you can accomplish through the `DataSet` model.

Another useful role for the `XmlDataDocument` is to provide a `DataSet` projection on an XML file. To use this approach, you create the `XmlDataDocument`, load a schema into the `DataSet` (this is a required step), and then load the XML file using the `XmlDataDocument.Load( )` method:

```
XmlDataDocument dataDoc = new XmlDataDocument();
dataDoc.DataSet.ReadXmlSchema("myschema.xsd");
dataDoc.Load("myfile.xml")
```

The primary advantage of this approach, versus just using the `DataSet` directly, is that you don't lose any information that isn't defined in the schema. The `DataSet` acts as a projection of a portion of the information. If you load a document with an extra element that's not included in the `DataSet` schema, you won't be able to access that column through the `XmlDocument.DataSet` object. However, you can access it directly through the `XmlDocument` nodes, and you won't lose the information when you call the `XmlDocument.Save( )` method.

Searching a DataSet with XPath

You can use the `XmlDataDocument` to perform an XPath query. Example 17-4 demonstrates how you can create the `XmlDataDocument` for an existing `DataSet` and then select nodes using an XPath query.

Example 17-4. Searching a DataSet with XPath

```
// ... create and populate a DataSet (ds) with the query:
// SELECT CategoryID, CategoryName, Description  FROM Categories

// Create the XML data document interface.
XmlDataDocument dataDoc = new XmlDataDocument(ds);

// Perform search for all Categories that have a
// CategoryName which starts with "C".
string XPath;
XPath = @"//Categories[starts-with(child::CategoryName, 'C')]";
XmlNodeList nodes = dataDoc.DocumentElement.SelectNodes(XPath);

foreach (XmlNode node in nodes)
{
    Console.Write("\nMatch: ");

    foreach (XmlNode child in node.ChildNodes)
    {
        Console.WriteLine(child.InnerText);
    }
}
```

The XPath query roughly translates into "get all the nodes named Categories where the contained CategoryName element has a value that starts with the letter 'C.'" The code then iterates through the results and produces the following console output:

```
Match: 2
Condiments
Sweet and savory sauces, relishes, spreads, and seasonings

Match: 3
Confections
Desserts, candies, and sweet breads
```

Transforming DataSet XML with XSLT

Another reason you might use the XmlDataDocument is so you can apply an XSL transformation. XSL is a language that defines transformations. These transformations allow you to convert an XML document into an XML document with a different format or an entirely different document (such as an HTML page). XSL documents are themselves written as XML documents that use a specialized XML grammar. This is usually called the XSL transformation document, and is given the extension *.xsl* or *.xslt*. Essentially, the XSL document maps the source XML to a new document. In .NET, XSL transformations are performed by the XslTransform class in the System.Xml.Xsl namespace.

The XSL standard (defined at *http://www.w3.org/TR/xslt*) is beyond the scope of this book. However, it's easy to illustrate the fundamentals with a quick example. Consider, for example, this simple XSL document:

```
<xsl:stylesheet xmlns:xsl="http://www.w3.org/1999/XSL/Transform"
                version="1.0">

<xsl:template match="CustomerDataSet">
This is the Customer DataSet.
(If this is an HTML document, we could insert opening tags here.)

Here's the customer list:
    <xsl:apply-templates select="Customers"/>

(Closing tags belong here.)
</xsl:template>

<xsl:template match="Customers">
Customer: <xsl:value-of select="ContactName"/>
Phone: <xsl:value-of select="Phone"/></xsl:template>

</xsl:stylesheet>
```

The document matches two elements in the XML document. First, it matches
CustomerDataSet as the root, which must be the name of the DataSet you create.
Once this match is made (on the fourth line), a few lines of ordinary text are
output into the new document. Then, the Customers element is matched, which is
the name of the table rows. Every time a customer row is found, the text from the
ContactName and Phone elements are output.

Example 17-5 shows a console application that uses this XSL document. Note
that the DataSet is carefully generated to use the matching element names
CustomerDataSet and Customers. If it doesn't, the XSL transform will fail. The
source XML for the transformation is supplied directly from the XmlDataDocument.
The target document is the output stream for the console window.

Example 17-5. Transforming a DataSet with XSL

```
using System;
using System.Data;
using System.Data.SqlClient;
using System.Xml;
using System.Xml.Xsl;

public class XslTransformDataSet
{
    private static string connectionString = "Data Source=localhost;" +
        "Initial Catalog=Northwind;Integrated Security=SSPI";

    public static void Main()
    {
        string SQL = "SELECT TOP 5 * FROM Customers";

        // Create ADO.NET objects.
        SqlConnection con = new SqlConnection(connectionString);
        SqlCommand com = new SqlCommand(SQL, con);
        SqlDataAdapter adapter = new SqlDataAdapter(com);
        DataSet ds = new DataSet("CustomerDataSet");
```

Example 17-5. Transforming a DataSet with XSL (continued)

```
        // Execute the command.
        try
        {
            con.Open();
            adapter.FillSchema(ds, SchemaType.Mapped, "Customers");
            adapter.Fill(ds, "Customers");
        }
        catch (Exception err)
        {
            Console.WriteLine(err.ToString());
        }
        finally
        {
            con.Close();
        }

        // Create the XML data document interface.
        XmlDataDocument dataDoc = new XmlDataDocument(ds);

        // Create the XSL transform object.
        XslTransform xsl = new XslTransform();
        xsl.Load("transform.xsl");

        // Perform the transformation.
        xsl.Transform(dataDoc, null, Console.Out);
    }
}
```

When this code is executed, you'll see the following output:

```
<?xml version="1.0" encoding="IBM437"?>
This is the Customer DataSet.
(If this is an HTML document, we could insert opening tags here.)

Here's the customer list:

Customer: Maria Anders, Phone: 030-0074321
Customer: Ana Trujillo, Phone: (5) 555-4729
Customer: Antonio Moreno, Phone: (5) 555-3932
Customer: Thomas Hardy, Phone: (171) 555-7788
Customer: Christina Berglund, Phone: 0921-12 34 65

(Closing tags belong here.)
```

Using the Data Objects to Edit XML

Editing relational tables through XML objects is rarely a good idea. You immediately introduce synchronization problems and lose the ability to enforce referential and identity integrity. There's a more useful side of the ADO.NET and XML, however: using the ADO.NET data objects to work with an ordinary XML file.

For example, your program might need to store user-specific settings. One choice for a location to store these settings is the registry, but this isn't always appropriate, particularly if users are regularly logging in to the program from different workstations. Another approach might be to use a central database server. However, you may not have the necessary database server in place, the program may need to support local (disconnected use), or you may not want to introduce additional network traffic. In these cases, you can adopt a different approach and assign a small XML configuration file to each user. To read and write the configuration file, use the DataSet.ReadXml( ) and DataSet.WriteXml( ) methods.

To evaluate this technique, here are a few considerations:

* This approach is best if you want to interact with the data using a table and row-based syntax. You don't interact natively with the XML.
* This approach has the same limitations as any other file-based storage. If you need to write large amounts of data, it's slow, and there is no way to manage concurrent updates. If you need these features, you need a full-fledged RDBMS.
* This approach works best if you create an XML schema to describe your data format. Otherwise, type conversion errors and other schema inference problems are possible.
* This approach works only if your XML document follows a DataSet-like organization of elements. This leads to problems for XML documents with deeply nested structures or XML documents that duplicate some elements to represent many-to-many relationships.

Inferring XML Structure

When using the ADO.NET objects to process an ordinary XML file, you should always create an associated schema. Otherwise, ADO.NET will attempt to infer a schema based on the structure of the XML document. This schema may not always be appropriate.

 If you load an XML document that has additional information (attributes or elements) beyond what the schema allows, ADO.NET will not throw an exception. However, ADO.NET will ignore the extra information. When you save the file later, it will not contain the additional information.

If you don't provide a schema, you can still load XML data into a DataSet. However, you're likely to discover a number of ADO.NET idiosyncrasies. The process ADO.NET uses to create a "best guess" schema by reading an XML document is called *schema inference*.

The DataSet follows a rigid set of inference rules:

* Elements with attributes become tables. Attributes are inferred as columns.
* Elements with child elements become tables. Elements that have no attributes or child elements and don't repeat are inferred as columns.
* Elements that repeat are inferred as a single table.

- If the document or root element has no attributes and no child elements that would be inferred as columns, it is inferred as a `DataSet`. Otherwise, the document element is inferred as a table.

- For elements that are inferred as tables and contain text, but have no child elements, a new column named `TableName_Text` is created. The text of each of the elements is placed in this column. If an element is inferred as a table and has text *and* child elements, any contained text is ignored.

- If ADO.NET infers that there is a table element nested with another table element, it automatically creates a nested `DataRelation` between the two tables. A new, primary key column named `TableName_Id` is added to both tables and used by the `DataRelation`. A `ForeignKeyConstraint` is created between the two tables using the `TableName_Id` column.

The last point is particularly interesting. With a nested table, ADO.NET always generates a new primary key column in the parent and a new foreign key column in the child, even if you already have elements that could serve this purpose.

Finally, note that schema inference has another major limitation: it doesn't detect data types. Even if you have numeric ID values, they are interpreted as strings.

 One easy way to create a schema for your custom XML files is to write a small utility that defines a new `DataSet`. You can then use the `WriteXml( )` method and the `WriteXmlSchema( )` method to generate the matching schema.

SQL Server 2000 XML

Finally, SQL Server also provides its own direct support for XML. By using the FOR XML clause in a SELECT query, you indicate that the results should be returned as XML. This technique is a bit of a compromise. Even though it provides XML-savvy development houses with an easy way to work natively with XML, it's also unavoidably specific to SQL Server, and therefore won't suit if you need the flexibility to migrate to (or incorporate data from) another platform such as Oracle or DB/2.

By default, the SQL Server XML representation isn't a full XML document. Instead, it simply returns the result of each record in a separate element, with all the fields as attributes (a marked different from ADO.NET's default, which includes all fields as elements).

For example, the query:

```
SELECT CategoryID, CategoryName, Description FROM Categories FOR XML AUTO
```

returns the following XML document:

```
<categories categoryID="1" categoryname="Beverages" description="Soft
drinks, coffees, teas, beers, and ales"/>
<categories categoryID="2" categoryname="Condiments" description="Sweet and
savory sauces, relishes, spreads, and seasonings"/>

<!-- Other categories omitted. -->
```

It's possible to reverse SQL Server's preference by adding the ELEMENTS keyword to the end of your query. For example, the query:

```
SELECT CategoryID, CategoryName, Description FROM Categories
FOR XML AUTO ELEMENTS
```

returns the following document:

```
<Categories>
  <CategoryID>1</CategoryID>
  <CategoryName>Beverages</CategoryName>
  <Description>Soft drinks, coffees, teas, beers, and ales</Description>
</Categories>
<Categories>
  <CategoryID>2</CategoryID>
  <CategoryName>Condiments</CategoryName>
  <Description>Sweet and savory sauces, relishes, spreads, and
    seasonings"/>
</Categories>

<!-- Other categories omitted. -->
```

Note that setting the format is an all-or-nothing decision. If you want to provide a more sophisticated XML document that follows a set format (i.e., some fields are represented as attributes, while others are columns) you must master the much more complex and much less compact FOR XML EXPLICIT syntax, which isn't described in this book. For more information, refer to *SQL Server Books Online*.

Finally, you can add the XMLDATA clause to return a pregenerated schema at the beginning of your document. However, this clause isn't of much use because the schema is based on Microsoft's XDR standard, which was proposed before the XSD standard was accepted. As a result, the schemas generated by SQL Server aren't recognized by most non-Microsoft XML parsers and will likely be replaced in future SQL Server versions.

If you want to retrieve a field with binary data, you can specify the BINARY BASE64 option at the end of your query. This returns the binary data as base-64 encoded text, rather than a reference. It also increases the size of the returned document.

In ADO.NET, you can retrieve this document using the SqlCommand. ExecuteXmlReader() method. This returns an XmlReader object that provides access to the returned XML.

Example 17-6 shows how to retrieve the query shown earlier and write it to a console window.

Example 17-6. Using SQL Server 2000 direct XML support

```
using System;
using System.Data;
using System.Data.SqlClient;
using System.Xml;
```

Example 17-6. Using SQL Server 2000 direct XML support (continued)

```
public class DirectXML
{
    private static string connectionString = "Data Source=localhost;" +
        "Initial Catalog=Northwind;Integrated Security=SSPI";

    public static void Main()
    {
        string SQL = "SELECT CategoryID, CategoryName, Description " +
                     "FROM Categories FOR XML AUTO";

        // Create ADO.NET objects.
        SqlConnection con = new SqlConnection(connectionString);
        SqlCommand com = new SqlCommand(SQL, con);

        // Execute the command.
        try
        {
            con.Open();
            XmlReader reader = com.ExecuteXmlReader();
            while (reader.Read())
            {

                Console.WriteLine("Element: " + reader.Name);

                if (reader.HasAttributes)
                {
                    for (int i = 0; i < reader.AttributeCount; i++)
                    {
                        reader.MoveToAttribute(i);
                        Console.Write("\t");
                        Console.Write(reader.Name + ": ");
                        Console.WriteLine(reader.Value);
                    }

                    // Move back to the element node.
                    reader.MoveToElement();

                    Console.WriteLine();
                }
            }
            reader.Close();
        }
        catch (Exception err)
        {
            Console.WriteLine(err.ToString());
        }
        finally
        {
            con.Close();
        }
    }
}
```

The results for the first two rows are shown here:

```
Element: Categories
        CategoryID: 1
        CategoryName: Beverages
        Description: Soft drinks, coffees, teas, beers, and ales

Element: Categories
        CategoryID: 2
        CategoryName: Condiments
        Description: Sweet and savory sauces, relishes, spreads
```

One other interesting ability of the `FOR XML AUTO` command is that it automatically infers relations with `JOIN` queries and creates XML documents with a nested structure. For example, the query:

```
SELECT CategoryName, ProductName Description FROM Categories INNER JOIN
Products ON Products.CategoryID = Categories.CategoryID FOR XML AUTO
```

creates the following XML document:

```
<Categories CategoryName="Beverages">
  <Products Description="Chai"/>
  <Products Description="Chang"/>
</Categories>
<Categories CategoryName="Condiments">
  <Products Description="Aniseed Syrup"/>

<!-- Other categories and products omitted. -->
```

To disable this behavior, use the `FOR XML RAW` syntax instead, which always returns a rigid single-grid XML result. The XML `RAW` option also gives every row element the name row instead of the name of the table (for example, `Categories`).

You can also use variations of the `FOR XML EXPLICIT` syntax to specify nearly every aspect of how the returned XML document should look, and the `OPENXML` statement to retrieve an XML document from a file and process it in a stored procedure. For more information about the direct support for XML in SQL Server, consult the SQL Server 2000 Books Online.

The SQLXML Provider

Microsoft also provides a special ADO.NET provider designed exclusively with SQL Server and its XML support in mind. This provider isn't included with .NET, although you can download it online from MSDN at *http://msdn.microsoft.com/downloads/sample.asp?url=/msdn-files/027/001/824/msdncompositedoc.xml*.

The SQLXML provider isn't in all respects a true ADO.NET provider. For example, it provides only three managed objects: `SqlXmlCommand`, `SqlXmlParameter`, and `SqlXmlAdapter`. These objects don't implement the standard interfaces, and there is no collection class (it is encapsulated by `SqlXmlCommand`).

The `SqlXmlCommand` class is the heart of the SQLXML provider. You choose the format of command by setting the `SqlXmlCommand.CommandType` property. Table 17-6 lists valid `CommandType` values.

Table 17-6. SqlXmlCommandType values

Property	Description
Sql	Uses SQL text (similar to the standard SQL Server provider), for example: SELECT * FROM Employees FOR XML AUTO
XPath	Uses an XPath query; for example, Employees[@EmployeeID=1]
Template	Executes a SQL command defined in an XML template document
TemplateFile	Executes a SQL command defined in an XML template document that's stored in a file
UpdateGram	Directly executes an UpdateGram, which is a predecessor to the DiffGram
Diffgram	Directly executes an ADO.NET DiffGram, which defines DataSet changes

When you use SQLXML with SQL Server and XML, you have several options. You can:

- Transform rowsets to XML on the client side, not the server side. This can lessen the work the server needs to perform.
- Submit XPath queries directly (rather than first retrieving the XML document and than searching it).
- Submit batch updates as a DiffGram.

We'll concentrate on these three features in the remainder of this chapter. In addition, the SQLXML provider duplicates some features provided by the standard SQL Server provider, such as the ability to execute a FOR XML query and capture the results with an XmlReader.

Converting to XML on the Client-Side

With FOR XML queries, SQL Server performs a query, converts it to XML, and returns the XML stream to the client. This has the potential for a minor performance penalty, and the network bandwidth required to send an XML document is always greater than that required for SQL Server's optimized TDS interface, which sends a stream of proprietary binary data. To reduce this effect in performance-sensitive applications, you can use the SQLXML provider's ability to convert a result set to XML on the client side. The resulting document takes the exact same form as if the server had performed the work.

The following code snippet shows this technique:

```
string connectionString = "Data Source=localhost;" +
  "Initial Catalog=Northwind;Integrated Security=SSPI";

// Create the command (which encapsulates a connection).
SqlXmlCommand cmd = new SqlXmlCommand(connectionString);

// Create the XML on the client.
cmd.ClientSideXml = true;

// Define the command.
cmd.CommandText = "SELECT * FROM Customers FOR XML AUTO";
```

```
// Get the XML document.
XmlReader r = cmd.ExecuteReader();
```

One reason to use the `ClientSideXml` property is to wrap a stored procedure that doesn't return an XML document; the data will convert to XML seamlessly. For example, consider the following stored procedure that retrieves a list of customers and the products they have ordered:

```
CREATE PROCEDURE CustOrderHist (@CustomerID nchar(5))
AS

SELECT ProductName, Total=SUM(Quantity)
 FROM Products P, [Order Details] OD, Orders O, Customers C
 WHERE C.CustomerID = @CustomerID
 AND C.CustomerID = O.CustomerID AND O.OrderID = OD.OrderID
 AND OD.ProductID = P.ProductID
 GROUP BY ProductName

GO
```

You can execute this stored procedure and convert the result to an XML document on the client side with the following code:

```
string connectionString = "Data Source=localhost;" +
  "Initial Catalog=Northwind;Integrated Security=SSPI";

SqlXmlCommand cmd = new SqlXmlCommand(connectionString);

SqlXmlParameter p = cmd.CreateParameter();
p.Value = "ALFKI";

// Define the command.
cmd.CommandText = "exec CustOrderHist ? FOR XML AUTO";
cmd.ClientSideXml = true;

// Get the XML document.
XmlReader r = cmd.ExecuteReader();
```

This example also illustrates the slightly different code used to call stored procedures with the SQLXML provider. Unlike other ADO.NET providers, you don't need to define the data type of the parameters used.

Submitting Direct XPath Queries

With the ordinary SQL Server provider, you must retrieve data using a SQL query before you can search it with XPath. The SQLXML provider removes this restriction. Performing an XPath query is as easy as setting the `SqlXmlCommand.XPath` property.

For example, consider the following XML document that defines an XPath query to select the `FirstName` and `LastName` fields from the `Customers` table:

```
<xsd:schema xmlns:xsd="http://www.w3.org/2001/XMLSchema"
            xmlns:sql="urn:schemas-microsoft-com:mapping-schema">
  <xsd:element name="Emp" sql:relation="Employees" >
```

```
<xsd:complexType>
  <xsd:sequence>
    <xsd:element name="FName"
                 sql:field="FirstName"
                 type="xsd:string" />
    <xsd:element name="LName"
                 sql:field="LastName"
                 type="xsd:string" />
  </xsd:sequence>
  <xsd:attribute name="EmployeeID" type="xsd:integer" />
</xsd:complexType>
  </xsd:element>
</xsd:schema>
```

You can use the defined Emp XPath query in a SqlXmlCommand as follows:

```
string connectionString = "Data Source=localhost;" +
  "Initial Catalog=Northwind;Integrated Security=SSPI";

SqlXmlCommand cmd = new SqlXmlCommand(connectionString);

SqlXmlParameter p = cmd.CreateParameter();
p.Value = "ALFKI";

// Define the command.
cmd.CommandText = "Emp";
cmd.CommandType = SqlXmlCommandType.XPath;
cmd.RootTag = "ROOT";
cmd.SchemaPath = "XPathDoc.xml";

// Get the XML document.
XmlReader r = cmd.ExecuteReader();
```

Note that the XPath document is loaded from the file identified by SqlXmlCommand. SchemaPath.

Batch Updates with the DiffGram

The SQLXML provider can also submit changes in a single batch operation using a DiffGram. In fact, if you use the SqlXmlAdatper to update a data source from a DataSet, this behavior takes place automatically, although you may not realize it.

For example, consider the following snippet of code that fills a DataSet and then applies changes to the data source:

```
SqlXmlCommand cmd = new SqlXmlCommand(connectionString);
cmd.CommandText = "SELECT * FROM Customers FOR XML AUTO";

SqlXmlAdapter adapter = new SqlXmlAdapter(cmd);

DataSet ds = new DataSet();

// Fill the DataSet.
adapter.Fill(ds);
```

```
// (Modify the DataSet here.)

// Apply changes using the DiffGram.
ad.Update(ds);
```

When the SqlXmlAdapter.Update( ) method is invoked, the SqlXmlAdapter doesn't step through the rows one by one looking for changes. Instead, it receives the Diff-Gram directly, and submits that document. The process is transparent to the .NET programmer.

II

ADO.NET Core Classes

18

The Connection Class

The Connection class is provided by all standard ADO.NET providers and represents a connection between your code and a data source. Connections require resources, so one hallmark of well-written ADO.NET code is that it opens a connection only when necessary and releases it as soon as possible. The Connection class is provided in several provider-specific varieties, including SqlConnection and OleDbConnection.

Most of the Connection properties are informational and can't be modified directly. Instead, before opening a connection, you use the ConnectionString property to set such information as the location of the data source, the authentication credentials, and the connection timeout. The Connection class is also the heart of client-side transactions with ADO.NET, connection pooling, and schema tables with the OLE DB provider.

Comments/Troubleshooting

All Connection objects implement the IDbConnection interface from the System. Data namespace and are thus quite similar. Provider-specific connection objects sometimes differ by adding new informational properties and slightly different methods for supporting transactions and connection pooling.

Some Connection classes for ADO.NET providers are shown in Table 18-1.

Table 18-1. Provider-specific Connection classes

Class	Data source
System.Data.SqlClient.SqlConnection	SQL Server
System.Data.OleDb.OleDbConnection	An OLE DB provider
System.Data.Odbc.OdbcConnection	An ODBC driver
System.Data.OleDb.OracleConnection	Oracle

Properties Reference

ConnectionString

```
string connectionString = Connection.ConnectionString;
```

Returns or sets a string that opens a database connection. The connection string is formatted as a collection of name/value pairs separated by semicolons. These settings can be provider-specific but typically follow certain conventions; they include basics such as the source database name, the location of the database server, and login information. The connection string is case-insensitive, and all blank characters are ignored.

Examples

The first example creates a SqlConnection that accesses a database on the local computer. Some properties of the connection string are set to connect to the Northwind database using integrated security.

```
SqlConnection conn = new SqlConnection();
conn.ConnectionString = "Data Source = localhost;" +
  "Integrated security = SSPI;Initial Catalog = Northwind";
```

The following example creates an OleDbConnection. Some properties of the connection string are set to connect to the Northwind database, using integrated security. Note that the information is identical, except for the addition of a Provider setting that specifies what underlying OLE DB provider should be used.

```
OleDbConnection conn = new OleDbConnection();
Conn.ConnectionString = "Provider = SQLOLEDB;Data Source = localhost;" +
  "Integrated Security = SSPI;Initial Catalog = northwind";
```

Notes

The ConnectionString property can be set only when the connection is closed. The Connection class provides many read-only properties that correspond to individual pieces of information from the connection string.

Values in the connection string can optionally be delimited by single or double quotes, e.g., name='value' or name="value"). The most common reason to use this approach is when you need to include blank or semicolon characters in a connection string value.

Any variation in a connection string can thwart connection pooling, so be sure to draw connection strings from a fixed location such as a configuration file to ensure consistency, rather than place them directly in code or construct them manually.

When retrieving the ConnectionString property, you will find that the user authentication information is automatically removed, unless you specifically submit the Persist Security Info setting in the connection string with a value of true.

 For a full list of connection string settings and examples of various provider-specific connection strings, see Chapter 3.

ConnectionTimeout

```
Int32 timeout = Connection.ConnectionTimeout;
```

Returns an integer containing the amount of time, in seconds, an attempt to establish a connection is allowed to run before timing out and throwing a provider-specific error such as `SqlException` or `OleDbException`.

Examples

This example creates a `SqlConnection` and stores the `ConnectionTimeout` property value to an `Integer` variable:

```
SqlConnection con = new SqlConnection();
int seconds = con.ConnectionTimeout;
```

The next example creates an `OleDbConnection` and stores the `ConnectionTimeout` property value to an integer variable:

```
OleDbConnection con = new OleDbConnection();
int seconds = con.ConnectionTimeout;
```

Note   To configure this setting, use the `Connection Timeout` parameter in the connection string.

Database

```
String databaseName = Connection.Database;
```

Returns the name of the database to be used for all commands (e.g., "Northwind"). If the connection isn't open, it's the name of the database that's initially used.

Note   To configure this setting, use the `Initial Catalog` parameter in the connection string. To change the database after connecting, use the `ChangeDatabase( )` method. This property isn't supported by Oracle databases.

DataSource

```
String serverName = Connection.DataSource;
```

Returns a string that specifies the location of the data source. This is almost always the name of the server running the database software (for example, "Production-SQLServer"). The value of (`local`) or `localhost` designates the current computer, regardless of its computer name.

Note   To configure this setting, use the `Data Source` parameter in the connection string.

Provider [OLE DB only]

```
String providerName = Connection.Provider;
```

Returns the name of the underlying OLE DB provider that this `OleDbConnection` is using to connect to the data source. This matches the name format used in the connection string. Table 18-2 lists some common examples.

Connection

Table 18-2. Commonly used OLE DB drivers

Name	Description
SQLOLEDB	OLE DB provider for SQL Server
MSDAORA	OLE DB provider for Oracle 7.3 and 8
Microsoft.Jet.OLEDB.4.0	OLE DB provider for Access (and other Jet data sources)

Note   To configure this setting, use the `Provider` parameter in the connection string.

PacketSize [SQL Server only]

```
Int32 packetSize = Connection.PacketSize;
```

Returns the size (in bytes) of the network packets that communicate with SQL Server. This value must fall between 512 and 32767 bytes and defaults to 512. Typically, a packet size of 512 bytes is ideal for small messages. However, if you know in advance that your application will primarily be used to transfer large amounts of data (e.g, it performs bulk copy operations or manipulates large text or image fields), larger packet sizes may improve performance because they require fewer network read and write operations.

Note   To configure this setting, use the `Packet Size` parameter in the connection string.

ServerVersion

```
String version = Connection.ServerVersion;
```

Returns a string with version information for the data source. This property is accessible only after a connection has been opened. This is typically in the format MM.mm. rrrr. The first two digits are the major version, the next two digits are the minor version, and the last four digits are the release version. Some providers may append a product-specific version, as in "08.01.0001 R3"

For OLE DB providers, this maps to the OLE DB `DBPROP_DBMSVER` property. If the OLE DB provider doesn't support this property, an empty string is returned.

State

```
ConnectionState state = Connection.State;
```

Returns the current state of the connection, as a bitwise combination of one or more values from the `ConnectionState` property. Currently most providers simply return `ConnectionState.Open` or `ConnectionState.Closed` and don't use other values such as `ConnectionState.Fetching`.

Retrieving this property incurs some slight overhead, because it requires a call to the OLE DB `DBPROP_CONNECTIONSTATUS` property. It is therefore not a good technique to poll this value repeatedly in a tight loop while performing database operations.

WorkstationId [SQL Server only]

`String id = Connection.WorkstationId;`

Returns a string with the name of the connecting client. By default, this setting returns the computer name of the client computer.

Note   You can configure this setting with the `Workstation ID` parameter in the connection string. If you set this value (with any value other than an empty string), it takes precedence over the computer name.

Methods Reference

BeginTransaction

```
IDbTransaction = Connection.BeginTransaction();
IDbTransaction = Connection.BeginTransaction(IsolationLevel iso);
IDbTransaction = Connection.BeginTransaction(String transactionName);
IDbTransaction = Connection.BeginTransaction(IsolationLevel iso,
 String transactionName);
```

Returns a strongly typed provider-specific `IDbTransaction` object that governs a client-initiated transaction (such as `SqlTransaction` or `OleDbTransaction`). You enlist operations within the scope of this transaction by setting the `Command.Transaction` property with the `IDbTransaction` object. Finally, you must use one of the methods of the `IDbTransaction` object to either commit or roll back the complete transaction.

Parameters

`IsolationLevel iso`
> Sets the isolation level for the transaction. The higher the isolation level, the less the chance of data errors or discrepancies such as phantom reads, and the greater the negative effect on user concurrency. See Table 16-3 for valid `IsolationLevel` values.

`String transactionName`
> Assigns a name to the transaction. This is useful if you are creating nested transactions or save points and want to selectively roll back a nested transaction. See Chapter 31 for more information about the methods of the `Transaction` class.

Example

Here is an example that starts a transaction, enlists two commands, and commits the entire transaction:

```
string connectionString = "Data Source=localhost;" +
    "Initial Catalog=Northwind;Integrated Security=SSPI";

string SQL1 = "INSERT INTO Categories (CategoryName, Description) " +
              "VALUES ('Beverages', 'Soft drinks')";
string SQL2 = "UPDATE Categories SET Description ='Coffee and tea' " +
              "WHERE CategoryName='Beverages'";
```

Connection

```
SqlConnection con = new SqlConnection(connectionString);
SqlCommand cmdA = new SqlCommand(SQL1, con);
SqlCommand cmdB = new SqlCommand(SQL2, con);

int rowsAffected;

SqlTransaction tran = null;
try
{
    con.Open();

    // Start the transaction.
    tran = con.BeginTransaction();

    // Enlist the commands.
    cmdA.Transaction = tran;
    cmdB.Transaction = tran;

    // Execute the commands.
    rowsAffected = cmdA.ExecuteNonQuery();
    rowsAffected += cmdB.ExecuteNonQuery();

    // Commit the transaction.
    tran.Commit();
}
catch
{
    tran.Rollback();
}
finally
{
    con.Close();
}
```

Notes

A client-initiated transaction requires a round trip over the network to inform the data source to start, commit, or rollback the transaction. This introduces some latency and means that a client-initiated transaction can never perform quite as well as a stored procedure transaction. When using the BeginTransaction( ) method, follow the same guidelines you would when coding a transaction in SQL, and try to enclose the least amount of critical commands into a short, well-encapsulated transaction.

If possible, consider replacing client-initiated transactions with stored procedure transactions. Client-initiated transactions are subject to coding errors that can inadvertently leave the transaction running longer than intended, which has a negative effect on user concurrency.

ChangeDatabase

Connection.ChangeDatabase(String *databaseName*);

Changes the current database used by the connection. This database is then used for all subsequent commands. This method corresponds to SQL Server's USE command. In order to invoke this method, the connection must be open.

Parameter

String *databaseName*

> The name of the new database to attach to (e.g., "Northwind"). A provider-specific exception such as SqlException is thrown if this database doesn't exist in the data source.

Example

The following code opens a connection and executes two commands. The first command uses the Northwind database; the second uses the pubs database.

```
string connectionString = "Data Source=localhost;" +
  "Initial Catalog=Northwind;Integrated Security=SSPI";

string SQL1 = "UPDATE Categories SET Description='Coffee and tea' " +
              "WHERE CategoryName='Beverages'";
string SQL2 = "UPDATE Titles SET Title='The Busy Executive' " +
              "WHERE Title_Id='BU1032'";

SqlConnection con = new SqlConnection(connectionString);
SqlCommand cmdA = new SqlCommand(SQL1, con);
SqlCommand cmdB = new SqlCommand(SQL2, con);

int rowsAffected;

try
{
    con.Open();

    // Execute the first command using the Northwind database.
    rowsAffected = cmdA.ExecuteNonQuery();

    // Execute the second command using the pubs database.
    con.ChangeDatabase("pubs");
    rowsAffected += cmdB.ExecuteNonQuery();
}
finally
{
    con.Close();
}
```

Note   You can set the initial database for a connection using the Initial Catalog parameter in the connection string. Oracle databases don't support this setting or the ChangeDatabase( ) method.

Close

Connection.Close();

Closes the connection. This method also rolls back any pending transactions, if necessary, and ends by releasing the connection to the connection pool (assuming connection pooling is enabled). No exception is thrown if the connection is already closed.

Note	The Close( ) method is preferred over the Dispose( ) method because the Dispose( ) method destroys the connection and doesn't return it to the connection pool. To ensure that connections are closed properly, even in the case of an unhandled error, you should close them in the finally block of an exception handler.

CreateCommand

```
IDbCommand cmd = Connection.CreateCommand();
```

Returns a strongly typed provider-specific IDbCommand that can execute a SQL statement. This method is primarily useful when writing generic database access code that can work with more than one provider. By generating an IDbCommand object with CreateCommand( ), you don't need to create a provider-specific Command object instance.

Example

The following code uses the CreateCommand( ) method and is completely provider-agnostic (aside from the first two lines, which create the provider-specific Connection object):

```
string connectionString = "Data Source=localhost;" +
  "Initial Catalog=Northwind;Integrated Security=SSPI";
IDbConnection con = new SqlConnection(connectionString);

IDbCommand cmd = con.CreateCommand();
cmd.CommandText = "SELECT * FROM Categories";

try
{
    con.Open();
    IDataReader r = cmd.ExecuteReader();

    // (Read the results here.)

    r.Close();
}
finally
{
    con.Close();
}
```

EnlistDistributedTransaction

```
EnlistDistributedTransaction(ITransaction transaction);
```

If auto-enlistment is disabled, this method enlists the Connection in the specified active distributed transaction. If the transaction is committed or rolled back, all modifications made to the data source using the Connection are also committed or rolled back.

Parameters

transaction
    The existing transaction in which to enlist.

Example

The following example shows how to enlist a Connection in a distributed transaction and how to vote to commit or abort the transaction based on the success or failure of a Command executed against the data source:

```
// create the connection with auto-enlistment disabled
SqlConnection conn = new SqlConnection(
    "Data Source=localhost;Integrated Security=SSPI;" +
    "Initial Catalog=Northwind;Enlist=false;");

SqlCommand cmd = new SqlCommand();

//... define the command to update the data source

conn.Open();

// get the current COM+ DTC transaction,
// and enlist the connection if the transaction exists
ITransaction tran = (ITransaction)ContextUtil.Transaction;
if(tran != null)
    conn.EnlistDistributedTransaction(tran);

try
{
    // execute the command against the data source
    cmd.ExecuteNonQuery();
    // vote to commit after successful command
    ContextUtil.SetComplete();
}
catch (SqlException ex)
{
    // vote to roll back if an error occurs
    ContextUtil.SetAbort();
}
finally
{
    conn.Close();
}
```

Notes

Auto-enlistment is disabled for the Connection using the connection string parameter Enlist=false for a SqlConnection or using the connection string parameter OLE DB Services=-7 for an OleDbConnection.

The Connection must be open prior to calling EnlistDistributedTransaction(). An exception is raised if the Connection has already started a transaction with BeginTransaction(). If, however, a local transaction at the data source exists, it's rolled back without notification, and the Connection is enlisted in the distributed transaction.

Connection

GetOleDbSchemaTable [OLE DB only]

```
DataTable = Connection.GetOleDbSchemaTable(Guid schema,
    Object restrictions);
```

This method allows you to retrieve a schema table that includes information about the structure of your database. This can include information such as column data types, constraint, table, and view names, database owners, and so on. This method is provided only by the OLE DB provider, but SQL Server provides similar functionality through its information views, which can be queried directly (see Chapter 5 for more information and a specific example).

This method returns the requested schema information in a DataTable object.

Parameters

Guid *schema*

> This is a globally unique identifier (GUID) that indicates the schema rowset to return. Each type of schema table is uniquely identified accordingly to OLE DB conventions. You can either create a Guid structure manually with the required value, or you can retrieve a GUID from one of the public fields of the OleDbSchemaGuid class. For example, the field OleDbSchemaGuid.Tables returns the Guid required to retrieve the list of tables and views that are accessible to the current user.

Object *restrictions*

> An array that contains restriction values. These values are objects usually containing strings that filter the results based on any one of the returned columns. They are applied in the order that the columns are returned. Thus, the first restriction value applies to the first returned column, the second restriction value applies to the second column, and so on.

Example

The following example retrieves and displays a list of tables defined in the current database using the GetOleDbSchemaTable( ) method:

```
string connectionString = "Data Source=localhost;" +
    "Provider=SQLOLEDB;Initial Catalog=Northwind;" +
    "Integrated Security=SSPI";

OleDbConnection con = new OleDbConnection(connectionString);
DataTable schema;

try
{
    con.Open();
    schema = con.GetOleDbSchemaTable(OleDbSchemaGuid.Tables,
            new object[] {null, null, null, "TABLE"});
}
finally
{
    con.Close();
}

// Display the schema table.
foreach (DataRow row in schema.Rows)
```

```
    {
        Console.WriteLine(row["TABLE_TYPE"] + ": " +
                          row["TABLE_NAME"]);
    }
```

Notes

For more information on schema rowsets, you can refer to Appendix B of the *OLE DB Programmer's Reference* (see it online on the MSDN at *http://msdn.microsoft.com/library/en-us/oledb/htm/oledbabout_the_ole_db_documentation.asp*). You can also refer to the fields of the OleDbSchemaGuid class in the MSDN class library reference. Each field has a list of the corresponding restriction columns.

Know that your OLE DB provider won't necessarily support all OLE DB schema rowset values. Consult your provider-specific documentation for more information.

Open

```
Connection.Open();
```

Opens a connection using the settings that are specified in the ConnectionString property. If you use connection pooling, this method retrieves the first available connection from the pool (or creates a new connection if none is available and the maximum pool size has not been reached).

Example

When opening a connection, you should always use exception handling to ensure that the connection is closed properly, even if an error occurs. This pattern is shown here:

```
try
{
    con.Open();

    // (Executed commands here)
}
finally
{
    con.Close();
}
```

ReleaseObjectPool [OLE DB only]

```
Connection.ReleaseObjectPool();
```

Releases the resources required for the connection pool. You can call this method if you know that no connections will be reused within the amount of time OLE DB normally keeps the connections alive. However, these resources are freed only if every connection is closed and has timed out of the pool.

Note Using this method can compromise the effectiveness of connection pooling and so is rarely used. The resources required for the connection pool are fairly minimal, and it's rare for an application to be able to predict that connections won't be used for a certain interval of time.

Events Reference

InfoMessage

`{Sql |OleDb}InfoMessageEventHandler InfoMessage`

Fires when a warning or informational messages is sent from a data source. If the message corresponds to an error, an exception is raised instead of this event being fired. Information about the message is stored in a provider-specific `EventArgs` object, such as `OleDbInfoMessageEventArgs` or `SqlInfoMessageEventArgs`.

This event isn't used to receive specific error messages (in SQL Server, these are messages with a severity greater than 10) that will cause an exception to be thrown.

Event Argument

`{Sql|OleDb}InfoMessageEventArgs e`
   The `InfoMessageEventArgs` object is provider-specific. Typically, it includes information such as the error number and message text, as well as the additional provider-specific information. For example, SQL Server provides information about the database, stored procedure, and line number from which the message originated.

Example

Here's an example event handler for the `InfoMessage` event. It displays some of the retrieved information in a console window:

```
private void OnInfoMessage(object sender, SqlInfoMessageEventArgs args)
{
    foreach (SqlError err in args.Errors)
    {
        Console.WriteLine("The {0} has received a severity {1}, " +
        "state {2} error number {3} on line {4} of procedure {5} " +
        "on server {6}", err.Source, err.Class, err.State, err.Number,
        err.LineNumber, err.Procedure, err.Server);
    }
}
```

StateChange

`StateChangeEventHandler StateChange`

Fires when the connection is opened or closed. This event provides a `StateChangeEventArgs` object with information about the current and previous state as a value from the `System.Data.ConnectionState` enumeration.

Event Argument

`StateChangeEventArgs e`
   Provides two properties. `CurrentState` indicates the current state of the connection (which triggered the `StateChange` event), and `OriginalState` indicates the state of the `Connection` object before the event was fired.

Example

Here's an example method that handles the StateChange event and displays some information to a console window:

```
private void OnStateChange(object sender, StateChangeEventArgs e)
{
    Console.WriteLine("Original State = " + e.OriginalState);
    Console.WriteLine("Current State = " + e.CurrentState);
}
```

19

The Command Class

The Command class is provided by all standard ADO.NET providers, and it almost always encapsulates a SQL statement or a stored procedure call that can be executed against a data source. Command objects can retrieve rows; directly insert, delete, or modify records; calculate totals and averages; alter the structure of a database; or fill a disconnected DataSet when used with a DataAdapter.

At a bare minimum, every Command must reference a Connection object, which it uses to communicate with the data source and define a few key properties, such as CommandText (the stored procedure or embedded SQL command) and CommandType. The Command class is provided in several provider-specific varieties, including SqlCommand and OleDbCommand.

To execute a Command, you use one of the Command object methods, including ExecuteNonQuery( ), ExecuteReader( ), and ExecuteScalar( ), depending on the type of Command. Occasionally, a provider may define an additional method, such as the ExecuteXmlReader( ) method offered by the SQL Server provider, which retrieves query results as an XML document. Other than this discrepancy, the Command objects provided by the core set of ADO.NET providers are virtually identical.

Comments/Troubleshooting

All Command objects implement the IDbCommand interface from the System.Data namespace, and are thus quite similar. In all basic ADO.NET providers, the Command object encapsulates a SQL statement or stored procedure call.

Some Command classes for ADO.NET providers are shown in Table 19-1.

Table 19-1. Provider-specific Command classes

Class	Data source
System.Data.SqlClient.SqlCommand	SQL Server
System.Data.OleDb.OleDbCommand	An OLE DB provider
System.Data.Odbc.OdbcCommand	An ODBC driver
System.Data.OleDb.OracleCommand	Oracle

Properties Reference

CommandText

```
String commandText = Command.CommandText;
Command.CommandText = commandText;
```

Defines the action that's taken when this command executes. The meaning of the CommandText property depends on the value of the CommandType property. If CommandType is Text (the default), it's the text of a SQL statement (such as SELECT * FROM Customers). If CommandType is StoredProcedure, it's the name of the stored procedure that's executed. If CommandType is TableDirect, it's the name of a table that's returned or a comma-delimited list of tables that's joined and returned.

Example

The following example defines a Command and sets the CommandText with a SQL INSERT statement. When executed, this Command creates a new row.

```
string connectionString = "Data Source=localhost;" +
    "Initial Catalog=Northwind;Integrated Security=SSPI";

string sQL = "INSERT INTO Categories (CategoryName, Description) " +
            "VALUES ('Beverages', 'Soft drinks')";

SqlConnection con = new SqlConnection(connectionString);
SqlCommand cmd = new SqlCommand();

cmd.Connection = con;
cmd.CommandText = sQL;

int rowsAffected;
try
{
    con.Open();

    // Execute the command.
    rowsAffected = cmd.ExecuteNonQuery();
}
finally
{
    con.Close();
}
```

Notes

You can set two properties of the Command object—the linked Connection and the CommandText—using an overloaded constructor when you create the Command:

```
SqlCommand cmd = new SqlCommand(commandText, con);
```

This is usually the easiest approach to setting these properties. You can then reuse the Command to perform a different task with the same data source by modifying the CommandText property.

Some providers support batch queries, in which case you can execute multiple commands at once and even return multiple result sets by separating each command with a semicolon:

```
cmd.CommandText = "SELECT * FROM Products;SELECT * FROM Orders";
```

For some exotic providers (those to a data source other than a database), the CommandText may not contain a SQL statement; in fact, it can contain something entirely different and proprietary. The only guarantee is that the CommandText property must contain a string.

CommandTimeout

```
Int32 timeout = Command.CommandTimeout;
Command.CommandTimeout = timeout;
```

Configures the time in seconds that a command will wait once you execute it. If the command hasn't completed once the timeout is reached, the attempt is aborted, and a provider-specific exception (such as SqlException or OleDbException) is thrown.

The default timeout is 30 seconds. You can set the timeout to 0 to specify an infinite timeout, but this isn't recommended because it can stall your application indefinitely. You can call the Command.Cancel() method from a separate thread to halt an in-progress command.

Example

The following code fragment defines a timeout of 15 seconds:

```
SqlCommand cmd = new SqlCommand(commandText, con);
cmd.CommandTimeout = 15;

try
{
    con.Open();
    // (Now execute the command)

}
catch (SqlException err)
{
    // This could indicate a timeout after 15 seconds.
}
finally
{
    con.Close();
}
```

CommandType

```
CommandType commandType = Command.CommandType;
Command.CommandType = commandType;
```

Indicates how the CommandText property should be interpreted, using the values from the System.Data.CommandType enumeration. Table 19-2 lists possible values.

Table 19-2. CommandType values

Value	Description
StoredProcedure	CommandText holds the name of the stored procedure that will be invoked. Input and output parameters for the stored procedure are contained in the Command.Parameters collection.
TableDirect	CommandText holds the name of the table that will be queried. All the columns and rows will be retrieved from this table when the command is executed. You can also use a comma-delimited list of tables that will be automatically joined together.
Text	CommandText holds the full text of the SQL command. The command may be a direct SQL statement, a stored procedure call with inline parameters, or a parameterized query, in which case the Command.Parameters collection holds the input and output parameters.

Example

The following code snippet configures a Command object to call a stored procedure called GetCustomers. The CommandText and Connection properties are set using a Command constructor.

```
SqlCommand cmd = new SqlCommand("GetCustomers", con);
cmd.CommandText = CommandType.StoredProcedure;
```

Note   TableDirect isn't supported by all providers and isn't suitable for an enterprise-level application because it returns all the information from all the rows of a table. This wastes bandwidth and server time retrieving information that may not be important. A much better approach is to selectively limit the rows you return with a WHERE clause and the columns of information you need. Ideally, database access should be performed through a stored procedure, which can be precompiled and optimized on the database server.

Connection

```
IDbConnection con = Command.Connection;
Command.Connection = con;
```

Identifies the connection that the Connection uses to execute the Command.

Note   You can't modify this property if the Command is enlisted in a client-initiated transaction that hasn't yet been committed or rolled back. (A command is enlisted in a client-initiated transaction by setting its Transaction property.)

Transaction

```
IDbTransaction tran = Command.Transaction;
Command.Transaction = tran;
```

Allows you to enlist the command in a client-initiated transaction. For example, if you set the Transaction property of three Command objects with the same Transaction object, and then invoke these commands, they all execute in the same transaction. When you commit or roll back the transaction, the work performed by all three Command objects are committed or rolled back as a unit.

The actual Transaction object is a provider-specific object that implements IDbTransaction and is created using the Connection.BeginTransaction( ) method.

Example

The following example creates two OleDbCommand objects and places them in the same client-initiated transaction using the Transaction property. Both commands are then executed, but their changes are rolled back immediately afterward.

```
string connectionString = "Data Source=localhost;Provider=SQLOLEDB;" +
    "Initial Catalog=Northwind;Integrated Security=SSPI ";

string SQL1 = "INSERT INTO Categories (CategoryName, Description) " +
              "VALUES ('Beverages', 'Soft drinks')";
string SQL2 = "UPDATE Categories SET Description ='Coffee and tea' " +
              "WHERE CategoryName='Beverages'";

OleDbConnection con = new OleDbConnection(connectionString);
OleDbCommand cmdA = new OleDbCommand(SQL1, con);
OleDbCommand cmdB = new OleDbCommand(SQL2, con);

con.Open();

// Start the transaction.
OleDbTransaction tran = con.BeginTransaction();

// Enlist the commands.
cmdA.Transaction = tran;
cmdB.Transaction = tran;

// Execute the commands.
cmdA.ExecuteNonQuery();
cmdB.ExecuteNonQuery();

// Roll back the transaction (cancelling the changes).
tran.Rollback();
con.Close();
```

Note   You will receive an exception if you attempt to execute a Command with a Transaction object created for a different Connection.

UpdatedRowSource

```
UpdateRowSource rowSource = Command.UpdateRowSource;
Command.UpdateRowSource = rowSource;
```

When this Command is used to commit changes with a DataAdapter, the UpdateRowSource property defines how the results from the Command will be applied to the original DataRow. This is primarily useful if your Command is invoking a stored procedure, and the stored procedure returns some type of generated information (such as a new value for a unique identifier column).

To specify how this returned information will be applied, use one of the values from the UpdateRowSource enumeration, as shown in Table 19-3.

Table 19-3. CommandType values

Value	Description
None	All output parameters and any returned rows are ignored.
FirstReturnedRecord	The column values from the first returned record are applied to the source DataRow. In other words, the stored procedure uses a SELECT statement to return the changed row after performing the update.
Parameters	The information from the output parameters is applied to the source DataRow, based on the Parameter.SourceColumn property.
Both	Information from the output parameters and the first returned record is applied to the source DataRow. This is the default. Note that it is uncommon for a stored procedure to return both types of information; the Both value simply ensures that the source information is updated no matter which approach you use.

Example

The following code snippet shows a Command that calls a CategoryAdd stored procedure when the DataAdapter inserts a new category record. This stored procedure returns an output parameter with the new unique CategoryID, which the Command maps to the source DataRow. For a full example of this technique, refer to Chapter 15.

```
// Create the command.
SqlCommand cmdInsert = new SqlCommand("CategoryAdd", con);
cmdInsert.CommandType = CommandType.StoredProcedure;
cmdInsert.UpdatedRowSource = UpdateRowSource.OutputParameters;

SqlParameter param;

// Add an input parameter to the command.
param = cmdInsert.Parameters.Add("@CategoryName", SqlDbType.NVarChar, 15);
param.SourceColumn = "CategoryName";
param.SourceVersion = DataRowVersion.Current;

// Add an output parameter to the command. The value returned by this
// parameter will be applied to the source DataRow once the insertion is
// complete.
param = cmdInsert.Parameters.Add("@CategoryID", SqlDbType.Int);
param.SourceColumn = "CategoryID";
```

```
param.SourceVersion = DataRowVersion.Original;
param.Direction = ParameterDirection.Output;

// Assign the command to the DataAdapter.
adapter.InsertCommand = cmdInsert;
```

Notes

You can also use this technique to map the information from a stored procedure return value. Remember, the return value is represented by a Parameter object with a Direction of ParameterDirection.ReturnValue. If you set the Command.UpdateRowSource property to Both or Parameters, this value updates the DataRow.

The UpdateRowSource property is almost always used with a stored procedure. Ordinary SQL statements simply returns the number of affected rows, not the new row. Similarly, parameterized queries use only input parameters, not output parameters. To use the UpdateRowSource property effectively, you must add stored procedure code to return the updated information you need.

Collections Reference

Parameters

```
ParameterCollection col = Command.Parameters;
```

If the Command contains a parameterized query or a stored procedure call, the Parameters collection will contain a group of Parameter objects, one for each input and output parameter. In addition, if the stored procedure uses a return value, this should be the first Parameter object in the collection. Parameter objects are described in Chapter 20.

Because the Parameter object is provider-specific, the Parameters collection is also provider-specific and implements IDataParameterCollection. The IDataParameterCollection defines a small set of members, including a default indexer that allows you to retrieve Parameter objects by their assigned names.

Example

The provider-specific versions of the Parameters collection (such as SqlParameterCollection and OleDbParameterCollection) typically include several overloaded versions of the Add( ) method, which allow you to create and insert a Parameter object in one step.

Here's how to create and set a SqlParameter using the SqlParameter constructor:

```
SqlParameter param = new SqlParameter("@Description", SqlDbType.VarChar,
                                      88, "Description");
param.Value = "This is the description";

cmd.Add(param);
```

Here's how to create and set the same `SqlParameter` using the `SqlParameterCollection`. `Add( )` method:

```
SqlParameter param = cmd.Add("@Description", SqlDbType.VarChar,
                             88, "Description");

param.Value = "This is the description";
```

Methods Reference

Cancel

`Cancel();`

Halts a `Command` that is currently executing. If the `Command` isn't executing, nothing happens. If the `Command` is in the middle of fetching results with a `DataReader`, the `DataReader` is closed. If the `Command` is in the middle of performing another time-consuming operation, an attempt is made to stop the operation. However, in this case, the `Cancel( )` method must be called from another thread because the main thread will be blocked, waiting for the operation to complete.

CreateParameter

`IDbDataParameter param = Command.CreateParameter();`

Returns a strongly typed provider-specific `IDbDataParameter` object. This method is primarily useful if you are writing generic code because it doesn't force you to explicitly differentiate your code based on the type of `Parameter` object. However, this approach can be restrictive because it prevents you from using data types that may be specific to your data source (you must use the closest type from the `System.Data.DbType` enumeration instead). Also, unlike the `Parameter` object constructors and the `ParameterCollection.Add()` method, the `CreateParameter( )` method doesn't accept any parameters, which means that you need to specify the name, data type, length, and so on, using separate property set statements.

Example

The following code snippet uses the `CreateParameter( )` method to generically create a `Parameter` object and then configures it accordingly:

```
IDbDataParameter param = cmd.CreateParameter();
param.Name = "@Description";
param.DbType = DbType.VarWChar;
param.Size = 88;
param.Value = "This is the description";

cmd.Add(param);
```

ExecuteNonQuery

```
int rowsAffected = Command.ExecuteNonQuery();
```

Executes a nonquery command (a command that doesn't return a set of rows). You can use ExecuteNonQuery() to modify data with the UPDATE, INSERT, or DELETE statements, in which case it returns the number of affected rows. You can also use the ExecuteNonQuery() method with other SQL statements, such as DDL commands that modify the structure of database tables. In this case, the ExecuteNonQuery() command returns −1.

Example

The following example executes an UPDATE command and displays the number of affected rows in a console window:

```
string cQL = "UPDATE Categories SET CategoryName='Beverages'" +
             "WHERE CategoryID=1";

SqlCommand cmd = new SqlCommand(SQL, con);

// Execute the command.
con.Open();
int rowsAffected = cmd.ExecuteNonQuery();
con.Close();

// Display the result of the operation.
Console.WriteLine(rowsAffected.ToString() + " row(s) affected");
```

ExecuteReader

```
IDataReader r = Command.ExecuteReader();
IDataReader r = Command.ExecuteReader(CommandBehavior cb);
```

Executes a query command, typically a SELECT statement or a stored procedure that uses a SELECT statement. The command returns a strongly typed provider-specific DataReader object (implementing IDataReader), which must be used to iterate through the results.

Parameter

CommandBehavior cb

> The CommandBehavior parameter can specify additional options detailing how the provider should handle the request. These options are indicated using a bitwise combination of values from the System.Data.CommandBehavior enumeration, as described in Table 19-4.

Table 19-4. CommandBehavior values

Value	Description
CloseConnection	When the DataReader returned by this method is closed, the underlying Connection object is also closed automatically.
Default	Specifies the default behavior. Using this value is equivalent to calling ExecuteReader() without supplying any CommandBehavior values.
KeyInfo	The query returns column and primary key information. When you use this option, the SQL Server provider automatically appends a FOR BROWSE clause to the statement.

Table 19-4. CommandBehavior values (continued)

Value	Description
SchemaOnly	The query returns column information only.
SequentialAccess	Instead of loading an entire row into memory each time you call the DataReader. Read( ) method, the information is read as a stream (and you can use DataReader. GetBytes( ) to access it). As a side effect, columns must be accessed in the order they are retrieved in the query, and you can't reread a column once you have read past its location.
	This value is typically used when retrieving large binary values because it lowers the memory footprint and can increase performance. See Chapter 5 for a complete example.
SingleResult	The query doesn't return more than one result set. Depending on the database, this information can theoretically allow the provider to optimize how it accesses the database.
SingleRow	The query returns a single row or multiple result sets that each contain a single row. Depending on the database, this information can theoretically allow the provider to optimize how it accesses the database. For example, when you specify SingleRow with the OLE DB provider, it uses the OLE DB IRow interface, if possible, instead of the IRowset interface.

Example

The following code snippet uses ExecuteReader( ) to retrieve a list of customers:

```
string SQL = "SELECT * FROM Customers";

SqlCommand cmd = new SqlCommand(SQL, con);
SqlDataReader r;

con.Open();
r = cmd.ExecuteReader();

// Iterate over the results.
while (r.Read())
{
    lstNames.Items.Add(r["ContactName"]);
}

con.Close();
```

Note   Some providers don't support the values of the CommandBehavior enumeration. In this case, they may ignore the values or throw a NotSupportedException.

ExecuteScalar

```
object result = Command.ExecuteScalar();
```

Executes a SQL command and returns the first value of the first row from the result set. One common use of this method is to return the results of an aggregate SQL function.

Example

Following is an example that uses the ExecuteScalar( ) method with the SQL aggregate function COUNT to determine how many rows match a specific criteria.

```
string SQL = "SELECT COUNT(*) FROM Orders WHERE " +
             "OrderDate >= '1996-01-01' AND OrderDate < '1997-01-01'";

SqlCommand cmd = new SqlCommand(SQL, con);

con.Open();
int result = (int)cmd.ExecuteScalar();
con.Close();

// Display the result of the operation.
Console.WriteLine(result.ToString() + " rows in 1996");
```

ExecuteXmlReader [SQL Server only]

```
XmlReader = Command.ExecuteXmlReader();
```

Executes a query command, typically a SELECT statement or a stored procedure that uses a SELECT statement. The command returns an XmlReader object, which must be used to iterate through the results.

In order for this method to work successfully, your query must return an XML document from the data source. In other words, your query should include the SQL Server FOR XML clause.

 The SQL Server 2000 XML extensions are described in Chapter 17, which also has information about the SQLXML provider.

Example

The following example retrieves category records as an XML document in which each row is a separate element and all column values are represented by element attributes. The code iterates through the results and prints out the returned information.

```
string SQL = "SELECT * FROM Categories FOR XML AUTO";

SqlCommand com = new SqlCommand(SQL, con);

con.Open();
XmlReader reader = com.ExecuteXmlReader();

while (reader.Read())
{
    Console.WriteLine("Element: " + reader.Name);

    // Print all column values.
    if (reader.HasAttributes)
    {
        for (int i = 0; i < reader.AttributeCount; i++)
        {
            reader.MoveToAttribute(i);
            Console.Write("\t");
            Console.Write(reader.Name + ": ");
            Console.WriteLine(reader.Value);
        }
```

```
            // Move back to the element node.
        reader.MoveToElement();
    }
}

reader.Close();
con.Close();
```

Note   As with the DataReader, you should read results as quickly as possible, and you must call XmlReader.Close() before attempting to use the Connection for another task.

Prepare

```
Command.Prepare();
```

Calling the Prepare() method creates a prepared version of a command in the data source, leading to improved performance if you want to reuse it multiple times with different values. However, some providers will not support this method, and others will not demonstrate any performance increase. Typically, SQL Server Version 6.5 or earlier may demonstrate an improvement, while SQL Server 7 databases perform all the necessary optimization automatically.

If you wish to use the Prepare() method, call it only after you have defined the Command and added all its parameters.

Example

The following example uses the Prepare() method before invoking a parameterized UPDATE command:

```
string SQL = "UPDATE Categories SET CategoryName=@CategoryName " +
            "WHERE CategoryID=@CategoryID";

SqlCommand cmd = new SqlCommand(SQL, con);

SqlParameter param;
param = cmd.Parameters.Add("@CategoryName", SqlDbType.NVarChar, 15);
param.Value = "Beverages";

param = cmd.Parameters.Add("@CategoryID", SqlDbType.Int);
param.Value = 1;

// Prepare and execute the command.
con.Open();
cmd.Prepare();
int rowsAffected = cmd.ExecuteNonQuery();
con.Close();
```

Notes

Because Prepare() requires an extra trip to the data source (to compile the initial command), it can actually reduce performance. It's recommended that you use this method only if you have tested it and confirmed it achieves a performance increase under your operating conditions.

When using Prepare( ), make sure each Parameter object has the correct value set for its Parameter.Size properties. Otherwise, data may be truncated, and no error will occur to inform you of the problem.

ResetCommandTimeout

```
Command.ResetCommandTimeout();
```

Resets the CommandTimeout property to the default value, which is usually 30 seconds. This method isn't defined by the IDbCommand interface and as such, isn't guaranteed to be supported by all ADO.NET providers.

20

The Parameter Class

The Parameter class works with the Command class to execute parameterized commands or call stored procedures. Every Command object exposes a Parameters collection. In this collection, there is one Parameter object for every input and output parameter, and an additional Parameter object to represent a return value, if required.

The Parameter object can also define a mapping between parameters and columns in a DataSet. This allows a column value to be submitted (copied from the DataSet into an input parameter) and refreshed (copied from an output parameter or return value into the DataSet) automatically when using the Update( ) method of the DataAdapter.

Comments/Troubleshooting

All Parameter objects implement the IDbDataParameter and IDataParameter interfaces from the System.Data namespace, and are thus quite similar. Because IDbDataParameter extends IDataParameter, you can use the IDataParameter to access all functionality when writing provider-agnostic data access code.

Provider-specific Parameter objects typically add a property that defines a database-specific data type for the parameter. Some Parameter classes for ADO.NET providers are shown in Table 20-1.

Table 20-1. Provider-specific Parameter classes

Class	Data source
System.Data.SqlClient.SqlParameter	SQL Server
System.Data.OleDb.OleDbParameter	An OLE DB provider
System.Data.Odbc.OdbcParameter	An ODBC driver
System.Data.OleDb.OracleParameter	Oracle

Properties Reference

DbType

```
DbType dataType = Parameter.DbType;
Parameter.DbType = dataType;
```

Specifies the data type of the parameter, using the DbType enumeration in the System. Data namespace. This enumeration includes values for common data types, such as strings and numbers of various sizes. If this property is set, the value of the Parameter is converted to this type before it is passed to the data source. If the type isn't specified, ADO.NET attempts to infer the data source type by looking at the .NET type.

Example

The following code snippet sets the Parameter.DbType property:

```
param.DbType = DbType.Int32;
```

Note   Every Parameter class includes a DbType property and a provider-specific data type property such as SqlDbType and OleDbType. These two properties are linked. When you set the provider-specific type, the DbType is adjusted to use a compatible type and vice versa. Usually, you will set this provider-specific type, but you may want to use the DbType when writing generic ADO.NET code.

Direction

```
ParameterDirection pd = Parameter.Direction;
Parameter.Direction = pd;
```

Specifies whether the parameter is input-only, output-only, bidirectional, or a return value. You set the Direction property using a value from the ParameterDirection enumeration, as shown in Table 20-2.

Table 20-2. ParameterDirection values

Value	Description
Input	The parameter value is submitted to the parameterized command or stored procedure.
Output	The parameter value is returned from the parameterized command or stored procedure.
InputOutput	The parameter can send information to a stored procedure and parameterized command and retrieve the new value if it is modified.
ReturnValue	The parameter represents a return value from a stored procedure or built-in function.

Note   If a value isn't returned for an output parameter or return value, the Value of the corresponding Parameter is null. With the OLE DB provider, make sure you add a parameter for the return value (if needed) before other parameters.

IsNullable

```
Boolean isNullable = Parameter.IsNulllable;
Parameter.IsNullable = isNullable;
```

This Boolean parameter indicates whether null values are accepted for the Parameter. Value property. The default is false.

Note   If your parameter accepts null values, you can test for them using the System.DBNull class. In this case, DBNull.Value equals Parameter.Value.

Offset [SQL Server only]

```
Int32 offset = Parameter.Offset;
Parameter.Offset = offset;
```

Sets an offset to use for the Value property, provided the Value property contains a binary or string type. For example, if you set the Offset to 5, the Parameter submits the content from the Value property, starting with the sixth character (in the case of a string) or sixth byte (in the case of binary data). The default is 0 (or no offset).

Note   The Offset property is rarely used, but it lets you submit a portion of a large byte array (for example, when dealing with image processing).

OleDbType [OLE DB only]

```
OleDbType oleDbType = Parameter.OleDbType
Parameter.OleDbType = OleDbType
```

Specifies the OLE DB data type of the parameter, using the OleDbType enumeration in the System.Data.OleDb namespace. The value of the Parameter is converted into this type before it is passed to the data source. The default is a DbType.VarWChar, a variable length string of Unicode characters.

Example

The following code snippet sets the Parameter.OleDbType property and then examines the linked DbType. In this case, the linked DbType value is DbType.Int32.

```
param.OleDbType = OleDbType.Integer;
Console.WriteLine(param.DbType.ToString());
```

Notes

Every OleDbParameter class includes a. DbType property and a provider-specific OleDbType property. These two properties are linked. When you set the OleDbType property, the DbType is adjusted to use a compatible type and vice versa.

For more information about valid OLE DB data types and their mappings to .NET framework types, see Appendix A.

ParameterName

```
string parameterName = Parameter.ParameterName;
Parameter.ParameterName = parameterName;
```

Names the parameter with a string. When calling a stored procedure, you must make sure that the ParameterName property exactly matches the parameter name defined in the data source. The ParameterName is also used as an indexer for the ParameterCollection (as is the ordinal position in the collection) and can retrieve Parameter objects, check if they exist in the collection, or remove them.

Example

The following code snippet creates a parameter named @Description, and then retrieves it from the collection by name.

```
cmd.Parameters.Add("@Description", SqlDbType.VarChar, 88);
SqlParameter param = cmd.Parameters["@Description"];
```

Notes

The ParameterName can also insert values into parameterized commands used with the SQL Server provider. However, the name doesn't play an important role when creating parameterized commands with the OLE DB provider. With the OLE DB provider, all parameters are identified with question-mark placeholders, and the order alone determines which parameters to substitute. For a full example of both SQL Server and OLE DB parameterized commands, refer to Chapter 4.

Parameter names typically begin with the @ character (as in @CustomerID). This is a common convention, but it isn't necessary.

Precision

```
byte precision = Parameter.Precision;
Parameter.Precision = precision;
```

Determines the maximum number of digits that represents the Value property, assuming it is a numeric type. For example, the number 1234.56 has a precision of 6. The default precision is 0, which indicates no maximum.

Note   You don't need to set the Precision property. The primary reason to set Precision is to ensure you don't accidentally submit a number that has a higher precision than allowed by the data source. In SQL Server, you can set a precision for all decimal data types when creating a table.

Scale

```
byte scale = Parameter.Scale;
Parameter.Scale = scale;
```

Determines the maximum number of digits to the right of the decimal in the Value property, assuming it is a numeric type. For example, the number 1234.56 has a scale of 2. The default scale is 0, which indicates no maximum.

Note   You don't need to set the Scale property. The primary reason to set Scale is to ensure you don't accidentally submit a number that has a higher scale than allowed by the data source. In SQL Server, you can set the scale for all decimal data types when creating a table.

Size

```
int size = Parameter.Size;
Parameter.Size = size;
```

Determines the maximum size of the Value property for a binary or string parameter. For fixed-width data types, the Size property is ignored. If not set, the actual size of the specified parameter value is used

In the case of a Unicode string, the Size corresponds to a number of characters, not including the final null termination. In the case of binary data or an ANSI string, the Size refers to a number of bytes. If you set the Size property to a value smaller than the parameter data, the Value is truncated.

SourceColumn

```
string columnName = Parameter.SourceColumn;
Parameter.SourceColumn = columnName;
```

Sets the name of the linked column from the DataSet. This property is important when using the DataAdapter to apply updates. In the case of an input parameter, the value from the source column in the DataSet is copied to the parameter value before the command is executed. In the case of an output parameter, the parameter value is copied to the DataSet column after the command is executed, assuming the Command. UpdateRowSource property allows it.

Example

The following code defines a linked @CategoryID output parameter. After the command is executed, the Value from the parameter is copied into the CategoryID column in the DataSet.

```
param = cmdInsert.Parameters.Add("@CategoryID", SqlDbType.Int);
param.SourceColumn = "CategoryID";
param.Direction = ParameterDirection.Output;
```

Note   When using the SourceColumn property with an input parameter, the SourceVersion property must indicate the version of the column data you want to use. Its default is DataRowVersion.Current.

SourceVersion

```
DataRowVersion version = Parameter.SourceVersion;
Parameter.SourceVersion = version;
```

Sets the DataRowVersion of the data that is used from the linked column in the DataSet. This property is used when the DataAdapter applies an update. In the case of an input parameter, the value from the source column in the DataSet is copied to the parameter value before the command is executed. The SourceVersion property doesn't apply to output or return-value parameters.

The list of valid DataRowVersion values is shown in Table 20-3. Typically, you use the Current value to apply a new change (for example, in the SET statement of a SQL

UPDATE command), and the Original value to find a specific row (for example, in the WHERE clause of a SQL command).

Table 20-3. DataRowVersion values

Value	Description
Current	Represents the current value. This may differ from the original value if any changes have been made to the row.
Original	Represents the value retrieved from the data source or the value that was committed the last time changes were applied.
Proposed	Represents an edited value that hasn't yet been committed. Rarely used with a parameter.

Example

The following code defines a linked @CategoryName input parameter. Before the command is executed, the current value from the CategoryName field is copied to the Parameter.Value property.

```
param = cmdInsert.Parameters.Add("@CategoryName", SqlDbType.NVarChar, 15);
param.SourceColumn = "CategoryName";

// The following line could be omitted, as this is the default.
param.SourceVersion = DataRowVersion.Current;
```

SqlDbType [SQL Server only]

```
SqlDbType dataType = Parameter.SqlDbType;
Parameter.SqlDbType = dataType;
```

Specifies the SQL Server data type of the parameter, using the SqlDbType enumeration in the System.Data namespace. If this property is set, the value of the Parameter is converted to this type before it's passed to the data source. The default is a SqlDbType.NVarChar, a variable-length string of Unicode characters.

Example

The following code snippet sets the Parameter.SqlDbType property and then examines the linked DbType. In this case, the linked DbType value is DbType.Int32.

```
param.SqlDbType = SqlDbType.Int;
Console.WriteLine(param.DbType.ToString());
```

Notes

Every SqlParameter class includes a DbType property and a provider-specific SqlDbType property. These two properties are linked. When you set the SqlDbType property, the DbType uses a compatible type and vice versa.

For more information about valid SQL Server data types, and their mappings to .NET framework types, see Appendix A.

Value

```
Object value = Parameter.Value;
Parameter.Value = value;
```

This is the actual content stored in the parameter. For output parameters, this is the information returned after the command is complete. For input parameters, this is the value that is sent to the data source when the command is executed.

The Value is stored as a loosely typed object, so it can accommodate any data type. When the command is executed, all input parameter values are converted to the appropriate type by examining the provider-specific type property (such as SqlDbType or OleDbType). This conversion can result in an error, particularly if the type doesn't support the IConvertible interface.

Example

The following code snippet creates a new parameter (as a variable-length Unicode string) and then sets the Value property using the .NET string type:

```
SqlParameter param;
param = new SqlParameter("@Description", SqlDbType.VarChar, 88);
param.Value = "This is the description";
```

Note   If you wish to specify a null value for a parameter, you must set the Parameter.Value property using the DBNull.Value property, which represents a null value. You can't set it directly to a null reference, or an error will occur.

21

The DataReader Class

The DataReader object represents a read-only, forward-only stream of data, which is ideal for quickly retrieving query results. The DataReader is useful if you don't need the full support for versioning and change tracking provided by the DataSet. Best of all, because the DataReader loads only a single row into memory at a time, it has a small in-memory footprint.

You can't create a DataReader directly. Instead, you must use the ExecuteReader( ) method of a Command object that returns a DataReader. Chapter 5 presents complete examples that show how to use the DataReader in various scenarios.

Comments/Troubleshooting

Most ADO.NET providers include a strongly typed DataReader. Every DataReader implements two interfaces: IDataReader (which defines the core reader functionality) and IDataRecord (which allows you to access the current record values). Because IDataReader extends IDataRecord, you can use the IDataReader to access all the IDataRecord and IDataReader functionality when writing provider-agnostic data access code.

Strongly typed DataReader objects typically add type-safe methods that allow you to retrieve column values as database-specific data types. Some DataReader classes for ADO.NET providers are shown in Table 21-1.

Table 21-1. Provider-specific DataReader classes

Class	Data source
System.Data.SqlClient.SqlDataReader	SQL Server
System.Data.OleDb.OleDbDataReader	An OLE DB provider

Table 21-1. Provider-specific DataReader classes (continued)

Class	Data source
System.Data.Odbc.OdbcDataReader	An ODBC driver
System.Data.OleDb.OracleDataReader	Oracle

Properties Reference

Depth

```
int32 depth = DataReader.Depth;
```

Indicates the depth of nesting for the current row. This is 0 by default. Many providers, including the SQL Server provider, always return 0 because they don't support nesting.

One case in which you might use nesting is when using the MSDataShape OLE DB provider to create a hierarchical result set, which use chapters (OLE DB type DBTYPE_HCHAPTER, ADO type adChapter). When returning a result set that includes chapters, the nested recordset is exposed as a column inside the first recordset.

Example

The following code shows a complete example that demonstrates nesting with a shaped record set. The custReader.Depth property returns 0; the ordReader.Depth property returns 1.

```
string connectionString = "Provider=MSDataShape;Data Provider=SQLOLEDB;" +
    "Data Source=localhost;Integrated Security=SSPI;" +
    "Initial Catalog=northwind";

string SQL = "SHAPE {SELECT CustomerID, CompanyName FROM Customers} " +
    "APPEND ({SELECT CustomerID, OrderID FROM Orders} AS CustomerOrders " +
    "RELATE CustomerID TO CustomerID)";

OleDbConnection con = new OleDbConnection(connectionString);
OleDbCommand cmd = new OleDbCommand(SQL, con);

con.Open();

OleDbDataReader custReader = cmd.ExecuteReader();
OleDbDataReader ordReader;

while (custReader.Read())
{
    Console.WriteLine("Orders for " + custReader.GetString(1));
    Console.WriteLine("Depth custReader: " + custReader.Depth.ToString());
    ordReader = (OleDbDataReader)custReader.GetValue(2);
    Console.WriteLine("Depth ordReader: " + ordReader.Depth.ToString());

    while (ordReader.Read())
    {
        Console.WriteLine(ordReader.Depth);
    }
}
```

DataReader

```
        ordReader.Close();
    }

    custReader.Close();
    con.Close();
```

Note   For more information on shaped recordsets and ADO.NET, you may
                want to refer to Microsoft Knowledge Base article Q308045 (see *http://
                support.microsoft.com*).

FieldCount

```
Int32 fieldCount = DataReader.FieldCount;
```

Returns the number of columns in the current row. If you aren't currently positioned
on a valid row, the `FieldCount` returns 0.

Example

The following code displays the number of rows, which is 2, because the query
includes only two columns:

```
string SQL = "SELECT CustomerID, ContactTitle FROM Customers";

SqlCommand cmd = new SqlCommand(SQL, con);
SqlDataReader r;

con.Open();
r = cmd.ExecuteReader();
r.Read();

Console.WriteLine(r.FieldCount.ToString() + " rows were returned.");

con.Close();
```

IsClosed

```
bool isClosed = DataReader.IsClosed;
```

Returns true if the `DataReader` has been closed, either by calling the `DataReader.Close( )`
method or calling `Close( )` on the underlying connection.

Note   `RecordsAffected` and `IsClosed` are the only two properties that can
                safely be called if the `DataReader` is closed.

HasRows

```
bool hasRows = DataReader.HasRows
```

Returns true if the `DataReader` has at least one row. This convenience feature (which
was added in the .NET Framework 1.1) is provided so you can quickly tell if there is a
result set without advancing to the first row. This is primarily useful when you need to
decide whether or not to pass the `DataReader` to another function or component that
will process it.

Item

```
object value = DataReader[int columnOrdinal];
object value = DataReader[string columnName];
```

The Item property is also the default indexer for the DataReader. It allows you to retrieve a value from any field by specifying the column name or column ordinal. This value is returned as an object and is stored in the native provider-specific format. You can cast this object to the desired type.

Example

Here is an example of how to retrieve a value from the OrderPrice field and convert it to the .NET decimal type:

```
decimal price = (decimal)r["OrderPrice"];
```

You can also retrieve the same information using a column ordinal. This is a zero-based number that corresponds to the order in which fields were retrieved. Assuming the OrderPrice field is the second field in the result set, use the following equivalent syntax:

```
decimal price = (decimal)r[1];
```

RecordsAffected

```
Int32 numRecords = DataReader.RecordsAffected;
```

Returns the number of rows that are changed, inserted, or deleted. It returns 0 if no rows are affected or −1 if the command simply corresponds to a SQL SELECT statement. This property is available only after all rows are read, and the DataReader is closed.

Note   RecordsAffected and IsClosed are the only two properties that can be retrieved safely if the DataReader is closed.

Methods Reference

Close

```
DataReader.Close();
```

Closes the DataReader, but leaves the connection open. You must call Close() before you can use the connection for another command. However, if you want to close the DataReader and the connection, simply call the Connection.Close() method instead.

Example

The following code shows how to close a DataReader and reuse the connection for another task:

```
con.Open();

SqlDataReader r = cmdA.ExecuteReader();
```

```
// (Process rows here.)

r.Close();

// Reuse the open connection for another query.
r = cmdB.ExecuteReader();

con.Close();
```

Get<TypeName>

```
Object value = DataReader.GetTypeName(Int32 columnOrdinal);
```

Every DataReader has a set of strongly typed accessors that allow you to retrieve column values without performing any sort of conversion, potentially improving performance. For example, you can use the GetInt32( ) method to retrieve a column value that holds a 32-bit integer. This call succeeds only if the column contains a 32-bit integer; otherwise, an exception occurs.

Many providers define additional accessor methods that are customized to use database-specific data types. You can recognize these because they will include .the provider abbreviation. For example, the SQL Server uses the abbreviation Sql and provides strongly typed accessors such as GetSqlGuid( ), GetSqlMoney( ), and GetSqlDateTime( ). These methods return values using the native SQL data types defined in the System.Data.SqlTypes namespace. For a complete example on how to use these types with a DataReader, refer to Chapter 5.

When using the strongly typed accessors, you must specify the column index. You can't look up a value by column name. However, you can use the GetOrdinal( ) method to retrieve the column ordinal for a column with a specific name.

Example

The following code retrieves the second column as a string:

```
string value = r.GetString(1);
```

Notes

It isn't necessary to use strongly typed accessors. You can use the indexer, unless you have reason to be concerned that the conversion to a .NET type could introduce a rounding error.

Before calling a strongly typed accessor on a field that can contain null values, you should use the IsDBNull( ) method.

GetDataTypeName

```
String typeName = DataReader.GetDataTypeName(Int32 columnOrdinal);
```

Retrieves the name of the native data type used for a specified column. In C#, you can also use the typeof( ) operator to retrieve type information.

Example

The following code displays the data type of the second column:

```
Console.WriteLine(r.GetDataTypeName(1));
```

GetName

```
String columnName = DataReader.GetName(Int32 columnOrdinal);
```

Returns the name of a column at a specified index. One reason to use this method is to display column headings when iterating through a result set by index number.

Example

The following code statement generically prints every column retrieved from a query and its column name:

```
con.Open();
r = cmd.ExecuteReader();

while (r.Read())
{
    for (int i = 1; i <= r.FieldCount - 1; i++)
    {
        Console.Write(r.GetName(i).ToString() + ": ");
        Console.WriteLine(r[i].ToString());
    }
    Console.WriteLine();
}

con.Close();
```

GetOrdinal

```
Int32 ordinal = DataReader.GetOrdinal(String columnName);
```

Retrieves the zero-based ordinal for the column with the specific name. This is useful for two reasons. First of all, many DataReader methods require the use of column ordinals, not field names. Second, access via a column ordinal is likely to perform faster. In fact, when you use a column name, ADO.NET performs a hashtable lookup behind the scenes to determine the correct column ordinal. Using GetOrdinal( ), you can perform this lookup once, rather than every time you need to access a field.

Example

The following code shows a simple example of how you might access a column using the column ordinal, even if you only know its column name:

```
// Perform the ordinal lookups.
int colID = r.GetOrdinal("CustomerID");
int colFirstName = r.GetOrdinal("FirstName");
int colSecondName = r.GetOrdinal("SecondName");

while (r.Read())
{
    // Use the ordinals far faster column value access.
    Console.WriteLine(r[colID].ToString());
    Console.WriteLine(r[colFirstName].ToString() + " " +
        r[colSecondName].ToString());
    Console.WriteLine();
}
```

Columns are returned in the same order they appear in a SELECT statement.

GetSchemaTable

```
DataTable dt = DataReader.GetSchemaTable();
```

Returns a DataTable that contains metadata for the current query. This table contains one row for each column in the result set and several fields that describe details such as column names and data types. Table 21-2 lists all columns returned in the schema DataTable, in order.

Table 21-2. Schema columns

Column	Description
ColumnName	The name of the column. If the query renamed the column using the AS keyword, this is the new name.
ColumnOrdinal	The ordinal number of the column.
ColumnSize	The maximum allowed length of values in the column or the size of the data type for fixed-length data type.
NumericPrecision	The maximum precision (number of digits) of the column for a numeric data type or null for all other data types.
NumericScale	The maximum scale (number of digits to the right of the decimal point) of the column for a numeric data type, or null for all other data types.
IsUnique	Indicates whether or not column values can be duplicated.
IsKey	Indicates whether or not this column is part of the primary key for the table.
BaseCatalogName	The name of the database that contains this table, or null if it can't be determined.
BaseColumnName	The name of the column in the data source. If the query renamed the column using the AS keyword, this is the original name.
BaseSchemaName	The name of the schema in the data source, or null if it can't be determined.
BaseTableName	The name of the table or view in the data source that contains this column, or null if it can't be determined.
DataType	The mapped .NET framework type.
AllowDBNull	Indicates whether null values are accepted for column values.
ProviderType	Indicates the provider-specific data type.
IsAliased	True if the column has been renamed using the AS keyword.
IsExpression	True if the column is calculated based on an expression.
IsIdentity	True if the column is an identity value generated by the data source.
IsAutoIncrement	True if column values are assigned by the data source in fixed increments.
IsRowVersion	True if the column contains a read-only row identifier.
IsHidden	True if the column is hidden.
IsLong	True if the column contains a binary long object (BLOB).
IsReadOnly	True if the column can't be modified.

Example

The following example retrieves a schema table and displays the returned information. The schema information describes the columns from the Customers table.

```
SqlCommand cmd = new SqlCommand("SELECT * FROM CUSTOMERS", con);

// Get the schema table.
con.Open();
SqlDataReader r = cmd.ExecuteReader();
DataTable schema = r.GetSchemaTable();
con.Close();

// Display schema table information.
foreach (DataRow row in schema.Rows)
{
    foreach (DataColumn col in schema.Columns)
    {
        Console.WriteLine(col.ColumnName + " = " + row[col].ToString());
    }
    Console.WriteLine();
}
```

GetValue

```
Object value = DataReader.GetValue(Int32 columnOrdinal);
```

Retrieves a single value from a column as a .NET framework type. This method is rarely needed because the indexer provides more convenient access.

Note　　　Some providers also provide strongly typed versions of the GetValue( ) method, which you can recognize based on the provider prefix. For example, SQL Server provides a GetSqlValue( ) method that retrieves a column values as a SQL Server-specific type.

GetValues

```
Int32 numberOfValues = DataReader.GetValues(Object[] values);
```

This method provides an efficient way to retrieve all the values in a row at once rather than access each column value separately. The values are retrieved into an array of objects, which you must supply as an argument. The GetValues( ) method returns the number of values used to fill the array.

Before you use the GetValues( ) method, you should make sure the array length is the correct size. If the array length is less than the number of required columns, all the values will not be retrieved. Instead, the available slots in the array are filled with the corresponding column values, and all additional column values are ignored. No exception is thrown. You can also pass an object array that has a length greater than the number of columns contained in the resulting row without generating an error.

Example

The following example retrieves all the column values for a row into an object array, and then adds this array to an ArrayList collection. The information for each row is added to the ArrayList in this fashion.

```
string SQL = "SELECT * FROM Customers";

SqlCommand cmd = new SqlCommand(SQL, con);
ArrayList rows = new ArrayList();
```

```
con.Open();
SqlDataReader r = cmd.ExecuteReader();

while (r.Read())
{
    object[] values = new object[r.FieldCount];
    r.GetValues(values);
    rows.Add(values);
}

con.Close();

Console.WriteLine("Data retrieved for " + rows.Count.ToString() + " rows");
```

Notes

Some providers also provide strongly typed versions of the GetValue( ) method, which you can recognize based on the provider prefix. For example, SQL Server provides a GetSqlValue( ) method.

There is no DataReader method that allows you to retrieve multiple rows into an array.

IsDBNull

```
Boolean = DataReader.IsDBNull(Int32 columnOrdinal);
```

Returns a Boolean value that indicates whether the indicated column contains a null value. You can call this method to check for a null value before you call a typed accessor method such as GetByte( ) or GetChar( ) and thereby avoid raising an error.

Example

The following code tests for a null value before attempting to retrieve an integer value:

```
int rowVal;

if (r.IsDbNull(i))
{
    // Use default value. Row is null.
    rowVal = 0;
}
else
{
    // Use database value.
    rowVal = (int)r[i];
}
```

NextResult

```
Boolean moreResultSets = DataReader.NextResult();
```

Moves the reader to the next result set. A DataReader returns multiple result sets only if you use a batch query or if you invoke a stored procedure that includes more than one SELECT query. By default, the DataReader begins on the first result set. NextResult( ) returns true if there are more result sets.

Example

Here's an example that retrieves multiple result sets using a batch query:

```
// Define a batch query.
string SQL = "SELECT * FROM Categories; SELECT * FROM Products";

SqlConnection con = new SqlConnection(connectionString);
SqlCommand cmd = new SqlCommand(SQL, con);

con.Open();

// Execute the batch query.
SqlDataReader reader = cmd.ExecuteReader();
while (reader.Read())
{
    // (Process the category rows here.)
}

reader.NextResult();

while (reader.Read())
{
    // (Process the product rows here.)
}
```

Read

```
Boolean moreRecords = DataReader.Read();
```

Moves to the next record. If no record can be found, it returns false. Otherwise, it returns true. When the DataReader is first created, it is positioned just before the first row. You must call Read( ) before you can retrieve information from the first row. (The first Read( ) call advances the DataReader to the first record, if any.)

Example

The following code shows the basic pattern of access for reading rows with the DataReader. The Read( ) method is invoked as part of a while loop, ensuring that the loop ends immediately when the Read( ) method returns false.

```
string SQL = "SELECT ContactName FROM Customers";

SqlCommand cmd = new SqlCommand(SQL, con);
SqlDataReader r;

try
{
    con.Open();
    r = cmd.ExecuteReader();

    // Iterate over the results.
    while (r.Read())
    {
        Console.WriteLine(r["ContactName"].ToString());
    }
}
```

```
finally
{
    con.Close();
}
```

Because the DataReader encapsulates a live connection, you should read all the information as quickly as possible and close the connection immediately after.

Note   The DataReader provides only a single record at a time. Once the DataReader has been moved forward, you can't retrieve a value from a previous row.

22

The DataSet Class

The DataSet is a memory-resident representation of data. It can contain the schema for one or more tables and relationships between those tables,

A DataSet is used for working with and transporting data in a disconnected environment. It can be filled with data from a data source and later reconciled with the data source using a DataAdapter object.

As with all disconnected data classes, the DataSet isn't specific to any data provider.

Comments/Troubleshooting

The DataSet class provides a consistent programming model, regardless of the actual data source. The DataSet schema can be created programmatically, read from a data source, read from an XML schema, or inferred from an XML document or stream.

The DataSet serves as a container for disconnected objects. It can contain DataTable objects in its DataTableCollection and can be accessed through its Tables property. These tables can be related to one another using DataRelation objects in the DataRelationCollection and are accessed through the Relations property of the DataSet. Data integrity can be maintained by adding ForeignKeyConstraint and UniqueConstraint objects to the DataTable objects.

The data in the DataSet can be populated from the data source, modified, and later reconciled back to a data source, using a DataAdapter. Alternatively, the data can be populated from XML documents or streams, modified, and saved as an XML document or stream. Finally, the data stored in the DataSet can be created and manipulated programmatically.

The DataSet and XML are tightly coupled, which permits the same data to be accessed and manipulated using either the DataSet and its contained objects or by using XML-based classes. This has two particularly important implications. First, XSLT templates can easily be applied to any DataSet to transform the data structure. Second, the schema, data, or both the schema and data within a DataSet can be persisted to memory or a file as an XML document.

DataSets exist as both untyped and strongly typed. Strongly typed DataSets are a collection of automatically generated classes that inherit from the DataSet, DataTable, and DataRow classes and provide additional properties, methods, and events based on the DataSet schema. Strongly typed DataSets are discussed in detail in Chapter 13.

The commonly used public properties of the DataSet class are listed in Table 22-1.

Table 22-1. DataSet properties

Property	Description
CaseSensitive	Gets or sets a value indicating whether string comparisons in the DataSet are treated as case-sensitive.
Locale	Gets or sets the locale information that is the basis for string comparisons in tables.
DataSetName	Gets or sets the name of the DataSet.
EnforceConstraints	Gets or sets a value indicating whether the constraint rules defined between tables in the DataSet are enforced when data is updated.
HasErrors	Gets a value indicating whether there are any errors in any rows within any of the tables within the DataSet.
Namespace	Gets or sets the namespace of the DataSet.
Prefix	Gets or sets an XML prefix that aliases the namespace of the DataSet.
DefaultViewManager	Gets a custom view of the data contained within the DataSet for filtering, sorting, and navigating using a DataViewManager.

The commonly used public collections of the DataSet class are listed in Table 22-2.

Table 22-2. DataSet collections

Collection	Description
Tables	Accesses the DataTableCollection that contains the tables for the DataSet as a collection of DataTable objects.
Relations	Accesses the DataRelationCollection that contains table relationships for the DataSet as a collection of DataRelation objects.
ExtendedProperties	Accesses the PropertyCollection that contains custom information for the DataSet as a collection of key-and-value pairs.

The commonly used public methods of the DataSet class are listed in Table 22-3.

Table 22-3. DataSet methods

Method	Description
AcceptChanges()	Commits all changes made to the DataSet since the last time it was loaded or since the last time changes were committed.
Clear()	Removes all data rows from the DataSet.

Table 22-3. DataSet methods (continued)

Method	Description
Clone( )	Creates a new DataSet with the same schema as the original but with none of the data.
Copy( )	Creates a new DataSet with the same schema and data as the original.
GetChanges( )	Gets a copy of the changes made to a DataSet since the last time it was loaded or since changes were last committed.
GetXml( )	Returns a string that is the XML representation of the data stored in the DataSet, optionally with XSD schema information.
GetXmlSchema( )	Returns a string that is the XSD schema for the XML representation of the data stored in the DataSet.
HasChanges( )	Returns a value indicating whether data in the DataSet has been modified, inserted, or deleted since it was last loaded or since changes were last committed.
InferXmlSchema( )	Infers an XML schema from the contents of a specified Stream, file, or TextReader into the DataSet.
Merge( )	Merges data from another DataSet, DataTable, or array of DataRows into the DataSet.
ReadXml( )	Reads XML schema information and data from a Stream, file, TextReader, or XmlReader into the DataSet.
ReadXmlSchema( )	Reads XML schema information from a Stream, file, TextReader, or XmlReader into the DataSet.
RejectChanges( )	Rejects all changes made to the DataSet since the last time it was loaded or since the last time changes were committed.
Reset( )	Discards the contents of the DataSet, resetting it to an uninitialized state.
WriteXml( )	Writes the data, and optionally the schema, from the DataSet to a Stream, file, TextReader, or XmlReader.
WriteXmlSchema( )	Writes the schema from the DataSet to a Stream, file, TextReader, or XmlReader.

The commonly used public events of the DataSet class are listed in Table 22-4.

Table 22-4. DataSet event

Event	Description
MergeFailed	Raised when the schema of the source DataSet and target DataSet being merged are in conflict.

The DataSet class is contained within the System.Data namespace. The DataSet class inherits from MarshalByValueComponent and implements the IListSource, ISupportInitialize, and ISerializable interfaces. It is safe for multithreaded read operations; multithreaded write operations must be synchronized. DataSet objects can be passed between different application domains.

Properties Reference

CaseSensitive

```
Boolean caseSensitive = DataSet.CaseSensitive;
DataSet.CaseSensitive = caseSensitive;
```

Gets or sets a value that indicates whether string comparisons within the DataTable objects in the DataSet are treated as case-sensitive.

Example

The following instructs the DataSet to treat string comparisons as case-sensitive:

```
DataSet ds = new DataSet();
ds.CaseSensitive = true;
```

Notes

The CaseSensitive property affects sorting, searching, and filtering within the DataSet.

The DataTable also has a CaseSensitive property. If the CaseSensitive property for a DataTable belonging to a DataSet has not been explicitly set, its value defaults to the value of the CaseSensitive property of the DataSet.

The default value of the CaseSenstive property is false.

DataSetName

```
String dataSetName = DataSet.DataSetName;
DataSet.DataSetName = dataSetName;
```

Gets or sets the name of the DataSet.

Example

The following example sets the name of a newly created DataSet:

```
DataSet ds = new DataSet();
ds.DataSetName = "MyDataSet";
```

Notes

The value for the DataSetName property can also be set using the DataSet constructor as shown in the following sample:

```
DataSet ds = new DataSet("MyDataSet");
```

If the contents of the DataSet are output as XML, the DataSetName is used as the name of the root node in the XML document.

The DataSetName property defaults to NewDataSet if it isn't explicitly specified.

DefaultViewManager

```
DataViewManager dvm = DataSet.DefaultViewManager;
```

Gets a reference to the default DataViewManager for the DataSet.

Example

The following example uses the DataViewManager property to access and set the property, which indicates that the default sort order should be used for all DataViews created from the DataViewManager:

```
DataViewManager dvm = ds.DefaultViewManager;
foreach(DataViewSetting dvs in dvm.DataViewSettings)
{
    dvs.ApplyDefaultSort = true;
}
```

Notes

The DataViewManager provides a convenient way to manage the default DataView settings for all tables in the DataSet and allows you to create new DataView objects for tables in the DataSet.

The DataViewManager contains a collection of DataViewSetting objects that can set the default values for the ApplyDefaultSort, Sort, RowFilter, and RowStateFilter properties for views on tables in the DataSet.

The public properties the DataViewManager class are described in Table 22-5.

Table 22-5. DataViewManager public properties

Property	Description
DataSet	Gets or sets the name of the DataSet to use with the DataViewManager.
DataViewSettings	Gets the DataViewSettingCollection for each DataTable in the DataSet.

The public methods of the DataViewManager class are described in Table 22-6.

Table 22-6. DataViewManager public methods

Method	Description
CreateDataView( )	Creates a DataView for the specified DataTable.

EnforceConstraints

```
Boolean enforceConstraints = DataSet.EnforceConstraints;
DataSet.EnforceConstraints = enforceConstraints;
```

Gets or sets a value indicating whether the constraints defined for the tables in the DataSet are enforced when data is edited or added. There are two types of constraints in ADO.NET: foreign key and unique. *Foreign key constraints* define how updates and deletes are propagated to related tables. *Unique constraints* ensure that the data in a column or columns is unique among all the rows in the table.

Example

The following example turns off constraint enforcement for the DataSet:

```
DataSet ds = new DataSet();
ds.EnforceConstraints = false;
```

Notes

If the EnforceConstraints property is true and a Constraint within the DataSet is violated, a ConstraintException error is raised.

The EnforceConstraint property can be set to false prior to filling the DataSet and set back to true after the data is loaded. This permits the data to be loaded in an arbitrary order.

The default value of the EnforceConstraints property is true.

HasErrors

```
Boolean hasErrors = DataSet.HasErrors;
```

Gets a value indicating whether there are errors in any of the rows in any of the tables in the DataSet.

Example

The following example shows how to use the HasErrors property to determine the success of the reconciliation of a modified DataSet with the data source:

```
DataSet ds = new DataSet();
SqlDataAdapter da = new SqlDataAdapter();

// ... define the DataAdapter

// fill the DataSet
da.Fill(ds);

// ... modify the data in the DataSet

da.Update(ds);
if (ds.HasErrors)
{
    // ... handle the errors
}
```

Notes

If the DataAdapter ContinueUpdateOnError property is true when the Update( ) method of the DataAdapter is called, and one or more rows fail the update attempt, the RowError property for the failed rows is set, and the operation continues with the next record. The HasErrors property can be called after the update attempt to determine whether any of the row update attempts has failed. To optimize performance, check this property before checking the HasErrors property of the DataTable and DataRow objects.

The DataTable and DataRow classes also expose a HasErrors property.

Locale

```
CultureInfo locale = DataSet.Locale;
DataSet.Locale = locale;
```

Gets or sets the locale information that is the basis of string comparisons in tables.

Example

The following code demonstrates how to set the Locale property of the DataSet to Spanish:

```
DataSet ds = new DataSet();
ds.Locale = new CultureInfo("es");
```

Notes

The Locale property determines how sorting, comparisons, and filtering will be performed within the DataSet. The CultureInfo class exists in the System. Globalization namespace.

If the Locale property for a DataTable contained in the DataSet isn't explicitly set, it defaults to the Locale value for the DataSet it belongs to.

The default for the Locale property is the current system CultureInfo.

Namespace

```
String namespace = DataSet.Namespace;
DataSet.Namespace = namespace;
```

Gets or sets the namespace for the XML representation of the data stored in the DataSet.

Example

The following example sets the Namespace property of the DataSet:

```
DataSet ds = new DataSet();
ds.Namespace = "AdoDotNetIan";
```

Note   The Namespace property scopes the XML attributes and elements when reading and writing the DataSet using the ReadXml( ), WriteXml( ), ReadXmlSchema( ), and WriteXmlSchema( ) methods.

Prefix

```
String prefix = DataSet.Prefix;
DataSet.Prefix = prefix;
```

Gets or sets an XML prefix that aliases the namespace of the DataSet.

Example

The following example sets the NameSpace and Prefix properties of the DataSet and uses them to scope the XML loaded into the DataSet using the ReadXml method:

```
DataSet ds = new DataSet();

ds.Namespace = "AdoDotNetIan";
ds.Prefix = "adni";

// read the XML from the file into the DataSet
ds.ReadXml("myXmlFile.xml");
```

Note	The Prefix is used within the XML document to identify attributes and elements that belong to the namespace of the DataSet object as defined by the Namespace property.

Collections Reference

ExtendedProperties

PropertyCollection *ep* = DataSet.ExtendedProperties;
DataSet.ExtendedProperties = *ep*;

Accesses the PropertyCollection object of the DataSet, which allows custom information about the DataSet to be stored.

Example

The following example shows how to set and retrieve custom information for the DataSet using ExtendedProperties:

```
// set
ds.ExtendedProperties.Add("MyKey", "MyCustomData");

// get
String customData = ds.ExtendedProperties["MyKey"].ToString();
```

Notes

Nonstring properties aren't persisted when the DataSet is written as XML.

The commonly used public properties of the PropertyCollection are listed and described in Table 22-7.

Table 22-7. PropertyCollection public properties

Property	Description
Count	Gets the number of items in the property collection.
Item	Gets an object containing the value for the specified key from the PropertyCollection. If the value isn't found, attempting to get it returns null. Attempting to set a value either creates a new key-value pair if the specified key isn't found or replaces the existing value for the key. In C#, the Item property is the indexer for the class.

The commonly used public methods of the PropertyCollection are listed and described in Table 22-8.

Table 22-8. PropertyCollection public methods

Method	Description
Add( )	Adds an item to the PropertyCollection with the specified key and value.
Clear( )	Removes all items from the PropertyCollection.
Clone( )	Creates a shallow copy of the PropertyCollection.

Table 22-8. PropertyCollection public methods (continued)

Method	Description
Contains( )	Returns a Boolean value indicating whether a specified key exists in the PropertyCollection.
ContainsKey( )	Returns a Boolean value indicating whether a specified key exists in the PropertyCollection.
CopyTo( )	Copies the items in the PropertyCollection to a one-dimensional array, starting at a specified index.
GetEnumerator( )	Returns an IDictionaryEnumerator that can be used to iterate through the PropertyCollection.
Remove( )	Removes the item with the specified key from the PropertyCollection.

Relations

```
DataRelationCollection drc = DataSet.Relations;
```

Accesses the DataRelationCollection contained in a DataSet that contains the child DataRelation objects belonging to the DataSet. These objects relate tables in the DataSet using their primary and foreign keys and allow navigation between parent and child tables in both directions.

Examples

The DataRelationCollection has two methods that are used to add relations to the DataSet. The first is the Add( ) method, which in its simplest form takes a single DataRelation argument as shown in the following example:

```
DataRelation dr = new DataRelation("MyDataRelation",
    parentTable.Columns["PrimaryKeyField"],
    childTable.Columns["ForeignKeyField"]);
ds.Relations.Add(dr);
```

The other overloaded versions of the Add( ) method allow a DataRelation object to be created and added to the DataSet in a single statement, as shown in the following example:

```
DataTable dt1;
DataColumn col1, col2;
// ... code to define columns col1 and col2 and add them to the table dt1

DataTable dt2;
DataColumn col3, col4;
// ... code to define columns col3 and col4 and add them to the table dt2

DataSet ds = new DataSet();
ds.Tables.Add(dt1);
ds.Tables.Add(dt2);

// add a relation to the DataRelationCollection called MyRelation
// and create the ForeignKey constraint between parent col1 and child col3
ds.Relations.Add("MyRelation", col1, col3, true);

// add the relation between parent columns col1 and col2 and child columns
// col3 and col4. Do not create the ForeignKey constraint.
```

```
ds.Relations.Add("MyRelation", new DataColumn[] {col1, col2},
    new DataColumn[] {col3, col4}, false);
```

More than one DataRelation can be added to a DataSet in a single statement using the AddRange( ) method. This method adds DataRelation objects from a DataRelation array to the end of the DataRelationCollection, as the following example illustrates:

```
// code to create DataRelations dr1 and dr2
ds.Relations.AddRange(new DataRelation[] {dr1, dr2});
```

The IndexOf( ) method allows the index of an existing relation to be retrieved from the DataRelationCollection. This method has two overloads that allow the relation to be located using either the relation name or a reference to the relation, as shown in the following examples:

```
Int32 index = ds.Relations.IndexOf("MyDataRelation");
```

```
Int32 index = ds.Relations.IndexOf(dr);
```

The value returned by the IndexOf( ) method is zero-based. A value of −1 is returned if the specified relation object doesn't exist within the collection.

There are also two methods that can remove a relation from the DataRelationCollection. The Remove( ) method removes a relation matching the relation name argument. The RemoveAt( ) method removes the relation at a specified index from the DataRelationCollection. The following examples illustrate both methods:

```
// remove the relation names MyDataRelation from the
// DataRelationCollection for the DataSet
ds.Relations.Remove("MyDataRelation");
```

```
// remove the first relation in the DataRelationCollection for the DataSet
ds.Relations.RemoveAt(0);
```

Finally, the Clear( ) method removes all the relations from the DataSet, as shown in the following example:

```
ds.Relations.Clear();
```

Notes

The commonly used public properties of the DataRelationCollection are listed and described in Table 22-9.

Table 22-9. DataRelationCollection public properties

Property	Description
Count	Gets the number of items in the DataRelationCollection.
Item	Gets the specified DataRelation from the DataRelationCollection. In C#, the Item property is the indexer for the class.

The commonly used public methods of the DataRelationCollection are listed and described in Table 22-10.

Table 22-10. DataRelationCollection public methods

Method	Description
Add( )	Adds a DataRelation object to the collection.
AddRange( )	Adds the objects in the array of DataRelation objects to the end of the collection.

Table 22-10. DataRelationCollection public methods (continued)

Method	Description
CanRemove( )	Returns a Boolean value indicating whether a specific item can be removed from the collection.
Clear( )	Removes all items from the collection.
Contains( )	Returns a Boolean value indicating whether a DataRelation with the specified name exists in the collection.
IndexOf( )	Returns the index of the specified DataRelation. A value of −1 is returned if the DataRelation doesn't exist in the collection.
Remove( )	Removes the specified DataRelation from the collection. An ArgumentException is generated if the specified DataRelation doesn't exist in the collection.
RemoveAt( )	Removes the DataRelation at the specified index from the collection. An ArgumentException is raised if the collection doesn't have a DataRelation at the specified index.

Tables

```
DataTableCollection dtc = DataSet.Tables;
```

Accesses the DataTableCollection contained by the DataSet that contains the DataTable objects belonging to the DataSet.

Example

The DataTableCollection has two methods that can add a table to a DataSet. The Add( ) method takes an optional table name argument and is used to add tables to the DataTableCollection. If this argument isn't supplied, the tables are automatically named Table, Table1, Table2, and so on. The following example adds a table to a DataSet:

```
DataSet ds = new DataSet("MyDataSet");
DataTable dt = new DataTable("MyTable");

// ... code to define the schema for the newly constructed DataTable

ds.Tables.Add(dt);
```

Alternatively, a DataTable can first be constructed within the DataTablesCollection and subsequently have its schema defined:

```
DataSet ds = new DataSet("MyDataSet");
DataTable dt = ds.Tables.Add("MyTable");

// ... code to define the schema for newly constructed DataTable
```

A reference to the table that already exists within the DataSet can be retrieved. Most commonly, this is done using the table name or the table ordinal as shown in these examples:

```
// using the table name
DataTable dt = ds.Tables("MyTable");

// using the table ordinal
DataTable dt = ds.Tables[0];
```

The Count property returns the number of tables in the DataSet, as shown here:

```
Int32 tableCount = ds.Tables.Count;
```

DataSet

The Contains() method returns whether a specific DataTable exists within a DataSet, as shown next:

```
bool tableExists = ds.Tables.Contains("MyTable");
```

Existing tables within the DataSet can be accessed by an indexer, which most commonly is passed the table name or the position of the table within the DataTableCollection as an argument as shown in these examples:

```
// using the table name
DataTable dt = ds.Tables["MyTable"];

// access the first table in the collection using the table ordinal
DataTable dt = ds.Tables[0];
```

The IndexOf() method allows the index of the table within the collection to be retrieved using either a reference to the table object or the table name. The following example demonstrates both techniques:

```
// get the index using the name of the table
Int32 tableIndex =  ds.Tables.IndexOf("MyTable");

// get the index using a reference to a table
DataTable dt = ds.Tables.Add("MyTable");

// ... build the table and do some work

// get the index of the table based on the table reference
Int32 tableIndex = ds.Tables.IndexOf(dt);
```

The DataTableCollection provides a number of other useful methods and properties. The AddRange() method allows more than one table to be added to the DataSet at the same time. The method takes an array of DataTable objects as the argument as the following examples show:

```
// create two new tables
DataTable dt1 = new DataTable();
DataTable dt2 = new DataTable();

// use the AddRange method to add them to the DataSet.
ds.Tables.AddRange(new DataTable[] {dt1, dt2});
```

There are also two methods that remove tables from a DataSet: the Remove() and RemoveAt() method. The Remove() method takes either the table name or a reference to the table to be removed as an argument as shown in the following example:

```
DataTable dt = ds.Tables.Add("MyTable");

// remove by table reference
ds.Tables.Remove(dt);

// remove using the table name
ds.Tables.Remove("MyTable");
```

The RemoveAt() method removes the table using the index of the table in the DataSetCollection of the DataSet as shown in the following example:

```
// removes the first table from the tables collection in the DataSet
ds.Tables.RemoveAt(0);
```

If you need to remove all tables from a DataSet, the Clear() method can be used. It takes no arguments and can be used as shown next:

```
ds.Tables.Clear();
```

Notes

The commonly used public properties of the DataTableCollection are listed and described in Table 22-11.

Table 22-11. DataTableCollection public properties

Property	Description
Count	Gets the number of table objects in the DataTableCollection.
Item	Gets the specified DataTable object from the DataTableCollection. In C#, the Item property is the indexer for the class.

The commonly used public methods of the DataTableCollection are listed and described in Table 22-12.

Table 22-12. DataTableCollection public methods

Method	Description
Add()	Adds a DataTable object to the collection.
AddRange()	Adds the objects in the array of DataTable objects to the end of the collection.
CanRemove()	Returns a Boolean value indicating whether a specific table can be removed from the collection.
Clear()	Removes all tables from the collection.
Contains()	Returns a Boolean value indicating whether a DataTable with the specified name exists in the collection.
IndexOf()	Returns the zero-based index of the specified DataTable. The value −1 is returned if the DataTable doesn't exist in the collection.
Remove()	Removes the specified DataTable from the collection. An ArgumentException is generated if the specified DataTable doesn't exist in the collection.
RemoveAt()	Removes the DataTable at the specified index from the collection. An ArgumentException is raised if the collection doesn't have a DataTable at the specified index.

Methods Reference

AcceptChanges

```
DataSet.AcceptChanges();
```

Commits all changes made to the DataSet since the last time it was loaded or since the last time AcceptChanges() was called.

Parameters   None.

Example

The following example demonstrates how to call the AcceptChanges() method of the DataSet:

```
DataSet ds = new DataSet();
// create a table with a single column
DataTable dt = ds.Tables.Add();
dt.Columns.Add("MyColumn", typeof(System.Int32));

DataRow row;
row = dt.NewRow();
row["MyColumn"] = 1;
dt.Rows.Add(row);        // RowState = Added

ds.AcceptChanges();      // RowState = Unchanged

row["MyColumn"] = 2;     // RowState = Modified
ds.AcceptChanges();      // RowState = Unchanged

row.Delete();            // RowState = Deleted
ds.AcceptChanges();      // Row is removed from the DataSet
```

Notes

Calling AcceptChanges() sets the RowState property of Added and Modified rows to Unchanged; the original values in the DataRow are set to the current values. Deleted rows are removed from the DataSet.

Calling the AcceptChanges() method on the DataSet causes AcceptChanges to be called on each DataTable belonging to the DataSet.

EndEdit() is implicitly called on any DataRow objects that are in edit mode as a result of calling the BeginEdit() method of the DataRow().

Calling AcceptChanges() clears all RowError information and sets the HasErrors property of the row to false.

Clear

```
DataSet.Clear();
```

Removes all data rows from the DataSet.

Parameters   None.

Example

The following example demonstrates the Clear() method of the DataSet:

```
DataSet ds = new DataSet();
DataTable dt1 = ds.Tables.Add("MyTable1");
DataTable dt2 = ds.Tables.Add("MyTable2");

// ... define the schema for the DataTables dt1 and dt2

// ... add some rows to each of the DataTables dt1 and dt2

ds.Clear();     // all rows removed from DataTables dt1 and dt2.
```

Clone

```
DataSet ds = DataSet.Clone();
```

Creates a new DataSet with the same schema as the current DataSet but which contains none of the data.

Parameter

ds   Returns the new DataSet with the same schema as the original but none of the data.

Example

The following example shows how to create a new empty DataSet with the same schema as an existing DataSet:

```
DataSet ds1 = new DataSet();
DataTable dt1 = ds1.Tables.Add("MyTable1");
DataTable dt2 = ds1.Tables.Add("MyTable2");

// ... define the schema for the DataTables dt1 and dt2

// ... add some rows to each of the DataTables dt1 and dt2

// Create DataSet ds2 with the same schema, but without any of the
// data in DataSet ds1.
DataSet ds2 = ds1.Clone();
```

Copy

```
DataSet ds = DataSet.Copy();
```

Creates a new DataSet having the same schema and containing the same data as the original DataSet.

Parameter

ds   Returns the new DataSet with the same schema and data as the original.

Example

The following example shows how to create a new DataSet with the same schema and data as an existing DataSet:

```
DataSet ds1 = new DataSet();
DataTable dt1 = ds1.Tables.Add("MyTable1");
DataTable dt2 = ds1.Tables.Add("MyTable2");

// ... define the schema for the DataTables dt1 and dt2

// ... add some rows to each of the DataTables dt1 and dt2

// Create DataSet ds2 with the same schema and data as DataSet ds1.
DataSet ds2 = ds1.Copy();
```

GetChanges

```
DataSet ds = DataSet.GetChanges();
DataSet ds = DataSet.GetChanges(DataRowState drs);
```

Returns a DataSet with the same schema as the original DataSet but which contains only the rows that have been modified since the last time the DataSet was loaded or since AcceptChanges( ) was last called. This overloaded method allows the changes to be filtered by the RowState of the DataRow objects.

Parameters

ds   Returns the DataSet with all changes made to the original since it was last loaded or AcceptChanges( ) was last called.

drs   A DataRowState enumeration value as described in Table 22-13 specifying the row state of the DataRow objects to return.

Table 22-13. DataRowState enumeration

Value	Description
Added	The row has been added to the DataRowCollection for the table, and AcceptChanges( ) has not been called.
Deleted	The row has been deleted from the DataRowCollection, and AcceptChanges( ) has not been called.
Detached	The row isn't part of a DataRowCollection.
Modified	The row has been modified, and AcceptChanges( ) has not been called.
Unchanged	The row has not been changed since AcceptChanges( ) was last called.

Example

The following example shows how to create a DataSet containing all changed rows and a DataSet containing all deleted rows from the original DataSet:

```
// return a DataSet containing all changed rows
DataSet dsChanges = dsOriginal.GetChanges();

// return a DataSet containing all deleted rows
DataSet dsDeleted = dsOriginal.GetChanges(DataRowState.Deleted);
```

Notes

Parent rows marked unchanged may be included in the rows returned if they are required because of relationship constraints.

The GetChanges( ) method can isolate the rows that have been changed so that the entire DataSet doesn't have to be passed to a method that reconciles DataSet changes with the data source.

A null reference is returned if there are no rows matching the specified criteria.

GetXml

```
String xmlString = DataSet.GetXml();
```

Returns a string that is the XML representation of the data stored in the DataSet, without the XSD schema information.

Parameter

xmlString

   A string containing an XML representation of the data stored in the DataSet.

Example

The following example shows how to use the GetXml() method to store the XML representation of a DataSet to a string:

```
DataSet ds = new DataSet();

// ... fill the DataSet

String xml = ds.GetXml();
```

Note   This method returns the same result as the WriteXml() method with the XmlWriteMode set to IgnoreSchema.

GetXmlSchema

```
String xmlSchemaString = DataSet.GetXmlSchema();
```

Returns a string that is the XSD schema for the XML representation of the data stored in the DataSet.

Parameter

xmlSchemaString

   A string that is the XSD schema for the XML representation of the data in the DataSet.

Example

The following example shows how to use the GetXml() method to store the XML representation of a DataSet schema to a string:

```
DataSet ds = new DataSet();

// ... fill the DataSet

String xmlSchema = ds.GetXmlSchema();
```

Note   This method returns the same result as the WriteXmlSchema() method except that only the primary schema is written.

HasChanges

```
Boolean hc = DataSet.HasChanges();
Boolean hc = DataSet.HasChanges(DataRowState drs);
```

Returns a value indicating whether data in the DataSet has been modified, inserted, or deleted since it was last loaded or since AcceptChanges() was last called. An optional DataRowState argument can be used to filter the results.

Parameters

hc Returns a Boolean value indicating whether data in the DataSet has been modified, inserted, or deleted since it was last loaded or since AcceptChanges() was last called.

drs One of the values from the DataRowState enumeration. See Table 22-13.

Example

The following example shows how to determine if any rows have been deleted from the DataSet:

```
bool hasDeleted = ds.HasChanges(DataRowState.Deleted);
```

Note   To maximize application performance, call this method to determine whether it is necessary to call the GetChanges() method.

InferXmlSchema

```
DataSet.InferXmlSchema(Stream xmlSource, String[] nsArray);
DataSet.InferXmlSchema(String xmlSource, String[] nsArray);
DataSet.InferXmlSchema(TextReader xmlSource, String[]nsArray);
DataSet.InferXmlSchema(XmlReader xmlSource, String[] nsArray);
```

Infers a schema from the specified XML source into the DataSet.

Parameters

xmlSource
    The Stream, filename, TextReader, or XmlReader containing the XML from which to infer the schema.

nsArray
    An array of namespace URI strings to be excluded from the inferred schema.

Example

The following example infers the schema from the XML representation of the DataSet:

```
DataSet ds1 = new DataSet();

// ... fill the DataSet

// write the XML representation of DataSet ds1 to a file, without schema.
String fileName = @"c:\MyFile.xml";
ds1.WriteXml(fileName, XmlWriteMode.IgnoreSchema);

// infer the schema and load the XML file into DataSet ds2, excluding a
// single namespace
DataSet ds2 = new DataSet();
ds1.InferXmlSchema(fileName, new String[] {"urn:my-schema:excludeddata"});
ds2.ReadXml(fileName);
```

Note   The InferXmlSchema() method functions the same as both the ReadXml() method with the XmlReadMode argument set to InferSchema and the ReadXmlSchema() method with an XML document containing only schema information without data. The InferXmlSchema()

method, however, optionally allows namespaces to be excluded from the inference process.

Merge

```
DataSet.Merge(DataRow[] dataSource);
DataSet.Merge(DataSet dataSource);
DataSet.Merge(DataTable dataSource);
DataSet.Merge(DataSet dataSource, Boolean preserveChanges);
DataSet.Merge(DataRow[] dataSource, Boolean preserveChanges,
    MissingSchemaAction msa);
DataSet.Merge(DataSet dataSource, Boolean preserveChanges,
    MissingSchemaAction msa);
DataSet.Merge(DataTable dataSource, Boolean preserveChanges,
    MissingSchemaAction msa);
```

The Merge( ) method combines the data and structure of a second, or source, DataSet, DataTable, or DataRow object array into a specified target DataSet with a similar structure.

Parameters

dataSource
> The array of DataRow objects, the DataSet, or the DataTable to be merged into the DataSet.

preserveChanges
> Indicates whether changes that have already been made to the target DataSet should be maintained when merging.

msa One of the values from the MissingSchemaAction enumeration described in Table 22-14.

Example

The following example demonstrates how to merge a source DataSet into a target DataSet:

```
// Merge DataSet mergeDs into DataSet ds
ds.Merge(mergeDs);
```

Notes

The Merge( ) method is typically used in a client application to update a DataSet with the latest changes to the underlying data in the data source.

When the Merge( ) method is called, the schemas of the source and target DataSet are compared. If there are schema differences, the MissingSchemaAction argument determines whether the target schema will be updated to include the missing schema and data. Table 22-14 describes the effect of the MissingSchemaAction values.

Table 22-14. MissingSchemaAction enumeration

Value	Description
Add	Adds information for new columns to the target DataSet and populates these columns with values from the source DataSet.
AddWithKey	Adds new schema and primary key information to the target DataSet and populates these columns with values from the source DataSet.

DataSet

Table 22-14. MissingSchemaAction enumeration (continued)

Value	Description
Error	Generates a SystemException when mismatched schemas are encountered.
Ignore	Ignores new schema information in the source DataSet.

During the merge operation, source rows with a RowState of Unchanged, Modified, or Deleted are matched to rows in the target DataSet with the same Current primary key values. Source rows with RowState of New are created in the target DataSet with the same primary key values as the Current value in the source, because the Original version doesn't exist in the source.

If the optional PreserveChanges argument is set to true, incoming values from the source don't overwrite Current values in the target DataSet rows. Data in the target Original row version is overwritten with the Original row version of the source row, and the target RowState is set to Modified. There are two exceptions. If the target RowState is Deleted, it remains deleted and isn't set to Modified. If the source RowState is Added, the target existing row isn't overwritten because it doesn't exist.

If PreserveChanges is false, both the Current and Original rows of the target are overwritten with the source data, and the RowState of the target row is set to the RowState of the source row. Again, there are two exceptions. If the source RowState is Unchanged, and the target RowState is Unchanged, Modified, Added, or Deleted, the RowState of the target row is set to Modified. If the source RowState is Added, the Original version of the target isn't overwritten because it doesn't exist.

During the merge operation, constraints are disabled. If constraints can't be enabled after the merge, the EnforceContraints property of the DataSet is set to false, and all invalid rows are marked as having errors.

ReadXml

```
DataSet.ReadXml(Stream xmlSource);
DataSet.ReadXml(String xmlSource);
DataSet.ReadXml(TextReader xmlSource);
DataSet.ReadXml(XmlReader xmlSource);
DataSet.ReadXml(Stream xmlSource, XmlReadMode xrm);
DataSet.ReadXml(String xmlSource, XmlReadMode xrm);
DataSet.ReadXml(TextReader xmlSource, XmlReadMode xrm);
DataSet.ReadXml(XmlReader xmlSource, XmlReadMode xrm);
```

Reads XML schema information and data from the specified source into the DataSet.

Parameters

xmlSource
> A Stream, filename, TextReader, or XmlReader containing the XML to read the schema and data from.

xrm One of the XmlReadMode enumeration values described in Table 22-15.

Table 22-15. XmlReadMode enumeration

Value	Description
Auto	Sets the XmlReadMode based on the data contained in the source. If the data is a Diffgram, the XmlReadMode is set to Diffgram. If either the DataSet has a schema defined or the XML document contains an inline XSD schema, the XmlReadMode is set to ReadSchema. If the DataSet doesn't have a schema and the XML document doesn't contain an inline XSD schema, the XmlReadMode is set to InferSchema. This is the default value.
Diffgram	Applies the changes specified by the Diffgram to the DataSet. The Diffgram for the source DataSet should be generated using the WriteXml() method specifying XmlWriteMode of Diffgram. An exception is thrown if the DataSet doesn't have the same schema as DataSet for which the DiffGram was generated.
Fragment	Reads an XML document using the default namespace as the inline schema.
IgnoreSchema	Reads the XML into the DataSet schema, ignoring any inline schema that might be present.
InferSchema	Reads the XML into the DataSet, inferring a schema and ignoring any inline schema that might be present. If the DataSet contains a schema that conflicts with the inferred schema, an exception is thrown.
ReadSchema	Reads the inline schema and loads data into the DataSet. If the DataSet contains a schema for tables defined in the inline schema, an exception is thrown.

Example

The following example shows how to use the ReadXml() and WriteXml() methods to read and write the XML representation of a DataSet along with the DataSet schema:

```
DataSet ds1 = new DataSet();

// ... fill the DataSet

// write the XML representation of DataSet ds1 to a file, with schema.
String fileName = @"c:\MyFile.xml";
ds1.WriteXml(fileName, XmlWriteMode.WriteSchema);

// load the XML file into DataSet ds2, with schema.
DataSet ds2 = new DataSet();
ds2.ReadXml(fileName, XmlReadMode.ReadSchema);
```

Note   The ReadXml() method can read the XML representation of the DataSet previously written using the WriteXml() method into a DataSet.

ReadXmlSchema

```
DataSet.ReadXmlSchema(Stream xmlSchemaSource);
DataSet.ReadXmlSchema(String xmlSchemaSource);
DataSet.ReadXmlSchema(TextReader xmlSchemaSource);
DataSet.ReadXmlSchema(XmlReader xmlSchemaSource);
```

Reads a XSD schema from the specified XML source into the DataSet schema.

Parameter

xmlSchemaSource

A Stream, filename, TextReader, or XmlReader containing the XML to read the schema and data from.

Example

The following example shows how to use the ReadXmlSchema( ) and WriteXmlSchema( ) methods to read and write the XML representation of the schema of a DataSet:

```
DataSet ds1 = new DataSet();

// ... fill the DataSet

String fileName = @"c:\MyFile.xml";

// create a FileStream and XmlTextWriter
System.IO.StreamWriter fsWrite = new System.IO.StreamWriter(fileName);
System.Xml.XmlTextWriter xw = new System.Xml.XmlTextWriter(fsWrite);

// write the XML schema of DataSet ds1 and close the XmlTextWriter.
ds1.WriteXmlSchema(xw);
xw.Close();

// create a FileStream and XmlTextReader
System.IO.StreamReader fsRead = new System.IO.StreamReader(fileName);
System.Xml.XmlTextReader xr = new System.Xml.XmlTextReader(fsRead);

// load the schema into DataSet ds2 and close the XmlTextReader.
DataSet ds2 = new DataSet();
ds2.ReadXmlSchema(xr);
xr.Close();
```

Note   The ReadXmlSchema( ) method can read the XSD schema of a DataSet previously written using the WriteXmlSchema( ) method back to a DataSet.

RejectChanges

```
DataSet.RejectChanges();
```

Rejects all changes made to the DataSet since the last time it was loaded or since the last time AcceptChanges( ) was called.

Parameters   None.

Example

The following example demonstrates how to call the RejectChanges( ) method of the DataSet and the effect of calling the RejectChanges( ) method on the row state:

```
DataSet ds = new DataSet();
// create a table with a single column
DataTable dt = ds.Tables.Add();
dt.Columns.Add("MyColumn", typeof(System.Int32));

DataRow row;
row = dt.NewRow();
row["MyColumn"] = 1;
dt.Rows.Add(row);       // RowState = Added

ds.AcceptChanges();     // RowState = Unchanged
```

```
row["MyColumn"] = 2;       // RowState = Modified
ds.RejectChanges();        // RowState = Unchanged, row["MyColumn"] = 1

row.Delete();              // RowState = Deleted
ds.RejectChanges();        // RowState = Unchanged
                           // The row isn't removed from the DataTable.
```

Notes

Calling RejectChanges( ) sets the RowState property of Deleted and Modified rows to Unchanged; the current values in the DataRow are set to the original values. Added rows are removed.

Calling the RejectChanges( ) method on the DataSet causes RejectChanges( ) to be called on each DataTable belonging to the DataSet.

When the RejectChanges( ) method is called, any rows in edit mode, as a result of calling BeginEdit( ), cancel their edits.

Calling RejectChanges( ) clears all RowError information and sets the HasErrors properties to false.

Reset

```
DataSet.Reset()
```

Discards the contents of the DataSet, resetting it to an uninitialized state.

Parameters   None.

Example

The following example shows how reset a DataSet to its original state:

```
ds.Reset();
```

Note   Calling Reset( ) on an existing DataSet is more efficient than instantiating a new DataSet.

WriteXml

```
DataSet.WriteXml(Stream xmlDest);
DataSet.WriteXml(String xmlDest);
DataSet.WriteXml(TextWriter xmlDest);
DataSet.WriteXml(XmlWriter xmlDest);
DataSet.WriteXml(Stream xmlDest, XmlWriteMode xwm);
DataSet.WriteXml(String xmlDest, XmlWriteMode xwm);
DataSet.WriteXml(TextWriter xmlDest, XmlWriteMode xwm);
DataSet.WriteXml(XmlWriter xmlDest, XmlWriteMode xwm);
```

Writes the data, and optionally the schema, from the DataSet to a specified destination.

Parameters

xmldest

The Stream, filename, TextReader, or XmlReader into which to write the XML representation of the DataSet.

xwm One of the values from the XmlWriteMode enumeration. See Table 22-16 for common XmlWriteMode enumeration values.

Table 22-16. XmlWriteMode enumeration

Value	Description
DiffGram	The entire DataSet is written as a DiffGram, including both original and current values for the data rows.
IgnoreSchema	An XML representation of the data in the DataSet is written without an XSD schema.
WriteSchema	An XML representation of the data in the DataSet is written together with its relational structure as an inline XSD schema. This is the default value.

Example   See the Example for the ReadXml( ) method in this chapter.

Note   The ReadXml( ) method can load the DataSet with the contents of XML previously written using the WriteXml( ) method.

WriteXmlSchema

```
DataSet.WriteXmlSchema(Stream xmlSchemaDest);
DataSet.WriteXmlSchema(String xmlSchemaDest);
DataSet.WriteXmlSchema(TextWrite xmlSchemaDest);
DataSet.WriteXmlSchema(XmlWriter xmlSchemaDest);
```

Writes the XSD schema from the DataSet to a specified destination.

Parameter

xmlSchemaDest
  The Stream, filename, TextReader, or XmlReader into which to write the XSD schema of the DataSet.

Example   See the Example for the ReadXmlSchema method in this chapter.

Note   The XSD schema written by the WriteXmlSchema( ) method can later be loaded back to a DataSet using the ReadXmlSchema( ) method.

Events Reference

MergeFailed

```
MergeFailedEventHandler MergeFailed;
```

The MergeFailed event is raised during a Merge( ) operation when the target table and source table contain a column with the same name but differing data types or when the source and target tables have primary keys defined on different columns.

Example

The following code demonstrates how to handle the MergeFailed event:

```
DataSet ds = new DataSet();
ds.MergeFailed += new MergeFailedEventHandler(ds_MergeFailed);

private void ds_MergeFailed(object sender, MergeFailedEventArgs e)
{
    MessageBox.Show("Failure in table: " + e.Table + Environment.NewLine +
        "Conflict = " + e.Conflict);
}
```

Notes

The event handler receives an argument of type MergeFailedEventArgs containing properties that provide specific information about the event as described in Table 22-17.

Table 22-17. MergeFailedEventArgs properties

Property	Description
Conflict	Gets the description of the merge conflict.
Table	Gets the DataTable object.

23

The DataTable Class

The `DataTable` is a memory-resident representation of a data table including columns, rows, and both unique and foreign key constraints. It's used for working with and transporting data in a disconnected environment.

As with all disconnected classes, the `DataTable` isn't specific to any data provider.

Comments/Troubleshooting

The `DataTable` class provides a consistent programming model regardless of the actual data source. The `DataTable` contains `DataColumn` and `Constraint` objects that define the schema of the data represented. The actual data is stored as a collection of `DataRows` within the `DataTable`.

The schema of the `DataTable` can be created entirely programmatically, retrieved as the result of a query against a data source using a .NET managed data provider or loaded from an XML document or stream through the `DataSet` the `DataTable` belongs to.

The data in the `DataTable` can be populated from the data source, modified, and later reconciled back to a data source using a `DataAdapter`. Alternatively, the data can be populated from XML documents or streams, modified, and saved as an XML document or stream through the `DataSet` the `DataTable` belongs to. Finally, the data stored in the `DataTable` can be manipulated programmatically.

There are similarities between the `DataTable` and the `DataReader` in that they both can store the results of a query, which can then be accessed through row and column objects. The primary difference is that the `DataTable` is a disconnected class that places little restriction on how the data within it is accessed and allows that data to be filtered, sorted, and modified; the `DataReader` is a connected class that provides little functionality beyond forward-only, read-only access to the result set, one row at a time.

The commonly used public properties of the DataTable class are listed in Table 23-1.

Table 23-1. DataTable properties

Property	Description
CaseSensitive	Gets or sets a value indicating whether string comparisons within the table are treated as case-sensitive.
DataSet	Gets a reference to the DataSet the table belongs to.
DefaultView	Gets the default DataView that is associated with the table.
DisplayExpression	Gets or sets the expression that represents the table in the user interface.
HasErrors	Gets a value that indicates whether there are errors in any rows of the table.
Locale	Gets or sets locale information that's used to compare strings stored in the table..
MinimumCapacity	Gets or sets the initial number of rows of the table.
Namespace	Gets or sets the XML namespace for the XML representation of the data stored in the table.
Prefix	Gets or sets the XML prefix that aliases the namespace of the table.
TableName	Gets or sets the name of the table.

The commonly used public collections of the DataTable class are listed in Table 23-2.

Table 23-2. DataTable collections

Collection	Description
ChildRelations	Accesses the DataRelationCollection that contains the child relations for the table as a collection of DataRelation objects.
Columns	Accesses the DataColumnCollection that contains the columns for the table as a collection of DataColumn objects.
Constraints	Accesses the ConstraintCollection that contains the constraints for the table as a collection of Constraint objects.
ExtendedProperties	Accesses the PropertyCollection that contains the extended properties for the table as a collection of key-and-value pairs.
ParentRelations	Accesses the DataRelationCollection that contains the parent relations for the table as a collection of DataRelation objects.
PrimaryKey	Accesses the array of DataColumn objects that make up the primary key of the table.
Rows	Accesses the DataRowCollection that contains the rows of data in the table as a collection of DataRow objects.

The commonly used public methods of the DataTable class are listed in Table 23-3.

Table 23-3. DataTable methods

Method	Description
AcceptChanges( )	Commits all changes made to the table since the last time it was loaded or since the last time changes were committed.
BeginLoadData( )	Turns off constraints, notifications, and index maintenance while loading data.
Clear( )	Removes all data rows from the table.

Table 23-3. DataTable methods (continued)

Method	Description
Clone( )	Creates a new table with the same schema as the original but contains none of the data.
Compute( )	Returns the result of an aggregate expression on a subset of rows meeting the filter criteria.
Copy( )	Creates a new table with the same schema and data as the original.
EndLoadData( )	Turns on constraints, notifications, and index maintenance after loading data.
GetChanges( )	Gets a copy of the changes made to a table since the last time it was loaded or since the last time changes were committed.
GetErrors( )	Gets an array of rows that contain errors.
ImportRow( )	Copies a specified row into the table.
LoadDataRow( )	Finds a row in the table and updates the values with the supplied array, or if the row isn't found, adds a new row to the table.
NewRow( )	Returns a new row with the same schema as the table.
RejectChanges( )	Rejects all changes made to the table since the last time it was loaded or the last time changes were committed.
Reset( )	Discards the contents of the table, resetting it to an uninitialized state.
Select( )	Returns an array of rows matching optionally specified filter and DataRowViewState criteria, optionally sorted according to specified criteria.

The commonly used public events of the DataTable class are listed in Table 23-4.

Table 23-4. DataTable events

Event	Description
ColumnChanged	Raised when a value has been changed for a column in a row.
ColumnChanging	Raised when a value is being changed for a column in a row.
RowChanged	Raised after a row has been successfully changed.
RowChanging	Raised when a row is about to be changed.
RowDeleted	Raised after a row has been deleted from the table.
RowDeleting	Raised when a row is about to be deleted from the table.

The DataTable class is contained within the System.Data namespace. The DataTable class inherits from MarshalByValueComponent and implements the IListSource, ISupportInitialize, and ISerializable interfaces. It is safe for multithreaded read operations; multithreaded write operations must be synchronized. DataTable objects can be passed between different application domains.

Properties Reference

CaseSensitive

```
Boolean caseSensitive = DataTable.CaseSensitive;
DataTable.CaseSensitive = caseSensitive;
```

Gets or sets a value indicating whether string comparisons within the DataTable are treated as case-sensitive.

Example

The following example instructs the DataTable to treat string comparisons as case-sensitive:

```
DataTable dt = new DataTable();
dt.CaseSensitive = true;
```

Notes

The CaseSensitive property affects sorting, searching, and filtering within the DataTable.

If the value of the CaseSensitive property isn't explicitly set, it defaults to the value of the CaseSensitive property of the DataSet the table belongs to.

DataSet

```
DataSet ds = DataTable.DataSet;
```

Gets a reference to the DataSet the DataTable belongs to.

Example

The following example shows how to retrieve a reference to the DataSet that the DataTable belongs to:

```
DataTable dt = new DataTable();

// ... code to define the DataTable dt and add it to the DataSet

DataSet ds = dt.DataSet;
```

Note   This property returns a null reference if the DataTable doesn't belong to a DataSet.

DefaultView

```
DataView dv = DataTable.DefaultView;
```

Gets the default DataView that is associated with the DataTable.

Example

The following example gets a reference to the default DataView for the DataTable and binds a DataGrid to that view:

```
DataTable dt = new DataTable();

// ... code to define the DataTable schema and populate it with data.
```

```
// returns the default DataView for the table.
DataView defaultView = dt.DefaultView;

// the next two statements both bind the DataGrid to
// the same default DataView
dataGrid.DataSource = defaultView ;
dataGrid.DataSource = dt;    // DefaultView is implied
```

Note   If a control is bound to the DataTable, the control actually binds to the DataView returned by the DefaultView property.

DisplayExpression

```
String displayExpression = DataTable.DisplayExpression;
DataTable.DisplayExpression = displayExpression;
```

Gets or sets the expression that represents the table in the user interface.

Example

The following example sets the DisplayExpression property of the DataTable:

```
DataTable dt = new DataTable();
dt.DisplayExpression = "MyDataTable";
```

HasErrors

```
Boolean hasErrors = DataTable.HasErrors;
```

Gets a value that indicates whether there are errors in any of the rows in the DataTable.

Example

The following example shows how to use the HasErrors property to determine whether there are errors in the DataTable after the reconciliation of the modified DataTable with the data source:

```
DataTable dt = new DataTable();
SqlDataAdapter da = new SqlDataAdapter();

// ... define the DataAdapter

// fill the DataTable
da.Fill(dt);

// ... modify the data in the DataTable

da.Update(dt);
if (dt.HasErrors)
{
    // ... handle the errors
}
```

Notes

If the DataAdapter ContinueUpdateOnError property is true when the Update( ) method of the DataAdapter is called, and one or more rows fail the update attempt, the RowError property for the failed rows is set. The HasErrors property can be called after the update attempt to determine whether any row update attempt has failed. To optimize performance, check the DataTable HasErrors property before checking the HasErrors property of the DataRow objects.

The DataSet and DataRow classes also expose a HasErrors property.

Locale

```
CultureInfo locale = DataTable.Locale;
DataTable.Locale = locale;
```

Gets or sets locale information that is used to compare strings stored in the DataTable.

Example

The following code demonstrates how to set the Locale property of the DataTable to Spanish:

```
DataTable ds = new DataTable();
dt.Locale = new CultureInfo("es");
```

Notes

The Locale property for the DataTable defaults to the Locale value of the DataSet that contains the table. If the DataTable doesn't belong to a DataSet, the Locale property defaults to the current value of the system CultureInfo.

The Locale property determines how sorting, comparisons, and filtering are performed within the DataTable.

MinimumCapacity

```
Int32 minimumCapacity = DataTable.MinimumCapacity;
DataTable.MinimumCapacity = minimumCapacity;
```

Gets or sets the initial starting size of the DataTable in rows.

Example

The following example shows how to set the MinimumCapacity of the DataTable:

```
DataTable dt = new DataTable();
dt.MinimumCapacity = 1000;
```

Notes

Setting this property can optimize performance by allocating an appropriate amount of resources to the table prior to retrieving data. If this value is set below the number of rows in the table, ADO.NET automatically requests additional memory.

The default value of the MinimumCapacity property is 50 rows.

Namespace

```
String namespace = DataTable.NameSpace;
DataTable.NameSpace = namespace;
```

Gets or sets the namespace for the XML representation of the data stored in the DataTable.

Example

The following example sets the Namespace property of the DataTable:

```
DataTable dt = new DataTable();
dt.Namespace = "AdoDotNetIan";
```

Note   The Namespace property scopes the XML attributes and elements when reading and writing the DataTable using the ReadXml( ), WriteXml( ), ReadXmlSchema( ), and WriteXmlSchema( ) methods of the DataSet the table belongs to.

Prefix

```
String prefix = DataTable.Prefix;
DataTable.Prefix = prefix;
```

Gets or sets the XML prefix that aliases the namespace of the DataTable.

Example

The following example sets the Prefix property of the DataTable:

```
DataTable dt = new DataTable();
dt.Prefix = "adni";
```

Note   The Prefix is used within the XML document to identify attributes and elements that belong to the namespace of the DataTable object defined by the Namespace property.

TableName

```
String tableName = DataTable.TableName;
DataTable.TableName = tableName;
```

Gets or sets the name of the DataTable.

Example

The following example sets the name of a newly created DataTable:

```
DataTable dt = new DataTable();
dt.TableName = "MyTable";
```

Notes

The value for the TableName property can also be set using the DataTable constructor as shown in the following example:

```
DataTable dt = new DataTable("MyDataTable");
```

If the contents of the DataSet containing the table are output as XML, the TableName is used as the element tag for each row in the DataTable.

By default, TableName property has no value. If the value has not been set when the table is added to the DataTableCollection of a DataSet, the table name defaults to Table, Table1, and so on.

Collections Reference

ChildRelations

```
DataRelationCollection cdrc = DataTable.ParentRelations;
```

Accesses the child `DataRelationCollection` for the `DataTable`, providing access to the child `DataRelation` objects belonging to the `DataTable`. The `ChildRelations` property can be used to add, remove, and examine the child `DataRelation` objects in a `DataTable`.

Example   See the Examples for the Relations collection in Chapter 22.

Note   See the Notes for the Relations collection in Chapter 22.

Columns

```
DataColumnCollection dcc = DataTable.Columns;
```

Accesses the `DataColumnCollection` for the `DataTable`, providing access to the `DataColumn` objects belonging to the `DataTable`. The `Columns` property can be used to add, remove, and examine the `DataColumn` objects in a `DataTable`.

Examples

There are two methods that can add a column to a table. The `Add()` method optionally takes arguments that specify the name, type, and expression of the column to be added. An existing column can be added by passing a reference to an existing column. If no arguments are passed, the default names `Column1`, `Column2`, and so on, are assigned to the new column. The following examples show how to create a column using the `Add()` method:

```
// adding a column using a reference to an existing column
DataColumn col = new DataColumn("MyColumn", typeof(System.Int32));
dt.Columns.Add(col);

// adding and creating a column in the same statement
dt.Columns.Add("MyColumn", typeof(System.Int32));
```

The second method is `AddRange()`, which allows more than one column stored in a `DataColumn` array to be added to the table in a single statement, as shown in the following example:

```
DataTable dt = new DataTable("MyTable");

// create and add two columns to the DataColumn array
DataColumn[] dca = new DataColumn[]
    {new DataColumn("Col1", typeof(System.Int32)),
     new DataColumn("Col2", typeof(System.Int32))};

// add the columns in the array to the table
dt.Columns.AddRange(dca);
```

There are several properties and methods that can interrogate the collection of columns within a table. The `Count()` method returns the number of columns in a table.

```
Int32 colCount = dt.Columns.Count;
```

The Contains( ) method returns a value indicating whether a column with a specified name exists in the collection. The method takes the column name as an argument.

```
bool colExists = dt.Columns.Contains("MyColumn");
```

The IndexOf( ) method returns the index of a column having a specified name within the collection. The method returns the zero-based index value for the column if it exists in the collection or the value of -1 if the column doesn't exist. The method takes a single argument containing the column name.

```
Int32 colIndex = dt.Columns.IndexOf("MyColumn");
```

Finally, there are three methods that remove columns from the collection. The Remove( ) method removes a column with a specified name from the collection. The method takes a single argument containing either the column name or a reference to a DataColumn object. If the column doesn't exist in the collection, an ArgumentException is raised.

```
// remove a column by specifying the name of the column
dt.Columns.Remove("MyColumn");

// remove a column by specifying a reference to the column
DataColumn col = new DataColumn("MyColumn");
dt.Columns.Add(col);

// ... do some work

dt.Columns.Remove(col);
```

The RemoveAt( ) method removes a column with a specified column index from the collection. The method takes a single argument containing the zero-based index of the column to be removed. If the column doesn't exist in the collection, an IndexOutOfRangeException is raised.

```
// remove the first column from the collection
dt.Columns.RemoveAt(0);
```

Finally, the Clear( ) method removes all columns from the column collection:

```
dt.Columns.Clear();
```

The DataColumnCollection raises a single event, CollectionChanged, when a column is either added or removed from the collection. The CollectionChangeEventArgs properties provide information about the nature of the change as described in Table 23-5.

Table 23-5. CollectionChangeEventArgs enumeration

Property	Description
Action	Describes how the collection changed. This is a value from the CollectionChangeAction enumeration as described in Table 23-6.
Element	Gets the column that was changed.

Table 23-6 describes the values of the CollectionChangeAction enumeration, one of which is assigned to the Action property of the CollectionChangeEventArgs argument passed to the event handling the change to the DataColumnCollection.

Table 23-6. CollectionChangeAction enumeration

Value	Description
Add	A column was added to the table.
Remove	A column was removed from the table.
Refresh	The column collection, as a whole, has changed. This is most commonly a result of adding or removing multiple columns or of removing all columns from the collection.

The following example demonstrates handling the ColumnChange event:

```
dt.Columns.CollectionChanged +=  new CollectionChangeEventHandler
    (dtColumns_CollectionChanged);

private void dtColumns_CollectionChanged(object sender,
  CollectionChangeEventArgs e)
{
    MessageBox.Show("Action = " + e.Action + Environment.NewLine +
    "Element = " + ((DataColumn) e.Element).ColumnName);
}
```

Notes

The DataColumnCollection class derives its standard functionality from the InternalDataCollectionBase class from which it inherits.

The commonly used public properties of the DataColumnCollection are listed and described in Table 23-7.

Table 23-7. DataColumnCollection public properties

Property	Description
Count	Gets the number of items in the DataColumnCollection.
Item	Gets the specified DataColumn from the DataColumnCollection. In C#, the Item property is the indexer for the class.

The commonly used public methods of the DataColumnCollection are listed and described in Table 23-8.

Table 23-8. DataColumnCollection public methods

Method	Description
Add( )	Adds a DataColumn object to the collection.
AddRange( )	Adds the objects in the array of DataColumn objects to the end of the collection.
CanRemove( )	Returns a Boolean value indicating whether a specific item can be removed from the collection.
Clear( )	Removes all items from the collection.
Contains( )	Returns a Boolean value indicating whether a DataColumn with the specified name exists in the collection.
IndexOf( )	Returns the index of the specified DataColumn. If the DataColumn doesn't exist in the collection, −1 is returned.
Remove( )	Removes the specified DataColumn from the collection. An ArgumentException is generated if the specified DataColumn doesn't exist in the collection.

Table 23-8. DataColumnCollection public methods (continued)

Method	Description
RemoveAt( )	Removes the DataColumn at the specified index from the collection. An ArgumentException is raised if the collection doesn't have a DataColumn at the specified index.

Constraints

```
ConstraintCollection cc = DataTable.Constraints;
```

Accesses the ConstraintCollection for the DataTable, providing access to the Constraint objects belonging to the DataTable. The Constraints property can be used to add, remove, and examine the UniqueConstraint and ForeignKeyConstraint objects in a DataTable.

Examples

There are two methods that can add a constraint to a table. The Add( ) method takes an argument specifying a reference to an existing constraint or takes arguments specifying whether a unique constraint or foreign key constraint is being added. The following example demonstrates adding a constraint by specifying a reference to an existing constraint:

```
// add a unique constraint by reference
UniqueConstraint uc = new UniqueConstraint(dt.Columns["MyColumn"]);
dt.Constraints.Add(uc);

// add a foreign key constraint by reference
ForeignKeyConstraint fc = new ForeignKeyConstraint(
    dtParent.Columns["ParentColumn"],
    dtChild.Columns["ChildColumn"]);
dt.Constraints.Add(fc);
```

Two overloads of the Add( ) method create and add a UniqueConstraint in one statement. The methods take a constraint name, either a reference to a DataColumn or a DataColumn array, and an argument indicating whether the column or columns are a primary key.

```
// add a unique constraint that is also a primary key
dt.Constraints.Add("MyUniqueConstraint", dt.Columns["MyColumn"], true);
```

The other two overloads of the Add( ) method create and add a ForeignKeyConstraint in one statement. The methods take a constraint name, and either two DataColumn references or two DataColumn arrays.

```
// add a foreign key constraint based on two columns
dt.Constraints.Add("MyForeignKeyConstraint",
    dtParent.Columns["ParentCol1"],
    dtChild.Columns["ChildCol2"]);
```

The AddRange( ) method adds an array of Constraint objects to the end of the constraint collection:

```
Constraint c1, c2;

// ... code to define constraints c1 and c2
```

```
// add the constraints c1 and c2 to the ConstraintCollection for the table
dt.Constraints.AddRange(new Constraint[] {c1, c2});
```

Notes

The `ConstraintCollection` class derives its standard functionality from the `InternalDataCollectionBase` class from which it inherits.

The commonly used public properties of the `ConstraintCollection` are listed and described in Table 23-9.

Table 23-9. ConstraintCollection public properties

Property	Description
Count	Gets the number of items in the `ConstraintCollection`.
Item	Gets the specified Constraint from the `ConstraintCollection`. In C#, the `Item` property is the indexer for the class.

The commonly used public methods of the `ConstraintCollection` are listed and described in Table 23-10.

Table 23-10. ConstraintCollection public methods

Method	Description
Add( )	Adds a `Constraint` object to the collection.
AddRange( )	Adds the objects in the array of `Constraint` objects to the end of the collection.
CanRemove( )	Returns a Boolean value indicating whether a specific item can be removed from the collection.
Clear( )	Removes all items from the collection.
IndexOf( )	Returns a Boolean value indicating whether a `Constraint` with the specified name exists in the collection.
Remove( )	Returns the index of the specified `Constraint`. A value of −1 is returned if the `Constraint` doesn't exist in the collection.
RemoveAt( )	Removes the specified `Constraint` from the collection. An `ArgumentException` is generated if the specified `Constraint` doesn't exist in the collection.

ExtendedProperties

```
PropertyCollection ep = DataTable.ExtendedProperties;
```

Accesses the `PropertyCollection` object of the `DataTable` that allows custom information related to the `DataTable` to be stored. Non-string properties aren't persisted when the `DataTable` is written as XML.

Example

The following example shows how to set and retrieve custom information for the `DataTable` using `ExtendedProperties`:

```
// set
dt.ExtendedProperties.Add("MyKey", "MyCustomData");

// get
String customData = dt.ExtendedProperties["MyKey"].ToString();
```

ParentRelations

```
DataRelationCollection pdrc = DataTable.ParentRelations;
```

Accesses the parent DataRelationCollection for the DataTable, providing access to the parent DataRelation objects belonging to the DataTable. The ParentRelations property be used to add, remove, and examine the parent DataRelation object in a DataTable.

Example   See the Examples for the Relations collection in Chapter 22.

Note   See the Notes for the Relations collection in Chapter 22.

PrimaryKey

```
DataColumn[] pka = DataTable.PrimaryKey;
DataTable.PrimaryKey = pka;
```

Accesses the array of DataColumn objects that make up the primary key of the table.

Example

The primary key for a table can be set by specifying an array of DataColumn objects from the table. The following example shows how to create a primary key based on two columns:

```
// set the primary key based on two columns in the DataTable
DataTable dt = new DataTable("MyTable");
dt.Columns.Add("PK_Field1", typeof(System.Int32));
dt.Columns.Add("PK_Field2", typeof(System.Int32));
// add other table columns
dt.PrimaryKey = new DataColumn[] {dt.Columns["PK_Field1"],
    dt.Columns["PK_Field2"]};
```

To remove the primary key, simply set the primary key to null, as shown in the following example:

```
// remove the primary key
dt.PrimaryKey = null;
```

Note   The PrimaryKey property accesses the DataColumn object or objects that make up the primary key of DataTable. The primary key acts as a unique constraint for the table and also allows records to be located using the Find() method of the DataTable rows collection.

Rows

```
DataRowCollection drc = DataTable.Rows;
```

Accesses the DataRowCollection for the DataTable, providing access to the DataRow objects belonging to the DataTable. The Rows property can be used to add, remove, and examine the DataRow objects in a DataTable.

Examples

There are two methods that can add a row to a table. The Add() method takes either a DataRow argument or an object array of columns of the row to be added:

```
DataTable dt = new DataTable("MyTable");
dt.Columns.Add("Column1", typeof(System.Int32));
dt.Columns.Add("Column2", typeof(System.String));

DataRow newRow = dt.NewRow();
newRow["Column1"] = 1;
newRow["Column2"] = "DataRow 1";

// add a row using a reference to a DataRow
dt.Rows.Add(newRow);

// add and create a DataRow in one statement
dt.Rows.Add(new Object[] {2, "DataRow 2"});
```

A DataRow can also be inserted at a specific point in the DataRowCollection using the InsertAt( ) method, which in addition to a reference to a DataRow, takes an argument specifying the zero-based index at which to insert the row.

```
// create a new row
DataRow row = dt.NewRow();
row.ItemArray = new Object[] {1, "DataRow 1"};

// insert a new row as the first item of the collection
dt.Rows.InsertAt(row,0);
```

The Contains( ) method returns a value that indicates whether the primary key exists in the collection of rows. The method has two overloads taking an object or an array of objects allowing primary keys based on one or more columns to be examined.

```
// look for a primary key that is based on a single column
bool exists = dt.Rows.Contains("PK Value 1");

// look for a primary key that is based on multiple columns
bool exists = dt.Rows.Contains(new Object[] {"PK Field1 Value",
    "PK Field2 Value"});
```

The Find( ) method is the second method available to locate a row based on the primary key. The Find( ) method differs from the Contains( ) method in that it returns the matching row rather than just indicating if a matching row exists. Like the Contains( ) method, the Find( ) method has two overloads taking an object or an array of objects allowing rows with primary keys based on a single or multiple columns to be returned. A null reference is returned if a matching row isn't found.

```
// get the row for a primary key that is based on a single column
DataRow row = dt.Rows.Find("PK Value 1");

// get the row for a primary key that is based on multiple columns
DataRow row = dt.Rows.Find(new Object[] {"PK Field1 Value",
    "PK Field2 Value"});
```

The Remove( ) method removes a row specified by a DataRow argument from the collection:

```
// remove the row matching the primary key value, if found
DataRow row = dt.Rows.Find("PK Value 1");
if(row != null)
    dt.Rows.Remove(row);
```

The RemoveAt() method removes the row specified by a zero-based index argument from the collection. If there no row at the index, an IndexOutOfRangeException is raised.

```
// remove the first row from the collection
dt.Rows.RemoveAt(0);
```

The Clear() method removes all rows from the collection:

```
// remove all rows from the table
dt.Rows.Clear();
```

Notes

The DataRowCollection class derives its standard functionality from the InternalDataCollectionBase class from which it inherits.

The commonly used public properties of the DataRowCollection are listed and described in Table 23-11.

Table 23-11. DataRowCollection public properties

Property	Description
Count	Gets the number of items in the DataRowCollection.
Item	Gets the specified DataRow from the DataRowCollection. In C#, the Item property is the indexer for the class.

The commonly used public methods of the DataRowCollection are listed and described in Table 23-12.

Table 23-12. DataRowCollection public methods

Method	Description
Add()	Adds a DataRow object to the collection.
Clear()	Removes all items from the collection.
Contains()	Returns a Boolean value indicating whether a DataRow with the specified name exists in the collection.
Find()	Returns a DataRow specified by the primary key value or values. If the primary key doesn't exist in the collection, a null reference is returned.
InsertAt()	Inserts the DataRow specified at the specified location in the collection. If the location specified is greater than the number of items in the collection, the DataRow is added to the end of the collection.
Remove()	Removes the specified DataRow from the collection. An ArgumentException is generated if the specified DataRow doesn't exist in the collection.
RemoveAt()	Removes the DataRow at the specified index from the collection. An ArgumentException is raised if the collection doesn't have a DataRow at the specified index.

Methods Reference

AcceptChanges

```
DataTable.AcceptChanges();
```

Commits all changes made to the DataTable since the last time it was loaded or the last time AcceptChanges() was called.

Parameters   None.

Example

The following example demonstrates how to call the AcceptChanges() method of the DataTable and the effect of calling AcceptChanges() on the row state:

```
// create a table with a single column
DataTable dt = new DataTable();
dt.Columns.Add("MyColumn", typeof(System.Int32));

DataRow row;
row = dt.NewRow();
row["MyColumn"] = 1;
dt.Rows.Add(row);        // RowState = Added

dt.AcceptChanges();      // RowState = Unchanged

row["MyColumn"] = 2;     // RowState = Modified
dt.AcceptChanges();      // RowState = Unchanged

row.Delete();            // RowState = Deleted
dt.AcceptChanges();      // Row is removed from the DataTable
```

Notes

Calling AcceptChanges() sets the RowState property of Added and Modified rows to Unchanged; the original values in the DataRow are set to the current values. Deleted rows are removed from the DataTable.

Calling the AcceptChanges() method on the DataTable causes AcceptChanges to be called on each DataRow belonging to the DataTable. Calling the AcceptChanges() method of a DataSet that the table belongs to implicitly calls the AcceptChanges() method of the table.

EndEdit() is implicitly called on any DataRow objects that are in edit mode as a result of calling the BeginEdit() method of the DataRow.

Calling AcceptChanges() clears all RowError information and sets the HasErrors property of the row to false.

BeginLoadData

```
DataTable.BeginLoadData();
```

Turns off constraints, notifications, and index maintenance for the DataTable.

Parameters   None.

Example

The following example shows how to use the `BeginLoadData()` and `EndLoadData()` methods to load data into a `DataTable`:

```
dt.BeginLoadData();

// load two rows to the DataTable dt
dt.LoadDataRow(new Object[]{1,"Row 1"}, false);
dt.LoadDataRow(new Object[]{2,"Row 2"}, false);

dt.EndLoadData();
```

Notes

Calling `BeginLoadData()` and `EndLoadData()` methods might result in performance improvements when adding multiple rows to a table with the `LoadDataRow()` method, although this isn't required.

The `EndLoadData()` method turns on constraints, notifications, and index maintenance for the `DataTable` after they have been turned off by `BeginLoadData()`.

Clear

```
DataTable.Clear();
```

Removes all rows from the `DataTable`.

Parameters   None.

Example

The following example demonstrates how to use the `Clear()` method of the `DataTable`:

```
DataTable dt = new DataTable();

// ... define the schema for the DataTable

// ... add some rows to the table

dt.Clear();     // all rows are removed from the table.
```

Note   An exception is generated if the `Clear()` operation deletes a parent row for a child row in an enforced relationship.

Clone

```
DataTable cloneTable = DataTable.Clone();
```

Creates a new `DataTable` with the same schema as the current `DataTable` but containing none of the data.

Parameter

cloneTable
    Returns a `DataTable` with the same schema but none of the data of the original `DataTable`.

Example

The following example shows how to create a new empty DataTable with the same schema as an existing DataTable:

```
DataSet dt1 = new DataTable();

// ... define the schema for the DataTable

// ... add some rows to the DataTable

// Create DataTable dt2 with the same schema, but without any of the
// data in DataTable dt1.
DataTable dt2 = dt1.Clone();
```

Compute

```
Object obj = DataTable.Compute(String expression, String filter);
```

Returns the result of an aggregate expression for a subset of rows in the table meeting the filter criteria.

Parameters

obj Returns an object containing the results computed.

expression
> The expression to calculate.

filter
> A filter that identifies a subset of rows for which the expression is computed.

Example

The following example demonstrates how to use the Compute() method to calculate the sum of a column for a subset of the rows filtered from the table:

```
DataTable dt = new DataTable();
dt.Columns.Add("OrderId", typeof(System.Int32));
dt.Columns.Add("OrderAmount", typeof(System.Decimal));

// ... add some rows

// computes the sum of order amounts for all orders with Id less than 10
Decimal totalOrderAmount=
    (Decimal) dt.Compute("SUM(OrderAmount)", "OrderId<10");
```

Note The expression must be set to an aggregate function. To compute a value based on an expression, create a DataColumn based on the expression and use that column in the expression.

Copy

```
DataTable copyTable = DataTable.Copy();
```

Creates a new DataTable with the same schema and data as the current DataTable.

Parameter

copyTable
> Returns a DataTable with the same schema and data as the original DataTable.

Example

The following example shows how to create a new empty DataTable with the same schema and data as an existing DataTable:

```
DataSet dt1 = new DataTable();

// ... define the schema for the DataTable

// ... add some rows to the DataTable

// Create DataTable dt2 with the same schema and data as DataTable dt1.
DataTable dt2 = dt1.Copy();
```

EndLoadData

```
DataTable.EndLoadData();
```

Turns on constraints, notifications, and index maintenance that were turned off by BeginLoadData().

Parameters   None.

Example   See the Example for the BeginLoadData() method in this chapter.

Notes

Calling BeginLoadData() and EndLoadData() methods might result in performance improvements when adding multiple rows to a table with the LoadDataRow() method.

The BeginLoadData() method turns off the constraints, notifications, and index maintenance for the DataTable.

If there are constraint violations when the EndLoadData() method is called, a ConstraintException event is raised.

GetChanges

```
DataTable changeTable = DataTable.GetChanges();
DataTable changeTable = DataTable.GetChanges(DataRowState drs);
```

Returns a DataTable with the same schema as the original DataTable, but containing only the rows that have been modified since the last time the DataSet was loaded or since AcceptChanges() was last called. This overloaded method allows the changes to be filtered by the RowState of the DataRow objects.

Parameters

changeTable
> Returns the DataTable with all changes made to the original since it was last loaded or since AcceptChanges() was last called.

drs   A value from the DataRowState enumeration described in Table 23-13 specifying the state of the DataRow objects to return.

Example

The following example shows how to create a DataTable containing only the changed rows from the original DataTable using the GetChanges() method:

```
DataSet dsChanges = dsOriginal.GetChanges();
```

Notes

The GetChanges() method can isolate the rows that have been changed so that the entire DataTable doesn't have to be passed to a method that reconciles DataTable changes with the data source.

A null reference is returned if there are no rows matching the specified criteria.

GetErrors

```
DataRow[] errorRows = DataTable.GetErrors();
```

Gets an array of DataRow objects that contain errors.

Parameter

errorRows
> Returns an array of DataRow objects that are the rows in the DataTable with errors.

Example

The following example demonstrates using the GetErrors() method to return the array of rows that have errors:

```
DataRow[] errorRows;
if(dt.HasErrors)
{
    errorRows = dt.GetErrors();
    for(Int32 i = 0; i<errorRows.Length; i++)
    {
        // ... resolve the error for the row

        // clear the error for resubmitting
        errorRows[i].ClearErrors();
    }
}
```

Notes

The GetErrors() method returns a DataRow array of the rows that contain errors, both constraint violations and failed update attempts.

To improve performance, call HasErrors() on the DataTable prior to calling GetErrors() to determine whether there are any errors.

ImportRow

```
DataTable.ImportRow(DataRow row);
```

Copies a DataRow to the DataTable.

Parameter

row The DataRow to import into the current DataTable.

Example

The following example demonstrates how to use the `ImportRow()` method to add a row to a table:

```
DataRow newRow = dt.NewRow();
newRow["Column1"] = 1;
newRow["Column2"] = "Row 1";

dt.Rows.ImportRow(newRow);
```

Notes

The `ImportRow()` can add rows from other tables or rows that were not created using the `NewRow()` method to the table.

The existing `DataRowState` and other values in the row are preserved.

LoadDataRow

```
DataRow row = DataTable.LoadDataRow(Object[] values,
    Boolean acceptChanges);
```

Finds a `DataRow` in the `DataTable` and updates the values with the values in the supplied array. If the row isn't found, a new row is added to the `DataTable`.

Parameters

row Returns the `DataRow` that has been loaded into the `DataTable`.

values
> An array of objects containing the column values for the row to load into the `DataSet`.

acceptChanges
> A value indicating whether `AcceptChanges()` should be called on the row loaded into the `DataTable`.

Example

This example demonstrates adding a new row to the `Northwind Shippers` table:

```
ds.Tables["Shippers"].BeginLoadData();

ds.Tables["Shippers"].LoadDataRow(new object[] {null,
    "NewShipperCompanyName", "NewShipperPhone"}, true);

// ... load some more rows

ds.Tables["Shippers"].EndLoadData();
```

Notice that a null value is passed for the array element corresponding to the `ShipperID` column that is an `AutoIncrement` column.

Notes

The `LoadDataRow()` method takes an array of values and attempts to find a row with a matching primary key. If the primary key is found, the values replace the existing data for the row; otherwise a new row is added.

If a column has a default value or is an `AutoIncrement` column, pass null in the array for that column.

While not required, using `LoadDataRow()` together with the `BeginLoadData()` and `EndLoadData()` methods might improve performance.

An `ArgumentException` is raised if the array is larger than the number of columns in the table. If a value in the array doesn't match the respective column type, an `InvalidCastException` is raised. A `ConstraintException` is raised if adding the row violates a constraint. Finally, `NoNullAllowedException` is raised if an attempt is made to set a column to `null` when `AllowDBNull` is `false` for that column.

NewRow

```
DataRow newRow = DataTable.NewRow();
```

Returns a new `DataRow` with the same schema as the `DataTable`.

Parameter

newRow

> Returns a new, empty `DataRow` with the same schema as the `DataTable`.

Example

The following example demonstrates how to create a new row and add the row to a `DataTable` using the `Add()` method of the `DataRowCollection`:

```
// create the target table
DataTable dt = new DataTable("MyTable");
dt.Columns.Add("Column1", typeof(System.Int32));
dt.Columns.Add("Column2", typeof(System.String));

// create and add a new row to the table
DataRow newRow=dt.NewRow();
newRow["Column1"] = 1;
newRow["Column2"] = "Row 1";
dt.Rows.Add(newRow);
```

RejectChanges

```
DataTable.RejectChanges();
```

Rejects all changes made to the `DataTable` since the last time it was loaded or since the last time `AcceptChanges()` was called.

Parameters   None.

Example

The following example demonstrates how to call the `RejectChanges()` method of the `DataTable`:

```
// create a table with a single column
DataTable dt = new DataTable();
dt.Columns.Add("MyColumn", typeof(System.Int32));

DataRow row;
row = dt.NewRow();
row["MyColumn"] = 1;
dt.Rows.Add(row);        // RowState = Added
```

```
dt.AcceptChanges();          // RowState = Unchanged

row["MyColumn"] = 2;         // RowState = Modified
dt.RejectChanges();          // RowState = Unchanged, row["MyColumn"] = 1

row.Delete();                // RowState = Deleted
dt.RejectChanges();          // RowState = Unchanged
                             // The row isn't removed from the DataTable.
```

Notes

Calling RejectChanges( ) sets the RowState property of Deleted and Modified rows to Unchanged; the current values in the DataRow are set to the original values. Added rows are removed.

Calling the RejectChanges( ) method on the DataTable causes RejectChanges( ) to be called on each DataRow belonging to the DataTable. Calling the RejectChanges( ) method of the DataSet that the table belongs to implicitly calls the RejectChanges( ) method of the table.

Any DataRows in edit mode as a result of calling BeginEdit( ) cancel their edits when RejectChanges( ) is called.

Calling RejectChanges( ) clears all RowError information and sets the HasErrors property to false.

Reset

```
DataTable.Reset();
```

Discards the contents of the DataTable, resetting it to an uninitialized state.

Parameters   None.

Example

The following example shows how reset a DataSet to its original state:

```
ds.Reset();
```

Note   Calling Reset( ) on an existing DataTable is more efficient than instan-
               tiating a new DataTable.

Select

```
DataRow[] selectRow = DataTable.Select();
DataRow[] selectRow = DataTable.Select(String filter);
DataRow[] selectRow = DataTable.Select(String filter, String sortOrder);
DataRow[] selectRow = DataTable.Select(String filter, String sortOrder,
    DataViewRowState dvrs);
```

Returns an array of DataRow objects that matches the optional filter and DataViewRowState specified. The sort criteria can be specified to control the order of the objects in the returned DataRow array.

Parameters

selectRow

Returns an array of DataRow objects matching the optional select criteria and row state, ordered as specified by the optional sort order parameter.

filter

The filter criteria used to select the rows.

sortOrder

The sort order and direction for the returned rows within the array.

dvrs

The row state of the rows to be returned. This is a value from the DataViewRowState enumeration described in Table 28-1.

Example

The following example demonstrates selecting rows from a data table specifying both a filter and sort order:

```
// all rows with order amount > 100, sorted on the order date descending
DataRow[] dra = dt.Select("OrderAmount>100.00", "OrderDate DESC");
```

Note   The arguments specifying both the filter and sort order follow standard rules for creating expression strings.

Events Reference

ColumnChanged

DataColumnChangeEventHandler ColumnChanged;

The ColumnChanged event is raised after the value for a column in the DataRow has been changed.

Example

The following code demonstrates how to handle the ColumnChanged event:

```
DataTable dt = new DataTable();
dt.ColumnChanged += new DataColumnChangeEventHandler(dt_ColumnChanged);

private void dt_ColumnChanged(object sender,
    DataColumnChangeEventArgs e)
{
    MessageBox.Show("ColumnChanged: Name = " + e.Column.ColumnName + "; " +
        "ProposedValue = " + e.ProposedValue.ToString() + "; " +
        "Row Id = " + e.Row["Id"].ToString());
}
```

Notes

The event handler receives an argument of type DataColumnChangeEventArgs containing properties that provide specific information about the event as described in Table 23-13.

Table 23-13. DataColumnChangeEventArgs properties

Property	Description
Column	Returns a reference to the DataColumn that changes.
ProposedValue	Gets or sets a reference to an object representing the proposed value for the column.
Row	Returns a reference to the DataRow of the column that changes.

ColumnChanging

DataColumnChangeEventHandler ColumnChanging;

The ColumnChanging event is raised when the value for column in the DataRow is being changed.

Example

The following code demonstrates how to handle the ColumnChanging event:

```
DataTable dt = new DataTable();
dt.ColumnChanging += new DataColumnChangeEventHandler(dt_ColumnChanging);

private void dt_ColumnChanging(object sender,
    DataColumnChangeEventArgs e)
{
    MessageBox.Show("ColumnChanging: Name = " + e.Column.ColumnName + "; " +
        "ProposedValue = " + e.ProposedValue.ToString() + "; " +
        "Row Id = " + e.Row["Id"].ToString());
}
```

Note   The event handler receives an argument of type DataColumnChangeEventArgs, which contains properties that provide specific information about the event as described in Table 23-13.

RowChanged

DataRowChangeEventHandler RowChanged;

The RowChanged event is raised after a DataRow is successfully changed.

Example

The following code demonstrates how to handle the RowChanged event:

```
DataTable dt = new DataTable();
dt.RowChanged += new DataRowChangeEventHandler(dt_RowChanged);

private void dt_RowChanged(object sender,
    DataRowChangeEventArgs e)
{
    MessageBox.Show("RowChanged: Action = " + e.Action + "; " +
        "Row Id = " + e.Row["Id"].ToString());
}
```

Notes

The event handler receives an argument of type DataRowChangeEventArgs, which contains properties that provide specific information about the event as described in Table 23-14. DataRowAction enumeration is covered in Table 23-15.

Table 23-14. DataRowChangeEventArgs properties

Property	Description
Action	Returns the action that has occurred on the DataRow. This value is from the DataRowAction enumeration as described in the next table.
Row	Returns a reference to the DataRow that is changing or being deleted.

Table 23-15. DataRowAction enumeration

Value	Description
Add	The row has been added to the table.
Change	The row has been modified.
Commit	The changes made to the row have been committed.
Delete	The row has been deleted from the table.
Nothing	The row has not been changed.
Rollback	The changes made to the row have been rolled back.

RowChanging

```
DataRowChangeEventHandler RowChanging;
```

The RowChanging event is raised when a DataRow is about to be changed.

Example

The following code demonstrates how to handle the RowChanging event:

```
DataTable dt = new DataTable();
dt.RowChanging += new DataRowChangeEventHandler(dt_RowChanging);

private void dt_RowChanging(object sender,
    DataRowChangeEventArgs e)
{
    MessageBox.Show("RowChanging: Action = " + e.Action + "; " +
        "Row Id = " + e.Row["Id"].ToString());
}
```

Note   The event handler receives an argument of type DataRowChangeEventArgs, which contains properties that provide specific information about the event as described in Table 23-14.

RowDeleted

```
DataRowChangeEventHandler RowDeleted;
```

The RowDeleted event is raised after a row is deleted from the table.

Example

The following code demonstrates how to handle the `RowDeleted` event:

```
DataTable dt = new DataTable();
dt.RowDeleted += new DataRowChangeEventHandler(dt_RowDeleted);

private void dt_RowDeleted(object sender,
    DataRowChangeEventArgs e)
{
    MessageBox.Show("RowDeleted: Action = " + e.Action + "; " +
        "Row Id = " + e.Row["Id"].ToString());
}
```

Note The event handler receives an argument of type `DataRowChangeEventArgs`, which contains properties that provide specific information about the event as described in Table 23-14.

RowDeleting

```
DataRowChangeEventHandler RowDeleting;
```

The `RowDeleting` event is raised when a row is about to be deleted from the table.

Example

The following code demonstrates how to handle the `RowDeleting` event:

```
DataTable dt = new DataTable();
dt.RowDeleting += new DataRowChangeEventHandler(dt_RowDeleting);

private void dt_RowDeleting(object sender,
    DataRowChangeEventArgs e)
{
    MessageBox.Show("RowDeleting: Action = " + e.Action + "; " +
        "Row Id = " + e.Row["Id"].ToString());
}
```

Note The event handler receives an argument of type `DataRowChangeEventArgs`, which contains properties that provide specific information about the event as described in Table 23-14.

24

The DataColumn Class

The DataColumn class defines the schema for a column in a DataTable. This schema defines the type of data that can be stored in the column, whether that data can be updated, any unique constraints on the data, and how values should be generated for new rows added to the table. Columns can be based on expressions that define a calculation or an aggregation for a column value.

As with all disconnected data classes, the DataColumn isn't specific to any data provider

Comments/Troubleshooting

The commonly used public properties of the DataColumn class are listed in Table 24-1.

Table 24-1. DataColumn properties

Property	Description
AllowDBNull	Gets or sets whether null values can be stored in the column.
AutoIncrement	Gets or sets whether the column automatically increments with each new row added to the table.
AutoIncrementSeed	Gets or sets the amount that an automatically incrementing column is incremented each time a row is added to the table.
AutoIncrementStep	Gets or sets the starting value for an automatically incrementing column.
Caption	Gets or sets the caption for the column used as the default value for the Caption property in controls that support its display.
ColumnMapping	Gets or sets how column data is written when it is saved as XML.
ColumnName	Gets or sets the name of the column.
DataType	Gets or sets the data type of the column data as one of the .NET Framework data types.
DefaultValue	Gets or sets the value that is automatically assigned to the column when a new row is created.

Table 24-1. DataColumn properties (continued)

Property	Description
Expression	Gets or sets an expression that calculates the value of the column.
MaxLength	Gets or sets the maximum length for a column with a text data type in characters.
Namespace	Gets or sets the XML namespace for the XML representation of the data stored in the column.
Ordinal	Gets the position of the column within the column collection of the table.
Prefix	Gets or sets the XML prefix for the XML representation of the data stored in the column.
ReadOnly	Gets or sets a value that indicates whether the data in the column can be changed once the row containing the column is added to a table.
Table	Gets the table that the column has been assigned to.
Unique	Gets or sets a value indicating whether the value for each row in the column must be unique.

The commonly used public collections of the DataColumn class are listed in Table 24-2.

Table 24-2. DataColumn collections

Collection	Description
ExtendedProperties	The ExtendedProperties property accesses the PropertyCollection collection that contains custom information for the DataColumn as a collection of key and value pairs.

The DataColumn class is contained within the System.Data namespace. The DataColumn class inherits from MarshalByValueComponent. It's safe for multi-threaded read operations; multithreaded write operations must be synchronized. DataColumn objects cannot be passed between different application domains.

Properties Reference

AllowDBNull

```
Boolean allowDBNull = DataColumn.AllowDBNull;
DataColumn.AllowDBNull = allowDBNull;
```

Gets or sets whether null values can be stored in the column.

Example
The following example creates a new DataColumn that doesn't allow null values:

```
DataColumn col = new DataColumn("MyColumn", typeof(System.String));
col.AllowDBNull = false;
```

Notes
The schema information to set the AllowDBNull property isn't retrieved from the data source using the Fill( ) method of the DataAdapter. The FillSchema( ) method of the DataAdapter does, however, set the AllowDBNull property based on the data source schema.

The AllowDBNull property is automatically set to false when a column is identified as the primary key or as part of the primary key.

A NoNullAllowedException is raised if an attempt is made to set the column value to null for a column in which the AllowDBNull property is set to false.

The default value for this property is true.

AutoIncrement

```
Boolean autoIncrement = DataColumn.AutoIncrement;
DataColumn.AutoIncrement = autoIncrement;
```

Gets or sets whether the column value automatically increments with each new row added to the table.

Example

The following example shows how to set the AutoIncrement, AutoIncrementSeed, and AutoIncrementStep properties of the DataColumn:

```
DataColumn col = new DataColumn("MyColumn", typeof(System.Int32));
col.AutoIncrement = true;
col.AutoIncrementSeed = -1;
col.AutoIncrementStep = -1;
```

Notes

The starting value for an AutoIncrement column in defined by the AutoIncrementSeed property. The subsequent values for the column are determined by the AutoIncrementStep property.

If the column type isn't an integer type (i.e., Int16, Int32, or Int64) and the AutoIncrement property is set to true, the DataType property of the column is coerced to Int32. If the column is computed (i.e., Expression property is set), and an attempt is made to set the AutoIncrement property to true, an exception is raised.

A new row can be created by using the ItemArray property of the DataRow and passing in an array of column values. Pass a null reference for AutoIncrement columns.

This property isn't set by calling either the Fill( ) or FillSchema( ) of the DataAdapter, regardless of the settings in the data source.

The default value of this property is false.

AutoIncrementSeed

```
Int64 autoIncrementSeed = DataColumn.AutoIncrementSeed;
DataColumn.AutoIncrementSeed = autoIncrementSeed;
```

Gets or sets the starting value for a column with its AutoIncrement property set to true.

Example   See the Example in the AutoIncrement property section of this chapter.

Note   The default value for this property is 0.

AutoIncrementStep

```
Int64 autoIncrementStep = DataColumn.AutoIncrementStep;
DataColumn.AutoIncrementStep = autoIncrementStep;
```

Gets or sets the amount that an AutoIncrement column is incremented each time a row is added to the table.

Example   See the Example in the AutoIncrement property section of this chapter.

Note   The default value of this property is 1.

Caption

```
String caption = DataColumn.Caption;
DataColumn.Caption = caption;
```

Gets or sets the caption for the column.

Example

The following example sets the caption for the DataColumn.

```
DataColumn col = new DataColumn("MyColumn", typeof(System.Int32));
col.Caption = "MyColumnCaption";
```

Notes

This value is used as the default value for the Caption of controls that support its display.

If not explicitly set, the Caption property defaults to the ColumnName value.

ColumnMapping

```
MappingType columnMapping = DataColumn.ColumnMapping;
DataColumn.ColumnMapping = columnMapping;
```

Gets or sets the MappingType for the column.

Example

The following example shows how to set the MappingType for a column so that the data for the column is output as an attribute.

```
DataColumn col = new DataColumn("MyColumn", typeof(System.String))
col.ColumnMapping = MappingType.Attribute;
```

Notes

The MappingType determines how the column data is written when it is saved to XML using the WriteXml method of the DataSet. It can be set to one of the MappingType enumeration values described in Table 24-3.

Table 24-3. MappingType enumeration

Value	Description
Attribute	XML attribute
Element	XML element

Table 24-3. MappingType enumeration (continued)

Value	Description
Hidden	A structure that isn't included in the output
SimpleContent	XmlText node

Using the first record in the Customers table in Northwind as an example, if the ColumnMapping for each column is set to Element, the following XML is produced:

```
<Customers>
    <CustomerID>ALFKI</CustomerID>
    <CompanyName>Alfreds Futterkiste</CompanyName>

    ...

    <Fax>030-0076545</Fax>
</Customers>
```

If, on the other hand, the ColumMapping for each column is set to Attribute, the following XML is produced:

```
<Customers CustomerID=" ALFKI" CompanyName="
    Alfreds Futterkiste" ... Fax="030-0076545" />
```

The ColumnMapping property must be set explicitly on each column to set it to a value other than the default value.

The default value for ColumnMapping is Element.

ColumnName

```
String columnName = DataColumn.ColumnName;
DataColumn.ColumnName = columnName;
```

Gets or sets the name of the column.

Example

The following example shows how to set the name of the column:

```
DataColumn col = new DataColumn();
col.ColumnName = "MyColumn";
```

Notes

The value for the ColumnName property can also be set using the DataColumn constructor as shown in this sample:

```
DataColumn col = new DataColumn("MyColumn");
```

If the contents of the DataColumn are output as XML, the ColumnName is used as the name element or attribute tag in the XML document.

By default, ColumnName property has no value. If the ColumnName property has not been set when the column is added to the DataColumnCollection of a DataTable, the column name defaults to Column1, Column2, and so on.

DataColumn

DataType

```
Type dataType = DataColumn.DataType;
DataColumn.DataType = dataType;
```

Gets or sets the data type of the column data as a .NET Framework data type.

Example

The following example demonstrates how to set the data type for a column:

```
DataColumn col = new DataColumn();
col.DataType = typeof(Int32);
```

Notes

This DataType property supports the base .NET Framework data types described in Table 24-4.

Table 24-4. NET Framework data types

Data type	Description
Boolean	A Boolean value. Instances of this type have the value true or false.
Byte	An 8-bit unsigned integer with values ranging from 0 to 255.
Char	A Unicode character with values ranging from hexadecimal 0x0000 to 0xFFFF.
DateTime	Represents dates and times with values ranging from January 1, 0001 12:00:00 midnight to December 31, 9999 11:59:50 P.M.
Decimal	A decimal number ranging from −79,228,162,514,264,337,593,543,950,335 through +79,228,162,514,264,337,593,543,950,335. The Decimal value type eliminates rounding errors in large numbers, typical in financial calculations.
Double	A double-precision 64-bit number ranging from −1.79769313486232e308 through +1.79769313486232e308. The Double type can also contain values −0, +0, PositiveInfinity, NegativeInfinity, and Not-a-Number (NaN).
Int16	A 16-bit signed integer with values ranging from −32,768 through +32,767.
Int32	A 32-bit signed integer with values ranging from −2,147,483,648 through +2,147,483,647.
Int64	A 64-bit signed integer with values ranging from −9,223,372,036,854,775,808 through +9,223,372,036,854,775,807.
SByte	An 8-bit signed integer with values ranging from −128 through +127.
Single	A single precision floating-point number with values ranging from −3.402823e38 through +3.402823e38. The Single type can also contain values −0, +0, PositiveInfinity, NegativeInfinity, and Not-a-Number (NaN).
String	An object representing an immutable series of characters.
TimeSpan	A 64-bit time interval measured in ticks.
UInt16	A 16-bit unsigned integer with values ranging from 0 to 65,535.
UInt32	A 32-bit unsigned integer with values ranging from 0 to 4,294,967,295.
UInt64	A 64-bit unsigned integer with values ranging from 0 to 184,467,440,737,095,551,615.

The value for the DataType property can also be set using the DataColumn constructor as shown in this sample:

```
DataColumn col = new DataColumn("MyColumn", typeof(System.String));
```

If the `AutoIncrement` property of the column is set to true, the `DataType` property must be set to an integer type; an `ArgumentException` is raised if an attempt is made to set the `DataType` property to a noninteger data type.

An `ArgumentException` is raised if the value of the `DataType` property is changed once there is data in the table.

The default value for this property is `String`.

DefaultValue

```
Object defaultValue = DataColumn.DefaultValue;
DataColumn.DefaultValue = defaultValue;
```

Gets or sets the value that is automatically assigned to the column when a new `DataRow` is created.

Example

The following example shows how to set the default value for a column:

```
DataColumn col = new DataColumn("MyColumn", typeof(System.String));
col.DefaultValue = "DefaultValue";
```

Notes

The default value is limited because it can only be set to a static value. There is no facility to, for example, set a `DefaultValue` that causes the date and time a column is created to be stored in the column.

If an attempt is made to set the `DefaultValue` to a value that isn't an instance of the data type of the column, an `InvalidCastException` is raised when a new row is added.

This value cannot be set if the `AutoIncrement` property is true.

Expression

```
String expression = DataColumn.Expression;
DataColumn.Expression = expression;
```

Gets or sets an expression that calculates the value of the column.

Example

The following example demonstrates how to create an expression column that returns the calculated `ExtendedPrice` based on the `Quantity` and `Price` columns:

```
DataColumn col1 = new DataColumn("Quantity", typeof(System.Int32));
DataColumn col2 = new DataColumn("Price", typeof(System.Decimal));

// create a column calculating the extended price
DataColumn col3 = new DataColumn("ExtendedPrice", typeof(System.Decimal));
col3.Expression = "Quantity * Price";
```

Notes

The value of an expression column is calculated each time the value of the column is requested.

If this property is set to anything other than an empty string, the `ReadOnly` property is automatically set to true.

MaxLength

```
Int32 maxLength = DataColumn.MaxLength;
DataColumn.MaxLength = maxLength;
```

Gets or sets the maximum length in characters for a column with a text data type.

Example

The following example creates a column with a data type of String and sets the maximum length to 50:

```
DataColumn col = new DataColumn("MyColumn", typeof(System.String));
col.MaxLength = 50;
```

Notes

This value is ignored for nontext columns.

The value for the MaxLength property can also be set using the DataColumn constructor as shown in this sample:

```
DataColumn col = new DataColumn("MyColumn", typeof(System.String), 50);
```

A value of −1, the default, indicates that the text column has no maximum length.

Namespace

```
String namespace = DataColumn.Namespace;
DataColumn.Namespace = namespace;
```

Gets or sets the XML namespace for the XML representation of the data stored in the DataColumn.

Example

The following example sets the Namespace property of the DataColumn:

```
DataColumn col = new DataColumn();
col.Namespace = "AdoDotNetIan";
```

Note   The Namespace property scopes the XML attributes and elements when reading and writing the DataColumn using the ReadXml( ), WriteXml( ), ReadXmlSchema( ), and WriteXmlSchema( ) methods of the Dataset the column belongs to.

Ordinal

```
Int32 ordinal = DataColumn.Ordinal;
```

Gets the position of the column in the DataColumnCollection of a DataTable.

Example

The following example demonstrates how to determine the position of the column in the table:

```
int colOrdinal;

DataColumn col = new DataColumn("MyColumn", typeof(System.Int32));
colOrdinal = col.Ordinal;     // colOrdinal=-1 after this statement
```

```
DataTable dt = new DataTable("MyTable");
dt.Columns.Add(col);
colOrdinal = col.Ordinal;     // colOrdinal=0 after this statement
```

Note   The Ordinal property is zero-based and returns −1 if the column doesn't belong to a table.

Prefix

```
String prefix = DataColumn.Prefix;
DataColumn.Prefix = prefix;
```

Gets or sets the XML prefix that aliases the namespace of the DataColumn.

Example

The following example sets the Prefix property of the DataColumn:

```
DataColumn col = new DataColumn();
col.Prefix = "adni";
```

Note   The Prefix is used within the XML document to identify attributes and elements that belong to the namespace of the DataColumn object defined by the Namespace property.

ReadOnly

```
Boolean readOnly = DataColumn.ReadOnly;
DataColumn.ReadOnly = readOnly;
```

Gets or sets a value indicating whether the data in the column can be changed once the DataRow containing the column is added to a DataTable.

Example

The following example creates a column and makes it read-only:

```
DataColumn col = new DataColumn("MyColumn");
col.ReadOnly = true;
```

Note   The default value of this property is false.

Table

```
DataTable table = DataColumn.Table;
```

Gets the DataTable to which the DataColumn belongs.

Example

The following example shows how to retrieve a reference to the DataTable object the DataColumn belongs to:

```
DataColumn col = new DataColumn();

// ... code to define the DataColumn col add it to the DataTable

DataTable dt = col.Table;
```

Table | 339

Note	This property returns a `null` reference if the `DataColumn` has not been assigned to a `DataTable`.

Unique

```
Boolean unique = DataColumn.Unique;
DataColumn.Unique = unique;
```

Gets or sets a value indicating whether the column value for each row in the column must be unique.

Example

The following example creates a column and makes it unique:

```
DataColumn col = new DataColumn("MyColumn", typeof(System.Int32));
col.Unique = true;
```

Notes

Setting this property to `true` creates a unique constraint on the column.

The `Fill()` method of the `DataAdapter` doesn't set this value based on the underlying data source schema; the `FillSchema()` method of the `DataAdapter` does.

The default value of this property is `false`.

Collections Reference

ExtendedProperties

```
PropertyCollection ep = DataColumn.ExtendedProperties;
```

Accesses the `PropertyCollection` object of the `DataColumn` that allows custom information related to the `DataColumn` to be stored. Nonstring properties aren't persisted when the `DataSet` is written as XML.

Example

The following example shows how to set and retrieve custom information for the `DataTable` using `ExtendedProperties`:

```
// set
col.ExtendedProperties.Add("MyKey", "MyCustomData");

// get
String customData = col.ExtendedProperties["MyKey"].ToString();
```

Note	See the Notes for the `ExtendedProperties` collection section in Chapter 22.

25

The DataRow Class

The `DataRow` class represents a single row of data in the `DataTable`. It retrieves, updates, inserts, and deletes a row of data from the `DataTable`. The `DataRow` object can access column values within the row.

As with all disconnected data classes, the `DataRow` isn't specific to any data provider.

Comments/Troubleshooting

The commonly used public properties of the `DataRow` class are listed in Table 25-1.

Table 25-1. DataRow properties

Property	Description
HasErrors	Gets a value indicating whether there are errors in the row.
RowError	Gets or sets a value containing the error description text for a row.
RowState	Gets the current row state.
Table	Gets the table that the row belongs to and has a schema for.

The commonly used public collections of the `DataRow` class are listed in Table 25-2.

Table 25-2. DataRow collection

Collection	Description
ItemArray	Gets or sets the values for the columns in the row as an object array.

The commonly used public methods of the `DataRow` class are listed in Table 25-3.

Table 25-3. DataRow methods

Method	Description
AcceptChanges( )	Commits all changes made to the row since the last time it was loaded or since the last time changes were committed.
BeginEdit( )	Puts the row into edit mode, suspending the events that trigger validation rules.
CancelEdit( )	Cancels the edit on the row, discarding any changes.
ClearErrors( )	Clears both row and column errors for the row.
Delete( )	If the row is newly added, it is removed from the table. Otherwise, the row is marked for deletion.
EndEdit( )	Ends the edit on the row, committing the changes made.
GetChildRows( )	Gets an array of child rows for the row, based on a specified relationship.
GetColumnError( )	Gets the error description for a specified column in the row.
GetColumnsInError( )	Gets the array of columns in the row having errors.
GetParentRow( )	Gets the parent row for the row, based on a relation.
GetParentRows( )	Gets an array of rows that are the parent rows of the row, based on a specified relationship.
HasVersion( )	Returns a value indicating whether the specified version of the row exists.
IsNull( )	Returns a value indicating whether the specified column in the row contains a null value.
RejectChanges( )	Rejects all changes made to the row since the last time it was loaded or since the last time changes were committed.
SetColumnError( )	Sets the error description for a specified column in the row.
SetParentRow( )	Sets the parent row of the row to the specified row.

The DataRow class is contained within the System.Data namespace. The DataRow class is safe for multithreaded read operations; multithreaded write operations must be synchronized. DataRow objects can't be passed between different application domains.

Properties Reference

HasErrors

```
Boolean hasErrors = DataRow.HasErrors;
```

Gets a value indicating whether there are errors in the DataRow.

Example

The following example shows how to use the HasErrors property to determine if there are any errors in the DataRow after the reconciliation of the modified DataTable with the data source:

```
DataTable dt = new DataTable();
SqlDataAdapter da = new SqlDataAdapter();

// ... define the DataAdapter
```

```
// fill the DataTable
da.Fill(dt);

// ... modify the data in the DataTable

da.Update(dt);
if (dt.HasErrors)
{
    foreach(DataRow row in dt.Rows)
    {
        if (row.HasErrors)
        {
         // ... handle the errors for the row
        }
    }
}
```

Notes

The SetColumnError method can set an error on a column in the row.

The GetColumnsInError methods can retrieve the columns in the row with errors. The GetColumnError can retrieve the error description for a column.

The ClearErrors method can clear all errors on the row.

Item

```
Object colValue = DataRow[String columnName];
DataRow[String columnName] = colValue;
Object colValue = DataRow[DataColumn col];
DataRow[DataColumn col] = colValue;
Object colValue = DataRow[Integer colIndex];
DataRow[Integer colIndex] = colValue;
Object colValue = DataRow[String columnName, DataRowVersion drv];
Object colValue = DataRow[DataColumn col, DataRowVersion drv];
Object colValue = DataRow[Integer colIndex, DataRowVersion drv];
```

The indexer for the class that gets or sets the data stored in the row for the specified column.

Parameters

colValue
> An object containing the data to get or set for the DataColumn.

columnName
> The name of the DataColumn.

col A reference to a DataColumn object.

colIndex
> The index of the column in the DataColumnCollection of the DataTable.

drv The DataRowVersion value of the column to retrieve. For more on the DataRowVersion value, see Table 25-5 in the HasVersion section of this chapter.

Example

The following examples show how to get and set the values for a column using the different versions of the Item property:

```
DataTable dt = new DataTable();
DataColumn col = dt.Columns.Add("MyColumn", typeof(System.String));
DataRow row = dt.NewRow();

// the next three statements have the same result
row["MyColumn"] = "My value";
row[col] = "My value";
row[0] = "My value";

String rowValue="";
// the next three statements return the same result
rowValue = (String) row["MyColumn", DataRowVersion.Current];
rowValue = (String) row[col, DataRowVersion.Current];
rowValue = (String) row[0, DataRowVersion.Current];
```

Notes

If the specified column can't be found, or the specified column index doesn't exist, an IndexOutOfRangeException is raised.

If the specified column reference is null, an ArgumentNullException is raised. If the column referenced doesn't belong to the table, an ArgumentException is raised.

If the data type of the column value specified doesn't match the DataType for the column, an InvalidCastException is raised.

If an attempt is made to set a value on a deleted row, a DeletedRowInaccessibleException is raised.

If an attempt is made to access a version of the row that doesn't exist, a VersionNot-FoundException is raised.

ItemArray

```
Object[] itemArray = DataRow.ItemArray;
DataRow.ItemArray = itemArray;
```

Gets or sets the values of the row using an object array. Each item in the object array corresponds to a column in the DataTable.

Example

The following example demonstrates how to get and set the values for columns in a row using the ItemArray property:

```
// create a table with two columns
DataTable dt = new DataTable();
DataColumn colId = new DataColumn("ProductId", typeof(System.Int32));
DataColumn colDesc = new DataColumn("Description", typeof(System.String));
dt.Columns.AddRange(new DataColumn[] {colId, colDesc});

dt.Rows.Add(new object[] {1, "Widget"});

// get the data for the row using the ItemArray property
object[] row = dt.Rows[0].ItemArray;
```

```
// set the ProductId to be AutoIncrement
colId.AutoIncrement = true;
// pass null for the AutoIncrement value
dt.Rows.Add(new object[] {null, "Thing"});

// let the description be null
colDesc.AllowDBNull = true;
// add a row with a null description, and AutoIncrement Id
dt.Rows.Add(new object[] {null, null});
```

Notes

When the ItemArray property is used, an attempt is made to locate the row matching the primary key. If the row is found, it is updated with the values in the ItemArray; otherwise, a new row is created.

Any columns with an array element set to null are set to the default value for a new column or the existing value for the column if the row is being updated.

The value for AutoIncrement columns should be set to null in the ItemArray.

RowError

```
String rowError = DataRow.RowError;
DataRow.RowError = rowError;
```

Gets or sets a value containing the error description text that applies to the entire DataRow.

Example

The following example shows how to set the error text for a DataRow:

```
DataTable dt = new DataTable();
DataColumn col = dt.Columns.Add("MyColumn", typeof(System.String));
DataRow row = dt.NewRow();

row.RowError = "This row has an error.";
```

Notes

The RowError property can be set when processing modified data against the business rules. Alternatively, when the Update() method of the DataAdapter is called and fails and the ContinueUpdateOnError property of the DataAdapter is set to true, the HasErrors property of the row is set to true and the RowError property is set to the error message. The RowUpdated event handler can be used to determine the status of the update attempt and set the error text for the row as necessary.

Use the GetColumnError() and SetColumnError() methods to get and set the error description for a particular column.

RowState

```
DataRowState rowState = DataRow.RowState;
```

Gets the current row state of a DataRow within the DataRowCollection. This value is one of the DataRowState values described in Table 25-4.

Table 25-4. DataRowState enumeration

Value	Description
Added	The row has been added to the DataRowCollection for the table, and AcceptChanges( ) hasn't been called.
Deleted	The row has been deleted, and AcceptChanges( ) hasn't called.
Detached	The row isn't part of a DataRowCollection.
Modified	The row has been modified, and AcceptChanges( ) hasn't been called.
Unchanged	The row hasn't been changed since AcceptChanges( ) was last called.

Example

The value of the RowState property can't be directly set. ADO.NET sets the row state in response to actions that affect the DataRow. The AcceptChanges( ) and RejectChanges( ) methods, whether explicitly or implicitly called, reset the RowState value for the row to Unchanged as illustrated in the following code:

```
// create a table with one column
DataTable dt = new DataTable();
dt.Columns.Add("MyColumn", typeof(System.String));

// create a new row
DataRow row = dt.NewRow();          // RowState = Detached

// add the row to the table
dt.Rows.Add(row);                   // RowState = Added
dt.AcceptChanges();                 // RowState = Unchanged

// modify the row
row["MyColumn"] = "MyFieldValue";   // RowState = Modified

// reject the changes
row.RejectChanges();                // RowState = Unchanged

// delete the row
row.Delete();                       // RowState = Deleted
row.AcceptChanges();                // row no longer exists
```

Note   The RowState property is used primarily by ADO.NET to track the changes that have been made to a disconnected row so that changes to the data while disconnected can be updated back to the data source

Table

```
DataTable table = DataRow.Table;
```

Gets the table that the row belongs to and has a schema for.

Example

The following example demonstrates how to retrieve the DataTable the row belongs to:

```
DataTable dt1 = new DataTable();
DataRow row = DataTable.NewRow();
```

```
// returns a reference to DataTable dt1
DataTable dt2 = row.Table;
```

Note   A row belongs to the DataTable once it is added to the DataRowCollection. If the DataRow doesn't belong to a table, a null reference is returned.

Collections Reference

ItemArray

```
Object[] itemArray = DataRow.ItemArray;
```

Gets or sets the values for the columns in the row as an object array.

Example

The following example demonstrates how to use the ItemArray collection property to set values for the columns in a row:

```
// create a table with two columns
DataTable dt = new DataTable();
DataColumn colId = new DataColumn("ProductId", typeof(System.Int32));
DataColumn colDesc = new DataColumn("Description", typeof(System.String));
dt.Columns.AddRange(new DataColumn[] {colId, colDesc});

// add a row using ItemArray
object[] rowArray = new object[] {1, "Widget"};
DataRow row = dt.NewRow();
row.ItemArray = rowArray;
dt.Rows.Add(row);

// get the data for the row using the ItemArray property
object[] row = dt.Rows[0].ItemArray;
```

Note   When the ItemArray property is used, an attempt is made to locate the row matching the primary key. If the row is found, it is updated with the values in the ItemArray; otherwise, a new row is created. Any columns with an array element set to null are set to the default value for the column. The value for AutoIncrement columns should also be set to null in the ItemArray.

DataRow

Methods Reference

AcceptChanges

```
DataRow.AcceptChanges();
```

Commits all changes made to the DataRow since the last time it was loaded or since the last time AcceptChanges() was called.

Parameters   None.

Example

The following example demonstrates how to call the AcceptChanges() method of the DataRow:

```
// create a table with a single column
DataTable dt = new DataTable();
dt.Columns.Add("MyColumn", typeof(System.Int32));

DataRow row;
row = dt.NewRow();
row["MyColumn"] = 1;
dt.Rows.Add(row);          // RowState = Added

row.AcceptChanges();       // RowState = Unchanged

row["MyColumn"] = 2;       // RowState = Modified
row.AcceptChanges();       // RowState = Unchanged

row.Delete();              // RowState = Deleted
row.AcceptChanges();       // Row is removed from the DataTable
```

Notes

Calling AcceptChanges() sets the RowState property of Added and Modified rows to Unchanged; the original values in the DataRow are set as the current values. Deleted rows are removed from the DataTable.

Calling the AcceptChanges() method of the table the row belongs to implicitly calls the AcceptChanges() method of the row.

If the DataRow is in edit mode, as a result of calling the BeginEdit() method, EndEdit() is implicitly called, ending the edit.

Calling AcceptChanges() clears all RowError information and sets the HasErrors property for the row to false.

BeginEdit

```
DataRow.BeginEdit();
```

Puts the DataRow into edit mode, suspending the events that trigger validations rules.

Parameters   None.

Example

The following example demonstrates how to use the BeginEdit( ), EndEdit( ), and CancelEdit( ) methods:

```
DataRow row;

// ... retrieve data into the DataRow object

row.BeginEdit();
foreach(DataColumn col in row.Table.Columns)
{
    // ... modify the column value
}

Boolean rowValid = true;

// check the values in the row to make sure that they are valid

if(rowValid)
{
    row.CancelEdit();
}
else
{
    row.EndEdit();
}
```

Notes

Updates to a row can be buffered by calling the BeginEdit( ), EndEdit( ), and CancelEdit( ) methods. The BeginEdit( ) method turns off all constraints and suspends events used to enforce validation rules. If CancelEdit( ) is called, the changes in the buffer are discarded. When EndEdit( ) is called, the data is validated against the constraints, and events are raised if any violations occur.

Prior to calling EndEdit( ), any changes made to values for the row are stored as a proposed value. Until EndEdit( ) is called, both the original value and the proposed value can be retrieved by specifying Original or Proposed as the optional DataRowVersion argument for the Item property. While the row is being edited, the proposed value is returned by default.

The HasVersion method can be called to determine whether the row has an Original or Proposed value.

BeginEdit( ) is called implicitly when a user changes the value of a data-bound control.

CancelEdit

DataRow.CancelEdit();

Cancels the edit on the DataRow, discarding the changes.

Parameters   None.

Example   See the Example for the BeginEdit( ) method in this chapter.

Notes

Updates to a row can be buffered by calling the BeginEdit( ), EndEdit( ), and CancelEdit( ) methods. The BeginEdit( ) method turns off all constraints and suspends events that enforce validation rules. If CancelEdit( ) is called, the changes in the buffer are discarded. When EndEdit( ) is called, the data is validated against the constraints, and events are raised if any violations occur.

Prior to EndEdit( ) being called, any changes made to values for the row are stored as a proposed value. Until EndEdit( ) is called, both the original value and the proposed value can be retrieved by specifying the Original or Proposed as the optional DataRowVersion argument for the Item property. While the row is being edited, the proposed value is returned by default.

The HasVersion( ) method can be called to determine whether the row has an Original or Proposed value.

ClearErrors

DataRow.ClearErrors();

Clears all errors for the DataRow.

Parameters   None.

Example

The following example demonstrates using the Clear( ) method to clear the errors for a row:

```
row.ClearErrors();
```

Note   The ClearErrors( ) method clears all errors set on the row and on the individual columns within the row, including the RowError and errors set on the columns using the SetColumnError( ) method.

Delete

DataRow.Delete();

If the RowState of the DataRow is Added, the row is removed from the table. Otherwise, the RowState of the DataRow is set to Deleted, effectively marking it for deletion.

Parameters   None.

Examples

Three examples follow that demonstrate how to use the Delete( ) method and that highlight the effect of the RowState property and of the AcceptChanges( ) and RejectChanges( ) methods. The first example shows the relationship between the Delete( ) method and the AcceptChanges( ) method:

```
// delete the first row from the table
DataRow row = dt.Rows[0];
row.Delete();           // RowState changed to Deleted
dt.AcceptChanges();     // row is removed from the DataTable
```

The next example shows the relationship between the Delete( ) method and the RejectChanges( ) method:

```
// delete the first row from the table
DataRow row = dt.Rows[0];
row.Delete();              // RowState changed to Deleted
dt.RejectChanges();        // RowState reverts to Unchanged
```

Finally, the following example shows the relationship between newly added rows and the Delete( ) method:

```
// Create a new row
row = dt.NewRow();

// ... code to set the data for the row

// add the row to the table
dt.Rows.Add(row);          // RowState is Added

// delete the newly added row
row.Delete();              // row is removed from the table
```

Note   A deleted row can be undeleted by calling the RejectChanges( ) method.

EndEdit

```
DataRow.EndEdit();
```

Ends the edit on the DataRow, committing the changes made.

Parameters   None.

Example   See the Example for the BeginEdit( ) method in this chapter.

Notes

Updates to a row can be buffered by calling the BeginEdit( ), EndEdit( ), and CancelEdit( ) methods. The BeginEdit( ) method turns off all constraints and suspends events that enforce validation rules. If CancelEdit( ) is called, the changes in the buffer are discarded. When EndEdit( ) is called, the data is validated against the constraints, and events are raised if any violations occur.

Prior to EndEdit( ) being called, any changes made to values for the row are stored as proposed values. Until EndEdit( ) is called, both the original value and the proposed value can be retrieved by specifying the Original or Proposed as the optional DataRowVersion argument for the Item property. While the row is being edited, the proposed value is returned by default.

The HasVersion method can be called to determine whether the row has an Original or Proposed value.

EndEdit( ) is called implicitly when AcceptChanges( ) is called.

GetChildRows

```
DataRow[] childRows = DataRow.GetChildRows(DataRelation dr);
DataRow[] childRows = DataRow.GetChildRows(String relationName);
```

```
DataRow[] childRows = DataRow.GetChildRows(DataRelation,
    DataRowVersion drv);
DataRow[] childRows = DataRow.GetChildRows(String relationName,
    DataRowVersion drv);
```

Gets an array of DataRow objects that are the child rows of the DataRow, based on a specified DataRelation.

Parameters

childRows
    Returns an array of DataRow objects containing the child rows.

dr The DataRelation object to use.

relationName
    The name of the DataRelation to use.

drv One of the DataRowVersion enumeration values described in Table 25-5, which is in the HasVersion section of this chapter.

Example

The following example uses the GetChildRows( ) method to retrieve the array of Orders for a Customer:

```
// iterate through all of the Customers rows
foreach(DataRow rowCustomer in ds.Tables["Customers"].Rows)
{
    // iterate through the orders rows for the customer
    foreach(DataRow rowOrder in rowCustomer.GetChildRows(
        "Customers_Orders"))
    {
        // ... code to process the order for the customer
    }
}
```

GetColumnError

```
String colErr = DataRow.GetColumnError(DataColumn col);
String colErr = DataRow.GetColumnError(Integer columnIndex);
String colErr = DataRow.GetColumnError(String columnName);
```

Gets the error description for a specified column in the DataRow.

Parameters

colErr
    Returns a string containing the error description for the specified DataColumn in the DataRow.

col The DataColumn object for which to return the error.

columnIndex
    The index of the DataColumn for which to return the error.

columnName
    The name of the DataColumn for which to return the error.

Example

The following example shows how to get the error description for a column named MyColumn using the GetColumnError( ) method:

```
String colError = row.GetColumnError("MyColumn");
```

Note   The SetColumnError( ) method can set the error description for a column in a row.

GetColumnsInError

```
DataColumn[] colInError = DataRow.GetColumnsInError();
```

Gets an array of DataColumn objects for the columns having errors in the DataRow.

Parameter

colInError
    Returns an array of DataColumn objects that have errors.

Example

The following example demonstrates using the GetColumnsInError( ) method to return the array of columns that have errors in the row:

```
DataColumn[] errorCols;
if(row.HasErrors)
{
    errorCols = row.GetColumnsInError();
    for(Int32 i = 0; i < errorCols.Length; i++)
    {
        // ... resolve the error for each column
    }
}

// clear all errors on the row after resolving
row.ClearErrors();
```

Notes

An error can be set on a specific column using the SetColumnError( ) method.

The ClearErrors( ) method clears errors for each column in the row and for the entire row.

Call HasErrors( ) on the DataRow prior to calling GetColumnsInError( ).

GetParentRow

```
DataRow parentRow = DataRow.GetParentRow(DataRelation dr);
DataRow parentRow = DataRow.GetParentRow(String relationName);
DataRow parentRow = DataRow.GetParentRow(DataRelation,
    DataRowVersion drv);
DataRow parentRow = DataRow.GetParentRow(String relationName,
    DataRowVersion drv);
```

Gets the parent DataRow of the current row, based on a DataRelation.

Parameters

parentRow
> Returns the parent DataRow.

dr The DataRelation to use when retrieving the parent row.

relationName
> The name of the DataRelation to use when retrieving the parent row.

drv One of the DataRowVersion enumeration values described in Table 25-5, which is in the HasVersion section later in this chapter.

Example

The following example uses the GetParentRow( ) method to retrieve the customer for each order:

```
// iterate through all of the Orders rows
foreach(DataRow rowOrder in ds.Tables["Orders"].Rows)
{
    // get the customer row for the specified order
    DataRow rowCustomer = rowOrder.GetParentRow("Customers_Orders");

    // ... code to process the customer row
}
```

GetParentRows

```
DataRow[] parentRows = DataRow.GetParentRows(DataRelation dr);
DataRow[] parentRows = DataRow.GetParentRows(String relationName);
DataRow[] parentRows = DataRow.GetParentRows(DataRelation,
    DataRowVersion drv);
DataRow[] parentRows = DataRow.GetParentRows(String relationName,
    DataRowVersion drv);
```

Gets an array of DataRow objects that are the parent rows of the current row, based on a DataRelation.

Parameters

parentRows
> Returns an array of DataRow objects.

dr The DataRelation to use when retrieving the parent row.

relationName
> The name of the DataRelation to use when retrieving the parent row.

drv One of the DataRowVersion enumeration values described in Table 25-5 in the next section.

Example

The following example uses the GetParentRow( ) method to retrieve the Cocktails in which each Ingredient is used:

```
// iterate through all of the Ingredient rows
foreach(DataRow rowIngredient in ds.Tables["Ingredient"].Rows)
{
    // iterate through the Cocktail rows for the specified Ingredient
    foreach(DataRow rowCocktail in rowIngredient.GetParentRows(
        "Cocktail_Ingredient"))
```

```
        {
            // ... code to process the Cocktail row
        }
    }
}
```

Note	Although the GetParentRows() returns the parent rows for a child row using many-to-many relationships, there is little RDBMS support for many-to-many relationships.

HasVersion

```
Boolean hasVersion = DataRow.HasVersion(DataRowVersion drv);
```

Returns a value that indicates whether the specified DataRowVersion for the DataRow exists.

Parameters

hv   Returns a Boolean value indicating whether the specified version of a DataRow exists.

drv One of the DataRowVersion enumeration values described in Table 25-5.

Table 25-5. DataRowVersion enumeration

Value	Description
Current	The row containing current values. Always available.
Default	The default row version. When the row is edited, the Proposed row is returned; otherwise the Current row is returned.
Original	The row containing the original values. Available only when the row has been retrieved and doesn't exist for newly added rows.
Proposed	The row containing the proposed values. Available only when the row is being edited using the BeginEdit() method.

Example

The following example shows how to check if a row has a proposed version that uses the HasVersion() method:

```
Boolean hasVersion = row.HasVersion(DataRowVersion.Proposed);
```

IsNull

```
Boolean isNull = DataRow.IsNull(DataColumn col)
Boolean isNull = DataRow.IsNull(Integer columnIndex)
Boolean isNull = DataRow.IsNull(String columnName)
Boolean isNull = DataRow.IsNull(DataColumn col, DataRowVersion drv)
```

Returns a value indicating whether the specified column contains a null value. An optional argument allows the DataRowVersion of the column to be specified.

Parameters

isNull
    Returns a Boolean indicating the specified DataColumn contains a null value.

col The DataColumn object tested for a null value.

columnIndex
The zero-based index of the `DataColumn` tested for a null value.

columnName
The name of the `DataColumn` tested for a null value.

drv One of the `DataRowVersion` enumeration values described in Table 25-5.

Example
The following example demonstrates how to check if the first column in the row contains a null value using an overload of the `IsNull()` method:

```
DataRow row;

// ... load data into the row

if(row.IsNull(0))
{
    // ... code to process the null value
}
```

Note   The `IsNull()` method can test data in situations in which null values are sometimes allowed in a column, thereby preventing the `AllowDBNull` property of the column from being set to `false`.

RejectChanges

```
DataRow.RejectChanges();
```

Rejects all changes made to the `DataRow` since the last time it was loaded or since the last time `AcceptChanges()` was called.

Parameters   None.

Example
This example demonstrates how to call the `RejectChanges()` method of the `DataRow`:

```
// create a table with a single column
DataTable dt = new DataTable();
dt.Columns.Add("MyColumn", typeof(System.Int32));

DataRow row;
row = dt.NewRow();
row["MyColumn"] = 1;
dt.Rows.Add(row);         // RowState = Added

row.AcceptChanges();      // RowState = Unchanged

row["MyColumn"] = 2;      // RowState = Modified
row.RejectChanges();      // RowState = Unchanged, row["MyColumn"] = 1

row.Delete();             // RowState = Deleted
row.RejectChanges();      // RowState = Unchanged
                          // The row isn't removed from the DataTable.
```

Notes

Calling RejectChanges( ) sets the RowState property of Deleted and Modified rows to Unchanged; the current values in the DataRow are set to the original values. Added rows are removed.

If the row is in edit mode as a result of calling BeginEdit( ), the edit is cancelled when RejectChanges( ) is called.

Calling RejectChanges( ) clears all RowError information and sets the HasErrors property to false.

SetColumnError

```
DataRow.SetColumnError(DataColumn col, String errorDesc);
DataRow.SetColumnError(Integer columnIndex, String errorDesc);
DataRow.SetColumnError(String columnName, String errorDesc);
```

Sets the error description for a specified column in the DataRow.

Parameters

col   The DataColumn object for which to set an error.

columnIndex
  The index of the DataColumn for which to set an error.

columnName
  The name of the DataColumn for which to set an error.

errorDesc
  The description of the error.

Example

The following example shows how to set the error description for a column using the SetColumnError( ) method:

```
row.SetColumnError("MyColumn", "Custom error message for the column");
```

Note   The GetColumnError( ) method can retrieve the error description for a column in a row.

SetParentRow

```
DataRow.SetParentRow(DataRow row);
DataRow.SetParentRow(DataRow row, DataRelation dr);
```

Sets the parent DataRow, optionally based on a DataRelation.

Parameters

row   The new parent DataRow.

dr   The DataRelation for the parent relationship.

Example

The following example shows how to use the SetParentRow( ):

```
row.SetParentRow(parentRow, "MyDataRelation");
```

DataRow

26

The Constraint Class

The Constraint class ensures data integrity in the disconnected DataSet. ADO.
NET includes two types of constraints, both of which derive from the abstract
Constraint class and aren't specific to any provider. The UniqueKeyConstraint
ensures that column values aren't repeated in a single table and can optionally
designate a specific column or group of columns as a primary key. The
ForeignKeyConstraint ensures that column values in a child table correspond to
values in the related parent table. In addition, the ForeignKeyConstraint can
define rules that affect how deletions and updates are propagated between parent
rows and their associated children.

Comments/Troubleshooting

Constraint objects are contained in a ConstraintCollection. Every DataTable
exposes a ConstraintCollection through its Constraints property, which can
contain UniqueKeyConstraint and ForeignKeyConstraint objects.

Both UniqueKeyConstraint and ForeignKeyConstraint classes can be created manually. In addition, a UniqueKeyConstraint may be created automatically when filling
a DataSet with schema information, and both a ForeignKeyConstraint and a
UniqueKeyConstraint may be generated when a DataRelation is defined and added
to a table. For more information, refer to Chapter 10.

Properties Reference

AcceptRejectRule [ForeignKeyConstraint only]

```
AcceptRejectRule rule = Constraint.AcceptRejectRule;
Constraint.AcceptRejectRule = rule;
```

Determines what happens to child rows when the `DataRow.AcceptChanges( )` method is called on a parent row (usually as part of a data source update). You can use any value from the `AcceptRejectRule` enumeration, as shown in Table 26-1. By default, this is `None`.

Table 26-1. AcceptRejectRule values

Value	Description
Cascade	When `AcceptChanges( )` is called on a parent record, `AcceptChanges( )` is also called on all linked child records.
None	No special action occurs when `AcceptChanges( )` is called on a parent record.

Note   Using a value of `Cascade` may prevent child rows from being updated when you merge changes back into the data source. Thus, it's strongly recommended that you use the default of `None`, unless you don't intend to commit `DataSet` changes.

Columns

```
DataColumn[] cols = Constraint.Columns;
```

This returns an array with all the `DataColumn` objects for this `Constraint`. In the case of a `UniqueConstraint`, this is a column or combination of columns that must be unique in the `DataTable`. In the case of a `ForeignKeyConstraint`, this typically includes the linked column (or group of columns) from the child `DataTable`.

Example

The following code snippet retrieves all the `Constraint` columns and displays their names:

```
foreach(DataColumn col in Constraint.Columns)
{
    Console.WriteLine(col.ColumnName);
}
```

ConstraintName

```
string constraintName = Constraint.ConstraintName;
Constraint.ConstraintName = constraintName;
```

This is the name that identifies a `Constraint`. It's primarily used to retrieve or remove a `Constraint` object by name from the `ConstraintCollection`.

Constraint

Example

The following code snippet displays the ConstraintName for every Constraint in a DataTable:

```
foreach(Constraint c in dt.Constraints)
{
    Console.WriteLine(c.ConstraintName);
}
```

DeleteRule [ForeignKeyConstraint only]

```
Rule rule = Constraint.DeleteRule;
Constraint.DeleteRule = rule;
```

Determines what happens to child rows when a parent is deleted. You can use any value from the Rule enumeration, as shown in Table 26-2. By default, this is Cascade, which means all child rows are deleted along with the parent.

Table 26-2. Rule values

Value	Description
Cascade	If the parent row is deleted, the child rows are also deleted.
None	No action is taken on child rows. Thus, if you try to delete a parent that has linked children, an exception is thrown. This is the traditional SQL Server behavior.
SetDefault	If the parent row is deleted, the child rows have the default value placed in their foreign key column, if allowed (otherwise an exception is thrown).
SetNull	If the parent row is deleted, the foreign key column of all children is set to null. If the DataColumn.AllowDbNull property disallows this, an exception is thrown.

Example

In this example, all the child order records are deleted when the customer parent record is deleted:

```
// This is the ForeignKeyConstraint for the Orders table.
fkc.DeleteRule = Rule.Cascade;

// Select the first row.
DataRow row = ds.Tables["Customers"].Rows[0];

Console.WriteLine("Deleting: " + row["CustomerID"].ToString());

// Delete this customer (and any linked order records).
row.Delete();
```

IsPrimaryKey [UniqueKeyConstraint only]

```
bool isPrimaryKey = Constraint.IsPrimaryKey;
Constraint.IsPrimaryKey = isPrimaryKey;
```

Indicates whether the UniqueKeyConstraint represents the primary key for the table.

Example

You can specify that a `UniqueKeyConstraint` should represent the primary key when creating the `UniqueKeyConstraint` by setting the `IsPrimaryKey` property to true. The following code snippet creates a `UniqueKeyConstraint` that represents a primary key defined on a first and last name column:

```
// Create an array with the two columns.
DataColumn[] cols = new DataColumn[] {dt.Columns["LastName"],
                                      dt.Columns["FirstName"]};

// Create the UniqueConstraint object to represent the primary key.
UniqueConstraint uc = new UniqueConstraint("FullName", cols, true);

// Add the UniqueConstraint to the table.
dt.Constraints.Add(uc);
```

Note   A primary key is created automatically when you use the `DataAdapter`. `FillSchema( )` method, as long as there is at least one unique column in the query. There can be only one primary key on a `DataTable` at a time. If you attempt to set a second primary key on a table, the original primary key is downgraded to a unique column.

RelatedColumns [ForeignKeyConstraint only]

```
DataColumn[] cols = Constraint.RelatedColumns;
```

This returns an array containing the parent `DataColumn` objects for this relationship. Typically, this is a single column from the parent `DataTable`. For example, if you define a `Customers.CustomerID → Orders.CustomerID` relationship, the `Orders` table contains the `ForeignKeyConstraint` object, and the `Customers` table is the related table. The `ForeignKeyConstraint.RelatedColumns` property then returns a single `DataColumn` representing the `Customers.CustomerID` field.

Example

The following code snippet retrieves the first parent `DataColumn` and displays its name:

```
DataColumn col = fkc.RelatedColumns[0];
Console.WriteLine("The linked column child is: " + col.ColumnName);
```

RelatedTable [ForeignKeyConstraint only]

```
DataTable ds = Constraint.RelatedTable;
```

Retrieves the parent `DataTable` object for this `ForeignKeyConstraint`. For example, in a `Customers → Orders` relationship, the `Orders` table contains the `ForeignKeyConstraint` object, and the `Customers` table is the related table. This property is primarily included for convenience; you can also retrieve the table directly from the `DataSet`.

Example

The following code retrieves the related `DataTable` and displays some basic information about it in a console window.

Constraint

```
DataTable dt = fkc.RelatedTable;

// Print the name and number of rows of the child table.
Console.WriteLine(dt.TableName, dt.Rows.Count.ToString());
```

Note You can also retrieve a reference to the child table in which the constraint is applied using the Constraint.Table property.

Table

```
DataTable ds = Constraint.Table;
```
Retrieves the DataTable object that the Constraint belongs to.

Example
The following code retrieves the containing DataTable and displays some basic information about it in a console window:

```
DataTable dt = dr.Table;

// Print the name and number of rows of the child table.
Console.WriteLine(dt.TableName, dt.Rows.Count.ToString());
```

Note In the case of a ForeignKeyConstraint, this is the child table in which the constraint is applied. The parent table can be retrieved through the ForeignKeyConstraint.RelatedTable property.

UpdateRule [ForeignKeyConstraint only]

```
Rule rule = Constraint.UpdateRule;
Constraint.UpdateRule = rule;
```

Determines what happens if the parent's key column is modified. You can use any value from the Rule enumeration, as shown in Table 26-3. The default is Cascade, which means that the child rows are updated to point to the new value.

Table 26-3. Rule values

Value	Description
Cascade	If the linked column is changed in the parent, the foreign key column in all child rows is updated accordingly.
None	No action is taken on child rows. Thus, if you change the linked column of a parent that has children, an exception is thrown. This is the traditional SQL Server behavior.
SetDefault	If the linked column of a parent row is changed, the foreign key column in the child rows is reset to the default value, if allowed (otherwise an exception is thrown).
SetNull	If the linked column of the parent row is changed, the foreign key column of all children is set to null. If the DataColumn.AllowDbNull property disallows this, an exception is thrown.

Example
In this example, all the child order records are updated to use the new CustomerID value:

```
// This is the ForeignKeyConstraint for the Orders table.
fkc.UpdateRule = Rule.Cascade;
```

```
// Select the first row.
DataRow row = ds.Tables["Customers"].Rows[0];

Console.WriteLine("Modifying: " + row["CustomerID"].ToString());

// Modify the CustomerID (all any linked order records will be updated).
row["CustomerID"] = "NEWCUST";
```

Collections Reference

ExtendedProperties

```
PropertyCollection props = Constraint.ExtendedProperties;
```

Contains a `PropertyCollection` that can store any amount of miscellaneous information about the `Constraint`. The information in the `ExtendedProperties` collection is for use by your code only; it isn't used by the .NET framework.

The `ProperyCollection` is derived from the `Hashtable` class. Most disconnected data objects provide an `ExtendedProperties` collection, including the `DataSet`, `DataColumn`, `DataTable`, and `DataRelation` classes.

Example

The following code snippet stores the name of a `DataRelation` object that relates to a `ForeignKeyConstraint`:

```
fkc.ExtendedProperties["RelationName"] = dr.RelationName;
```

Note   Items in the `PropertyCollection` must be strings if you want them to persist when the `DataSet` is written to XML.

Constraint

27

The DataRelation Class

The DataRelation class represents a parent-child relationship between two DataTable objects in the same DataSet. The DataRelation can be used as a navigational aid, or it can enforce relational integrity and cascade deletes or updates. In the latter case, the constraints are actually applied by the ForeignKeyConstraint class, which the DataRelation creates automatically when added to a DataSet.

As with all disconnected data classes, the DataRelation isn't specific to any provider. DataRelation objects must be created manually; the provider can't generate them based on the information in the data source.

Comments/Troubleshooting

DataRelation objects are contained in a DataRelationCollection. Every DataSet exposes a DataRelationCollection through its Relations property. In addition, you can access the DataRelation objects that pertain to a specific table through the DataTable.ChildRelations and DataTable.ParentRelations properties.

The DataRelation links two matching DataColumn objects from different tables. Thus, the data type of both columns must be identical. When a DataRelation object is created, the relationship is verified. Once you add the DataRelation to the DataSet.Relations collection, a ForeignKeyConstraint is generated for the child table, preventing changes that would violate relational integrity.

The following code creates and adds a DataRelation:

```
DataColumn parentCol = ds.Tables["Categories"].Columns["CategoryID"];
DataColumn childCol = ds.Tables["Products"].Columns["CategoryID"];
DataRelation dr = new DataRelation("Cat_Prod", parentCol, childCol);

ds.Relations.Add(dr);
```

Properties Reference

ChildKeyConstraint

```
ForeignKeyConstraint fc = DataRelation.ForeignKeyConstraint;
```

Retrieves the `ForeignKeyConstraint` object that is associated with this relationship, if it exists. This constraint is applied to one or more `DataColumns` in the child table.

Example

The following code retrieves the associated `ForeignKeyConstraint` and uses it to ensure that cascading deletes are configured for this relationship. This means that a delete operation that affects the parent row automatically removes all related child rows as well.

```
ForeignKeyConstraint fk = dr.ChildKeyConstraint;
fk.DeleteRule = Rule.Cascade;
```

ChildTable

```
DataTable dt = DataRelation.ChildTable;
```

Retrieves the `DataTable` object for the child table in the relationship. For example, in a Customer → Orders relationship, this is the Orders table.

Example

The following code retrieves the child `DataTable` and displays some basic information about it in a console window:

```
DataTable dt = dr.ChildTable;

// Print the name and number of rows of the child table.
Console.WriteLine(dt.TableName, dt.Rows.Count.ToString());
```

DataSet

```
DataSet ds = DataRelation.DataSet;
```

Retrieves the `DataSet` that the `DataRelation` belongs to.

Example

The following code retrieves the appropriate `DataSet` and displays some basic information about it in a console window:

```
DataSet ds = dr.DataSet;

// Print the name and number of tables of the DataSet.
Console.WriteLine(ds.DataSetName, ds.Tables.Count.ToString());
```

Nested

```
Boolean nested = DataRelation.Nested;
DataRelation.Nested = nested;
```

Determines whether the XML output for this `DataSet` uses nesting for this relationship. If true, the XML elements that represent child rows appear inside the XML element that represents the corresponding parent row. For more information on XML and nesting rows, refer to Chapter 17.

Example

The following example displays the XML for a DataSet, both with and without nesting:

```
DataColumn parentCol = ds.Tables["Categories"].Columns["CategoryID"];
DataColumn childCol = ds.Tables["Products"].Columns["CategoryID"];
DataRelation dr = new DataRelation("Cat_Prod", parentCol, childCol);

ds.Relations.Add(dr);

// Write output without nesting.
ds.WriteXml(Console.Out);

// Writer output with nesting.
dr.Nested = true;
ds.WriteXml(Console.Out);
```

Without nesting, the XML output has this structure:

```
<?xml version="1.0" standalone="yes"?>
<Northwind>

  <Categories />
  <Categories />
  ...

  <Products />
  <Products />
  ...

</Northwind>
```

With nesting, the XML output has this form:

```
<?xml version="1.0" standalone="yes"?>
<Northwind>

  <Categories>
    <Products />
  </Categories>

  <Categories>
    <Products />
  </Categories>

  ...

</Northwind>
```

For more information about the XML representation of a DataSet, refer to Chapter 17.

Note   You can't nest more than one level deep because it can introduce row duplication. Thus, you can't nest the multiple levels of a many-to-many relationship.

ParentKeyConstraint

```
UniqueConstraint uc = DataRelation.ParentKeyConstraint;
```

Retrieves the `UniqueKeyConstraint` object that is associated with this relationship, if it exists. This constraint is applied to the `DataColumn` in the parent table.

Example

The following code retrieves the associated `UniqueKeyConstraint` and displays some basic information about it in a console window:

```
UniqueConstraint uc = dr.ParentKeyConstraint;

// Does this constraint represent a primary key?
Console.WriteLine(uc.IsPrimaryKey.ToString());
```

ParentTable

```
DataTable dt = DataRelation.ParentTable;
```

Retrieves the `DataTable` object for the parent table in the relationship. For example, in a `Customer` → `Orders` relationship, this is the `Customers` table. This property is primarily included for convenience; you can also retrieve the table directly from the `DataSet`.

Example

The following code retrieves the parent `DataTable` and displays some basic information about it in a console window:

```
DataTable dt = dr.ParentTable;

// Print the name and number of rows of the child table.
Console.WriteLine(dt.TableName, dt.Rows.Count.ToString());
```

RelationName

```
string relationName = DataRelation.RelationName;
DataRelation.RelationName = relationName;
```

This is the name of the `DataRelation`. It's primarily used to retrieve or remove a `DataRelation` object by name from the `DataRelationCollection`.

Example

The following code snippet retrieves a relation by its `RelationName`:

```
DataRelation dr = ds.Relations["Cat_Prod"];
```

Note   Often, the `RelationName` incorporates the parent and child column names, as in `Customers_Orders`. This convention isn't required, however.

Collections Reference

ChildColumns

```
DataColumn[] cols = DataRelation.ChildColumns;
```

This returns an array with all the child DataColumn objects for this relationship. Usually, this is a single column from the child DataTable. However, if they are all a part of the same relationship, you can relate multiple columns using one of the overloaded DataRelation constructors.

Example

The following code snippet retrieves the first child DataColumn and displays its name:

```
DataColumn col = dr.ChildColumns[0];
Console.WriteLine("The linked column child is: " + col.ColumnName);
```

ExtendedProperties

```
PropertyCollection props = DataRelation.ExtendedProperties;
```

Contains a PropertyCollection that can store any amount of miscellaneous information about the DataRelation. For example, you can store information about the parent and child columns or how the relationship should be validated according to custom validation functions you may have created. The information in the ExtendedProperties collection is for use by your code only; it isn't used by the .NET framework (although any strings you add to the PropertyCollection are retained in serialized DataSet XML.

The ProperyCollection is a name/value dictionary that derives from the Hashtable class. Most disconnected data objects provide an ExtendedProperties collection, including the DataSet, DataColumn, DataTable, and Constraint classes.

Example

The following code snippet stores the data type of the child DataColumn in the PropertyCollection:

```
// Determine the data type for the linked column.
Type dataType = dr.ChildColumns[0].DataType;

// Store it in the extended properties for future reference.
dr.ExtendedProperties["ColumnDataType"] = dataType.ToString();
```

Note   Items in the PropertyCollection must be strings if you want them to persist when the DataSet is written to XML.

ParentColumns

```
DataColumn[] cols = DataRelation.ParentColumns;
```

This returns an array with all the parent DataColumn objects for this relationship. Typically, this is a single column from the parent DataTable. However, if they are all a part of the same relationship, you can relate multiple columns using one of the overloaded DataRelation constructors.

Example

The following code snippet retrieves the first parent DataColumn and displays its name:

```
DataColumn col = dr.ParentColumns[0];
Console.WriteLine("The linked column parent is: " + col.ColumnName);
```

28

The DataView Class

The DataView class is a view onto a DataTable. Using the DataView, you can apply sort or filter conditions without modifying the underlying data. You can even create multiple DataView objects to show different representations of the same DataTable. The DataView also provides methods for searching for specific rows.

As with all disconnected data classes, the DataView isn't specific to any provider. DataView objects can be created programmatically, but every DataTable also provides a DefaultView property that contains a default DataView. If you bind directly to a DataTable, .NET automatically uses the DataView contained in the DefaultView property to determine what data should be displayed. In addition, every DataSet provides a DefaultViewManager property, which provides a default DataViewManager. The DataViewManager is primarily used when binding an entire DataSet to a control (like the Windows DataGrid). In this case, the control can use the presets stored in the DataViewManager to generate individual DataView objects for each DataTable as required.

Comments/Troubleshooting

In most cases, the DataView is used with ASP.NET or Windows Forms data binding, as described in Chapter 12. However, you can also use a DataView when programmatically modifying or manipulating a subset of data from a DataTable. In this case, you can access each row in the DataView through a DataRowView object. The DataRowView is a view on a single row and is similar to the DataRow class, with an overloaded indexer that allows you to retrieve column values by name or index number.

 The DataRowView doesn't provide any ability to customize the formatting of individual values. To apply custom formatting, you may need to handle data binding events, as described in Chapter 12.

Properties Reference

AllowDelete

```
Boolean allowDelete = DataView.AllowDelete;
DataView.AllowDelete = allowDelete;
```

Specifies whether it is possible to delete rows in the underlying DataTable using this DataView. It is the responsibility of the control or application to heed this setting; .NET doesn't enforce it in any way.

Example

The following example checks the AllowDelete property before removing a row:

```
DataView view = new DataView(ds.Tables["Customers"]);

// Select the first row.
DataRowView row = view[0];

// Delete it if allowed.
if (view.AllowDelete)
{
    row.Delete();
}
```

AllowEdit

```
Boolean allowEdit = DataView.AllowEdit;
DataView.AllowEdit = allowEdit;
```

Specifies whether it is possible to modify rows in the underlying DataTable using this DataView. It is the responsibility of the control or application to heed this setting; .NET doesn't enforce it in any way.

Example

The following example checks the AllowEdit property before modifying a row:

```
DataView view = new DataView(ds.Tables["Customers"]);

// Select the first row.
DataRowView row = view[0];

// Modify it if allowed.
if (view.AllowEdit)
{
    row["CustomerID"] = "NEWCUST";
}
```

AllowNew

```
Boolean allowNew = DataView.AllowNew;
DataView.AllowNew = allowNew;
```

Specifies whether it is possible to add new rows to the underlying DataTable using this DataView. It is the responsibility of the control or application to heed this setting; .NET doesn't enforce it in any way.

Example

The following example checks the AllowNew property before inserting a row:

```
DataView view = new DataView(ds.Tables["Customers"]);

// Add a row if allowed.
if (view.AllowNew)
{
    DataRowView row = view.AddNew();

    // (Configure columns here.)

    // Commit the new row.
    row.EndEdit();
}
```

ApplyDefaultSort

```
Boolean applyDefaultSort = DataView.ApplyDefaultSort;
DataView.ApplyDefaultSort = applyDefaultSort;
```

If true, the DataView sets a sort order to ascend based on the primary key column of the underlying DataTable. If set to false, this property has no effect. The ApplyDefaultSort property is ignored if the DataView.Sort property isn't a null reference or an empty string. ApplyDefaultSort also has no effect if the underlying DataTable doesn't have a primary key defined.

Example

This example configures a primary key column for a table and uses the column for DataView sorting:

```
DataTable dt = ds.Tables["Customers"];

// Create a UniqueConstraint object that represents the primary key.
UniqueConstraint uc = new UniqueConstraint("ID", dt.Columns["CustomerID"],
    true);

// Add the UniqueConstraint to the table's Constraints collection.
dt.Constraints.Add(uc);

view = new DataView(dt);

// Use the CustomerID column for sorting.
view.ApplyDefaultSort = true;
```

Count

```
Int32 Count = DataView.Count;
```

Returns the number of rows in the DataView. This may not be the same as the number of rows in the underlying DataTable, depending on the DataView.RowFilter or DataView.RowStateFilter properties.

Example

Here's an example that sets filter selection criteria, and checks how many rows meet the condition:

```
DataView view = new DataView(ds.Tables["Customers"]);

Console.WriteLine("There are " + view.Count.ToString() + " rows.");

// Find all the rows where a Country isn't specified.
view.RowFilter = "Country IS NULL";

Console.WriteLine("There are " + view.Count.ToString() +
    " rows that have no specified Country.");
```

DataViewManager

```
DataViewManager dvm = DataView.DataViewManager;
```

Returns the DataViewManager that created this DataTable. If this is the DataTable. DefaultView, this will be the DataSet.DefaultViewManager. If you created the DataView programmatically, the DataViewManager property returns a null reference.

Example

The following code example finds the DataViewManager that created a DataView and then uses that DataViewManager to create a new DataView:

```
// Retrieve the DataViewManager.
DataViewManager viewManager = view.DataViewManager;

// Use the DataViewManager to create a new DataView.
DataView newView = viewManager.CreateDataView(ds.Tables["Customers"]);
```

Item

```
DataRowView row = DataView[Int32 rowIndex];
```

Retrieves a DataRowView object using the zero-based row index. The Item property is the default indexer for the DataView class.

Example

The following code retrieves the first row and then modifies a field in that DataRow using the DataRowView:

```
// Retrieve the first row from the view.
DataRowView row = view[0];

// Modify a field in the first row through the DataRowView.
// Because the DataRowView is a window onto the DataView,
```

```
// both objects will reflect the changed value.
row["CustomerID"] = "NEWCUST";
```

Notes

The DataView class also implements the IEnumerable interface, which means you can iterate over its collection of DataRowView objects using the foreach syntax:

```
DataView view = new DataView(ds.Tables["Customers"]);

// (Configure DataView sorting and filtering here.)

foreach (DataRowView row in view)
{
    // (Do something with the row here.)
}
```

Remember, you will see only rows from the underlying DataTable that meet the DataView filter conditions.

RowFilter

```
String filter = DataView.RowFilter;
DataView.RowFilter = filter;
```

Gets or sets a filter expression that limits the rows that are included in the DataView. The filter expression resembles the WHERE clause of a SQL SELECT statement, so a filter expression of Country = 'Germany' selects only those records in which the Country field contains the string "Germany."

However, you aren't limited to simply equality testing: ADO.NET supports a rich subset of the SQL language for filter expressions, complete with support for aggregate functions, relationships, mathematical operations, and string handling. For a full list of supported operators and several examples, refer to Chapter 12.

Example

The following code statement filters a DataView to include only those rows in which the UnitPrice field is greater than 10:

```
view.RowFilter = "UnitPrice > 10";
```

Note   Every time you change the RowFilter property, the contents of the DataView are dynamically updated. Similarly, if you change column values, a row may appear or disappear from the DataView, depending on the filter condition.

RowStateFilter

```
DataViewRowState state = DataView.RowStateFilter;
DataView.RowStateFilter = state;
```

Gets or sets a value that determines how rows are filtered based on their DataRowState. You set the RowStateFilter property using one of the values from the DataViewRowState enumeration (or a bitwise combination of values). These values are shown in Table 28-1. By default, the RowStateFilter is set to CurrentRows and shows everything except rows that are scheduled for deletion.

Table 28-1. DataViewRowState values

Value	Description
Added	A new row that is inserted into the data source when the next update is performed.
CurrentRows	Current rows, including unchanged, new, and modified rows. This is the default.
Deleted	A deleted row that is removed from the data source when the next update is performed.
ModifiedCurrent	A row that exists in the DataSet but has been modified.
ModifiedOriginal	The original version (although it has since been modified and is available as ModifiedCurrent).
None	No rows will be shown.
OriginalRows	Original rows including unchanged and deleted rows.
Unchanged	A row that exists in the DataSet and has not been modified.

Example

The following code snippet configures a view to display only deleted and added rows:

```
// Show deleted and added rows.
view.RowStateFilter =
    DataViewRowState.Deleted | DataViewRowState.Added;
```

Note
The values in the DataViewRowState enumeration don't exactly correspond to the values in the DataRowState enumeration. This is because the DataViewRowState must take into account the state of rows (deleted, added, and so on) and indicate which version of the information should be used for display purposes (the current information or the original data queried from the data source).

Sort

```
String sort = DataView.Sort;
DataView.Sort = sort;
```

Gets or sets a sort expression that determines how rows are ordered in a DataView. The sort expression resembles the ORDER BY clause of a SQL SELECT statement, so a filter expression of Country ASC orders records alphabetically by country name. If you sort with a numeric data type, numeric sorting is used. If you sort with a character-based data type, alphanumeric sorting applies instead.

ADO.NET supports a rich subset of the SQL language for sort expressions. For a full listing of supported operators and several examples, refer to Chapter 12.

Example

The following code statement orders a DataView by Country and then (if two records have the same Country) by City:

```
view.Sort = "Country ASC, City ASC";
```

Notes

Every time you change the Sort property, the contents of the DataView is refreshed. Similarly, if you change a column value that affects sorting, rows may move to new positions in the DataView.

To use the primary key for a sort without defining a Sort expression, set the ApplyDefaultSort property to true.

Table

```
DataTable dt = DataView.Table;
DataView.Table = dt;
```

Provides a reference to the underlying DataTable that this DataView exposes. You can read this property to access the full DataTable, or you can modify this property to "point" a DataView to a different DataTable.

Example

The following code retrieves the underlying DataTable and displays some basic information about it in a console window:

```
DataTable dt = view.Table;

// Print the name and number of rows of the child table.
Console.WriteLine(dt.TableName, dt.Rows.Count.ToString());
```

Methods Reference

AddNew

```
DataRowView = DataView.AddNew();
```

Inserts a new row into the underlying DataTable and returns a DataRowView object that represents the new row. The DataView.AddNew() method immediately adds the new row to the DataTable and implicitly calls BeginEdit() on the row. You must set all required values (values for columns that don't allow nulls and don't have default values) and then call DataRowView.EndEdit() to commit changes.

Example

Here's an example that creates a new row for the Categories table using the DataView. AddNew() method:

```
DataRowView row = view.AddNew();

// Set all required values.
row["CategoryName"] = "Fruit";
row["Description"] = "Pears, kiwis, and oranges";

// Commit the new row.
view.EndEdit();
```

Note   It's possible that the new DataRowView won't be visible in the DataView you used to create it, depending on the value of the DataView. RowFilter and DataView.RowStateFilter properties.

Delete

```
DataView.Delete(Int32 rowIndex);
```

Removes a row at the specified index. This affects both the DataView and the under-lying DataTable. As with the DataRow.Delete( ) method, the DataView.Delete( ) method marks a row for deletion by setting the DataRow.RowState property. The change doesn't become final until you call the DataTable.AcceptChanges( ) method (either directly or implicitly through the DataAdapter.Update( ) method).

Example

This code snippet deletes all order records in which the UnitPrice field is equal to 0.

```
DataView view = new DataView(ds.Tables["Orders"]);
view.RowFilter = "UnitPrice = 0";

// Delete these rows.
foreach (DataRowView row in view)
{
    row.Delete();
}
```

Find

```
Int32 rowIndex = DataView.Find(Object sortKey);
Int32 rowIndex = DataView.Find(Object[] sortKey);
```

Returns the index of a single matching row, using the current DataView sort order. For example, if you have a sort defined on the ContactName column of the Customers table, you can use the Find( ) method to search for a row with a specific ContactName. If no match is found, the Find( ) method returns −1. If there are multiple matches, only the first is returned.

The Find( ) method requires exact matches. You can't perform a partial match (for example, by supplying just a first name for the ContactName) or use a wildcard.

Parameters

```
Object sortKey
Object[] sortKey
```
The sortKey specifies the value you are searching for. The data type you use should match the data type of the column used for the search criteria. If you create a sort expression that incorporates information from multiple columns, you must use the overloaded version of the Find( ) method that accepts an array with search values for all columns, in the same order.

Example

The following code snippet searches for an exact match of the ContactName field:

```
DataView view = new DataView(ds.Tables["Customers"]);
view.Sort = "ContactName";

int rowIndex = view.Find("Roland Mendel");

if (rowIndex == -1)
{
```

```
            Console.WriteLine("No match found.");
    }
    else
    {
            Console.WriteLine(view[rowIndex]["CustomerID"].ToString() +
                            " is a match.");
    }
```

Notes

To use the Find( ) method, you must have defined a sort order for a DataView, either by
setting the RowFilter property or the ApplyDefaultSort property. If it's possible that
your search will match more than one row, use the FindRows( ) method instead of the
Find( ) method.

The case-sensitivity of search values for the Find( ) method is determined by the
CaseSensitive property of the underlying DataTable.

FindRows

```
DataRowView[] rows = DataView.FindRows(Object sortKey);
DataRowView[] rows = DataView.FindRows(Object[] sortKey);
```

Returns an array with every DataRowView object that matches a specified search expression in a given DataView. If no match is found, FindRows( ) returns an empty array.

The FindRows( ) method requires exact matches. You can't perform a partial match
(for example, by supplying just a first name for the ContactName).

Parameters

Object *sortKey*
Object[] *sortKey*

> The *sortKey* specifies that value you are searching for. The data type you use must
> match the data type of the column used for the search criteria. If you create a sort
> expression that incorporates information from multiple columns, you must use
> the overloaded version of the FindRows( ) method that accepts an array with
> search values for all columns. These search values must use the same order as the
> columns in the sort expression.

Example

The following code snippet searches for an exact match of the Country field and
displays the information for all matching rows:

```
DataView view = new DataView(ds.Tables["Customers"]);
view.Sort = "Country";

DataRowView[] rows = view.FindRows("Germany");

if (rows.Length == 0)
{
    Console.WriteLine("No match found.");
}
else
{
    foreach (DataRowView row in rows)
    {
```

```
            Console.WriteLine(row["CustomerID"].ToString() + " is a match.");
        }
    }
}
```

Notes

To use the FindRows() method, you must define a sort order for a DataView, either by setting the RowFilter property or the ApplyDefaultSort property. If you want to search a unique column, you can use the Find() method instead of the FindRows() method for slightly easier coding.

The case-sensitivity of search values for the FindRows() method is determined by the CaseSensitive property of the underlying DataTable.

Events Reference

ListChanged

ListChangedEventHandler ListChanged;

Fires when the information in a DataView changes, including when DataRowView objects are added, deleted, modified, or moved. This event provides a ListChangedEventArgs object with information about the type of change, and the old and new index of the item, if appropriate. This event is rarely used in application programming (in which case the DataTable events are much more useful) but is typically reserved for creating custom data bound controls.

Event Argument

ListChangedEventArgs e

Exposes three properties. ListChangedType provides an enumerated value that indicates how the list changed. NewIndex and OldIndex indicate where an item moved, if the event is in response to a single row change. For example, if an item is moved from position 0 to position 1, NewIndex is 1, and OldIndex is 0. If an item is deleted, NewIndex contains the former index of the deleted item, and OldIndex isn't used.

Table 28-2 lists the valid values for the ListChangedType enumeration.

Table 28-2. ListChangedType values

Value	Description
ItemAdded	An item was added to the list at position NewIndex.
ItemChanged	The item at NewIndex was changed.
ItemDeleted	The item at NewIndex was deleted.
ItemMoved	An item moved in the list from OldIndex to NewIndex.
PropertyDescriptorAdded, PropertyDescriptorChanged, and PropertyDescriptorDeleted	A PropertyDescriptor was added, changed, or deleted, and this changed the schema.
Reset	The list has changed substantially. Any listeners should reread the entire DataView.

Example

Here's an example that handles the ListChanged event and displays some information to a debug window:

```
private void OnListChanged(object sender, ListChangedEventArgs args)
{
    Debug.WriteLine("ListChanged:");
    Debug.WriteLine("\t    Type = " + args.ListChangedType);
    Debug.WriteLine("\tOldIndex = " + args.OldIndex);
    Debug.WriteLine("\tNewIndex = " + args.NewIndex);
}
```

Note   If you make a change that affects multiple rows, such as changing the Sort order, the DataView doesn't fire one ListChanged event for each row. Instead, it fires a ListChanged event with a ListChangedType of Reset.

29

The DataAdapter Class

The DataAdapter class serves as a bridge between a DataSet and a data source. The DataAdapter both retrieves a DataSet from a data source and updates any changes made to the DataSet back to the data source.

Comments/Troubleshooting

No reference is maintained between the DataSet, the DataAdapter, and the Connection. After the DataAdapter retrieves data from a data source into a DataSet, the DataSet has no information about the connection, database, tables, columns, or any other details about the source of the data.

Because the DataAdapter is a connected class, each .NET data provider implements its own DataAdapter, with a similar interface and function to other DataAdapter classes but in its own unique namespace. The DataAdapter class namespaces for several ADO.NET data providers are listed in Table 29-1.

Table 29-1. Provider-specific DataAdapter classes

Class	Data source
System.Data.SqlClient.SqlDataAdapter	SQL Server
System.Data.OleDb.OleDbDataAdapter	OLE DB provider
Microsoft.Data.Odbc.OdbcDataAdapter	ODBC driver
System.Data.OracleClient.OracleDataAdapter	Oracle

The commonly used public properties of the DataAdapter class are listed in Table 29-2.

Table 29-2. DataAdapter properties

Property	Description
AcceptChangesDuringFill	Gets or sets a value indicating whether the row is committed when added to a table using the Fill( ) method.
ContinueUpdateOnError	Gets or sets a value indicating whether the DataAdapter should raise an exception and stop processing remaining updates when an error is encountered.
DeleteCommand	Gets or sets the command, either a SQL statement or a stored procedure, that deletes the DataSet records marked for deletion from the data source when using the Update( ) method.
InsertCommand	Gets or sets the command, either a SQL statement or a stored procedure, that inserts new DataSet records into the data source when using the Update( ) method.
MissingMappingAction	Specifies the action to take when columns or tables in the incoming data from the data source don't have matching columns or tables in the DataSet.
MissingSchemaAction	Specifies the action to take when the schema of the data source doesn't match the DataSet schema.
SelectCommand	Gets or sets the command, either a SQL statement or a stored procedure, that selects records from the data source when using the Fill( ) method.
UpdateCommand	Gets or sets the command, either a SQL statement or a stored procedure, that updates modified Dataset records in the data source when using the Update( ) method.

The commonly used public collections of the DataAdapter class are listed in Table 29-3.

Table 29-3. DataAdapter collections

Collection	Description
TableMappings	Accesses the DataTableMappingCollection, which contains table and column name mapping information for reconciling the disconnected data with the data source, as a collection of DataTableMapping objects.

The commonly used public methods of the DataAdapter class are listed in Table 29-4.

Table 29-4. DataAdapter methods

Method	Description
Fill( )	Adds new rows or refreshes rows in the DataSet with data from the data source.
FillSchema( )	Adds an empty table to the DataSet and configures its schema to match the data source.
GetFillParameters( )	Returns an array of parameter objects for the SelectCommand.
Update( )	Submits changes in the DataSet to the data source for reconciliation.

The commonly used public events of the DataAdapter class are listed in Table 29-5.

Table 29-5. DataAdapter events

Event	Description
FillError	Raised when an error is encountered during a Fill( ) operation.
RowUpdating	Raised before the command to reconcile a DataSet row with the data source row has been executed.
RowUpdated	Raised after the command to reconcile a DataSet row with the data source row has been executed.

The DataAdapter class inherits from Component and implements the IDataAdapter interface. Public static members of this class are safe for multithreaded operations; instance members aren't guaranteed to be thread-safe.

Properties Reference

AcceptChangesDuringFill

```
Boolean acceptChangesDuringFill = DataAdapter.AcceptChangesDuringFill;
DataAdapter.AcceptChangesDuringFill = acceptChangesDuringFill;
```

Gets or sets a value that indicates whether AcceptChanges( ) is called on a DataRow after the row is added to a DataTable using the Fill( ) method.

Example

The following example demonstrates the effect of setting the AcceptChangesDuringFill property to both true and false using the Orders table in the Northwind database:

```
// connection and select command strings
String connString = "Data Source = (local);Integrated security = SSPI;" +
    "Initial Catalog = Northwind;";
String sqlSelect = "SELECT * FROM Orders";

// create a new DataSet to receive the data
DataSet ds = new DataSet();

SqlDataAdapter da = new SqlDataAdapter(sqlSelect, connString);

da.AcceptChangesDuringFill = true;
da.Fill(ds, "Orders");
// each row in the Orders table has RowState = Unchanged

// remove all rows from the Orders table
ds.Tables["Orders"].Clear();

da.AcceptChangesDuringFill = false;
da.Fill(ds, "Orders");
// each row in the Orders table has RowState = Inserted

// manually call AcceptChanges
ds.AcceptChanges();
// each row in the Orders table has RowState = Unchanged
```

DataAdapter

Notes

If `AcceptChangesDuringFill` property is `false`, and `AcceptChanges()` isn't called, newly added rows have a `RowState` of `Inserted`.

The default value of the `AcceptChangesDuringFill` property is `true`.

ContinueUpdateOnError

```
Boolean continueUpdateOnError = DataAdapter.ContinueUpdateOnError;
DataAdapter.ContinueUpdateOnError = continueUpdateOnError;
```

Gets or sets a value indicating whether the `DataAdapter` should raise an exception and stop processing remaining updates when an error is encountered.

Example

The following example demonstrates how to set the `ContinueUpdateOnError` property:

```
SqlDataAdapter da = new SqlDataAdapter();
da.ContinueUpdateOnError = true;
```

Notes

If this value if `true`, and an error occurs while updating a row, the `RowError` property of that row is set to the error information, the update of the row isn't performed, and processing continues with the next row.

The default value of the `ContinueUpdateOnError` property `false`.

DeleteCommand

```
SqlCommand deleteCommand = DataAdapter.DeleteCommand;
DataAdapter.DeleteCommand = deleteCommand;
```

Gets or sets the command, either a SQL statement or a stored procedure, that deletes the `DataSet` records marked for deletion from the data source when the `Update()` method is called.

Example

The following example shows how to set the `DeleteCommand`, `InsertCommand`, `SelectCommand`, and `UpdateCommand` properties using the `Shippers` table in the `Northwind` database:

```
// the SQL statements for delete, insert, select, and update
String sqlSelect = "SELECT ShipperID, CompanyName, Phone FROM Shippers";
String sqlDelete = "DELETE FROM Shippers WHERE ShipperID=@ShipperID";
String sqlInsert = "INSERT Shippers (CompanyName, Phone) " +
    "VALUES (@CompanyName, @Phone)";
String sqlUpdate = "UPDATE Shippers SET CompanyName=@CompanyName, " +
    "Phone=@Phone WHERE ShipperID=@ShipperID";

// build the connection
String connString = "Data Source = (local);Integrated security = SSPI;" +
    "Initial Catalog = Northwind;";
SqlConnection conn = new SqlConnection(connString);

// create the update command objects using SQL statements
SqlCommand selectCommand = new SqlCommand(sqlSelect, conn);
```

```
SqlCommand deleteCommand = new SqlCommand(sqlDelete, conn);
SqlCommand insertCommand = new SqlCommand(sqlInsert, conn);
SqlCommand updateCommand = new SqlCommand(sqlUpdate, conn);

// set up the parameters for the command objects
SqlParameterCollection cparams;

// delete command parameters
cparams = deleteCommand.Parameters;
cparams.Add("@ShipperID", SqlDbType.Int, 0, "ShipperID");

// insert command parameters
cparams = insertCommand.Parameters;
cparams.Add("@ShipperID", SqlDbType.Int, 0, "ShipperID");
cparams["@ShipperID"].Direction = ParameterDirection.Output;
cparams.Add("@CompanyName", SqlDbType.NVarChar, 40, "CompanyName");
cparams.Add("@ShipperPhone", SqlDbType.NVarChar, 24, "ShipperPhone");

// update command parameters
cparams = updateCommand.Parameters;
cparams.Add("@ShipperID", SqlDbType.Int, 0, "ShipperID");
cparams.Add("@CompanyName", SqlDbType.NVarChar, 40, "CompanyName");
cparams.Add("@ShipperPhone", SqlDbType.NVarChar, 24, "ShipperPhone");

// create the DataAdapter
SqlDataAdapter da  = new SqlDataAdapter(sqlSelect, connString);

// set the command objects for the DataAdapter
da.DeleteCommand = deleteCommand;
da.InsertCommand = insertCommand;
da.UpdateCommand = updateCommand;
```

This example uses dynamic SQL statements rather than stored procedures. To use stored procedures, set the command text for each update command object to the name of the stored procedure and set each CommandType property to StoredProcedure. The affected lines for the delete command are shown here:

```
// replace line 3 with the following line - the stored procedure
// DeleteShipper must exist on the server.
String SqlDelete = "DeleteShipper";

// insert after deleteCommand is instantiated.
deleteCommand.CommandType = CommandType.StoredProcedure;
```

Note   If the DeleteCommand property isn't set, and the DataSet has a primary key, the DeleteCommand can be generated automatically using the CommandBuilder after specifying the SelectCommand property.

InsertCommand

```
SqlCommand insertCommand = DataAdapter.InsertCommand
DataAdapter.InsertCommand = insertCommand;
```

Gets or sets the command, either a SQL statement or a stored procedure, used to insert new DataSet records into the data source when the Update( ) method is called.

Example	See the Example for the DeleteCommand property in this chapter.
Note	If the InsertCommand property isn't set, and the DataSet has a primary key, the InsertCommand can be automatically generated using the CommandBuilder after specifying the SelectCommand property.

MissingMappingAction

```
MissingMappingAction mma = DataAdapter.MissingMappingAction;
DataAdapter.MissingMappingAction = mma;
```

Specifies the action to take when columns or tables in the incoming data don't have matching columns or tables in the DataSet. The value is one of the MissingMappingAction enumeration values described on Table 29-6.

Table 29-6. MissingMappingAction enumeration

Value	Description
Passthrough	Create missing objects in the DataSet using the column and table names from the data source. This is the default value.
Ignore	Ignore table and columns in the data source that don't exist in the DataSet.
Error	If the data source contains tables or columns that don't appear in the DataSet, a SytemException is raised.

Example

The following example shows how to set the MissingMappingAction and MissingSchemaAction properties so that an error is raised if columns or tables in the incoming schema or data from the data source don't have matching columns in the DataSet.

```
// connection and select command strings
String connString = "Data Source=(local);Integrated security=SSPI;" +
    "Initial Catalog=Northwind;";
String selectCommand = "SELECT * FROM Orders";

SqlDataAdapter da = new sqlDataAdapter(selectCommand, connString);
da.MissingMappingAction = MissingMappingAction.Error;
da.MissingSchemaAction = MissingSchemaAction.Error;
```

Note	An ArgumentException is raised if an attempt is made to set the value of this property to a value other than one of the MissingMappingAction values.

MissingSchemaAction

```
MissingSchemaAction msa = DataAdapter.MissingSchemaAction;
DataAdapter.MissingSchemaAction = msa;
```

Specifies the action to take when the columns or tables in the incoming schema data don't have matching columns or tables in the DataSet. The value is one of the MissingSchemaAction enumeration values described in Table 29-7. The default value is Add.

Table 29-7. MissingSchemaAction enumeration

Value	Description
Add	If the data source contains columns or tables that don't exist in the DataSet, DataColumn, and DataTable, objects required to complete the schema are added to the DataSet. This is the default value.
AddWithKey	In addition to the behavior of the MissingSchemaAction.Add, this causes key information to be added.
Error	If the data source contains tables or columns that don't appear in the DataSet, a SytemException is raised.
Ignore	Tables and columns in the data source that don't exist in the DataSet are ignored.

Example   See the Example for the MissingMappingAction property in this chapter.

Note   An ArgumentException is raised if an attempt is made to set the value of this property to a value other than one of the MissingSchemaAction values.

SelectCommand

```
SqlCommand selectCommand = DataAdapter.SelectCommand;
DataAdapter.SelectCommand = selectCommand;
```

Gets or sets the command, either a SQL statement or a stored procedure, that selects records from the data source when using the Fill( ) method.

Example   See the Example for the DeleteCommand property in this chapter.

Note   If the SelectCommand doesn't return any rows, no tables are added to the DataSet during the Fill( ) operation, and no exception is raised.

UpdateCommand

```
SqlCommand updateCommand = DataAdapter.UpdateCommand;
DataAdapter.UpdateCommand = updateCommand;
```

Gets or sets the command, either a SQL statement or a stored procedure, that updates modified DataSet records in the data source when the Update( ) method is called.

Example   See the Example for the DeleteCommand property in this chapter.

Note   If the UpdateCommand property isn't set, and the DataSet has a primary key, the UpdateCommand can be generated automatically using the CommandBuilder after specifying the SelectCommand property.

Collections Reference

TableMappings

```
DataTableMappingCollection dtmc = DataAdapter.TableMappings;
```

Accesses a collection of DataTableMapping objects that map the data source table names to DataSet table names. This allows different table names to be used during change reconciliation. An empty collection is returned if no mappings exist.

Example

The following example shows how to set up a TableMapping and a ColumnMapping:

```
SqlDataAdapter da;

// ... code to set up the data adapter

// map the DataSet table MyOrders to the data source table Orders
DataTableMapping dtm = da.TableMappings.Add("Orders", "MyOrders");

// map the DataSet column MyOrderID (in the DataSet MyOrders table)
// to the data source column OrderID (in the data source Orders table)
dtm.ColumnMappings.Add("MyOrderID", "OrderID");
```

The DataTableMappingCollection and DataColumnMappingCollection collections have an AddRange( ) method that allows an array of mappings to be added in a single statement, as shown in the following example:

```
// map the CustomerID and EmployeeID columns from the data source
dtm.ColumnMappings.AddRange(new DataColumnMapping[] {
    new DataColumnMapping("MyCustomerID", "CustomerID"),
    new DataColumnMapping("MyEmployeeID", "EmployeeID")});
```

Mappings can be removed from both the DataTableMappingCollection and DataColumnMappingCollection objects using the Remove( ), RemoveAt( ), or Clear( ) methods. The following example demonstrates using these methods with the DataTableMappingCollection; using the methods with the DataColumnMappingCollection is similar.

```
SqlDataAdapter da;

// ... code to set up the DataAdapter da

// map the DataSet table MyOrders to the data source table Orders
DataTableMapping dtm = da.TableMappings.Add("Orders", "MyOrders");

// The next three commands remove the mapping just added

// remove the table mapping just added, using a reference to the
// DataTableMapping object
da.TableMappings.Remove(dtm);

// use RemoveAt to remove the DataTableMapping s
da.TableMappings.RemoveAt(0);
```

```
// use RemoveAt with the data source table name
da.TableMappings.RemoveAt("Orders");

// use Clear method to remove all mappings
da.TableMappings.Clear();
```

DataAdapter

Notes

A mapping is created by adding a DataTableMapping object to the DataTableMappingCollection collection. This maps a table in the data source to a table with different name in the DataSet.

Each DataTableMapping object contains a DataColumnMappingCollection object that is accessed through its ColumnMappings property. The collection controls how columns in the data source are mapped to DataColumn objects in the DataTable. The column mapping applies only for the table mapped by the DataTableMapping. A column mapping is created by adding a DataColumnMapping object to the DataColumnMappingCollection collection. This maps a column in the data source to a column with a different name in the DataSet.

Both table and column mappings can be used by the Fill() and FillSchema() methods when retrieving data, and by the Update() method when submitting DataSet changes back to the data source. The Fill() method always uses mapping information if it's available; the FillSchema() method lets you choose whether to use the mapping information.

If incoming data source table and column names don't match DataSet object names, and mapping isn't performed, the MissingMappingAction property of the DataAdapter determines what action is taken when data is retrieved using the Fill() method. Similarly, if incoming data source table and column names don't match DataSet object names, and mapping isn't performed, the MissingSchemaAction property of the data adapter determines what action is taken when the schema is retrieved using the FillSchema() or Fill() method.

DataTableMappingCollection

The commonly used public properties of the DataTableMappingCollection are listed and described in Table 29-8.

Table 29-8. DataTableMappingCollection public properties

Property	Description
Count	Gets the number of items in the DataTableMappingCollection.
Item	Gets the DataTableMapping for the specified index. If the value isn't found, null is returned. In C#, the Item property is the indexer of the class.

The commonly used public methods of the DataTableMappingCollection are listed and described in Table 29-9.

Table 29-9. DataTableMappingCollection public methods

Method	Description
Add()	Adds a DataTableMapping object to the collection.
AddRange()	Adds the objects in the array of DataTableMapping objects to the end of the collection.

TableMappings | 389

Table 29-9. DataTableMappingCollection public methods (continued)

Method	Description
Clear( )	Removes all items from the collection.
Contains( )	Returns a Boolean value indicating whether a DataTableMapping with the specified name exists in the collection.
CopyTo( )	Copies the elements of the collection to the specified array.
GetByDataSetTable( )	Returns the DataTableMapping object from the collection matching the specified DataSet table name.
GetTableMappingBy-SchemaAction( )	Returns a reference to a DataColumnMapping object with the specified source and DataSet table names, and with the specified MissingMappingAction.
IndexOf( )	Returns the index of the specified DataTableMapping. A value of −1 is returned if the DataTableMapping doesn't exist in the collection.
IndexOfDataSetTable( )	Returns the index of the DataTableMapping object with the specified DataSet table name.
Insert( )	Inserts a DataTableMapping object at the end of the collection.
Remove( )	Removes the specified DataTableMapping from the collection. An ArgumentException is generated if the specified DataTableMapping doesn't exist in the collection.
RemoveAt( )	Removes the DataTableMapping at the specified index from the collection. An ArgumentException is raised if the collection doesn't have a DataTableMapping at the specified index.

DataTableMapping class

The commonly used public properties of the DataTableMapping class are listed and described in Table 29-10.

Table 29-10. DataTableMapping public properties

Property	Description
ColumnMappings	Gets the DataColumnMappingCollection for the DataTable.
DataSetTable	Gets or sets the table name in the DataSet to map to.
SourceTable	Gets or sets the table name in the data source to map from.

The commonly used public methods of the DataTableMapping class are listed and described in Table 29-11.

Table 29-11. DataTableMapping public methods

Method	Description
GetColumnMappingBy-SchemaAction( )	Returns a DataColumnMapping for the specified DataTable using the given MissingMappingAction and DataColumnName arguments.
GetDataTableBySchema-Action( )	Returns a DataTable for the specified DataSet and MissingMappingAction arguments.

DataColumnMappingCollection

The DataColumnMappingCollection is returned by the ColumnMappings collection property of the TableMappings class. It maps the names of columns in the DataSet to columns in the data source with different names.

The commonly used public properties of the DataColumnMappingCollection are listed and described in Table 29-12.

Table 29-12. DataColumnMappingCollection public properties

Property	Description
Count	Gets the number of items in the DataColumnMappingCollection.
Item	Gets an object containing the value for the specified index. If the value isn't found, attempting to get it returns null. In C#, the Item property is the indexer of the class.

The commonly used public methods of the DataColumnMappingCollection are listed and described in Table 29-13.

Table 29-13. DataColumnMappingCollection public methods

Method	Description
Add( )	Adds a DataColumnMapping object to the collection.
AddRange( )	Adds the objects in the array of DataColumnMapping objects to the end of the collection.
Clear( )	Removes all items from the collection.
Contains( )	Returns a Boolean value indicating whether a DataColumnMapping with the specified name exists in the collection.
CopyTo( )	Copies the elements of the collection to the specified array.
GetByDataSetColumn( )	Returns the DataColumnMapping object from the collection matching the specified DataSet table name.
GetColumnMappingBy-SchemaAction( )	Returns a DataColumnMapping for the specified DataColumnMappingCollection for the specified source column name and MissingMappingAction arguments.
IndexOf( )	Returns the index of the specified DataColumnMapping. A value of −1 is returned if the DataColumnMapping doesn't exist in the collection.
IndexOfDataSetColumn( )	Returns the zero-based index of the DataColumnMapping object with the specified DataSet table name.
Insert( )	Inserts a DataColumnMapping object at the end of the collection.
Remove( )	Removes the specified DataColumnMapping from the collection. An ArgumentException is generated if the specified DataColumnMapping doesn't exist in the collection.
RemoveAt( )	Removes the DataColumnMapping at the specified index from the collection. An ArgumentException is raised if the collection doesn't have a DataColumnMapping at the specified index.

DataColumnMapping class

The commonly used public properties of the DataColumnMapping class are listed and described in Table 29-14.

Table 29-14. DataColumnMapping public properties

Property	Description
DataSetColumn	Gets or sets the name of the column in the DataSet to map to.
SourceColumn	Gets or sets the name of the column in the data source to map from.

The commonly used public methods of the DataColumnMapping class are listed and described in Table 29-15.

Table 29-15. DataColumnMapping public method

Method	Description
GetDataColumnBySchemaAction( )	Returns a DataColumn from the given DataTable for the specified DataColumn data type and the MissingSchemaAction arguments.

Methods Reference

Fill

```
Int32 rowCount = DataAdapter.Fill(DataSet ds);
Int32 rowCount = DataAdapter.Fill(DataTable dt);
Int32 rowCount = DataAdapter.Fill(DataSet ds, String tableName);
Int32 rowCount = DataAdapter.Fill(DataSet ds, Int32 startRecord,
    Int32 maxRecords, String tableName);
```

Adds new rows or refreshes rows with changed data from the data source to the DataSet.

Parameters

rowCount
> Returns the number of rows successfully created or refreshed from the data source.

ds The DataSet to fill with records, and optionally, schema information.

dt The DataTable to fill with records, and optionally, schema information.

tableName
> The name of the DataTable in the DataSet to fill with the returned records.

startRecord
> The zero-based record number, from the result set returned by the SQL statement, to start adding.

maxRecords
> The number of records, from the result set returned by the SQL statement, to add.

Example

The following example demonstrates how to fill both a table within a DataSet object and a DataTable object using the Fill( ) method:

```
// connection string and select statement
String connString = "Data Source=(local);Integrated security=SSPI;" +
    "Initial Catalog=Northwind;";
String selectSql = "SELECT * FROM Orders";
```

```
    // create the data adapter
    SqlDataAdapter da = new SqlDataAdapter(selectSql, connString);

    // create a new DataSet to receive the Orders data
    DataSet ds = new DataSet();
    // read all of the Orders data into a table named Orders in the DataSet
    da.Fill(ds, "Orders");

    // create a new DataTable to receive the Orders data
    DataTable dt = new DataTable("Orders");
    // read all of the Orders data into table
    da.Fill(dt);
```

Notes

The Fill() method returns data from the data source using the SQL statement or stored procedure in the SelectCommand. The Connection object associated with the SelectCommand must be valid but doesn't need to be open. If it is open prior to calling Fill(), it's left open. If it isn't open prior to calling fill, the DataAdapter opens it when required and closes it when the data has been retrieved.

The Fill() method adds rows to the specified DataTable, creating the table if it doesn't exist. When creating a DataTable, column metadata for the table is created, and if the MissingSchemaAction property is set to AddWithKey, the primary key and constraints are created as well.

If duplicate columns are encountered while populating a DataTable, column names ColumnName1, ColumnName2, and so on, are generated for the duplicate columns. If unnamed columns are returned, default column names Column1, Column2, and so on, are generated. Avoid using these default column names.

If the SelectCommand doesn't return any rows, no tables are added to the DataSet, and no exceptions are raised.

If multiple result sets are returned, a table is created in the DataSet for each result set. If a table name isn't specified, the DataAdapter generates the table names Table, Table1, Table2, and so on, for the tables and assign them to the result sets in the order in which they were returned. Avoid using these default table names. If a table name is specified, MyTable for example, the DataAdapter generates table names MyTable, MyTable1, MyTable2, and so on, and assigns them to the result sets in the order in which they were returned.

The DataSet can contain DataTables whose names differ only by case. If the argument specifying the table name differs only by case from a table name in the DataSet, two outcomes are possible. If the DataSet contains only one table with a table name that differs only by case, the records are added to that table. If, on the other hand, the DataSet contains more than one table with the table name that differs only by case, the records are added to the table with the name that matches based on a case-sensitive comparison or to a newly created table, if no match is found.

When executing a subsequent Fill() operation to refresh data, a primary key must exist on the table being refreshed. Rows from the data source are matched with existing rows in the DataSet based on this key and are used to update the existing rows.

If an error is encountered during the Fill() operation, all records added up to the error remain in the DataSet, and the remainder of the operation is aborted. Also, if multiple result sets are returned, any result set after the error is skipped.

In the case of the overload `Fill()` method accepting arguments specifying the starting record and the number of records to return, if zero is specified as the maximum number of records to return, all records after the starting record are returned. If the specified maximum number of records to return is greater than the number of remaining rows in the result set, all remaining rows are returned without raising an exception. If the `SelectCommand` returns multiple result sets, values specified for the start record and the maximum number of records to return are applied only to the first result set.

It's important to understand that when the start record and the maximum number of records are specified, the underlying mechanism that retrieves the matching subset of records selects all records based on the `SelectCommand` query and then discards records outside of the specified range of records. This can result in poor performance and resource utilization when retrieving a small number of records from the result set of a `SelectCommand` query that retrieves a large number of records, such as in some paging scenarios.

FillSchema

```
DataTable[] dta = DataAdapter.FillSchema(DataSet ds,
    SchemaType schemaType);
DataTable[] dta = DataAdapter.FillSchema(DataTable dt,
    SchemaType schemaType);
DataTable[] dta = DataAdapter.FillSchema(DataSet ds,
    SchemaType schemaType, String tableName);
```

Creates a schema in the DataSet based on the data source. The schema information retrieved is based on the query in the `SelectCommand`.

Parameters

dta Returns an array of DataTable objects added to the DataSet.

ds The DataSet in which to create the schema.

dt The DataTable in which to create the schema.

schemaType
> One of the SchemaType enumeration values described in Table 29-16, which specifies how table mappings are treated during the FillSchema operation.

Table 29-16. SchemaType enumeration

Value	Description
Mapped	Table mappings in the data adapter are applied to the incoming schema. This transformed schema is used.
Source	Ignores table mappings in the data adapter. The data source schema is used.

tableName
> The name of the DataTable in which to create the schema.

Example

The following example demonstrates how to get the schema for both a table within a
DataSet object and a DataTable object using the DataAdapter FillSchema( ) method:

```
// connection string and select statement
String connString = "Data Source=(local);Integrated security=SSPI;" +
    "Initial Catalog=Northwind;";
String selectSql = "SELECT * FROM Orders";

// create the data adapter
SqlDataAdapter da = new SqlDataAdapter(selectSql, connString);

// create a new DataSet to receive the Orders data
DataSet ds = new DataSet();
// read Orders table schema into the Orders table in the DataSet
da.FillSchema(ds, SchemaType.Mapped, "Orders");

// create a new DataTable to receive the Orders data
DataTable dt = new DataTable("Orders");
// read the schema for the Orders table into the DataTable
da.FillSchema(dt, SchemaType.Mapped);
```

Notes

The FillSchema( ) method creates tables in the DataSet from the data source using the
SQL statement or stored procedure in the SelectCommand. The Connection object associated with the SelectCommand must be valid but doesn't need to be open. If it is open
prior to calling FillSchema( ), it is left open. If it isn't open prior to calling FillSchema(
), the DataAdapter opens it when required and closes it when the schema information
has been retrieved.

In addition to creating tables in the data source, the FillSchema method configures the
columns within the tables. The AllowDBNull, AutoIncrement, Maxlength, ReadOnly, and
Unique properties are set for each column as they exist at the data source. The
AutoIncrementSeed and AutoIncrementStep properties must be set programmatically, as
does the DefaultValue property.

The primary key for the table is set to the primary key information from the data
source, if it exists. If no primary key information exists in the data source, but unique
columns are returned, those unique columns are used as the primary key if none of the
unique columns allow null values. Unique constraints are set on columns based on the
information returned from the data source. Other constraint types aren't added.

If duplicate columns are encountered while creating a DataTable, column names
ColumnName1, ColumnName2, ColumnName3, and so on, are generated for the duplicate
columns. If unnamed columns are returned, default column names Column1, Column2,
Column3, and so on, are generated. Avoid using these default column names.

If multiple result sets are returned, a table is created in the DataSet for each result set.
The DataAdapter generates the table names Table, Table1, Table2, and so on, for the
tables and assigns them to the result sets in the order in which they were returned.
Avoid using theses default table names. If a table name is specified, MyTable for
example, the DataAdapter generates table names MyTable, MyTable1, MyTable2, and so
on, and assigns them to the result sets in the order in which they were returned.

The DataSet can contain DataTables whose names differ only by case. If the table-name
argument specifies a table name that differs only by case from a table name in the

DataSet, two outcomes are possible. If the DataSet contains only one table with a table name that differs only by case, that table is created or updated. If, on the other hand, the DataSet contains more than one table with a table name that differs only by case, the table with the matching name based on a case-sensitive comparison is updated or created, if no match is found.

GetFillParameters

```
IDataParameter[] idp = DataRow.GetFillParameters();
```

Returns an array of parameter objects set by the user for the SelectCommand.

Parameters   None.

Example

```
// connection string and select statement
String connString = "Data Source=(local);Integrated security=SSPI;" +
    "Initial Catalog=Northwind;";
String selectSql = "SELECT * FROM Orders WHERE OrderID=@OrderID";

// create the data adapter
SqlDataAdapter da = new SqlDataAdapter(selectSql, connString);
da.SelectCommand.Parameters.Add("@OrderID", SqlDbType.Int);

da.GetFillParameters()[0].Value = 10248;
```

Note   An array of IDataParameter objects is returned rather than the .NET data provider Parameter class that implements IDataParameter. Cast the IDataParameter interface to the provider-specific Parameter class to access provider-specific functionality.

Update

```
Int32 rowCount = DataAdapter.Update(DataRow[] dra);
Int32 rowCount = DataAdapter.Update(DataSet ds);
Int32 rowCount = DataAdapter.Update(DataTable dt);
Int32 rowCount = DataAdapter.Update(DataRow[] dra, DataTableMapping dtm);
Int32 rowCount = DataAdapter.Update(DataSet ds, String mappingTableName);
```

Submits changed data in the DataSet to the data source. The method calls the respective DeleteCommand, InsertCommand, or UpdateCommand objects for each deleted, inserted, or modified DataRow to perform the reconciliation.

Parameters

rowCount
  Returns the number of rows successfully updated in the data source.

dra An array of DataRow objects to reconcile with the data source.

ds A DataSet to reconcile with the data source.

dt A DataTable to reconcile with the data source.

dtm Specifies the action to take whenever a column or table in the data to be reconciled does have a matching column or table in the data source. The value is one of the MissingMappingAction enumeration values as described in Table 29-6 .

Example

The following example demonstrates how to use the Update() method of the DataAdapter to reconcile changes made to a DataSet with the underlying data source:

```
// connection and select command strings
String connString = "Data Source=(local);Integrated security=SSPI;" +
    "Initial Catalog=Northwind;";
String sqlSelect = "SELECT * FROM Orders";

// create a new DataSet to receive the data
DataSet ds = new DataSet();

SqlDataAdapter da = new SqlDataAdapter(sqlSelect, connString);

// create the command builder
SqlCommandBuilder cb = new SqlCommandBuilder(da);

// load data from the Orders table into the Orders table in the DataSet
da.Fill(ds, "Orders");

// ... code to modify the data in the DataSet

// update the data in the Orders table in the DataSet to the data source
da.Update(ds, "Orders");
```

Notes

The Update() method submits changes to the DataSet back to the data source. The Update() method uses the DeleteCommand, InsertCommand, and UpdateCommand objects to attempt to update the data source with records that have been respectively deleted, inserted, or updated in the DataSet. The rows are updated one at a time and not as part of a batch process. The order that the rows are processed as part of the update is determined by the indexes on the DataTable and not by the type of update being performed.

The UpdatedRowSource property of each Command object that submits updates to the data source determines how data is returned back to the DataSet. Table 29-3 lists the possible values for UpdatedRowSource and describes the effect of each on data returned back to the updated row in the DataSet.

Parameter values for each update command are mapped to the current row through the SourceColumn and SourceVersion properties of the Parameter class. If the SourceColumn refers to a column that doesn't exist, the MissingMappingAction dictates what happens. The SourceColumn property also maps updated data-source values in the data source, back to the DataSet. An exception is raised if a nonexistent column is specified.

If an error occurs when a row is being updated, any updates made to rows before the error occurred are kept. If the ContinueUpdateOnError property is true, the row in error is skipped, and processing continues with the next record. If ContinueUpdateOnError is set to false, an exception is raised, and the remaining records aren't processed.

Events Reference

FillError

```
FillErrorEventHandler FillError;
```

The FillError event is raised when an error is encountered during a Fill( ) operation.

Example

The following code demonstrates how to handle the FillError event:

```
SqlDataAdapter da;

// ... code to set up the data adapter

da.FillError += new FillErrorEventHandler(da_FillError);

DataSet ds = new DataSet();

da.Fill(ds);


private void da_FillError(object sender, FillErrorEventArgs e);
{
    MessageBox.Show("RowUpdating");

    // continue the Fill with the rows remaining in the data source
    // despite the error
    e.Continue = true;
}
```

Notes

The event handler receives an argument of type FillErrorEventArgs containing properties that provide specific information about the event as described in Table 29-17.

Table 29-17. FillErrorEventArgs properties

Property	Description
Continue	Gets or sets a value that controls whether the Fill( ) operation continues despite the error.
DataTable	The DataTable being filled when the error occurred.
Errors	The Exception being handled.
Values	An object array containing the values for the row being filled when the error occurred.

This information can be used to handle the event appropriately and determine if the Fill( ) operation should continue processing the DataAdapter Fill( ) operation. To continue processing, set the Continue property of the FillErrorEventArgs argument to true; this results in the Fill( ) operation resuming with the next row in the data source.

If an error is encountered while processing the Fill( ) operation, and the FillError( ) event isn't handled, an exception is raised.

RowUpdated

{Sql | OleDb}RowUpdatingEventHandler RowUpdating;

The RowUpdated event is raised after the command to reconcile a row with the data source row has been executed.

Example

The following code demonstrates how to handle the RowUpdated event:

```
SqlDataAdapter da;

// ... code to set up the data adapter

da.RowUpdated + =new SqlRowUpdatedEventHandler(da_RowUpdated);

private void da_RowUpdated(object sender, SqlRowUpdatedEventArgs e);
{
    MessageBox.Show("RowUpdated");
}
```

Notes

The event handler receives an argument of type RowUpdatedEventArgs containing properties that provide specific information about the event as described in Table 29-18.

Table 29-18. RowUpdatedEventArgs properties

Property	Description
Command	Gets the Command executed to perform the Update( ).
Errors	Gets any errors generated by the .NET data provider when the Command executes to perform the Update( ).
RecordsAffected	Gets the number of rows that deleted, changed, or inserted as a result of executing the Command.
Row	Gets the DataRow used in the Update( ).
StatementType	Gets the type of SQL statement (DELETE, INSERT, or UPDATE) executed in the Update( ).
Status	Gets or sets the UpdateStatus of the Command as described in Table 29-19.
TableMapping	Gets the DataTableMapping used in the Update( ).

Table 29-19 lists and describes the values in the UpdateStatus enumeration.

Table 29-19. UpdateStatus enumeration

Value	Description
Continue	Continue processing rows.
ErrorsOccurred	Raise an error as a result of the update.
SkipAllRemainingRows	Do not update the current and remaining rows.
SkipCurrentRow	Do not update the current row and continue processing the remaining rows.

RowUpdating

```
{Sql | OleDb}RowUpdatedEventHandler RowUpdated;
```

The RowUpdating event is raised before the command to reconcile a row with the data source row has been executed.

Example

The following code demonstrates how to handle the RowUpdating event:

```
SqlDataAdapter da;

// ... code to set up the data adapter

da.RowUpdating += new SqlRowUpdatingEventHandler(da_RowUpdating);

private void da_RowUpdating(object sender, SqlRowUpdatingEventArgs e);
{
    MessageBox.Show("RowUpdating");
}
```

Notes

The event handler receives an argument of type RowUpdatingEventArgs containing properties that provide specific information about the event as described in Table 29-20.

Table 29-20. RowUpdatingEventArgs

Property	Description
Command	Gets or sets the Command that executes to perform the update.
Errors	Gets any errors generated by the .NET provider when the Command executes to perform the update.
Row	Gets the DataRow that is used in the update.
StatementType	Gets the type of SQL statement (DELETE, INSERT, or UPDATE) that is executed in the update.
Status	Gets or sets the UpdateStatus of the Command as described in Table 29-19.
TableMapping	Gets the DataTableMapping that is used in the update.

30

The CommandBuilder Class

The `CommandBuilder` class can automatically generate single-table commands for the `DataAdapter` to use when reconciling changes made to disconnected data with the underlying data source The `CommandBuilder` can also update the data source with changes made to the `DataSet` using very little code. It creates all of the updating logic: the UPDATE, INSERT, and DELETE SQL statements.

Comments/Troubleshooting

The `CommandBuilder` has poorer performance compared to custom update logic because of the time it takes to request metadata and construct the updating logic. The update logic the `CommandBuilder` generates is limited to simple single-table scenarios and provides no support for stored procedures.

To generate update commands for the `DataAdapter` using a `CommandBuilder` object, you must set the `SelectCommand` property of the `DataAdapter` to the SQL statement that retrieves data into the `DataSet`. The `CommandBuilder` uses the SELECT statement to retrieve the metadata needed to generate the DELETE, INSERT, and UPDATE statements. The update logic is generated for the `DeleteCommand`, `InsertCommand`, and `UpdateCommand` objects of the `DataAdapter` when the `Update()` method of the `DataAdapter` is called or when the commands are explicitly retrieved.

If the `SelectCommand` is changed after the metadata is retrieved, the `RefreshSchema()` method of the `CommandBuilder` should be called to update the metadata that generates the update logic; otherwise, the `DeleteCommand`, `InsertCommand`, and `UpdateCommand` retain the values based on the original metadata.

The `SelectCommand` must return a primary key or at least one unique column. Otherwise, an `InvalidOperationException` is raised.

Because the `CommandBuilder` is a connected class, each .NET data provider implements its own `CommandBuilder`, with a similar interface and function as other

CommandBuilder classes but in its own unique namespace. The CommandBuilder class namespaces for several ADO.NET data providers are listed in Table 30-1.

Table 30-1. Provider-specific CommandBuilder classes

Class	Data source
System.Data.SqlClient.SqlCommandBuilder	SQL Server
System.Data.OleDb.OleDbCommandBuilder	OLE DB provider
Microsoft.Data.Odbc.OdbcCommandBuilder	ODBC driver
System.Data.OracleClient.OracleCommandBuilder	Oracle

Table 30-2 describes the commonly used public properties of the CommandBuilder class.

Table 30-2. CommandBuilder properties

Property	Description
DataAdapter	Gets or sets the DataAdapater for which the updating logic is automatically generated.
QuotePrefix	Sets the character or characters that are prefixed to column, table, and other object names within automatically generated SQL statements.
QuoteSuffix	Sets the character or characters that are appended to column, table, and other object names within automatically generated SQL statements.

The commonly used public methods of the CommandBuilder class are listed in Table 30-3.

Table 30-3. CommandBuilder methods

Method	Description
DeriveParameters()	Populates the collection of parameters for a stored procedure Command object from the data source.
GetDeleteCommand()	Returns a reference to the automatically generated Command object that performs deletions on the data source when the Update method of the data adapter is called.
GetInsertCommand()	Returns a reference to the automatically generated Command object that performs inserts into the data source when the Update method of the data adapter is called.
GetUpdateCommand()	Returns a reference to the automatically generated Command object that performs updates on the data source when the Update method of the data adapter is called.
RefrreshSchema()	Refreshes the metadata that automatically generates the updating logic.

Public static members of the CommandBuilder class are safe for multithreaded operations; instance members aren't guaranteed to be thread-safe.

Properties Reference

DataAdapter

```
DataAdapter dataAdapter = CommandBuilder.DataAdapter;
CommandBuilder.DataAdapter = dataAdapter;
```

Gets or sets the DataAdapter for which the SQL statements are automatically generated.

Example

The following example sets the DataAdapter property for a newly created CommandBuilder object:

```
SqlDataAdapter da = new SqlDataAdapter(sqlSelect, connString);
SqlCommandBuilder cb = new SqlCommandBuilder();
cb.DataAdapter = da;
```

Notes

The DataAdapter property can be set for the CommandBuilder object in the constructor, as shown in this example:

```
SqlDataAdapter da = new SqlDataAdapter(sqlSelect, connString);
SqlCommandBuilder cb = new SqlCommandBuilder(da);
```

When a new CommandBuilder is associated with a DataAdapter, any commands from a previous associated CommandBuilder object are released.

QuotePrefix

```
String quotePrefix = CommandBuilder.QuotePrefix;
CommandBuilder.QuotePrefix = quotePrefix;
```

Gets or sets the character or characters that are prefixed to column, table, and other object names. Together with the QuoteSuffix property, this permits characters such as spaces to be used when naming objects. The default value is an empty string.

Example

The following example sets the QuotePrefix and QuoteSuffix property to allow a SQL Server table containing spaces to be specified:

```
SqlCommandBuilder cb = new SqlCommandBuilder();
cb.QuotePrefix = "[";
cd.QuoteSuffix = "]";
```

When the update statements are generated by the CommandBuilder, the SQL Server object names within the updating logic statements are delimited by open and close square brackets.

Notes

Although any valid character can be accommodated by setting the QuotePrefix and QuoteSuffix property, the values of QuotePrefix and QuoteSuffix must be valid delimiters in the data source server. The characters used in the object name must be valid for naming objects in the data source server.

The `QuotePrefix` property can't be changed after the DELETE, INSERT, or UPDATE command has been generated. Attempting to do so raises an `InvalidOperationException` exception.

QuoteSuffix

```
String quoteSuffix = CommandBuilder.QuoteSuffix;
CommandBuilder.QuoteSuffix = quoteSuffix;
```

Gets or sets the character or characters that are appended to column, table, and other object names. Together with the `QuotePrefix` property, this permits characters such as spaces to be used when naming objects. The default value is an empty string.

Example   See the Example for the `QuotePrefix` in this chapter.

Notes

Although any valid character can be accommodated by setting the `QuotePrefix` and `QuoteSuffix` property, the values of `QuotePrefix` and `QuoteSuffix` must be valid delimiters in the data source server. The characters used in the object name must be valid for naming objects in the data source server.

The `QuoteSuffix` property can't be changed after the DELETE, INSERT, or UPDATE command has been generated. Attempting to do so raises an `InvalidOperationException` exception.

Methods Reference

DeriveParameters

```
CommandBuilder.DeriveParameters(Command cmd);
```

Populates the `Parameters` collection for the stored procedure `Command` object from the data source.

Parameters

cmd The `Command` object referencing the stored procedure for which the parameters are to be derived.

Example

The following example shows how to use the `DeriveParameters( )` method to retrieve parameters for a stored procedure command:

```
String connString = "Data Source=(local);Integrated security=SSPI;" +
    "Initial Catalog=Northwind;";

SqlConnection conn = new SqlConnection(connString);
SqlCommand cmd = new SqlCommand("CustOrderHist", conn);
cmd.CommandType = CommandType.StoredProcedure;
```

```
conn.Open();
SqlCommandBuilder.DeriveParameters(cmd);
conn.Close();

foreach(SqlParameter param in cmd.Parameters)
{
    // ... do something with the SqlParameter param
}
```

Notes

The Command must be a stored procedure. Attempting to call this method on any other type of command, or on a stored procedure that doesn't exist in the data source, results in an InvalidOperationException.

Calling this method overwrites any existing information in the Parameters collection for the Command.

This method shouldn't be used when maximum performance is required. Because this method requires a round trip to the data source, it's better to specify the Parameters collection for stored procedure explicitly.

GetDeleteCommand

```
SqlCommand deleteCommand = CommandBuilder.GetDeleteCommand();
```

Returns a reference to the automatically generated Command object, which deletes data from the data source when the Update( ) method of the data adapter is called.

Parameters   None.

Example

The following example demonstrates how to retrieve the automatically generated DeleteCommand, InsertCommand, and UpdateCommand objects using the CommandBuilder:

```
// connection and select command strings
String connString = "Data Source=(local);Integrated security=SSPI;" +
    "Initial Catalog=Northwind;";
String sqlSelect = "SELECT * FROM Orders";

SqlDataAdapter da=new SqlDataAdapter(sqlSelect, connString);

// create the command builder
SqlCommandBuilder cb = new SqlCommandBuilder(da);

// retrieve the Command objects
SqlCommand deleteCommand = cb.GetDeleteCommand();
SqlCommand insertCommand = cb.GetInsertCommand();
SqlCommand updateCommand = cb.GetUpdateCommand();
```

Notes

If the SELECT command that is the basis of the automatically generated DELETE command is changed, the RefreshSchema( ) method must be called. Otherwise the GetDeleteCommand( ) method returns a statement for the previous schema.

Calling one of the GetDeleteCommand( ), GetInsertCommand( ), or GetUpdateCommand( ) methods, or the Update( ) method of the DataAdapter generates all delete, insert, and update command logic.

GetInsertCommand

```
SqlCommand insertCommand = CommandBuilder.GetInsertCommand();
```

Returns a reference to the automatically generated Command object, which inserts data into the data source when the Update( ) method of the data adapter is called.

Parameters   None.

Example   See the Example for the GetDeleteCommand( ) method in this chapter.

Notes

If the select command that is the basis of the automatically generated INSERT command is changed, the RefreshSchema( ) method must be called. Otherwise the GetInsertCommand( ) method returns a statement for the previous schema.

Calling one of the GetDeleteCommand( ), GetInsertCommand( ), or GetUpdateCommand( ) methods or the Update( ) method of the DataAdapter, generates all delete, insert, and update command logic.

GetUpdateCommand

```
SqlCommand updateCommand = CommandBuilder.GetUpdateCommand();
```

Returns a reference to the automatically generated Command object, which updates data within the data source when the Update( ) method of the data adapter is called.

Parameters   None.

Example   See the Example for the GetDeleteCommand( ) method in this chapter.

Notes

If the SELECT command that is the basis of the automatically generated UPDATE command is changed, the RefreshSchema( ) method must be called. Otherwise the GetUpdateCommand( ) method returns a statement for the previous schema.

Calling one of the GetDeleteCommand( ), GetInsertCommand( ), or GetUpdateCommand( ) methods or the Update( ) method of the DataAdapter, generates all delete, insert, and update command logic.

RefreshSchema

```
CommandBuilder.RefreshSchema();
```

Refreshes the schema that automatically generates the DeleteCommand, InsertCommand, and UpdateCommand.

Parameters   None.

Example

The following example demonstrates how to use the RefreshSchema( ) method:

```
// connection and select command strings
String connString = "Data Source=(local);Integrated security=SSPI;" +
    "Initial Catalog=Northwind;";
SqlConnection conn = new SqlConnection(connString);

String sqlSelect = "SELECT * FROM Orders";
SqlCommand selectCommand = new SqlCommand(sqlSelect, conn);

SqlDataAdapter da = new SqlDataAdapter(selectCommand);

// create the command builder
SqlCommandBuilder cb = new SqlCommandBuilder(da);
// retrieve the DeleteCommand
SqlCommand deleteCommand = cb.GetDeleteCommand();

// change the select statement
sqlSelect = "SELECT OrderID, CustomerID, EmployeeID FROM Orders";
selectCommand = new SqlCommand(sqlSelect, conn);
// have to call RefreshSchema before retrieving the DeleteCommand again
cb.RefreshSchema();
deleteCommand = cb.GetDeleteCommand();
```

Notes

The RefreshSchema( ) method should be called whenever the SELECT statement associated with the CommandBuilder changes.

The RefreshSchema( ) method doesn't cause the updating logic in the DeleteCommand, InsertCommand, and UpdateCommand objects to be regenerated immediately. The updating logic is regenerated when the DataAdapter Update( ) method is called or when the GetDeleteCommand( ), GetInsertCommand( ), or GetUpdateCommand( ) method is called.

31

The Transaction Class

Transactions ensure that a set of related operations are all completed or are aborted, leaving the involved resources in the state that they were in when the transaction was started. Transactions are most commonly used in data-oriented situations in which all related operations must be completed successfully (e.g., debiting and crediting respective bank accounts when funds are transferred from one to the other). The related operations are bound together into a transactional unit of work that must either completely succeed or completely fail; this is referred to as committing or aborting the transaction.

Transactions can occur within a single data resource, with the data resource providing transaction functionality and controlling the transaction. Transactions can also span multiple data resources. These distributed transactions are generally managed by an external transaction processing system.

Comments/Troubleshooting

A .NET transaction is created by calling the BeginTransaction( ) method on the Connection object. All subsequent operations associated with the transaction, such as committing or aborting the transaction, are performed using the Transaction object.

Transactions should be used only when required. Using transactions imposes a performance penalty due to the system overhead in managing the transaction. Transactions can also block work of other users in the system, which causes performance problems. For that reason, if transactions are required, the isolation level of the transactions should be carefully considered.

Because the Transaction is a connected class, each .NET data provider implements its own Transaction class, with a similar interface and function as other Transaction classes but in its own unique namespace. The Transaction class namespaces for several ADO.NET data providers are listed in Table 31-1.

Table 31-1. Provider-specific transaction classes

Class	Data source
System.Data.SqlClient.SqlTransaction	SQL Server
System.Data.OleDb.OleDbTransaction	OLE DB provider
Microsoft.Data.Odbc.OdbcTransaction	ODBC driver
System.Data.OracleClient.OracleTransaction	Oracle

The commonly used public properties of the Transaction class are listed in Table 31-2.

Table 31-2. Transaction properties

Property	Description
Connection	Gets the connection associated with the transaction.
IsolationLevel	Gets the isolation level for the transaction.

The commonly used public methods of the Transaction class are listed in Table 31-3.

Table 31-3. Transaction methods

Method	Description
Begin( )	Starts a nested transaction (OLE DB only).
Commit( )	Commits the transaction.
Rollback( )	Rolls back a transaction from a pending state.
Save( )	Creates a savepoint in the transaction that can be used to roll back a portion of the transaction (SQL Server only).

The Transaction class inherits from MarshalByRefObject and implements the IDbTransaction and IDisposable interfaces. Public static members of this class are safe for multithreaded operations; instance members aren't guaranteed thread-safe.

Properties Reference

Connection

```
SqlConnection sqlConnection = Transaction.Connection;
```
Gets the connection object associated with the transaction.

Example

The following example demonstrates how to retrieve the connection object for a transaction:

```
String connString = "Data Source=(local);Integrated security=SSPI;" +
    "Initial Catalog=Northwind;";
```

```
SqlConnection conn = new SqlConnection(connString);
conn.Open();
SqlTransaction tran = conn.BeginTransaction();

// returns a reference to the SqlConnection conn
SqlConnection conn2 = tran.Connection;
```

Note　　　　This value is null if the connection is no longer valid.

IsolationLevel

```
IsolationLevel isolationLevel = Transaction.IsolationLevel;
```

Gets the isolation level for the transaction. This value is one of the IsolationLevel enumeration values described in Table 31-4.

Table 31-4. IsolationLevelEnumeration

Name	Description
ReadUncommitted	No shared locks are issued, and exclusive locks aren't honored. A dirty read is possible.
ReadCommitted	Shared locks are held while data is being read by the transaction. Dirty reads aren't possible, but non-repeatable reads or phantom rows can occur because data can be changed before it is committed.
RepeatableRead	Shared locks are placed on all data used in a query, preventing other users from updating the data. Nonrepeatable reads are prevented, but phantom reads are still possible.
Serializable	A range lock, in which the individual records and the ranges between records are covered, is placed on the data preventing other users from updating or inserting rows until the transaction is complete. Phantom reads are prevented.
Chaos	Pending changes from more highly isolated transactions can't be overwritten. Not supported by SQL Server.
Unspecified	A different isolation level than the one specified is used, but that level can't be determined.

Example

The following example demonstrates how to set the IsolationLevel for a new transaction:

```
String connString = "Data Source=(local);Integrated security=SSPI;" +
    "Initial Catalog=Northwind;";

SqlConnection conn = new SqlConnection(connString);
conn.Open();
SqlTransaction tran =
    conn.BeginTransaction(IsolationLevel.RepeatableRead);

// returns IsolationLevel.RepeatableRead
IsolationLevel il = tran.IsolationLevel;
```

Note　　　　The default value of the IsolationLevel property is ReadCommitted.

Methods Reference

Begin [OLE DB only]

```
Transaction nestTran = Transaction.Begin();
Transaction nestTran = Transaction.Begin(IsolationLevel il);
```

Starts a nested database transaction.

Parameters

nestTran
> Returns a reference to the nested database transaction.

il   The isolation level to use for the new transaction.

Example

This example demonstrates how to start a nested transaction using the Begin method:

```
String connString = "Data Source=(local);Integrated security=SSPI;" +
    "Initial Catalog=Northwind;";

OleDbConnection conn = new OleDbConnection(connString);
conn.Open();
OleDbTransaction tran = conn.BeginTransaction();

// start a nested transaction
OleDbTransaction nestTran = tran.Begin();
```

Notes

This method is available only in the OLE DB .NET data provider.

An InvalidOperationException is raised if the data source doesn't support nested transactions.

Commit

```
Transaction.Commit();
```

Commits the database transaction.

Parameters   None.

Example

The following example demonstrates how to start a transaction and either commit the transaction or roll the transaction back, depending on the outcome of commands executed against the data source:

```
String connString = "Data Source=(local);Integrated security=SSPI;" +
    "Initial Catalog=Northwind;";

SqlConnection conn = new SqlConnection(connString);
conn.Open();
```

```
SqlTransaction tran = conn.BeginTransaction();
try
{
    // ... execute some commands against the data source

    tran.Commit();
}
catch (Exception e)
{
    tran.Rollback();
}
finally
{
    conn.Close();
}
```

Rollback

```
Transaction.Rollback();
Transaction.Rollback(String savePointName);
```

Rolls back a transaction from a pending state. A savepoint can optionally be specified as the point to roll the transaction back to with the SQL Server .NET data provider.

Parameters   None.

Example   See the Example for the Commit( ) method in this chapter.

Note   The overloaded Rollback( ) method with the savepoint name argument is available only in the SQL Server .NET data provider.

Save [SQL Server only]

```
void = Transaction.Save(String savePointName);
```

Creates a savepoint in the transaction that can roll back a portion of the transaction.

Parameters   None.

Example

The following example demonstrates how to create and use a savepoint to partially roll back a transaction:

```
String connString = "Data Source=(local);Integrated security=SSPI;" +
    "Initial Catalog=Northwind;";

SqlConnection conn = new SqlConnection(connString);
conn.Open();

SqlTransaction tran = conn.BeginTransaction();

try
{
```

```
    // ... execute some commands against the data source
}
catch (Exception ex)
{
    // roll back the transaction, close the connection, and leave
    tran.Rollback();
    conn.Close();

    return;
}

// create a save point called SavePoint1
tran.Save("SavePoint1");

try
{
    // ... execute some commands against the data source

    tran.Commit();
}
catch (SqlException ex)
{
    // roll back the transaction to the save point
    tran.Rollback("SavePoint1");
    // commit all processing up to the save point
    tran.Commit();
}
finally
{
    conn.Close();
}
```

Note   This method is available only in the SQL Server .NET data provider.

API Quick Reference

32

How to Use This
Quick Reference

The quick-reference section that follows packs a lot of information into a small space. This introduction explains how to get the most out of that information. It describes how the quick reference is organized and how to read the individual quick-reference entries.

Finding a Quick-Reference Entry

The quick reference is organized into chapters, one per namespace. Each chapter begins with an overview of the namespace and includes a hierarchy diagram for the types (classes, interfaces, enumerations, delegates, and structs) in the namespace. Following the overview are quick-reference entries for all the types in the namespace.

Figure 32-1 is a sample diagram showing the notation used in this book. This notation is similar to that used in *Java in a Nutshell*, but borrows some features from UML. Abstract classes are shown as a slanted rectangle, and sealed classes as an octagonal rectangle. Inheritance is shown as a solid line from the subtype, ending with a hollow triangle that points to the supertype. There are two notations that indicate interface implementation. The lollipop notation is used most of the time because it is easier to read. In some cases, especially where many types implement a given interface, the shaded box notation with a dashed line is used.

Important relationships between types (associations) are shown with a dashed line ending with an arrow. The figures don't show every possible association.

Entries are organized alphabetically by type and namespace, so that related types are grouped near each other. Thus, in order to look up a quick reference entry for a particular type, you must also know the name of the namespace that contains that type. Usually, the namespace is obvious from the context, and you should have no trouble looking up the quick-reference entry you want. Use the tabs on

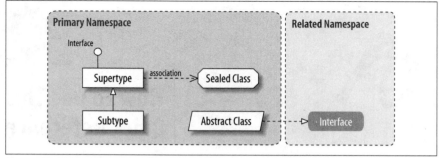

Figure 32-1. Class hierarchy notation

the outside edge of the book and the dictionary-style headers on the upper outside corner of each page to help you find the namespace and type you are looking for.

Occasionally, you may need to look up a type for which you don't already know the namespace. In this case, refer to Appendix D. This index allows you to look up a type by its name and find out what namespace it is part of.

Reading a Quick-Reference Entry

Each quick-reference entry contains quite a bit of information. The sections that follow describe the structure of a quick-reference entry, explaining what information is available, where it is found, and what it means. While reading the descriptions that follow, you will find it helpful to flip through the reference section itself to find examples of the features being described.

Type Name, Namespace, Assembly, Type Category, and Flags

Each quick-reference entry begins with a four-part title that specifies the name, namespace (followed by the assembly in parentheses), and type category of the type. It may also specify various additional flags that describe the type. The type name appears in bold at the upper left of the title. The namespace and assembly appear, in smaller print, in the lower left, below the type name.

In the upper-right corner of the title, you may find a list of flags that describe the type. The possible flags and their meanings are as follows:

ECMA
The type is part of the ECMA CLI specification.

serializable
The type, or a supertype, implements System.Runtime.Serialization.ISerializable or has been flagged with the System.Serializable attribute.

marshal by reference
This class, or a superclass, derives from System.MarshalByRefObject.

context bound
This class, or a superclass, derives from System.ContextBoundObject.

disposable
> The type implements the System.IDisposable interface.

flag
> The enumeration is marked with the System.FlagsAttribute.

The lower-right portion of the title indicates the **type** category of the type (**class**, **delegate**, **enum**, **interface**, or **struct**). The class category may include modifiers such as **sealed** or **abstract**.

Description

The title of each quick-reference entry is followed by a short description of the most important features of the type. This description may be anywhere from a couple of sentences to several paragraphs long.

Synopsis

The most important part of every quick-reference entry is the synopsis, which follows the title and description. The synopsis for a type looks a lot like its source code, except that the member bodies are omitted, and some additional annotations are added. If you know C# syntax, you can read the type synopsis.

The first line of the synopsis contains information about the type itself. It begins with a list of type modifiers, such as **abstract** and **sealed**. These modifiers are followed by the **class**, **delegate**, **enum**, **interface**, or **struct** keyword, and then by the name of the type. The type name may be followed by a colon (:) and a supertype or interfaces that the type implements.

The type definition line is followed by a list of the members that the type defines. This list includes only those members that are explicitly declared in the type, are overridden from a base class, or are implementations of an interface member. Members that are simply inherited from a base class aren't shown; you will need to look up the base class definition to find those members. Once again, if you understand basic C# syntax, you should have no trouble making sense of these lines. The listing for each member includes the modifiers, type, and name of the member. For methods, the synopsis also includes the type and name of each method parameter. The member names are in boldface, so it is easy to scan the list of members looking for the one you want. The names of method parameters are in italics to indicate that they aren't to be used literally. The member listings are printed on alternating gray and white backgrounds to keep them visually separate.

Member availability and flags

Each member listing is a single line that defines the API for that member. These listings use C# syntax, so their meaning is immediately clear to any C# programmer. There is some auxiliary information associated with each member synopsis, however, that requires explanation.

The area to the right of the member synopsis displays a variety of flags that provide additional information about the member. Some of these flags indicate additional specification details that don't appear in the member API itself.

The following flags may be displayed to the right of a member synopsis:

Overrides
> Indicates that a method overrides a method in one of its supertypes. The flag is followed by the name of the supertype that the method overrides.

Implements
> Indicates that a method implements a method in an interface. The flag is followed by the name of the interface that is implemented.

=
> For enumeration fields and constant fields, this flag is followed by the constant value of the field. Only constants of primitive and String types and constants with the value null are displayed. Some constant values are specification details, while others are implementation details. The reason symbolic constants are defined, however, is so you can write code that doesn't rely directly upon the constant value. Use this flag to help you understand the type, but don't rely upon the constant values in your own programs.

Functional grouping of members

Within a type synopsis, the members aren't listed in strict alphabetical order. Instead, they are broken into functional groups and listed alphabetically within each group. Constructors, events, fields, methods, and properties are all listed separately. Instance methods are kept separate from static (class) methods. Public members are listed separately from protected members. Grouping members by category breaks a type down into smaller, more comprehensible segments, making the type easier to understand. This grouping also makes it easier for you to find a desired member.

Functional groups are separated from one another in a type synopsis with C# comments, such as // Public Constructors, // Protected Instance Properties, and // Events. The various functional categories are as follows (in the order in which they appear in a type synopsis):

Constructors
> Displays the constructors for the type. Public constructors and protected constructors are displayed separately in subgroupings. If a type defines no constructor at all, the C# compiler adds a default no-argument constructor that is displayed here. If a type defines only private constructors, it can't be instantiated, so no constructor appears. Constructors are listed first because the first thing you do with most types is instantiate them by calling a constructor.

Fields
> Displays all fields defined by the type, including constants. Public and protected fields are displayed in separate subgroups. Fields are listed here, near the top of the synopsis, because constant values are often used throughout the type as legal values for method parameters and return values.

Properties
> Lists all the properties of the type, breaking them down into subgroups for public and protected static properties and public and protected instance properties. After the property name, its accessors (**get** or **set**) are shown.

Static Methods
> Lists the static methods (class methods) of the type, broken into subgroups for public static methods and protected static methods.

Public Instance Methods
> Contains all public instance methods.

Protected Instance Methods
> Contains all protected instance methods.

Class Hierarchy

For any type that has a nontrivial inheritance hierarchy, the synopsis is followed by a Hierarchy section. This section lists all the supertypes of the type, as well as any interfaces implemented by those supertypes. It also lists any interfaces implemented by an interface. In the hierarchy listing, arrows indicate supertype-to-subtype relationships, while the interfaces implemented by a type follow the type name in parentheses. For example, the following hierarchy indicates SomeClass implements IDisposable and extends MarshalByRefObject, which itself extends Object:

```
System.Object→System.MarshalByRefObject→SomeClass(System.IDisposable)
```

If a type has subtypes, the Hierarchy section is followed by a Subtypes section that lists those subtypes. If an interface has implementations, the Hierarchy section is followed by an Implementations section that lists those implementations. While the Hierarchy section shows ancestors of the type, the Subtypes or Implementations section shows descendants.

Cross References

The Hierarchy section of a quick-reference entry is followed by a number of optional cross-reference sections that indicate related types and methods that may be of interest. These sections are the following:

Passed To
> This section lists all the members (from other types) that are passed an object of this type as an argument, including properties whose values can be set to this type. This is useful when you have an object of a given type and want to know where it can be used.

Returned By
> This section lists all the members that return an object of this type, including properties whose values can take on this type. This is useful when you want to work with an object of this type but don't know how to obtain one.

Valid On

For attributes, this lists the attribute targets the attribute can be applied to.

Associated Events

For delegates, lists the events it can handle.

A Note About Type Names

Throughout the quick reference, you'll notice that types are sometimes referred to by type name alone and at other times referred to by type name and namespace. If namespaces were always used, the type synopses would become long and hard to read. On the other hand, if namespaces were never used, it would sometimes be difficult to know what type was being referred to. The rules for including or omitting the namespace name are complex. They can be summarized approximately as follows, however:

- If the type name alone is ambiguous, the namespace name is always used.
- If the type is part of the System namespace or is a commonly used type such as System.Collection.ICollection, the namespace is omitted.
- If the type being referred to is part of the current namespace (and has a quick-reference entry in the current chapter), the namespace is omitted. The namespace is also omitted if the type being referred to is part of a namespace that contains the current namespace.

33

Converting from C# to VB Syntax

Although information on all types and their members is shown using C# syntax, it is easy to mentally convert to Visual Basic syntax. This appendix will provide the information you need to convert the documentation for each type into the syntax used by Visual Basic.

This chapter doesn't try to completely cover the syntax for each language element it discusses. Instead, it focuses on direct translation of the syntax of the types used in ADO.NET programming from C# to VB.

General Considerations

The most evident difference between C# and VB syntax is that C# uses the semicolon (;) as a statement terminator, whereas VB uses a line break. As a result, a statement in C# can occupy multiple lines as long as it is terminated with a semicolon; a VB statement must occupy only a single line. Multiline statements in VB must appear with the VB line continuation character (a space followed by an underscore) on all but the last line.

A second, and not quite so evident, difference is that C# is case sensitive, whereas VB isn't. (Uniform casing for VB code is enforced by the Visual Studio environment, but it is by no means required.)

Finally, all types and their members have access modifiers that determine the type or member's accessibility. The keywords for these access modifiers are nearly identical in VB and C#, as Table 33-1 shows.

Table 33-1. Access modifiers in C# and VB

C# keyword	VB keyword
public	Public
private	Private
protected	Protected
internal	Friend
protected internal	Protected Friend

Classes

C# uses the class statement along with opening and closing braces to indicate the beginning and end of a class definition. For example:

```
public class DataException : SystemException {
    // member definitions
}
```

In VB, a class definition is indicated by the Class... End Class construct:

```
Public Class DataException
    Inherits SystemException
    ' member definitions
End Class
```

In addition, C# classes can be marked as abstract or sealed; these correspond to the VB MustInherit and NonInheritable keywords, as shown in Table 33-2.

Table 33-2. C# and equivalent VB class modifiers

C# keyword	VB keyword
abstract	MustInherit
sealed	NonInheritable

C# uses the colon to indicate either inheritance or interface implementation. Both the base class and the implemented interfaces are part of the class statement. For example:

```
public class DataSet : MarshalByValueComponent, IListSource,
    ISupportInitialize, ISerializable
```

In VB, a base class and any implemented interfaces are specified on separate lines immediately following the Class statement. A class's base class is indicated by preceding its name with the Inherits keyword; any implemented interfaces are indicated by the Implements keyword. Hence, the previous definition of the DataSet class in C# would appear as follows in VB:

```
Public Class DataSet
    Inherits MarshalByValueComponent
    Implements IListSource, ISupportInitalize, ISerializable
```

Structures

C# uses the struct statement along with opening and closing braces to indicate the beginning and end of a structure definition. For example, System.Windows.Forms.DataGridCell is defined in C# as follows:

```
public struct DataGridCell {
    // member definitions
}
```

In VB, a structure definition is indicated by the Structure... End Interface construct:

```
Public Structure DataGridCell
    ' member definitions
End Structure
```

C# uses the colon with structures to indicate interface implementation. Any implemented interfaces are part of the class statement. In VB, any implemented interfaces are specified by an Implements statement on the line immediately following the Structure statement. However, none of the structures documented in the reference section of this book use interface inheritance.

Interfaces

C# uses the interface statement along with opening and closing braces to indicate the beginning and end of an interface definition. For example:

```
public interface IDataAdapter {
    // member definitions
}
```

In VB, an interface definition is indicated by the Interface... End Structure construct:

```
Public Interface IDataAdapter
    ' member definitions
End Interface
```

C# uses the colon with interfaces to specify any implemented interfaces. For example:

```
public interface IDataReader : IDisposable, IDataRecord
```

In VB, any implemented interfaces are specified by an Implements statement on the line immediately following the Interface statement. The previous definition of IDataReader in C# would appear as follows in VB:

```
Public Interface IDataReader
    Implements IDisposable, IDataRecord
```

Class, Structure, and Interface Members

Classes, structures, and interfaces can contain one or more fields, methods, properties, and events. This section discusses converting the C# syntax for each of these constructs to VB.

Note that .NET supports both static (or shared) members (which apply to the type as a whole, and typically don't require that an object of that type be instantiated) and instance members (which apply only to an instance of that type). Shared or static members are indicated by using the static keyword in C#. For example:

```
public static string ToString(long value);
```

The corresponding VB keyword is Shared, so the FromResource method, when converted to VB, has the following syntax:

```
Public Shared Function ToString(value As Long) As String
```

Fields

A field is simply a constant or a variable that is exposed as a publicly accessible member of a type. In C#, for example, the Value field of the System.DBNull class has the syntax:

```
public static readonly DBNull Value;
```

Note that C# indicates the data type of a field before the name of the field. (For C# data types and their VB equivalents, see Table 33-3.) Also note that fields are frequently read-only. Constant fields, in fact, are always read-only. As a result, the use of the C# readonly keyword and the VB ReadOnly keyword with fields is quite common.

The syntax for the Value field in Visual Basic then becomes:

```
Public Shared ReadOnly Value As DBNull
```

Methods

In C#, all methods have a return value, which appears before the name of the function; in contrast, VB differentiates between function and subprocedures. C# functions without an explicit return value return void. For example, one of the overloads of the DataSet class's AcceptChanges method has the following syntax in C#:

```
public void AcceptChanges( );
```

C# methods that return void are expressed as subprocedures in VB. Here's the corresponding syntax of the AcceptChanges method:

```
Public Sub AcceptChanges( )
```

All C# methods other than those returning void are functions in VB. The function's return value appears in an As clause at the end of the function declaration. C# data types and their VB equivalents are shown in Table 33-3. Methods that return arrays are indicated by adding braces ([]) to the return data type in C# and parentheses (())to the return data type in VB.

For example, the Copy method of the DataSet class has the C# syntax:

```
public bool Copy( );
```

The VB equivalent is:

```
Public Function Copy( ) As Boolean
```

Table 33-3. C# data types and their VB equivalents

C# data type	VB data type
bool	Boolean
byte	Byte
char	Char
decimal	Decimal
double	Double
float	Single
int	Integer
long	Long
object	Object
sbyte	System.SByte
short	Short
string	String
System.Currency	Currency
System.DateTime	Date
uint	System.UInt32
ulong	System.UInt64
ushort	System.UInt16
<class_name>	<class_name>
<delegate_name>	<delegate_name>
<interface_name>	<interface_name>
<structure_name>	<structure_name>

Method parameters in C# take the general form:

```
<data_type> <parameter_name>
```

In VB, method parameters take the form:

```
<parameter_name> As <data_type>
```

where *<data_type>* is any of the data types listed in Table 33-3. If a parameter is an array, its data type is followed by braces in C# (e.g., string[] Name), while the parameter name is followed by parentheses in VB (e.g., Name( ) As String).

For example, one of the versions of the DataTable class's Select method has the following syntax in C#:

```
public DataRow[] Select(string filterExpression, string sort,
    DataViewRowState recordStates);
```

Its VB equivalent is:

```
Overloads Public Function Select(ByVal filterExpression As String, _
    ByVal sort As String, ByVal recordStates As DataViewRowState _
    ) As DataRow( )
```

VB allows methods to be called using either named and positional parameters. If named parameters are used, the parameter name must correspond to that shown in the documentation. For instance, DataTable.Select can be called as follows using named parameters:

```
dr = DataTable.Select(filterexpression:=flt, _
        sort:=sd, _
        recordstates:=DataViewRowState.CurrentRows)
```

C# also uses a number of object-oriented qualifiers with methods. These, and their VB equivalents, are shown in Table 33-4.

Table 33-4. C# keywords used with methods and their VB equivalents

C# keyword	VB keyword
abstract	MustOverride
override	Overrides
sealed	NotOverridable
virtual	Overridable

In both C# and VB, constructors have a special syntax. In C#, constructors have the same name as the classes whose objects they instantiate and don't indicate a return value. For example, the default constructor for the SqlCommand class is:

```
public SqlCommand( );
```

In VB, the constructor is represented by a call to a class's New subprocedure. The equivalent call to the SqlCommand class constructor in VB is:

```
Public Sub New( )
```

Properties

The SqlCommand.CommandText property provides a more or less typical example of a property definition using C# syntax:

```
public string CommandText {get; set;}
```

Like all C# type definitions, the property's data type precedes the property name. The get; and set; property accessors indicate that this is a read-write property. Read-only properties are indicated with a get; only, while write-only properties are indicated with a set; only.

The equivalent VB property definition is:

```
Public Property CommandText As String
```

Note that read-write properties aren't decorated with additional keywords in VB. Read-only properties, on the other hand, are indicated with the ReadOnly keyword in front of the Property keyword, while write-only properties have the WriteOnly keyword before the Property keyword.

Note that properties, like methods, can use the object-oriented modifiers listed in Table 33-4.

Events

Events are declared in C# using the **event** keyword, which is followed by the delegate type returned by the event and the name of the event. For example, the **RowUpdated** event of the **SqlDataAdapter** class has the following syntax:

```
public event SqlRowUpdatedEventHandler RowUpdated;
```

The equivalent VB syntax is:

```
Public Event RowUpdated As SqlRowUpdatedEventHandler
```

In addition, the C# **event** and the VB **Event** keywords can be preceded by the object modifiers listed in Table 33-4.

Delegates

The syntax for a delegate in C# closely follows the syntax for a method. The **delegate** statement is followed by the delegate's return type (or void, if there is none) and the delegate name. This in turn is followed by the delegate's parameter list, in which each parameter takes the form:

```
<parameter_type> <parameter_name>
```

For example:

```
public delegate void StateChangeEventHandler(object sender,
    StateChangeEventArgs e);
```

In a VB **Delegate** statement, the **Delegate** keyword is followed by the **Sub** keyword (if the delegate returns a void in C#) or the **Function** keyword (if the delegate returns some other value). For example, in VB, the **StateChangeEventHandler** delegate has the following syntax:

```
Public Delegate Sub StateChangeEventHandler( _
    ByVal sender As Object, ByVal e As StateChangeEventArgs)
```

Enumerations

C# uses the **enum** statement along with opening and closing braces to indicate the beginning and end of an enumeration definition. For example:

```
public enum CommandType {
    // enumeration members
}
```

In VB, an enumeration is defined by the **Enum... End Enum** construct. For example, the VB version of the **CommandType** enum declaration is:

```
Public Enum CommandType
    ' enumeration members
End Enum
```

In both C# and VB, the member listing consists of the name of the enumerated member and its value. These are identical in C# and VB, except that C# adds a comma to separate one member of the enumeration from another, whereas VB requires that they be on separate lines. For example, the full declaration of the CommandType enumeration in C# is:

```csharp
public enum CommandType {
    Text = 1,
    StoredProcedure = 4,
    TableDirect = 512
}
```

The VB equivalent is:

```vb
Public Enum CommandType
    Text = 1
    StoredProcedure = 4
    TableDirect = 512
End Enum
```

34

The System.Data Namespace

The System.Data namespace represents the core of ADO.NET. It contains the fundamental data container classes such as DataSet. Every DataSet contains a collection of DataTable instances. Each DataTable holds a collection of DataRow objects, each of which contains the data for a single row. These data classes are independent of any ADO.NET provider. They simply store disconnected data. In addition, the DataSet also contains objects that describe structural information about your data. This structural information, which is also known as *metadata*, includes column-specific settings such as data type (found in DataColumn), foreign key and unique column constraints (represented by ForeignKeyConstraint and UniqueConstraint), and relations that link columns in different tables (represented by DataRelation).

Taken together, these objects act like an in-memory relational database, complete with versioning, column and table information, XML output, and automatic enforcement of identity and relational integrity rules. However, these classes are only part of the System.Data namespace. You'll also find the interfaces that must be implemented by every ADO.NET provider. These interfaces define connections (IDbConnection), commands (IDbCommand), data readers (IDataReader), parameters (IDbDataParameter), transactions (IDbTransaction), and data adapters (IDbDataAdapter and IDataAdapter). These interfaces aren't just a low-level part of ADO.NET. You'll need to use them if you want to write generic provider-agnostic data code (as described in Chapter 2). You'll also need to use them to create your own custom provider.

Figure 34-1 shows many of the types in this namespace. Figure 34-2 highlights the exceptions, delegates, and event arguments. See Figure 34-3 for components and other types.

AcceptRejectRule   serializable

System.Data (system.data.dll)   enum

This enumeration sets values for the ForeignKeyConstraint.AcceptRejectRule property. It determines what happens to child rows when you call the DataRow.AcceptChanges( ) method of

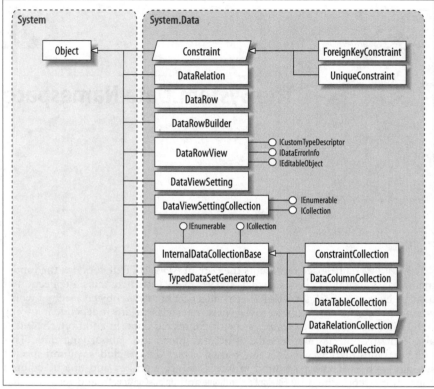

Figure 34-1. The System.Data namespace

the parent row. With the default value (None) nothing happens. If you select Cascade, the DataRow.AcceptChanges( ) method is called automatically on all child rows when it is called on the parent.

The DataRow.AcceptChanges( ) method can be triggered in several ways. For example, if you call the DataTable.AcceptChanges( ) or DataSet.AcceptChanges( ) method, the AcceptChanges( ) method is called for every contained row. Also, if you update a data source using a data adapter, the DataRow.AcceptChanges( ) method is also called implicitly on each row once the change is committed to the data source.

```
public enum AcceptRejectRule {
  None = 0,
  Cascade = 1
}
```

Hierarchy   System.Object → System.ValueType → System.Enum(System.IComparable, System.IFor-
                   mattable, System.IConvertible) → AcceptRejectRule

Returned By   ForeignKeyConstraint.AcceptRejectRule

Passed To   ForeignKeyConstraint.{AcceptRejectRule, ForeignKeyConstraint( )}

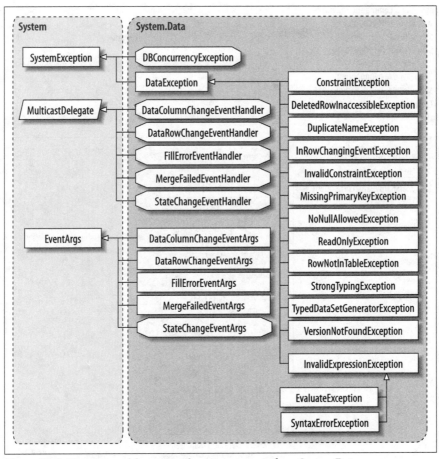

Figure 34-2. Exceptions, delegates, and event arguments from System.Data

CommandBehavior

serializable, flag

System.Data (system.data.dll)   enum

This enumeration is used with an overload of the IDbCommand.ExecuteReader() method. Typically, you don't use this method directly but will instead use the IDbCommand. ExecuteReader() method that requires no arguments, which is functionally equivalent to calling IDbCommand.ExecuteReader() with Default. One notable exception is when you access BLOB information (a column that contains a binary large object). In this case, the SequentialAccess value is useful because it instructs .NET not to load the entire row into memory at once. Rather, the row is read as a stream, and you can use the IDataRecord. GetBytes() method (exposed by most DataReader objects) to specify a byte location to start the read operation and the number of bytes to read for the data returned. This technique is demonstrated in Chapter 5. You can also use other CommandBehavior enumeration values to specify the command to return a single value, a single row, column schema information, or column and primary key information.

```
public enum CommandBehavior {
 Default = 0x00000000,
 SingleResult = 0x00000001,
 SchemaOnly = 0x00000002,
 KeyInfo = 0x00000004,
 SingleRow = 0x00000008,
 SequentialAccess = 0x00000010,
 CloseConnection = 0x00000020
}
```

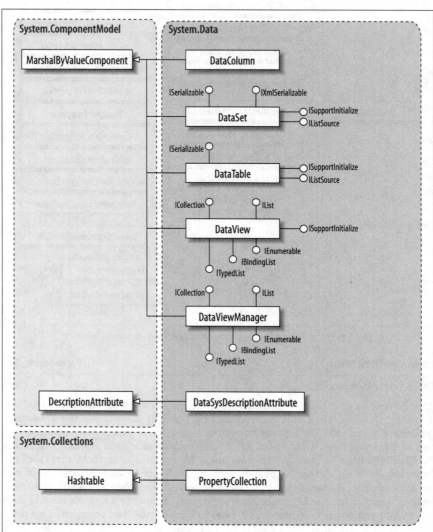

Figure 34-3. System.Data's components and miscellaneous types

Hierarchy	System.Object → System.ValueType → System.Enum(System.IComparable, System.IFor-mattable, System.IConvertible) → CommandBehavior
Passed To	System.Data.Common.DbDataAdapter.{Fill( ), FillSchema( )}, IDbCommand. ExecuteReader( ), System.Data.OleDb.OleDbCommand.ExecuteReader( ), System.Data. OracleClient.OracleCommand.ExecuteReader( ), System.Data.SqlClient.SqlCommand. ExecuteReader( )

CommandType   serializable

System.Data (system.data.dll)   enum

This enumeration sets the IDbCommand.CommandType property, which defines how the IDbCommand.CommandText property is interpreted. If you use Text (the default), the IDbCommand.CommandText is interpreted as a SQL command (e.g., a direct UPDATE, DELETE, INSERT, or SELECT command). If you use StoredProcedure, IDbCommand.CommandText is the name of the stored procedure you want to execute. Some providers support the use of the TableDirect CommandType. In this case, the IDbCommand.CommandText is interpreted as the name of a table from which rows will be retrieved (in a SELECT * FROM TableName style). You can also use a comma-delimited list of tables on which a join is performed. TableDirect isn't supported by all data providers.

```
public enum CommandType {
  Text = 1,
  StoredProcedure = 4,
  TableDirect = 512
}
```

Hierarchy	System.Object → System.ValueType → System.Enum(System.IComparable, System.IFor-mattable, System.IConvertible) → CommandType
Returned By	IDbCommand.CommandType, System.Data.OleDb.OleDbCommand.CommandType, System.Data.OracleClient.OracleCommand.CommandType, System.Data.SqlClient.SqlCom-mand.CommandType
Passed To	IDbCommand.CommandType, System.Data.OleDb.OleDbCommand.CommandType, System.Data.OracleClient.OracleCommand.CommandType, System.Data.SqlClient.SqlCom-mand.CommandType

ConnectionState   serializable, flag

System.Data (system.data.dll)   enum

Used for the IDbConnection.State property, which describes the connection state. Fetching, Executing, Connecting, and Broken aren't currently used by ADO.NET and are included to use when creating a custom provider and for future upgrades to the .NET framework.

```
public enum ConnectionState {
  Closed = 0x00000000,
  Open = 0x00000001,
  Connecting = 0x00000002,
  Executing = 0x00000004,
```

```
Fetching = 0x00000008,
Broken = 0x00000010
}
```

Hierarchy	System.Object → System.ValueType → System.Enum(System.IComparable, System.IFormattable, System.IConvertible) → ConnectionState
Returned By	IDbConnection.State, System.Data.OleDb.OleDbConnection.State, System.Data.OracleClient.OracleConnection.State, System.Data.SqlClient.SqlConnection.State, StateChangeEventArgs.{CurrentState, OriginalState}
Passed To	StateChangeEventArgs.StateChangeEventArgs( )

Constraint   serializable

System.Data (system.data.dll)   abstract class

This abstract class represents a rule that can be placed on one or more DataColumn objects. ADO.NET includes two derived constraint classes: ForeignKeyConstraint and Unique-Constraint. Constraints aren't enforced unless the EnforceConstraints property of the DataSet is true.

```
public abstract class Constraint {
// Protected Constructors
  protected Constraint( );
// Public Instance Properties
  public virtual string ConstraintName{set; get; }
  public PropertyCollection ExtendedProperties{get; }
  public abstract DataTable Table{get; }
// Protected Instance Properties
  protected internal virtual DataSet _DataSet{get; }
// Public Instance Methods
  public override string ToString( );                                                // overrides object
// Protected Instance Methods
  protected void CheckStateForProperty( );
  protected internal void SetDataSet( DataSet dataSet);
}
```

Subclasses	ForeignKeyConstraint, UniqueConstraint
Returned By	ConstraintCollection.{Add( ), this}
Passed To	ConstraintCollection.{Add( ), AddRange( ), CanRemove( ), IndexOf( ), Remove( )}

ConstraintCollection   serializable

System.Data (system.data.dll)   class

This collection stores the constraints for a table, which it exposes through the DataTable.Constraints property. It can contain any class that derives from Constraint, including Foreign-KeyConstraint and UniqueConstraint objects. You can retrieve an individual constraint by index or name.

```
public class ConstraintCollection : InternalDataCollectionBase {
// Public Instance Properties
  public virtual Constraint this[string name]{get; }
  public virtual Constraint this[int index]{get; }
// Protected Instance Properties
  protected override ArrayList List{get; }                                    // overrides InternalDataCollectionBase
// Public Instance Methods
  public virtual Constraint Add(string name, DataColumn[ ] columns, bool primaryKey);
  public virtual Constraint Add(string name, DataColumn[ ] primaryKeyColumns, DataColumn[ ] foreignKeyColumns);
  public virtual Constraint Add(string name, DataColumn column, bool primaryKey);
  public virtual Constraint Add(string name, DataColumn primaryKeyColumn, DataColumn foreignKeyColumn);
  public void Add( Constraint constraint);
  public void AddRange( Constraint[ ] constraints);
  public bool CanRemove( Constraint constraint);
  public void Clear( );
  public bool Contains( string name);
  public int IndexOf( Constraint constraint);
  public virtual int IndexOf( string constraintName);
  public void Remove( Constraint constraint);
  public void Remove( string name);
  public void RemoveAt( int index);
// Protected Instance Methods
  protected virtual void OnCollectionChanged(System.ComponentModel.CollectionChangeEventArgs ccevent);
// Events
  public event CollectionChangeEventHandler CollectionChanged;
}
```

Hierarchy System.Object → InternalDataCollectionBase(System.Collections.ICollection, System. Collections.IEnumerable) → ConstraintCollection

Returned By DataTable.Constraints

ConstraintException   serializable

System.Data (system.data.dll)   class

This exception is thrown if you attempt an action that violates a constraint or if you try to apply a constraint to a DataTable that contains rows that violate it. For example, you might try to create more than one row with the same value in a unique column or a child record that references a nonexistent parent.

```
public class ConstraintException : DataException {
// Public Constructors
  public ConstraintException( );
  public ConstraintException(string s);
// Protected Constructors
  protected ConstraintException(System.Runtime.Serialization.SerializationInfo info,
    System.Runtime.Serialization.StreamingContext context);
}
```

Hierarchy System.Object → System.Exception(System.Runtime.Serialization.ISerializable) → System. SystemException → DataException → ConstraintException

The DataColumn represents a column schema within a table. The DataTable stores the Data-Column objects in its DataTable.Columns collection. The DataColumn object doesn't contain data. Instead, it defines the properties of a column such as the .NET data type (DataType), whether it allows null values (AllowDBNull), whether it is read-only (ReadOnly), whether values in each row of the column must be unique (Unique), the column name (ColumnName), the default value when a new row is created (DefaultValue), the maximum length for text fields (MaxLength), and the position relative to other columns in the table (Ordinal). If you retrieve data without schema information, some of these values (such as MaxLength) aren't initialized. However, even if you do retrieve schema information, you'll find that some information, such as DefaultValue, is never retrieved from the data source.

The DataColumn class provides additional properties, such as ExtendedProperties, which is a collection you can use to store miscellaneous information, and ColumnMapping, which allows you to configure the XML representation for each column in a DataTable using a value from the MappingType enumeration. Finally, the Expression property allows you to define a calculated or aggregate column or one that is stored as an expression or calculation. For example, you use a statement such as:

```
dt.Columns("Total").Expression = "Price * 1.15";
```

to define an expression for a column that shows the tax-adjusted value from the Price column. It assumes you've created and added the Total column. For a complete example, as well as information about the syntax used for expression functions, operators, and table relations, refer to Chapter 8.

```
public class DataColumn : System.ComponentModel.MarshalByValueComponent {
// Public Constructors
  public DataColumn( );
  public DataColumn( string columnName);
  public DataColumn( string columnName, Type dataType);
  public DataColumn(string columnName, Type dataType, string expr);
  public DataColumn(string columnName, Type dataType, string expr, MappingType type);
// Public Instance Properties
  public bool AllowDBNull{set; get; }
  public bool AutoIncrement{set; get; }
  public long AutoIncrementSeed{set; get; }
  public long AutoIncrementStep{set; get; }
  public string Caption{set; get; }
  public virtual MappingType ColumnMapping{set; get; }
  public string ColumnName{set; get; }
  public Type DataType{set; get; }
  public object DefaultValue{set; get; }
  public string Expression{set; get; }
  public PropertyCollection ExtendedProperties{get; }
  public int MaxLength{set; get; }
  public string Namespace{set; get; }
  public int Ordinal{get; }
  public string Prefix{set; get; }
  public bool ReadOnly{set; get; }
  public DataTable Table{get; }
```

```
  public bool Unique{set; get; }
```
// Public Instance Methods
```
  public override string ToString( );                              // overrides System.ComponentModel.MarshalByValueComponent
```
// Protected Instance Methods
```
  protected internal void CheckNotAllowNull( );
  protected void CheckUnique( );
  protected internal virtual void OnPropertyChanging(System.ComponentModel.PropertyChangedEventArgs pcevent);
  protected internal void RaisePropertyChanging(string name);
}
```

Hierarchy   System.Object → System.ComponentModel.MarshalByValueComponent(System.Compo-
                   nentModel.IComponent, System.IDisposable, System.IServiceProvider) → DataColumn

Returned By   System.Data.Common.DataColumnMapping.GetDataColumnBySchemaAction( ), DataCol-
                   umnChangeEventArgs.Column, DataColumnCollection.{Add( ), this}, DataRelation.
                   {ChildColumns, ParentColumns}, DataRow.GetColumnsInError( ), DataTable.PrimaryKey,
                   ForeignKeyConstraint.{Columns, RelatedColumns}, UniqueConstraint.Columns

Passed To   Multiple types

DataColumnChangeEventArgs

System.Data (system.data.dll)   class

Provides an argument containing data for the DataTable.ColumnChanging event. This information includes the affected DataRow (Row), and the DataColumn that is changing (Column),
and the new value (ProposedValue).

```
public class DataColumnChangeEventArgs : EventArgs {
// Public Constructors
  public DataColumnChangeEventArgs(DataRow row, DataColumn column, object value);
// Public Instance Properties
  public DataColumn Column{get; }
  public object ProposedValue{set; get; }
  public DataRow Row{get; }
}
```

Hierarchy   System.Object → System.EventArgs → DataColumnChangeEventArgs

Passed To   DataColumnChangeEventHandler.{BeginInvoke( ), Invoke( )}, DataTable.
                   {OnColumnChanged( ), OnColumnChanging( )}

DataColumnChangeEventHandler   serializable

System.Data (system.data.dll)   delegate

Represents the method that handles the DataTable.ColumnChanging event. This event fires
when any field is changed in any row of a DataTable, just before the change is made.

```
public delegate void DataColumnChangeEventHandler(object sender, DataColumnChangeEventArgs e);
```

Associated Events   DataTable.{ColumnChanged( ), ColumnChanging( )}

System.Data

DataColumnCollection

System.Data (system.data.dll)   class

This collection contains **DataColumn** objects for a **DataTable**. This collection is accessed using the **DataTable.Columns** property. You can retrieve an individual **DataColumn** by name or index.

```
public class DataColumnCollection : InternalDataCollectionBase {
// Public Instance Properties
  public virtual DataColumn this[string name]{get; }
  public virtual DataColumn this[int index]{get; }
// Protected Instance Properties
  protected override ArrayList List{get; }                                    // overrides InternalDataCollectionBase
// Public Instance Methods
  public virtual DataColumn Add( );
  public virtual DataColumn Add( string columnName);
  public virtual DataColumn Add(string columnName, Type type);
  public virtual DataColumn Add(string columnName, Type type, string expression);
  public void Add( DataColumn column);
  public void AddRange( DataColumn[ ] columns);
  public bool CanRemove( DataColumn column);
  public void Clear( );
  public bool Contains( string name);
  public virtual int IndexOf( DataColumn column);
  public int IndexOf( string columnName);
  public void Remove( DataColumn column);
  public void Remove( string name);
  public void RemoveAt( int index);
// Protected Instance Methods
  protected virtual void OnCollectionChanged(System.ComponentModel.CollectionChangeEventArgs ccevent);
  protected internal virtual void OnCollectionChanging(System.ComponentModel.CollectionChangeEventArgs ccevent);
// Events
  public event CollectionChangeEventHandler CollectionChanged;
}
```

Hierarchy   System.Object → InternalDataCollectionBase(System.Collections.ICollection, System.
                     Collections.IEnumerable) → DataColumnCollection

Returned By   DataTable.Columns

DataException

System.Data (system.data.dll)   class

This is the base class for all exceptions in this namespace. Provider-specific exception classes (such as System.Data.SqlClient.SqlException), which represent errors that are raised when executing a command or accessing a connection, don't derive from this class.

```
public class DataException : SystemException {
// Public Constructors
  public DataException( );
  public DataException(string s);
  public DataException(string s, Exception innerException);
```

```
// Protected Constructors
    protected DataException(System.Runtime.Serialization.SerializationInfo info,
        System.Runtime.Serialization.StreamingContext context);
}
```

Hierarchy   System.Object → System.Exception(System.Runtime.Serialization.ISerializable) → System.
                   SystemException → DataException

Subclasses   Multiple types

DataRelation   serializable

System.Data (system.data.dll)   class

A DataRelation represents a parent-child relation between two tables. A DataSet stores
DataRelation objects in its DataRelationCollection object. These DataRelation objects must be
created programmatically, even if they are defined in the data source. ADO.NET data
providers automatically determine relationships from the data source.

There are two reasons to add a DataRelation object. The first is make navigation easier.
Once you have created the relation, you can use methods such as DataRow.GetChildRows()
and DataRow.GetParentRow() to retrieve related rows. The second reason is to enforce relational constraints. When you create a relation, a corresponding ForeignKeyConstraint is
generated by default and added to the table. As long as DataSet.EnforceConstraints is set to
true, an exception is thrown when you attempt to perform an action that violates the
relationship (such as adding a child that refers to a nonexistent parent).

The easiest way to create a DataRelation is to use the constructor that requires the relation name, the parent DataColumn, and the child DataColumn. Alternatively, you can relate
multiple columns or use an overloaded version that allows you to prevent the creation
of the ForeignKeyConstraint.

```
public class DataRelation {
// Public Constructors
    public DataRelation(string relationName, DataColumn[ ] parentColumns, DataColumn[ ] childColumns);
    public DataRelation(string relationName,  DataColumn[ ] parentColumns, DataColumn[ ] childColumns,
        bool createConstraints);
    public DataRelation(string relationName, DataColumn parentColumn, DataColumn childColumn);
    public DataRelation(string relationName, DataColumn parentColumn, DataColumn childColumn, bool createConstraints);
    public DataRelation(string relationName, string parentTableName, string childTableName, string[ ] parentColumnNames,
        string[ ] childColumnNames, bool nested);
// Public Instance Properties
    public virtual DataColumn[ ] ChildColumns{get; }
    public virtual ForeignKeyConstraint ChildKeyConstraint{get; }
    public virtual DataTable ChildTable{get; }
    public virtual DataSet DataSet{get; }
    public PropertyCollection ExtendedProperties{get; }
    public virtual bool Nested{set; get; }
    public virtual DataColumn[ ] ParentColumns{get; }
    public virtual UniqueConstraint ParentKeyConstraint{get; }
    public virtual DataTable ParentTable{get; }
    public virtual string RelationName{set; get; }
// Public Instance Methods
    public override string ToString( );                                    // overrides object
```

```
// Protected Instance Methods
  protected void CheckStateForProperty( );
  protected internal void OnPropertyChanging(System.ComponentModel.PropertyChangedEventArgs pcevent);
  protected internal void RaisePropertyChanging( string name);
}
```

Returned By   DataRelationCollection.{Add( ), this}

Passed To   Multiple types

DataRelationCollection   serializable

System.Data (system.data.dll)   abstract class

This collection contains all DataRelation objects for a DataSet. This collection is accessed through the DataSet.Relations property. You can look up a DataRelation object by index or by name.

```
public abstract class DataRelationCollection : InternalDataCollectionBase {
// Protected Constructors
  protected DataRelationCollection( );
// Public Instance Properties
  public abstract DataRelation this[string name]{get; }
  public abstract DataRelation this[int index]{get; }
// Public Instance Methods
  public virtual DataRelation Add(DataColumn[ ] parentColumns, DataColumn[ ] childColumns);
  public virtual DataRelation Add(DataColumn parentColumn, DataColumn childColumn);
  public virtual DataRelation Add(string name, DataColumn[ ] parentColumns, DataColumn[ ] childColumns);
  public virtual DataRelation Add(string name,  DataColumn[ ] parentColumns, DataColumn[ ] childColumns,
    bool createConstraints);
  public virtual DataRelation Add(string name, DataColumn parentColumn, DataColumn childColumn);
  public virtual DataRelation Add(string name, DataColumn parentColumn, DataColumn childColumn, bool createConstraints);
  public void Add( DataRelation relation);
  public virtual void AddRange( DataRelation[ ] relations);
  public virtual bool CanRemove( DataRelation relation);
  public virtual void Clear( );
  public virtual bool Contains( string name);
  public virtual int IndexOf( DataRelation relation);
  public virtual int IndexOf( string relationName);
  public void Remove( DataRelation relation);
  public void Remove( string name);
  public void RemoveAt( int index);
// Protected Instance Methods
  protected virtual void AddCore( DataRelation relation);
  protected abstract DataSet GetDataSet( );
  protected virtual void OnCollectionChanged(System.ComponentModel.CollectionChangeEventArgs ccevent);
  protected internal virtual void OnCollectionChanging(
    System.ComponentModel.CollectionChangeEventArgs ccevent);
  protected virtual void RemoveCore( DataRelation relation);
// Events
  public event CollectionChangeEventHandler CollectionChanged;
}
```

Hierarchy	System.Object → InternalDataCollectionBase(System.Collections.ICollection, System. Collections.IEnumerable) → DataRelationCollection
Returned By	DataSet.Relations, DataTable.{ChildRelations, ParentRelations}

DataRow

serializable

System.Data (system.data.dll)

class

The DataRow class represents a single record in a database. You can access the columns of the record using the indexer, which is also the indexer for the class. You can retrieve or set a column value using a zero-based index or the column name. Using the name is slightly slower because it requires a behind-the-scenes hashtable lookup. The indexer has two overloads that allow you to specify the row version to retrieve using the DataRowVersion enumeration. For example:

```
Console.Write(row["ID"], DataRowVersion.Original);
```

retrieves the original data source value, even if it has been modified. If you omit the version, you receive the current (DataRowVersion.Current) value.

Alternatively, you can get or set values for all the rows at one time using the ItemArray property. The ItemArray is a one-dimensional array, in which each item contains the value for a field, in the same order as the DataRow. The ItemArray doesn't include the names of the field. You can also retrieve the state of the row (indicating if it has been added, deleted, and so on), using the RowState property.

The DataRow allocates space for error information. You can set or retrieve a string that describes an error using the SetColumnError() or GetColumnError() methods. To determine if the row has any errors, simply inspect the Boolean HasErrors property or retrieve the Data-Column objects with errors using the GetColumnsInError() method.

The GetParentRow() and GetChildRows() methods allow you to retrieve related rows if you have defined a parent-child relationship using a DataRelation object.

The DataRow also includes methods for managing the editing process, including BeginEdit(), EndEdit(), and CancelEdit(). BeginEdit() suspends row validation until either EndEdit() or CancelEdit() is called, allowing the rows to temporarily violate referential integrity.

```
public class DataRow {
// Protected Constructors
  protected internal DataRow( DataRowBuilder builder);
// Public Instance Properties
  public bool HasErrors{get; }
  public object[ ] ItemArray{set; get; }
  public string RowError{set; get; }
  public DataRowState RowState{get; }
  public DataTable Table{get; }
  public object this[string columnName, DataRowVersion version]{get; }
  public object this[DatraColumn column, DataRowVersion version]{get; }
  public object this[string columnName]{set; get; }
  public object this[int columnIndex]{set; get; }
  public object this[int columnIndex, DataRowVersion version]{get; }
  public object this[DataColumn column]{set; get; }
// Public Instance Methods
  public void AcceptChanges( );
```

```
public void BeginEdit( );
public void CancelEdit( );
public void ClearErrors( );
public void Delete( );
public void EndEdit( );
public DataRow[ ] GetChildRows( DataRelation relation);
public DataRow[ ] GetChildRows(DataRelation relation, DataRowVersion version);
public DataRow[ ] GetChildRows( string relationName);
public DataRow[ ] GetChildRows(string relationName, DataRowVersion version);
public string GetColumnError( DataColumn column);
public string GetColumnError( int columnIndex);
public string GetColumnError( string columnName);
public DataColumn[ ] GetColumnsInError( );
public DataRow GetParentRow( DataRelation relation);
public DataRow GetParentRow(DataRelation relation, DataRowVersion version);
public DataRow GetParentRow( string relationName);
public DataRow GetParentRow(string relationName, DataRowVersion version);
public DataRow[ ] GetParentRows( DataRelation relation);
public DataRow[ ] GetParentRows(DataRelation relation, DataRowVersion version);
public DataRow[ ] GetParentRows( string relationName);
public DataRow[ ] GetParentRows(string relationName, DataRowVersion version);
public bool HasVersion( DataRowVersion version);
public bool IsNull( DataColumn column);
public bool IsNull(DataColumn column, DataRowVersion version);
public bool IsNull( int columnIndex);
public bool IsNull( string columnName);
public void RejectChanges( );
public void SetColumnError(DataColumn column, string error);
public void SetColumnError(int columnIndex, string error);
public void SetColumnError(string columnName, string error);
public void SetParentRow( DataRow parentRow);
public void SetParentRow(DataRow parentRow, DataRelation relation);
// Protected Instance Methods
protected void SetNull( DataColumn column);
```

Returned By	Multiple types

Passed To	Multiple types

DataRowAction   serializable, flag

System.Data (system.data.dll)   enum

This enumeration describes an action performed on a row that causes an event to be
raised. It is used by the Action property of the DataRowChangeEventArgs class to indicate what
caused the event to be raised.

```
public enum DataRowAction {
  Nothing = 0x00000000,
  Delete = 0x00000001,
  Change = 0x00000002,
```

```
    Rollback = 0x00000004,
    Commit = 0x00000008,
    Add = 0x00000010
}
```

Hierarchy   System.Object → System.ValueType → System.Enum(System.IComparable, System.IFor-
                 mattable, System.IConvertible) → DataRowAction

Returned By DataRowChangeEventArgs.Action

Passed To   DataRowChangeEventArgs.DataRowChangeEventArgs( )

DataRowChangeEventArgs

System.Data (system.data.dll)   class

This class provides extra information for four DataTable events: DataTable.RowChanging,
DataTable.RowChanged, DataTable.RowDeleting, and DataTable.RowDeleted. This information consists
of the affected DataRow (Row) and the action that occurred on the row (Action).

```
public class DataRowChangeEventArgs : EventArgs {
// Public Constructors
    public DataRowChangeEventArgs(DataRow row, DataRowAction action);
// Public Instance Properties
    public DataRowAction Action{get; }
    public DataRow Row{get; }
}
```

Hierarchy   System.Object → System.EventArgs → DataRowChangeEventArgs

Passed To   DataRowChangeEventHandler.{BeginInvoke( ), Invoke( )}, DataTable.{OnRowChanged( ),
                 OnRowChanging( ), OnRowDeleted( ), OnRowDeleting( )}

DataRowChangeEventHandler   serializable

System.Data (system.data.dll)   delegate

This delegate represents the method that handles one of four DataTable events: DataTable.
RowChanging, DataTable.RowChanged, DataTable.RowDeleting, or DataTable.RowDeleted. These events
fire during and after data edits. Those that fire before a change is committed
(DataTable.RowChanging and DataTable.RowDeleting) are useful for validation. In the case of an
edit, you can evaluate the proposed change by examining the DataRowVersion.Proposed
value for the DataRow. The events that fire after a change is committed (DataTable.
RowChanged and DataTable.RowDeleted) are useful for tasks such as synchronizing controls
or providing information in a status bar.

```
public delegate void DataRowChangeEventHandler(object sender, DataRowChangeEventArgs e);
```

Associated Events
DataTable.{RowChanged( ), RowChanging( ), RowDeleted( ), RowDeleting( )}

DataRowCollection

serializable

System.Data (system.data.dll)

class

This collection contains DataRow objects. It's accessed through the DataTable.Rows property and contains the data for a table. You can use the Find() method and Contains() method to locate records. Both methods accept a column value and search for it in the primary key field. If a matching row is found, the Contains() method returns true, and the Find() method returns the DataRow object.

```
public class DataRowCollection : InternalDataCollectionBase {
// Public Instance Properties
  public DataRow this[int index]{get; }
// Protected Instance Properties
  protected override ArrayList List{get; }                          // overrides InternalDataCollectionBase
// Public Instance Methods
  public virtual DataRow Add( object[ ] values);
  public void Add( DataRow row);
  public void Clear( );
  public bool Contains( object key);
  public bool Contains( object[ ] keys);
  public DataRow Find( object key);
  public DataRow Find( object[ ] keys);
  public void InsertAt( DataRow row, int pos);
  public void Remove( DataRow row);
  public void RemoveAt( int index);
}
```

Hierarchy   System.Object → InternalDataCollectionBase(System.Collections.ICollection, System. Collections.IEnumerable) → DataRowCollection

Returned By   DataTable.Rows

DataRowState

serializable, flag

System.Data (system.data.dll)

enum

This enumeration indicates the state of a row (returned by the DataRow.RowState property). Added indicates a row inserted into the DataTable but not yet committed to the data source. Deleted indicates the row was deleted, but the change has not been applied to the data source, and Modified indicates the row has been edited but the changes have not been committed. Detached indicates a new row (created with DataTable.NewRow()) but not yet inserted into the table (with DataRowCollection.Add()).

```
public enum DataRowState {
  Detached = 0x00000001,
  Unchanged = 0x00000002,
  Added = 0x00000004,
  Deleted = 0x00000008,
  Modified = 0x00000010
}
```

Hierarchy	System.Object → System.ValueType → System.Enum(System.IComparable, System.IFormattable, System.IConvertible) → DataRowState
Returned By	DataRow.RowState
Passed To	DataSet.{GetChanges( ), HasChanges( )}, DataTable.GetChanges( )

DataRowVersion

System.Data (system.data.dll)   enum

This enumeration represents the different versions of a DataRow. You can access this enumeration with the indexer for the DataRow class. For example:

```
Console.Write(row["ID", DataRowVersion.Original]);
```

displays the original value of a row, which is the value retrieved from the data source. The Proposed value contains a value while the row is in edit mode (after DataRow.BeginEdit( ) has been called, or when a DataTable edit event is fired).

```
public enum DataRowVersion {
  Original = 256,
  Current = 512,
  Proposed = 1024,
  Default = 1536
}
```

Hierarchy	System.Object → System.ValueType → System.Enum(System.IComparable, System.IFormattable, System.IConvertible) → DataRowVersion
Returned By	DataRowView.RowVersion, IDataParameter.SourceVersion, System.Data.OleDb.OleDbParameter.SourceVersion, System.Data.OracleClient.OracleParameter.SourceVersion, System.Data.SqlClient.SqlParameter.SourceVersion
Passed To	Multiple types

DataRowView

System.Data (system.data.dll)   class

It represents a customized view of a DataRow that is shown in a control when using data binding. For example, if you bind a DataTable to a System.Windows.Forms.DataGrid control, .NET displays the data using the table's default DataView, which contains one DataRowView instance for every DataRow that should be displayed. Unlike a DataRow, the DataRowView can display only one version of the underlying data. This version is determined by the RowVersion property, which is modified automatically during an editing operation to show the proposed value instead of the current value.

You can access the DataRow instance that corresponds to a DataRowView through the Row property. Many DataRowView methods and properties are similar to those of the DataRow. For example, you can programmatically place multiple rows into edit mode using BeginEdit( ), finish the operation with EndEdit( ) or CancelEdit( ), or delete a row with Delete( ). You can also retrieve field values using the column name or the indexer of the DataRowView class. Two read-only properties can be used to determine if a DataRowView is being edited (IsEdit) or is newly added (IsNew).

```
public class DataRowView : System.ComponentModel.ICustomTypeDescriptor, System.ComponentModel.IEditableObject,
System.ComponentModel.IDataErrorInfo {
// Public Instance Properties
  public DataView DataView{get; }
  public bool IsEdit{get; }
  public bool IsNew{get; }
  public DataRow Row{get; }
  public DataRowVersion RowVersion{get; }
  public object this[int ndx]{set; get; }
  public object this[string property]{set; get; }
// Public Instance Methods
  public void BeginEdit( );                                    // implements System.ComponentModel.IEditableObject
  public void CancelEdit( );                                   // implements System.ComponentModel.IEditableObject
  public DataView CreateChildView( DataRelation relation);
  public DataView CreateChildView( string relationName);
  public void Delete( );
  public void EndEdit( );                                      // implements System.ComponentModel.IEditableObject
  public override bool Equals( object other);                  // overrides object
  public override int GetHashCode( );                          // overrides object
}
```

Returned By   DataView.{AddNew( ), FindRows( ), this}

DataSet
serializable, disposable

System.Data (system.data.dll)   class

The DataSet contains a collection of DataTable objects that define the schema and contain
the data for each table (Tables). The DataSet also contains a collection of DataRelation objects
that define the relationships between the tables (Relations). The DataSet references a Data-
ViewManager that specifies how views should be created when data binding to a control
(DefaultViewManager). The DataSet is often described as an in-memory cache of relational
data.

The DataSet is the only ADO.NET object with the ability to serialize its content to an
XML file (using the WriteXml( ) and WriteXmlSchema( ) methods) or to populate itself from an
existing schema or XML file (using the ReadXmlSchema( ) and ReadXml( ) methods). Alternatively, you can use GetXml( ) and GetXmlSchema( ) to retrieve the XML data and schema
information as a string.

You can delete the data in a DataSet without affecting the schema (using Clear( )), create a
duplicate DataSet with the same table structure and meta data (using Clone( )) or with the
same structure and content (using Copy( )), merge two DataSet objects (using Merge( )), or
check the entire DataSet for errors (using HasErrors).

One of the most important features of the DataSet is its version-tracking ability. By
default, each DataRow object in the DataSet stores enough information to track any modifications made to it, and whether it is scheduled for insertion or deletion when
reconciled with the data source. The DataAdapter uses this information to reconcile
changes and then calls AcceptChanges( ) on each DataRow to replace the original values with
the current values. You can retrieve a DataSet with the same schema that contains only
modified, deleted, or inserted rows using the GetChanges( ) method.

```
public class DataSet : System.ComponentModel.MarshalByValueComponent , System.ComponentModel.IListSource,
System.Xml.Serialization.IXmlSerializable, System.ComponentModel.ISupportInitialize, System.Runtime.Serialization.
ISerializable {
// Public Constructors
  public DataSet( );
  public DataSet( string dataSetName);
// Protected Constructors
  protected DataSet(System.Runtime.Serialization.SerializationInfo info,
    System.Runtime.Serialization.StreamingContext context);
// Public Instance Properties
  public bool CaseSensitive{set; get; }
  public string DataSetName{set; get; }
  public DataViewManager DefaultViewManager{get; }
  public bool EnforceConstraints{set; get; }
  public PropertyCollection ExtendedProperties{get; }
  public bool HasErrors{get; }
  public CultureInfo Locale{set; get; }
  public string Namespace{set; get; }
  public string Prefix{set; get; }
  public DataRelationCollection Relations{get; }
  public override ISite Site{set; get; }                       // overrides System.ComponentModel.MarshalByValueComponent
  public DataTableCollection Tables{get; }
// Public Instance Methods
  public void AcceptChanges( );
  public void BeginInit( );                                    // implements System.ComponentModel.ISupportInitialize
  public void Clear( );
  public virtual DataSet Clone( );
  public DataSet Copy( );
  public void EndInit( );                                      // implements System.ComponentModel.ISupportInitialize
  public DataSet GetChanges( );
  public DataSet GetChanges( DataRowState rowStates);
  public string GetXml( );
  public string GetXmlSchema( );
  public bool HasChanges( );
  public bool HasChanges( DataRowState rowStates);
  public void InferXmlSchema(System.IO.Stream stream, string[ ] nsArray);
  public void InferXmlSchema(string fileName, string[ ] nsArray);
  public void InferXmlSchema(System.IO.TextReader reader, string[ ] nsArray);
  public void InferXmlSchema(System.Xml.XmlReader reader, string[ ] nsArray);
  public void Merge( DataRow[ ] rows);
  public void Merge(DataRow[ ] rows, bool preserveChanges, MissingSchemaAction missingSchemaAction);
  public void Merge( DataSet dataSet);
  public void Merge( DataSet dataSet, bool preserveChanges);
  public void Merge(DataSet dataSet, bool preserveChanges, MissingSchemaAction missingSchemaAction);
  public void Merge( DataTable table);
  public void Merge(DataTable table, bool preserveChanges, MissingSchemaAction missingSchemaAction);
  public XmlReadMode ReadXml( System.IO.Stream stream);
  public XmlReadMode ReadXml(System.IO.Stream stream, XmlReadMode mode);
  public XmlReadMode ReadXml( string fileName);
  public XmlReadMode ReadXml(string fileName, XmlReadMode mode);
  public XmlReadMode ReadXml( System.IO.TextReader reader);
```

```
    public XmlReadMode ReadXml(System.IO.TextReader reader, XmlReadMode mode);
    public XmlReadMode ReadXml( System.Xml.XmlReader reader);
    public XmlReadMode ReadXml(System.Xml.XmlReader reader, XmlReadMode mode);
    public void ReadXmlSchema( System.IO.Stream stream);
    public void ReadXmlSchema( string fileName);
    public void ReadXmlSchema( System.IO.TextReader reader);
    public void ReadXmlSchema( System.Xml.XmlReader reader);
    public virtual void RejectChanges( );
    public virtual void Reset( );
    public void WriteXml( System.IO.Stream stream);
    public void WriteXml(System.IO.Stream stream, XmlWriteMode mode);
    public void WriteXml( string fileName);
    public void WriteXml( string fileName, XmlWriteMode mode);
    public void WriteXml( System.IO.TextWriter writer);
    public void WriteXml(System.IO.TextWriter writer, XmlWriteMode mode);
    public void WriteXml( System.Xml.XmlWriter writer);              // implements System.Xml.Serialization.IXmlSerializable
    public void WriteXml(System.Xml.XmlWriter writer, XmlWriteMode mode);
    public void WriteXmlSchema( System.IO.Stream stream);
    public void WriteXmlSchema( string fileName);
    public void WriteXmlSchema( System.IO.TextWriter writer);
    public void WriteXmlSchema( System.Xml.XmlWriter writer);
// Protected Instance Methods
    protected virtual XmlSchema GetSchemaSerializable( );
    protected void GetSerializationData(System.Runtime.Serialization.SerializationInfo info,
        System.Runtime.Serialization.StreamingContext context);
    protected internal virtual void OnPropertyChanging(System.ComponentModel.PropertyChangedEventArgs pcevent);
    protected virtual void OnRemoveRelation(DataRelation relation);
    protected virtual void OnRemoveTable( DataTable table);
    protected internal void RaisePropertyChanging(string name);
    protected virtual void ReadXmlSerializable(System.Xml.XmlReader reader);
    protected virtual bool ShouldSerializeRelations( );
    protected virtual bool ShouldSerializeTables( );
// Events
    public event MergeFailedEventHandler MergeFailed;
}
```

Hierarchy	System.Object → System.ComponentModel.MarshalByValueComponent(System.Compo-nentModel.IComponent, System.IDisposable, System.IServiceProvider) → DataSet(System.ComponentModel.IListSource, System.Xml.Serialization.IXmlSerializable, System.Compo-nentModel.ISupportInitialize, System.Runtime.Serialization.ISerializable)
Returned By	DataRelation.DataSet, DataRelationCollection.GetDataSet( ), DataTable.DataSet, DataView-Manager.DataSet, System.Xml.XmlDataDocument.DataSet
Passed To	Multiple types

DataSysDescriptionAttribute

System.Data (system.data.dll)   class

This class marks a property, event, or extender with a description (Description). Visual designers such as the Visual Studio .NET IDE can display this description when you reference the member.

```
public class DataSysDescriptionAttribute : System.ComponentModel.DescriptionAttribute {
// Public Constructors
    public DataSysDescriptionAttribute( string description);
// Public Instance Properties
    public override string Description{get; }                        // overrides System.ComponentModel.DescriptionAttribute
}
```

Hierarchy   System.Object → System.Attribute → System.ComponentModel.DescriptionAttribute → DataSysDescriptionAttribute

Valid On   All

DataTable   serializable, disposable

System.Data (system.data.dll)   class

The DataTable object contains the schema and data for a single table. Column settings, such as column names and data types are specified using the DataColumn objects contained in the table and accessed using the Columns property. Each row of data is encapsulated within a separate DataRow object, which is accessed using the Rows property. Also, ForeignKeyConstraint and UniqueConstraint objects can be added to the ConstraintCollection for the table, which is accessed using the Constraints property.

The DataTable provides many of the same methods as the DataSet. For example, you can use Copy(), Clone(), Clear(), GetChanges(), HasErrors, and AcceptChanges() in the same way as described for the DataSet. In addition, you can use the Select() method to retrieve an array of DataRow objects that match a specified SQL filter expression. There are four overloaded versions of the Select() method, some of which allow you to specify a sort order and filter based on the DataRowState of the DataRow. Finally, you can use the NewRow() method to generate a new DataRow object that has the same schema as the DataTable. This is detached row; once you have finished entering the required information you must add it to the RowCollection.

The DataTable has six events that allow you to react when column values are changed. You can handle RowChanging to implement row-specific validation rules or handle Column-Changing to implement column-specific validation rules. Both events fire during the course of a column edit; the difference is that ColumnChanging provides a reference to a DataColumn object. RowChanged, ColumnChanged, and RowDeleted occur after a change has been applied. They are most useful if you need to log the change or update part of the user interface.

```
public class DataTable : System.ComponentModel.MarshalByValueComponent , System.ComponentModel.IListSource,
System.ComponentModel.ISupportInitialize, System.Runtime.Serialization.ISerializable {
// Public Constructors
    public DataTable( );
    public DataTable( string tableName);
```

```
// Protected Constructors
  protected DataTable(
    System.Runtime.Serialization.SerializationInfo info,
    System.Runtime.Serialization.StreamingContext context);
// Public Instance Properties
  public bool CaseSensitive{set; get; }
  public DataRelationCollection ChildRelations{get; }
  public DataColumnCollection Columns{get; }
  public ConstraintCollection Constraints{get; }
  public DataSet DataSet{get; }
  public DataView DefaultView{get; }
  public string DisplayExpression{set; get; }
  public PropertyCollection ExtendedProperties{get; }
  public bool HasErrors{get; }
  public CultureInfo Locale{set; get; }
  public int MinimumCapacity{set; get; }
  public string Namespace{set; get; }
  public DataRelationCollection ParentRelations{get; }
  public string Prefix{set; get; }
  public DataColumn[ ] PrimaryKey{set; get; }
  public DataRowCollection Rows{get; }
  public override ISite Site{set; get; }                   // overrides System.ComponentModel.MarshalByValueComponent
  public string TableName{set; get; }
// Public Instance Methods
  public void AcceptChanges( );
  public void BeginInit( );                                // implements System.ComponentModel.ISupportInitialize
  public void BeginLoadData( );
  public void Clear( );
  public virtual DataTable Clone( );
  public object Compute( string expression, string filter);
  public DataTable Copy( );
  public void EndInit( );                                  // implements System.ComponentModel.ISupportInitialize
  public void EndLoadData( );
  public DataTable GetChanges( );
  public DataTable GetChanges( DataRowState rowStates);
  public DataRow[ ] GetErrors( );
  public void ImportRow( DataRow row);
  public DataRow LoadDataRow(object[ ] values, bool fAcceptChanges);
  public DataRow NewRow( );
  public void RejectChanges( );
  public virtual void Reset( );
  public DataRow[ ] Select( );
  public DataRow[ ] Select( string filterExpression);
  public DataRow[ ] Select(string filterExpression, string sort);
  public DataRow[ ] Select(string filterExpression, string sort, DataViewRowState recordStates);
  public override string ToString( );                      // overrides System.ComponentModel.MarshalByValueComponent
// Protected Instance Methods
  protected virtual DataTable CreateInstance( );
  protected virtual Type GetRowType( );
  protected internal DataRow[ ] NewRowArray( int size);
  protected virtual DataRow NewRowFromBuilder(DataRowBuilder builder);
```

```
    protected virtual void OnColumnChanged(
      DataColumnChangeEventArgs e);
    protected virtual void OnColumnChanging(DataColumnChangeEventArgs e);
    protected internal virtual void OnPropertyChanging(System.ComponentModel.PropertyChangedEventArgs pcevent);
    protected internal virtual void OnRemoveColumn(DataColumn column);
    protected virtual void OnRowChanged(DataRowChangeEventArgs e);
    protected virtual void OnRowChanging(DataRowChangeEventArgs e);
    protected virtual void OnRowDeleted(DataRowChangeEventArgs e);
    protected virtual void OnRowDeleting(DataRowChangeEventArgs e);
// Events
    public event DataColumnChangeEventHandler ColumnChanged;
    public event DataColumnChangeEventHandler ColumnChanging;
    public event DataRowChangeEventHandler RowChanged;
    public event DataRowChangeEventHandler RowChanging;
    public event DataRowChangeEventHandler RowDeleted;
    public event DataRowChangeEventHandler RowDeleting;
}
```

Hierarchy	System.Object → System.ComponentModel.MarshalByValueComponent(System.Compo-nentModel.IComponent, System.IDisposable, System.IServiceProvider) → DataTable(System.ComponentModel.IListSource, System.ComponentModel.ISupportIni-tialize, System.Runtime.Serialization.ISerializable)
Returned By	Multiple types
Passed To	Multiple types

DataTableCollection   serializable

System.Data (system.data.dll)   class

This class contains a collection of **DataTable** objects and is accessed using the **DataSet.Tables** property. **DataTable** objects can be retrieved by table name or index.

```
public class DataTableCollection : InternalDataCollectionBase {
// Public Instance Properties
  public DataTable this[string name]{get; }
  public DataTable this[int index]{get; }
// Protected Instance Properties
  protected override ArrayList List{get; }                    // overrides InternalDataCollectionBase
// Public Instance Methods
  public virtual DataTable Add( );
  public virtual DataTable Add( string name);
  public virtual void Add( DataTable table);
  public void AddRange( DataTable[ ] tables);
  public bool CanRemove( DataTable table);
  public void Clear( );
  public bool Contains( string name);
  public virtual int IndexOf( DataTable table);
  public virtual int IndexOf( string tableName);
  public void Remove( DataTable table);
  public void Remove( string name);
```

```
    public void RemoveAt( int index);
// Protected Instance Methods
    protected virtual void OnCollectionChanged(System.ComponentModel.CollectionChangeEventArgs ccevent);
    protected internal virtual void OnCollectionChanging(System.ComponentModel.CollectionChangeEventArgs ccevent);
// Events
    public event CollectionChangeEventHandler CollectionChanged;
    public event CollectionChangeEventHandler CollectionChanging;
}
```

Hierarchy	System.Object → InternalDataCollectionBase(System.Collections.ICollection, System. Collections.IEnumerable) → DataTableCollection
Returned By	DataSet.Tables

DataView   disposable

System.Data (system.data.dll)   class

The DataView represents a custom view of a DataTable that can be bound to controls. It allows you to apply row sorting and filtering without affecting the underlying data. All DataTable binding takes place through a DataView. When you bind to a DataTable object, you are actually binding to the DataTable.DefaultView, which is an automatically created DataView object. You can configure this DataView or create a new DataView. In fact, you can even create multiple DataView objects for the same DataTable and use them to display different views of the same data in different user interface controls.

Some significant properties of the DataView are Sort, RowFilter, and RowStateFilter. Sort is a SQL expression that sets column-based sorting (as in CustomerID ASC). RowFilter is a SQL expression that works like a WHERE clause, including only rows that match certain criteria (such as CustomerID > 100). Finally, RowStateFilter shows only rows that have a specified DataViewRowState. For more information about the DataView objects and the syntax you can use to filter and sort data within them, refer to Chapter 28. Much as with a Data-Table, you can add new rows (using AddNew()) and select existing ones (using Find()) through a DataView.

```
public class DataView : System.ComponentModel.MarshalByValueComponent , System.ComponentModel.IBindingList, IList,
ICollection, IEnumerable, System.ComponentModel.ITypedList, System.ComponentModel.ISupportInitialize {
// Public Constructors
    public DataView( );
    public DataView( DataTable table);
    public DataView(DataTable table, string RowFilter, string Sort, DataViewRowState RowState);
// Public Instance Properties
    public bool AllowDelete{set; get; }
    public bool AllowEdit{set; get; }                                    // implements System.ComponentModel.IBindingList
    public bool AllowNew{set; get; }                                     // implements System.ComponentModel.IBindingList
    public bool ApplyDefaultSort{set; get; }
    public int Count{get; }                                              // implements ICollection
    public DataViewManager DataViewManager{get; }
    public virtual string RowFilter{set; get; }
    public DataViewRowState RowStateFilter{set; get; }
    public string Sort{set; get; }
    public DataTable Table{set; get; }
    public DataRowView this[int recordIndex]{get; }
```

```
// Protected Instance Properties
  protected bool IsOpen{get; }
// Public Instance Methods
  public virtual DataRowView AddNew( );
  public void BeginInit( );                                    // implements System.ComponentModel.ISupportInitialize
  public void CopyTo( Array array, int index);                 // implements ICollection
  public void Delete( int index);
  public void EndInit( );                                      // implements System.ComponentModel.ISupportInitialize
  public int Find( object key);
  public int Find( object[ ] key);
  public DataRowView[ ] FindRows( object key);
  public DataRowView[ ] FindRows( object[ ] key);
  public IEnumerator GetEnumerator( );                         // implements IEnumerable
// Protected Instance Methods
  protected void Close( );
  protected virtual void ColumnCollectionChanged(object sender, System.ComponentModel.CollectionChangeEventArgs e);
  protected override void Dispose( bool disposing);            // overrides System.ComponentModel.MarshalByValueComponent
  protected virtual void IndexListChanged(object sender, System.ComponentModel.ListChangedEventArgs e);
  protected virtual void OnListChanged(System.ComponentModel.ListChangedEventArgs e);
  protected void Open( );
  protected void Reset( );
  protected void UpdateIndex( );
  protected virtual void UpdateIndex( bool force);
// Events
  public event ListChangedEventHandler ListChanged;            // implements System.ComponentModel.IBindingList
}
```

Hierarchy   System.Object → System.ComponentModel.MarshalByValueComponent(System.Compo-
nentModel.IComponent, System.IDisposable, System.IServiceProvider) →
DataView(System.ComponentModel.IBindingList, System.Collections.IList, System.Collec-
tions.ICollection, System.Collections.IEnumerable, System.ComponentModel.ITypedList,
System.ComponentModel.ISupportInitialize)

Returned By   DataRowView.{CreateChildView( ), DataView}, DataTable.DefaultView, DataViewManager.
CreateDataView( )

DataViewManager   disposable

System.Data (system.data.dll)   class

The DataViewManager is used when binding an entire DataSet to a control. When binding a
DataSet to a control, you have two choices. You can explicitly create a DataViewManager
object and bind that, or you can bind to the DataSet that contains the data. In the latter
case, ADO.NET automatically uses the default DataViewManager accessed using the DataSet.
DefaultViewManager property.

Understanding this process becomes important if you want to control the display of
data (for example, applying a sort of filter expression). When binding an entire DataSet,
ADO.NET doesn't use the default DataView objects that are associated with each table
and accessed using the DataTable.DefaultView property. Instead, it uses the DataViewSetting.
The default DataViewManager for a DataSet contains one DataViewSetting for each DataTable. You

can access this collection and modify individual **DataViewSetting** objects through the **Data-ViewSettings** property.

```
public class DataViewManager : System.ComponentModel.MarshalByValueComponent , System.ComponentModel.
IBindingList, IList, ICollection, IEnumerable, System.ComponentModel.ITypedList {
// Public Constructors
  public DataViewManager( );
  public DataViewManager( DataSet dataSet);
// Public Instance Properties
  public DataSet DataSet{set; get; }
  public string DataViewSettingCollectionString{set; get; }
  public DataViewSettingCollection DataViewSettings{get; }
// Public Instance Methods
  public DataView CreateDataView( DataTable table);
// Protected Instance Methods
  protected virtual void OnListChanged(System.ComponentModel.ListChangedEventArgs e);
  protected virtual void RelationCollectionChanged(object sender,
    System.ComponentModel.CollectionChangeEventArgs e);
  protected virtual void TableCollectionChanged(object sender, System.ComponentModel.CollectionChangeEventArgs e);
// Events
  public event ListChangedEventHandler ListChanged;                    // implements System.ComponentModel.IBindingList
}
```

Hierarchy   System.Object → System.ComponentModel.MarshalByValueComponent(System.Compo-nentModel.IComponent, System.IDisposable, System.IServiceProvider) → DataViewManager(System.ComponentModel.IBindingList, System.Collections.IList, System.Collections.ICollection, System.Collections.IEnumerable, System.ComponentModel.ITypedList)

Returned By   DataSet.DefaultViewManager, DataView.DataViewManager, DataViewSetting.DataViewManager

DataViewRowState   serializable, flag

System.Data (system.data.dll)   enum

This enumeration is similar to the **DataRowState** enumeration, but it is used with the **Data-View.RowStateFilter** property to select the versions of rows that are displayed in a **DataView**. By default, the current version of the data is shown, and the **DataView.RowStateFilter** is set to **CurrentRows**. Alternatively, you can display only rows that have been deleted, added, modified, or unchanged. You can even use a bitwise combination of **Data-ViewRowState** values to show several versions of rows.

```
public enum DataViewRowState {
  None = 0x00000000,
  Unchanged = 0x00000002,
  Added = 0x00000004,
  Deleted = 0x00000008,
  ModifiedCurrent = 0x00000010,
  CurrentRows = 0x00000016,
  ModifiedOriginal = 0x00000020,
  OriginalRows = 0x0000002A
}
```

Hierarchy	System.Object → System.ValueType → System.Enum(System.IComparable, System.IFormattable, System.IConvertible) → DataViewRowState
Returned By	DataView.RowStateFilter, DataViewSetting.RowStateFilter
Passed To	DataTable.Select( ), DataView.{DataView( ), RowStateFilter}, DataViewSetting.RowStateFilter

DataViewSetting

serializable

System.Data (system.data.dll)   class

This class encapsulates the settings that create a DataView from a DataViewManager.

```
public class DataViewSetting {
// Public Instance Properties
  public bool ApplyDefaultSort{set; get; }
  public DataViewManager DataViewManager{get; }
  public string RowFilter{set; get; }
  public DataViewRowState RowStateFilter{set; get; }
  public string Sort{set; get; }
  public DataTable Table{get; }
}
```

Returned By	DataViewSettingCollection.this
Passed To	DataViewSettingCollection.this

DataViewSettingCollection

serializable

System.Data (system.data.dll)   class

This class contains a collection of DataViewSetting objects and is used by the DataViewManager class. The DataViewManager provides one DataViewSetting instance for each DataTable in a DataSet. These DataViewSetting objects can then be used to set default values when creating DataView instances. You can locate an individual DataViewSetting object in this collection using its index, table name, or corresponding DataTable object.

```
public class DataViewSettingCollection : ICollection, IEnumerable {
// Public Instance Properties
  public virtual int Count{get; }                                                      // implements ICollection
  public bool IsReadOnly{get; }
  public bool IsSynchronized{get; }                                                    // implements ICollection
  public object SyncRoot{get; }                                                        // implements ICollection
  public virtual DataViewSetting this[string tableName]{get; }
  public virtual DataViewSetting this[int index]{set; get; }
  public virtual DataViewSetting this[DataTable table]{set; get; }
// Public Instance Methods
  public void CopyTo( Array ar, int index);                                            // implements ICollection
  public IEnumerator GetEnumerator( );                                                 // implements IEnumerable
}
```

System.Data

Returned By	DataViewManager.DataViewSettings

DBConcurrencyException
System.Data (system.data.dll)

serializable

sealed class

The exception is thrown by a DataAdapter if an attempt to update, delete, or insert a row results in zero affected rows. For example, if a data adapter attempts to execute a SQL DELETE statement to remove the record corresponding to a deleted DataRow from the data source, and no rows are deleted, this exception will be thrown. This exception usually indicates that another user has already modified the row you are attempting to update and a matching row can't be found. You can suppress the DBConcurrencyException by setting the System.Data.Common.DataAdapter.ContinueUpdateOnError property to true, in which case invalid rows are skipped, and the error information is placed in the DataRow.RowError property of rows having errors. Alternatively, you can respond to concurrency errors during the update (and suppress them if needed) by handling the data adapter's RowUpdating event.

```
public sealed class DBConcurrencyException : SystemException {
// Public Constructors
   public DBConcurrencyException( );
   public DBConcurrencyException( string message);
   public DBConcurrencyException(string message, Exception inner);
// Public Instance Properties
   public DataRow Row{set; get; }
// Public Instance Methods
   public override void GetObjectData(System.Runtime.Serialization.SerializationInfo si,
      System.Runtime.Serialization.StreamingContext context);
                                                                  // overrides Exception
}
```

Hierarchy   System.Object → System.Exception(System.Runtime.Serialization.ISerializable) → System. SystemException → DBConcurrencyException

DbType
System.Data (system.data.dll)

serializable

enum

This enumeration specifies a data type of a field, property, or parameter in the data source. It sets the IDataParameter.DbType property, which identifies the data type of a Command parameter, typically for a stored procedure. Most ADO.NET providers include an enumeration for the data types supported by the data source. For example, the OLE DB provider includes a System.Data.OleDb.OleDbType enumeration, which can be used to set the System.Data.OleDb.OleDbParameter.OleDbType property. When you set the System.Data.OleDb. OleDbParameter.OleDbType property, the System.Data.OleDb.OleDbParameter.DbType property is updated automatically with the closest compatible type from the DbType enumeration.

```
public enum DbType {
   AnsiString = 0,
   Binary = 1,
   Byte = 2,
   Boolean = 3,
   Currency = 4,
   Date = 5,
   DateTime = 6,
   Decimal = 7,
```

```
    Double = 8,
    Guid = 9,
    Int16 = 10,
    Int32 = 11,
    Int64 = 12,
    Object = 13,
    SByte = 14,
    Single = 15,
    String = 16,
    Time = 17,
    UInt16 = 18,
    UInt32 = 19,
    UInt64 = 20,
    VarNumeric = 21,
    AnsiStringFixedLength = 22,
    StringFixedLength = 23
}
```

Hierarchy   System.Object → System.ValueType → System.Enum(System.IComparable, System.IFormattable, System.IConvertible) → DbType

Returned By   IDataParameter.DbType, System.Data.OleDb.OleDbParameter.DbType, System.Data.OracleClient.OracleParameter.DbType, System.Data.SqlClient.SqlParameter.DbType

Passed To   IDataParameter.DbType, System.Data.OleDb.OleDbParameter.DbType, System.Data.OracleClient.OracleParameter.DbType, System.Data.SqlClient.SqlParameter.DbType

DeletedRowInaccessibleException   serializable

System.Data (system.data.dll)   class

This exception occurs when you attempt to retrieve data from a DataRow that has been deleted. Remember, deleted rows are not removed until you commit changes back to the data source. To avoid a DeletedRowInaccessibleException, check the DataRow.RowState property before attempting to retrieve data when iterating through all the rows in a table.

```
public class DeletedRowInaccessibleException : DataException {
// Public Constructors
  public DeletedRowInaccessibleException( );
  public DeletedRowInaccessibleException( string s);
// Protected Constructors
  protected DeletedRowInaccessibleException(System.Runtime.Serialization.SerializationInfo info,
    System.Runtime.Serialization.StreamingContext context);
}
```

Hierarchy   System.Object → System.Exception(System.Runtime.Serialization.ISerializable) → System.SystemException → DataException → DeletedRowInaccessibleException

DuplicateNameException

System.Data (system.data.dll)   class

This exception occurs when you attempt to add a database object with a duplicate name to a DataSet-related object.

```
public class DuplicateNameException : DataException {
// Public Constructors
  public DuplicateNameException( );
  public DuplicateNameException( string s);
// Protected Constructors
  protected DuplicateNameException(System.Runtime.Serialization.SerializationInfo info,
    System.Runtime.Serialization.StreamingContext context);
}
```

Hierarchy   System.Object → System.Exception(System.Runtime.Serialization.ISerializable) → System.
                       SystemException → DataException → DuplicateNameException

EvaluateException   serializable

System.Data (system.data.dll)   class

This exception is thrown when you specify a DataColumn.Expression property that can't be evaluated. A related exception is SyntaxErrorException.

```
public class EvaluateException : InvalidExpressionException {
// Public Constructors
  public EvaluateException( );
  public EvaluateException( string s);
// Protected Constructors
  protected EvaluateException(System.Runtime.Serialization.SerializationInfo info,
    System.Runtime.Serialization.StreamingContext context);
}
```

Hierarchy   System.Object → System.Exception(System.Runtime.Serialization.ISerializable) → System.
                       SystemException → DataException → InvalidExpressionException → EvaluateException

FillErrorEventArgs

System.Data (system.data.dll)   class

This class provides data for the System.Data.Common.DbDataAdapter.FillError event. This includes the DataTable that was being updated (DataTable), and the exception that occurred (Errors). You can also set the Continue property to specify whether the update should continue despite an error.

```
public class FillErrorEventArgs : EventArgs {
// Public Constructors
  public FillErrorEventArgs(DataTable dataTable, object[ ] values);
// Public Instance Properties
  public bool Continue{set; get; }
  public DataTable DataTable{get; }
```

```
    public Exception Errors{set; get; }
    public object[ ] Values{get; }
}
```

Hierarchy   System.Object → System.EventArgs → FillErrorEventArgs

Passed To   System.Data.Common.DbDataAdapter.OnFillError( ), FillErrorEventHandler.{BeginInvoke( ),
                   Invoke( )}

FillErrorEventHandler   serializable

System.Data (system.data.dll)   delegate

This delegate represents the method that will handle the System.Data.Common.DbDataAdapter.
FillError event. This error can occur for many reasons: for example, if the data can't be
converted into a CLR data type without losing precision or an enforced constraint is
violated. The System.Data.Common.DbDataAdapter.FillError event allows the user to decide
whether the fill operation should continue after the error occurs. A System.Data.Common.
DbDataAdapter.FillError event isn't fired if the error occurs at the data source. If you don't
handle the System.Data.Common.DbDataAdapter.FillError event, a System.InvalidCastException is thrown.

```
public delegate void FillErrorEventHandler(object sender, FillErrorEventArgs e);
```

Associated Events   System.Data.Common.DbDataAdapter.FillError( ), System.Data.OleDb.OleDbDataAdapter.
                        FillError( ), System.Data.OracleClient.OracleDataAdapter.FillError( ), System.Data.SqlClient.
                        SqlDataAdapter.FillError( )

ForeignKeyConstraint   serializable

System.Data (system.data.dll)   class

The ForeignKeyConstraint represents a restriction on a set of related columns. Usually, you
don't create a ForeignKeyConstraint directly. Instead, you define and add a DataRelation to the
DataSet.Relations collection. A corresponding ForeignKeyConstraint is added automatically to
the DataTable.Constraints collection of the child table. When you have a ForeignKeyConstraint on
a DataTable, certain actions are not allowed (such as creating a parent that references a
nonexistent parent row). You can disable checking for constraint violations by setting
DataSet.EnforceConstraints to false.

The ForeignKeyConstraint allows you to configure what happens when the parent column is
updated (UpdateRule), or when the parent row is deleted (DeleteRule) or has AcceptChanges( )
called on it (AcceptRejectRule). Out of these three options, the DeleteRule is the most
commonly used. If you set the DeleteRule to Rule.Cascade, all child rows are deleted when
the parent row is deleted. If you use Rule.SetNull, however, the foreign key field in the
child record is set to a null value. If you use Rule.SetDefault, the foreign key field is set to a
default value when the parent record is deleted. Finally, if you use Rule.None (the
default), no action is taken. This results in an error when you attempt to remove a
parent with child rows, when you have the DataSet.EnforceConstraints property set to true.

```
public class ForeignKeyConstraint : Constraint {
// Public Constructors
    public ForeignKeyConstraint(DataColumn[ ] parentColumns, DataColumn[ ] childColumns);
    public ForeignKeyConstraint(DataColumn parentColumn, DataColumn childColumn);
    public ForeignKeyConstraint(string constraintName, DataColumn[ ] parentColumns, DataColumn[ ] childColumns);
```

```
        public ForeignKeyConstraint(string constraintName, DataColumn parentColumn, DataColumn childColumn);
        public ForeignKeyConstraint(string constraintName, string parentTableName, string[ ] parentColumnNames,
            string[ ] childColumnNames, AcceptRejectRule acceptRejectRule, Rule deleteRule, Rule updateRule);
// Public Instance Properties
        public virtual AcceptRejectRule AcceptRejectRule{set; get; }
        public virtual DataColumn[ ] Columns{get; }
        public virtual Rule DeleteRule{set; get; }
        public virtual DataColumn[ ] RelatedColumns{get; }
        public virtual DataTable RelatedTable{get; }
        public override DataTable Table{get; }                                          // overrides Constraint
        public virtual Rule UpdateRule{set; get; }
// Public Instance Methods
        public override bool Equals( object key);                                       // overrides object
        public override int GetHashCode( );                                             // overrides object
}
```

Hierarchy   System.Object → Constraint → ForeignKeyConstraint

Returned By   DataRelation.ChildKeyConstraint

IColumnMapping

System.Data (system.data.dll)   interface

This interface represents a mapping between a column name in the data source and a
column name in the DataSet, which may be different. This interface is implemented by
the System.Data.Common.DataColumnMapping class.

```
public interface IColumnMapping {
// Public Instance Properties
        public string DataSetColumn{set; get; }
        public string SourceColumn{set; get; }
}
```

Implemented By   System.Data.Common.DataColumnMapping

Returned By   IColumnMappingCollection.{Add( ), GetByDataSetColumn( )}

IColumnMappingCollection

System.Data (system.data.dll)   interface

Contains a collection of IColumnMapping instances. This interface is implemented by the
System.Data.Common.DataColumnMappingCollection class.

```
public interface IColumnMappingCollection : IList, ICollection, IEnumerable {
// Public Instance Properties
        public object this[string index]{set; get; }
// Public Instance Methods
        public IColumnMapping Add(string sourceColumnName, string dataSetColumnName);
        public bool Contains( string sourceColumnName);
        public IColumnMapping GetByDataSetColumn(string dataSetColumnName);
```

```
public int IndexOf( string sourceColumnName);
public void RemoveAt( string sourceColumnName);
}
```

IDataAdapter

System.Data (system.data.dll)   interface

This interface represents a data adapter that bridges a data source and a DataSet or Data-
Table object. Every ADO.NET provider defines its own provider-specific class that
implements this interface (such as System.Data.SqlClient.SqlDataAdapter). Data adapters play
two roles: they transfer data from the data source to the DataSet when you invoke Fill(),
and they apply all DataSet or DataTable changes to a data source when you invoke Update().
In addition, you can use the FillSchema() method before you use the Fill() method to
configure schema information such as column names, data types, and primary key
information. The TableMappings property accesses the collection of ITableMapping objects
that map data source tables to DataTable objects in the DataSet. You can use the
MissingSchemaAction property to indicate what action should be taken if you use Fill() on a
DataSet that doesn't contain the relevant schema information (by default, the data
adapter will add the required DataColumn objects with primary key information). You can
also use the MissingMappingAction to configure what will happen if a table is inserted
without a matching ITableMapping existing in the TableMappings collection (by default, the
table name from the data source is used for the DataSet).

```
public interface IDataAdapter {
// Public Instance Properties
    public MissingMappingAction MissingMappingAction{set; get; }
    public MissingSchemaAction MissingSchemaAction{set; get; }
    public ITableMappingCollection TableMappings{get; }
// Public Instance Methods
    public int Fill( DataSet dataSet);
    public DataTable[ ] FillSchema(DataSet dataSet, SchemaType schemaType);
    public IDataParameter[ ] GetFillParameters( );
    public int Update( DataSet dataSet);
}
```

IDataParameter

System.Data (system.data.dll)   interface

This class represents a parameter for a Command object. Parameters are accessed using
the IDbCommand.Parameters collection. Parameters are identified using the ParameterName
property. With the SQL Server provider, parameter names are required, and the SQL
statement takes the form:

```
SELECT * FROM Customers WHERE CustomerID = @CustomerID
```

and the parameter must be named **@CustomerID**. With the OLE DB provider, however, a question mark placeholder is used instead. Order is important, but the parameter name isn't. The SQL statement takes the form:

```
SELECT * FROM Customers WHERE CustomerID = ?
```

(and the **CustomerID** value must be first in the parameter collection).

The **IDataParameter** interface also defines several other important properties. **DbType** indicates the underlying database data type (although individual ADO.NET providers usually provide an enumeration specific to the data source), and **Direction** determines whether the parameter is sent to the stored procedure, retrieve from it, or both. You can set the value for the parameter directly using the **Value** property. You can map it to a column in the **DataSet** by setting the name of the column in the **SourceColumn** property. This is primarily useful when you are defining a generic update, insert, or delete command for use with a data adapter. Because this command must work with any modified row, you can't directly code a parameter value. Instead, the value must be retrieved from the appropriate **DataRow**. You can also specify the version of the value using the **SourceVersion** property. For example, if the parameter corresponds to a WHERE clause that selects the row that needs to be updated, you use the original value. If the parameter corresponds to the SET clause in an UPDATE statement, use the current value to apply the new information to the data source.

```
public interface IDataParameter {
// Public Instance Properties
  public DbType DbType{set; get; }
  public ParameterDirection Direction{set; get; }
  public bool IsNullable{get; }
  public string ParameterName{set; get; }
  public string SourceColumn{set; get; }
  public DataRowVersion SourceVersion{set; get; }
  public object Value{set; get; }
}
```

Implemented By   IDbDataParameter, System.Data.OleDb.OleDbParameter, System.Data.OracleClient. OracleParameter, System.Data.SqlClient.SqlParameter

Returned By   System.Data.Common.DataAdapter.GetFillParameters( ), IDataAdapter. GetFillParameters( )

IDataParameterCollection

System.Data (system.data.dll)   interface

This collection contains all parameters and their mappings to **DataSet** columns used by a command and is accessed using the **IDbCommand.Parameters** property.

```
public interface IDataParameterCollection : IList, ICollection, IEnumerable {
// Public Instance Properties
  public object this{set; get; }
// Public Instance Methods
  public bool Contains( string parameterName);
  public int IndexOf( string parameterName);
  public void RemoveAt( string parameterName);
}
```

Implemented By	System.Data.OleDb.OleDbParameterCollection, System.Data.OracleClient.OracleParameter-Collection, System.Data.SqlClient.SqlParameterCollection
Returned By	IDbCommand.Parameters

IDataReader

disposable

System.Data (system.data.dll)

interface

The **IDataReader** interface is implemented by all data readers. A data reader provides a way to read a command-only stream of data from a data source. You can't create a data reader directly. Instead, an open **IDataReader** instance is returned from the **IDbCommand.ExecuteReader( )** method. You can then use the **Read( )** method to move from one row to the next. The **Read( )** method returns **true** if it can successfully read a row or **false** if there are no more rows remaining, and it has moved beyond the bounds of the result set. There is no way to move backward. When it is first created, the **IDataReader** doesn't yet point to a row. You must call **Read( )** to move to the first row before you attempt to read any information. You can use **NextResult( )** to move to the next result set if you are using a command or stored procedure that returns multiple result sets.

You retrieve data from a row (the row the **IDataReader** is currently positioned on) by column name or index. The **IDataReader** acquires this functionality through the **IDataRecord** interface, which it extends.

```
public interface IDataReader : IDisposable, IDataRecord {
// Public Instance Properties
  public int Depth{get; }
  public bool IsClosed{get; }
  public int RecordsAffected{get; }
// Public Instance Methods
  public void Close( );
  public DataTable GetSchemaTable( );
  public bool NextResult( );
  public bool Read( );
}
```

Implemented By	System.Data.OleDb.OleDbDataReader, System.Data.OracleClient.OracleDataReader, System.Data.SqlClient.SqlDataReader
Returned By	System.Data.Common.DbDataRecord.GetData( ), IDataRecord.GetData( ), IDbCommand. ExecuteReader( ), System.Data.OracleClient.OracleDataReader.GetData( ), System.Data. SqlClient.SqlDataReader.GetData( )
Passed To	System.Data.Common.DbDataAdapter.Fill( ), System.Data.Common.DbEnumerator. DbEnumerator( )

IDataRecord

System.Data (system.data.dll)

interface

This interface provides access to column values when you use a data reader. You can retrieve a value from a column using the indexer for **IDataRecord** with the column name or index. Alternatively, you can use one of the typed accessor methods to retrieve a column value by index and convert it to the specified type in one step. For example,

GetInt32( ) retrieves the specified column value and casts it to the System.Int32 type. Provider-specific data readers add methods that return data using source-specific data types. You can use the FieldCount property to determine how many columns are in a table. However, if you aren't positioned on a record (for example, you haven't called IDataReader.Read( )), this property returns 0.

```
public interface IDataRecord {
// Public Instance Properties
  public int FieldCount{get; }
  public object this[string name]{get; }
  public object this[int i]{get; }
// Public Instance Methods
  public bool GetBoolean( int i);
  public byte GetByte( int i);
  public long GetBytes(int i, long fieldOffset, byte[ ] buffer, int bufferoffset, int length);
  public char GetChar( int i);
  public long GetChars(int i, long fieldoffset, char[ ] buffer, int bufferoffset, int length);
  public IDataReader GetData( int i);
  public string GetDataTypeName( int i);
  public DateTime GetDateTime( int i);
  public decimal GetDecimal( int i);
  public double GetDouble( int i);
  public Type GetFieldType( int i);
  public float GetFloat( int i);
  public Guid GetGuid( int i);
  public short GetInt16( int i);
  public int GetInt32( int i);
  public long GetInt64( int i);
  public string GetName( int i);
  public int GetOrdinal( string name);
  public string GetString( int i);
  public object GetValue( int i);
  public int GetValues( object[ ] values);
  public bool IsDBNull( int i);
}
```

Implemented By   IDataReader, System.Data.Common.DbDataRecord, System.Data.OleDb.OleDbDataReader, System.Data.OracleClient.OracleDataReader, System.Data.SqlClient.SqlDataReader

IDbCommand   disposable

System.Data (system.data.dll)   interface

The IDbCommand interface represents a command that can be executed against a data source. Some examples include queries that retrieve rows (a SQL SELECT statement), statements that retrieve a single piece of information (such as SQL aggregate functions), or statements designed to modify rows (such as a SQL UPDATE, DELETE, or INSERT statement). ADO.NET providers that access relational data implement this interface.

Before, using the command, you must set the Connection property to a valid IDbConnection and open the connection. You can then execute the command in one of three ways. Use ExecuteNonQuery( ) to execute a statement such as INSERT, DELETE, or UPDATE, which returns the number of rows affected. Use ExecuteScalar( ) to execute a statement that returns a single value, such as an aggregate SQL function (SUM, MAX, MIN, AVG, and so on). Finally, use ExecuteReader( ) to perform a query and return a IDataReader that provides access to the result set. The CommandTimeout property identifies the number of seconds ADO.NET will wait while trying to execute the command before throwing a provider-specific exception. The default is 30, and 0 represents an infinite wait. Finally, if you are using a stored procedure, you can use the Prepare( ) method to compile the stored procedure in the data source, which may improve performance with some providers if you are executing the same stored procedure multiple times with different parameters. (It's recommended that you profile this approach to gauge if it offers any improvement.)

There are three types of commands (as identified by the CommandType property). The default is CommandType.Text, which represents a SQL text statement set in the CommandText property). You can also use CommandType.TableDirect to directly retrieve a single table (if the provider supports it) or CommandType.StoredProcedure to invoke a stored procedure. In either case, you identify the table or stored procedure by name in the CommandText property. For stored procedures that use parameters, you must add a single IDataParameter object for each parameter to the Parameters collection. The order is sometimes important with parameterized queries. See the description for the IDataParameter type for more information. Commands can be enlisted in a client-initiated transaction by setting the Transaction property to an IDbTransaction instance.

The UpdatedRowSource property specifies how command results are applied to the DataRow when a DataSet is reconciled with the data source using the Update( ) method of a DbData-Adapter. The default value, UpdateRowSource.None, does nothing. However, you can use UpdateRowSource.OutputParameters to ensure that the values set in the output parameters of a stored procedure are applied automatically to the changed DataRow when the row update is completed. Alternatively, you can use UpdateRowSource.FirstReturnedRecord to map an entire row returned by a stored procedure to the DataRow. This technique is useful if you are inserting a record that has an identity (or timestamp) value, which was set or changed during the update.

```
public interface IDbCommand : IDisposable {
// Public Instance Properties
    public string CommandText{set; get; }
    public int CommandTimeout{set; get; }
    public CommandType CommandType{set; get; }
    public IDbConnection Connection{set; get; }
    public IDataParameterCollection Parameters{get; }
    public IDbTransaction Transaction{set; get; }
    public UpdateRowSource UpdatedRowSource{set; get; }
// Public Instance Methods
    public void Cancel( );
    public IDbDataParameter CreateParameter( );
    public int ExecuteNonQuery( );
    public IDataReader ExecuteReader( );
    public IDataReader ExecuteReader(
        CommandBehavior behavior);
    public object ExecuteScalar( );
    public void Prepare( );
}
```

Implemented By	System.Data.OleDb.OleDbCommand, System.Data.OracleClient.OracleCommand, System.Data.SqlClient.SqlCommand
Returned By	System.Data.Common.RowUpdatedEventArgs.Command, System.Data.Common.RowUpdatingEventArgs.Command, IDbConnection.CreateCommand( ), IDbDataAdapter.{DeleteCommand, InsertCommand, SelectCommand, UpdateCommand}
Passed To	Multiple types

IDbConnection

disposable

System.Data (system.data.dll)

interface

This class represents a connection to a data source, which can be opened using the Open( ) method or closed using Close( ). No work can be performed while a connection is closed; however, some objects (such as data adapters) automatically open and close their connection as required. A data provider derives its own Connection class (such as System.Data.SqlClient.SqlConnection) that implements this interface.

With most data providers, you need to set some basic information (such as the initial database, server, and user login account) in the ConnectionString property before you attempt to open a connection. The connection string information differs from provider to provider. All connection strings arrange their information in a series of name-value pairs delimited by semicolons. Other than ConnectionString, the other IDbConnection properties are read-only. Chapter 3 provides connection string examples for several provider types and a list of supported parameters.

The IDbConnection interface also defines a BeginTransaction( ) method, which initiates a SQL transaction and returns an IDbTransaction object that allows you to commit or roll back the transaction. You can also use ChangeDatabase( ) to work with the tables in a different database in the same data source, and CreateCommand( ) to generate a generic IDbCommand instance linked to the current connection. You don't need to use CreateCommand( ); you can instantiate the appropriate provider-specific Command object. However, the CreateCommand( ) method is useful when you need to write provider-agnostic ADO.NET code. Even though it returns the appropriate provider-specific Command object, you can interact with it solely through the IDbConnection and IDbCommand interfaces, freeing your code from provider-specific details.

```
public interface IDbConnection : IDisposable {
// Public Instance Properties
  public string ConnectionString{set; get; }
  public int ConnectionTimeout{get; }
  public string Database{get; }
  public ConnectionState State{get; }
// Public Instance Methods
  public IDbTransaction BeginTransaction( );
  public IDbTransaction BeginTransaction(IsolationLevel il);
  public void ChangeDatabase( string databaseName);
  public void Close( );
  public IDbCommand CreateCommand( );
  public void Open( );
}
```

Implemented By	System.Data.OleDb.OleDbConnection, System.Data.OracleClient.OracleConnection, System.Data.SqlClient.SqlConnection
Returned By	IDbCommand.Connection, IDbTransaction.Connection
Passed To	IDbCommand.Connection

IDbDataAdapter

System.Data (system.data.dll)   interface

This interface represents a data adapter that bridges a data source and a DataSet object. This interface extends the IDataAdapter, which provides basic methods for transferring data to and from a data source by adding four properties that are specific to relational database use. These include DeleteCommand (the SQL statement used to delete records from the data source), InsertCommand (the SQL statement used to insert new records in the data source), UpdateCommand (the SQL statement used to update records in the data source), and SelectCommand (the SQL query used to retrieve records from the data source).

```
public interface IDbDataAdapter : IDataAdapter {
// Public Instance Properties
   public IDbCommand DeleteCommand{set; get; }
   public IDbCommand InsertCommand{set; get; }
   public IDbCommand SelectCommand{set; get; }
   public IDbCommand UpdateCommand{set; get; }
}
```

Implemented By	System.Data.OleDb.OleDbDataAdapter, System.Data.OracleClient.OracleDataAdapter, System.Data.SqlClient.SqlDataAdapter

IDbDataParameter

System.Data (system.data.dll)   interface

This interface represents a parameter for a parameterized query or stored procedure Command. A provider implements this interface in a provider-specific parameter object, such as System.Data.SqlClient.SqlParameter. The properties include Precision (the maximum number of digits for numeric values), Scale (the maximum number of decimal places), and Size (the maximum size of the value, in bytes). Other properties are inherited from the IDataParameter interface, which this interface implements.

```
public interface IDbDataParameter : IDataParameter {
// Public Instance Properties
   public byte Precision{set; get; }
   public byte Scale{set; get; }
   public int Size{set; get; }
}
```

Implemented By	System.Data.OleDb.OleDbParameter, System.Data.OracleClient.OracleParameter, System.Data.SqlClient.SqlParameter
Returned By	IDbCommand.CreateParameter( )

IDbTransaction

disposable

System.Data (system.data.dll)

interface

This class encapsulates a relational database transaction. You can start a transaction, provided you have an open connection, by calling the IDbConnection.BeginTransaction() method, which returns an IDbTransaction instance. You can enlist commands in a transaction by setting their IDbCommand.Transaction property to the appropriate IDbTransaction object. You end the transaction by calling the Commit() method to complete the transaction and accept all changes, or the Rollback() method to cancel all changes. Different providers have different ways to support nested transactions. A relational database provider defines a provider-specific transaction object that implements IDbTransaction, such as System.Data.SqlClient.SqlTransaction.

One important fact is that the IDbTransaction class represents a data provider transaction; it's analogous to executing the BEGIN TRANSACTION SQL statement in SQL Server (or a similar statement in other data sources). It has nothing in common with COM+ services.

When creating a transaction, be sure that you understand the isolation level it uses, which determines how other users can interact with the same data. The default transaction level (set by the IsolationLevel property) is IsolationLevel.ReadCommitted, which means that shared locks are held while the data is being read to avoid dirty reads, but the data can be changed before the end of the transaction, resulting in nonrepeatable reads or phantom data.

```
public interface IDbTransaction : IDisposable {
// Public Instance Properties
  public IDbConnection Connection{get; }
  public IsolationLevel IsolationLevel{get; }
// Public Instance Methods
  public void Commit( );
  public void Rollback( );
}
```

Implemented By   System.Data.OleDb.OleDbTransaction, System.Data.OracleClient.OracleTransaction, System.Data.SqlClient.SqlTransaction

Returned By   IDbCommand.Transaction, IDbConnection.BeginTransaction( )

Passed To   IDbCommand.Transaction

InRowChangingEventException

serializable

System.Data (system.data.dll)

class

This exception occurs only if you call the DataRow.EndEdit() method within the DataTable.RowChanging event handler. (The row is automatically placed into edit mode before the DataTable.RowChanging event is called, and the edit is committed at the end of the DataTable.RowChanging event.)

```
public class InRowChangingEventException : DataException {
// Public Constructors
  public InRowChangingEventException( );
  public InRowChangingEventException( string s);
```

    protected **InRowChangingEventException**(System.Runtime.Serialization.SerializationInfo *info*,
        System.Runtime.Serialization.StreamingContext *context*);
}

Hierarchy   System.Object → System.Exception(System.Runtime.Serialization.ISerializable) → System.
                       SystemException → DataException → InRowChangingEventException

InternalDataCollectionBase

System.Data (system.data.dll)   class

This class provides the base functionality used by many of the ADO.NET collection
types, such as ConstraintCollection, DataColumnCollection. DataRelationCollection, DataRowCollection, and
DataTableCollection.

```
public class InternalDataCollectionBase : ICollection, IEnumerable {
// Public Constructors
  public InternalDataCollectionBase( );
// Public Instance Properties
  public virtual int Count{get; }                                               // implements ICollection
  public bool IsReadOnly{get; }
  public bool IsSynchronized{get; }                                             // implements ICollection
  public object SyncRoot{get; }                                                 // implements ICollection
// Protected Instance Properties
  protected virtual ArrayList List{get; }
// Public Instance Methods
  public void CopyTo( Array ar, int index);                                     // implements ICollection
  public IEnumerator GetEnumerator( );                                          // implements IEnumerable
}
```

Subclasses   ConstraintCollection, DataColumnCollection, DataRelationCollection, DataRowCollection,
                       DataTableCollection

InvalidConstraintException   serializable

System.Data (system.data.dll)   class

This exception is thrown when incorrectly attempting to create or access a DataRelation
object. For example, if you attempt to remove a DataRelation when a corresponding
ForeignKeyConstraint exists on a table, or if you try to specify DataRelation parent-and-child
columns with incompatible data types or in tables from different DataSet objects, this
exception is thrown.

```
public class InvalidConstraintException : DataException {
// Public Constructors
  public InvalidConstraintException( );
  public InvalidConstraintException( string s);
// Protected Constructors
  protected InvalidConstraintException(System.Runtime.Serialization.SerializationInfo info,
      System.Runtime.Serialization.StreamingContext context);
}
```

System.Data

Hierarchy	System.Object → System.Exception(System.Runtime.Serialization.ISerializable) → System. SystemException → DataException → InvalidConstraintException

InvalidExpressionException   serializable

System.Data (system.data.dll)   class

This exception occurs when you try to set an invalid SQL expression for the DataColumn. Expression property. The exception description may indicate more information about the problem.

```
public class InvalidExpressionException : DataException {
// Public Constructors
  public InvalidExpressionException( );
  public InvalidExpressionException( string s);
// Protected Constructors
  protected InvalidExpressionException(System.Runtime.Serialization.SerializationInfo info,
    System.Runtime.Serialization.StreamingContext context);
}
```

Hierarchy	System.Object → System.Exception(System.Runtime.Serialization.ISerializable) → System. SystemException → DataException → InvalidExpressionException
Subclasses	EvaluateException, SyntaxErrorException

IsolationLevel   serializable, flag

System.Data (system.data.dll)   enum

This enumeration specifies the isolation level that is used for a transaction. The isolation level is a measure of the degree that a transaction is isolated from other database activity. Higher isolation levels provide better data integrity, but they also slow performance because of required locking. For example, the highest isolation level, Serializable, places a lock on all the tables a transaction accesses, which prevents other users from updating or inserting rows while the transaction is in process. Their requests are still processed when the transaction ends, provided their commands don't time out. RepeatableRead is the next highest isolation level; it uses locking to prevent another user from updating or deleting the rows that are being used in the transaction, but it doesn't guarantee that new rows won't be inserted. ReadCommitted is often a good compromise with shared locks held while the data is being read, thereby avoiding dirty reads (reads that retrieve information from a transaction that has not yet been committed). However, the data can be changed by another user before the end of the transaction, resulting in nonrepeatable reads or phantom data. This is SQL Server's default. ReadUncommitted doesn't use any locking, and dirty reads are possible.

You specify the isolation level when creating a transaction with the IDbConnection. BeginTransaction( ) method. Not all providers support all levels (for example, Chaos isn't supported by SQL Server).

```
public enum IsolationLevel {
  Chaos = 0x00000010,
  ReadUncommitted = 0x00000100,
  ReadCommitted = 0x00001000,
  RepeatableRead = 0x00010000,
```

```
Serializable = 0x00100000,
Unspecified = 0xFFFFFFFF
}
```

Hierarchy	System.Object → System.ValueType → System.Enum(System.IComparable, System.IFormattable, System.IConvertible) → IsolationLevel
Returned By	IDbTransaction.IsolationLevel, System.Data.OleDb.OleDbTransaction.IsolationLevel, System.Data.OracleClient.OracleTransaction.IsolationLevel, System.Data.SqlClient. SqlTransaction.IsolationLevel
Passed To	IDbConnection.BeginTransaction( ), System.Data.OleDb.OleDbConnection. BeginTransaction( ), System.Data.OleDb.OleDbTransaction.Begin( ), System.Data. OracleClient.OracleConnection.BeginTransaction( ), System.Data.SqlClient.SqlConnection. BeginTransaction( )

ITableMapping

System.Data (system.data.dll)   interface

This interface represents a mapping between a table in the data source and a table in the DataSet, which may have a different name. This interface is implemented by the System.Data.Common.DataTableMapping class.

```
public interface ITableMapping {
// Public Instance Properties
  public IColumnMappingCollection ColumnMappings{get; }
  public string DataSetTable{set; get; }
  public string SourceTable{set; get; }
}
```

Implemented By	System.Data.Common.DataTableMapping
Returned By	ITableMappingCollection.{Add( ), GetByDataSetTable( )}

ITableMappingCollection

System.Data (system.data.dll)   interface

Contains a collection of ITableMapping instances. This interface is implemented by the System.Data.Common.DataTableMappingCollection class.

```
public interface ITableMappingCollection : IList, ICollection, IEnumerable {
// Public Instance Properties
  public object this[string index]{set; get; }
// Public Instance Methods
  public ITableMapping Add(string sourceTableName, string dataSetTableName);
  public bool Contains( string sourceTableName);
  public ITableMapping GetByDataSetTable(string dataSetTableName);
  public int IndexOf( string sourceTableName);
  public void RemoveAt( string sourceTableName);
}
```

Returned By   IDataAdapter.TableMappings

MappingType   serializable

System.Data (system.data.dll)   enum

This enumeration specifies the DataColumn.ColumnMapping property, which determines how a column's value is written when the DataSet.WriteXml( ) method is called. Each column can be mapped to an element (Element), which is the default; an attribute of the row element (Attribute); omitted (Hidden); or set to a text node within the element (SimpleContent). There can be only one SimpleContent column in a table.

```
public enum MappingType {
  Element = 1,
  Attribute = 2,
  SimpleContent = 3,
  Hidden = 4
}
```

Hierarchy   System.Object → System.ValueType → System.Enum(System.IComparable, System.IFormattable, System.IConvertible) → MappingType

Returned By   DataColumn.ColumnMapping

Passed To   DataColumn.{ColumnMapping, DataColumn( )}

MergeFailedEventArgs

System.Data (system.data.dll)   class

This class provides data for the DataSet.MergeFailed event. This includes the DataTable in which the problem occurred (Table) and a descriptive error message (Conflict).

```
public class MergeFailedEventArgs : EventArgs {
// Public Constructors
  public MergeFailedEventArgs(DataTable table, string conflict);
// Public Instance Properties
  public string Conflict{get; }
  public DataTable Table{get; }
}
```

Hierarchy   System.Object → System.EventArgs → MergeFailedEventArgs

Passed To   MergeFailedEventHandler.{BeginInvoke( ), Invoke( )}

MergeFailedEventHandler   serializable

System.Data (system.data.dll)   delegate

This delegate represents the method that will handle the DataSet.MergeFailed event. This event occurs if you invoke DataSet.Merge( ) to combine two DataSet objects where source and target rows have a different primary key. Note that this event occurs only if DataSet.

EnforceConstraints is set to true, and it doesn't occur if the schemas are invalid (in which case an exception is thrown before the merge process is started). When a merge fails, the DataSet.EnforceConstraints property is set to false, all the data is retained, and the rows that are invalid are marked with a descriptive DataRow.RowError. You can't reenable constraint checking until these conflicts are resolved.

```
public delegate void MergeFailedEventHandler(object sender, MergeFailedEventArgs e);
```

Associated Events   DataSet.MergeFailed( )

MissingMappingAction   serializable

System.Data (system.data.dll)   enum

This enumeration is used to specify the IDataAdapter.MissingMappingAction property, which determines what happens when a DataSet is filled using columns or tables that don't have corresponding System.Data.Common.DataColumnMapping or System.Data.Common.DataTableMapping. The default value, Passthrough, simply means that the original name will be used. You can also use Ignore, in which case the column or table aren't added, or Error, in which case a System.SystemException is thrown. Mapping information must be added to a data adapter manually, as described in Chapter 14.

```
public enum MissingMappingAction {
  Passthrough = 1,
  Ignore = 2,
  Error = 3
}
```

Hierarchy   System.Object → System.ValueType → System.Enum(System.IComparable, System.IFor-
                     mattable, System.IConvertible) → MissingMappingAction

Returned By   System.Data.Common.DataAdapter.MissingMappingAction, IDataAdapter.
                     MissingMappingAction

Passed To   System.Data.Common.DataAdapter.MissingMappingAction, System.Data.Common.Data-
                     ColumnMappingCollection.GetColumnMappingBySchemaAction( ), System.Data.Common.
                     DataTableMapping.GetColumnMappingBySchemaAction( ), System.Data.Common.Data-
                     TableMappingCollection.GetTableMappingBySchemaAction( ), IDataAdapter.
                     MissingMappingAction

MissingPrimaryKeyException   serializable

System.Data (system.data.dll)   class

This exception is thrown when you attempt to invoke the DataRowCollection.Contains( ) or DataRowCollection.Find( ) method on a DataTable that has no primary key. To retrieve primary key information, you can use the IDataAdapter.FillSchema( ) method when accessing a data source. To programmatically set a primary key, you must add a UniqueConstraint (typically by setting the DataColumn.Unique property of the primary key field to true) and then set the UniqueConstraint.IsPrimaryKey property to true.

```
public class MissingPrimaryKeyException : DataException {
// Public Constructors
  public MissingPrimaryKeyException( );
```

```
    public MissingPrimaryKeyException( string s);
// Protected Constructors
    protected MissingPrimaryKeyException(System.Runtime.Serialization.SerializationInfo info,
        System.Runtime.Serialization.StreamingContext context);
}
```

Hierarchy   System.Object → System.Exception(System.Runtime.Serialization.ISerializable) → System.
                 SystemException → DataException → MissingPrimaryKeyException

MissingSchemaAction   serializable

System.Data (system.data.dll)   enum

This enumeration specifies what happens when adding information to a DataSet and the
schema information can't be found. This enumeration is used when merging two
DataSet objects (with the DataSet.Merge( ) method) and when filling a DataSet from a data
source using the IDataAdapter.Fill( ) method. In the first case, a MissingSchemaAction value is
specified as a parameter. In the second case, a MissingSchemaAction value is set using the
IDataAdapter.MissingSchemaAction property.

If set to Add, the new missing DataColumn objects are added to the DataSet. If set to
AddWithKey (the default when filling a DataSet), the required DataColumn objects are added,
and ADO.NET tries to determine the primary key. In the case of the SQL Server
provider, this involves appending the FOR BROWSE clause on the SQL statement and
parsing out the additional information. In the case of an OLE DB provider, this
involves setting the DBPROP_UNIQUEROWS property, and then determining which columns
are primary key columns by examining DBCOLUMN_KEYCOLUMN in the IColumnsRowset. (Not all
OLE DB providers support this technique. If you experience problems, use Add instead
of AddWithKey and set the primary key manually.) Finally, you can specify Ignore, in which
case data in a missing column will not be added, or Error, in which case a System.SystemEx-
ception is thrown if data is encountered for a column that doesn't exist.

```
public enum MissingSchemaAction {
    Add = 1,
    Ignore = 2,
    Error = 3,
    AddWithKey = 4
}
```

Hierarchy   System.Object → System.ValueType → System.Enum(System.IComparable, System.IFor-
                  mattable, System.IConvertible) → MissingSchemaAction

Returned By   System.Data.Common.DataAdapter.MissingSchemaAction, IDataAdapter.
                  MissingSchemaAction

Passed To   System.Data.Common.DataAdapter.MissingSchemaAction, System.Data.Common.
                  DataColumnMapping.GetDataColumnBySchemaAction( ), System.Data.Common.
                  DataTableMapping.GetDataTableBySchemaAction( ), DataSet.Merge( ), IDataAdapter.
                  MissingSchemaAction

NoNullAllowedException

System.Data (system.data.dll)   class

This exception is thrown if you try to insert a null value into a column that has Data-Column.AllowDBNull set to false.

```
public class NoNullAllowedException : DataException {
// Public Constructors
  public NoNullAllowedException( );
  public NoNullAllowedException( string s);
// Protected Constructors
  protected NoNullAllowedException(System.Runtime.Serialization.SerializationInfo info,
     System.Runtime.Serialization.StreamingContext context);
}
```

Hierarchy   System.Object → System.Exception(System.Runtime.Serialization.ISerializable) → System.
                     SystemException → DataException → NoNullAllowedException

ParameterDirection

serializable

System.Data (system.data.dll)   enum

This enumeration specifies the IDataParameter.Direction property. Input, the default, indicates a parameter passed into a stored procedure. Output specifies a parameter passed back from a stored procedure. InputOutput specifies a parameter that is passed in to and back from the stored procedure. Finally, ReturnValue specifies a parameter that is the return value of the stored procedure.

```
public enum ParameterDirection {
  Input = 1,
  Output = 2,
  InputOutput = 3,
  ReturnValue = 6
}
```

Hierarchy   System.Object → System.ValueType → System.Enum(System.IComparable, System.IFor-
                     mattable, System.IConvertible) → ParameterDirection

Returned By   IDataParameter.Direction, System.Data.OleDb.OleDbParameter.Direction, System.Data.
                     OracleClient.OracleParameter.Direction, System.Data.SqlClient.SqlParameter.Direction

Passed To   IDataParameter.Direction, System.Data.OleDb.OleDbParameter.{Direction,
                     OleDbParameter( )}, System.Data.OracleClient.OracleParameter.{Direction,
                     OracleParameter( )}, System.Data.SqlClient.SqlParameter.{Direction, SqlParameter( )}

PropertyAttributes

serializable, flag

System.Data (system.data.dll)   enum

This enumeration can be used when creating a custom provider to indicate whether a specific property is required or supported, and how it should be set. You can use bitwise combinations of the values in this enumeration. Optional indicates that the user doesn't need to specify a value for this property before the data source is initialized, while Required indicates that it must be set first. Read and Write indicate whether the value can be read or modified.

```
public enum PropertyAttributes {
  NotSupported = 0x00000000,
  Required = 0x00000001,
  Optional = 0x00000002,
  Read = 0x00000200,
  Write = 0x00000400
}
```

Hierarchy System.Object → System.ValueType → System.Enum(System.IComparable, System.IFormattable, System.IConvertible) → PropertyAttributes

PropertyCollection

System.Data (system.data.dll)   class

This class is accessed using the ExtendedProperties property of the DataColumn, DataTable, DataSet, Constraint, and DataRelation. It can store additional information about the object. For example, you might want to store an expiration date for a DataSet.

```
public class PropertyCollection : Hashtable {
// Public Constructors
  public PropertyCollection( );
}
```

Hierarchy System.Object → System.Collections.Hashtable(System.Collections.IDictionary, System.Collections.ICollection, System.Collections.IEnumerable, System.Runtime.Serialization.ISerializable, System.Runtime.Serialization.IDeserializationCallback, System.ICloneable) → PropertyCollection

Returned By Constraint.ExtendedProperties, DataColumn.ExtendedProperties, DataRelation.ExtendedProperties, DataSet.ExtendedProperties, DataTable.ExtendedProperties

ReadOnlyException   serializable

System.Data (system.data.dll)   class

This exception occurs when you attempt to modify a value in a read-only field (a column that has DataColumn.ReadOnly set to true).

```
public class ReadOnlyException : DataException {
// Public Constructors
  public ReadOnlyException( );
  public ReadOnlyException( string s);
// Protected Constructors
  protected ReadOnlyException(System.Runtime.Serialization.SerializationInfo info,
    System.Runtime.Serialization.StreamingContext context);
}
```

Hierarchy System.Object → System.Exception(System.Runtime.Serialization.ISerializable) → System.SystemException → DataException → ReadOnlyException

RowNotInTableException
serializable

System.Data (system.data.dll)   class

This exception is thrown if you attempt to perform an operation on a row that is not in the DataSet. For example, if you use a method such as DataRow.AcceptChanges( ), DataRow. GetChildRows( ), or DataRow.GetParentRow( ) on a deleted row, this exception results. Another related exception is DeletedRowInaccessibleException.

```
public class RowNotInTableException : DataException {
// Public Constructors
  public RowNotInTableException( );
  public RowNotInTableException( string s);
// Protected Constructors
  protected RowNotInTableException(System.Runtime.Serialization.SerializationInfo info,
    System.Runtime.Serialization.StreamingContext context);
}
```

Hierarchy   System.Object → System.Exception(System.Runtime.Serialization.ISerializable) → System. SystemException → DataException → RowNotInTableException

Rule
serializable

System.Data (system.data.dll)   enum

This enumeration is used to specify two properties of the ForeignKeyConstraint class: Foreign-KeyConstraint.UpdateRule and ForeignKeyConstraint.DeleteRule. The value from this enumeration indicates what will happen to the related child rows when a change is made to a parent row. For example, by using a ForeignKeyConstraint.DeleteRule or Cascade, all child rows are removed when the parent row is deleted. If you use SetNull, the foreign key field in the child record is set to a null value. SetDefault restores the default value for the foreign key field; None performs no action.

```
public enum Rule {
  None = 0,
  Cascade = 1,
  SetNull = 2,
  SetDefault = 3
}
```

Hierarchy   System.Object → System.ValueType → System.Enum(System.IComparable, System.IFor-mattable, System.IConvertible) → Rule

Returned By   ForeignKeyConstraint.{DeleteRule, UpdateRule}

Passed To   ForeignKeyConstraint.{DeleteRule, ForeignKeyConstraint( ), UpdateRule}

SchemaType
serializable

System.Data (system.data.dll)   enum

This enumeration is used with the IDataAdapter.FillSchema( ) method. It specifies whether schema information should use table and column mappings applied to the data adapter. If you specify Source, mappings are ignored. If you specify Mapped, the schema is

System.Data

retrieved using mappings, if they exist. For example, if the Customers data source table is mapped to the CustomerTable DataSet table, the schema is applied to CustomerTable. If the table doesn't exist, it's created. Note that if you aren't using table mappings, both options are equivalent.

```
public enum SchemaType {
   Source = 1,
   Mapped = 2
}
```

Hierarchy   System.Object → System.ValueType → System.Enum(System.IComparable, System.IFormattable, System.IConvertible) → SchemaType

Passed To   System.Data.Common.DataAdapter.FillSchema( ), System.Data.Common.DbDataAdapter.FillSchema( ), IDataAdapter.FillSchema( )

SqlDbType   serializable

System.Data (system.data.dll)   enum

This enumeration is used to specify the SQL Server data types. For information about what .NET type each SQL Server data type maps, refer to Appendix A.

```
public enum SqlDbType {
   BigInt = 0,
   Binary = 1,
   Bit = 2,
   Char = 3,
   DateTime = 4,
   Decimal = 5,
   Float = 6,
   Image = 7,
   Int = 8,
   Money = 9,
   NChar = 10,
   NText = 11,
   NVarChar = 12,
   Real = 13,
   UniqueIdentifier = 14,
   SmallDateTime = 15,
   SmallInt = 16,
   SmallMoney = 17,
   Text = 18,
   Timestamp = 19,
   TinyInt = 20,
   VarBinary = 21,
   VarChar = 22,
   Variant = 23
}
```

Hierarchy   System.Object → System.ValueType → System.Enum(System.IComparable, System.IFormattable, System.IConvertible) → SqlDbType

Returned By	System.Data.SqlClient.SqlParameter.SqlDbType

Passed To	System.Data.SqlClient.SqlParameter.{SqlDbType, SqlParameter( )}, System.Data.SqlClient. SqlParameterCollection.Add( )

StateChangeEventArgs

System.Data (system.data.dll)   sealed class

This class provides data for the method that handles the StateChanged event of a provider-specific Connection object. It indicates the state of the Connection before (Current-State) and after (OriginalState) the state change.

```
public sealed class StateChangeEventArgs : EventArgs {
// Public Constructors
  public StateChangeEventArgs(ConnectionState originalState, ConnectionState currentState);
// Public Instance Properties
  public ConnectionState CurrentState{get; }
  public ConnectionState OriginalState{get; }
}
```

Hierarchy	System.Object → System.EventArgs → StateChangeEventArgs

Passed To	StateChangeEventHandler.{BeginInvoke( ), Invoke( )}

StateChangeEventHandler   serializable

System.Data (system.data.dll)   delegate

This delegate represents the method that will handle the StateChanged event of a provider-specific Connection object. This event typically fires when the connection state changes from open to closed or vice versa.

```
public delegate void StateChangeEventHandler(object sender, StateChangeEventArgs e);
```

Associated Events	System.Data.OleDb.OleDbConnection.StateChange( ), System.Data.OracleClient.OracleCon-nection.StateChange( ), System.Data.SqlClient.SqlConnection.StateChange( )

StatementType   serializable

System.Data (system.data.dll)   enum

This enumeration is used to specify the StatementType property of the System.Data.Common. RowUpdatingEventArgs and System.Data.Common.RowUpdatedEventArgs classes. These objects are provided to clients when handling row update events for a data adapter, allowing your code to determine whether the action for the current row corresponds to a SQL SELECT, DELETE, INSERT, or UPDATE command.

```
public enum StatementType {
  Select = 0,
  Insert = 1,
  Update = 2,
  Delete = 3
}
```

Hierarchy	System.Object → System.ValueType → System.Enum(System.IComparable, System.IFormattable, System.IConvertible) → StatementType
Returned By	System.Data.Common.RowUpdatedEventArgs.StatementType, System.Data.Common. RowUpdatingEventArgs.StatementType
Passed To	System.Data.Common.DbDataAdapter.{CreateRowUpdatedEvent( ), CreateRowUpdatingEvent( )}, System.Data.Common.RowUpdatedEventArgs. RowUpdatedEventArgs( ), System.Data.Common.RowUpdatingEventArgs. RowUpdatingEventArgs( ), System.Data.OleDb.OleDbRowUpdatedEventArgs. OleDbRowUpdatedEventArgs( ), System.Data.OleDb.OleDbRowUpdatingEventArgs. OleDbRowUpdatingEventArgs( ), System.Data.OracleClient.OracleRowUpdatedEventArgs. OracleRowUpdatedEventArgs( ), System.Data.OracleClient.OracleRowUpdatingEventArgs. OracleRowUpdatingEventArgs( ), System.Data.SqlClient.SqlRowUpdatedEventArgs. SqlRowUpdatedEventArgs( ), System.Data.SqlClient.SqlRowUpdatingEventArgs. SqlRowUpdatingEventArgs( )

StrongTypingException   serializable

System.Data (system.data.dll)   class

This exception is thrown when you try to access a null value in a column of a strongly typed DataSet. This exception isn't generated by the .NET runtime. Instead, the strongly typed DataSet class catches an System.InvalidCastException and then throws a StrongTypingException to notify your code of the problem. This code takes place in the get property accessor for a strongly typed DataRow.

```
public class StrongTypingException : DataException {
// Public Constructors
  public StrongTypingException( );
  public StrongTypingException(string s, Exception innerException);
// Protected Constructors
  protected StrongTypingException(System.Runtime.Serialization.SerializationInfo info,
    System.Runtime.Serialization.StreamingContext context);
}
```

Hierarchy	System.Object → System.Exception(System.Runtime.Serialization.ISerializable) → System. SystemException → DataException → StrongTypingException

SyntaxErrorException   serializable

System.Data (system.data.dll)   class

This exception is thrown if there is a syntax error in the SQL used for the DataColumn. Expression property typically used to filter rows, calculate the values in a column, or create an aggregate column. Note that other SQL syntax problems (such as invalid syntax in a Command) generally lead to provider-specific errors such as System.Data.SqlClient. SqlException and System.Data.OleDb.OleDbException when you execute the Command. A related exception is EvaluateException.

```
public class SyntaxErrorException : InvalidExpressionException {
// Public Constructors
  public SyntaxErrorException( );
```

```
    public SyntaxErrorException( string s);
// Protected Constructors
    protected SyntaxErrorException(System.Runtime.Serialization.SerializationInfo info,
        System.Runtime.Serialization.StreamingContext context);
}
```

Hierarchy   System.Object → System.Exception(System.Runtime.Serialization.ISerializable) → System.
                  SystemException → DataException → InvalidExpressionException → SyntaxErrorException

TypedDataSetGenerator

System.Data (system.data.dll)   class

This class allows you to programmatically generate a typed DataSet. However, it's
extremely unlikely that you'll ever use this class. Instead, you'll almost always rely on
Visual Studio .NET or the *xsd.exe* command-line utility to create a set of classes for a
typed DataSet using a schema file. This process is described in Chapter 13.

```
public class TypedDataSetGenerator {
// Public Constructors
    public TypedDataSetGenerator( );
// Public Static Methods
    public static void Generate(DataSet dataSet, System.CodeDom.CodeNamespace codeNamespace,
        System.CodeDom.Compiler.ICodeGenerator codeGen);
    public static string GenerateIdName(string name,
        System.CodeDom.Compiler.ICodeGenerator codeGen);
}
```

TypedDataSetGeneratorException   serializable

System.Data (system.data.dll)   class

This exception is thrown when an error is encountered by the TypedDataSetGenerator.

```
public class TypedDataSetGeneratorException : DataException {
// Public Constructors
    public TypedDataSetGeneratorException( );
    public TypedDataSetGeneratorException(System.Collections.ArrayList list);
// Protected Constructors
    protected TypedDataSetGeneratorException(System.Runtime.Serialization.SerializationInfo info,
        System.Runtime.Serialization.StreamingContext context);
// Public Instance Properties
    public ArrayList ErrorList{get; }
// Public Instance Methods
    public override void GetObjectData(System.Runtime.Serialization.SerializationInfo info,
        System.Runtime.Serialization.StreamingContext context);          // overrides Exception
}
```

Hierarchy   System.Object → System.Exception(System.Runtime.Serialization.ISerializable) → System.
                  SystemException → DataException → TypedDataSetGeneratorException

UniqueConstraint

serializable

System.Data (system.data.dll) class

The UniqueConstraint is a rule that prevents duplicate values in a column. There are two ways to create a UniqueConstraint: by setting the DataColumn.Unique property to true for one or more columns, or by using the IDataAdapter.FillSchema() method when retrieving a row set that includes a primary key column. You could also create a UniqueConstraint object using the new keyword, however, you need to add it to the DataTable.Constraints collection before it takes effect; simply specifying the column and table information isn't enough. As with all constraints, the UniqueConstraint is enforced only when the DataSet.EnforceConstraints is true (the default).

```
public class UniqueConstraint : Constraint {
// Public Constructors
   public UniqueConstraint( DataColumn column);
   public UniqueConstraint( DataColumn[ ] columns);
   public UniqueConstraint(DataColumn[ ] columns, bool isPrimaryKey);
   public UniqueConstraint(DataColumn column, bool isPrimaryKey);
   public UniqueConstraint( string name, DataColumn column);
   public UniqueConstraint(string name, DataColumn[ ] columns);
   public UniqueConstraint(string name, DataColumn[ ] columns, bool isPrimaryKey);
   public UniqueConstraint(string name, DataColumn column, bool isPrimaryKey);
   public UniqueConstraint(string name, string[ ] columnNames, bool isPrimaryKey);
// Public Instance Properties
   public virtual DataColumn[ ] Columns{get; }
   public bool IsPrimaryKey{get; }
   public override DataTable Table{get; }                              // overrides Constraint
// Public Instance Methods
   public override bool Equals( object key2);                          // overrides object
   public override int GetHashCode( );                                 // overrides object
}
```

Hierarchy System.Object → Constraint → UniqueConstraint

Returned By DataRelation.ParentKeyConstraint

UpdateRowSource

serializable

System.Data (system.data.dll) enum

This enumeration is used to specify the IDbCommand.UpdatedRowSource property (and the same property for provider-specific Command objects). It's relevant only when DataSet changes are committed using a data adapter. This value specifies whether updated values in the data source are used to update the source row in the DataSet. It eliminates the need to use a query to retrieve the updated data and to subsequently update the DataSet.

This technique can be used only when updating the data source with a stored procedure. That's because by default, after an update operation, a database won't return any information beside the number of rows affected. However, you can create a stored procedure that returns one or more updated values (use OutputParameters) or one that returns the updated row (use FirstReturnedRecord). The default is Both.

```
public enum UpdateRowSource {
  None = 0,
  OutputParameters = 1,
  FirstReturnedRecord = 2,
  Both = 3
}
```

Hierarchy	System.Object → System.ValueType → System.Enum(System.IComparable, System.IFor-mattable, System.IConvertible) → UpdateRowSource
Returned By	IDbCommand.UpdatedRowSource, System.Data.OleDb.OleDbCommand. UpdatedRowSource, System.Data.OracleClient.OracleCommand.UpdatedRowSource, System.Data.SqlClient.SqlCommand.UpdatedRowSource
Passed To	IDbCommand.UpdatedRowSource, System.Data.OleDb.OleDbCommand. UpdatedRowSource, System.Data.OracleClient.OracleCommand.UpdatedRowSource, System.Data.SqlClient.SqlCommand.UpdatedRowSource

UpdateStatus   serializable

System.Data (system.data.dll)   enum

This enumeration is used to specify the Status property of the System.Data.Common.RowUp-datingEventArgs and System.Data.Common.RowUpdatedEventArgs classes. These objects are provided to clients when handling row update events for a data adapter. The UpdateStatus enumeration specifies whether to continue the update, raise an error, skip the current row (usually because the update failed), or skip all the remaining rows.

```
public enum UpdateStatus {
  Continue = 0,
  ErrorsOccurred = 1,
  SkipCurrentRow = 2,
  SkipAllRemainingRows = 3
}
```

Hierarchy	System.Object → System.ValueType → System.Enum(System.IComparable, System.IFor-mattable, System.IConvertible) → UpdateStatus
Returned By	System.Data.Common.RowUpdatedEventArgs.Status, System.Data.Common. RowUpdatingEventArgs.Status
Passed To	System.Data.Common.RowUpdatedEventArgs.Status, System.Data.Common. RowUpdatingEventArgs.Status

VersionNotFoundException   serializable

System.Data (system.data.dll)   class

This exception is thrown if you try to access a DataRow after it has been marked deleted, but before changes have been accepted. Typically, it occurs when you try to retrieve the current value of a deleted row. To prevent this exception, check the DataRow.RowState property before attempting to read the value, and skip the task if the row is in the DataRowState. Deleted state. A related exception that has the same cause is DeletedRowInaccessibleException.

```
public class VersionNotFoundException : DataException {
// Public Constructors
  public VersionNotFoundException( );
  public VersionNotFoundException( string s);
// Protected Constructors
  protected VersionNotFoundException(System.Runtime.Serialization.SerializationInfo info,
     System.Runtime.Serialization.StreamingContext context);
}
```

Hierarchy   System.Object → System.Exception(System.Runtime.Serialization.ISerializable) → System.
                     SystemException → DataException → VersionNotFoundException

XmlReadMode   serializable

System.Data (system.data.dll)   enum

This enumeration is used to specify how a serialized DataSet file is interpreted using the
DataSet.ReadXml( ) method. Generally, Auto is the most convenient option. It uses DiffGram if
the file is in a DiffGram format (with versioning information), ReadSchema if the file
includes an inline XSD schema, or InferSchema if the file contains only data. In addition,
you can specify Fragment read mode to read an XML document such as the kind created
with a FOR XML query in SQL Server 2000.

Different read modes imply different schema rules. For example, if you use DiffGram
mode to try to read a serialized file into a DataSet that doesn't match the original
schema, an exception is thrown. However, you can use InferSchema on a DataSet that
already has a schema, provided there are no conflicting tables and columns. The
existing schema is simply extended. ReadSchema is a little more restrictive; it throws an
exception if it finds any duplicate tables in the DataSet schema, even if it is compatible
with the serialized file. Otherwise, it extends the existing schema with new tables.
Finally, IgnoreSchema ignores any inline schemas and discards data that doesn't match
the existing schema. IgnoreSchema doesn't work with the DiffGram format; instead, the
DiffGram behavior applies.

```
public enum XmlReadMode {
  Auto = 0,
  ReadSchema = 1,
  IgnoreSchema = 2,
  InferSchema = 3,
  DiffGram = 4,
  Fragment = 5
}
```

Hierarchy   System.Object → System.ValueType → System.Enum(System.IComparable, System.IFor-
                     mattable, System.IConvertible) → XmlReadMode

Returned By   DataSet.ReadXml( )

Passed To   DataSet.ReadXml( )

XmlWriteMode

System.Data (system.data.dll)   **enum**

This enumeration is used to specify the type of XML output generated by the DataSet. WriteXml() method. IgnoreSchema writes the data only. In this case, you can use the DataSet. WriteXmlSchema() method to create a separate schema file for the DataSet. If you choose WriteSchema, an inline XSD schema is written at the beginning of the file, followed by the XML data. Finally, you can use DiffGram to write the data indicating which rows have been added, deleted, and modified (along with the original value for changed rows). When a DataSet is serialized as part of a SOAP message sent to or from a web service, the DiffGram format is used automatically, and the DataSet schema is prepended to the data.

```
public enum XmlWriteMode {
  WriteSchema = 0,
  IgnoreSchema = 1,
  DiffGram = 2
}
```

Hierarchy   System.Object → System.ValueType → System.Enum(System.IComparable, System.IFor-
                     mattable, System.IConvertible) → XmlWriteMode

Passed To   DataSet.WriteXml()

35

The System.Data.Common Namespace

This namespace includes some of the base classes that define common ADO.NET functionality for provider-specific objects. For example, you'll find DataAdapter, which is the root for classes such as System.Data.SqlClient.SqlDataAdapter and System.Data. OleDb.OleDbDataAdapter. However, many connection-specific classes don't derive from a base class. Instead, they implement a common interface, such as System.Data.IDbConnection (implemented by System.Data.SqlClient.SqlConnection and System.Data.OleDb. OleDbConnection).

The System.Data.Common namespace does include a few classes that are generic to all data providers. Namely, these are the DataColumnMapping and DataTableMapping classes, which allow you to map table names and column names in the DataSet. These classes are used by the provider-specific objects but are completely generic. Figure 35-1 shows the types in this namespace.

DataAdapter   marshal by reference, disposable

System.Data.Common (system.data.dll)   abstract class

DataAdapter classes are provider-specific types that act as a bridge between a data source (such as a SQL Server database) and the ADO.NET System.Data.DataSet. DataAdapters have two responsibilities: to retrieve the results of a query and place it in a System.Data.DataSet (when you call the Fill() method), and to reconcile changes in the System.Data.DataSet and apply changes back to the data source (when you call the Update() method.

An ADO.NET provider includes its own custom DataAdapter (such as System.Data.SqlClient. SqlDataAdapter). Unfortunately, DataAdapter classes have a complex inheritance hierarchy. The base functionality is defined by two interfaces: System.Data.IDataAdapter (which defines the Update() and Fill() methods) and, for relational database providers, a System.Data.IDbDataAdapter (which defines the command properties used for interacting with the data source). The relational database provider-specific DataAdapter implements only one of these interfaces directly (System.Data.IDbDataAdapter). It implements the other indirectly by deriving from DbDataAdapter, which in turn derives from this class. This situation is illustrated more clearly in Figure 36-2. This allows some basic DataAdapter functionality to be

488

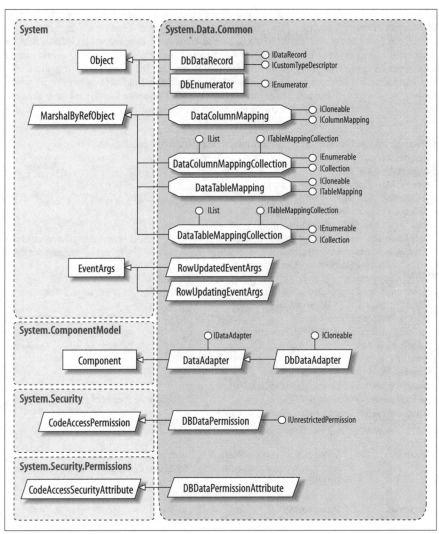

Figure 35-1. The System.Data.Common namespace

implemented in this class (so the provider-specific DataAdapter doesn't need to). It also allows the provider-specific class to use strongly typed Command properties but still support generic access to these properties as System.Data.IDbCommand objects (thanks to the interface).

Generally, you won't ever use the DataAdapter class directly. If you want to create generic data-access code that can use different provider-specific ADO.NET objects, you always cast the DataAdapter to the System.Data.IDbDataAdapter interface. Note that the Data-Adapter class contains a mix of abstract members the provider-specific class must override and members that need no alteration (mainly, its properties). Some properties that are implemented in this class include TableMappings (which maps data source table and field names to table and field names in the System.Data.DataSet) and ContinueUpdateOnError (which, if true, continues updating even if some changes can't be committed and stores an error message in the corresponding System.Data.DataRow.RowError property). You can also set MissingMappingAction to tell the DataAdapter what to do if it finds a column or table that doesn't have a mapping (by default, it adds it using the name used in the data source) and MissingSchemaAction to tell the DataAdapter what to do when adding tables to a System.Data.DataSet that doesn't have a schema (it can retrieve schema information automatically, throw an exception, or simply add the table without schema information, which is the default).

```
public abstract class DataAdapter : System.ComponentModel.Component , System.Data.IDataAdapter {
// Protected Constructors
    protected DataAdapter( );
    protected DataAdapter( DataAdapter adapter);
// Public Instance Properties
    public bool AcceptChangesDuringFill{set; get; }
    public bool ContinueUpdateOnError{set; get; }
    public MissingMappingAction MissingMappingAction{set; get; }          // implements System.Data.IDataAdapter
    public MissingSchemaAction MissingSchemaAction{set; get; }            // implements System.Data.IDataAdapter
    public DataTableMappingCollection TableMappings{get; }
// Public Instance Methods
    public abstract int Fill( System.Data.DataSet dataSet);               // implements System.Data.IDataAdapter
    public abstract DataTable[ ] FillSchema(System.Data.DataSet dataSet,
        System.Data.SchemaType schemaType);                              // implements System.Data.IDataAdapter
    public abstract IDataParameter[ ] GetFillParameters( );              // implements System.Data.IDataAdapter
    public abstract int Update( System.Data.DataSet dataSet);            // implements System.Data.IDataAdapter
// Protected Instance Methods
    protected virtual DataAdapter CloneInternals( );
    protected virtual DataTableMappingCollection CreateTableMappings();
    protected override void Dispose( bool disposing);                    // overrides System.ComponentModel.Component
    protected virtual bool ShouldSerializeTableMappings( );
}
```

Hierarchy	System.Object → System.MarshalByRefObject → System.ComponentModel.Compo-nent(System.ComponentModel.IComponent, System.IDisposable) → DataAdapter(System.Data.IDataAdapter)
Subclasses	DbDataAdapter

DataColumnMapping

marshal by reference

System.Data.Common (system.data.dll)   sealed class

This class represents a mapping between a field (or column) name in the data source (SourceColumn) and the field name in the System.Data.DataSet (DataSetColumn). The data source column name is case-sensitive, while the System.Data.DataSet column name isn't.

Column mappings are applied to the DataAdapter you use to transfer information. Column mappings work in both directions: in other words, the DataAdapter automatically maps the column when filling it with the appropriate data and can apply any changes back to the original data source column during updates. Column mappings are never added independently to a DataAdapter; instead, they are added to a DataTableMapping, which can then be added to the DataAdapter.TableMappings collection.

```
public sealed class DataColumnMapping : MarshalByRefObject , System.Data.IColumnMapping, ICloneable {
// Public Constructors
  public DataColumnMapping( );
  public DataColumnMapping(string sourceColumn, string dataSetColumn);
// Public Instance Properties
  public string DataSetColumn{set; get; }                          // implements System.Data.IColumnMapping
  public string SourceColumn{set; get; }                           // implements System.Data.IColumnMapping
// Public Instance Methods
  public DataColumn GetDataColumnBySchemaAction(System.Data.DataTable dataTable, Type dataType,
    System.Data.MissingSchemaAction schemaAction);
  public override string ToString( );                                          // overrides object
}
```

Hierarchy	System.Object → System.MarshalByRefObject → DataColumnMapping(System.Data. IColumnMapping, System.ICloneable)
Returned By	DataColumnMappingCollection.{GetByDataSetColumn( ), GetColumnMappingBySchemaAction( ), this}, DataTableMapping. GetColumnMappingBySchemaAction( )
Passed To	DataColumnMappingCollection.{AddRange( ), this}, DataTableMapping. DataTableMapping( )

DataColumnMappingCollection   marshal by reference

System.Data.Common (system.data.dll)   sealed class

This class contains a collection of DataColumnMapping objects and is typically used for the DataTableMapping.ColumnMappings property. You can look up an individual DataColumnMapping by index or data source column name using the indexer. You can also use the GetByDataSetColumn( ) to retrieve a DataColumnMapping using the System.Data.DataSet name.

```
public sealed class DataColumnMappingCollection : MarshalByRefObject , System.Data.IColumnMappingCollection, IList,
  ICollection, IEnumerable {
// Public Constructors
  public DataColumnMappingCollection( );
// Public Instance Properties
  public int Count{get; }                                                   // implements ICollection
  public DataColumnMapping this[string SourceColumn]{set; get; }
  public DataColumnMapping this[int index]{set; get; }
// Public Static Methods
  public static DataColumnMapping GetColumnMappingBySchemaAction(
    DataColumnMappingCollection columnMappings, string sourceColumn,
    System.Data.MissingMappingAction mappingAction);
// Public Instance Methods
  public DataColumnMapping Add(string sourceColumn, string dataSetColumn);
  public int Add( object value);                                            // implements IList
  public void AddRange( DataColumnMapping[ ] values);
  public void Clear( );                                                     // implements IList
  public bool Contains( object value);                                      // implements IList
  public bool Contains( string value);                    // implements System.Data.IColumnMappingCollection
  public void CopyTo( Array array, int index);                             // implements ICollection
```

```
public DataColumnMapping GetByDataSetColumn(string value);
public IEnumerator GetEnumerator( );                                    // implements IEnumerable
public int IndexOf( object value);                                              // implements IList
public int IndexOf( string sourceColumn);          // implements System.Data.IColumnMappingCollection
public int IndexOfDataSetColumn( string dataSetColumn);
public void Insert( int index, object value);                                   // implements IList
public void Remove( object value);                                              // implements IList
public void RemoveAt( int index);                                               // implements IList
public void RemoveAt( string sourceColumn);        // implements System.Data.IColumnMappingCollection
}
```

Hierarchy   System.Object → System.MarshalByRefObject → DataColumnMappingCollection(System.
              Data.IColumnMappingCollection, System.Collections.IList, System.Collections.ICollection,
              System.Collections.IEnumerable)

Returned By   DataTableMapping.ColumnMappings

DataTableMapping   marshal by reference

System.Data.Common (system.data.dll)   sealed class

This class represents a mapping between a table name in the data source (SourceTable)
and the table name in the System.Data.DataSet (DataSetTable). The data source table name is
case-sensitive, while the System.Data.DataSet table name isn't. A third property, DataColumn-
MappingCollection, contains all field-name mappings for the table. Column and table name
mappings aren't required (by default, ADO.NET simply uses the data source names),
but they do add that an extra layer of indirection.

Table mappings are applied to the DataAdapter. Table mappings work in both directions:
when filling a table and when updating it. You add a table mapping to a DataAdapter by
inserting the appropriate DataTableMapping into the DataAdapter.TableMappings collection.

```
public sealed class DataTableMapping : MarshalByRefObject , System.Data.ITableMapping, ICloneable {
// Public Constructors
  public DataTableMapping( );
  public DataTableMapping(string sourceTable, string dataSetTable);
  public DataTableMapping(string sourceTable, string dataSetTable, DataColumnMapping[ ] columnMappings);
// Public Instance Properties
  public DataColumnMappingCollection ColumnMappings{get; }
  public string DataSetTable{set; get; }                           // implements System.Data.ITableMapping
  public string SourceTable{set; get; }                            // implements System.Data.ITableMapping
// Public Instance Methods
  public DataColumnMapping GetColumnMappingBySchemaAction(string sourceColumn,
     System.Data.MissingMappingAction mappingAction);
  public DataTable GetDataTableBySchemaAction(System.Data.DataSet dataSet,
     System.Data.MissingSchemaAction schemaAction);
  public override string ToString( );                                        // overrides object
}
```

Hierarchy   System.Object → System.MarshalByRefObject → DataTableMapping(System.Data.
                  ITableMapping, System.ICloneable)

DataTableMappingCollection.{GetByDataSetTable( ), GetTableMappingBySchemaAction( ), this}, RowUpdatedEventArgs.TableMapping, RowUpdatingEventArgs.TableMapping

Passed To   Multiple types

DataTableMappingCollection

marshal by reference

System.Data.Common (system.data.dll)

sealed class

This class contains a collection of DataTableMapping objects for the collection exposed by the DataAdapter.TableMappings property. You can access DataTableMapping by index or data source table name using the indexer. You can also use the GetByDataSetTable( ) to retrieve a DataTableMapping using the System.Data.DataSet name.

```
public sealed class DataTableMappingCollection : MarshalByRefObject , System.Data.ITableMappingCollection, IList,
    ICollection, IEnumerable {
// Public Constructors
  public DataTableMappingCollection( );
// Public Instance Properties
  public int Count{get; }                                                    // implements ICollection
  public DataTableMapping this[string sourceTable]{set; get; }
  public DataTableMapping this[int index]{set; get; }
// Public Static Methods
  public static DataTableMapping GetTableMappingBySchemaAction(DataTableMappingCollection tableMappings,
    string sourceTable, string dataSetTable, System.Data.MissingMappingAction mappingAction);
// Public Instance Methods
  public DataTableMapping Add(string sourceTable, string dataSetTable);
  public int Add( object value);                                             // implements IList
  public void AddRange( DataTableMapping[ ] values);
  public void Clear( );                                                      // implements IList
  public bool Contains( object value);                                       // implements IList
  public bool Contains( string value);           // implements System.Data.ITableMappingCollection
  public void CopyTo( Array array, int index);                               // implements ICollection
  public DataTableMapping GetByDataSetTable(
    string dataSetTable);
  public IEnumerator GetEnumerator( );                                       // implements IEnumerable
  public int IndexOf( object value);                                         // implements IList
  public int IndexOf( string sourceTable);       // implements System.Data.ITableMappingCollection
  public int IndexOfDataSetTable( string dataSetTable);
  public void Insert( int index, object value);                             // implements IList
  public void Remove( object value);                                        // implements IList
  public void RemoveAt( int index);                                        // implements IList
  public void RemoveAt( string sourceTable);    // implements System.Data.ITableMappingCollection
}
```

Hierarchy   System.Object → System.MarshalByRefObject → DataTableMappingCollection(System. Data.ITableMappingCollection, System.Collections.IList, System.Collections.ICollection, System.Collections.IEnumerable)

Returned By   DataAdapter.{CreateTableMappings( ), TableMappings}

DbDataAdapter

marshal by reference, disposable

System.Data.Common (system.data.dll)   abstract class

This class in an intermediate step in the **DataAdapter** hierarchy. Relational database provider-specific **DataAdapter** objects inherit from this class, which extends the **DataAdapter**. Note that this class doesn't implement the **System.Data.IDbDataAdapter** interface. If it did, classes that derive from **DbDataAdapter** would be forced to use weakly typed commands (in other words, allow any **System.Data.IDbCommand** object for properties such as **SelectCommand** instead of provider-specific objects such as **System.Data.SqlClient.SqlCommand**). A more complete description of the inheritance chain is provided in the **DataAdapter** description.

You probably won't ever use the **DbDataAdapter** class directly. If you write generic client-side code that works with any provider-specific object, refer to the **DataAdapter** using the **System.Data.IDbDataAdapter** interface, which includes all important members in one package.

```
public abstract class DbDataAdapter : DataAdapter , ICloneable {
// Protected Constructors
   protected DbDataAdapter( );
   protected DbDataAdapter( DbDataAdapter adapter);
// Public Static Fields
   public const string DefaultSourceTableName;                                             // =Table
// Public Instance Methods
   public override int Fill( System.Data.DataSet dataSet);                        // overrides DataAdapter
   public int Fill(System.Data.DataSet dataSet, int startRecord, int maxRecords, string srcTable);
   public int Fill(System.Data.DataSet dataSet, string srcTable);
   public int Fill( System.Data.DataTable dataTable);
   public override DataTable[ ] FillSchema(System.Data.DataSet dataSet, System.Data.SchemaType schemaType);
                                                                                 // overrides DataAdapter
   public DataTable[ ] FillSchema(System.Data.DataSet dataSet, System.Data.SchemaType schemaType, string srcTable);
   public DataTable FillSchema(System.Data.DataTable dataTable, System.Data.SchemaType schemaType);
   public override IDataParameter[ ] GetFillParameters( );                        // overrides DataAdapter
   public int Update( System.Data.DataRow[ ] dataRows);
   public override int Update( System.Data.DataSet dataSet);                      // overrides DataAdapter
   public int Update(System.Data.DataSet dataSet, string srcTable);
   public int Update( System.Data.DataTable dataTable);
// Protected Instance Methods
   protected abstract RowUpdatedEventArgs CreateRowUpdatedEvent( System.Data.DataRow dataRow,
      System.Data.IDbCommand command, System.Data.StatementType statementType,
      DataTableMapping tableMapping);
   protected abstract RowUpdatingEventArgs CreateRowUpdatingEvent(System.Data.DataRow dataRow,
      System.Data.IDbCommand command, System.Data.StatementType statementType, DataTableMapping tableMapping);
   protected override void Dispose( bool disposing);                             // overrides DataAdapter
   protected virtual int Fill(System.Data.DataSet dataSet, nt startRecord, int maxRecords, string srcTable,
      System.Data.IDbCommand command, System.Data.CommandBehavior behavior); string srcTable,
      System.Data.IDataReader dataReader, int startRecord, int maxRecords);
   protected virtual int Fill(System.Data.DataTable dataTable, System.Data.IDataReader dataReader);
   protected virtual int Fill(System.Data.DataTable dataTable, System.Data.IDbCommand command,
      System.Data.CommandBehavior behavior);
   protected virtual DataTable[ ] FillSchema(System.Data.DataSet dataSet, System.Data.SchemaType schemaType,
      System.Data.IDbCommand command, string srcTable, System.Data.CommandBehavior behavior);
```

494 | Chapter 35: The System.Data.Common Namespace

```
protected virtual DataTable FillSchema(System.Data.DataTable dataTable, System.Data.SchemaType schemaType,
    System.Data.IDbCommand command, System.Data.CommandBehavior behavior);
protected virtual void OnFillError(System.Data.FillErrorEventArgs value);
protected abstract void OnRowUpdated(RowUpdatedEventArgs value);
protected abstract void OnRowUpdating(RowUpdatingEventArgs value);
protected virtual int Update(System.Data.DataRow[ ] dataRows, DataTableMapping tableMapping);
// Events
public event FillErrorEventHandler FillError;
}
```

Hierarchy	System.Object → System.MarshalByRefObject → System.ComponentModel.Compo-nent(System.ComponentModel.IComponent, System.IDisposable) → DataAdapter(System.Data.IDataAdapter) → DbDataAdapter(System.ICloneable)
Subclasses	System.Data.OleDb.OleDbDataAdapter, System.Data.OracleClient.OracleDataAdapter, System.Data.SqlClient.SqlDataAdapter

DBDataPermission   serializable

System.Data.Common (system.data.dll)   abstract class

DBDataPermission represents the security level access to a database. It's an abstract class
(providers derive their own specific permission class), which allows you to ensure that
the current user has required code access security permissions. For example, if you use
the Demand( ) method before attempting to open a connection and the current user lacks
the required security permissions, your code receives a System.Security.SecurityException to be
handled gracefully. If you don't call Demand( ), System.Security.SecurityException is still raised,
but it won't occur until your code attempts the disallowed action.

Remember that this setting pertains only to code access security. It has to do with
authentication. By default, any client running .NET code is allowed to open a connection. However, you can modify code access permissions (for example, denying users
permission to use a connection string with a blank password) using the .NET Framework Configuration Tool.

You can also use the Deny( ) to programmatically revoke the client's ability to access the
data source. This will remain in effect until the current method returns (and will apply
to any methods further down the call stack).

```
public abstract class DBDataPermission : System.Security.CodeAccessPermission , System.Security.Permissions
    IUnrestrictedPermission {
// Public Constructors
public DBDataPermission(System.Security.Permissions.PermissionState state, bool allowBlankPassword);
// Protected Constructors
protected DBDataPermission( );
protected DBDataPermission( DBDataPermission permission);
protected DBDataPermission(DBDataPermissionAttribute permissionAttribute);
protected DBDataPermission(System.Security.Permissions.PermissionState state);
// Public Instance Properties
public bool AllowBlankPassword{set; get; }
// Public Instance Methods
public virtual void Add(string connectionString, string restrictions, System.Data.KeyRestrictionBehavior behavior);
public override IPermission Copy( );                                              // overrides CodeAccessPermission
public override void FromXml(System.Security.SecurityElement securityElement);    // overrides CodeAccessPermission
```

```
public override IPermission Intersect(System.Security.IPermission target);        // overrides CodeAccessPermission
public override bool IsSubsetOf(System.Security.IPermission target);              // overrides CodeAccessPermission
public bool IsUnrestricted( );                                                    // implements IUnrestrictedPermission
public override SecurityElement ToXml( );                                         // overrides CodeAccessPermission
public override IPermission Union(System.Security.IPermission target);            // overrides CodeAccessPermission
// Protected Instance Methods
protected void Clear( );
protected virtual DBDataPermission CreateInstance( );
}
```

Hierarchy	System.Object → System.Security.CodeAccessPermission(System.Security.IPermission, System.Security.ISecurityEncodable, System.Security.IStackWalk) → DBDataPermission(System.Security.Permissions.IUnrestrictedPermission)
Subclasses	System.Data.OleDb.OleDbPermission, System.Data.SqlClient.SqlClientPermission

DBDataPermissionAttribute   serializable

System.Data.Common (system.data.dll)   abstract class

Provider-specific attributes that derive from this class identify custom security attributes for certain actions. This is how it works: by default, .NET code has full access to attempt any actions using managed providers. However, using the .NET Framework Configuration tool (installed to the Administrative Tools group), you can modify these permissions. Currently, there are only two additional restrictions you can impose: denying the right to use blank passwords in a connection string, and restricting the allowed OLE DB drivers that managed OLE DB provider can use. (These settings are translated to specific entries in the *machine.config* file for your computer.) If you use impose these restrictions, you may want to identify an area of your code that requires a certain permission (such as the ability to use a blank password). You identify these areas using an attribute derived from DBDataPermissionAttribute. By identifying these areas, you ensure only one thing: if the required privilege isn't allowed, an exception will be thrown before .NET attempts to run the identified code.

You can apply an attribute derived from DBDataPermissionAttribute to an assembly, class, struct, constructor, or method.

```
public abstract class DBDataPermissionAttribute : System.Security.Permissions.CodeAccessSecurityAttribute {
// Protected Constructors
  protected DBDataPermissionAttribute(System.Security.Permissions.SecurityAction action);
// Public Instance Properties
  public bool AllowBlankPassword{set; get; }
  public string ConnectionString{set; get; }
  public KeyRestrictionBehavior KeyRestrictionBehavior{set; get; }
  public string KeyRestrictions{set; get; }
}
```

Hierarchy	System.Object → System.Attribute → System.Security.Permissions.SecurityAttribute → System.Security.Permissions.CodeAccessSecurityAttribute → DBDataPermissionAttribute
Subclasses	System.Data.OleDb.OleDbPermissionAttribute, System.Data.SqlClient.SqlClientPermissionAttribute

Passed To   DBDataPermission.DBDataPermission( )

Valid On   Assembly, Class, Struct, Constructor, Method

DbDataRecord

System.Data.Common (system.data.dll)   class

This type supports the .NET framework. It provides data binding support for DbEnumerator. You never need to use it directly in your code.

```
public class DbDataRecord : System.Data.IDataRecord, System.ComponentModel.ICustomTypeDescriptor {
// Public Instance Properties
  public int FieldCount{get; }                                    // implements System.Data.IDataRecord
  public object this{get; }                                       // implements System.Data.IDataRecord
  public object this{get; }                                       // implements System.Data.IDataRecord
// Public Instance Methods
  public bool GetBoolean( int i);                                 // implements System.Data.IDataRecord
  public byte GetByte( int i);                                    // implements System.Data.IDataRecord
  public long GetBytes(int i, long dataIndex, byte[ ] buffer,int bufferIndex, int length);
                                                                  // implements System.Data.IDataRecord
  public char GetChar( int i);                                    // implements System.Data.IDataRecord
  public long GetChars(int i, long dataIndex, char[ ] buffer,  int bufferIndex, int length);
                                                                  // implements System.Data.IDataRecord
  public IDataReader GetData( int i);                             // implements System.Data.IDataRecord
  public string GetDataTypeName( int i);                          // implements System.Data.IDataRecord
  public DateTime GetDateTime( int i);                            // implements System.Data.IDataRecord
  public decimal GetDecimal( int i);                              // implements System.Data.IDataRecord
  public double GetDouble( int i);                                // implements System.Data.IDataRecord
  public Type GetFieldType( int i);                               // implements System.Data.IDataRecord
  public float GetFloat( int i);                                  // implements System.Data.IDataRecord
  public Guid GetGuid( int i);                                    // implements System.Data.IDataRecord
  public short GetInt16( int i);                                  // implements System.Data.IDataRecord
  public int GetInt32( int i);                                    // implements System.Data.IDataRecord
  public long GetInt64( int i);                                   // implements System.Data.IDataRecord
  public string GetName( int i);                                  // implements System.Data.IDataRecord
  public int GetOrdinal( string name);                            // implements System.Data.IDataRecord
  public string GetString( int i);                                // implements System.Data.IDataRecord
  public object GetValue( int i);                                 // implements System.Data.IDataRecord
  public int GetValues( object[ ] values);                        // implements System.Data.IDataRecord
  public bool IsDBNull( int i);                                   // implements System.Data.IDataRecord
}
```

DbEnumerator

System.Data.Common (system.data.dll)   class

This type supports the .NET framework. It supports simple iteration over a data provider collection. You never need to use it directly in your code.

```
public class DbEnumerator : IEnumerator {
// Public Constructors
  public DbEnumerator( System.Data.IDataReader reader);
  public DbEnumerator(System.Data.IDataReader reader, bool closeReader);
```

System.Data.
Common

```
// Public Instance Properties
  public object Current{get; }                                                  // implements IEnumerator
// Public Instance Methods
  public bool MoveNext( );                                                      // implements IEnumerator
  public void Reset( );                                                         // implements IEnumerator
}
```

RowUpdatedEventArgs

System.Data.Common (system.data.dll)   abstract class

This System.EventArgs class provides data for event handlers for the RowUpdated event of the DataAdapter. This includes the command that was just completed (Command); any errors that were encountered (Errors); the number of rows that were changed, inserted, or deleted in response to the command (RecordsAffected); the type of SQL statement the command executed (StatementType); and the relevant System.Data.DataRow object (Row). You can set the Status property to System.Data.UpdateStatus.SkipCurrentRow to bypass a row if there was an error. One easy way to determine if an error occurred is simply to check the number of records affected. If this value is 0, the statement did not complete as expected.

Each provider derives a provider-specific version of the RowUpdatedEventArgs class. Although the RowUpdated event is supported by most DataAdapter objects. It isn't part of any interface or either base class (DataAdapter or System.Data.IDbDataAdapter). Hence, you can't attach a generic event handler to this event.

```
public abstract class RowUpdatedEventArgs : EventArgs {
// Protected Constructors
  protected RowUpdatedEventArgs(System.Data.DataRow dataRow, System.Data.IDbCommand command,
     System.Data.StatementType statementType, DataTableMapping tableMapping);
// Public Instance Properties
  public IDbCommand Command{get; }
  public Exception Errors{set; get; }
  public int RecordsAffected{get; }
  public DataRow Row{get; }
  public StatementType StatementType{get; }
  public UpdateStatus Status{set; get; }
  public DataTableMapping TableMapping{get; }
}
```

Hierarchy	System.Object → System.EventArgs → RowUpdatedEventArgs
Subclasses	System.Data.OleDb.OleDbRowUpdatedEventArgs, System.Data.OracleClient.OracleRowUpdatedEventArgs, System.Data.SqlClient.SqlRowUpdatedEventArgs
Returned By	DbDataAdapter.CreateRowUpdatedEvent( )
Passed To	DbDataAdapter.OnRowUpdated( )

RowUpdatingEventArgs

System.Data.Common (system.data.dll)   abstract class

This System.EventArgs class provides data for event handlers that react to the RowUpdating event of the DataAdapter. This includes the command that is about to be executed (Command), the type of SQL statement the command will execute (StatementType), and the relevant System.Data.DataRow object (Row). You can set the Status property to System.Data. UpdateStatus.SkipCurrentRow to bypass a row or System.Data.UpdateStatus.SkipAllRemainingRows to abort the update.

Each provider derives a provider-specific version of the RowUpdatingEventArgs class. Although the RowUpdating event is supported by most DataAdapter objects, it isn't part of any interface or either base class (DataAdapter or System.Data.IDbDataAdapter). Hence, you can't attach a generic event handler.

```
public abstract class RowUpdatingEventArgs : EventArgs {
// Protected Constructors
  protected RowUpdatingEventArgs(System.Data.DataRow dataRow, System.Data.IDbCommand command,
    System.Data.StatementType statementType, DataTableMapping tableMapping);
// Public Instance Properties
  public IDbCommand Command{set; get; }
  public Exception Errors{set; get; }
  public DataRow Row{get; }
  public StatementType StatementType{get; }
  public UpdateStatus Status{set; get; }
  public DataTableMapping TableMapping{get; }
}
```

Hierarchy	System.Object → System.EventArgs → RowUpdatingEventArgs
Subclasses	System.Data.OleDb.OleDbRowUpdatingEventArgs, System.Data.OracleClient.OracleRowUpdatingEventArgs, System.Data.SqlClient.SqlRowUpdatingEventArgs
Returned By	DbDataAdapter.CreateRowUpdatingEvent( )
Passed To	DbDataAdapter.OnRowUpdating( )

36

The System.Data.SqlClient Namespace

The System.Data.SqlClient namespace contains the provider-specific ADO.NET objects used to connect to a SQL Server 7 or SQL Server 2000 database, execute a command, and transfer information to and from a DataSet. The SQL Server .NET provider is optimized for accessing the SQL Server data source protocol; it doesn't use an intermediate OLE DB provider or ODBC driver. The classes in this namespace can also be used with MSDE databases. If you need to connect to a version of SQL Server earlier than 7.0, you need to instead use the .NET OLE DB data provider.

Many types in this namespace implement a common interface from the System.Data namespace or inherit from a class in the System.Data.Common namespace. This ensures a high degree of commonality between these types and those supplied with other ADO.NET data providers. The documentation for this namespace refers to these inherited classes and implemented interfaces where appropriate, and notes any SQL Server-specific functionality. Figure 36-1 and Figure 36-2 show the types in this namespace.

SqlClientPermission serializable

System.Data.SqlClient (system.data.dll) sealed class

With this class, you can ensure that the current process has the required code access security permission to access the SQL Server provider before you attempt to open a connection. If it doesn't, a System.Security.SecurityException will be thrown. You can also use this class to programmatically revoke the permission to access the SQL Server provider for the current method call.

This class pertains only to code access security (the policy of allowed and disallowed actions you have configured using the .NET Framework Configuration Tool or the *caspol.exe* command-line utility). It has nothing to do with the authentication process SQL Server uses. For more information, refer to the reference for the base class System.

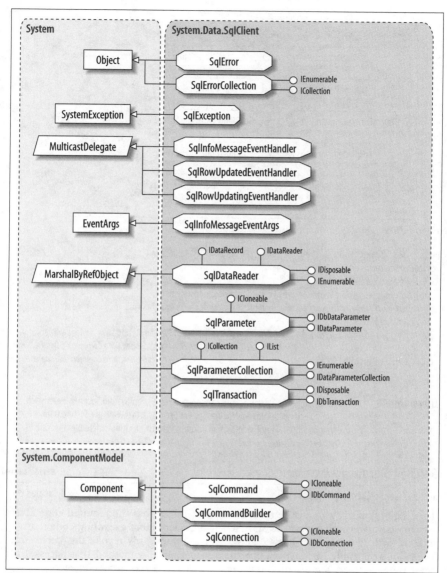

Figure 36-1. The System.Data.SqlClient namespace

Data.Common.DBDataPermission. Currently, the only code access security restriction you can apply to the SQL Server data provider is denying permission to use blank passwords in the connection string.

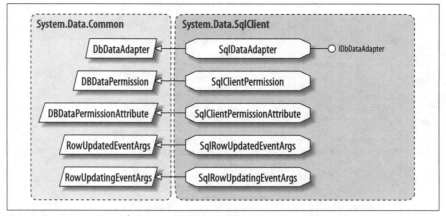

Figure 36-2. More types from System.Data.SqlClient

```
public sealed class SqlClientPermission : System.Data.Common.DBDataPermission {
// Public Constructors
  public SqlClientPermission( );
  public SqlClientPermission(System.Security.Permissions.PermissionState state);
  public SqlClientPermission(System.Security.Permissions.PermissionState state, bool allowBlankPassword);
// Public Instance Methods
  public override void Add(string connectionString, string restrictions, System.Data.KeyRestrictionBehavior behavior);
                                              // overrides System.Data.Common.DBDataPermission
  public override IPermission Copy( );           // overrides System.Data.Common.DBDataPermission
}
```

Hierarchy   System.Object → System.Security.CodeAccessPermission(System.Security.IPermission,
System.Security.ISecurityEncodable, System.Security.IStackWalk) → System.Data.
Common.DBDataPermission(System.Security.Permissions.IUnrestrictedPermission) →
SqlClientPermission

SqlClientPermissionAttribute   serializable

System.Data.SqlClient (system.data.dll)   sealed class

This class allows you to ensure that the current process has the required code access
security permission to access the SQL Server provider before executing code that will
interact with the database. It also allows you to temporarily revoke this permission.
Typically, you apply this attribute to the declaration of a method that accesses the
database or to the definition of a class that contains data access code in every method.
You can also apply the attribute to an assembly, struct, or constructor. The SqlClientPermissionAttribute provides essentially the same functionality as the SqlClientPermission class, but
it allows you to add declarative security code instead of explicit (inline) code.

Note that this attribute pertains only to code access security (the policy of allowed and
disallowed actions you have configured using the .NET Framework Configuration
Tool). It has nothing to do with the authentication process that SQL Server will use.
For more information, refer to the reference for the base class System.Data.Common.
DBDataPermissionAttribute. Currently, the only code access security restriction that you can

apply to the SQL Server managed provider is denying the permission to use blank passwords in the connection string.

```
public sealed class SqlClientPermissionAttribute : System.Data.Common.DBDataPermissionAttribute {
// Public Constructors
   public SqlClientPermissionAttribute(System.Security.Permissions.SecurityAction action);
// Public Instance Methods
   public override IPermission CreatePermission( );              // overrides System.Security.Permissions.SecurityAttribute
}
```

Hierarchy	System.Object → System.Attribute → System.Security.Permissions.SecurityAttribute → System.Security.Permissions.CodeAccessSecurityAttribute → System.Data.Common. DBDataPermissionAttribute → SqlClientPermissionAttribute
Valid On	Assembly, Class, Struct, Constructor, Method

SqlCommand   marshal by reference, disposable

System.Data.SqlClient (system.data.dll)   sealed class

This class represents a Transact-SQL command or stored procedure that can be executed against a SQL Server data source. For information about the basic SqlCommand methods and properties, refer to the reference for the System.Data.IDbCommand interface, which SqlCommand implements. SqlCommand errors result in a SqlException being thrown.

The order of parameters isn't important with the SqlCommand when you create a parameterized query or stored procedure. To create a parameterized query, set CommandType to System.Data.CommandType.Text and name all parameters. For example, you can set the CommandText to:

```
SELECT * FROM Customers WHERE CustomerID = @CustomerID
```

to specify that a CustomerID value will be supplied as a parameter with the name @CustomerID.

The SqlCommand class also adds an ExecuteXmlReader( ) method, which executes a SELECT query that uses the FOR XML clause to return the results in an XML document. You can access the nodes of this document in a forward-only, node-by-node basis using the System.Xml.XmlReader instance that ExecuteXmlReader( ) returns. For more information about the FOR XML clause, refer to Chapter 17 or SQL Server 2000 Books Online.

```
public sealed class SqlCommand : System.ComponentModel.Component , System.Data.IDbCommand, ICloneable {
// Public Constructors
   public SqlCommand( );
   public SqlCommand( string cmdText);
   public SqlCommand(string cmdText, SqlConnection connection);
   public SqlCommand(string cmdText, SqlConnection connection, SqlTransaction transaction);
// Public Instance Properties
   public string CommandText{set; get; }                         // implements System.Data.IDbCommand
   public int CommandTimeout{set; get; }                         // implements System.Data.IDbCommand
   public CommandType CommandType{set; get; }                    // implements System.Data.IDbCommand
   public SqlConnection Connection{set; get; }
   public bool DesignTimeVisible{set; get; }
   public SqlParameterCollection Parameters{get; }
   public SqlTransaction Transaction{set; get; }
   public UpdateRowSource UpdatedRowSource{set; get; }           // implements System.Data.IDbCommand
```

```
// Public Instance Methods
  public void Cancel( );                                                  // implements System.Data.IDbCommand
  public SqlParameter CreateParameter( );
  public int ExecuteNonQuery( );                                          // implements System.Data.IDbCommand
  public SqlDataReader ExecuteReader( );
  public SqlDataReader ExecuteReader(System.Data.CommandBehavior behavior);
  public object ExecuteScalar( );                                         // implements System.Data.IDbCommand
  public XmlReader ExecuteXmlReader( );
  public void Prepare( );                                                 // implements System.Data.IDbCommand
  public void ResetCommandTimeout( );
}
```

Hierarchy	System.Object → System.MarshalByRefObject → System.ComponentModel.Compo-nent(System.ComponentModel.IComponent, System.IDisposable) → SqlCommand(System.Data.IDbCommand, System.ICloneable)
Returned By	SqlCommandBuilder.{GetDeleteCommand( ), GetInsertCommand( ), GetUpdateCom-mand(), SqlConnection.CreateCommand( ), SqlDataAdapter.{DeleteCommand, InsertCommand, SelectCommand, UpdateCommand}, SqlRowUpdatedEventArgs. Command, SqlRowUpdatingEventArgs.Command
Passed To	SqlCommandBuilder.DeriveParameters( ), SqlDataAdapter.{DeleteCommand, InsertCom-mand, SelectCommand, SqlDataAdapter( ), UpdateCommand}, SqlRowUpdatingEventArgs. Command

SqlCommandBuilder
marshal by reference, disposable

System.Data.SqlClient (system.data.dll)   *sealed class*

This class serves two functions. It can automatically retrieve information about the parameters used by a stored procedure (through the DeriveParameters( ) method), and it can automatically generate matching UPDATE, INSERT, and DELETE SQL commands based on a SELECT query. Note that both features, while convenient, suffer from some problems. First of all, the DeriveParameters( ) method requires an extra call to the database. The command-generation methods don't produce optimal SQL syntax: by default they select records by matching every field, not just a single key value; they don't support join queries; and they can't use stored procedures. Chapter 30 explains how to use the SqlCommandBuilder.

Note that if you want to derive update commands, you don't supply the SELECT command directly. Instead, you supply a SqlDataAdapter, either by setting the DataAdapter property or using the constructor that accepts a SqlDataAdapter. The SqlCommandBuilder uses the SqlDataAdapter.SelectCommand property to retrieve the required meta data from the data source. Note that, in order for the commands to be generated, this Select command must return at least one primary key or unique column. If you change the SqlDataAdapter. SelectCommand after the meta data has been retrieved, you should call the RefreshSchema( ) method.

```
public sealed class SqlCommandBuilder : System.ComponentModel.Component {
// Public Constructors
  public SqlCommandBuilder( );
  public SqlCommandBuilder( SqlDataAdapter adapter);
```

Hierarchy   System.Object → System.MarshalByRefObject → System.ComponentModel.Compo-
                     nent(System.ComponentModel.IComponent, System.IDisposable) → SqlCommandBuilder

SqlConnection   **marshal by reference, disposable**

System.Data.SqlClient (system.data.dll)   **sealed class**

This class represents a connection to a SQL Server database, which can be opened (to
execute a SQL command) or closed. For information about the basic SqlConnection
methods and properties, refer to the reference for the System.Data.IDbConnection interface,
which SqlCommand implements. If an error is generated by SQL Server when performing
a operation over a connection, a SqlException is thrown.

In addition, the SqlConnection provides some additional provider-specific read-only properties, such as ServerVersion (a string with the SQL Server version in the format xx.xx.
xxxx), PacketSize (the size in bytes of the network packets used to communicate with
SQL Server), and WorkstationId (a name identifying the client, which defaults to the
computer network name). The PacketSize property can be configured using the Packet Size
connection string setting. You can use a value from 512 to 32767 (the default is 8192).
If your application sends or receives large amounts of text or binary data, a larger
packet size may improve efficiency by requiring less network activity. If applications
send and receive small amounts of information, a smaller packet size (such as 512
bytes) is more efficient. The WorkstationId property can also be set through the connection string as the Workstation ID setting.

The SQL Server provider implements connection pooling automatically, allowing
connections to be reused on the same computer, provided clients use an identical
connection string.

```
public sealed class SqlConnection : System.ComponentModel.Component , System.Data.IDbConnection, ICloneable {
// Public Constructors
  public SqlConnection( );
  public SqlConnection( string connectionString);
// Public Instance Properties
  public string ConnectionString{set; get; }                    // implements System.Data.IDbConnection
  public int ConnectionTimeout{get; }                           // implements System.Data.IDbConnection
  public string Database{get; }                                 // implements System.Data.IDbConnection
  public string DataSource{get; }
  public int PacketSize{get; }
```

```
public string ServerVersion{get; }
public ConnectionState State{get; }                                       // implements System.Data.IDbConnection
public string WorkstationId{get; }
// Public Instance Methods
public SqlTransaction BeginTransaction( );
public SqlTransaction BeginTransaction(System.Data.IsolationLevel iso);
public SqlTransaction BeginTransaction(System.Data.IsolationLevel iso, string transactionName);
public SqlTransaction BeginTransaction(string transactionName);
public void ChangeDatabase( string database);                             // implements System.Data.IDbConnection
public void Close( );                                                     // implements System.Data.IDbConnection
public SqlCommand CreateCommand( );
public void EnlistDistributedTransaction(System.EnterpriseServices.ITransaction transaction);
public void Open( );                                                      // implements System.Data.IDbConnection
// Protected Instance Methods
protected override void Dispose( bool disposing);                         // overrides System.ComponentModel.Component
// Events
public event SqlInfoMessageEventHandler InfoMessage;
public event StateChangeEventHandler StateChange;
}
```

Hierarchy	System.Object → System.MarshalByRefObject → System.ComponentModel.Component(System.ComponentModel.IComponent, System.IDisposable) → SqlConnection(System.Data.IDbConnection, System.ICloneable)
Returned By	SqlCommand.Connection, SqlTransaction.Connection
Passed To	SqlCommand.{Connection, SqlCommand( )}, SqlDataAdapter.SqlDataAdapter( )

SqlDataAdapter   marshal by reference, disposable

System.Data.SqlClient (system.data.dll)   sealed class

This class represents a data adapter that can retrieve information from a SQL Server database to a System.Data.DataSet and update that database with changes made to the DataSet. For information about the basic SqlDataAdapter methods and properties, refer to the reference for the System.Data.IDbDataAdapter and System.Data.IDataAdapter interfaces, which SqlDataAdapter implements.

```
public sealed class SqlDataAdapter : System.Data.Common.DbDataAdapter , System.Data.IDbDataAdapter {
// Public Constructors
public SqlDataAdapter( );
public SqlDataAdapter( SqlCommand selectCommand);
public SqlDataAdapter(string selectCommandText, SqlConnection selectConnection);
public SqlDataAdapter(string selectCommandText, string selectConnectionString);
// Public Instance Properties
public SqlCommand DeleteCommand{set; get; }
public SqlCommand InsertCommand{set; get; }
public SqlCommand SelectCommand{set; get; }
public SqlCommand UpdateCommand{set; get; }
```

// Protected Instance Methods
```
    protected override RowUpdatedEventArgs CreateRowUpdatedEvent(System.Data.DataRow dataRow,
        System.Data.IDbCommand command, System.Data.StatementType statementType,
        System.Data.Common.DataTableMapping tableMapping);          // overrides System.Data.Common.DbDataAdapter
    protected override RowUpdatingEventArgs CreateRowUpdatingEvent(System.Data.DataRow dataRow,
        System.Data. DataRow dataRow, System.Data.IDbCommand command, System.Data.StatementType statementType,
        System.Data.Common.DataTableMapping tableMapping);          // overrides System.Data.Common.DbDataAdapter
    protected override void Dispose( bool disposing);               // overrides System.Data.Common.DbDataAdapter
    protected override void OnRowUpdated( System.Data.Common.RowUpdatedEventArgs value);
                                                                    // overrides System.Data.Common.DbDataAdapter
    protected override void OnRowUpdating(System.Data.Common.RowUpdatingEventArgs value);
                                                                    // overrides System.Data.Common.DbDataAdapter
// Events
    public event SqlRowUpdatedEventHandler RowUpdated;
    public event SqlRowUpdatingEventHandler RowUpdating;
}
```

Hierarchy	System.Object → System.MarshalByRefObject → System.ComponentModel.Component(System.ComponentModel.IComponent, System.IDisposable) → System.Data.Common.DataAdapter(System.Data.IDataAdapter) → System.Data.Common.DbDataAdapter(System.ICloneable) → SqlDataAdapter(System.Data.IDbDataAdapter)
Returned By	SqlCommandBuilder.DataAdapter
Passed To	SqlCommandBuilder.{DataAdapter, SqlCommandBuilder( )}

SqlDataReader   marshal by reference, disposable

System.Data.SqlClient (system.data.dll)   sealed class

This class represents a forward-only, read-only cursor that reads data from a SQL Server database and allows you to access it one record at a time. For information about the basic SqlDataReader methods and properties, refer to the reference for the System.Data.IDataReader and System.Data.IDataRecord interfaces, which SqlDataReader implements. In addition, you'll find that SqlDataReader adds many methods that retrieve data in native SQL Server data types.

```
public sealed class SqlDataReader : MarshalByRefObject , IEnumerable, System.Data.IDataReader, IDisposable, System.Data.
    IDataRecord {
// Public Instance Properties
    public int Depth{get; }                                         // implements System.Data.IDataReader
    public int FieldCount{get; }                                    // implements System.Data.IDataRecord
    public bool HasRows{get; }
    public bool IsClosed{get; }                                     // implements System.Data.IDataReader
    public int RecordsAffected{get; }                               // implements System.Data.IDataReader
    public object this[int i]{get; }                                // implements System.Data.IDataRecord
    public object this[string name]{get; }                          // implements System.Data.IDataRecord
// Public Instance Methods
    public void Close( );                                           // implements System.Data.IDataReader
    public bool GetBoolean( int i);                                 // implements System.Data.IDataRecord
    public byte GetByte( int i);                                    // implements System.Data.IDataRecord
    public long GetBytes(int i, long dataIndex, byte[ ] buffer, int bufferIndex, int length);
                                                                    // implements System.Data.IDataRecord
```

```
public char GetChar( int i);                                              // implements System.Data.IDataRecord
public long GetChars(int i, long dataIndex, char[ ] buffer, int bufferIndex, int length);
                                                                          // implements System.Data.IDataRecord
public IDataReader GetData( int i);                                       // implements System.Data.IDataRecord
public string GetDataTypeName( int i);                                    // implements System.Data.IDataRecord
public DateTime GetDateTime( int i);                                      // implements System.Data.IDataRecord
public decimal GetDecimal( int i);                                        // implements System.Data.IDataRecord
public double GetDouble( int i);                                          // implements System.Data.IDataRecord
public Type GetFieldType( int i);                                         // implements System.Data.IDataRecord
public float GetFloat( int i);                                            // implements System.Data.IDataRecord
public Guid GetGuid( int i);                                              // implements System.Data.IDataRecord
public short GetInt16( int i);                                            // implements System.Data.IDataRecord
public int GetInt32( int i);                                              // implements System.Data.IDataRecord
public long GetInt64( int i);                                             // implements System.Data.IDataRecord
public string GetName( int i);                                            // implements System.Data.IDataRecord
public int GetOrdinal( string name);                                      // implements System.Data.IDataRecord
public DataTable GetSchemaTable( );                                       // implements System.Data.IDataReader
public SqlBinary GetSqlBinary( int i);
public SqlBoolean GetSqlBoolean( int i);
public SqlByte GetSqlByte( int i);
public SqlDateTime GetSqlDateTime( int i);
public SqlDecimal GetSqlDecimal( int i);
public SqlDouble GetSqlDouble( int i);
public SqlGuid GetSqlGuid( int i);
public SqlInt16 GetSqlInt16( int i);
public SqlInt32 GetSqlInt32( int i);
public SqlInt64 GetSqlInt64( int i);
public SqlMoney GetSqlMoney( int i);
public SqlSingle GetSqlSingle( int i);
public SqlString GetSqlString( int i);
public object GetSqlValue( int i);
public int GetSqlValues( object[ ] values);
public string GetString( int i);                                         // implements System.Data.IDataRecord
public object GetValue( int i);                                          // implements System.Data.IDataRecord
public int GetValues( object[ ] values);                                 // implements System.Data.IDataRecord
public bool IsDBNull( int i);                                            // implements System.Data.IDataRecord
public bool NextResult( );                                               // implements System.Data.IDataReader
public bool Read( );                                                     // implements System.Data.IDataReader
}
```

Hierarchy   System.Object → System.MarshalByRefObject → SqlDataReader(System.Collections.IEnu-
                       merable, System.Data.IDataReader, System.IDisposable, System.Data.IDataRecord)

Returned By   SqlCommand.ExecuteReader( )

SqlError   serializable

System.Data.SqlClient (system.data.dll)   sealed class

This class represents one or more data source errors, but it isn't an exception. Instead,
the data source may report multiple errors, and multiple SqlError instances may be added

to a single SqlErrorCollection, which are then accessed using the SqlException.Errors property of the exception that is raised.

SQL Server errors contain information about the command causing the error (Procedure provides the procedure name, and LineNumber indicates which statement failed), the instance of SQL Server where the error occurred (Server), and a descriptive text message (Message). Additional numeric information is provided, such as the error code (State) that can be "translated" using the SQL Server 2000 Books Online, a number that indicates the type of error and maps to an entry in the master.dbo.sysmessages table (Number), and a severity level from 1 to 25 (Class). Messages with a severity level of 10 or less are informational. All errors of level 16 or less are probably generated by the user (for example, invalid input or a miscoded stored procedure) and can be corrected by the user. Severity levels from 17 through 25 indicate software or hardware errors. The SqlConnection remains open if the severity level is 19 or less; if the severity level is 20 or greater, the server usually closes the connection. However, you can reopen the connection and attempt to continue. Severity levels of 20 or above are fatal and usually prevent any work from being accomplished with SQL Server. For information on SQL Server's warning and informational messages, refer to the Troubleshooting section of the SQL Server 2000 Books Online documentation.

```
public sealed class SqlError {
// Public Instance Properties
  public byte Class{get; }
  public int LineNumber{get; }
  public string Message{get; }
  public int Number{get; }
  public string Procedure{get; }
  public string Server{get; }
  public string Source{get; }
  public byte State{get; }
// Public Instance Methods
  public override string ToString( );                                    // overrides object
}
```

Returned By   SqlErrorCollection.this

SqlErrorCollection   serializable

System.Data.SqlClient (system.data.dll)   sealed class

Contains a collection of SqlError instances, which are stored in the collection accessed by the SqlException.Errors property to indicate all the errors that have occurred with the SQL Server provider. This collection always contains at least one SqlError object.

```
public sealed class SqlErrorCollection : ICollection, IEnumerable {
// Public Instance Properties
  public int Count{get; }                                                // implements ICollection
  public SqlError this[int index]{get; }
// Public Instance Methods
  public void CopyTo( Array array, int index);                          // implements ICollection
  public IEnumerator GetEnumerator( );                                  // implements IEnumerable
}
```

SqlException   serializable

System.Data.SqlClient (system.data.dll)   sealed class

This exception represents a data source error. For example, if you attempt to execute a
SQL statement that is syntactically incorrect or try to open a connection to a database
server that can't be found, this exception is thrown. Every SqlException contains at least
one SqlError, identifying the problem, in the SqlErrorCollection object. Errors that happen
while disconnected from the data source (such as violating a System.Data.DataSet constraint
or attempting to access a deleted row) result in a more specific exception from the
System.Data namespace.

```
public sealed class SqlException : SystemException {
// Public Instance Properties
  public byte Class{get; }
  public SqlErrorCollection Errors{get; }
  public int LineNumber{get; }
  public override string Message{get; }                                      // overrides Exception
  public int Number{get; }
  public string Procedure{get; }
  public string Server{get; }
  public override string Source{get; }                                       // overrides Exception
  public byte State{get; }
// Public Instance Methods
  public override void GetObjectData(System.Runtime.Serialization.SerializationInfo si,
    System.Runtime.Serialization.StreamingContext context);                  // overrides Exception
}
```

Hierarchy   System.Object → System.Exception(System.Runtime.Serialization.ISerializable) → System.
SystemException → SqlException

SqlInfoMessageEventArgs

System.Data.SqlClient (system.data.dll)   sealed class

This class provides data to the event handler for the SqlConnection.InfoMessage event. It
provides a collection of warnings or messages in the SqlErrorCollection object as SqlError
instances. In addition, the Message property wraps the SqlError.Message property, and the
Source property wraps the SqlError.Source property.

```
public sealed class SqlInfoMessageEventArgs : EventArgs {
// Public Instance Properties
  public SqlErrorCollection Errors{get; }
  public string Message{get; }
  public string Source{get; }
// Public Instance Methods
  public override string ToString( );                                        // overrides object
}
```

Hierarchy   System.Object → System.EventArgs → SqlInfoMessageEventArgs

SqlInfoMessageEventHandler

serializable

System.Data.SqlClient (system.data.dll)   delegate

This delegate defines the method that will handle the SqlConnection.InfoMessage event. This event fires whenever a message is received from the data source that has a severity of 10 or less (and is thus an informational message, not an error). Messages with higher severities are interpreted as errors and cause a SqlException to be thrown instead.

```
public delegate void SqlInfoMessageEventHandler(object sender, SqlInfoMessageEventArgs e);
```

Associated Events   SqlConnection.InfoMessage( )

SqlParameter

marshal by reference

System.Data.SqlClient (system.data.dll)   sealed class

This class represents a parameter for a stored procedure or parameterized query. For information about the basic SqlParameter members, refer to the reference for the System. Data.IDbDataParameter and System.Data.IDataParameter interfaces, which SqlParameter implements.

In addition, the SqlParameter class adds two members. SqlDbType sets the SQL Server data type of a parameter. When you set SqlDbType, DbType is updated automatically with the most compatible value. The other member is the Offset property, which is used for binary and string types. It returns the offset in bytes for a binary parameter and in characters for a string parameter.

```
public sealed class SqlParameter : MarshalByRefObject , System.Data.IDbDataParameter, System.Data.IDataParameter,
    ICloneable {
// Public Constructors
  public SqlParameter( );
  public SqlParameter( string parameterName, object value);
  public SqlParameter(string parameterName,  System.Data.SqlDbType dbType);
  public SqlParameter(string parameterName, System.Data.SqlDbType dbType, int size);
  public SqlParameter(string parameterName, System.Data.SqlDbType dbType, int size,
      System.Data.ParameterDirection direction, bool isNullable, byte precision, byte scale, string sourceColumn,
      System.Data.DataRowVersion sourceVersion, object value);
  public SqlParameter(string parameterName, System.Data.SqlDbType dbType, int size, string sourceColumn);
  public DbType DbType{set; get; }                                          // implements System.Data.IDataParameter
  public ParameterDirection Direction{set; get; }                           // implements System.Data.IDataParameter
  public bool IsNullable{set; get; }                                        // implements System.Data.IDataParameter
  public int Offset{set; get; }
  public string ParameterName{set; get; }                                   // implements System.Data.IDataParameter
  public byte Precision{set; get; }                                         // implements System.Data.IDbDataParameter
  public byte Scale{set; get; }                                             // implements System.Data.IDbDataParameter
  public int Size{set; get; }                                               // implements System.Data.IDbDataParameter
  public string SourceColumn{set; get; }                                    // implements System.Data.IDataParameter
  public DataRowVersion SourceVersion{set; get; }                           // implements System.Data.IDataParameter
  public SqlDbType SqlDBType{set; get; }
  public object Value{set; get; }                                           // implements System.Data.IDataParameter
```

```
// Public Instance Methods
  public override string ToString( );                                                        // overrides object
}
```

Hierarchy   System.Object → System.MarshalByRefObject → SqlParameter(System.Data.IDbData-
Parameter, System.Data.IDataParameter, System.ICloneable)

Returned By   SqlCommand.CreateParameter( ), SqlParameterCollection.this

Passed To   SqlParameterCollection.{Add( ), this}

SqlParameterCollection   marshal by reference

System.Data.SqlClient (system.data.dll)   sealed class

A collection of SqlParameter objects representing the set of parameters for a stored procedure or parameterized query (and set through the SqlCommand.Parameters property). This
class also provides an overloaded Add( ) method that allows you to create and add a
SqlParameter object to the collection in one step.

```
public sealed class SqlParameterCollection : MarshalByRefObject , System.Data.IDataParameterCollection, IList, ICollection,
    IEnumerable {
// Public Instance Properties
  public int Count{get; }                                                            // implements ICollection
  public SqlParameter this[string parameter]{set; get; }
  public SqlParameter this[int index]{set; get; }
// Public Instance Methods
  public int Add( object value);                                                        // implements IList
  public SqlParameter Add( SqlParameter value);
  public SqlParameter Add(string parameterName, object value);
  public SqlParameter Add(string parameterName, System.Data.SqlDbType sqlDbType);
  public SqlParameter Add(string parameterName, System.Data.SqlDbType sqlDbType, int size);
  public SqlParameter Add(string parameterName,  System.Data.SqlDbType sqlDbType, int size, string sourceColumn);
  public void Clear( );                                                                 // implements IList
  public bool Contains( object value);                                                  // implements IList
  public bool Contains( string value);                              // implements System.Data.IDataParameterCollection
  public void CopyTo( Array array, int index);                                         // implements ICollection
  public IEnumerator GetEnumerator( );                                               // implements IEnumerable
  public int IndexOf( object value);                                                    // implements IList
  public int IndexOf( string parameterName);                        // implements System.Data.IDataParameterCollection
  public void Insert( int index, object value);                                         // implements IList
  public void Remove( object value);                                                    // implements IList
  public void RemoveAt( int index);                                                     // implements IList
  public void RemoveAt( string parameterName);                      // implements System.Data.IDataParameterCollection
}
```

Hierarchy   System.Object → System.MarshalByRefObject → SqlParameterCollection(System.Data.
IDataParameterCollection, System.Collections.IList, System.Collections.ICollection, System.
Collections.IEnumerable)

Returned By   SqlCommand.Parameters

SqlRowUpdatedEventArgs

sealed class

This System.EventArgs class provides data for the SqlDataAdapter.RowUpdated event. For more information, refer to the abstract base class System.Data.Common.RowUpdatedEventArgs, which defines all members.

```
public sealed class SqlRowUpdatedEventArgs : System.Data.Common.RowUpdatedEventArgs {
// Public Constructors
    public SqlRowUpdatedEventArgs(System.Data.DataRow row, System.Data.IDbCommand command,
        System.Data.StatementType statementType, System.Data.Common.DataTableMapping tableMapping);
// Public Instance Properties
    public SqlCommand Command{get; }
}
```

Hierarchy   System.Object → System.EventArgs → System.Data.Common.RowUpdatedEventArgs → SqlRowUpdatedEventArgs

Passed To   SqlRowUpdatedEventHandler.{BeginInvoke( ), Invoke( )}

SqlRowUpdatedEventHandler   serializable

System.Data.SqlClient (system.data.dll)   delegate

This delegate defines the method that handles the System.Data.Common.RowUpdatingEventArgs event. This event occurs for each row that must be deleted, inserted, or modified when you use the SqlDataAdapter.Update( ) method, after the change has been attempted. This event provides information about whether the command succeeded or encountered an error.

```
public delegate void SqlRowUpdatedEventHandler(
    object sender, SqlRowUpdatedEventArgs e);
```

Associated Events   SqlDataAdapter.RowUpdated( )

SqlRowUpdatingEventArgs

System.Data.SqlClient (system.data.dll)   sealed class

This System.EventArgs class provides data for the SqlDataAdapter.RowUpdating event. For more information, refer to the abstract base class System.Data.Common.RowUpdatingEventArgs, which defines all members.

```
public sealed class SqlRowUpdatingEventArgs : System.Data.Common.RowUpdatingEventArgs {
// Public Constructors
    public SqlRowUpdatingEventArgs(System.Data.DataRow row, System.Data.IDbCommand command,
        System.Data.StatementType statementType, System.Data.Common.DataTableMapping tableMapping);
// Public Instance Properties
    public SqlCommand Command{set; get; }
}
```

Hierarchy   System.Object → System.EventArgs → System.Data.Common.RowUpdatingEventArgs → SqlRowUpdatingEventArgs

SqlRowUpdatingEventHandler   serializable

System.Data.SqlClient (system.data.dll)   delegate

This delegate defines the method that handles the System.Data.Common.RowUpdatingEventArgs event. This event occurs for each row that must be deleted, inserted, or modified when you use the SqlDataAdapter.Update( ) method before the change occurs.

```
public delegate void SqlRowUpdatingEventHandler(object sender, SqlRowUpdatingEventArgs e);
```

Associated Events   SqlDataAdapter.RowUpdating( )

SqlTransaction   marshal by reference, disposable

System.Data.SqlClient (system.data.dll)   sealed class

This class encapsulates a client-initiated database transaction. You can start a transaction, provided you have an open connection, by calling the SqlConnection.BeginTransaction( ) method, which returns a SqlTransaction object. The SqlTransaction class implements the System.Data.IDbTransaction interface, and its members are described in that section of the reference.

You can also use the Save( ) method to create a savepoint, which is similar to a nested transaction. (This method is equivalent to Transact-SQL SAVE TRANSACTION statement.) You must supply a string that names the savepoint. You can then roll back the transaction to an intermediate point using the overloaded version of the Rollback( ) method that accepts the savepoint name. Savepoints are useful when you want to be able to roll back part of the transaction without canceling the entire transaction.

```
public sealed class SqlTransaction : MarshalByRefObject , System.Data.IDbTransaction, IDisposable {
// Public Instance Properties
  public SqlConnection Connection{get; }
  public IsolationLevel IsolationLevel{get; }                      // implements System.Data.IDbTransaction
// Public Instance Methods
  public void Commit( );                                           // implements System.Data.IDbTransaction
  public void Dispose( );                                          // implements IDisposable
  public void Rollback( );                                         // implements System.Data.IDbTransaction
  public void Rollback( string transactionName);
  public void Save( string savePointName);
}
```

Hierarchy   System.Object → System.MarshalByRefObject → SqlTransaction(System.Data.IDbTransaction, System.IDisposable)

Returned By   SqlCommand.Transaction, SqlConnection.BeginTransaction( )

Passed To   SqlCommand.{SqlCommand( ), Transaction}

37

The System.Data.OleDb Namespace

The System.Data.OleDb namespace contains the provider-specific ADO.NET classes used to connect to an OLE DB data source, execute a command, and transfer data to and from a System.Data.DataSet. The OLE DB provider uses COM interop to access the OLE DB interfaces, so performance will not equal a native provider optimized for a specific data source. Most OLE DB providers are supported, including the OLE DB provider for SQL Server (SQLOLEDB) (which is required if you are using SQL Server 6.5 or earlier), the OLE DB provider for Oracle (MSDAORA), and the OLE DB provider for Microsoft Access (Microsoft.Jet.OLEDB.4.0). The OLE DB provider for ODBC (MSDASQL) isn't supported; you have to use the ODBC .NET provider instead. The OLE DB provider for Exchange (ExOLEDB), Internet Publishing (MSDAIPP), and any other provider that uses OLE DB Version 2.5 interfaces isn't supported. The MSDN framework lists the specific COM interfaces an OLE DB provider must support to be available through the OLE DB data provider.

Many of the types in this namespace implement an interface from the System.Data namespace or inherit from a class in the System.Data.Common namespace. This ensures a high degree of commonality between these types and those supplied with other ADO.NET data providers. The documentation on this namespace refers to these inherited classes and implemented interfaces where appropriate, and notes any OLE DB-specific functionality. Figures 37-1 and 37-2 show the types in this namespace.

OleDbCommand

marshal by reference, disposable

System.Data.OleDb (system.data.dll)

sealed class

This class represents a SQL command that can be executed against a data source through the .NET OLE DB provider. For information about the basic OleDbCommand methods and properties, refer to the reference for the System.Data.IDbCommand interface, which OleDbCommand implements. OleDbCommand errors result in a OleDbException being thrown.

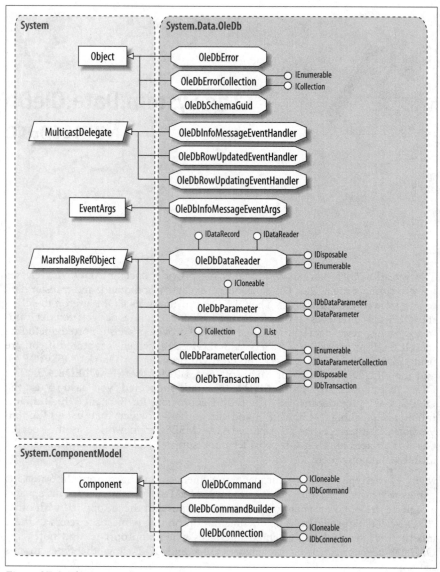

Figure 37-1. The System.Data.OleDb namespace

When `CommandType` is set to `System.Data.CommandType.Text`, named parameters aren't supported. This differs from the SQL Server provider. In this case, you must use a question mark (?) placeholder for parameters in the SQL statement. For example, you can set the `CommandType` to `System.Data.CommandType.Text`, and set the `CommandText` to:

```
SELECT * FROM Customers WHERE CustomerID = ?
```

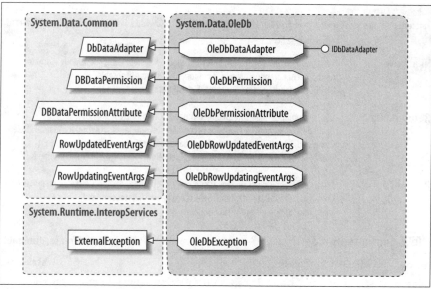

Figure 37-2. More types from System.Data.OleDb

to specify that a CustomerID value will be supplied as a parameter. If there is more than one parameter, the order in which you insert the OleDbParameter to the Parameters collection must match the order of the placeholders.

```
public sealed class OleDbCommand : System.ComponentModel.Component , ICloneable, System.Data.IDbCommand {
// Public Constructors
   public OleDbCommand( );
   public OleDbCommand( string cmdText);
   public OleDbCommand(string cmdText, OleDbConnection connection);
   public OleDbCommand(string cmdText, OleDbConnection connection, OleDbTransaction transaction);
// Public Instance Properties
   public string CommandText{set; get; }                              // implements System.Data.IDbCommand
   public int CommandTimeout{set; get; }                              // implements System.Data.IDbCommand
   public CommandType CommandType{set; get; }                         // implements System.Data.IDbCommand
   public OleDbConnection Connection{set; get; }
   public bool DesignTimeVisible{set; get; }
   public OleDbParameterCollection Parameters{get; }
   public OleDbTransaction Transaction{set; get; }
   public UpdateRowSource UpdatedRowSource{set; get; }                // implements System.Data.IDbCommand
// Public Instance Methods
   public void Cancel( );                                             // implements System.Data.IDbCommand
   public OleDbParameter CreateParameter( );
   public int ExecuteNonQuery( );                                     // implements System.Data.IDbCommand
   public OleDbDataReader ExecuteReader( );
   public OleDbDataReader ExecuteReader(System.Data.CommandBehavior behavior);
   public object ExecuteScalar( );                                    // implements System.Data.IDbCommand
   public void Prepare( );                                            // implements System.Data.IDbCommand
   public void ResetCommandTimeout( );
```

  protected override void **Dispose**(bool *disposing*);   // overrides System.ComponentModel.Component
}

Hierarchy	System.Object → System.MarshalByRefObject → System.ComponentModel.Component(System.ComponentModel.IComponent, System.IDisposable) → OleDbCommand(System.ICloneable, System.Data.IDbCommand)
Returned By	OleDbCommandBuilder.{GetDeleteCommand( ), GetInsertCommand( ), GetUpdateCommand( )}, OleDbConnection.CreateCommand( ), OleDbDataAdapter.{DeleteCommand, InsertCommand, SelectCommand, UpdateCommand}, OleDbRowUpdatedEventArgs.Command, OleDbRowUpdatingEventArgs.Command
Passed To	OleDbCommandBuilder.DeriveParameters( ), OleDbDataAdapter.{DeleteCommand, InsertCommand, OleDbDataAdapter( ), SelectCommand, UpdateCommand}, OleDbRowUpdatingEventArgs.Command

OleDbCommandBuilder
                                                   marshal by reference, disposable

System.Data.OleDb (system.data.dll)   **sealed class**

This class serves two functions. It can automatically retrieve information about the parameters used by a stored procedure (through the DeriveParameters( ) method), and it can automatically generate matching UPDATE, INSERT, and DELETE SQL commands based on a SELECT query. Note that both features, while convenient, suffer from some problems. First of all, the DeriveParameters( ) method requires an extra call to the database. The command-generation methods don't produce optimal SQL syntax. For example, by default they select records by matching every field, not just a single key value; they don't support join queries; and they can't use stored procedures.

Note that if you want to derive update commands, you don't supply the SELECT command directly. Instead, you supply a OleDbDataAdapter, either by setting the DataAdapter property or using the constructor that accepts a OleDbDataAdapter. The OleDbCommandBuilder uses the OleDbDataAdapter.SelectCommand property to retrieve the required meta data from the data source. Note that the SELECT command must return at least one primary key or unique column to generate the commands. If you change the OleDbDataAdapter.SelectCommand after the meta data has been retrieved, you should call the RefreshSchema( ) method.

```
public sealed class OleDbCommandBuilder : System.ComponentModel.Component {
// Public Constructors
  public OleDbCommandBuilder( );
  public OleDbCommandBuilder( OleDbDataAdapter adapter);
// Public Instance Properties
  public OleDbDataAdapter DataAdapter{set; get; }
  public string QuotePrefix{set; get; }
  public string QuoteSuffix{set; get; }
// Public Static Methods
  public static void DeriveParameters(OleDbCommand command);
// Public Instance Methods
  public OleDbCommand GetDeleteCommand( );
  public OleDbCommand GetInsertCommand( );
  public OleDbCommand GetUpdateCommand( );
  public void RefreshSchema( );
```

```
// Protected Instance Methods
  protected override void Dispose( bool disposing);                          // overrides System.ComponentModel.Component
}
```

Hierarchy   System.Object → System.MarshalByRefObject → System.ComponentModel.Compo-
                      nent(System.ComponentModel.IComponent, System.IDisposable) →
                      OleDbCommandBuilder

OleDbConnection   marshal by reference, disposable

System.Data.OleDb (system.data.dll)   sealed class

This class represents a connection to an OLE DB data source, which can be opened (in
order to execute a SQL command) or closed. For information about the basic OleDbConnection methods and properties, refer to the reference for the System.Data.IDbConnection
interface, which OleDbCommand implements. If an error is generated by the data source
when performing an operation over a connection, an OleDbException is thrown.

In addition, the OleDbConnection provides some additional provider-specific read-only
properties, such as Provider (the name of the provider, as in MSDASQL), and ServerVersion
(a string with the data source version in the format xx.xx.xxxx). The version maps to
the OLE DB DBPROP_DBMSVER property. If this isn't supported by the underlying OLE
DB provider, an empty string is returned.

The OLE DB provider implements connection pooling through COM+, which allow
connections to be reused on the same computer, provided clients use an identical
connection string.

```
public sealed class OleDbConnection : System.ComponentModel.Component , ICloneable, System.Data.IDbConnection {
// Public Constructors
  public OleDbConnection( );
  public OleDbConnection( string connectionString);
// Public Instance Properties
  public string ConnectionString{set; get; }                                // implements System.Data.IDbConnection
  public int ConnectionTimeout{get; }                                       // implements System.Data.IDbConnection
  public string Database{get; }                                             // implements System.Data.IDbConnection
  public string DataSource{get; }
  public string Provider{get; }
  public string ServerVersion{get; }
  public ConnectionState State{get; }                                       // implements System.Data.IDbConnection
// Public Static Methods
  public static void ReleaseObjectPool( );
// Public Instance Methods
  public OleDbTransaction BeginTransaction( );
  public OleDbTransaction BeginTransaction(System.Data.IsolationLevel isolationLevel);
  public void ChangeDatabase( string value);                                // implements System.Data.IDbConnection
  public void Close( );                                                     // implements System.Data.IDbConnection
  public OleDbCommand CreateCommand( );
  public void EnlistDistributedTransaction(System.EnterpriseServices.ITransaction transaction);
  public DataTable GetOleDbSchemaTable(Guid schema, object[ ] restrictions);
  public void Open( );                                                      // implements System.Data.IDbConnection
// Protected Instance Methods
  protected override void Dispose( bool disposing);                         // overrides System.ComponentModel.Component
```

```
// Events
  public event OleDbInfoMessageEventHandler InfoMessage;
  public event StateChangeEventHandler StateChange;
}
```

Hierarchy	System.Object → System.MarshalByRefObject → System.ComponentModel.Compo-nent(System.ComponentModel.IComponent, System.IDisposable) → OleDbConnection(System.ICloneable, System.Data.IDbConnection)
Returned By	OleDbCommand.Connection, OleDbTransaction.Connection
Passed To	OleDbCommand.{Connection, OleDbCommand( )}, OleDbDataAdapter.OleDbDataAdapter( )

OleDbDataAdapter   marshal by reference, disposable

System.Data.OleDb (system.data.dll)   sealed class

This class represents a data adapter that can transfer information from an OLE DB data source to a System.Data.DataSet and update a data source with changes made to the DataSet. For information about the basic OleDbDataAdapter methods and properties, refer to the reference for the System.Data.IDbDataAdapter and System.Data.IDataAdapter interfaces, which OleDbDataAdapter implements.

```
public sealed class OleDbDataAdapter : System.Data.Common.DbDataAdapter , System.Data.IDbDataAdapter {
// Public Constructors
  public OleDbDataAdapter( );
  public OleDbDataAdapter( OleDbCommand selectCommand);
  public OleDbDataAdapter(string selectCommandText, OleDbConnection selectConnection);
  public OleDbDataAdapter(string selectCommandText, string selectConnectionString);
// Public Instance Properties
  public OleDbCommand DeleteCommand{set; get; }
  public OleDbCommand InsertCommand{set; get; }
  public OleDbCommand SelectCommand{set; get; }
  public OleDbCommand UpdateCommand{set; get; }
// Public Instance Methods
  public int Fill(System.Data.DataSet dataSet, object ADODBRecordSet, string srcTable);
  public int Fill(System.Data.DataTable dataTable, object ADODBRecordSet);
// Protected Instance Methods
  protected override RowUpdatedEventArgs CreateRowUpdatedEvent(System.Data.DataRow dataRow,
    System.Data.IDbCommand command, System.Data.StatementType statementType,
    System.Data.Common. DataTableMapping tableMapping);          // overrides System.Data.Common.DbDataAdapter
  protected override RowUpdatingEventArgs CreateRowUpdatingEvent(System.Data.DataRow dataRow,
    System.Data.DataRow dataRow, System.Data.IDbCommand command, System.Data.StatementType statementType,
    System.Data.Common.DataTableMapping tableMapping);           // overrides System.Data.Common.DbDataAdapter
  protected override void Dispose( bool disposing);              // overrides System.Data.Common.DbDataAdapter
  protected override void OnRowUpdated(
    System.Data.Common.RowUpdatedEventArgs value);               // overrides System.Data.Common.DbDataAdapter
  protected override void OnRowUpdating(                          // overrides System.Data.Common.DbDataAdapter
    System.Data.Common.RowUpdatingEventArgs value);
// Events
  public event OleDbRowUpdatedEventHandler RowUpdated;
```

```
public event OleDbRowUpdatingEventHandler RowUpdating;
}
```

Hierarchy   System.Object → System.MarshalByRefObject → System.ComponentModel.Compo-
nent(System.ComponentModel.IComponent, System.IDisposable) → System.Data.
Common.DataAdapter(System.Data.IDataAdapter) → System.Data.Common.DbData-
Adapter(System.ICloneable) → OleDbDataAdapter(System.Data.IDbDataAdapter)

Returned By   OleDbCommandBuilder.DataAdapter

Passed To   OleDbCommandBuilder.{DataAdapter, OleDbCommandBuilder( )}

OleDbDataReader
marshal by reference, disposable

System.Data.OleDb (system.data.dll)
sealed class

This class represents a forward-only, read-only cursor that reads data from an OLE DB
data source and allows you to access it one record at a time. For information about the
basic OleDbDataReader methods and properties, refer to the reference for the System.Data.
IDataReader and System.Data.IDataRecord interfaces, which OleDbDataReader implements.

```
public sealed class OleDbDataReader : MarshalByRefObject , System.Data.IDataReader, IDisposable, System.Data.
    IDataRecord, IEnumerable {
// Public Instance Properties
  public int Depth{get; }                                              // implements System.Data.IDataReader
  public int FieldCount{get; }                                         // implements System.Data.IDataRecord
  public bool HasRows{get; }
  public bool IsClosed{get; }                                          // implements System.Data.IDataReader
  public int RecordsAffected{get; }                                    // implements System.Data.IDataReader
  public object this[string name]{get; }                               // implements System.Data.IDataRecord
  public object this[int index]{get; }                                 // implements System.Data.IDataRecord
// Public Instance Methods
  public void Close( );                                                // implements System.Data.IDataReader
  public bool GetBoolean( int ordinal);                               // implements System.Data.IDataRecord
  public byte GetByte( int ordinal);                                   // implements System.Data.IDataRecord
  public long GetBytes(int ordinal, long dataIndex, byte[ ] buffer, int bufferIndex, int length);
                                                                       // implements System.Data.IDataRecord
  public char GetChar( int ordinal);                                   // implements System.Data.IDataRecord
  public long GetChars(int ordinal, long dataIndex, char[ ] buffer, int bufferIndex, int length);
                                                                       // implements System.Data.IDataRecord
  public OleDbDataReader GetData( int ordinal);
  public string GetDataTypeName( int index);                          // implements System.Data.IDataRecord
  public DateTime GetDateTime( int ordinal);                          // implements System.Data.IDataRecord
  public decimal GetDecimal( int ordinal);                            // implements System.Data.IDataRecord
  public double GetDouble( int ordinal);                              // implements System.Data.IDataRecord
  public Type GetFieldType( int index);                               // implements System.Data.IDataRecord
  public float GetFloat( int ordinal);                                // implements System.Data.IDataRecord
  public Guid GetGuid( int ordinal);                                  // implements System.Data.IDataRecord
  public short GetInt16( int ordinal);                                // implements System.Data.IDataRecord
  public int GetInt32( int ordinal);                                  // implements System.Data.IDataRecord
  public long GetInt64( int ordinal);                                 // implements System.Data.IDataRecord
  public string GetName( int index);                                  // implements System.Data.IDataRecord
```

public int **GetOrdinal**(string *name*);	// implements System.Data.IDataRecord
public DataTable **GetSchemaTable**( );	// implements System.Data.IDataReader
public string **GetString**(int *ordinal*);	// implements System.Data.IDataRecord
public TimeSpan **GetTimeSpan**(int *ordinal*);	
public object **GetValue**(int *ordinal*);	// implements System.Data.IDataRecord
public int **GetValues**(object[ ] *values*);	// implements System.Data.IDataRecord
public bool **IsDBNull**(int *ordinal*);	// implements System.Data.IDataRecord
public bool **NextResult**( );	// implements System.Data.IDataReader
public bool **Read**( );	// implements System.Data.IDataReader
// Protected Instance Methods	
protected override void **Finalize**( );	// overrides object
}	

Hierarchy   System.Object → System.MarshalByRefObject → OleDbDataReader(System.Data.
IDataReader, System.IDisposable, System.Data.IDataRecord, System.Collections.
IEnumerable)

Returned By   OleDbCommand.ExecuteReader( )

OleDbError   serializable

System.Data.OleDb (system.data.dll)   sealed class

This class represents one or more data source errors, but it isn't an exception. Instead,
the data source may report multiple errors, and multiple OleDbError instances may be
added to a single OleDbErrorCollection, which are then accessed using the OleDbException.Errors
property of the exception that is raised.

OLE DB errors contain information including a database-specific error code (NativeError),
a five-character code following the ANSI SQL standard (SQLState), and a descriptive text
message (Message).

public sealed class **OleDbError** {	
// Public Instance Properties	
public string **Message**{get; }	
public int **NativeError**{get; }	
public string **Source**{get; }	
public string **SQLState**{get; }	
// Public Instance Methods	
public override string **ToString**( );	// overrides object
}	

Returned By   OleDbErrorCollection.this

OleDbErrorCollection   serializable

System.Data.OleDb (system.data.dll)   sealed class

Contains a collection of OleDbError instances, which is used by the OleDbException.Errors property to indicate all errors that have occurred while using the OLE DB data provider.
This collection always contains at least one OleDbError object.

```
public sealed class OleDbErrorCollection : ICollection, IEnumerable {
// Public Instance Properties
  public int Count{get; }                                                    // implements ICollection
  public OleDbError this[int index]{get; }
// Public Instance Methods
  public void CopyTo( Array array, int index);                               // implements ICollection
  public IEnumerator GetEnumerator( );                                       // implements IEnumerable
}
```

Returned By   OleDbException.Errors, OleDbInfoMessageEventArgs.Errors

OleDbException   serializable

System.Data.OleDb (system.data.dll)   sealed class

This exception represents a data source error. For example, if you attempt to execute a
SQL statement that is syntactically incorrect or open a connection to a database server
that can't be found, this exception is thrown. Every OleDbException contains at least one
OleDbError object with data about the problem in the OleDbErrorCollection object. Errors that
happen while disconnected from the data source (such as violating a System.Data.DataSet
constraint or attempting to access a deleted row) result in a more specific exception
from the System.Data namespace.

```
public sealed class OleDbException : System.Runtime.InteropServices.ExternalException {
// Public Instance Properties
  public override int ErrorCode{get; }               // overrides System.Runtime.InteropServices.ExternalException
  public OleDbErrorCollection Errors{get; }
  public override string Message{get; }                                      // overrides Exception
  public override string Source{get; }                                       // overrides Exception
// Public Instance Methods
  public override void GetObjectData(System.Runtime.Serialization.SerializationInfo si,
    System.Runtime.Serialization.StreamingContext context);                  // overrides Exception
}
```

Hierarchy   System.Object → System.Exception(System.Runtime.Serialization.ISerializable) → System.
                    SystemException → System.Runtime.InteropServices.ExternalException → OleDbException

OleDbInfoMessageEventArgs

System.Data.OleDb (system.data.dll)   sealed class

This class provides data to the event handler for the OleDbConnection.InfoMessage event. It
also provides a collection of messages in the OleDbErrorCollection object as OleDbError
instances. The Message property wraps the OleDbError.Message property, and the Source property wraps the OleDbError.Source property.

```
public sealed class OleDbInfoMessageEventArgs : EventArgs {
// Public Instance Properties
  public int ErrorCode{get; }
  public OleDbErrorCollection Errors{get; }
  public string Message{get; }
  public string Source{get; }
```

```
// Public Instance Methods
  public override string ToString( );                                                    // overrides object
}
```

Hierarchy   System.Object → System.EventArgs → OleDbInfoMessageEventArgs

Passed To   OleDbInfoMessageEventHandler.{BeginInvoke( ), Invoke( )}

OleDbInfoMessageEventHandler   serializable

System.Data.OleDb (system.data.dll)   delegate

This delegate represents the method that will be used to handle the InfoMessage event of
an OleDbConnection.

```
public delegate void OleDbInfoMessageEventHandler(object sender, OleDbInfoMessageEventArgs e);
```

Associated Events   OleDbConnection.InfoMessage( )

OleDbParameter   marshal by reference

System.Data.OleDb (system.data.dll)   sealed class

This class represents a parameter for a stored procedure or parameterized query. For
information about the basic OleDbParameter members, refer to the reference for the System.
Data.IDbDataParameter and System.Data.IDataParameter interfaces, which OleDbParameter
implements.

In addition, the OleDbParameter class adds a new property: OleDbType. This property sets the
OLE DB data type of a parameter. You should always set this value (explicitly, or
through one of the constructors) rather than the more general DbType. When you set
OleDbType, DbType is updated automatically with the most compatible System.Data.DbType
value.

```
public sealed class OleDbParameter : MarshalByRefObject , System.Data.IDbDataParameter, System.Data.IDataParameter,
    ICloneable {
// Public Constructors
  public OleDbParameter( );
  public OleDbParameter( string name, object value);
  public OleDbParameter( string name, OleDbType dataType);
  public OleDbParameter(string name, OleDbType dataType, int size);
  public OleDbParameter(string parameterName, OleDbType dbType, int size, System.Data.ParameterDirection direction,
      bool isNullable, byte precision, byte scale, string srcColumn, System.Data.DataRowVersion srcVersion, object value);
  public OleDbParameter(string name, OleDbType dataType, int size, string srcColumn);
// Public Instance Properties
  public DbType DbType{set; get; }                                      // implements System.Data.IDataParameter
  public ParameterDirection Direction{set; get; }                       // implements System.Data.IDataParameter
  public bool IsNullable{set; get; }                                    // implements System.Data.IDataParameter
  public OleDbType OleDbType{set; get; }
  public string ParameterName{set; get; }                               // implements System.Data.IDataParameter
  public byte Precision{set; get; }                                     // implements System.Data.IDbDataParameter
  public byte Scale{set; get; }                                         // implements System.Data.IDbDataParameter
```

public int **Size**{set; get; }	// implements System.Data.IDbDataParameter
public string **SourceColumn**{set; get; }	// implements System.Data.IDataParameter
public DataRowVersion **SourceVersion**{set; get; }	// implements System.Data.IDataParameter
public object **Value**{set; get; }	// implements System.Data.IDataParameter

// Public Instance Methods

public override string **ToString**( );	// overrides object

}

Hierarchy   System.Object → System.MarshalByRefObject → OleDbParameter(System.Data.IDbData-
Parameter, System.Data.IDataParameter, System.ICloneable)

Returned By   OleDbCommand.CreateParameter( ), OleDbParameterCollection.this

Passed To   OleDbParameterCollection.{Add( ), this}

OleDbParameterCollection   marshal by reference

System.Data.OleDb (system.data.dll)   sealed class

Represents a collection of OleDbParameter objects that are used with a single stored procedure or parameterized query and are added to the collection accessed using
OleDbCommand.Parameters. You can retrieve an individual OleDbCommand object by its index or
by its parameter name. This class also provides an overloaded Add( ) method that lets
you create and add an OleDbParameter object to the collection in one step.

```
public sealed class OleDbParameterCollection : MarshalByRefObject , System.Data.IDataParameterCollection, IList,
    ICollection, IEnumerable {
```

// Public Instance Properties

public int **Count**{get; }	// implements ICollection
public OleDbParameter **this**[string *parameterName*]{set; get; }	
public OleDbParameter **this**[int *index*]{set; get; }	

// Public Instance Methods

public int **Add**(object *value*);	// implements IList
public OleDbParameter **Add**(OleDbParameter *value*);	
public OleDbParameter **Add**(string *parameterName*, object *value*);	
public OleDbParameter **Add**(string *parameterName*, OleDbType *oleDbType*);	
public OleDbParameter **Add**(string *parameterName*, OleDbType *oleDbType*, int *size*);	
public OleDbParameter **Add**(string *parameterName*, OleDbType *oleDbType*, int *size*, string *sourceColumn*);	
public void **Clear**( );	// implements IList
public bool **Contains**(object *value*);	// implements IList
public bool **Contains**(string *value*);	// implements System.Data.IDataParameterCollection
public void **CopyTo**(Array *array*, int *index*);	// implements ICollection
public IEnumerator **GetEnumerator**( );	// implements IEnumerable
public int **IndexOf**(object *value*);	// implements IList
public int **IndexOf**(string *parameterName*);	// implements System.Data.IDataParameterCollection
public void **Insert**(int *index*, object *value*);	// implements IList
public void **Remove**(object *value*);	// implements IList
public void **RemoveAt**(int *index*);	// implements IList
public void **RemoveAt**(string *parameterName*);	// implements System.Data.IDataParameterCollection

}

Hierarchy	System.Object → System.MarshalByRefObject → OleDbParameterCollection(System.Data. IDataParameterCollection, System.Collections.IList, System.Collections.ICollection, System. Collections.IEnumerable)
Returned By	OleDbCommand.Parameters

OleDbPermission   serializable

System.Data.OleDb (system.data.dll)   sealed class

With this class, you can ensure that the current process has the required security level to access the OLE DB .NET provider before you attempt to open a connection. If it doesn't, a System.Security.SecurityException will be thrown. You can also use this class to programmatically revoke the permission to access the OLE DB .NET provider for the current method call.

Note that this class pertains only to code access security (the policy of allowed and disallowed actions you have configured using the .NET Framework Configuration Tool or the *caspol.exe* command-line utility). For more information, refer to the reference for the base class System.Data.Common.DBDataPermission. Currently, there are only two additional restrictions you can impose: denying the right to use blank passwords in a connection string and restricting the allowed OLE DB drivers.

```
public sealed class OleDbPermission : System.Data.Common.DBDataPermission {
// Public Constructors
  public OleDbPermission( );
  public OleDbPermission(System.Security.Permissions.PermissionState state);
  public OleDbPermission(System.Security.Permissions.PermissionState state, bool allowBlankPassword);
// Public Instance Properties
  public string Provider{set; get; }
// Public Instance Methods
  public override IPermission Copy( );                              // overrides System.Data.Common.DBDataPermission
  public override void FromXml(System.Security.SecurityElement securityElement);
                                                                   // overrides System.Data.Common.DBDataPermission
  public override IPermission Intersect(System.Security.IPermission target);
                                                                   // overrides System.Data.Common.DBDataPermission
  public override SecurityElement ToXml( );                        // overrides System.Data.Common.DBDataPermission
  public override IPermission Union(System.Security.IPermission target);        // overrides System.Data.Common.
                                                                                         DBDataPermission
}
```

Hierarchy	System.Object → System.Security.CodeAccessPermission(System.Security.IPermission, System.Security.ISecurityEncodable, System.Security.IStackWalk) → System.Data. Common.DBDataPermission(System.Security.Permissions.IUnrestrictedPermission) → OleDbPermission

OleDbPermissionAttribute   serializable

System.Data.OleDb (system.data.dll)   sealed class

This class allows you to ensure that the current process has the required code-access security permission to access the OLE DB provider before executing code that interacts with the database. It also allows you to temporarily revoke this permission. Typically, you apply this attribute to the declaration of a method that accesses the database or to the definition of a class that contains data access code in every method. You can also apply the attribute to an assembly, struct, or constructor. The OleDbPermissionAttribute provides essentially the same functionality as the OleDbPermission class, but it allows you to add declarative security code instead of explicit (inline) code.

Note that this attribute pertains only to code access security (the policy of allowed and disallowed actions you have configured using the .NET Framework Configuration Tool). For more information, refer to the reference for the base class System.Data.Common. DBDataPermissionAttribute. Currently, there are only two additional restrictions you can impose: denying the right to use blank passwords in a connection string and restricting the allowed OLE DB drivers.

```
public sealed class OleDbPermissionAttribute : System.Data.Common.DBDataPermissionAttribute {
// Public Constructors
  public OleDbPermissionAttribute(System.Security.Permissions.SecurityAction action);
// Public Instance Properties
  public string Provider{set; get; }
// Public Instance Methods
  public override IPermission CreatePermission( );        // overrides System.Security.Permissions.SecurityAttribute
}
```

Hierarchy System.Object → System.Attribute → System.Security.Permissions.SecurityAttribute → System.Security.Permissions.CodeAccessSecurityAttribute → System.Data.Common. DBDataPermissionAttribute → OleDbPermissionAttribute

Valid On Assembly, Class, Struct, Constructor, Method

OleDbRowUpdatedEventArgs

System.Data.OleDb (system.data.dll)   sealed class

This System.EventArgs class provides data for the OleDbDataAdapter.RowUpdated event. For more information, refer to the abstract base class System.Data.Common.RowUpdatedEventArgs, which defines all members.

```
public sealed class OleDbRowUpdatedEventArgs : System.Data.Common.RowUpdatedEventArgs {
// Public Constructors
  public OleDbRowUpdatedEventArgs(System.Data.DataRow dataRow, System.Data.IDbCommand command,
    System.Data.StatementType statementType, System.Data.Common.DataTableMapping tableMapping);
// Public Instance Properties
  public OleDbCommand Command{get; }
}
```

Hierarchy System.Object → System.EventArgs → System.Data.Common.RowUpdatedEventArgs → OleDbRowUpdatedEventArgs

Passed To OleDbRowUpdatedEventHandler.{BeginInvoke( ), Invoke( )}

OleDbRowUpdatedEventHandler   serializable

System.Data.OleDb (system.data.dll)   delegate

This delegate represents the method that will handle the OleDbDataAdapter.RowUpdated event, which fires for each row that is updated (inserted, deleted, or modified) just after the appropriate command is executed, whether it has succeeded or failed. This event gives you the chance to inspect the row and skip over a failed update or cancel processing entirely using the OleDbRowUpdatedEventArgs class.

```
public delegate void OleDbRowUpdatedEventHandler(object sender, OleDbRowUpdatedEventArgs e);
```

Associated Events   OleDbDataAdapter.RowUpdated( )

OleDbRowUpdatingEventArgs

System.Data.OleDb (system.data.dll)   sealed class

This System.EventArgs class provides data for the OleDbDataAdapter.RowUpdating event. For more information, refer to the abstract base class System.Data.Common.RowUpdatingEvent-Args, which defines all members.

```
public sealed class OleDbRowUpdatingEventArgs : System.Data.Common.RowUpdatingEventArgs {
// Public Constructors
  public OleDbRowUpdatingEventArgs(System.Data.DataRow dataRow, System.Data.IDbCommand command,
    System.Data.StatementType statementType, System.Data.Common.DataTableMapping tableMapping);
// Public Instance Properties
  public OleDbCommand Command{set; get; }
}
```

Hierarchy   System.Object → System.EventArgs → System.Data.Common.RowUpdatingEventArgs →
                       OleDbRowUpdatingEventArgs

Passed To   OleDbRowUpdatingEventHandler.{BeginInvoke( ), Invoke( )}

OleDbRowUpdatingEventHandler   serializable

System.Data.OleDb (system.data.dll)   delegate

This delegate represents the method that handles the OleDbDataAdapter.RowUpdating event, which fires for each row that's updated (inserted, deleted, or modified), just before the appropriate command is executed. This event lets you inspect the row and skip or cancel processing using the OleDbRowUpdatingEventArgs class.

```
public delegate void OleDbRowUpdatingEventHandler(object sender, OleDbRowUpdatingEventArgs e);
```

Associated Events   OleDbDataAdapter.RowUpdating( )

OleDbSchemaGuid

System.Data.OleDb (system.data.dll)   sealed class

The OleDbSchemaGuid class is used to specify the type of schema table used by the OleDbConnection.GetOleDbSchemaTable( ) method. This class is used to indicate the information you want to retrieve. For example, you can retrieve the tables in a database using code like this:

```
DataTable dt = con.GetOleDbSchemaTable(OleDbSchemaGuid.Tables, new object[ ]
    {null, null, null, "TABLE"});
```

After executing this code, the System.Data.DataTable object dt will contain a list of all tables in the current database. You can also retrieve information such as a list of views, stored procedures, constraints, keys, indexes, and so on by using a different OleDbSchemaGuid. Note that when you use a System.Data.DataSet, you can use the OleDbDataAdapter.FillSchema( ) method to retrieve some of the required schema information.

```
public sealed class OleDbSchemaGuid {
// Public Constructors
  public OleDbSchemaGuid( );
// Public Static Fields
  public static readonly Guid Assertions;                          // =c8b52210-5cf3-11ce-ade5-00aa0044773d
  public static readonly Guid Catalogs;                            // =c8b52211-5cf3-11ce-ade5-00aa0044773d
  public static readonly Guid Character_Sets;                      // =c8b52212-5cf3-11ce-ade5-00aa0044773d
  public static readonly Guid Check_Constraints;                   // =c8b52215-5cf3-11ce-ade5-00aa0044773d
  public static readonly Guid Check_Constraints_By_Table;          // =c8b52301-5cf3-11ce-ade5-00aa0044773d
  public static readonly Guid Collations;                          // =c8b52213-5cf3-11ce-ade5-00aa0044773d
  public static readonly Guid Column_Domain_Usage;                 // =c8b5221b-5cf3-11ce-ade5-00aa0044773d
  public static readonly Guid Column_Privileges;                   // =c8b52221-5cf3-11ce-ade5-00aa0044773d
  public static readonly Guid Columns;                             // =c8b52214-5cf3-11ce-ade5-00aa0044773d
  public static readonly Guid Constraint_Column_Usage;             // =c8b52216-5cf3-11ce-ade5-00aa0044773d
  public static readonly Guid Constraint_Table_Usage;              // =c8b52217-5cf3-11ce-ade5-00aa0044773d
  public static readonly Guid DbInfoLiterals;                      // =f3264c9d-1860-4dfe-b71b-2961b2ea91bd
  public static readonly Guid Foreign_Keys;                        // =c8b522c4-5cf3-11ce-ade5-00aa0044773d
  public static readonly Guid Indexes;                             // =c8b5221e-5cf3-11ce-ade5-00aa0044773d
  public static readonly Guid Key_Column_Usage;                    // =c8b52218-5cf3-11ce-ade5-00aa0044773d
  public static readonly Guid Primary_Keys;                        // =c8b522c5-5cf3-11ce-ade5-00aa0044773d
  public static readonly Guid Procedure_Columns;                   // =c8b522c9-5cf3-11ce-ade5-00aa0044773d
  public static readonly Guid Procedure_Parameters;                // =c8b522b8-5cf3-11ce-ade5-00aa0044773d
  public static readonly Guid Procedures;                          // =c8b52224-5cf3-11ce-ade5-00aa0044773d
  public static readonly Guid Provider_Types;                      // =c8b5222c-5cf3-11ce-ade5-00aa0044773d
  public static readonly Guid Referential_Constraints;             // =c8b52219-5cf3-11ce-ade5-00aa0044773d
  public static readonly Guid Schemata;                            // =c8b52225-5cf3-11ce-ade5-00aa0044773d
  public static readonly Guid Sql_Languages;                       // =c8b52226-5cf3-11ce-ade5-00aa0044773d
  public static readonly Guid Statistics;                          // =c8b52227-5cf3-11ce-ade5-00aa0044773d
  public static readonly Guid Table_Constraints;                   // =c8b5221a-5cf3-11ce-ade5-00aa0044773d
  public static readonly Guid Table_Privileges;                    // =c8b52222-5cf3-11ce-ade5-00aa0044773d
  public static readonly Guid Table_Statistics;                    // =c8b522ff-5cf3-11ce-ade5-00aa0044773d
  public static readonly Guid Tables;                              // =c8b52229-5cf3-11ce-ade5-00aa0044773d
  public static readonly Guid Tables_Info;                         // =c8b522e0-5cf3-11ce-ade5-00aa0044773d
  public static readonly Guid Translations;                        // =c8b5222a-5cf3-11ce-ade5-00aa0044773d
  public static readonly Guid Trustee;                             // =c8b522ef-5cf3-11ce-ade5-00aa0044773d
  public static readonly Guid Usage_Privileges;                    // =c8b52223-5cf3-11ce-ade5-00aa0044773d
  public static readonly Guid View_Column_Usage;                   // =c8b5222e-5cf3-11ce-ade5-00aa0044773d
  public static readonly Guid View_Table_Usage;                    // =c8b5222f-5cf3-11ce-ade5-00aa0044773d
  public static readonly Guid Views;                               // =c8b5222d-5cf3-11ce-ade5-00aa0044773d
}
```

OleDbTransaction

marshal by reference, disposable

System.Data.OleDb (system.data.dll)   sealed class

This class encapsulates a client-initiated database transaction. If you have an open connection, you can start a transaction by calling the OleDbConnection.BeginTransaction() method, which returns an OleDbTransaction object. The OleDbTransaction class implements the System.Data.IDbTransaction interface, and its members are described in that section of the reference.

You can also use the Begin() method to start a nested transaction (a transaction within the bounds of another transaction). This returns a second OleDbTransaction instance, which can be used to manage the nested transaction. The actions in the nested transaction can be committed or rolled back independently; however, if you roll back the parent transaction, the actions in the nested transaction are also rolled back (even if you committed the nested transaction).

```
public sealed class OleDbTransaction : MarshalByRefObject , System.Data.IDbTransaction, IDisposable {
// Public Instance Properties
  public OleDbConnection Connection{get; }
  public IsolationLevel IsolationLevel{get; }                      // implements System.Data.IDbTransaction
// Public Instance Methods
  public OleDbTransaction Begin( );
  public OleDbTransaction Begin(System.Data.IsolationLevel isolevel);
  public void Commit( );                                           // implements System.Data.IDbTransaction
  public void Rollback( );                                         // implements System.Data.IDbTransaction
// Protected Instance Methods
  protected override void Finalize( );                             // overrides object
}
```

Hierarchy	System.Object → System.MarshalByRefObject → OleDbTransaction(System.Data.IDbTransaction, System.IDisposable)
Returned By	OleDbCommand.Transaction, OleDbConnection.BeginTransaction( )
Passed To	OleDbCommand.{OleDbCommand( ), Transaction}

OleDbType

serializable

System.Data.OleDb (system.data.dll)   enum

This enumeration specifies values for common OLE DB data types. For information about the mapping between these enumerated values, the underlying OLE DB type, and the compatible .NET framework type, refer to Appendix A.

```
public enum OleDbType {
  Empty = 0,
  SmallInt = 2,
  Integer = 3,
  Single = 4,
  Double = 5,
  Currency = 6,
  Date = 7,
  BSTR = 8,
```

```
    IDispatch = 9,
    Error = 10,
    Boolean = 11,
    Variant = 12,
    IUnknown = 13,
    Decimal = 14,
    TinyInt = 16,
    UnsignedTinyInt = 17,
    UnsignedSmallInt = 18,
    UnsignedInt = 19,
    BigInt = 20,
    UnsignedBigInt = 21,
    Filetime = 64,
    Guid = 72,
    Binary = 128,
    Char = 129,
    WChar = 130,
    Numeric = 131,
    DBDate = 133,
    DBTime = 134,
    DBTimeStamp = 135,
    PropVariant = 138,
    VarNumeric = 139,
    VarChar = 200,
    LongVarChar = 201,
    VarWChar = 202,
    LongVarWChar = 203,
    VarBinary = 204,
    LongVarBinary = 205
}
```

Hierarchy   System.Object → System.ValueType → System.Enum(System.IComparable, System.IFormattable, System.IConvertible) → OleDbType

Returned By   OleDbParameter.OleDbType

Passed To   OleDbParameter.{OleDbParameter( ), OleDbType}, OleDbParameterCollection.Add( )

38

The System.Data.SqlTypes Namespace

The System.Data.SqlTypes namespace contains classes for SQL Server's native data types, such as money, tinyint, and varchar. These classes can provide faster access (because typecasting isn't required), and eliminate conversion errors. Chapter 5 describes the DataReader methods you can use to retrieve database values in their native format. However, this technique is rarely required. Figure 38-1 shows the types in this namespace.

INullable

System.Data.SqlTypes (system.data.dll)   interface

.NET system types can't contain the value null. However, database values can because this value can; a null value indicates the absence of a value. All SQLTypes implement the INullable interface to enable them to contain the null value.

```
public interface INullable {
// Public Instance Properties
  public bool IsNull{get; }
}
```

Implemented By   Multiple types

SqlBinary

System.Data.SqlTypes (system.data.dll)   struct

A structure that represents a variable-length stream of bytes, which corresponds to the SQL Server binary or varbinary data types. You can retrieve the number of bytes using the Length property.

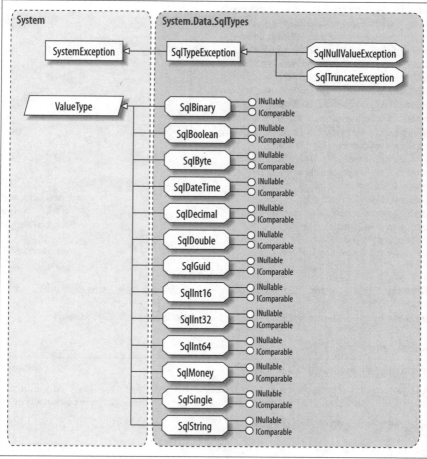

Figure 38-1. The System.Data.SqlTypes namespace

```
public struct SqlBinary : INullable, IComparable {
// Public Constructors
  public SqlBinary( byte[ ] value);
// Public Static Fields
  public static readonly SqlBinary Null;                              // =Null
// Public Instance Properties
  public bool IsNull{get; }                                   // implements INullable
  public int Length{get; }
  public byte this[int index] {get;}
  public byte[ ] Value{get; }
// Public Static Methods
  public static SqlBinary Concat( SqlBinary x, SqlBinary y);
  public static SqlBoolean Equals(SqlBinary x, SqlBinary y);
  public static SqlBoolean GreaterThan(SqlBinary x, SqlBinary y);
  public static SqlBoolean GreaterThanOrEqual(SqlBinary x, SqlBinary y);
```

```
    public static SqlBoolean LessThan(SqlBinary x, SqlBinary y);
    public static SqlBoolean LessThanOrEqual(SqlBinary x, SqlBinary y);
    public static SqlBoolean NotEquals(SqlBinary x, SqlBinary y);
    public static SqlBinary operator +(SqlBinary x, SqlBinary y);
    public static SqlBoolean operator !=(SqlBinary x, SqlBinary y);
    public static SqlBoolean operator <(SqlBinary x, SqlBinary y);
    public static SqlBoolean operator <=(SqlBinary x,  SqlBinary y);
    public static SqlBoolean operator ==(SqlBinary x, SqlBinary y);
    public static SqlBoolean operator >(SqlBinary x, SqlBinary y);
    public static SqlBoolean operator >=(SqlBinary x, SqlBinary y);
    public static explicit operator Byte( SqlBinary x);
    public static explicit operator SqlBinary( SqlGuid x);
    public static implicit operator SqlBinary( byte[ ] x);
// Public Instance Methods
    public int CompareTo( object value);                                    // implements IComparable
    public override bool Equals( object value);                             // overrides ValueType
    public override int GetHashCode( );                                     // overrides ValueType
    public SqlGuid ToSqlGuid( );
    public override string ToString( );                                     // overrides ValueType
}
```

Hierarchy   System.Object → System.ValueType → SqlBinary(INullable, System.IComparable)

Returned By   System.Data.SqlClient.SqlDataReader.GetSqlBinary( ), SqlGuid.ToSqlBinary( )

SqlBoolean

System.Data.SqlTypes (system.data.dll)   struct

A structure that represents an integer that is either a 1 (**true**) or 0 (**false**). Any nonzero
value is interpreted as 1. This structure can be used with the SQL Server bit data type.

```
public struct SqlBoolean : INullable, IComparable {
// Public Constructors
    public SqlBoolean( bool value);
    public SqlBoolean( int value);
// Public Static Fields
    public static readonly SqlBoolean False;                                // =False
    public static readonly SqlBoolean Null;                                 // =Null
    public static readonly SqlBoolean One;                                  // =True
    public static readonly SqlBoolean True;                                 // =True
    public static readonly SqlBoolean Zero;                                 // =False
// Public Instance Properties
    public byte ByteValue{get; }
    public bool IsFalse{get; }
    public bool IsNull{get; }                                               // implements INullable
    public bool IsTrue{get; }
    public bool Value{get; }
// Public Static Methods
    public static SqlBoolean And( SqlBoolean x, SqlBoolean y);
    public static SqlBoolean Equals(SqlBoolean x, SqlBoolean y);
```

```
public static SqlBoolean NotEquals(SqlBoolean x, SqlBoolean y);
public static SqlBoolean OnesComplement( SqlBoolean x);
public static SqlBoolean operator &(SqlBoolean x, SqlBoolean y);
public static SqlBoolean operator |(SqlBoolean x, SqlBoolean y);
public static SqlBoolean operator ^(SqlBoolean x, SqlBoolean y);
public static bool operator op_False( SqlBoolean x);
public static SqlBoolean operator !(SqlBoolean x);
public static SqlBoolean operator ~(SqlBoolean x);
public static bool operator op_True( SqlBoolean x);
public static SqlBoolean Or( SqlBoolean x, SqlBoolean y);
public static SqlBoolean Parse( string s);
public static SqlBoolean Xor( SqlBoolean x, SqlBoolean y);
public static SqlBoolean operator !=(SqlBoolean x, SqlBoolean y);
public static SqlBoolean operator ==(SqlBoolean x, SqlBoolean y);
public static explicit operator bool( SqlBoolean x);
public static explicit operator SqlBoolean( SqlByte x);
public static explicit operator SqlBoolean( SqlDecimal x);
public static explicit operator SqlBoolean( SqlDouble x);
public static explicit operator SqlBoolean( SqlInt16 x);
public static explicit operator SqlBoolean( SqlInt32 x);
public static explicit operator SqlBoolean( SqlInt64 x);
public static explicit operator SqlBoolean( SqlMoney x);
public static explicit operator SqlBoolean( SqlSingle x);
public static explicit operator SqlBoolean( SqlString x);
public static implicit operator SqlBoolean( bool x);
// Public Instance Methods
public int CompareTo( object value);                    // implements IComparable
public override bool Equals( object value);             // overrides ValueType
public override int GetHashCode( );                     // overrides ValueType
public SqlByte ToSqlByte( );
public SqlDecimal ToSqlDecimal( );
public SqlDouble ToSqlDouble( );
public SqlInt16 ToSqlInt16( );
public SqlInt32 ToSqlInt32( );
public SqlInt64 ToSqlInt64( );
public SqlMoney ToSqlMoney( );
public SqlSingle ToSqlSingle( );
public SqlString ToSqlString( );
public override string ToString( );                     // overrides ValueType
}
```

Hierarchy   System.Object → System.ValueType → SqlBoolean(INullable, System.IComparable)

Returned By   Multiple types

SqlByte

System.Data.SqlTypes (system.data.dll)   struct

A structure that represents a single byte (8-bit unsigned integer), which can store an integer value from 0 to 255. This maps to the SQL Server **tinyint** data type. This structure has methods for conversion to .NET numeric types and mathematical operations such as Mod( ) and Xor( ).

```
public struct SqlByte : INullable, IComparable {
// Public Constructors
   public SqlByte( byte value);
// Public Static Fields
   public static readonly SqlByte MaxValue;                                    // =255
   public static readonly SqlByte MinValue;                                    // =0
   public static readonly SqlByte Null;                                        // =Null
   public static readonly SqlByte Zero;                                        // =0
// Public Instance Properties
   public bool IsNull{get; }                                    // implements INullable
   public byte Value{get; }
// Public Static Methods
   public static SqlByte Add( SqlByte x, SqlByte y);
   public static SqlByte BitwiseAnd( SqlByte x, SqlByte y);
   public static SqlByte BitwiseOr( SqlByte x, SqlByte y);
   public static SqlByte Divide( SqlByte x, SqlByte y);
   public static SqlBoolean Equals( SqlByte x, SqlByte y);
   public static SqlBoolean GreaterThan(SqlByte x, SqlByte y);
   public static SqlBoolean GreaterThanOrEqual(SqlByte x, SqlByte y);
   public static SqlBoolean LessThan( SqlByte x, SqlByte y);
   public static SqlBoolean LessThanOrEqual(SqlByte x, SqlByte y);
   public static SqlByte Mod( SqlByte x, SqlByte y);
   public static SqlByte Multiply( SqlByte x, SqlByte y);
   public static SqlBoolean NotEquals( SqlByte x, SqlByte y);
   public static SqlByte OnesComplement( SqlByte x);
   public static SqlByte operator &(SqlByte x, SqlByte y);
   public static SqlByte operator |(SqlByte x, SqlByte y);
   public static SqlByte operator ^(SqlByte x, SqlByte y);
   public static SqlByte operator ~(SqlByte x);
   public static SqlByte Parse( string s);
   public static SqlByte Subtract( SqlByte x, SqlByte y);
   public static SqlByte Xor( SqlByte x, SqlByte y);
   public static SqlByte operator %(SqlByte x, SqlByte y);
   public static SqlByte operator *(SqlByte x, SqlByte y);
   public static SqlByte operator /(SqlByte x, SqlByte y);
   public static SqlByte operator −(SqlByte x, SqlByte y);
   public static SqlByte operator +(SqlByte x, SqlByte y);
   public static SqlBoolean operator !=(SqlByte x, SqlByte y);
   public static SqlBoolean operator <(SqlByte x, SqlByte y);
   public static SqlBoolean operator <=(SqlByte x, SqlByte y);
   public static SqlBoolean operator ==(SqlByte x, SqlByte y);
   public static SqlBoolean operator >(SqlByte x, SqlByte y);
   public static SqlBoolean operator >=(SqlByte x, SqlByte y);
   public static explicit operator byte( SqlByte x);
   public static explicit operator SqlByte( SqlBoolean x);
   public static explicit operator SqlByte( SqlDecimal x);
   public static explicit operator SqlByte( SqlDouble x);
   public static explicit operator SqlByte( SqlInt16 x);
   public static explicit operator SqlByte( SqlInt32 x);
```

```
public static explicit operator SqlByte( SqlInt64 x);
public static explicit operator SqlByte( SqlMoney x);
public static explicit operator SqlByte( SqlSingle x);
public static explicit operator SqlByte( SqlString x);
public static implicit operator SqlByte( byte x);
// Public Instance Methods
public int CompareTo( object value);                              // implements IComparable
public override bool Equals( object value);                       // overrides ValueType
public override int GetHashCode( );                               // overrides ValueType
public SqlBoolean ToSqlBoolean( );
public SqlDecimal ToSqlDecimal( );
public SqlDouble ToSqlDouble( );
public SqlInt16 ToSqlInt16( );
public SqlInt32 ToSqlInt32( );
public SqlInt64 ToSqlInt64( );
public SqlMoney ToSqlMoney( );
public SqlSingle ToSqlSingle( );
public SqlString ToSqlString( );
public override string ToString( );                               // overrides ValueType
}
```

Hierarchy   System.Object → System.ValueType → SqlByte(INullable, System.IComparable)

Returned By   System.Data.SqlClient.SqlDataReader.GetSqlByte( ), SqlBoolean.ToSqlByte( ), SqlDecimal.
ToSqlByte( ), SqlDouble.ToSqlByte( ), SqlInt16.ToSqlByte( ), SqlInt32.ToSqlByte( ), SqlInt64.
ToSqlByte( ), SqlMoney.ToSqlByte( ), SqlSingle.ToSqlByte( ), SqlString.ToSqlByte( )

SqlCompareOptions   serializable, flag

System.Data.SqlTypes (system.data.dll)   enum

Specifies how SqlString instances are compared. You can use any bitwise combination of
these values. BinarySort specifies that sorts should be based on the character's numeric
value, rather than its alphabetic value. IgnoreCase specifies that SqlString comparison won't
take capitalization into account. The other values apply primarily to extended character sets. For example, IgnoreKanaType specifies that SqlString comparisons must ignore the
Kana type (the Kana type refers to Japanese hiragana and katakana characters, which
represent phonetic sounds in the Japanese language). IgnoreNonSpace specifies that SqlString
comparisons must ignore nonspace combining characters, such as diacritics. The
Unicode Standard (see *http://www.unicode.org*) defines combining characters as characters that are combined with base characters to produce a new character. Finally,
IgnoreWidth specifies that SqlString comparisons must ignore the character width (which
can apply to languages such as Japanese where some characters can be written an full
or half width).

```
public enum SqlCompareOptions {
  None = 0x00000000,
  IgnoreCase = 0x00000001,
  IgnoreNonSpace = 0x00000002,
  IgnoreKanaType = 0x00000008,
```

```
IgnoreWidth = 0x00000010,
BinarySort = 0x00008000
}
```

Hierarchy   System.Object → System.ValueType → System.Enum(System.IComparable, System.IFor-
                         mattable, System.IConvertible) → SqlCompareOptions

Returned By   SqlString.SqlCompareOptions

Passed To   SqlString.{CompareOptionsFromSqlCompareOptions( ), SqlString( )}

SqlDateTime

System.Data.SqlTypes (system.data.dll)   struct

A structure that represents a date and time that can range in value from January 1, 1753
to December 31, 9999, with an accuracy of 3.33 milliseconds. This maps directly to the
SQL Server datetime data type. It can also be used for the smalldatetime data type, which can
store a date and time from January 1, 1900 to June 6, 2079 with an accuracy of one
minute.

```
public struct SqlDateTime : INullable, IComparable {
// Public Constructors
  public SqlDateTime( DateTime value);
  public SqlDateTime( int dayTicks, int timeTicks);
  public SqlDateTime( int year, int month, int day);
  public SqlDateTime(int year, int month, int day, int hour, int minute, int second);
  public SqlDateTime(int year, int month, int day, int hour, int minute, int second, double millisecond);
  public SqlDateTime(int year, int month, int day, int hour,  int minute, int second, int bilisecond);
// Public Static Fields
  public static readonly SqlDateTime MaxValue;                          // =12/31/9999 11:59:59 PM
  public static readonly SqlDateTime MinValue;                          // =1/1/1753 12:00:00 AM
  public static readonly SqlDateTime Null;                                             // =Null
  public static readonly int SQLTicksPerHour;                                      // =1080000
  public static readonly int SQLTicksPerMinute;                                      // =18000
  public static readonly int SQLTicksPerSecond;                                        // =300
// Public Instance Properties
  public int DayTicks{get; }
  public bool IsNull{get; }                                                 // implements INullable
  public int TimeTicks{get; }
  public DateTime Value{get; }
// Public Static Methods
  public static SqlBoolean Equals(SqlDateTime x, SqlDateTime y);
  public static SqlBoolean GreaterThan(SqlDateTime x, SqlDateTime y);
  public static SqlBoolean GreaterThanOrEqual(SqlDateTime x, SqlDateTime y);
  public static SqlBoolean LessThan(SqlDateTime x, SqlDateTime y);
  public static SqlBoolean LessThanOrEqual(SqlDateTime x, SqlDateTime y);
  public static SqlBoolean NotEquals(SqlDateTime x, SqlDateTime y);
  public static SqlDateTime Parse( string s);
  public static SqlDateTime operator −(SqlDateTime x, TimeSpan t);
  public static SqlDateTime operator +(SqlDateTime x, TimeSpan t);
  public static SqlBoolean operator !=(SqlDateTime x, SqlDateTime y);
```

```
    public static SqlBoolean operator <(SqlDateTime x, SqlDateTime y);
    public static SqlBoolean operator <=(SqlDateTime x, SqlDateTime y);
    public static SqlBoolean operator ==(SqlDateTime x, SqlDateTime y);
    public static SqlBoolean operator >(SqlDateTime x, SqlDateTime y);
    public static SqlBoolean operator >=(SqlDateTime x, SqlDateTime y);
    public static explicit operator DateTime( SqlDateTime x);
    public static explicit operator SqlDateTime( SqlString x);
    public static implicit operator SqlDateTime(DateTime value);
// Public Instance Methods
    public int CompareTo( object value);                                    // implements IComparable
    public override bool Equals( object value);                             // overrides ValueType
    public override int GetHashCode( );                                     // overrides ValueType
    public SqlString ToSqlString( );
    public override string ToString( );                                     // overrides ValueType
}
```

Hierarchy   System.Object → System.ValueType → SqlDateTime(INullable, System.IComparable)

Returned By   System.Data.SqlClient.SqlDataReader.GetSqlDateTime( ), SqlString.ToSqlDateTime( )

SqlDecimal

System.Data.SqlTypes (system.data.dll)   struct

A structure that represents a numeric value with a fixed precision and scale and a value between $-10^{38}-1$ and $10^{38}-1$. You can set the precision through the Precision property (which represents the maximum number of digits used), and the scale through the Scale property (which represents the number of decimal places to which the value is resolved).

```
public struct SqlDecimal : INullable, IComparable {
// Public Constructors
    public SqlDecimal(byte bPrecision, byte bScale, bool fPositive, int[ ] bits);
    public SqlDecimal(byte bPrecision, byte bScale, bool fPositive, int data1, int data2, int data3, int data4);
    public SqlDecimal( decimal value);
    public SqlDecimal( double dVal);
    public SqlDecimal( int value);
    public SqlDecimal( long value);
// Public Static Fields
    public static readonly byte MaxPrecision;                                       // =38
    public static readonly byte MaxScale;                                           // =38
    public static readonly SqlDecimal MaxValue;           // =99999999999999999999999999999999999999
    public static readonly SqlDecimal MinValue;           // =-99999999999999999999999999999999999999
    public static readonly SqlDecimal Null;                                         // =Null
// Public Instance Properties
    public byte[ ] BinData{get; }
    public int[ ] Data{get; }
    public bool IsNull{get; }                                                       // implements INullable
    public bool IsPositive{get; }
    public byte Precision{get; }
    public byte Scale{get; }
    public decimal Value{get; }
```

```
// Public Static Methods
   public static SqlDecimal Abs( SqlDecimal n);
   public static SqlDecimal Add( SqlDecimal x, SqlDecimal y);
   public static SqlDecimal AdjustScale(SqlDecimal n, int digits, bool fRound);
   public static SqlDecimal Ceiling( SqlDecimal n);
   public static SqlDecimal ConvertToPrecScale(SqlDecimal n, int precision, int scale);
   public static SqlDecimal Divide(SqlDecimal x, SqlDecimal y);
   public static SqlBoolean Equals(SqlDecimal x, SqlDecimal y);
   public static SqlDecimal Floor( SqlDecimal n);
   public static SqlBoolean GreaterThan(SqlDecimal x, SqlDecimal y);
   public static SqlBoolean GreaterThanOrEqual(SqlDecimal x, SqlDecimal y);
   public static SqlBoolean LessThan(SqlDecimal x, SqlDecimal y);
   public static SqlBoolean LessThanOrEqual(SqlDecimal x, SqlDecimal y);
   public static SqlDecimal Multiply(SqlDecimal x, SqlDecimal y);
   public static SqlBoolean NotEquals(SqlDecimal x, SqlDecimal y);
   public static SqlDecimal Parse( string s);
   public static SqlDecimal Power( SqlDecimal n, double exp);
   public static SqlDecimal Round(SqlDecimal n, int position);
   public static SqlInt32 Sign( SqlDecimal n);
   public static SqlDecimal Subtract(SqlDecimal x, SqlDecimal y);
   public static SqlDecimal Truncate(SqlDecimal n, int position);
   public static SqlDecimal operator *(SqlDecimal x, SqlDecimal y);
   public static SqlDecimal operator /(SqlDecimal x, SqlDecimal y);
   public static SqlDecimal operator −( SqlDecimal x);
   public static SqlDecimal operator −(SqlDecimal x, SqlDecimal y);
   public static SqlDecimal operator +(SqlDecimal x, SqlDecimal y);
   public static SqlBoolean operator !=(SqlDecimal x, SqlDecimal y);
   public static SqlBoolean operator <(SqlDecimal x, SqlDecimal y);
   public static SqlBoolean operator <=(SqlDecimal x, SqlDecimal y);
   public static SqlBoolean operator ==(SqlDecimal x, SqlDecimal y);
   public static SqlBoolean operator >(SqlDecimal x, SqlDecimal y);
   public static SqlBoolean operator >=(SqlDecimal x, SqlDecimal y);
   public static explicit operator decimal( SqlDecimal x);
   public static explicit operator SqlDecimal( SqlBoolean x);
   public static explicit operator SqlDecimal( SqlDouble x);
   public static explicit operator SqlDecimal( SqlSingle x);
   public static explicit operator SqlDecimal( SqlString x);
   public static implicit operator SqlDecimal( decimal x);
   public static implicit operator SqlDecimal( SqlByte x);
   public static implicit operator SqlDecimal( SqlInt16 x);
   public static implicit operator SqlDecimal( SqlInt32 x);
   public static implicit operator SqlDecimal( SqlInt64 x);
   public static implicit operator SqlDecimal( SqlMoney x);
// Public Instance Methods
   public int CompareTo( object value);                                    // implements IComparable
   public override bool Equals( object value);                             // overrides ValueType
   public override int GetHashCode( );                                     // overrides ValueType
   public double ToDouble( );
   public SqlBoolean ToSqlBoolean( );
   public SqlByte ToSqlByte( );
   public SqlDouble ToSqlDouble( );
   public SqlInt16 ToSqlInt16( );
```

```
public SqlInt32 ToSqlInt32( );
public SqlInt64 ToSqlInt64( );
public SqlMoney ToSqlMoney( );
public SqlSingle ToSqlSingle( );
public SqlString ToSqlString( );
public override string ToString( );                                    // overrides ValueType
}
```

Hierarchy   System.Object → System.ValueType → SqlDecimal(INullable, System.IComparable)

Returned By   System.Data.SqlClient.SqlDataReader.GetSqlDecimal( ), SqlBoolean.ToSqlDecimal( ),
                    SqlByte.ToSqlDecimal( ), SqlDouble.ToSqlDecimal( ), SqlInt16.ToSqlDecimal( ), SqlInt32.
                    ToSqlDecimal( ), SqlInt64.ToSqlDecimal( ), SqlMoney.ToSqlDecimal( ), SqlSingle.
                    ToSqlDecimal( ), SqlString.ToSqlDecimal( )

SqlDouble

System.Data.SqlTypes (system.data.dll)   struct

A structure that represents a floating-point number from -1.79E+308 to 1.79E+308.
This maps to the SQL Server **float** data type.

```
public struct SqlDouble : INullable, IComparable {
// Public Constructors
  public SqlDouble( double value);
// Public Static Fields
  public static readonly SqlDouble MaxValue;                           // =1.79769313486232E+308
  public static readonly SqlDouble MinValue;                          // =-1.79769313486232E+308
  public static readonly SqlDouble Null;                                            // =Null
  public static readonly SqlDouble Zero;                                            // =0
// Public Instance Properties
  public bool IsNull{get; }                                            // implements INullable
  public double Value{get; }
// Public Static Methods
  public static SqlDouble Add( SqlDouble x, SqlDouble y);
  public static SqlDouble Divide( SqlDouble x, SqlDouble y);
  public static SqlBoolean Equals(SqlDouble x, SqlDouble y);
  public static SqlBoolean GreaterThan(SqlDouble x, SqlDouble y);
  public static SqlBoolean GreaterThanOrEqual(SqlDouble x, SqlDouble y);
  public static SqlBoolean LessThan(SqlDouble x, SqlDouble y);
  public static SqlBoolean LessThanOrEqual(SqlDouble x, SqlDouble y);
  public static SqlDouble Multiply(SqlDouble x, SqlDouble y);
  public static SqlBoolean NotEquals(SqlDouble x, SqlDouble y);
  public static SqlDouble Parse( string s);
  public static SqlDouble Subtract(SqlDouble x, SqlDouble y);
  public static SqlDouble operator *(SqlDouble x, SqlDouble y);
  public static SqlDouble operator /(SqlDouble x, SqlDouble y);
  public static SqlDouble operator –( SqlDouble x);
  public static SqlDouble operator –(SqlDouble x, SqlDouble y);
  public static SqlDouble operator +(SqlDouble x, SqlDouble y);
  public static SqlBoolean operator !=(SqlDouble x, SqlDouble y);
```

```
public static SqlBoolean operator <(SqlDouble x, SqlDouble y);
public static SqlBoolean operator <=(SqlDouble x, SqlDouble y);
public static SqlBoolean operator ==(SqlDouble x, SqlDouble y);
public static SqlBoolean operator >(SqlDouble x, SqlDouble y);
public static SqlBoolean operator >=(SqlDouble x, SqlDouble y);
public static explicit operator double( SqlDouble x);
public static explicit operator SqlDouble( SqlBoolean x);
public static explicit operator SqlDouble( SqlString x);
public static implicit operator SqlDouble( double x);
public static implicit operator SqlDouble( SqlByte x);
public static implicit operator SqlDouble( SqlDecimal x);
public static implicit operator SqlDouble( SqlInt16 x);
public static implicit operator SqlDouble( SqlInt32 x);
public static implicit operator SqlDouble( SqlInt64 x);
public static implicit operator SqlDouble( SqlMoney x);
public static implicit operator SqlDouble( SqlSingle x);
// Public Instance Methods
public int CompareTo( object value);                              // implements IComparable
public override bool Equals( object value);                       // overrides ValueType
public override int GetHashCode( );                              // overrides ValueType
public SqlBoolean ToSqlBoolean( );
public SqlByte ToSqlByte( );
public SqlDecimal ToSqlDecimal( );
public SqlInt16 ToSqlInt16( );
public SqlInt32 ToSqlInt32( );
public SqlInt64 ToSqlInt64( );
public SqlMoney ToSqlMoney( );
public SqlSingle ToSqlSingle( );
public SqlString ToSqlString( );
public override string ToString( );                             // overrides ValueType
}
```

Hierarchy System.Object → System.ValueType → SqlDouble(INullable, System.IComparable)

Returned By System.Data.SqlClient.SqlDataReader.GetSqlDouble( ), SqlBoolean.ToSqlDouble( ), SqlByte.
ToSqlDouble( ), SqlDecimal.ToSqlDouble( ), SqlInt16.ToSqlDouble( ), SqlInt32.
ToSqlDouble( ), SqlInt64.ToSqlDouble( ), SqlMoney.ToSqlDouble( ), SqlSingle.
ToSqlDouble( ), SqlString.ToSqlDouble( )

SqlGuid

System.Data.SqlTypes (system.data.dll)   struct

A structure that represents a GUID, which maps to the SQL Server **uniqueidentifier** data type. Any generated GUID is statistically unique. A GUID converts to strings in the format xxxxxxxx-xxxx-xxxx-xxxx-xxxxxxxxxxxx, in which each x is a hexadecimal digit in the range 0–9 or A–F, e.g., 6F9619FF-8B86-D011-B42D-00C04FC964FF.

```
public struct SqlGuid : INullable, IComparable {
// Public Constructors
  public SqlGuid( byte[ ] value);
  public SqlGuid( Guid g);
```

```
    public SqlGuid(int a, short b, short c, byte d, byte e, byte f, byte g, byte h, byte i, byte j, byte k);
    public SqlGuid( string s);
// Public Static Fields
    public static readonly SqlGuid Null;                                            // =Null
// Public Instance Properties
    public bool IsNull{get; }                                                       // implements INullable
    public Guid Value{get; }
// Public Static Methods
    public static SqlBoolean Equals( SqlGuid x, SqlGuid y);
    public static SqlBoolean GreaterThan(SqlGuid x, SqlGuid y);
    public static SqlBoolean GreaterThanOrEqual(SqlGuid x, SqlGuid y);
    public static SqlBoolean LessThan( SqlGuid x, SqlGuid y);
    public static SqlBoolean LessThanOrEqual(SqlGuid x,  SqlGuid y);
    public static SqlBoolean NotEquals( SqlGuid x, SqlGuid y);
    public static SqlGuid Parse( string s);
    public static SqlBoolean operator !=(SqlGuid x, SqlGuid y);
    public static SqlBoolean operator <(SqlGuid x, SqlGuid y);
    public static SqlBoolean operator <=(SqlGuid x, SqlGuid y);
    public static SqlBoolean operator ==(SqlGuid x, SqlGuid y);
    public static SqlBoolean operator >(SqlGuid x, SqlGuid y);
    public static SqlBoolean operator >=(SqlGuid x, SqlGuid y);
    public static explicit operator Guid( SqlGuid x);
    public static explicit operator SqlGuid( SqlBinary x);
    public static explicit operator SqlGuid( SqlString x);
    public static implicit operator SqlGuid( Guid x);
// Public Instance Methods
    public int CompareTo( object value);                                           // implements IComparable
    public override bool Equals( object value);                                    // overrides ValueType
    public override int GetHashCode( );                                            // overrides ValueType
    public byte[ ] ToByteArray( );
    public SqlBinary ToSqlBinary( );
    public SqlString ToSqlString( );
    public override string ToString( );                                           // overrides ValueType
}
```

Hierarchy   System.Object → System.ValueType → SqlGuid(INullable, System.IComparable)

Returned By   System.Data.SqlClient.SqlDataReader.GetSqlGuid( ), SqlBinary.ToSqlGuid( ), SqlString.
                   ToSqlGuid( )

SqlInt16

System.Data.SqlTypes (system.data.dll)   struct

A structure that represents a 16-bit signed integer that can contain a value ranging from 2^{15} (-32,768) to 2^{15}-1 (32,767). It maps to the SQL Server **smallint** data type.

```
public struct SqlInt16 : INullable, IComparable {
// Public Constructors
    public SqlInt16( short value);
// Public Static Fields
    public static readonly SqlInt16 MaxValue;                                      // =32767
    public static readonly SqlInt16 MinValue;                                      // =-32768
```

```
public static readonly SqlInt16 Null;                                          // =Null
public static readonly SqlInt16 Zero;                                          // =0
// Public Instance Properties
public bool IsNull{get; }                                                      // implements INullable
public short Value{get; }
// Public Static Methods
public static SqlInt16 Add( SqlInt16 x, SqlInt16 y);
public static SqlInt16 BitwiseAnd(SqlInt16 x, SqlInt16 y);
public static SqlInt16 BitwiseOr( SqlInt16 x, SqlInt16 y);
public static SqlInt16 Divide( SqlInt16 x, SqlInt16 y);
public static SqlBoolean Equals( SqlInt16 x, SqlInt16 y);
public static SqlBoolean GreaterThan(SqlInt16 x, SqlInt16 y);
public static SqlBoolean GreaterThanOrEqual(SqlInt16 x, SqlInt16 y);
public static SqlBoolean LessThan(SqlInt16 x, SqlInt16 y);
public static SqlBoolean LessThanOrEqual(SqlInt16 x, SqlInt16 y);
public static SqlInt16 Mod( SqlInt16 x, SqlInt16 y);
public static SqlInt16 Multiply( SqlInt16 x, SqlInt16 y);
public static SqlBoolean NotEquals(SqlInt16 x, SqlInt16 y);
public static SqlInt16 OnesComplement( SqlInt16 x);
public static SqlInt16 operator &(SqlInt16 x, SqlInt16 y);
public static SqlInt16 operator |(SqlInt16 x, SqlInt16 y);
public static SqlInt16 operator ^(SqlInt16 x, SqlInt16 y);
public static SqlInt16 operator ~(SqlInt16 x);
public static SqlInt16 Parse( string s);
public static SqlInt16 Subtract( SqlInt16 x, SqlInt16 y);
public static SqlInt16 Xor( SqlInt16 x, SqlInt16 y);
public static SqlInt16 operator %(SqlInt16 x, SqlInt16 y);
public static SqlInt16 operator *(SqlInt16 x, SqlInt16 y);
public static SqlInt16 operator /(SqlInt16 x, SqlInt16 y);
public static SqlInt16 operator −( SqlInt16 x);
public static SqlInt16 operator −(SqlInt16 x, SqlInt16 y);
public static SqlInt16 operator +(SqlInt16 x, SqlInt16 y);
public static SqlBoolean operator !=(SqlInt16 x, SqlInt16 y);
public static SqlBoolean operator <(SqlInt16 x, SqlInt16 y);
public static SqlBoolean operator <=(SqlInt16 x, SqlInt16 y);
public static SqlBoolean operator ==(SqlInt16 x, SqlInt16 y);
public static SqlBoolean operator >(SqlInt16 x, SqlInt16 y);
public static SqlBoolean operator >=(SqlInt16 x, SqlInt16 y);
public static explicit operator short( SqlInt16 x);
public static explicit operator SqlInt16( SqlBoolean x);
public static explicit operator SqlInt16( SqlDecimal x);
public static explicit operator SqlInt16( SqlDouble x);
public static explicit operator SqlInt16( SqlInt32 x);
public static explicit operator SqlInt16( SqlInt64 x);
public static explicit operator SqlInt16( SqlMoney x);
public static explicit operator SqlInt16( SqlSingle x);
public static explicit operator SqlInt16( SqlString x);
public static implicit operator SqlInt16( short x);
public static implicit operator SqlInt16( SqlByte x);
```

```
// Public Instance Methods
  public int CompareTo( object value);                                          // implements IComparable
  public override bool Equals( object value);                                   // overrides ValueType
  public override int GetHashCode( );                                           // overrides ValueType
  public SqlBoolean ToSqlBoolean( );
  public SqlByte ToSqlByte( );
  public SqlDecimal ToSqlDecimal( );
  public SqlDouble ToSqlDouble( );
  public SqlInt32 ToSqlInt32( );
  public SqlInt64 ToSqlInt64( );
  public SqlMoney ToSqlMoney( );
  public SqlSingle ToSqlSingle( );
  public SqlString ToSqlString( );
  public override string ToString( );                                          // overrides ValueType
}
```

Hierarchy   System.Object → System.ValueType → SqlInt16(INullable, System.IComparable)

Returned By   System.Data.SqlClient.SqlDataReader.GetSqlInt16( ), SqlBoolean.ToSqlInt16( ), SqlByte.
ToSqlInt16( ), SqlDecimal.ToSqlInt16( ), SqlDouble.ToSqlInt16( ), SqlInt32.ToSqlInt16( ),
SqlInt64.ToSqlInt16( ), SqlMoney.ToSqlInt16( ), SqlSingle.ToSqlInt16( ), SqlString.
ToSqlInt16( )

SqlInt32

System.Data.SqlTypes (system.data.dll)   struct

A structure that represents a 32-bit signed integer that can contain a value ranging from
-2^{31} (-2,147,483,648) to $2^{31}-1$ (2,147,483,647). It maps to the SQL Server int data type.

```
public struct SqlInt32 : INullable, IComparable {
// Public Constructors
  public SqlInt32( int value);
// Public Static Fields
  public static readonly SqlInt32 MaxValue;                                     // =2147483647
  public static readonly SqlInt32 MinValue;                                     // =-2147483648
  public static readonly SqlInt32 Null;                                         // =Null
  public static readonly SqlInt32 Zero;                                         // =0
// Public Instance Properties
  public bool IsNull{get; }                                                     // implements INullable
  public int Value{get; }
// Public Static Methods
  public static SqlInt32 Add( SqlInt32 x, SqlInt32 y);
  public static SqlInt32 BitwiseAnd(SqlInt32 x, SqlInt32 y);
  public static SqlInt32 BitwiseOr( SqlInt32 x, SqlInt32 y);
  public static SqlInt32 Divide( SqlInt32 x, SqlInt32 y);
  public static SqlBoolean Equals( SqlInt32 x, SqlInt32 y);
  public static SqlBoolean GreaterThan(SqlInt32 x, SqlInt32 y);
  public static SqlBoolean GreaterThanOrEqual(SqlInt32 x, SqlInt32 y);
  public static SqlBoolean LessThan(SqlInt32 x, SqlInt32 y);
  public static SqlBoolean LessThanOrEqual(SqlInt32 x, SqlInt32 y);
  public static SqlInt32 Mod( SqlInt32 x, SqlInt32 y);
```

```
    public static SqlInt32 Multiply( SqlInt32 x, SqlInt32 y);
    public static SqlBoolean NotEquals(SqlInt32 x, SqlInt32 y);
    public static SqlInt32 OnesComplement( SqlInt32 x);
    public static SqlInt32 operator &(SqlInt32 x, SqlInt32 y);
    public static SqlInt32 operator |(SqlInt32 x, SqlInt32 y);
    public static SqlInt32 operator ^(SqlInt32 x, SqlInt32 y);
    public static SqlInt32 operator ~(SqlInt32 x);
    public static SqlInt32 Parse( string s);
    public static SqlInt32 Subtract( SqlInt32 x, SqlInt32 y);
    public static SqlInt32 Xor( SqlInt32 x, SqlInt32 y);
    public static SqlInt32 operator %(SqlInt32 x, SqlInt32 y);
    public static SqlInt32 operator *(SqlInt32 x, SqlInt32 y);
    public static SqlInt32 operator /(SqlInt32 x, SqlInt32 y);
    public static SqlInt32 operator -( SqlInt32 x);
    public static SqlInt32 operator -(SqlInt32 x, SqlInt32 y);
    public static SqlInt32 operator +(SqlInt32 x, SqlInt32 y);
    public static SqlBoolean operator !=(SqlInt32 x, SqlInt32 y);
    public static SqlBoolean operator <(SqlInt32 x, SqlInt32 y);
    public static SqlBoolean operator <=(SqlInt32 x, SqlInt32 y);
    public static SqlBoolean operator ==(SqlInt32 x, SqlInt32 y);
    public static SqlBoolean operator >(SqlInt32 x, SqlInt32 y);
    public static SqlBoolean operator >=(SqlInt32 x, SqlInt32 y);
    public static explicit operator int( SqlInt32 x);
    public static explicit operator SqlInt32( SqlBoolean x);
    public static explicit operator SqlInt32( SqlDecimal x);
    public static explicit operator SqlInt32( SqlDouble x);
    public static explicit operator SqlInt32( SqlInt64 x);
    public static explicit operator SqlInt32( SqlMoney x);
    public static explicit operator SqlInt32( SqlSingle x);
    public static explicit operator SqlInt32( SqlString x);
    public static implicit operator SqlInt32( int x);
    public static implicit operator SqlInt32( SqlByte x);
    public static implicit operator SqlInt32( SqlInt16 x);
// Public Instance Methods
    public int CompareTo( object value);                              // implements IComparable
    public override bool Equals( object value);                       // overrides ValueType
    public override int GetHashCode( );                               // overrides ValueType
    public SqlBoolean ToSqlBoolean( );
    public SqlByte ToSqlByte( );
    public SqlDecimal ToSqlDecimal( );
    public SqlDouble ToSqlDouble( );
    public SqlInt16 ToSqlInt16( );
    public SqlInt64 ToSqlInt64( );
    public SqlMoney ToSqlMoney( );
    public SqlSingle ToSqlSingle( );
    public SqlString ToSqlString( );
    public override string ToString( );                              // overrides ValueType
}
```

Hierarchy   System.Object → System.ValueType → SqlInt32(INullable, System.IComparable)

Returned By   System.Data.SqlClient.SqlDataReader.GetSqlInt32( ), SqlBoolean.ToSqlInt32( ), SqlByte.
ToSqlInt32( ), SqlDecimal.{Sign( ), ToSqlInt32( )}, SqlDouble.ToSqlInt32( ), SqlInt16.
ToSqlInt32( ), SqlInt64.ToSqlInt32( ), SqlMoney.ToSqlInt32( ), SqlSingle.ToSqlInt32( ),
SqlString.ToSqlInt32( )

SqlInt64

System.Data.SqlTypes (system.data.dll)   struct

A structure that represents a 64-bit signed integer that can contain a value ranging from
-2^{63} (-9223372036854775808) to $2^{63}-1$ (9223372036854775807). It maps to the SQL
Server bigint data type.

```
public struct SqlInt64 : INullable, IComparable {
// Public Constructors
  public SqlInt64( long value);
// Public Static Fields
  public static readonly SqlInt64 MaxValue;                              // =9223372036854775807
  public static readonly SqlInt64 MinValue;                             // =-9223372036854775808
  public static readonly SqlInt64 Null;                                                // =Null
  public static readonly SqlInt64 Zero;                                                   // =0
// Public Instance Properties
  public bool IsNull{get; }                                             // implements INullable
  public long Value{get; }
// Public Static Methods
  public static SqlInt64 Add( SqlInt64 x, SqlInt64 y);
  public static SqlInt64 BitwiseAnd(SqlInt64 x, SqlInt64 y);
  public static SqlInt64 BitwiseOr( SqlInt64 x, SqlInt64 y);
  public static SqlInt64 Divide( SqlInt64 x, SqlInt64 y);
  public static SqlBoolean Equals( SqlInt64 x, SqlInt64 y);
  public static SqlBoolean GreaterThan(SqlInt64 x, SqlInt64 y);
  public static SqlBoolean GreaterThanOrEqual(SqlInt64 x, SqlInt64 y);
  public static SqlBoolean LessThan(SqlInt64 x, SqlInt64 y);
  public static SqlBoolean LessThanOrEqual(SqlInt64 x, SqlInt64 y);
  public static SqlInt64 Mod( SqlInt64 x, SqlInt64 y);
  public static SqlInt64 Multiply( SqlInt64 x, SqlInt64 y);
  public static SqlBoolean NotEquals(SqlInt64 x, SqlInt64 y);
  public static SqlInt64 OnesComplement( SqlInt64 x);
  public static SqlInt64 operator &(SqlInt64 x, SqlInt64 y);
  public static SqlInt64 operator |(SqlInt64 x, SqlInt64 y);
  public static SqlInt64 operator ^(SqlInt64 x, SqlInt64 y);
  public static SqlInt64 operator ~(SqlInt64 x);
  public static SqlInt64 Parse( string s);
  public static SqlInt64 Subtract( SqlInt64 x, SqlInt64 y);
  public static SqlInt64 Xor( SqlInt64 x, SqlInt64 y);
  public static SqlInt64 operator %(SqlInt64 x, SqlInt64 y);
  public static SqlInt64 operator *(SqlInt64 x, SqlInt64 y);
  public static SqlInt64 operator /(SqlInt64 x, SqlInt64 y);
  public static SqlInt64 operator -( SqlInt64 x);
  public static SqlInt64 operator -(SqlInt64 x, SqlInt64 y);
  public static SqlInt64 operator +(SqlInt64 x, SqlInt64 y);
  public static SqlBoolean operator !=(SqlInt64 x, SqlInt64 y);
```

```
  public static SqlBoolean operator <(SqlInt64 x, SqlInt64 y);
  public static SqlBoolean operator <=(SqlInt64 x, SqlInt64 y);
  public static SqlBoolean operator ==(SqlInt64 x, SqlInt64 y);
  public static SqlBoolean operator >(SqlInt64 x, SqlInt64 y);
  public static SqlBoolean operator >=(SqlInt64 x, SqlInt64 y);
  public static explicit operator long( SqlInt64 x);
  public static explicit operator SqlInt64( SqlBoolean x);
  public static explicit operator SqlInt64( SqlDecimal x);
  public static explicit operator SqlInt64( SqlDouble x);
  public static explicit operator SqlInt64( SqlMoney x);
  public static explicit operator SqlInt64( SqlSingle x);
  public static explicit operator SqlInt64( SqlString x);
  public static implicit operator SqlInt64( long x);
  public static implicit operator SqlInt64( SqlByte x);
  public static implicit operator SqlInt64( SqlInt16 x);
  public static implicit operator SqlInt64( SqlInt32 x);
// Public Instance Methods
  public int CompareTo( object value);                                  // implements IComparable
  public override bool Equals( object value);                           // overrides ValueType
  public override int GetHashCode( );                                   // overrides ValueType
  public SqlBoolean ToSqlBoolean( );
  public SqlByte ToSqlByte( );
  public SqlDecimal ToSqlDecimal( );
  public SqlDouble ToSqlDouble( );
  public SqlInt16 ToSqlInt16( );
  public SqlInt32 ToSqlInt32( );
  public SqlMoney ToSqlMoney( );
  public SqlSingle ToSqlSingle( );
  public SqlString ToSqlString( );
  public override string ToString( );                                   // overrides ValueType
}
```

Hierarchy   System.Object → System.ValueType → SqlInt64(INullable, System.IComparable)

Returned By   System.Data.SqlClient.SqlDataReader.GetSqlInt64( ), SqlBoolean.ToSqlInt64( ), SqlByte.
                   ToSqlInt64( ), SqlDecimal.ToSqlInt64( ), SqlDouble.ToSqlInt64( ), SqlInt16.ToSqlInt64( ),
                   SqlInt32.ToSqlInt64( ), SqlMoney.ToSqlInt64( ), SqlSingle.ToSqlInt64( ), SqlString.
                   ToSqlInt64( )

SqlMoney

System.Data.SqlTypes (system.data.dll)   struct

A structure that represents a currency value ranging from -2^{63} (-922,337,203,685,477.
5808) to 2^{63-1} (922,337,203,685,477.5807) with an accuracy to a ten-thousandth of a
unit. It maps to the SQL Server money data type.

```
public struct SqlMoney : INullable, IComparable {
// Public Constructors
  public SqlMoney( decimal value);
  public SqlMoney( double value);
  public SqlMoney( int value);
```

```
    public SqlMoney( long value);
```

// Public Static Fields
```
    public static readonly SqlMoney MaxValue;                                    // =922337203685477.5807
    public static readonly SqlMoney MinValue;                                    // =-922337203685477.5808
    public static readonly SqlMoney Null;                                        // =Null
    public static readonly SqlMoney Zero;                                        // =0
```
// Public Instance Properties
```
    public bool IsNull{get; }                                                    // implements INullable
    public decimal Value{get; }
```
// Public Static Methods
```
    public static SqlMoney Add( SqlMoney x, SqlMoney y);
    public static SqlMoney Divide( SqlMoney x, SqlMoney y);
    public static SqlBoolean Equals( SqlMoney x, SqlMoney y);
    public static SqlBoolean GreaterThan(SqlMoney x, SqlMoney y);
    public static SqlBoolean GreaterThanOrEqual(SqlMoney x, SqlMoney y);
    public static SqlBoolean LessThan(SqlMoney x, SqlMoney y);
    public static SqlBoolean LessThanOrEqual(SqlMoney x, SqlMoney y);
    public static SqlMoney Multiply( SqlMoney x, SqlMoney y);
    public static SqlBoolean NotEquals(SqlMoney x, SqlMoney y);
    public static SqlMoney Parse( string s);
    public static SqlMoney Subtract( SqlMoney x, SqlMoney y);
    public static SqlMoney operator *(SqlMoney x, SqlMoney y);
    public static SqlMoney operator /(SqlMoney x, SqlMoney y);
    public static SqlMoney operator −( SqlMoney x);
    public static SqlMoney operator −(SqlMoney x, SqlMoney y);
    public static SqlMoney operator +(SqlMoney x, SqlMoney y);
    public static SqlBoolean operator !=(SqlMoney x, SqlMoney y);
    public static SqlBoolean operator <(SqlMoney x, SqlMoney y);
    public static SqlBoolean operator <=(SqlMoney x, SqlMoney y);
    public static SqlBoolean operator ==(SqlMoney x, SqlMoney y);
    public static SqlBoolean operator >(SqlMoney x, SqlMoney y);
    public static SqlBoolean operator >=(SqlMoney x, SqlMoney y);
    public static explicit operator decimal( SqlMoney x);
    public static explicit operator SqlMoney( SqlBoolean x);
    public static explicit operator SqlMoney( SqlDecimal x);
    public static explicit operator SqlMoney( SqlDouble x);
    public static explicit operator SqlMoney( SqlSingle x);
    public static explicit operator SqlMoney( SqlString x);
    public static implicit operator SqlMoney( decimal x);
    public static implicit operator SqlMoney( SqlByte x);
    public static implicit operator SqlMoney( SqlInt16 x);
    public static implicit operator SqlMoney( SqlInt32 x);
    public static implicit operator SqlMoney( SqlInt64 x);
```
// Public Instance Methods
```
    public int CompareTo( object value);                                         // implements IComparable
    public override bool Equals( object value);                                  // overrides ValueType
    public override int GetHashCode( );                                          // overrides ValueType
    public decimal ToDecimal( );
    public double ToDouble( );
    public int ToInt32( );
    public long ToInt64( );
```

```
public SqlBoolean ToSqlBoolean( );
public SqlByte ToSqlByte( );
public SqlDecimal ToSqlDecimal( );
public SqlDouble ToSqlDouble( );
public SqlInt16 ToSqlInt16( );
public SqlInt32 ToSqlInt32( );
public SqlInt64 ToSqlInt64( );
public SqlSingle ToSqlSingle( );
public SqlString ToSqlString( );
public override string ToString( );                                          // overrides ValueType
}
```

Hierarchy   System.Object → System.ValueType → SqlMoney(INullable, System.IComparable)

Returned By   System.Data.SqlClient.SqlDataReader.GetSqlMoney( ), SqlBoolean.ToSqlMoney( ), SqlByte.
                       ToSqlMoney( ), SqlDecimal.ToSqlMoney( ), SqlDouble.ToSqlMoney( ), SqlInt16.
                       ToSqlMoney( ), SqlInt32.ToSqlMoney( ), SqlInt64.ToSqlMoney( ), SqlSingle.ToSqlMoney( ),
                       SqlString.ToSqlMoney( )

SqlNullValueException   serializable

System.Data.SqlTypes (system.data.dll)   sealed class

This exception is thrown when you set the Value property of a SQL structure to null. To
prevent throwing this exception, you should check the IsNull property of the structure
before accessing the Value property.

```
public sealed class SqlNullValueException : SqlTypeException {
// Public Constructors
  public SqlNullValueException( );
  public SqlNullValueException( string message);
  public SqlNullValueException(string message, Exception e);
}
```

Hierarchy   System.Object → System.Exception(System.Runtime.Serialization.ISerializable) → System.
                       SystemException → SqlTypeException → SqlNullValueException

SqlSingle

System.Data.SqlTypes (system.data.dll)   struct

A structure that represents a floating-point value ranging from -3.40E38 to 3.40E38. It
maps to the SQL Server real data type.

```
public struct SqlSingle : INullable, IComparable {
// Public Constructors
  public SqlSingle( double value);
  public SqlSingle( float value);
// Public Static Fields
  public static readonly SqlSingle MaxValue;                              // =3.402823E+38
  public static readonly SqlSingle MinValue;                              // =-3.402823E+38
  public static readonly SqlSingle Null;                                  // =Null
  public static readonly SqlSingle Zero;                                  // =0
```

```
// Public Instance Properties
  public bool IsNull{get; }                                                            // implements INullable
  public float Value{get; }
// Public Static Methods
  public static SqlSingle Add( SqlSingle x, SqlSingle y);
  public static SqlSingle Divide( SqlSingle x, SqlSingle y);
  public static SqlBoolean Equals(SqlSingle x, SqlSingle y);
  public static SqlBoolean GreaterThan(SqlSingle x, SqlSingle y);
  public static SqlBoolean GreaterThanOrEqual(SqlSingle x, SqlSingle y);
  public static SqlBoolean LessThan(SqlSingle x, SqlSingle y);
  public static SqlBoolean LessThanOrEqual(SqlSingle x, SqlSingle y);
  public static SqlSingle Multiply(SqlSingle x, SqlSingle y);
  public static SqlBoolean NotEquals(SqlSingle x, SqlSingle y);
  public static SqlSingle Parse( string s);
  public static SqlSingle Subtract(SqlSingle x, SqlSingle y);
  public static SqlSingle operator *(SqlSingle x, SqlSingle y);
  public static SqlSingle operator /(SqlSingle x, SqlSingle y);
  public static SqlSingle operator −( SqlSingle x);
  public static SqlSingle operator −(SqlSingle x, SqlSingle y);
  public static SqlSingle operator +(SqlSingle x, SqlSingle y);
  public static SqlBoolean operator !=(SqlSingle x, SqlSingle y);
  public static SqlBoolean operator <(SqlSingle x, SqlSingle y);
  public static SqlBoolean operator <=(SqlSingle x, SqlSingle y);
  public static SqlBoolean operator ==(SqlSingle x, SqlSingle y);
  public static SqlBoolean operator >(SqlSingle x, SqlSingle y);
  public static SqlBoolean operator >=(SqlSingle x, SqlSingle y);
  public static explicit operator float( SqlSingle x);
  public static explicit operator SqlSingle( SqlBoolean x);
  public static explicit operator SqlSingle( SqlDouble x);
  public static explicit operator SqlSingle( SqlString x);
  public static implicit operator SqlSingle( float x);
  public static implicit operator SqlSingle( SqlByte x);
  public static implicit operator SqlSingle( SqlDecimal x);
  public static implicit operator SqlSingle( SqlInt16 x);
  public static implicit operator SqlSingle( SqlInt32 x);
  public static implicit operator SqlSingle( SqlInt64 x);
  public static implicit operator SqlSingle( SqlMoney x);
// Public Instance Methods
  public int CompareTo( object value);                                                 // implements IComparable
  public override bool Equals( object value);                                          // overrides ValueType
  public override int GetHashCode( );                                                  // overrides ValueType
  public SqlBoolean ToSqlBoolean( );
  public SqlByte ToSqlByte( );
  public SqlDecimal ToSqlDecimal( );
  public SqlDouble ToSqlDouble( );
  public SqlInt16 ToSqlInt16( );
  public SqlInt32 ToSqlInt32( );
  public SqlInt64 ToSqlInt64( );
  public SqlMoney ToSqlMoney( );
```

```
public SqlString ToSqlString( );
public override string ToString( );                                           // overrides ValueType
}
```

Hierarchy   System.Object → System.ValueType → SqlSingle(INullable, System.IComparable)

Returned By   System.Data.SqlClient.SqlDataReader.GetSqlSingle( ), SqlBoolean.ToSqlSingle( ), SqlByte.
                       ToSqlSingle( ), SqlDecimal.ToSqlSingle( ), SqlDouble.ToSqlSingle( ), SqlInt16.ToSqlSingle( ),
                       SqlInt32.ToSqlSingle( ), SqlInt64.ToSqlSingle( ), SqlMoney.ToSqlSingle( ), SqlString.
                       ToSqlSingle( )

SqlString

System.Data.SqlTypes (system.data.dll)   struct

A structure that represents a variable-length stream of characters. You can use this
structure for the following SQL Server data types: char, nchar, varchar, nvarchar, ntext, text,
and sysname. You can configure how SqlString instances should be compared by setting a
combination of values from the SqlCompareOptions enumeration for the SqlCompareOptions
property.

The built-in methods include one for string concatenation (Concat( )). To determine the
geographical locale and language for this structure, use the LCID property, and for information about culture-specific settings (such as culture name, writing system, and
calendar) use the CultureInfo property.

```
public struct SqlString : INullable, IComparable {
// Public Constructors
  public SqlString(int lcid, SqlCompareOptions compareOptions, byte[ ] data);
  public SqlString(int lcid, SqlCompareOptions compareOptions, byte[ ] data, bool fUnicode);
  public SqlString(int lcid, SqlCompareOptions compareOptions, byte[ ] data, int index, int count);
  public SqlString(int lcid, SqlCompareOptions compareOptions, byte[ ] data, int index, int count, bool fUnicode);
  public SqlString( string data);
  public SqlString( string data, int lcid);
  public SqlString(string data, int lcid, SqlCompareOptions compareOptions);
// Public Static Fields
  public static readonly int BinarySort;                                                // =32768
  public static readonly int IgnoreCase;                                                 // =1
  public static readonly int IgnoreKanaType;                                             // =8
  public static readonly int IgnoreNonSpace;                                             // =2
  public static readonly int IgnoreWidth;                                                // =16
  public static readonly SqlString Null;                                                 // =Null
// Public Instance Properties
  public CompareInfo CompareInfo{get; }
  public CultureInfo CultureInfo{get; }
  public bool IsNull{get; }                                                         // implements INullable
  public int LCID{get; }
  public SqlCompareOptions SqlCompareOptions{get; }
  public string Value{get; }
// Public Static Methods
  public static CompareOptions CompareOptionsFromSqlCompareOptions(SqlCompareOptions compareOptions);
  public static SqlString Concat( SqlString x, SqlString y);
  public static SqlBoolean Equals(SqlString x, SqlString y);
```

```
    public static SqlBoolean GreaterThan(SqlString x, SqlString y);
    public static SqlBoolean GreaterThanOrEqual(SqlString x, SqlString y);
    public static SqlBoolean LessThan(SqlString x, SqlString y);
    public static SqlBoolean LessThanOrEqual(SqlString x, SqlString y);
    public static SqlBoolean NotEquals(SqlString x, SqlString y);
    public static SqlString operator +(SqlString x, SqlString y);
    public static SqlBoolean operator !=(SqlString x, SqlString y);
    public static SqlBoolean operator <(SqlString x, SqlString y);
    public static SqlBoolean operator <=(SqlString x, SqlString y);
    public static SqlBoolean operator ==(SqlString x, SqlString y);
    public static SqlBoolean operator >(SqlString x, SqlString y);
    public static SqlBoolean operator >=(SqlString x, SqlString y);
    public static explicit operator SqlString( SqlBoolean x);
    public static explicit operator SqlString( SqlByte x);
    public static explicit operator SqlString( SqlDateTime x);
    public static explicit operator SqlString( SqlDecimal x);
    public static explicit operator SqlString( SqlDouble x);
    public static explicit operator SqlString( SqlGuid x);
    public static explicit operator SqlString( SqlInt16 x);
    public static explicit operator SqlString( SqlInt32 x);
    public static explicit operator SqlString( SqlInt64 x);
    public static explicit operator SqlString( SqlMoney x);
    public static explicit operator SqlString( SqlSingle x);
    public static explicit operator string( SqlString x);
    public static implicit operator SqlString( string x);
// Public Instance Methods
    public SqlString Clone( );
    public int CompareTo( object value);                          // implements IComparable
    public override bool Equals( object value);                   // overrides ValueType
    public override int GetHashCode( );                           // overrides ValueType
    public byte[ ] GetNonUnicodeBytes( );
    public byte[ ] GetUnicodeBytes( );
    public SqlBoolean ToSqlBoolean( );
    public SqlByte ToSqlByte( );
    public SqlDateTime ToSqlDateTime( );
    public SqlDecimal ToSqlDecimal( );
    public SqlDouble ToSqlDouble( );
    public SqlGuid ToSqlGuid( );
    public SqlInt16 ToSqlInt16( );
    public SqlInt32 ToSqlInt32( );
    public SqlInt64 ToSqlInt64( );
    public SqlMoney ToSqlMoney( );
    public SqlSingle ToSqlSingle( );
    public override string ToString( );                          // overrides ValueType
}
```

Hierarchy   System.Object → System.ValueType → SqlString(INullable, System.IComparable)

Returned By   System.Data.SqlClient.SqlDataReader.GetSqlString( ), SqlBoolean.ToSqlString( ), SqlByte.
                     ToSqlString( ), SqlDateTime.ToSqlString( ), SqlDecimal.ToSqlString( ), SqlDouble.

ToSqlString( ), SqlGuid.ToSqlString( ), SqlInt16.ToSqlString( ), SqlInt32.ToSqlString( ),
SqlInt64.ToSqlString( ), SqlMoney.ToSqlString( ), SqlSingle.ToSqlString( )

SqlTruncateException
serializable

System.Data.SqlTypes (system.data.dll)
sealed class

This exception is thrown if you try to set a value that doesn't fit in a structure (e.g., a
string that is longer than the maximum character length allowed for SqlString).

```
public sealed class SqlTruncateException : SqlTypeException {
// Public Constructors
  public SqlTruncateException( );
  public SqlTruncateException( string message);
  public SqlTruncateException( string message, Exception e);
}
```

Hierarchy   System.Object → System.Exception(System.Runtime.Serialization.ISerializable) → System.
SystemException → SqlTypeException → SqlTruncateException

SqlTypeException
serializable

System.Data.SqlTypes (system.data.dll)
class

This is the base class for exceptions with the SQL Server .NET data structures. Both
SqlTruncateException and SqlNullValueException derive from this class.

```
public class SqlTypeException : SystemException {
// Public Constructors
  public SqlTypeException( );
  public SqlTypeException( string message);
  public SqlTypeException( string message, Exception e);
// Protected Constructors
  protected SqlTypeException(System.Runtime.Serialization.SerializationInfo si,
    System.Runtime.Serialization.StreamingContext sc);
}
```

Hierarchy   System.Object → System.Exception(System.Runtime.Serialization.ISerializable) → System.
SystemException → SqlTypeException

Subclasses   SqlNullValueException, SqlTruncateException

IV

Appendixes

ADO.NET Providers

This appendix gives a thumbnail view of the ADO.NET providers discussed in this book. It also describes where you can find some additional ADO.NET providers, including ODBC .NET, Oracle .NET, ODP.NET, and SQLXML. All these providers are freely downloadable. (Version 1.1 of the .NET Framework SDK includes ODBC .NET and Oracle .NET).

If you can't locate a managed provider for your data source, the next best option is to use an OLE DB driver with the .NET OLE DB provider classes. If your data source doesn't provide an OLE DB driver, your final resort is to use a lower-level ODBC driver in conjunction with the ODBC .NET provider. Many data sources, and nearly all database products include an OLE DB or ODBC driver.

The SQL Server Provider

The SQL Server provider provides access to a SQL Server database (Version 7.0 or later) through the optimized Tabular Data Stream (TDS) interface (see Table A-1). To connect to the pre-7.0 version of SQL Server, use the OLE DB .NET data provider with the SQL Server OLE DB provider (SQLOLEDB). The connection-specific types are found in the System.Data.SqlClient namespace.

Table A-1. SQL Server provider classes

Interface	Implementing class
IDbConnection	SqlConnection
IDbCommand	SqlCommand
IDataParameter, IDbDataParameter	SqlParameter
IDataReader, IDataRecord	SqlDataReader
IDataAdapter, IDbDataAdapter	SqlDataAdapter
IDbTransaction	SqlTransaction

The SQL Server provider also provides .NET structures that map exactly to SQL Server types in the System.Data.SqlTypes namespace (see Table A-2). You can use SqlDataReader methods such as GetSqlMoney() and GetSqlDataTime() to retrieve values using these types (as described in Chapter 2).

Table A-2. Native SQL Server data types

SQL Server data type	Mapped .NET Type (System namespace)	Underlying .NET type (SqlTypes namespace)
Binary	Byte[]	SqlBinary
Bigint	Int64	SqlInt64
Char	String	SqlString
Datetime	DateTime	SqlDateTime
Decimal	Decimal	SqlDecimal
Float	Double	SqlDouble
Image	Byte[]	SqlBinary
Int	Int32	SqlInt32
Money	Decimal	SqlMoney
Nchar	String	SqlString
Ntext	String	SqlString
Nvarchar	String	SqlString
Numeric	Decimal	SqlDecimal
Real	Single	SqlSingle
Smalldatetime	DateTime	SqlDateTime
Smallint	Int16	SqlInt16
Smallmoney	Decimal	SqlMoney
sql_variant	Object	System.Object (base class)
Sysname	String	SqlString
Text	String	SqlString
Timestamp	DateTime	SqlBinary
Tinyint	Byte	SqlByte
Varbinary	Byte[]	SqlBinary
Varchar	String	SqlString
Uniqueidentifier	Guid	SqlGuid

The OLE DB Provider

The OLE DB provider interface provides access to a database through an OLE DB provider installed on your computer. Most OLE DB providers are supported, but those that use OLE DB Version 2.5 interfaces aren't supported. Some unsupported OLE DB interfaces include:

- OLE DB provider for ODBC (MSDASQL)
- OLE DB provider for Exchange (ExOLEDB)
- OLE DB for Internet Publishing (MSDAIPP)

Table A-3 lists some commonly used OLE DB drivers.

Table A-3. Commonly used OLE DB drivers

Name	Description
SQLOLEDB	OLE DB provider for SQL Server
MSDAORA	OLE DB provider for Oracle 7.3 and Oracle 8.
Microsoft.Jet.OLEDB.4.0	OLE DB provider for Access (and other Jet data sources)

All OLE DB types are contained in the System.Data.OleDb namespace (see Table A-4). For low-level information about OLE DB providers, you can refer to the OLE DB programmer's reference on MSDN at *http://msdn.microsoft.com/ library/en-us/oledb/htm/oledboverview_of_ole_db.asp*.

Table A-4. OLE DB .NET provider classes

Interface	Implementing class
IDbConnection	OleDbConnection
IDbCommand	OleDbCommand
IDataParameter, IDbDataParameter	OleDbParameter
IDataReader, IDataRecord	OleDbDataReader
IDataAdapter, IDbDataAdapter	OleDbDataAdapter
IDbTransaction	OleDbTransaction

The OLE DB managed provider doesn't include any structures for OLE DB types. However, the OleDbDataReader does include additional methods that allow you to specify the data type when retrieving a column value. Table A-5 shows the mapping between OLE DB types and .NET framework types (although it doesn't include types used exclusively for stored procedure parameters).

Table A-5. OLE DB type mappings

OLE DB data type	Mapped .NET type	Name in OleDBType enumeration
DBTYPE_I8	Int64	BigInt
DBTYPE_BYTES	Byte[]	Binary
DBTYPE_BOOL	Boolean	Boolean
DBTYPE_BSTR	String	BSTR
DBTYPE_STR	String	Char
DBTYPE_CY	Decimal	Currency
DBTYPE_DATE	DateTime	Date
DBTYPE_DBDATE	DateTime	DBDate
DBTYPE_DBTIME	TimeSpan	DBTime
DBTYPE_DBTIMESTAMP	DateTime	DBTimeStamp
DBTYPE_DECIMAL	Decimal	Decimal
DBTYPE_R8	Double	Double
DBTYPE_EMPTY	Not applicable	Empty
DBTYPE_ERROR	Exception	Error
DBTYPE_FILETIME	DateTime	Filetime
DBTYPE_GUID	Guid	Guid

Table A-5. OLE DB type mappings (continued)

OLE DB data type	Mapped .NET type	Name in OleDBType enumeration
DBTYPE_IDISPATCH	Not supported	IDispatch
DBTYPE_I4	Int32	Integer
DBTYPE_UNKNOWN	Not supported	IUnknown
DBTYPE_NUMERIC	Decimal	Numeric
DBTYPE_PROPVARIANT	Object	PropVarian
DBTYPE_R4	Single	Single
DBTYPE_I2	Int16	SmallInt
DBTYPE_I1	SByte	TinyInt
DBTYPE_UI8	UInt64	UnsignedBitInt
DBTYPE_UI4	UInt32	UnsignedInt
DBTYPE_UI2	UInt16	UnsignedSmallInt
DBTYPE_UI1	Byte	UnsignedTinyInt
DBTYPE_VARIANT	Object	Variant
DBTYPE_WSTR	String	WChar

The ODBC .NET Provider

The ODBC .NET provider is a set of managed classes (see Table A-6) that provides access to a database through any ODBC driver installed on your computer. To find the ODBC .NET driver, navigate to *http://msdn.microsoft.com* and search for ODBC .NET. If you have Version 1.1 of the .NET Framework SDK, ODBC .NET is included.

Table A-6. ODBC .NET provider classes

Interface	Implementing class
IDbConnection	OdbcConnection
IDbCommand	OdbcCommand
IDataParameter, IDbDataParameter	OdbcParameter
IDataReader, IDataRecord	OdbcDataReader
IDataAdapter, IDbDataAdapter	OdbcDataAdapter
IDbTransaction	OdbcTransaction

In .NET 1.1, these types are defined in the *SystemData.dll* assembly and contained in the System.Data.Odbc namespace. With earlier versions of .NET, you need to install the *Microsoft.Data.Odbc.dll* assembly (available form the MSDN site as a separate download), reference it, and import the Microsoft.Data.Odbc namespace.

The Oracle .NET Provider

There are currently two native Oracle providers. Microsoft provides a native Oracle provider that uses the Oracle Call Interface (OCI), provides structures that represent basic Oracle data types, and is optimized for Oracle 8i. This provider can be downloaded from *http://msdn.microsoft.com* (search for Oracle .NET) but is included with the .NET Framework 1.1 (see Table A-7). It doesn't support Oracle 7.3. To use these types, add a reference to the `System.Data.OracleClient.dll` assembly in your Visual Studio .NET project, or use the following *csc.exe* command line:

```
csc /r:System.Data.OracleClient.dll codeFile.cs
```

Table A-7. Oracle .NET provider classes

Interface	Implementing class
IDbConnection	OracleConnection
IDbCommand	OracleCommand
IDataParameter, IDbDataParameter	OracleParameter
IDataReader, IDataRecord	OracleDataReader
IDataAdapter, IDbDataAdapter	OracleDataAdapter
IDbTransaction	OracleTransaction

The ODP.NET Provider

Oracle also provides its own native provider called ODP.NET (see Table A-8). It can connect to an Oracle 8*i* or later database and be downloaded from *http://otn.oracle.com/tech/windows/odpnet* with documentation and code samples. The ODP.NET provider provides the standard connection-based and type-specific classes, and is actually quite similar in structure to the Microsoft provider for Oracle.

To use the ODP.NET types, add the reference to the *Oracle.DataAccess.dll* assembly in your Visual Studio .NET project, or use the following command line when compiling:

```
csc /r:Oracle.DataAccess.dll codeFile.cs
```

Table A-8. ODP.NET provider classes

Interface	Implementing class
IDbConnection	OraConnection
IDbCommand	OraCommand
IDataParameter, IDbDataParameter	OraParameter
IDataReader, IDataRecord	OraDataReader
IDataAdapter, IDbDataAdapter	OraDataAdapter
IDbTransaction	OraTransaction

B

ADO.NET XML Extensions

Microsoft defines two namespaces for configuring DataSet schema files: codegen (*urn:schemas-microsoft-com:xml-msprop*) and msdata (*urn:schemas-microsoft-com:xml-msdata*). These namespaces extend the XSD format, allowing it to represent additional database-specific properties and allowing you to configure how typed DataSets are generated. In addition, the diffgr, or DiffGram namespace (*urn:schemas-microsoft-com:xml-diffgram-v1*), defines attributes that provide a way for XML documents to track DataSet changes and row insertions and deletions.

The structure of the XSD file for a DataSet is as follows:

```
<?xml version="1.0" encoding="utf-8"?>
<xs:schema id="DataSetName">

  <xs:element name="DataSetName" >
    <xs:complexType>
      <xs:choice maxOccurs="unbounded">

        <xs:element name="DataTableName" >
          <xs:complexType>
            <xs:sequence>

              <xs:element name="FieldName" />

          </xs:complexType>
        </xs:element>

      </xs:choice>
    </xs:complexType>

    <xs:unique name="ConstraintName" />
    <xs:keyref name="RelationName" />
```

```
    </xs:element>
  </xs:schema>
```

The structure of the DiffGram format is shown next. All DiffGrams contains three sections: the current data, the original data, and any errors.

```
<?xml version="1.0"?>
<diffgr:diffgram
        xmlns:msdata="urn:schemas-microsoft-com:xml-msdata"
        xmlns:diffgr="urn:schemas-microsoft-com:xml-diffgram-v1"
        xmlns:xsd="http://www.w3.org/2001/XMLSchema">

  <!-- Data goes here. Changed rows are flagged. -->

  <diffgr:before>
      <!-- Contains the original data. -->
  </diffgr:before>

  <diffgr:errors>
      <!-- Contains error information. -->
  </diffgr:errors>

</diffgr:diffgram>
```

For specific examples that show how you can create a typed DataSet and refine its schema, refer to Chapter 4. For an introduction to the DiffGram format and XML serialization with the DataSet, refer to Chapter 7.

codegen Namespace

The codegen namespace gives you fine-grained control of a typed DataSet. By adding codegen attributes, you can configure the names that are used for methods, properties, relations, and constraints. When using the codegen namespace, it should be imported as shown:

```
<xs:schema id="DataSetName" xmlns=""
    xmlns:xs="http://www.w3.org/2001/XMLSchema"
    xmlns:msdata="urn:schemas-microsoft-com:xml-msdata"
    xmlns:codegen="urn:schemas-microsoft-com:xml-msprop" >
```

 codegen attributes configure the names used in strongly typed DataSet objects. They do not have any effect on the functionality of the generated DataSet class.

Table B-1 indicates where the various codegen attributes can be used and what they accomplish. Table B-2 briefly describes each attribute.

Table B-1. codegen attribute use

Typed DataSet object/method/event	Default name	codegen attribute
DataTable	TableNameDataTable	typedPlural
DataTable Methods	NewTableNameRow AddTableNameRow DeleteTableNameRow	typedName

Table B-1. codegen attribute use (continued)

Typed DataSet object/method/event	Default name	codegen attribute
DataRowCollection	TableName	typedPlural
DataRow	TableNameRow	typedName
DataColumn	DataTable.ColumnNameColumn DataRow.ColumnName	typedName
Property	PropertyName	typedName
Child Accessor	GetChildTableNameRows	typedChildren
Parent Accessor	TableNameRow	typedParent
DataSet Events	TableNameRowChangeEvent TableNameRowChangeEventHandler	typedName

Table B-2. codegen atttributes

Attribute	Description
typedName	Name of the object in the generated class.
typedPlural	The name of the object in a collection of objects. For example, if you specify Category for typedName and Categories for typedPlural, you generate a Categories collection and a Category row (instead of a CategoriesRow).
typedParent	Name of the object when referred to in a parent relationship. Typed datasets automatically generate methods that provide access to parent and child rows. For example, if you specify Category for the typedParent of an order record, use a Order.Category( ) method instead of Order.GetCategoriesRow( ).
typedChildren	Name of the method to return objects from a child relationship. For example, if you specify Order for the typedChild of a category record, use a Category.Orders( ) method instead of Category.GetOrdersRows( ).
nullValue	Indicates the behavior when null values are encountered. See Table B-3 for possible values.

Finally, Table B-3 identifies possible values for the nullValue attribute.

Table B-3. Values for nullValue

Value	Description
[Replacement Value]	Specifies a value to be returned. For example, use nullValue="0" to set null integer fields to 0.
_throw	Throws an exception when a null value is encountered. This is the default.
_null	Returns a null reference (or throws an exception if a primitive type is encountered).
_empty	For strings, returns String.Empty. For objects, returns the default uninitialized object (created from the zero-parameter constructor). If a primitive type is encountered, ADO.NET generates an exception.

msdata Namespace

The msdata namespace extends a XSD document so that it can represent an ADO.NET DataSet. The msdata namespace is also used in XML documents: namely in the DiffGram representation of a DataSet (along with the diffgr namespace). Here's an example of how the msdata namespace is imported in an XSD file:

```
<xs:schema id="DataSetName" xmlns=""
    xmlns:xs="http://www.w3.org/2001/XMLSchema"
    xmlns:msdata="urn:schemas-microsoft-com:xml-msdata" >
```

One place where you'll see the `msdata` namespace is in the element tag containing the XSD structure. Here, an `IsDataSet` attribute indicates that the schema is used to represent an ADO.NET `DataSet`:

```
<xs:element name="DataSetName" msdata:IsDataSet="true" >
```

The element tag also supports optional `CaseSensitive` and `Local` attributes:

```
<xs:element name="DataSetName"
    msdata:CaseSensitive="true" msdata:Locale="en">
```

More importantly, the `msdata` namespace represents various `DataColumn` properties that don't have direct XSD mappings. Table B-4 lists these.

Table B-4. msdata column attributes

Attribute	Description
AutoIncrement, AutoIncrementSeed, AutoIncrementStep	Sets the auto-incrementing options for unique identity fields. These attributes map to corresponding DataColumn properties.
Caption	Specifies the display caption for the column. Maps to DataColumn.Caption.
Expression	Sets the expression used to filter rows, calculate the values in a column, or create an aggregate column. Maps to DataColumn.Expression.
ReadOnly	Indicates (true or false) whether the value can be changed. This maps to DataColumn.ReadOnly.

The `msdata` namespace is also used with `unique` elements (to specify a unique constraint for a field), `key` elements (to specify the primary key for a table), and `keyref` elements (to specify relations between two tables). These elements are introduced in Chapter 4. See Tables B-5 and B-6.

Table B-5. msdata unique and key attributes

Attribute	Description
ConstraintName	If this attribute is specified, its value is used as the constraint name in the DataSet.Contraints collection. Otherwise, the name attribute provides the constraint name.
PrimaryKey	If set to true, the indicated field is identified as a primary key for the table.

Table B-6. msdata keyref attributes

Attribute	Description
ConstraintOnly	When set to true, a constraint is created on the DataSet but no relation is created. If this attribute isn't specified (or is set to false), both the constraint and the relation are created.
ConstraintName	Maps to ForeignKeyConstraint.ConstraintName. If it is not specified, name attribute of the keyref element is used instead.
UpdateRule	Maps to ForeignKeyConstraint.UpdateRule. If it is not specified, Cascade is used by default.

Table B-6. msdata keyref attributes (continued)

Attribute	Description
DeleteRule	Maps to ForeignKeyConstraint.DeleteRule. If it is not specified, Cascade is used by default.
AcceptRejectRule	Maps to ForeignKeyConstraint.AcceptRejectRule. If it is not specified, None is used by default.
IsNested	This is true if the relationship is nested (meaning the elements of the child table are grouped under the appropriate parent row in the XML file).

When you use a keyref element in a schema, there will be one of two results:

- If the ConstraintOnly attribute is false, a ForeignKeyConstraint and a DataRelation object are created and added to the DataSet.
- If the ConstraintOnly attribute is true, a ForeignKeyConstraint object is created an added to the DataSet, but a DataRelation isn't.

If you want to create a DataRelation without a ForeignKeyConstraint, you need to add an entirely new element to the schema document: msdata:Relationship. This element is shown below and in Table B-7.

```
<msdata:Relationship name="RelationshipName"
      msdata:parent="ParentElement"
      msdata:child="ChildElement"
      msdata:parentkey="ParentColumnElement"
      msdata:childkey="ChildColumnElement" />
```

Table B-7. msdata:Relationship attributes

Attribute	Description
parent	The name of the complex type element that represents the parent row
child	The name of the complex type element that represents the child row
parentkey	The name of the element that represents the parent column
childkey	The name of the element that represents the child column

Finally, the msdata namespace is used with the DiffGram if you want to set a specific column order or hide a row. There are two valid msdata attributes that you can apply to row elements in a DiffGram, and they are described in Table B-8.

Table B-8. msdata DiffGram row attributes

Attribute	Description
rowOrder	A zero-based index number that can specify a column ordering other than the one in which the columns are listed in the DiffGram. For example, the row with rowOrder="0" automatically becomes the first column in the DataSet.
hidden	This attribute is used if the DataColumn.ColumnMapping property for a column is set to MappingType.Hidden. In this case, the column value is written in the DiffGram as a special hidden attribute, using the syntax msdata:hiddenColumnName="value". An example might be msdata:hiddenContactTitle="Owner". If a hidden column is empty, its value isn't written to the DiffGram.

diffgr Namespace

The `diffgr` namespace contains XML attributes used to mark up a DiffGram document with versioning information. Here's how the `diffgr` namespace is imported in a DiffGram document:

```
<xs:schema id="DataSetName" xmlns=""
    xmlns:msdata="urn:schemas-microsoft-com:xml-msdata"
    xmlns:diffgr="urn:schemas-microsoft-com:xml-diffgram-v1"
    xmlns:xsd="http://www.w3.org/2001/XMLSchema" >
```

The `diffgr` namespace includes several attributes that can be applied to row elements, as described in Table B-9. The values `hasChanges` can take on are listed in Table B-10.

Table B-9. diffgr row attributes

Attribute	Description
id	Uniquely identifies a row. This pairs the elements in the `<diffgr:before>` and `<diffgr:errors>` sections to the current data. This value is generated using the table name and row identifier (for example, `diffgr:id="Customers1"`).
parentId	Used with relationships. Identifies the element that's the parent for the current row, using the parent's `diffgr:id` attribute.
hasChanges	Flags a row, identifying that is has been modified. This attribute is used only in the `<DataInstance>` section and can take one of the three values described in Table B-10.
hasErrors	If set to `true`, the row is flagged as having an error (which is described in the `<diffgr:errors>` section).
Error	Contains the text of the `DataRow.RowError` property. This is used only in the `<diffgr:errors>` section.

Table B-10. Values for hasChanges

Attribute	Description
Inserted	Represents a newly added row.
modified	Represents a row in which at least some data has changed from the data in the `<diffgr:before>` section. This doesn't include the deleted row, which appears in the `<diffgr:before>` section but nowhere else.
descent	Identifies an element in which one or more children from a parent-child relationship have been modified.

C

Microsoft Data Engine (MSDE)

MSDE is a scaled-down version of the SQL Server engine that's free to install and distribute. It's similar to SQL Server, except for a few limitations:

- It supports only five simultaneous users.
- It doesn't include any graphical tools to help you design tables, monitor performance, and perform general database maintenance. However, you can use Visual Studio .NET and its Server Explorer to gain some basic database manipulation abilities.
- It can't host a database larger than 2 GB.

MSDE is an ideal platform for testing ADO.NET code if you don't have a SQL Server database handy. You can even install it alongside an instance of SQL Server if you don't want to test with a production server. Best of all, databases created in MSDE can be easily migrated to a SQL Server installation.

Installing MSDE

MSDE is included with the Visual Studio .NET and the .NET Framework SDK. You must complete its setup after you run the main software installation. You do this by running the *setup.exe* program from the *\Setup\MSDE* subfolder under the main Visual Studio .NET or the *Samples\Setup\MSDE* directory under the main Framework SDK installation folder.

To connect to an MSDE instance, use the SQL Server provider. Remember, MSDE is simply a client-limited version of SQL Server. The connection string is similar but requires a slightly different Data Source parameter. If you use MSDE on the local machine, and you installed it with the .NET SDK, use the following connection string:

```
Data Source=localhost\\NetSDK
```

If you installed MSDE with Visual Studio .NET, use the following instead:

```
Data Source=localhost\\VSdotNET
```

You can also replace localhost with the name of an MSDE server. To view the MSDE service, and start, stop, or pause it, run the Computer Management utility (from the Administrative Tools section of the Control Panel), and browse to the Services and Applications → Microsoft SQL Servers node (see Figure C-1).

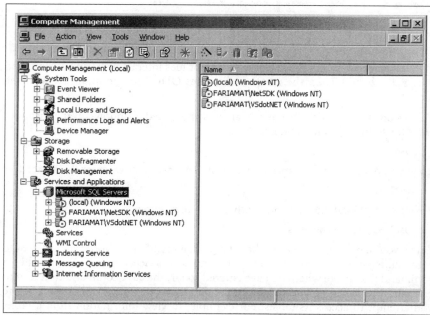

Figure C-1. Installed SQL and MSDE services

MSDE Essentials

MSDE has been around since Visual Studio 6, and you can find additional information about using it from Microsoft at *http://www.microsoft.com/sql/techinfo/development/2000/MSDE2000.asp*. Table C-1 lists the differences between SQL Server and MSDE.

Table C-1. MSDE versus SQL Server

Feature	SQL Server	MSDE
Storage limit	None	2 GB
Concurrent user limit	None	5
CPU limit	Depends on the version, typically 4 to 32.	2
Clustering	Yes	No
OLAP	Yes	No
Replication	Snapshot, merge, and transactional	Merge and transactional (subscriber only)

Table C-1. MSDE versus SQL Server (continued)

Feature	SQL Server	MSDE
Graphical tools	A full suite, including tools for database design, performance tracing, and running queries	None, although you can perform some tasks through Visual Studio .NET or Microsoft Access. You can also use the command-line *OSQL.exe* utility or the SQL Server Enterprise Manager if it's installed.
Licensing	Server license plus concurrent user license	Free.

Though MSDE lacks a graphical tool for executing SQL queries and commands, you can use the OSQL command-line utility. It allows you to execute Transact-SQL statements, system procedures, and script files interactively from a command line. Behind the scenes, the OSQL utility uses ODBC to communicate with the server.

To log on to an MSDE instance that uses integrated Windows authentication, enter the following command line:

```
osql -E
```

To log on to an MSDE instance that uses SQL authentication, enter this instead:

```
osql –U sa
```

To access an MSDE instance on another computer, enter:

```
osql –S serverName –U sa
```

Once you have logged on to the OSQL command line, you can enter SQL commands, store procedure statements, and so on (see Figure C-2). Use the go command to execute what you have entered so far, the quit command to return to exit, and the use command to specify the database you want to work with before you attempt to access its tables. For example, to view information from a table, you might enter the following commands in OSQL:

```
USE Northwind
SELECT * FROM Customers
GO
```

More information about OSQL can be found online at *http://msdn.microsoft.com/library/en-us/coprompt/cp_osql_1wxl.asp*.

Adding the Northwind Data

When first installed, MSDE doesn't contain any data except the standard set of system tables such as master, model, msdb, and tempdb. Fortunately, the .NET framework includes SQL scripts to install several sample databases:

- The Northwind database: *instnwnd.sql*
- The pubs database: *instpubs.sql*
- The IBuySpy portal database: *portal.sql*

Look for these files in a directory such as *C:\Program Files\Microsoft Visual Studio .NET\FrameworkSDK\Samples\Setup*. The *instnwnd.sql* installs the database,

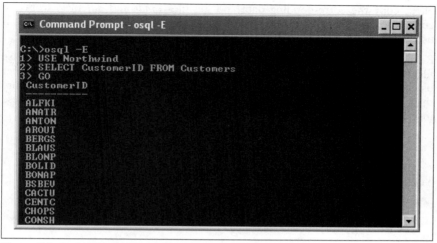

Figure C-2. Performing a query with OSQL

tables, and sample rows you need to run all the examples in this book. To install it, you can use the OSQL command-line utility.

Here's the code required to install the Northwind table to the instance of MSDE that is installed with Visual Studio .NET (assuming the *instnwnd.sql* file is in the current directory).

```
osql -E /i instnwnd.sql
```

Alternatively, you can use SQL authentication with the –U parameter:

```
osql -U sa /i instnwnd.sql
```

If MSDE is installed on another computer, or if your computer also has SQL Server installed, you must explicitly identify the MSDE instance you want to use by adding the –S parameter. The following command assumes you are using the version of MSDE installed with Visual Studio .NET:

```
osql -S serverName\VSdotNET -E /i instnwnd.sql
```

Migrating MSDE to SQL Server

If you decide to migrate an MSDE database to SQL Server, you have several options. One is to simply install SQL Server on top of MSDE. If you install SQL Server on a separate computer (a more likely approach), you can detach the MSDE database file and reattach it on a SQL Server machine using the *sp_detach_db* and *sp_attach_db* stored procedures that are provided in all SQL Server and MSDE databases.

To start, log on to your MSDE instance, and use the following commands (in OSQL) to remove the database:

```
USE Master
sp_detach_db 'databaseName'
GO
```

Next, copy the corresponding data and log files (*.mdf* and *.ldf* files) from the current location to the new computer. They should be placed in the data path used by your SQL Server.

Reattach the database to SQL Server using the database name and the database filename (with full path). These commands can be entered on the SQL Server using Query Analyzer or OSQL (which SQL Server also supports). Just make sure that you log on to the correct SQL Server first before you execute these instructions.

```
USE master
sp_attach_db 'database name','databaseFile'
GO
```

You can verify the change in file location using the *sp_helpfile* stored procedure:

```
USE databaseName
sp_helpfile
GO
```

D

Type, Method, Property, and Field Index

Use this index to locate a type or member and see where it's defined. For a type (a class or interface), you can find the enclosing namespace. If you know the name of a member (a method, property, event, or field), you can find all the types that define it.

Handler, OleDbRowUpdatedEvent-Handler, OleDbRowUpdatingEvent-Handler, SqlInfoMessageEventHandler, SqlRowUpdatedEventHandler, SqlRow-UpdatingEventHandler, StateChange-EventHandler

BeginLoadData( ): DataTable

BeginTransaction( ): IDbConnection, Ole-DbConnection, SqlConnection

BigInt: OleDbType, SqlDbType

Binary: DbType, OleDbType, SqlDbType

Binary_Literal: OleDbLiteral

BinarySort: SqlCompareOptions, SqlString

BinData: SqlDecimal

Bit: SqlDbType

BitwiseAnd( ): SqlByte, SqlInt16, SqlInt32, SqlInt64

BitwiseOr( ): SqlByte, SqlInt16, SqlInt32, Sql-Int64

Boolean: DbType, OleDbType

Both: UpdateRowSource

Broken: ConnectionState

BSTR: OleDbType

Byte: DbType

ByteValue: SqlBoolean

C

Cancel( ): IDbCommand, OleDbCommand, SqlCommand

CancelEdit( ): DataRow, DataRowView

CanRemove( ): ConstraintCollection, DataColumnCollection, DataRelation-Collection, DataTableCollection

Caption: DataColumn

Cascade: AcceptRejectRule, Rule

CaseSensitive: DataSet, DataTable

Catalog_Name: OleDbLiteral

Catalog_Separator: OleDbLiteral

Catalogs: OleDbSchemaGuid

Ceiling( ): SqlDecimal

Change: DataRowAction

ChangeDatabase( ): IDbConnection, Ole-DbConnection, SqlConnection

Chaos: IsolationLevel

Char: OleDbType, SqlDbType

Char_Literal: OleDbLiteral

Character_Sets: OleDbSchemaGuid

Check_Constraints: OleDbSchemaGuid

Check_Constraints_By_Table: OleDbSchema-Guid

CheckStateForProperty( ): Constraint, Data-Relation

CheckUnique( ): DataColumn

ChildColumns: DataRelation

ChildKeyConstraint: DataRelation

ChildRelations: DataTable

ChildTable: DataRelation

Class: SqlError, SqlException

Clear( ): ConstraintCollection, Data-ColumnCollection, DataColumn-MappingCollection, DataRelation-Collection, DataRowCollection, DataSet, DataTable, DataTableCollection, Data-TableMappingCollection, DBData-Permission, OleDbParameterCollection, SqlParameterCollection

ClearErrors( ): DataRow

ClearFunctionCalled: DataSet

Clone( ): DataSet, DataTable, SqlString

CloneInternals( ): DataAdapter

Close( ): DataView, IDataReader, IDb-Connection, OleDbConnection, OleDb-DataReader, SqlConnection, SqlData-Reader

CloseConnection: CommandBehavior

Closed: ConnectionState

Collations: OleDbSchemaGuid

CollectionChanged: ConstraintCollection, DataColumnCollection, DataRelation-Collection, DataTableCollection

CollectionChanging: DataColumnCollection, DataRelationCollection, DataTable-Collection

Column: DataColumnChangeEventArgs

Column_Alias: OleDbLiteral

Column_Domain_Usage: OleDbSchemaGuid

Column_Name: OleDbLiteral

Column_Privileges: OleDbSchemaGuid

ColumnChanged: DataTable

ColumnChanging: DataTable

ColumnCollectionChanged( ): DataView

ColumnMapping: DataColumn

ColumnMappings: DataTableMapping, ITableMapping

ColumnName: DataColumn

ColumnPropertyChanged: DataColumn-Collection

Class Index

D

Data: SqlDecimal

DataAdapter: OleDbCommandBuilder, SqlCommandBuilder, System.Data.Common

Database: IDbConnection, OleDbConnection, SqlConnection

DataColumn: System.Data

DataColumnChangeEventArgs: System.Data

DataColumnChangeEventHandler: System.Data

DataColumnCollection: System.Data

DataColumnMapping: System.Data.Common

DataColumnMappingCollection: System.Data.Common

DataException: System.Data

DataRelation: System.Data

DataRelationCollection: System.Data

DataRow: System.Data

DataRowAction: System.Data

DataRowBuilder: System.Data

DataRowChangeEventArgs: System.Data

DataRowChangeEventHandler: System.Data

DataRowCollection: System.Data

DataRowCreated: DataSet

DataRowState: System.Data

DataRowVersion: System.Data

DataRowView: System.Data

DataSet: DataRelation, DataTable, DataViewManager, System.Data

DataSetColumn: DataColumnMapping, IColumnMapping

DataSetName: DataSet

DataSetTable: DataTableMapping, ITableMapping

DataSource: OleDbConnection, SqlConnection

DataSysDescriptionAttribute: System.Data

DataTable: FillErrorEventArgs, System.Data

DataTableCollection: System.Data

DataTableMapping: System.Data.Common

DataTableMappingCollection: System.Data.Common

DataType: DataColumn

DataView: DataRowView, System.Data

DataViewManager: DataView, DataViewSetting, System.Data

DataViewRowState: System.Data

DataViewSetting: System.Data

DataViewSettingCollection: System.Data

DataViewSettingCollectionString: DataViewManager

DataViewSettings: DataViewManager

Date: DbType, OleDbType

DateTime: DbType, SqlDbType

DayTicks: SqlDateTime

DBConcurrencyException: System.Data

DbDataAdapter: System.Data.Common

DBDataPermission: System.Data.Common

DBDataPermissionAttribute: System.Data.Common

DbDataRecord: System.Data.Common

DBDate: OleDbType

DbEnumerator: System.Data.Common

DbInfoLiterals: OleDbSchemaGuid

DBTime: OleDbType

DBTimeStamp: OleDbType

DbType: IDataParameter, OleDbParameter, SqlParameter, System.Data

Decimal: DbType, OleDbType, SqlDbType

Default: CommandBehavior, DataRowVersion

DefaultSourceTableName: DbDataAdapter

DefaultValue: DataColumn

DefaultView: DataTable

DefaultViewManager: DataSet

Delete: DataRowAction, StatementType

Delete( ): DataRow, DataRowView, DataView

DeleteCommand: IDbDataAdapter, OleDbDataAdapter, SqlDataAdapter

Deleted: DataRowState, DataViewRowState

DeletedRowInaccessibleException: System.Data

DeleteRule: ForeignKeyConstraint

Depth: IDataReader, OleDbDataReader, SqlDataReader

DeriveParameters( ): OleDbCommandBuilder, SqlCommandBuilder

Description: DataSysDescriptionAttribute

DesignTimeVisible: OleDbCommand, SqlCommand

Detached: DataRowState

DiffGram: XmlReadMode, XmlWriteMode

Dimension_Name: OleDbLiteral

Direction: IDataParameter, OleDbParameter, SqlParameter

DisplayExpression: DataTable

Dispose( ): DataAdapter, DataView, DbDataAdapter, OleDbCommand, OleDbCommandBuilder, OleDbConnection, OleDbDataAdapter, SqlCommandBuilder, SqlConnection, SqlDataAdapter, SqlTransaction

Divide( ): SqlByte, SqlDecimal, SqlDouble, SqlInt16, SqlInt32, SqlInt64, SqlMoney, SqlSingle

Double: DbType, OleDbType

DuplicateNameException: System.Data

E

Element: MappingType

Empty: OleDbType

EndEdit( ): DataRow, DataRowView

EndInit( ): DataSet, DataTable, DataView

EndInvoke( ): DataColumnChangeEventHandler, DataRowChangeEventHandler, FillErrorEventHandler, MergeFailedEventHandler, OleDbInfoMessageEventHandler, OleDbRowUpdatedEventHandler, OleDbRowUpdatingEventHandler, SqlInfoMessageEventHandler, SqlRowUpdatedEventHandler, SqlRowUpdatingEventHandler, StateChangeEventHandler

EndLoadData( ): DataTable

EnforceConstraints: DataSet

EnlistDistributedTransaction( ): OleDbConnection, SqlConnection

Equals( ): DataRowView, ForeignKeyConstraint, SqlBinary, SqlBoolean, SqlByte, SqlDateTime, SqlDecimal, SqlDouble, SqlGuid, SqlInt16, SqlInt32, SqlInt64, SqlMoney, SqlSingle, SqlString, UniqueConstraint

Error: MissingMappingAction, MissingSchemaAction, OleDbType

ErrorCode: OleDbException, OleDbInfoMessageEventArgs

ErrorList: TypedDataSetGeneratorException

Errors: FillErrorEventArgs, OleDbException, OleDbInfoMessageEventArgs, RowUpdatedEventArgs, RowUpdatingEventArgs, SqlException, SqlInfoMessageEventArgs

ErrorsOccurred: UpdateStatus

Escape_Percent_Prefix: OleDbLiteral

Escape_Percent_Suffix: OleDbLiteral

Escape_Underscore_Prefix: OleDbLiteral

Escape_Underscore_Suffix: OleDbLiteral

EvaluateException: System.Data

ExecuteNonQuery( ): IDbCommand, OleDbCommand, SqlCommand

ExecuteReader( ): IDbCommand, OleDbCommand, SqlCommand

ExecuteScalar( ): IDbCommand, OleDbCommand, SqlCommand

ExecuteXmlReader( ): SqlCommand

Executing: ConnectionState

Expression: DataColumn

ExtendedProperties: Constraint, DataColumn, DataRelation, DataSet, DataTable

F

False: SqlBoolean

Fetching: ConnectionState

FieldCount: DbDataRecord, IDataRecord, OleDbDataReader, SqlDataReader

Filetime: OleDbType

Fill( ): DataAdapter, DbDataAdapter, IDataAdapter, OleDbDataAdapter

FillError: DbDataAdapter

FillErrorEventArgs: System.Data

FillErrorEventHandler: System.Data

FillSchema( ): DataAdapter, DbDataAdapter, IDataAdapter

Finalize( ): OleDbDataReader, OleDbTransaction

Find( ): DataRowCollection, DataView

FindRows( ): DataView

FirstReturnedRecord: UpdateRowSource

Float: SqlDbType

Floor( ): SqlDecimal

Foreign_Keys: OleDbSchemaGuid

ForeignKeyConstraint: System.Data

Fragment: XmlReadMode

FromXml( ): DBDataPermission, OleDbPermission

G

Generate( ): TypedDataSetGenerator

GenerateIdName( ): TypedDataSetGenerator

GetBoolean( ): DbDataRecord, IDataRecord, OleDbDataReader, SqlDataReader

GetByDataSetColumn( ): DataColumnMappingCollection, IColumnMappingCollection

GetByDataSetTable( ): DataTableMappingCollection, ITableMappingCollection

GetByte( ): DbDataRecord, IDataRecord, OleDbDataReader, SqlDataReader

GetBytes( ): DbDataRecord, IDataRecord, OleDbDataReader, SqlDataReader

GetChanges( ): DataSet, DataTable

GetChar( ): DbDataRecord, IDataRecord, OleDbDataReader, SqlDataReader

GetChars( ): DbDataRecord, IDataRecord, OleDbDataReader, SqlDataReader

GetChildRows( ): DataRow

GetColumnError( ): DataRow

GetColumnMappingBySchemaAction( ): DataColumnMappingCollection, DataTableMapping

GetColumnsInError( ): DataRow

GetData( ): DbDataRecord, IDataRecord, OleDbDataReader, SqlDataReader

GetDataColumnBySchemaAction( ): DataColumnMapping

GetDataSet( ): DataRelationCollection

GetDataTableBySchemaAction( ): DataTableMapping

GetDataTypeName( ): DbDataRecord, IDataRecord, OleDbDataReader, SqlDataReader

GetDateTime( ): DbDataRecord, IDataRecord, OleDbDataReader, SqlDataReader

GetDecimal( ): DbDataRecord, IDataRecord, OleDbDataReader, SqlDataReader

GetDeleteCommand( ): OleDbCommandBuilder, SqlCommandBuilder

GetDouble( ): DbDataRecord, IDataRecord, OleDbDataReader, SqlDataReader

GetEnumerator( ): DataColumnMappingCollection, DataTableMappingCollection, DataView, DataViewSettingCollection, InternalDataCollectionBase, OleDbErrorCollection, OleDbParameterCollection, SqlErrorCollection, SqlParameterCollection

GetErrors( ): DataTable

GetFieldType( ): DbDataRecord, IDataRecord, OleDbDataReader, SqlDataReader

GetFillParameters( ): DataAdapter, DbDataAdapter, IDataAdapter

GetFloat( ): DbDataRecord, IDataRecord, OleDbDataReader, SqlDataReader

GetGuid( ): DbDataRecord, IDataRecord, OleDbDataReader, SqlDataReader

GetHashCode( ): DataRowView, ForeignKeyConstraint, SqlBinary, SqlBoolean, SqlByte, SqlDateTime, SqlDecimal, SqlDouble, SqlGuid, SqlInt16, SqlInt32, SqlInt64, SqlMoney, SqlSingle, SqlString, UniqueConstraint

GetInsertCommand( ): OleDbCommandBuilder, SqlCommandBuilder

GetInt16( ): DbDataRecord, IDataRecord, OleDbDataReader, SqlDataReader

GetInt32( ): DbDataRecord, IDataRecord, OleDbDataReader, SqlDataReader

GetInt64( ): DbDataRecord, IDataRecord, OleDbDataReader, SqlDataReader

GetName( ): DbDataRecord, IDataRecord, OleDbDataReader, SqlDataReader

GetNonUnicodeBytes( ): SqlString

GetObjectData( ): DBConcurrencyException, OleDbException, SqlException, TypedDataSetGeneratorException

GetOleDbSchemaTable( ): OleDbConnection

GetOrdinal( ): DbDataRecord, IDataRecord, OleDbDataReader, SqlDataReader

GetParentRow( ): DataRow

GetParentRows( ): DataRow

GetRowType( ): DataTable

GetSchemaSerializable( ): DataSet

GetSchemaTable( ): IDataReader, OleDbDataReader, SqlDataReader

GetSerializationData( ): DataSet

GetSqlBinary( ): SqlDataReader

GetSqlBoolean( ): SqlDataReader

GetSqlByte( ): SqlDataReader

GetSqlDateTime( ): SqlDataReader

GetSqlDecimal( ): SqlDataReader

GetSqlDouble( ): SqlDataReader

GetSqlGuid( ): SqlDataReader

GetSqlInt16( ): SqlDataReader

GetSqlInt32( ): SqlDataReader

GetSqlInt64( ): SqlDataReader

Int32: DbType

Int64: DbType

Integer: OleDbType

InternalDataCollectionBase: System.Data

Intersect( ): DBDataPermission, OleDb-
Permission

INullable: System.Data.SqlTypes

Invalid: OleDbLiteral

InvalidConstraintException: System.Data

InvalidExpressionException: System.Data

Invoke( ): DataColumnChangeEventHandler,
DataRowChangeEventHandler, Fill-
ErrorEventHandler, MergeFailedEvent-
Handler, OleDbInfoMessageEvent-
Handler, OleDbRowUpdatedEvent-
Handler, OleDbRowUpdatingEvent-
Handler, SqlInfoMessageEventHandler,
SqlRowUpdatedEventHandler, SqlRow-
UpdatingEventHandler, StateChange-
EventHandler

IsClosed: IDataReader, OleDbDataReader,
SqlDataReader

IsDBNull( ): DbDataRecord, IDataRecord,
OleDbDataReader, SqlDataReader

IsEdit: DataRowView

IsFalse: SqlBoolean

IsNew: DataRowView

IsNull: INullable, SqlBinary, SqlBoolean, Sql-
Byte, SqlDateTime, SqlDecimal, Sql-
Double, SqlGuid, SqlInt16, SqlInt32, Sql-
Int64, SqlMoney, SqlSingle, SqlString

IsNull( ): DataRow

IsNullable: IDataParameter, OleDb-
Parameter, SqlParameter

IsolationLevel: IDbTransaction, OleDb-
Transaction, SqlTransaction, System.Data

IsPositive: SqlDecimal

IsPrimaryKey: UniqueConstraint

IsReadOnly: DataViewSettingCollection,
InternalDataCollectionBase

IsSubsetOf( ): DBDataPermission

IsSynchronized: DataViewSettingCollection,
InternalDataCollectionBase

IsTrue: SqlBoolean

IsUnrestricted( ): DBDataPermission

ITableMapping: System.Data

ITableMappingCollection: System.Data

Item: ConstraintCollection, Data-
ColumnCollection, DataColumn-
MappingCollection, DataRelation-
Collection, DataRow, DataRow-
Collection, DataRowView, DataTable-
Collection, DataTable-
MappingCollection, DataView, Data-
ViewSettingCollection, DbDataRecord,
IColumnMappingCollection, IData-
ParameterCollection, IDataRecord,
ITableMappingCollection, OleDbData-
Reader, OleDbErrorCollection, OleDb-
ParameterCollection, SqlBinary, SqlData-
Reader, SqlErrorCollection, SqlParameter-
Collection

ItemArray: DataRow

IUnknown: OleDbType

K

Key_Column_Usage: OleDbSchemaGuid

KeyInfo: CommandBehavior

KeyRestrictionBehavior: DBDataPermission-
Attribute, System.Data

KeyRestrictions: DBDataPermissionAttribute

L

LCID: SqlString

Length: SqlBinary

LessThan( ): SqlBinary, SqlByte, SqlDate-
Time, SqlDecimal, SqlDouble, SqlGuid,
SqlInt16, SqlInt32, SqlInt64, SqlMoney,
SqlSingle, SqlString

LessThanOrEqual( ): SqlBinary, SqlByte, Sql-
DateTime, SqlDecimal, SqlDouble, Sql-
Guid, SqlInt16, SqlInt32, SqlInt64, Sql-
Money, SqlSingle, SqlString

Level_Name: OleDbLiteral

Like_Percent: OleDbLiteral

Like_Underscore: OleDbLiteral

LineNumber: SqlError, SqlException

ListChanged: DataView, DataViewManager

LoadDataRow( ): DataTable

Locale: DataSet, DataTable

LongVarBinary: OleDbType

LongVarChar: OleDbType

LongVarWChar: OleDbType

M

Mapped: SchemaType

MappingType: System.Data

MaxLength: DataColumn

MaxPrecision: SqlDecimal

MaxScale: SqlDecimal

MaxValue: SqlByte, SqlDateTime, Sql-
Decimal, SqlDouble, SqlInt16, SqlInt32,
SqlInt64, SqlMoney, SqlSingle

Member_Name: OleDbLiteral

Merge( ): DataSet

MergeFailed: DataSet

MergeFailedEventArgs: System.Data

MergeFailedEventHandler: System.Data

Message: OleDbError, OleDbException,
OleDbInfoMessageEventArgs, SqlError,
SqlException, SqlInfoMessageEventArgs

MinimumCapacity: DataTable

MinValue: SqlByte, SqlDateTime, Sql-
Decimal, SqlDouble, SqlInt16, SqlInt32,
SqlInt64, SqlMoney, SqlSingle

MissingMappingAction: DataAdapter, IData-
Adapter, System.Data

MissingPrimaryKeyException: System.Data

MissingSchemaAction: DataAdapter, IData-
Adapter, System.Data

Mod( ): SqlByte, SqlInt16, SqlInt32, SqlInt64

Modified: DataRowState

ModifiedCurrent: DataViewRowState

ModifiedOriginal: DataViewRowState

Money: SqlDbType

MoveNext( ): DbEnumerator

Multiply( ): SqlByte, SqlDecimal, SqlDouble,
SqlInt16, SqlInt32, SqlInt64, SqlMoney,
SqlSingle

N

Namespace: DataColumn, DataSet, Data-
Table

NativeError: OleDbError

NChar: SqlDbType

Nested: DataRelation

NewRow( ): DataTable

NewRowFromBuilder( ): DataTable

NextResult( ): IDataReader, OleDb-
DataReader, SqlDataReader

None: AcceptRejectRule, DataView-
RowState, Rule, SqlCompareOptions,
UpdateRowSource

NoNullAllowedException: System.Data

NotEquals( ): SqlBinary, SqlBoolean, SqlByte,
SqlDateTime, SqlDecimal, SqlDouble,
SqlGuid, SqlInt16, SqlInt32, SqlInt64,
SqlMoney, SqlSingle, SqlString

Nothing: DataRowAction

NotSupported: PropertyAttributes

NText: SqlDbType

Null: SqlBinary, SqlBoolean, SqlByte, Sql-
DateTime, SqlDecimal, SqlDouble, Sql-
Guid, SqlInt16, SqlInt32, SqlInt64, Sql-
Money, SqlSingle, SqlString

Number: SqlError, SqlException

Numeric: OleDbType

NVarChar: SqlDbType

O

Object: DbType

Offset: SqlParameter

OleDbCommand: System.Data.OleDb

OleDbCommandBuilder: System.Data.OleDb

OleDbConnection: System.Data.OleDb

OleDbDataAdapter: System.Data.OleDb

OleDbDataReader: System.Data.OleDb

OleDbError: System.Data.OleDb

OleDbErrorCollection: System.Data.OleDb

OleDbException: System.Data.OleDb

OleDbInfoMessageEventArgs: System.Data.
OleDb

OleDbInfoMessageEventHandler: System.Data.
OleDb

OleDbLiteral: System.Data.OleDb

OleDbParameter: System.Data.OleDb

OleDbParameterCollection: System.Data.OleDb

OleDbPermission: System.Data.OleDb

OleDbPermissionAttribute: System.Data.OleDb

OleDbRowUpdatedEventArgs: System.Data.
OleDb

OleDbRowUpdatedEventHandler: System.Data.
OleDb

OleDbRowUpdatingEventArgs: System.Data.
OleDb

OleDbRowUpdatingEventHandler: System.Data.
OleDb

OleDbSchemaGuid: System.Data.OleDb

OleDbTransaction: System.Data.OleDb

OleDbType: OleDbParameter, System.Data.
OleDb

OnCollectionChanged( ): ConstraintCollection,
DataColumnCollection, DataRelation-
Collection, DataTableCollection

OnColumnChanged( ): DataTable

OnColumnChanging( ): DataTable

One: SqlBoolean

OnesComplement( ): SqlBoolean, SqlByte, Sql-Int16, SqlInt32, SqlInt64

OnFillError( ): DbDataAdapter

OnListChanged( ): DataView, DataView-Manager

OnRemoveRelation( ): DataSet

OnRemoveTable( ): DataSet

OnRowChanged( ): DataTable

OnRowChanging( ): DataTable

OnRowDeleted( ): DataTable

OnRowDeleting( ): DataTable

OnRowUpdated( ): DbDataAdapter, Ole-DbDataAdapter, SqlDataAdapter

OnRowUpdating( ): DbDataAdapter, Ole-DbDataAdapter, SqlDataAdapter

Open: ConnectionState

Open( ): DataView, IDbConnection, Ole-DbConnection, SqlConnection

Optional: PropertyAttributes

Or( ): SqlBoolean

Ordinal: DataColumn

Original: DataRowVersion

OriginalRows: DataViewRowState

OriginalState: StateChangeEventArgs

Output: ParameterDirection

OutputParameters: UpdateRowSource

P

PacketSize: SqlConnection

ParameterDirection: System.Data

ParameterName: IDataParameter, OleDb-Parameter, SqlParameter

Parameters: IDbCommand, OleDb-Command, SqlCommand

ParentColumns: DataRelation

ParentKeyConstraint: DataRelation

ParentRelations: DataTable

ParentTable: DataRelation

Parse( ): SqlBoolean, SqlByte, SqlDateTime, SqlDecimal, SqlDouble, SqlGuid, Sql-Int16, SqlInt32, SqlInt64, SqlMoney, Sql-Single

Passthrough: MissingMappingAction

Power( ): SqlDecimal

Precision: IDbDataParameter, OleDb-Parameter, SqlDecimal, SqlParameter

Prefix: DataColumn, DataSet, DataTable

Prepare( ): IDbCommand, OleDbCommand, SqlCommand

PreventUsage: KeyRestrictionBehavior

Primary_Keys: OleDbSchemaGuid

PrimaryKey: DataTable

Procedure: SqlError, SqlException

Procedure_Columns: OleDbSchemaGuid

Procedure_Name: OleDbLiteral

Procedure_Parameters: OleDbSchemaGuid

Procedures: OleDbSchemaGuid

Property_Name: OleDbLiteral

PropertyAttributes: System.Data

PropertyChanging: DataColumn, Data-Relation, DataSet, DataTable

PropertyCollection: System.Data

Proposed: DataRowVersion

ProposedValue: DataColumnChangeEvent-Args

PropVariant: OleDbType

Provider: OleDbConnection, OleDb-Permission, OleDbPermissionAttribute

Provider_Types: OleDbSchemaGuid

Q

Quote_Prefix: OleDbLiteral

Quote_Suffix: OleDbLiteral

QuotePrefix: OleDbCommandBuilder, SqlCommandBuilder

QuoteSuffix: OleDbCommandBuilder, SqlCommandBuilder

R

Read: PropertyAttributes

Read( ): IDataReader, OleDbDataReader, SqlDataReader

ReadCommitted: IsolationLevel

ReadOnly: DataColumn

ReadOnlyException: System.Data

ReadSchema: XmlReadMode

ReadUncommitted: IsolationLevel

ReadXml( ): DataSet

ReadXmlSchema( ): DataSet

ReadXmlSerializable( ): DataSet

Real: SqlDbType

RecordsAffected: IDataReader, OleDb-
DataReader, RowUpdatedEventArgs, Sql-
DataReader

Referential_Constraints: OleDbSchemaGuid

RefreshSchema( ): OleDbCommandBuilder,
SqlCommandBuilder

RejectChanges( ): DataRow, DataSet, Data-
Table

RelatedColumns: ForeignKeyConstraint

RelatedTable: ForeignKeyConstraint

RelationCollectionChanged( ): DataView-
Manager

RelationName: DataRelation

Relations: DataSet

ReleaseObjectPool( ): OleDbConnection

Remove( ): ConstraintCollection, Data-
ColumnCollection, DataColumn-
MappingCollection, DataRelation-
Collection, DataRowCollection, Data-
TableCollection, DataTableMapping-
Collection, OleDbParameterCollection,
SqlParameterCollection

RemoveAt( ): ConstraintCollection, Data-
ColumnCollection, DataColumn-
MappingCollection, DataRelation-
Collection, DataRowCollection, Data-
TableCollection, DataTableMapping-
Collection, IColumnMappingCollection,
IDataParameterCollection, ITable-
MappingCollection, OleDbParameter-
Collection, SqlParameterCollection

RemoveCore( ): DataRelationCollection

RepeatableRead: IsolationLevel

Required: PropertyAttributes

Reset( ): DataSet, DataTable, DataView,
DbEnumerator

ResetCommandTimeout( ): OleDbCommand,
SqlCommand

ReturnValue: ParameterDirection

Rollback: DataRowAction

Rollback( ): IDbTransaction, OleDb-
Transaction, SqlTransaction

Round( ): SqlDecimal

Row: DataColumnChangeEventArgs, Data-
RowChangeEventArgs, DataRowView,
DBConcurrencyException, RowUpdated-
EventArgs, RowUpdatingEventArgs

RowChanged: DataTable

RowChanging: DataTable

RowDeleted: DataTable

RowDeleting: DataTable

RowError: DataRow

RowFilter: DataView, DataViewSetting

RowNotInTableException: System.Data

Rows: DataTable

RowState: DataRow

RowStateFilter: DataView, DataViewSetting

RowUpdated: OleDbDataAdapter, Sql-
DataAdapter

RowUpdatedEventArgs: System.Data.Common

RowUpdating: OleDbDataAdapter, Sql-
DataAdapter

RowUpdatingEventArgs: System.Data.Com-
mon

RowVersion: DataRowView

Rule: System.Data

S

Save( ): SqlTransaction

SByte: DbType

Scale: IDbDataParameter, OleDbParameter,
SqlDecimal, SqlParameter

Schema_Name: OleDbLiteral

Schema_Separator: OleDbLiteral

SchemaOnly: CommandBehavior

Schemata: OleDbSchemaGuid

SchemaType: System.Data

Select: StatementType

Select( ): DataTable

SelectCommand: IDbDataAdapter, Ole-
DbDataAdapter, SqlDataAdapter

SequentialAccess: CommandBehavior

Serializable: IsolationLevel

Server: SqlError, SqlException

ServerVersion: OleDbConnection, Sql-
Connection

SetColumnError( ): DataRow

SetDefault: Rule

SetNull: Rule

SetNull( ): DataRow

SetParentRow( ): DataRow

ShouldSerializeRelations( ): DataSet

ShouldSerializeTableMappings( ): DataAdapter

ShouldSerializeTables( ): DataSet

Sign( ): SqlDecimal

SimpleContent: MappingType

Single: DbType, OleDbType

SingleResult: CommandBehavior

SingleRow: CommandBehavior

Site: DataSet, DataTable

Size: IDbDataParameter, OleDbParameter, SqlParameter

SkipAllRemainingRows: UpdateStatus

SkipCurrentRow: UpdateStatus

SmallDateTime: SqlDbType

SmallInt: OleDbType, SqlDbType

SmallMoney: SqlDbType

Sort: DataView, DataViewSetting

Source: OleDbError, OleDbException, OleDbInfoMessageEventArgs, SchemaType, SqlError, SqlException, SqlInfoMessageEventArgs

SourceColumn: DataColumnMapping, IColumnMapping, IDataParameter, OleDbParameter, SqlParameter

SourceTable: DataTableMapping, ITableMapping

SourceVersion: IDataParameter, OleDbParameter, SqlParameter

Sql_Languages: OleDbSchemaGuid

SqlBinary: System.Data.SqlTypes

SqlBoolean: System.Data.SqlTypes

SqlByte: System.Data.SqlTypes

SqlClientPermission: System.Data.SqlClient

SqlClientPermissionAttribute: System.Data.SqlClient

SqlCommand: System.Data.SqlClient

SqlCommandBuilder: System.Data.SqlClient

SqlCompareOptions: SqlString, System.Data.SqlTypes

SqlConnection: System.Data.SqlClient

SqlDataAdapter: System.Data.SqlClient

SqlDataReader: System.Data.SqlClient

SqlDateTime: System.Data.SqlTypes

SqlDbType: SqlParameter, System.Data

SQLDebugging: System.Data.SqlClient

SqlDecimal: System.Data.SqlTypes

SqlDouble: System.Data.SqlTypes

SqlError: System.Data.SqlClient

SqlErrorCollection: System.Data.SqlClient

SqlException: System.Data.SqlClient

SqlGuid: System.Data.SqlTypes

SqlInfoMessageEventArgs: System.Data.SqlClient

SqlInfoMessageEventHandler: System.Data.SqlClient

SqlInt16: System.Data.SqlTypes

SqlInt32: System.Data.SqlTypes

SqlInt64: System.Data.SqlTypes

SqlMoney: System.Data.SqlTypes

SqlNullValueException: System.Data.SqlTypes

SqlParameter: System.Data.SqlClient

SqlParameterCollection: System.Data.SqlClient

SqlRowUpdatedEventArgs: System.Data.SqlClient

SqlRowUpdatedEventHandler: System.Data.SqlClient

SqlRowUpdatingEventArgs: System.Data.SqlClient

SqlRowUpdatingEventHandler: System.Data.SqlClient

SqlSingle: System.Data.SqlTypes

SQLState: OleDbError

SqlString: System.Data.SqlTypes

SQLTicksPerHour: SqlDateTime

SQLTicksPerMinute: SqlDateTime

SQLTicksPerSecond: SqlDateTime

SqlTransaction: System.Data.SqlClient

SqlTruncateException: System.Data.SqlTypes

SqlTypeException: System.Data.SqlTypes

State: IDbConnection, OleDbConnection, SqlConnection, SqlError, SqlException

StateChange: OleDbConnection, SqlConnection

StateChangeEventArgs: System.Data

StateChangeEventHandler: System.Data

StatementType: RowUpdatedEventArgs, RowUpdatingEventArgs, System.Data

Statistics: OleDbSchemaGuid

Status: RowUpdatedEventArgs, RowUpdatingEventArgs

StoredProcedure: CommandType

String: DbType

StringFixedLength: DbType

StrongTypingException: System.Data

Subtract( ): SqlByte, SqlDecimal, SqlDouble, SqlInt16, SqlInt32, SqlInt64, SqlMoney, SqlSingle

SyncRoot: DataViewSettingCollection, InternalDataCollectionBase

SyntaxErrorException: System.Data

T

Table: Constraint, DataColumn, DataRow, DataView, DataViewSetting, ForeignKeyConstraint, MergeFailedEventArgs, UniqueConstraint

Table_Constraints: OleDbSchemaGuid

Table_Name: OleDbLiteral

Table_Privileges: OleDbSchemaGuid

Table_Statistics: OleDbSchemaGuid

TableCollectionChanged( ): DataViewManager

TableDirect: CommandType

TableMapping: RowUpdatedEventArgs, RowUpdatingEventArgs

TableMappings: DataAdapter, IDataAdapter

TableName: DataTable

Tables: DataSet, OleDbSchemaGuid

Tables_Info: OleDbSchemaGuid

Text: CommandType, SqlDbType

Text_Command: OleDbLiteral

Time: DbType

Timestamp: SqlDbType

TimeTicks: SqlDateTime

TinyInt: OleDbType, SqlDbType

ToByteArray( ): SqlGuid

ToDecimal( ): SqlMoney

ToDouble( ): SqlDecimal, SqlMoney

ToInt32( ): SqlMoney

ToInt64( ): SqlMoney

ToSqlBinary( ): SqlGuid

ToSqlBoolean( ): SqlByte, SqlDecimal, SqlDouble, SqlInt16, SqlInt32, SqlInt64, SqlMoney, SqlSingle, SqlString

ToSqlByte( ): SqlBoolean, SqlDecimal, SqlDouble, SqlInt16, SqlInt32, SqlInt64, SqlMoney, SqlSingle, SqlString

ToSqlDateTime( ): SqlString

ToSqlDecimal( ): SqlBoolean, SqlByte, SqlDouble, SqlInt16, SqlInt32, SqlInt64, SqlMoney, SqlSingle, SqlString

ToSqlDouble( ): SqlBoolean, SqlByte, SqlDecimal, SqlInt16, SqlInt32, SqlInt64, SqlMoney, SqlSingle, SqlString

ToSqlGuid( ): SqlBinary, SqlString

ToSqlInt16( ): SqlBoolean, SqlByte, SqlDecimal, SqlDouble, SqlInt32, SqlInt64, SqlMoney, SqlSingle, SqlString

ToSqlInt32( ): SqlBoolean, SqlByte, SqlDecimal, SqlDouble, SqlInt16, SqlInt64, SqlMoney, SqlSingle, SqlString

ToSqlInt64( ): SqlBoolean, SqlByte, SqlDecimal, SqlDouble, SqlInt16, SqlInt32, SqlMoney, SqlSingle, SqlString

ToSqlMoney( ): SqlBoolean, SqlByte, SqlDecimal, SqlDouble, SqlInt16, SqlInt32, SqlInt64, SqlSingle, SqlString

ToSqlSingle( ): SqlBoolean, SqlByte, SqlDecimal, SqlDouble, SqlInt16, SqlInt32, SqlInt64, SqlMoney, SqlString

ToSqlString( ): SqlBoolean, SqlByte, SqlDateTime, SqlDecimal, SqlDouble, SqlGuid, SqlInt16, SqlInt32, SqlInt64, SqlMoney, SqlSingle

ToString( ): Constraint, DataColumn, DataColumnMapping, DataRelation, DataTable, DataTableMapping, OleDbError, OleDbInfoMessageEventArgs, OleDbParameter, SqlBinary, SqlBoolean, SqlByte, SqlDateTime, SqlDecimal, SqlDouble, SqlError, SqlGuid, SqlInfoMessageEventArgs, SqlInt16, SqlInt32, SqlInt64, SqlMoney, SqlParameter, SqlSingle, SqlString

ToXml( ): DBDataPermission, OleDbPermission

Transaction: IDbCommand, OleDbCommand, SqlCommand

Translations: OleDbSchemaGuid

True: SqlBoolean

Truncate( ): SqlDecimal

Trustee: OleDbSchemaGuid

TypedDataSetGenerator: System.Data

TypedDataSetGeneratorException: System.Data

U

UInt16: DbType

UInt32: DbType

UInt64: DbType

Unchanged: DataRowState, DataViewRowState

Union( ): DBDataPermission, OleDbPermission

Unique: DataColumn

UniqueConstraint: System.Data

UniqueIdentifier: SqlDbType

UnsignedBigInt: OleDbType

UnsignedInt: OleDbType

UnsignedSmallInt: OleDbType
UnsignedTinyInt: OleDbType
Unspecified: IsolationLevel
Update: StatementType
Update( ): DataAdapter, DbDataAdapter,
   IDataAdapter
UpdateCommand: IDbDataAdapter, Ole-
   DbDataAdapter, SqlDataAdapter
UpdatedRowSource: IDbCommand, Ole-
   DbCommand, SqlCommand
UpdateIndex( ): DataView
UpdateRowSource: System.Data
UpdateRule: ForeignKeyConstraint
UpdateStatus: System.Data
Usage_Privileges: OleDbSchemaGuid
User_Name: OleDbLiteral

V

Value: IDataParameter, OleDbParameter,
   SqlBinary, SqlBoolean, SqlByte, SqlDate-
   Time, SqlDecimal, SqlDouble, SqlGuid,
   SqlInt16, SqlInt32, SqlInt64, SqlMoney,
   SqlParameter, SqlSingle, SqlString
value__: AcceptRejectRule, Command-
   Behavior, CommandType, Connection-
   State, DataRowAction, DataRowState,
   DataRowVersion, DataViewRowState,
   DbType, IsolationLevel, Key-
   RestrictionBehavior, MappingType,
   MissingMappingAction, MissingSchema-
   Action, OleDbLiteral, OleDbType,
   ParameterDirection, PropertyAttributes,
   Rule, SchemaType, SqlCompareOptions,
   SqlDbType, StatementType, Update-
   RowSource, UpdateStatus, XmlRead-
   Mode, XmlWriteMode
Values: FillErrorEventArgs
VarBinary: OleDbType, SqlDbType
VarChar: OleDbType, SqlDbType
Variant: OleDbType, SqlDbType
VarNumeric: DbType, OleDbType
VarWChar: OleDbType
VersionNotFoundException: System.Data
View_Column_Usage: OleDbSchemaGuid
View_Name: OleDbLiteral
View_Table_Usage: OleDbSchemaGuid
Views: OleDbSchemaGuid

W

WChar: OleDbType
WorkstationId: SqlConnection
Write: PropertyAttributes
WriteSchema: XmlWriteMode
WriteXml( ): DataSet
WriteXmlSchema( ): DataSet

X

XmlReadMode: System.Data
XmlWriteMode: System.Data
Xor( ): SqlBoolean, SqlByte, SqlInt16, Sql-
   Int32, SqlInt64

Z

Zero: SqlBoolean, SqlByte, SqlDouble, Sql-
   Int16, SqlInt32, SqlInt64, SqlMoney, Sql-
   Single

Index

Symbols

[ ] brackets, not supported in
    ADO.NET, 122
_ character, not supported in
    ADO.NET, 122
: colon, 424
% percent sign, 122
; semicolon, 14, 423
@ symbol, 33

A

AcceptChanges( ) method
    for DataRows, 92, 342, 431
    for DataSets, 72, 280
    for DataTables, 82, 305
    EndEdit( ) method and, 90
AcceptChangesDuringFill( )
    method, 169
AcceptChangesDuringFill property, 382
AcceptRejectRule enumeration, 431
AcceptRejectRule property, 101, 102
access modifiers, 423
Add( ) method
    for columns, 76
    for constraints, 77
    for relations, 69
    for rows, 79

single-value binding and, 132
    for tables in DataSets, 67
AddRange( ) method
    for columns, 76
    for tables in DataSets, 68
AddTableNameRow( ) method, 153
ADO.NET providers (see data
    providers)
ADOX, 44
aggregate calculations, 83
aggregate commands, 32
aggregate functions, 123
AllowDBNull property, 88, 331
annotations, 158
application domains, connection
    pooling and, 24–26
ApplyDefaultSort property, 128
ASP.NET data binding, 140–148
ASP.NET list binding, 140–142
at (@) symbol, preceding SQL
    parameter object names, 33
AutoIncrement columns
    creating, 87
    data source and, 181–190
    updating rows and, 90
AutoIncrement property, 331
AutoIncrementSeed property, 331
AutoIncrementStep property, 331
automatic transactions, 199–202

We'd like to hear your suggestions for improving our indexes. Send email to *index@oreilly.com*.

B

batch queries, using to retrieve updated
   values from data source, 181
Begin( ) method, for nested
   transactions, 197, 409
BeginEdit( ) method, for DataRows, 90,
   92, 342
BeginLoadData( ) method, for
   DataTables, 81, 305
BeginTransaction( ) method, 14, 193,
   408
bidirectional parameters, 33
binary large objects (BLOBs), 56–58
binding, 131–134
BindingContext objects, 131–140
   creating new, 139
BLOBs (binary large objects), 56–58
brackets [ ], not supported in
   ADO.NET, 122

C

C# syntax, converting to Visual Basic
   syntax, 423–430
C# using statement, 21
calculated columns, 112–114
Cancel( ) method, 29
CancelEdit( ) method, for
   DataRows, 90, 92, 342
Caption property, 331
case sensitivity
   C# and, 423
   connection strings and, 14
CaseSensitive property
   for DataSets, 280
   for DataTables, 305
ChangeDatabase( ) method, 14
changes, committing/discarding
   for DataRows, 93
      in DataSets, 72–74
      in DataTables, 82
   UniqueConstraint and, 98
child rows, 93
   ForeignKeyConstraint class and, 100
ChildRelations collection, 305
classes
   connected/disconnected, 4–7
   C#/Visual Basic and, 424
   included in .NET data providers, 3

namespace quick reference and, 417
   for ODBC .NET provider, 560
   for ODP.NET data provider, 561
   for OLE DB .NET provider, 559
   for SQL Server .NET provider, 557
Clear( ) method
   for columns, 77
   for constraints, 79
   for rows, removing
      from DataSets, 280, 72
      from DataTables, 81, 83, 305
   for tables, removing from
      DataSets, 69
ClearErrors( ) method, 342
Clone( ) method
   for DataSets, 67, 70, 281
   for DataTables, 82, 306
Close( ) method
   for connections, 14
   for DataReaders, 47
codegen namespace, 562–564
   annotations and, 158
CollectionChangeEventArgs
   enumeration, 312
collections reference
   Command class, 254
   Constraint class, 363
   DataAdapter class, 382, 388–392
   DataColumn class, 340
   DataRelation class, 368
   DataRow class, 341, 347
   DataSet class, 286–291
   DataTable class, 311–318
colon (:), in C# syntax, 424
column mappings, 168
column ordinals, 49
ColumnChanged event, 84, 306
ColumnChanging event, 84, 306
ColumnMapping property, 331
ColumnName property, 331
columns, 77–79
   DataTable events and, 84
   expression, 112–114
   filtering by, 120
   showing all with DataReaders, 54
   strongly typed DataSets and, 156
   UniqueConstraint and, 98
   (see also DataColumn objects)
Columns collection, 305

About the Authors

Bill Hamilton is a software architect who specializes in designing, developing, and implementing distributed applications using .NET and J2EE technologies. Over the last 10 years, he has provided consulting services in B2B, B2C, B2E, data integration, and portal initiatives for banking, retail, accounting, manufacturing, and financial services. An early technology adopter, he frequently evaluates, recommends, and helps his clients use new technologies effectively. Bill has designed and helped build several award-winning software packages.

Matthew MacDonald is an MCSD developer, author, and educator. He is the author of several books about .NET, including *Microsoft .NET Distributed Applications* (Microsoft Press), *The Book of VB .NET* (No Starch), and *ASP.NET: The Complete Reference* (McGraw-Hill). He's also worked on several O'Reilly projects: he's contributed to *C# in a Nutshell*, written the reference for *ASP.NET in a Nutshell*, and coauthored *Programming .NET Web Services*.

Colophon

Our look is the result of reader comments, our own experimentation, and feedback from distribution channels. Distinctive covers complement our distinctive approach to technical topics, breathing personality and life into potentially dry subjects.

The animal on the cover of *ADO.NET in a Nutshell* is an African spoonbill (*Platalea alba*). The African spoonbill a long-legged wading bird distinguished by a bare red face and legs, all-white plumage, and a long spatulate bill, the inside of which reacts to touch, causing the bill to snap shut on its prey. It feeds by fishing in shallow water, swinging its open bill from side to side.

The African spoonbill's habitat includes the lakes, marshes, rivers, and estuaries of southern Africa. A shy and alert bird, it's usually found singly but can also be encountered in pairs or in groups. It is usually silent except for an occasional grunt when alarmed. It flies with its neck and legs extended, flapping its wings steadily in the air.

At birth, this bird's beak is short; it gradually develops into its spoon-like shape. Following a spring courtship, eggs are laid in a nest platform of sticks or reeds in a tree near water; however, nests can also be found in swamp reeds, among rocks, marsh plants, or on cliffs. Males and females share incubation and feeding the young for about 20 to 30 days. Young birds begin to fly after another four weeks.

Mary Anne Weeks Mayo was the production editor and copyeditor for *ADO.NET in a Nutshell*. Ann Schirmer proofread the book. Matt Hutchinson and Claire Cloutier provided quality control. Reg Aubry, Sue Willing, Genevieve d'Entremont, and Judy Hoer provided production assistance. Brenda Miller wrote the index.

Emma Colby designed the cover of this book, based on a series design by Edie Freedman. The cover image is an illustration from the 1898 edition of *Animate*

Creation Illustrated. Bret Kerr produced the cover layout with QuarkXPress 4.1 using Adobe's ITC Garamond font. David Futato designed and produced the CD label with QuarkXPress 4.1 using Adobe's ITC Garamond font.

Bret Kerr designed the interior layout, based on a series design by David Futato. This book was converted by Mike Sierra to FrameMaker 5.5.6 with a format conversion tool created by Erik Ray, Jason McIntosh, Neil Walls, and Mike Sierra that uses Perl and XML technologies. The text font is Linotype Birka; the heading font is Adobe Myriad Condensed; and the code font is LucasFont's TheSans Mono Condensed. The illustrations that appear in the book were produced by Robert Romano and Jessamyn Read using Macromedia FreeHand 9 and Adobe Photoshop 6. The tip and warning icons were drawn by Christopher Bing. This colophon was compiled by Mary Anne Weeks Mayo.

Other Titles Available from O'Reilly

Microsoft .NET Programming

Mastering Visual Studio .NET

*By Ian Griffiths, Jon Flanders
& Chris Sells
1st Edition March 2003
352 pages, ISBN 0-596-00360-9*

Mastering Visual Studio .NET
provides you, as an experienced
programmer, with all the information needed to get the most out of the latest and
greatest development tool from Microsoft. Written
by experienced developers and trainers John Flanders,
Ian Griffiths, and Chris Sells, this book not only covers
the fundamentals, but also shows how to customize
and extend the toolkit to your specific needs.

Programming C#, 2nd Edition

*By Jesse Liberty
2nd Edition February 2002
650 pages, ISBN 0-596-00309-9*

The first part of *Programming
C#*, 2nd Edition introduces C#
fundamentals, then goes on to
explain the development of desk-
top and Internet applications, including Windows
Forms, ADO.NET, ASP.NET (including Web
Forms), and Web Services. Next, this book gets to
the heart of the .NET Framework, focusing on
attributes and reflection, remoting, threads and
synchronization, streams, and finally, it illustrates
how to interoperate with COM objects.

Learning Visual Basic .NET

*By Jesse Liberty
1st edition October 2002
320 pages, ISBN 0-596-00386-2*

Learning Visual Basic .NET is a
complete introduction to
VB.NET and object-oriented programming. By using hundreds of
examples, this book demonstrates how to develop
various kinds of applications—including those that
work with databases—and web services. *Learning
Visual Basic .NET* will help you build a solid foundation in .NET.

Programming ASP.NET

*By Jesse Liberty & Dan Hurwitz
1st Edition February 2002
960 pages, ISBN 0-596-00171-1*

The ASP.NET technologies are so
complete and flexible; your main
difficulty may lie simply in weav-
ing the pieces together for maxi-
mum efficiency. *Programming ASP.NET* shows you
how to do just that. Jesse Liberty and Dan Hurwitz
teach everything you need to know to write web
applications and web services using both C# and
Visual Basic .NET.

C# in a Nutshell

*By Peter Drayton & Ben
Albarhari
1st Edition March 2002
856 pages, ISBN 0-596-00181-9*

C# is likely to become one of the
most widely used languages for
building .NET applications. *C#
in a Nutshell* contains a concise
introduction to the language and its syntax, plus
brief tutorials used to accomplish common programming tasks. It also includes O'Reilly's classic-
style, quick-reference material for all the types and
members in core .NET namespaces, including System, System.Text, System.IO, and System.Collec-
tions.

ASP.NET in a Nutshell

*By G. Andrew Duthie &
Matthew MacDonald
1st Edition June 2002
816 pages, ISBN 0-596-00116-9*

As a quick reference and tutorial
in one, *ASP.NET in a Nutshell*
goes beyond the published documentation to highlight little-
known details, stress practical uses for particular
features, and provide real-world examples that
show how features can be used in a working application. This book covers application and web service development, custom controls, data access,
security, deployment, and error handling. There is
also an overview of web-related class libraries.

O'REILLY®

To order: *800-998-9938* • *order@oreilly.com* • *www.oreilly.com*
Online editions of most O'Reilly titles are available by subscription at *safari.oreilly.com*
Also available at most retail and online bookstores.

How to stay in touch with O'Reilly

1. Visit our award-winning web site

http://www.oreilly.com/

★ "Top 100 Sites on the Web"—PC Magazine
★ CIO Magazine's Web Business 50 Awards

Our web site contains a library of comprehensive product information (including book excerpts and tables of contents), downloadable software, background articles, interviews with technology leaders, links to relevant sites, book cover art, and more. File us in your bookmarks or favorites!

2. Join our email mailing lists

Sign up to get email announcements of new books and conferences, special offers, and O'Reilly Network technology newsletters at:

http://elists.oreilly.com

It's easy to customize your free elists subscription so you'll get exactly the O'Reilly news you want.

3. Get examples from our books

To find example files for a book, go to:

http://www.oreilly.com/catalog

select the book, and follow the "Examples" link.

4. Work with us

Check out our web site for current employment opportunites:

http://jobs.oreilly.com/

5. Register your book

Register your book at:
http://register.oreilly.com

6. Contact us

O'Reilly & Associates, Inc.
1005 Gravenstein Hwy North
Sebastopol, CA 95472 USA
TEL: 707-827-7000 or 800-998-9938
     (6am to 5pm PST)
FAX: 707-829-0104

order@oreilly.com
For answers to problems regarding your order or our products. To place a book order online visit:

http://www.oreilly.com/order_new/

catalog@oreilly.com
To request a copy of our latest catalog.

booktech@oreilly.com
For book content technical questions or corrections.

corporate@oreilly.com
For educational, library, government, and corporate sales.

proposals@oreilly.com
To submit new book proposals to our editors and product managers.

international@oreilly.com
For information about our international distributors or translation queries. For a list of our distributors outside of North America check out:

http://international.oreilly.com/distributors.html

adoption@oreilly.com
For information about academic use of O'Reilly books, visit:

http://academic.oreilly.com

O'REILLY®

To order: *800-998-9938* • *order@oreilly.com* • *www.oreilly.com*
Online editions of most O'Reilly titles are available by subscription at *safari.oreilly.com*
Also available at most retail and online bookstores.